THE FLAT
Flat Racing in Britain since 1939

THE
FLAT

Flat Racing in Britain
since 1939

by
ROGER MORTIMER

London
GEORGE ALLEN & UNWIN
Boston   Sydney

First published 1979

GEORGE ALLEN & UNWIN LTD
40 Museum Street, London WC1A 1LU

British Library Cataloguing in Publication Data

Mortimer, Roger
   The flat,
   1. Horse-racing – Great Britain – History –
  20th century
   I. Title
   798 .43'0941   SF335.G7

   ISBN 0-04-798002-8

Typeset in 11 on 12 point Imprint
and printed in Great Britain
by Cox and Wyman Ltd,
London, Fakenham and Reading

CONTENTS

1976—French successes—Doping—the Trepan affair—Wollow wins The Two Thousand Guineas—Empery wins substandard Derby—Flying Water—M. Wildenstein's three classic victories—Sagaro wins The Gold Cup—Lochnager the crack sprinter of 1976— J. O. Tobin and The Minstrel the best two-year-olds—Noel Murless retires—Woodrow Wyatt becomes Chairman of the Tote—1977 continues influence of American thoroughbred in Europe—National Stud closed—the Jockey Club elects three women members—deaths of Sam Hall and Staff Ingham—Nebbiolo and Mrs McArdy win The Guineas—The Minstrel wins The Derby—Jubilee Year victories for the Queen's Dunfermline—Alleged takes revenge and The Arc—Sagaro's Gold Cup—Gentilhombre wins The Diadem Stakes and the Prix de l'Abbaye—Lady Beaverbrook's Boldboy—Artaius—Relkino—North Stoke—Dominance of American-bred two-year-olds—Mr Robert Sangster the most successful owner—the prospects for English racing.

LIST OF ILLUSTRATIONS

Acknowledgements and thanks for help with assembling the pictures are due to *The British Racehorse* and to the following copyright owners:

Gerry Cranham: 1, 2, 29, 50, 59, 60, 62, 64, 65, 66, 67, 68
London News Agency Photos: 3
Horses in Action (Michael Joseph Ltd): 4, 6, 10, 26
W. W. Rouch & Co.: 5, 53
Radio Times Hulton Picture Library: 7, 8, 12, 13, 16, 17
Sport and General Press Agency Ltd: 9, 11, 14, 18, 21, 23, 24, 27, 31, 33, 36, 37, 39, 40, 41, 45, 46, 47, 48, 51, 58, 61, 63
Central Press Photos Ltd: 15, 19, 22, 25, 30, 35, 38, 49, 56
British Movietonews Ltd: 20
Barratts Press Agency: 28
Press Association: 32, 42, 43, 44, 55, 57
Fox Photos: 34
Mrs Ian Balding: 52, 54

THE FLAT
Flat Racing in Britain since 1939

I

THE changes in racing that have taken place since the beginning of World War II reflect the profundity of the changes that have occurred in the life of this country as a whole.

Between 1914 and 1939, under the undisputed control of the Jockey Club, a far more autocratic and self-confident body than it is today, flat-racing sailed placidly along on a smooth and rarely troubled sea. The outstanding innovation was the introduction of totalisator betting. For this Lord Hamilton of Dalzell was largely responsible.

Lord Hamilton was never a rich man and he neither bred nor owned horses on a large scale. He was, though, unquestionably one of the Jockey Club's most able administrators, far-sighted and progressive at a time when most of his fellow members were content to slumber peacefully and displayed singularly little enthusiasm for change. It was his firm resolve that betting should be compelled to contribute towards the maintenance of the sport. In 1927 he was appointed Senior Steward in place of Lord Penhryn whose health prevented him from taking office. At the next Jockey Club meeting the Stewards submitted a resolution that a committee be appointed to 'institute without delay an inquiry into the means by which betting may best be made to contribute to the maintenance of the sport'. Lord Hamilton himself was chairman of that committee and in 1928 the Chancellor of the Exchequer, Mr Winston Churchill, promised facilities in the House of Commons for a private member's Bill to legalise the totalisator. Lord Hamilton was in close touch with Sir Ralph Glyn, who introduced the Bill, and he made no secret of his disappointment when it received such rough handling in the committee stage as to emerge barely recognisable. The original Bill had placed the Jockey Club in control of the tote. The Racecourse Betting Act of 1928 vested control in a statutory body, the Racecourse Betting Control Board, responsible to the Home Office. The first chairman of the Board was Sir Clement Hindley, whose apparent qualification for an exacting task was the administrative experience gained when Chief Commissioner of Railways to the Government of India.

The tote has never proved to be the financial prop to racing that its advocates had hoped. This is hardly surprising in view of the fact that the Racecourse Betting

Control Board was launched, without funds or guarantee, to perform duties imposed by Act of Parliament and involving heavy expenditure. It was not long before the tote was in grave financial difficulties and, although it did not actually founder, its subsequent activities, particularly as regards expansion, have always been hampered by lack of capital. From the start the tote faced daunting problems. The bookmakers, who have always possessed a powerful parliamentary lobby, were of course bitterly opposed to it. When, during the 1960s, there was much talk of the desirability of establishing a tote monopoly, the bookmakers rose up and demanded freedom of choice for punters. They had not appeared noticeably keen on freedom of choice when the tote first came into operation. In any case it is difficult to alter the betting habits of a nation and the bookmakers had been firmly entrenched for a century. Moreover no provision had been made in the Act for credit betting on the tote, or for gaining a share of the immense volume of money that was wagered off the course. However, chiefly through the energy and enterprise of Lord Milford, Tote Investors Ltd was founded, this firm providing facilities for credit betting on the tote both on the course and off it.

The Racecourse Betting Control Board naturally took advice from experienced tote operators throughout the world. Unfortunately the conditions under which racing is run in this country tend to be unique, and much well-meant advice proved not only misleading but involved the Board in heavy expenditure to no purpose.

The tote's first operations were on the July Course at Newmarket on July 2, 1929. The bookmakers, needlessly as it turned out, were apprehensive of the effect the tote might have on their own business and retaliated by offering extravagant odds. In consequence Lord Rosebery's The Bastard, who won an event of no particular significance, was returned at 100/1. The Bastard was eventually exported to Australia, where, under the more refined name of The Buzzard, he proved an outstanding success as a sire.

A notable weakness in English racing between the wars lay in the poor quality of many local stewards. All too often they were old gentlemen resident in the locality who wanted a good lunch and no trouble afterwards. Mr Sidney Galtrey, for many years the racing correspondent of the Daily Telegraph, wrote as follows in his *Memoirs of a Racing Journalist* published in 1934:

> I subscribe to the view that local stewardship is a real weakness in the administrative system of English racing. For all I know it may always have been a weakness. Even if it served generations ago it does not follow that haphazard voluntary stewardship is the best possible principle today.
>
> The local executives are primarily to blame and the Jockey Club in a lesser degree, for not being firm with the executives and insisting on efficient stewardship. Here and there at the more prominent meetings certain members of the Jockey Club, whose names command respect, will officiate, though some may not have been racing for some time and may not be in touch with the form. They may not even know the colours so as to follow the racing closely. There are men

who have grown old, with their faculties impaired through age, who, nevertheless, expect as a right to be invited to officiate. They will expect it until they die. Some of them are notorious as backers. They like to back winners, which means they must accept confidences from individuals whose horses must come under their notice. How is it possible in human nature for them to be impartial?

A few favoured trainers are persona grata in stewards' luncheon rooms. The hospitality is at the expense of the shareholders of the meeting. Again it is not in human nature to question the morale of those who have been your guests and whose mind has possibly been opened to you. There are occasions when I think stewards are asked to act because they are less likely than anyone else on the course to be familiar with the form. They listen to the evidence of the judge and some of the jockeys, whose evidence I would never ask for except to hear them in their defence or as complainants. I long for the day when there will be a raising of the standard of local stewardship, and when it comes we might expect some regard being paid to an age limit while recognising the potential value of the man of shrewd understanding with no axes to grind and with a limited number of friends.

The inept nature of much stewarding was the subject of frequent adverse comment. At one meeting the stewards were commonly referred to as 'The Three Blind Mice', at another as 'The Unburied Dead'. Demands for the appointment of stewards' secretaries to advise and assist the local stewards were made in Gimcrack Dinner speeches and in the columns of responsible journalists. The Jockey Club of those days was never in a hurry to accede to popular demand but at length, in 1936, the first stewards' secretaries, commonly but inaccurately referred to as 'stipes', were appointed. Some local stewards took umbrage at what they took to be a reflection on their own capabilities and made scant attempt to make life easy or agreeable for the new officials. During those early days a stewards' secretary at a northern meeting was adamant on the need for an inquiry, much to the annoyance of one of the local stewards. Later that afternoon the official was standing outside the weighing room close to the steward in question and the trainer of the horse concerned in the inquiry. The steward jerked his thumb towards the official and observed in a penetrating voice: 'That's the bastard that caused all the trouble.'

Ruff's Guide for 1976 listed ten stewards' secretaries. The value of the work of these officials is now generally appreciated by the local stewards and the racing public. Brigadier 'Roscoe' Harvey, certainly one of the best liked men in the racing world, was elected a member of the Jockey Club following his retirement at the end of 1969 as Senior Stewards' Secretary.

As for local stewards, the standard is now very much higher than it was and those who were notorious for punting when on duty are a memory of the past. There is certainly no modern steward as bizarre as the late Captain 'Wiggie' Weyland, with his breeches and cloth gaiters and his grey curls peeping coyly from beneath an auburn wig. The story goes that when acting as a steward at Windsor he delayed the hearing of an objection because he was down on the rails with the bookmakers betting away happily on the result of it. Today all local stewards, though appointed by the executive concerned, have to be approved by the Stewards of the Jockey Club. There is an age limit of seventy-five. Of course the work of the local stewards has been greatly assisted by the introduction of the patrol camera which, within a few minutes of the horses' passing the post, can provide both lateral and head-on films of the race.

Nearly every man nowadays has to work for his living and it is not always easy to secure the services of local stewards with the appropriate qualities. Such individuals frequently simply lack the time to spare. In addition, the once rich supply of retired army officers with at least a knowledge of horses and perhaps some experience in race riding has more or less dried up. Recently, and quite rightly, a number of women—Lavinia, Duchess of Norfolk, Lady Halifax and Mrs P. Hastings—have been invited to act as stewards. There are a lot of intelligent, well-informed women connected with racing, and if a woman can lead a great political party or carry out the duties of a High Court judge, there is surely no reason why a woman should fail to function efficiently as a steward.[1]

Occasionally a voice is heard demanding the appointment of paid stewards. Bearing in mind the economic climate, the demand is unrealistic. The cost would be heavy indeed, taking into account the large amount of racing that takes place in this country, the number of paid stewards required, their salaries, expenses and pensions. Moreover, in the end it might merely mean paying much the same type of person, who, by and large, does the job with reasonable competence today for no reward other than a few fringe benefits. If the same salaried stewards officiated at meeting after meeting, there would almost certainly be dire complaints from a few trainers and jockeys that so-and-so had a down on him and was unfair.

One other pre-war reform is worth noting. The Jockey Club had for years been worried by the question of nominations rendered void by an owner's death. Advised by the highest legal opinion, the Jockey Club had acted under the assumption that fees and forfeits incurred by horses entered under Jockey Club rules could not be recovered under process of law since they were contracts by way of gambling and wagering and possessed no legal sanction. If a living owner evaded forfeit liabilities, his name appeared in the forfeit list in the Racing Calendar but that deterrent could hardly be applied with decency in respect of a dead man or of his executors. The 'Void Nomination' rule thus came into existence, stipulating that when an owner died, all entries for his horses ceased to exist.

It so happened that in 1927 the matter was under discussion and among those interested was Mr Edgar Wallace, the well-known author and journalist. Mr Wallace, whose enthusiasm for racing was unfortunately accompanied by almost total lack of success as an owner, suggested a 'friendly' action between himself and the Jockey Club. It was accordingly agreed for Mr Wallace to be sued in the High

---

[1] In 1977 Lady Halifax, Mrs Hastings and Mrs Helen Johnson Houghton were elected members of the Jockey Club.

Court for the recovery of £4 in respect of a horse of his entered at Newmarket. To the chagrin of all concerned, the verdict in the Chancery Court went in favour of Mr Wallace, who, while the action was pending, was unable to run any of his horses since in the unlikely event of one of them winning a race Mr Wallace would have had a credit balance at Weatherbys and the £4 in dispute would have been appropriated.

It was decided to take the case to the Court of Appeal and in the meantime Mr Wallace wrote a racing play, which proved highly successful, called *The Calendar*. The play itself was the subject of legal action since a certain Mr Goldflam, who wrote under the name of L. G. Gould Fleme, repeatedly accused Mr Wallace of plagiarism. In the end Mr Wallace felt compelled to sue for libel and was awarded damages of £1,000.

In the Court of Appeal the Master of the Rolls and Lords Justices Lawrence and Russell found in favour of the Jockey Club. This judgment enabled the rule to be changed in 1929 and permitted Cameronian, whose owner-breeder Lord Dewar died in 1930, to win the 1931 Two Thousand Guineas and Derby for Lord Dewar's nephew, Mr J. A. Dewar.

In general it could be said that up till 1939 racing, conducted in a manner that was somewhat amateurish by modern standards, was still essentially a sport rather than a business or an industry. It was all the more enjoyable because of that. There was no shortage of wealthy men and women who had no cause to worry unduly if their racing activities showed an adverse balance at the end of the year more often than not. The scene was still dominated by the great owner-breeders such as the 17th Earl of Derby, the 2nd Viscount Astor, the 6th Earl of Rosebery and the Aga Khan. Owners who enjoyed betting could do so without having their winnings scaled down by taxation.

Costs were still comparatively low, though a bit higher than earlier in the century when a member of the Jockey Club declared that racing would be finished if training fees at Newmarket ever rose beyond £2 10s a week. In the 1920s the famous Alec Taylor of Manton charged his owners £3 10s a week and sent his bill in once a year, a week before Christmas. He was clearly not robbing himself since he left over £500,000.

It was rare for a stable to contain more than forty horses, and trainers were thus required to cope with fewer horses, fewer owners and a compact labour force. In 1975 Peter Walwyn, a man of immense energy, had 105 horses and more than sixty owners. A lad used to look after two horses whereas today he may have to look after four. Certainly a trainer's life was easier in those days with freedom from labour troubles and a far lighter burden of office work. In general, horses were out at exercise for a longer period than they are today. At Manton the preparation of the Cup horses began the previous autumn with long periods of walking and trotting every afternoon. Those methods would not be easy to accomplish with modern labour. The best horses today are no doubt trained as well as they ever were but the less talented ones perhaps receive a less thorough preparation. In nearly all the top stables the lads used to be impeccably turned-out, well disciplined and highly efficient. That stern martinet the late Fred Darling would surely rotate in his grave if he could see certain strings at work on Newmarket Heath today with the lads looking as if they were members of a No. 2 touring company of that lively entertainment *Hair*.

In 1938, the last completed season before the war, the top-priced yearling was a Bahram colt that made 13,000 guineas. Only nine other yearlings realised 3,000 guineas or more. It was a very long way from the Mill Reef colt that made 202,000 guineas at Newmarket in 1975. Stallions such as Hyperion, Fairway and Windsor Lad stood at 400 guineas. At 500 guineas there were only Bahram, winner of the Triple Crown in 1935, and the St Leger winner Solario, who had created a record in 1932 when sold as a stallion by Tattersalls for 47,000 guineas.

Of course there was less money to be won. Top trainer was Captain (later Sir) Cecil Boyd-Rochfort with £51,350. In 1975 the leading owner was Dr C. Vittadini with £209,492, while the leading trainer, Peter Walwyn, had won £382,257. Moreover, Dr Vittadini's total does not include the money won by Grundy in the Irish Two Thousand Guineas and the Irish Sweeps Derby, while Walwyn won an additional £100,000 in Ireland and on the Continent.

If English jockeyship was at a low ebb from 1900 to 1914, the inter-war period represented a golden age with Sir Gordon Richards, Steve Donoghue, Bernard Carslake, Joe Childs, Frank Bullock, Charles Smirke, Freddy Fox, Dick Perryman, the Smith brothers, Charles Elliott, Victor Smyth, Michael Beary, Rufus Beasley, Harry Wragg and Tommy Weston. Sir Gordon in his prime faced far fiercer competition than Lester Piggott has ever done.

Justice was liable to be rough and ready. Smirke lost his licence in 1928 after his mount Welcome Gift had been left at the post at Gatwick. He did not get his licence back for five years. Possibly the authorities were gunning for Smirke, but in view of Welcome Gift's subsequent racing record it hardly appears that the occasion was well chosen.

A notorious case of neglect of duty by the local stewards occurred at Doncaster in 1931. The Derby winner Cameronian was an odds-on favourite for the St Leger. Normally placid, he was in a state of the wildest excitement both before the race, when he kicked Orpen savagely, and during it when he fought like a mad thing for his head and ran himself out long before the turn for home had been reached. He finished last. Incredible as it may seem, no form of veterinary test was ordered. Cameronian ran a slight but persistent temperature for nearly a year afterwards. Orpen, belonging to Sir J. Rutherford, was third in The Two Thousand Guineas, second in The Derby, second in The St Leger.

The Stewards of the Jockey Club nearly caught a nasty cold over a doping case in 1930. Don Pat, trained by Charles Chapman, a young man with a small stable at Lavant, near Goodwood, won The Bedfont High Weight Handicap at Kempton Park on August 30. The Stewards at Kempton ordered a test to be taken and this proved positive, caffeine being the drug employed. On September 29 Chapman appeared before the Stewards of the Jockey Club, Lords Rosebery, Harewood and Ellesmere. No suggestion was made that Chapman had been a party to the

3. Three jockeys of the inter-war era: Steve Donoghue (*left*), Henri Jellis, Joe Childs

4.   Charlie Smirke is riding with his hands only, whereas the centre jockey is picking up his whip and the outside one is resorting to more desperate measures

doping or knew anything about it. However, after a brief retirement the Stewards communicated their verdict to Chapman in these words: 'We have given most careful thought to this case. We have come to the conclusion that Don Pat was doped and he is disqualified for life. We consider you, as trainer, were directly responsible for the care of the horse. Your licence to train is revoked and you are warned off Newmarket Heath.'

This was a harsh sentence in view of the fact that there had been no accusation, let alone proof, that Chapman was personally involved in the doping. However, the words used by the Stewards did seem to make it clear that there was nothing against Chapman except a breach of the duty cast upon every trainer to ensure the safety of all horses under his care.

Unfortunately, the notice of the case published in the Racing Calendar was worded differently. It entirely failed to indicate that the reason for Chapman having been 'warned off' was that the Stewards judged him to be directly responsible for the care of the horse. The notice in the Racing Calendar ran as follows: 'The Stewards of the Jockey Club (Lord Ellesmere acting for Lord Zetland) after further investigation satisfied themselves that a drug had been administered to the horse for the purpose of the race. They disqualified Don Pat for all future races under their rules and warned C. Chapman, the trainer of the horse, off Newmarket Heath.'

The news agencies circulated this statement, which naturally received wide publicity. It was repeated in The Times under the heading:

Racing
Another Trainer Warned Off
The Doping of Don Pat

Chapman thus found himself in an unenviable position. His career had been ruined and most people who followed racing had gained the impression that he himself had been party to the doping. He had very little money and in fact was compelled to take a job as chauffeur-groom in order that his family should not become destitute. Fortunately he was not without friends—among whom was the Duke of Richmond, one of his patrons—and sympathisers. With their support and encouragement he set out to win back his good name. He accordingly issued writs for libel against the three Stewards of the Jockey Club, Messrs Weatherby Ltd, publishers of the Racing Calendar which was owned by the Jockey Club, and also against the news agencies and The Times.

The case came up in November 1931 before Mr Justice Horridge and a special jury. The judge, an occasional racegoer, was a somewhat disconcerting individual since his features gave the impression that he was smiling away merrily whereas in fact he was very far indeed from feeling amused. Chapman, represented by Sir Patrick Hastings K.C., proved an excellent witness, whereas the Stewards of the Jockey Club were not seen to advantage, not even the usually quick-witted Lord Rosebery.

On the third and last day of the trial the judge ruled out the plea of privilege on the part of the defendants but at the same time he said there was no evidence of malice on their part. In his summing up he stated that it did not matter what the Stewards of the Jockey Club intended their notice to mean; the test was what a reasonable-minded person would say that it meant.

Answering questions put to them by the judge, the jury found that the words complained of were not true in their ordinary meaning, and that the words meant that Chapman was a party to the actual doping of Don Pat. The jury awarded damages as follows:

(a) In respect of the publication by the Stewards to the press agencies, £3,000.
(b) In respect of the publication by The Times, £3,000.
(c) In respect of the publication in the Racing Calendar, £10,000.

It is perhaps interesting to note that one of Chapman's counsel was Mr D. N. Pritt K.C., later a left-wing Labour Member of Parliament; while for the Jockey Club Mr Norman Birkett K.C. led Mr Geoffrey Lawrence K.C. who later became the 1st Lord Oaksey.

Thus Chapman was vindicated and his supporters were naturally delighted. Their jubilation, though, was of comparatively brief duration. The defendants decided to appeal. The Court of Appeal held that the Stewards and Messrs Weatherby were protected, since this decision was the bona fide decision of an agreed domestic tribunal, that the publication of the Racing Calendar was privileged, and that this privilege was not lost because the jury put on the words an interpretation different from that which was honestly intended by the tribunal; but that the privilege did not extend to the news agencies and The Times. The Stewards and Weatherbys were accordingly dismissed from the action, but a new trial was ordered in respect of the other parties on the grounds that the amounts awarded against them were excessive. There was, in fact, no trial since the parties concerned came to terms.

Mr H. Montgomery Hyde's book *Sir Patrick Hastings : His Life and Cases* tells of the uneasiness Hastings expressed over this particular case: 'There is somewhere a defect in our legal system when a completely innocent person may have to suffer from the public belief that he is guilty and when there exists no means of proving his innocence except by bringing an action that he cannot win.'

Chepstow was the only course constructed between the wars where flat-racing takes place. For many years Chepstow, largely because of its comparative inaccessibility, lacked public support and sport there, both on the flat and under National Hunt rules, was of mediocre quality. Nowadays the picture is very much brighter, thanks to the Severn Bridge and the M4 which have brought the course to within little more than an hour's car journey from Lambourn. Certain courses were absurdly underemployed. For instance Ascot had only four days' racing a year, Goodwood four, Epsom seven and Chester three.

Racing was without the technical aids that are generally accepted today. With no photograph to assist them, judges sometimes perpetrated mistakes, a notable case in point being that of Insight II who was placed third in the 1927 Cambridgeshire, a race that he had very clearly won. One amiable official observed after a verdict at Windsor that had caused a lively hostile demonstration: 'Oh dear, I'm afraid my spectacles may have let me down again.' He added: 'I never really wanted to be a judge but Weatherbys invited me and I did not like to hurt their feelings by refusing.' The result of an objection was liable to be a matter of chance. There was no patrol camera and stewards had to rely on their own fleeting impression of an incident that lasted not more than a few seconds; and on the evidence of jockeys who might or might not be without bias or self-interest in the matter under jurisdiction.

There were no twenty-four-hour declarations but the list of probable runners, at any rate at the major meetings, that was supplied by the Press Association was laudably accurate. Just occasionally some individual who enjoyed being a trifle 'hot' would pop up with a surprise runner, which, if it won, naturally caused resentment among off-course punters. It was at the lesser fixtures that the list of 'probables' was liable to degenerate into guesswork, and at a secondary jumping meeting it was not unknown for fifty horses listed as 'probables' to fail to take the field. There was guesswork, too, in respect of jockeys, and sometimes a horse would be down to be ridden by 'owner' although for many a year that individual had not climbed up on anything more demanding than a bar-stool at the Cavalry Club.

Class distinctions gave the lie to the old saying that 'on the turf and under it all men are equal'. Many courses were very fussy over admission to the members' enclosure and at Newmarket it was made deliberately difficult for a visitor to obtain a badge for the Private Stand. Such an attitude was in those days taken for granted and caused comparatively little resentment. Certainly on a hot day at Goodwood what is now the Richmond Stand would not have included a portly racegoer without a shirt, his badge attached to his hirsute and perspiring chest with a strip of Sellotape.

In one respect at least, racegoers were better off then than now. The train service was on the whole quite excellent and those who could afford to travel first class enjoyed a standard of comfort, for example on the Pullman Car service to Lingfield, that has long ceased to exist.

2

AS Lord Rosebery's handsome chestnut colt Blue Peter swept past the post to win the 1939 Derby by four lengths, a good many of those present at Epsom must have pondered gloomily on whether there would be a Derby in 1940. Younger racegoers, mindful of the fearful casualties of World War I, wondered if they would ever see a Derby again. There remains the still vivid memory of emerging from race meetings in the summers of 1938 and 1939, perhaps in a happy mood after a winning day, and then buying an evening newspaper which, with a disconcerting jerk, brought the reader back to the dread imminence of war.

The outbreak of war occurred a few days before the Doncaster St Leger meeting and the Doncaster Yearling Sales were to have taken place. Racing was cancelled and so were the Sales, breeders thus being left with valuable bloodstock on their hands. Some of the leading breeders, such as Lord Furness, Lord Adare, Mr Ernest Bellaney and Mr Frank Tuthill, did not send any yearlings to the sale held by Tattersalls at Newmarket in October, while the Sledmere Stud sold all its yearling colts privately to Mr J. V. Rank. The top price for a yearling at the October Sales was 1,550 guineas. Captain Terence Watt, who was to lose his life in the war, wore Life Guards uniform in the rostrum.

The abandonment of The St Leger caused much disappointment on account of the keen interest taken in the prospective clash between Blue Peter, a son of Fairway, and M. M. Boussac's Pharis II, by Fairway's brother Pharos. Pharis was unbeaten and had won the Prix du Jockey Club and the Grand Prix. Whatever the comparative merits of these two fine horses, Blue Peter possessed the better conformation and it is doubtful if Pharis II would have taken the field had the going been firm.

Because of fear of massive air attacks, there was no racing at all till mid-October. By then the war had settled down more or less comfortably into the 'phoney' stage. Flat-racing continued till the middle of November when as usual The Manchester November Handicap was run. This was won by Lord Rosebery's three-year-old Tutor, who carried 8 st. 3 lb. In a trial at Newmarket over a mile and three-quarters in August, Blue Peter had given Tutor 28 lb. and finished a dozen lengths in front of him.

5. Blue Peter

A number of courses were taken over by the military, the Scots Guards for example going to Kempton Park and the Coldstream to Sandown. Living conditions there were reasonably agreeable until the long spell of exceptionally cold weather began in December. Then fortunate indeed was the officer who secured a pitch in the ladies' loo of the Royal Pavilion at Sandown, since a gas fire there was still in operation. Among the company commanders at Sandown was Sir Humphrey de Trafford who had ridden winners there and had also officiated as steward.

Until the frost came, race meetings had been well attended. Uniforms became increasingly thick on the ground and an officer in the Coldstream, sporting his best service dress and blue cap, was not noticeably pleased when Eph Smith congratulated him on having joined the National Fire Service. Doubtless it was in the higher interests of national security that uniformed racegoers whose picture appeared in The Tatler or in similar publications had their cap badges erased. Several well-known Newmarket racing personalities joined a locally formed A.A. battery. There was an apparent lack of military uniform in this particular unit and Battery Sergeant-Major Hugh Sidebottom could be observed on the racecourse wearing a forage cap, a tweed overcoat with a fur collar, and gumboots.

Among the first trainers to be commissioned were Geoffrey Barling and his brother-in-law George Colling. The latter, never robust and not in the least military by inclination, was not cut out for a soldier's life. A photograph depicting

6.   In the paddock at Epsom. A two-year-old plays up

him at the head of a column of troops during 'Salute the Soldier' Week at Blackpool does little to convey the impression of a happy warrior. Not long afterwards his health gave way and he was invalided out. Many jockeys simply lacked the appropriate physique for service in the armed forces. Bill Rickaby, though, attained the rank of Major in the Royal Artillery. His immediate post-war reward was to experience considerable difficulty in obtaining any riding at all. He gradually fought his way back, though, and it delighted his many friends when he won The One Thousand Guineas and The Oaks on Sweet Solera trained by the veteran Reg Day. Sadly, Bill suffered a crippling car crash in Hong Kong where he had just gone out to take up a racing appointment following his retirement from being a jockey.

On February 15, 1940 the Racing Calendar published the following notice:

The Stewards of the Jockey Club have decided to close a New Two Thousand Guineas and a New One Thousand Guineas to be run over the Bunbury Mile if the Rowley Mile is not available. These races will close on February 27. It is, however, probable that the Rowley Mile will be available for the Craven Meeting and for at least three days of the First Spring Meeting. In that event these two new races become void. The Stewards of the Jockey Club have decided that the substitute Derby and Oaks for 1940 shall, if possible, be run at Newbury on June 12 and 13. These races will close on February 27. Should the course at Newbury not be available, these races will be run at Newmarket.

Kingsclere, where John Porter trained seven Derby winners and where in 1937 Fred Butters trained Mid-day Sun, the first Epsom Derby winner to carry the colours of a woman owner, closed down a few weeks after the outbreak of war, Butters returning to Newmarket where he and members of his family had lived for many years.

The cold weather prevented racing under National Hunt rules till late in February. On February 22 there was a contretemps after The United Services Steeplechase at Newbury, won by Mr Tom Hanbury on Gowran Ranger. Gowran Ranger was disqualified as Hanbury, who had been walking about before the race in trooper's uniform, was not a commissioned officer. Later in the war Hanbury, father of the Newmarket trainer Ben Hanbury, was awarded the M.C. when serving in the Household Cavalry.

The Lincoln and The Grand National were run as usual. Mervyn Jones, who rode the Grand National winner Bogskar was subsequently killed while serving with the R.A.F. The Two Thousand Guineas and The One Thousand Guineas were run at Newmarket during the first week in May. The Rowley Mile course was no longer available so both races took place on the July Course.

The Two Thousand Guineas resulted in a victory for France, the winner, and a very good one too, being M. M. Boussac's Djebel, trained at Chantilly by A. Swann. A smallish, active bay with an arab-like head, Djebel was by Tourbillon out of the Gay Crusader mare Loika. In 1936 Loika, carrying Djebel, had been sent to the Newmarket December Sales but had failed to find a purchaser. The course of racing history might have been very different if Loika had been bought by a British breeder, since Djebel proved an outstanding sire, his winners in this country including Galcador (Derby), My Babu (Two Thousand Guineas), Hugh Lupus (Champion Stakes), Arbar (Gold Cup) and Djeddah (Eclipse and Champion Stakes).

It had been intended to send Djebel back to England for The Derby but the war situation rendered that plan impossible. Wisely M. Boussac sent him down to the South of France until conditions in France began to look a bit more settled. Djebel, who also won the French Two Thousand Guineas, won fifteen races altogether including the Prix de l'Arc de Triomphe. He improved with age and was unbeaten at five. M. Boussac was fortunate in that the Germans did not steal Djebel as they stole other good horses in France. They did take M. Boussac's good mare Corrida, twice winner of the 'Arc' and the best winner ever sired by the Derby winner Coronach. Moreover she was never recovered.

Lord Astor's Golden Penny was an odds-on favourite for The One Thousand Guineas but this daughter of Hyperion was beaten by five lengths by another Hyperion filly, Mr Esmond Harmsworth's Godiva. Trained by William Jarvis, Godiva had been bred by her owner and was a young lady of lively and somewhat unpredictable disposition whose way of life caused Jarvis many moments of acute anxiety. She got on best with one of the stable apprentices, Douglas Marks, who rode her in all her races following the death of the stable jockey John Crouch in a flying accident in 1939. Marks, who later became a successful trainer and is one of racing's 'characters', was born in Grimsby and is said to have owed his introduction to racing to the Duke of Windsor, to whom his father had written hoping for a recommendation. Inquiries were made and in due course young Marks was apprenticed to Jarvis who had succeeded Richard Marsh as royal trainer.

It only remains to add that Godiva won The New Oaks at Newmarket by three lengths after losing lengths at the start and being tailed off in the early stages of the contest. Later that summer she was sent to the Fort Union Stud, Co. Limerick. She completed the journey safely but soon afterwards she had an accident there. She contracted septicaemia and it was found necessary to put her down at the end of August, a sad end to a really brilliant filly.

The terrible events during May 1940 failed to disturb the racing programme which, unbelievably, was carried on without interruption. I myself was serving in a battalion that formed part of the spearhead of the advance of the British Expeditionary Force into Belgium. It soon became apparent that the role was not altogether an enviable one. However the weather was perfect for outdoor activities and somehow it restored morale when, during a brief lull in the conflict, the post was delivered to the bank of the canal which the Germans had been so busily trying to cross. My share included a copy of the Sporting Life which gave the results from Fontwell Park where I noticed that one or two of my friends had been riding. This information led me to believe, only temporarily and certainly mistakenly, that the position must be rather less serious than I had imagined.

As the war situation continued to deteriorate in June, refugees began to arrive from France, including Jack Watts senior, William Pratt and Claud Halsey. Racing in England went on, though, as if nothing really important was happening and there were 10,000 people at Newmarket to watch The Derby, special trains being run from King's Cross.

The Derby was won by Pont l'Évêque, owned and trained by Fred Darling. It was the sixth Derby winner he had trained. Pont l'Évêque had been bred by Mr H. E. Morriss who was a patron of Darling and had won The Derby with Manna. A son of the Grand Prix winner Barneveldt, Pont l'Évêque was an unprepossessing individual when he first arrived at Beckhampton. He failed to win at two and Darling was requested to find a purchaser for him. He bought the colt himself for £500. During the winter Pont l'Évêque made notable physical improvement and on his first appearance, at Newbury in the spring, he won with the utmost ease. Darling then sent a cable to Mr Morriss, who was in the Far East, offering him a half share for £2,500. Perhaps not altogether surprisingly, he did not receive a reply. After being beaten in The Newmarket Stakes, Pont l'Évêque won a minor race at Salisbury. In The Derby, ridden by Sam Wragg, he started at 10/1 and won by three lengths from Turkhan. In his only other race, the Champion Stakes, he finished third behind Stardust, subsequently disqualified, and Hippius. In 1942 he was exported to Argentina where he made no great mark as a sire.

The Derby, what with the special trains and the long stream of cars and coaches, aroused a suspicion in some minds that the nation as a whole was not treating the war with the seriousness it unfortunately deserved. Inevitably questions were asked in the House of Commons, one being 'whether the Home Secretary would take steps to avoid the squandering of war resources by prohibiting motor-coach tours, horse racing and hunting'. However, on June 19 the Stewards of the Jockey Club announced, none too soon, that there would be no more racing until further notice. In view of the frighteningly critical situation the decision was clearly the right one, but it left people professionally engaged in racing in a condition of complete uncertainty with regard to the future.

Meanwhile the Aga Khan had incurred the displeasure of British breeders by selling his Derby winners Blenheim, Bahram and Mahmoud for export to America. It was rumoured that he took a somewhat disenchanted view as to the probable outcome of the war. During his racing career he had the felicity of seeing his colours carried five times to victory in The Derby. Not one of these five winners ever ran as a four-year-old and all were eventually sold. Blenheim and Mahmoud were both extremely successful in America. The Aga Khan had more than once declared that never, never would he part with Bahram. However, he did not take much persuading when an American syndicate offered him £40,000. Unfortunately Bahram was not in good health when he landed in America and breeders there never took to him. In 1946 he was sent to Argentina where he died ten years later. In England his best winners were Big Game (Two Thousand Guineas); Turkhan (St Leger); and Persian Gulf (Coronation Cup; sire of the 1959 Derby winner

7–8.   During World War II The Derby was run at Newmarket. (**Above**) 1940, Pont L'Évêque leading the field at the distance, watched by Army and Air Force men. (**Below**) 1941, runners leaving the saddling ring to go to the start

Parthia). In selling Blenheim, Mahmoud and Bahram, the Aga Khan certainly dealt the British bloodstock industry a damaging blow.

As regards the Aga Khan's two post-war Derby winners, My Love, after five stud seasons in France, was exported to Argentina where he was not a success. Tulyar was sold for approximately £250,000 to the Irish National Stud. In 1956 the Irish National Stud passed him on to an American syndicate. His career as a stallion in the United States was checked by a grave illness and he never fulfilled expectations there.

From June 1940 until victory was virtually assured, there was a good deal of opposition to the continuance of racing even on a very limited scale. The Jockey Club, therefore, was faced with the tricky task of keeping the pulse of the sport beating without incurring criticism for impeding the war effort. The Times, having given up its role of leading appeaser, was in bellicose mood and published a stream of letters demanding the cessation of racing 'for the duration', while a leading article warned of 'widespread resentment' if racing were resumed. There were some admirable replies giving the opposite point of view, notably from the veteran trainer the Hon. George Lambton and from Lord Ilchester, who had just given up being Senior Steward and was a man who combined intelligence with tact.

The Times would not let the matter rest and correspondence condemning racing reappeared in 1941. Members of Parliament applied pressure, too, and one importunate individual was eventually informed that if all the oats provided for racehorses were given to poultry instead the saving would provide one egg per head of the population once every four years. Mr Emmanuel Shinwell M.P. (later Lord Shinwell), still at an early stage on the path leading from middle-aged *enfant terrible* of the left to respected elder statesman, described racing as 'an insane and unseemly spectacle'. An element of class resentment began to creep in. People who saw nothing wrong in big crowds at football matches and dog racing, had the strongest objection to anyone going to a race meeting, racing in their eyes being the pastime of the rich.

The Stewards of the Jockey Club did their utmost to persuade owners to get rid of moderate animals, particularly geldings, while agreement was reached with the Ministry of Agriculture to reduce the number of brood mares after the next covering season by twenty-five per cent. Despite the difficulties encountered and continued opposition, it remained just possible to keep racing ticking over, thanks in no small measure to the two joint Parliamentary Secretaries to the Ministry of Agriculture, the Duke of Norfolk and Mr Tom Williams M.P., who became Labour's Minister of Agriculture in the 1945 government.

Racing in 1940 had been resumed at Ripon on September 14. The war-substitute St Leger, though, did not take place till November 23. Named The Yorkshire St Leger and run at Thirsk, it was won by the Aga Khan's Turkhan from his stable-companion Stardust, who started favourite. Turkhan subsequently made quite a name for himself as a sire of brood mares.

The inevitable slump in bloodstock was illustrated with painful clarity at Tattersalls' October Sales at Newmarket. The Sales lasted two days and the total turnover was 7,596 guineas. The turnover for the December Sales was 75,008 guineas, more than half of this coming from the dispersal of all the late Sir Abe Bailey's bloodstock with the exception of old Son-in-Law who had won the Cesarewitch during the previous war.

It was becoming increasingly difficult to make hard and fast plans for the future and the Jockey Club modified the Rules as follows:

Every race closing after November 1st 1940 may be ordered to be run:
(a) On any course selected by the Stewards of the Jockey Club.
(b) On any date subsequent to and within 28 days of the advertised date.

On December 9 the Stewards of the Jockey Club ordered the abandonment of all fixtures arranged for 1941, and of all races that had closed for that year. Particulars were also announced of the five substitute classics and other important races for 1941. These were all to close on January 14.

In 1941 the war became a world-wide conflict which looked likely to go on for several years. Victories for British arms were depressingly rare and the shipping situation was becoming extremely grave. Nevertheless racing, albeit on a reduced scale, was carried on without a break. Some thought this was in the tradition of Sir Francis Drake before the Armada; others were inclined to take a less charitable view.

A return made to Weatherbys in July showed there were 5,985 stallions, mares, yearlings and foals on stud farms. There were about 1,500 horses in training for the flat, 700 for jumping. The total number of horses in training in 1939 had been just short of 4,000. Till the middle of 1941 it was still possible to export horses to many countries abroad. Trainers found life becoming less agreeable and there was an inconvenient shortage of stable labour. At Newmarket, Fred Wood, who had ridden a Cesarewitch winner during the reign of Queen Victoria, began riding work again, while Jack Jarvis was happy to employ the lad who had looked after Cyllene, winner of The Gold Cup and sire of four Derby winners, forty-two years previously. A lone German bomber dropped eight bombs on Newmarket in daylight, causing a number of deaths and demolishing The White Hart. The Jockey Club decided that the time was opportune to look ahead and set up a committee to look into the whole future of racing with particular attention to the encouragement of owners, combined with the greater comfort and convenience of the racegoing public. Known as the Racing Reorganisation Committee, it consisted of Lord Ilchester, who acted as Chairman; the Duke of Norfolk, who had narrowly escaped capture at Dunkirk while serving with the Royal Sussex Regiment; Viscount Portal; Lord Harewood; and Sir Humphrey de Trafford.

The two-day National Hunt Meeting at Cheltenham was well attended but there was no Grand National. The flat made its traditional start at Lincoln where the Clerk of the Course, Captain Malcolm Hancock, wore Coldstream Guards uniform. By April plans to run The Derby and The Oaks at Newbury had to be given up, both races being transferred to Newmarket. Certain races normally run at Royal

Ascot—The St James's Palace Stakes, The Coventry Stakes, The Queen Mary Stakes and The Gold Cup—were moved to Newmarket as well. News from the Middle East indicated that Bruce Hobbs, later awarded the M.C., had added to his riding triumphs by winning the Palestine Grand National at Tel Aviv.

The Derby was won by the Hon. Mrs Macdonald-Buchanan's Owen Tudor, by Hyperion. Bred by his owner, whose father, Lord Woolavington, won The Derby with Captain Cuttle and Coronach, and trained by Fred Darling, Owen Tudor was hardly famed for consistency but was a very good horse on his day and other successes included the Newmarket St Leger and a war-substitute Gold Cup run at Newmarket. He was admirably ridden in The Derby by Private W. Nevett of the Royal Army Ordnance Corps. As a sire, too, Owen Tudor tended to be inconsistent but he got a number of top-class winners and his versatility was undeniable. Among his offspring were Abernant, one of the outstanding sprinters of this century; Tudor Minstrel, a horse of exceptional brilliance up to a mile; Right Royal V, who won the Prix du Jockey Club and then cut the dual classic winner St Paddy down to size in The King George VI and Queen Elizabeth Stakes; and Elpenor, who not only won The Ascot Gold Cup for M. Boussac, but also the Prix du Cadran, its French equivalent.

Owen Tudor was Darling's seventh and last Derby winner. Darling also trained the 1941 Oaks winner, Commotion, by Mieuxcé out of Riot, a half-sister to Fair Trial by Colorado and thus a descendant of the famous Lady Josephine. Commotion did well as a brood mare. Among her eight winners were Combat, unbeaten in nine races and sire of Aggressor, who defeated Petite Étoile in The King George VI and Queen Elizabeth Stakes; Faux Tirage, a full brother to Combat, whose five victories included The St James's Palace Stakes and who did well as a sire in New Zealand; and Aristophanes, a son of Hyperion who won eight races and was sold for 22,000 guineas to go to Argentina, where he sired that highly successful stallion Forli.

The 2nd Duke of Westminster had enjoyed his first classic success in 1906 when the Kingsclere-trained Troutbeck won The St Leger ridden by George Stern, who rode a deplorably rough race and was lucky not to earn disqualification. The Duke's second and last classic victory came in 1941 when his Fair Trial colt Lambert Simnel, trained by Fred Templeman, won The Two Thousand Guineas. Lambert Simnel was a substandard winner of that race. The St Leger, run at Manchester, went to Lord Portal's Sun Castle trained by Boyd-Rochfort and ridden by George Bridgland. Bridgland, born in France of English parents, had sought refuge in England on the collapse of France. Sun Castle died in 1942 before he could take up stud duties. The One Thousand Guineas provided a final classic winner for Lord Glanely in the form of Dancing Time, a filly by Colombo. Trained by Basil Jarvis, Dancing Time stayed well and finished close up third in The St Leger.

The following year Lord Glanely was killed in an air raid. He was in his seventy-fifth year. Born William James Tatem at Appledore in Devonshire—the names of many of his horses bore West Country associations—his origins were rather different from those of most members of the Jockey Club, to which he was elected in 1929. By a combination of shrewdness and sheer hard work, he made a fortune in the shipping business. His first interest in horses lay with show hunters and hackneys; in due course he transferred his enthusiasm to racing and became an increasingly lavish patron of the turf. He was a breeder on a large scale and in addition during his life he spent a vast amount of money on yearlings. At the Sales he used to bid himself from the gateway and once he got started he was rarely vanquished. In 1919, when Frank Barling was his trainer, he won The Derby with Grand Parade and seven races at Royal Ascot. For many years his trainer was Captain Thomas Hogg who won for him The Two Thousand Guineas with Colombo, The Oaks with Rose of England, and The St Leger with Singapore and Chulmleigh.

An intensely patriotic man—his colours typically included a red, white and blue sash—and at heart an extremely kind and charitable one, Lord Glanely was affectionately known on the racecourse as 'Old Guts and Gaiters'. He was certainly easy to recognise with his portly figure, rubicund features, walrus moustache and large buttonhole. In the summer he was apt to favour white ducks and a panama hat. 'Which end would you like to bowl, my lord?' asked Major Gerald Deane politely from the rostrum as Lord Glanely approached the sale-ring one sultry evening at Newmarket. In 1933 Lord Glanely, always a man of great determination, earned the gratitude of bloodstock breeders for his successful appeal to the House of Lords concerning the taxation of stallion fees.

With the exception of Colombo, who was acquired privately by a syndicate of breeders, all Lord Glanely's horses were sold by auction before the year was out. A total of 135,570 guineas was realised. The top price was 17,000 guineas for Olein, a mare in foal to Hyperion. Dancing Time was bought for the Brownstown Stud in Ireland for 4,600 guineas. No one was keen to buy the stallions. Chulmleigh went for 2,500 guineas, the Gold Cup winner Tiberius for 1,050, Singapore for 500 and Navigator, winner of the Stewards' Cup, for 70 guineas.

At least until the autumn, 1942 was a terrible year for the allied cause with disaster following upon humiliating disaster. The shipping situation was appalling and ultimate victory, if attainable at all, looked a depressingly long way distant. Under the circumstances it is not surprising that the continuance of racing hung upon an extremely slender thread.

On March 12 the Racing Calendar announced plans for racing to be conducted on a regional basis. The only courses permitted to stage racing were Newmarket, Salisbury, Windsor, Pontefract and Stockton. To save travelling, Newmarket-trained horses could run only at Newmarket. Northern horses were allowed to race only at Stockton and Pontefract, while those trained south of the Trent, Newmarket excluded, were confined to Salisbury and Windsor. To reduce the number of horses in training, handicaps were barred for horses aged five years or older. Furthermore, there was to be no racing at all under National Hunt Rules in 1942–3.

More and more training establishments were closed down and the Arundel Castle stables, destined to play an ever-increasing part in the sport, came into being when those at Michel Grove ceased to function. In general race meetings were still well attended. Racegoers, though, had to be prepared to put up with inconveniences. At Newmarket, for example, there were no buses and taxis, and racegoers had to walk to the July Course and back again afterwards. Enviable indeed was the position of the starter who rode on his grey cob from the town to the racecourse.

As regards the horses, 1942 is chiefly remembered for two three-year-olds that carried the royal colours, Big Game and Sun Chariot. Both had been bred by the National Stud, were leased for racing to King George VI, and were trained by Fred Darling. Between them they won all the classic races bar The Derby.

Big Game was a big, handsome, strongly made bay by Bahram out of the brilliant Myrobella, by Tetratema. At two he won all his five races. He won the five-furlongs Coventry Stakes, run over the Chesterfield Course at Newmarket, by four lengths from Lord Derby's Watling Street. There was, however, only a short head between them at the conclusion of the six-furlongs Champagne Stakes at Newbury, a result that raised certain doubts on the score of the winner's stamina.

In 1942 Big Game, who had wintered exceptionally well, won his preliminary race at Salisbury ridden by Gordon Richards, fully recovered from a nasty accident at Salisbury the previous May. He started at 11/8 on for The Two Thousand Guineas and won with ease by four lengths from Watling Street.

Big Game looked a picture in the paddock before The Derby, for which he was favourite at 6/4 on. Meyrick Good of the Sporting Life, an excellent judge of a horse, wrote: 'I have seen every Derby candidate for forty-four years and never have I beheld a three year old of such strength and maturity.' Alas, Big Game ran all too freely, Richards being quite unable to settle him down. He was in front two furlongs from home but he was tiring and in the end he was only fourth behind Watling Street, Hyperides and Ujiji. His failure was all the more disappointing as the King, in uniform, and the Queen had come to see him run. In the autumn he concluded his racing career by winning the ten-furlongs Champion Stakes.

As a sire Big Game was not quite the success anticipated. His colts were apt to be heavy-topped and not easy to train, particularly when the ground was on the firm side. His fillies were more successful than his colts and included Queenpot (One Thousand Guineas) and Ambiguity (Oaks and Jockey Club Cup).

Watling Street was bred by his owner, whose third Derby winner he was. He was a rangy bay by Fairway out of Ranai, a Rabelais mare who also bred Garden Path, a sister to Watling Street that won the 1944 Two Thousand Guineas. Harry Wragg, most thoughtful of jockeys, had ridden Big Game the previous season after Richards had been injured and had no faith in Big Game's stamina. He was confident that if he rode a waiting race on Watling Street, tactics at which he excelled, Watling Street's superior stamina would prove the decisive factor in the closing stages.

Wragg's timing had to be carefully adjusted as Watling Street was highly strung and might well have resented a prolonged struggle under the whip.

Watling Street was no match for Sun Chariot in The St Leger and was retired to the stud at the end of the season. He was not a success as a sire, too many of his offspring being distinctly temperamental. In 1952 he was exported to America where he died soon afterwards.

Trainer of Watling Street was the genial and highly competent Walter Earl. Born in what used to be called Bohemia, his father being for over forty years a trainer in Austria-Hungary, he was sent to England as a boy and apprenticed to Willie Waugh at Kingsclere. He rode his first winner in 1906 at Goodwood. He soon became too heavy for the flat and for some years rode with success under National Hunt Rules. He began training in 1920 and eventually succeeded Colledge Leader as Lord Derby's trainer. No doubt he found Lord Derby a bit different from previous patrons such as Mr Bob Sievier and Mr 'Solly' Joel.

Sun Chariot, for sheer racing ability, was worthy to be ranked with great fillies such as Pretty Polly, Sceptre and Meld. She had a will of her own, though, and could at times be very difficult indeed. Sir Gordon Richards had this to say of her: 'She was a machine and what a character! I've a few grey hairs and she gave them to me. She was probably the greatest racehorse I've ever been across. You never knew what she would do. In The Oaks she let them go a furlong at the start; then decided to go after them and won in a canter. In The St Leger she made a hack of the Derby winner. She was only defeated once but should never have been beaten.'[1]

Sun Chariot was a long, low, brown filly of beautiful quality, and standing 15.2¼ hands, by Hyperion out of Clarence, by Diligence out of Nun's Veil, by Friar Marcus. Clarence never ran and was covered at three by Diligence (by Hurry On), a moderate sire that ended his days in Russia. Diligence had a full brother called Feridoon who, together with another National Stud yearling, was sold privately to the Aga Khan, the price for the pair being £20,000. Feridoon's share in the transaction was £17,000, a huge sum for a yearling in those days. As a racehorse Feridoon was a lamentable failure and was eventually sold in France for the equivalent of £17. His name had been long forgotten in this country when it appeared in the pedigree of that great French racehorse Tantième. Diligence and Feridoon were members of the Cheshire Cat family that had earned a reputation for bloody-mindedness. Clarence also bred Calash and Sister Clara. Calash, a sister of Sun Chariot, was dam of the Oaks winner Carrozza; Sister Clara was dam of the Derby winner Santa Claus.

On arrival at Beckhampton Sun Chariot gave scant indication of promise and in fact Darling made arrangements for her to be returned to the National Stud which at that date was still in Ireland. By sheer good fortune a delay occurred in securing the required export licence. A day or two before the licence turned up, Sun Chariot for the first time pleased her exacting trainer by the manner in which she worked. Plans were swiftly changed. On June 6, ridden by Wragg as Richards

---

[1] Comments made by Sir Gordon Richards to Mr Eric Rickman for inclusion in the latter's book *Come Racing With Me*.

was *hors de combat*, she took the field in the five-furlongs Acorn Plate at Newbury and won with ease.

She then won The Queen Mary Stakes at Newmarket and The Amesbury Stakes at Salisbury, the former only by a head as she came down the hill very badly. In the autumn Darling felt sufficient confidence in her ability to take on the colts in The Middle Park Stakes, a race that had not been won by a filly since the victory of Golden Corn in 1921. Sun Chariot won without the slightest difficulty by three lengths from Ujiji with Gold Nib third. Watling Street had probably not recovered from his tough battle against Big Game in The Champagne Stakes. He sweated up beforehand and was only fourth. In The Free Handicap Sun Chariot and Big Game both received 9 st. 7 lb. Next came Watling Street with 9 st. 2 lb.

In her first race as a three-year-old, the six-furlongs Southern Stakes at Salisbury on April 25, Sun Chariot met with the one defeat of her career. She simply declined to co-operate and dead-heated for third place behind Ujiji and Mehrali. On May 2 she went to Salisbury again, this time for the seven-furlongs Sarum Stakes. She duly won but her conduct was by no means exemplary. She was reluctant to go down to the post and in addition gave Richards uncomfortable moments in the race itself.

Despite her unreliable temperament, she was a hot favourite for The One Thousand Guineas. She was inclined to play up at the start but was well enough away in the end. Richards had a tight hold of her head and kept her completely under control for as long as he wanted. Close home he asked her to go and she at once accelerated to win easily from Perfect Peace and Light of Day in a time slightly faster than that taken by Big Game the previous day in similar conditions.

Though temperamental, Sun Chariot was tough, tougher by far than Big Game who could not stand up to nearly as much hard work and in fact was very tenderly treated by Darling at home. On no occasion were the filly and the colt worked together. Sun Chariot possessed no undue respect for royalty. The King and Queen came down to Beckhampton to see the horses work. Sun Chariot was in one of her less tractable moods. She refused to start and when Richards gave her a tap with his whip she bolted into a ploughed field, went down on her knees and roared like a bull from sheer temper. It was anything but a happy morning for all concerned.

In The Oaks Sun Chariot started at 4/1 on. She gave trouble at the start and ruined three attempts by the starter to get them off. When the gate did go up, she darted away to the left and by the time her opponents had gone a furlong, she herself had covered about fifty yards. The situation then looked bleak, to say the least, as far as she was concerned but suddenly she straightened herself out and began to run on. She did not help her cause by running wide at the entrance of the straight but from that point, with Richards sitting quite still and doing nothing to upset her, she began to make up ground with extraordinary rapidity. Approaching the final furlong she headed the leader, Lord Rosebery's Afterthought, and looked sure to win easily. At that point, though, she decided she had had sufficient exertion for one day and in the end Richards had to ride her out to beat Afterthought by a length. The King, in R.A.F. uniform, led her in.

Sun Chariot's final appearance was in The St Leger. She took on Watling Street, Hyperides and Ujiji, first, second and third respectively in The Derby, and treated them as if they were the humblest of selling platers. The Newmarket crowd gave her a wonderful reception.

At the stud Sun Chariot never bred a colt or a filly anything like as good as herself but her stud career was by no means a total failure. She was barren three times, slipped her foal three times, and had a colt that died young. Of her eleven surviving foals, ten ran and seven were winners, gaining eighteen victories between them. Blue Train, by Blue Peter, won all his three races and was potentially a high-class horse but because of a ring-bone he was not a sound one. Gigantic, by Big Game, won The Imperial Produce Stakes at Kempton and did well as a sire in New Zealand. Landau, by Dante, won The Sussex Stakes at Goodwood and The Rous Memorial Stakes at Royal Ascot; he sired plenty of winners in Australia. Pindari, by Pinza, was third in The St Leger and won The Solario, Craven, King Edward VII and The Great Voltigeur Stakes.

3

BY 1943 the tide had at long last begun to turn in favour of the Allies even though little hope existed of the war drawing to a speedy conclusion. Racing was still on a very restricted scale but Ascot was added to the list of courses where sport was permitted. Attendances at race meetings tended to be large even though there was a desperate shortage of transport, and often a good deal of pluck and perseverance was required from racegoers to get to the course. With the improvement in the war situation the bloodstock market began to pick up and in particular there were good prices for foals. Lord Sefton's term of office as Senior Steward was extended to cover a third year. The dearth of labour in stables grew ever more acute and veterans who were riding work included Mr Percy Whitaker who had ridden in The Grand National as far back as 1906. Captain Cecil Boyd-Rochfort became trainer to the King following the death of William Jarvis after an operation. Notable turf figures who died during the year included the Duke of Portland, who had owned the mighty St Simon as well as the Derby winners Donovan and Ayrshire; and Alec Taylor of Manton, one of the most distinguished of trainers. A link with the past vanished with the death of Mrs Julia Tunbridge at the age of 102. She was a granddaughter of Sam Arnull who won the first Derby on Sir Charles Bunbury's Diomed in 1780.

The Jockey Club committee set up in 1941 to inquire into the whole future of racing finally concluded its labours and presented its report. It had certainly taken a long time to complete it but the report was nothing if not thorough. Detailed evidence had been taken from every organised body connected with the sport and from many individuals as well. Moreover, the members of the committee could hardly have been expected to devote their entire time to racing's problems while the war was at its very peak.

By and large the report was well received. There was not the slightest sign in it of a desire to cling to the past or a reluctance to accept some radical changes. A true sense of responsibility was shown not merely to racing but to the racing public as well. The report comprised five separate sections: (a) The Owner; (b) The Breeder; (c) The Public; (d) The Racecourse Executives; and (e) The Horse. Under each section faults and weaknesses were pointed out and recommendations made for improvements.

The committee certainly did not dodge disturbing facts. For example, the report stated:

> There is little doubt that in attractiveness, from the point of view of the general public, as distinct from the regular racegoer, racing in England has fallen far behind that in other countries, in which it is of far more recent origin. Racecourse Executives, with few exceptions, have shown little disposition to cater for the individual—man or woman—outside the fringe of those directly concerned with the business of racing. Yet from this reservoir must be drawn the increased attendances which we seek, for from it must come a large part of the new money required to bring about the improvements which are called for, particularly during the early years of reorganization.
>
> It may be urged that the alterations needed to bring the majority of the existing racecourses up to the necessary standard would constitute drastic innovations in a country tenacious of its traditions and essentially conservative in its outlook. This may be so; but we would urge that now is the time when changes will be most easily effected. Yet we realize that there are racecourses where some of the alterations may be impracticable; further, that the circumstances vary in the case of different racecourses, and that any attempt at complete standardization is undesirable.

It was all too true that little thought had been expended in the past on the needs and comfort of the average racegoer. In particular no attempt had been made to render the various enclosures, other than the members', acceptable to women. In the members' enclosure, women usually formed a high percentage of those present. The percentage dropped steeply in the other enclosures and there were very few women indeed in the Silver Ring. What was there to attract them? They were barred from the paddock and thus had no sight of the horses or, what was possibly more important to them, of the leading personalities in the sport. Catering and lavatory facilities were too often verging on the primitive. There was nothing to do between races but watch the bookmakers altering the prices on their boards. Certain cheap enclosures looked less like a place of entertainment than a collecting cage for prisoners of war.

Even after World War II, when social and class distinctions were becoming blurred if not actually erased, there were courses, not invariably major ones, that put up ludicrous barriers against individuals wanting a day badge for the members' enclosure. Many people naturally resented having to queue up to fill in a card demanding the name of their club or their regiment. This boring practice did not even possess the virtue of being effective. One Londoner from the south side of the Thames and of not totally unblemished reputation invariably obtained admission by declaring himself 'President of Boodles'. The Jockey Club itself set a lamentable example and that important word 'welcome' was certainly not written on the mat at the entrance to the Rowley Mile and the July Courses. Little was done to gratify owners or to make them wish to run their horses there again. Quite to the contrary in fact. A member of the Private Stand at Newmarket who wished to obtain a day badge for a friend had to have the friend's voucher backed first by a member of the Jockey Club, a tiresome and idiotic procedure. The time was to come, though, when the sheer need to attract customers compelled Newmarket to play a very different tune. It is only fair to say that the take-it-or-leave-it attitude that caused many potential racegoers to prefer to leave it has entirely vanished. An entirely different and much pleasanter spirit exists and there is now no course in the country, and rightly so, more solicitous of the needs of the average racegoer.

At some important courses, one being Goodwood, there is no longer a members' enclosure. Some reckon this an improvement, others the reverse. Among those holding the latter view can be included an elderly owner who, expostulating mildly with a racegoer who had trodden heavily but without apology on his goutier foot, received as reply two orange pips spat with unerring accuracy into his left eye.

The Reorganisation Committee stated clearly that some courses were no longer required and ought to be abolished forthwith. That desirable outcome did not immediately take place but since then a number of courses, one or two regrettably, have vanished from the fixture list. Those where flat-racing took place were Alexandra Park, Birmingham, Bogside, Hurst Park, Lewes, Lincoln and Manchester. Edinburgh looked a 'goner' at one stage but was rescued at the eleventh hour, chiefly through the determined resistance offered by Lord Rosebery. Worcester has survived as a jumping course but there is no longer any flat-racing there.

At the time of the report the only racecourses in the country that were being conducted on a non-dividend basis were Ascot, Newmarket, Salisbury, Stockton and York. The report stated:

It is obvious that the ideal is the racecourse which has no equity shareholders to consider and where the whole of the revenue, subject to fixed charges in respect of borrowed money, is available to be put back into racing. We feel that something can be arranged on those lines for the attainment of our objects. We seek to acquire on fair terms the control of a selected number of racecourses which would be taken over. We have examined the organization which would be necessary to operate such an undertaking, and are perfectly satisfied that it will fit readily into the present system of horse-racing.

What was visualised, in short, was that the Jockey Club should form a trust to enable them to purchase a number of racecourses which would then be run for the good of racing as a whole rather than for the financial benefit of directors and shareholders. Lord Rosebery, with Lord Zetland seconding, proposed that measures should be taken to put this important suggestion into force. It was a step forward that would surely have been for the good of racing. Furthermore it would have obviated the danger, that appeared later, of the bulk of the shares in a racecourse company being acquired by individuals with not the slightest concern for racing but intent on 'developing' the land to the maximum financial advantage. Hurst Park, a favourite racecourse with many Londoners, was 'developed' and Sandown had a narrowish squeak from suffering a similar fate, apart from being placed in peril by plans to drive a new road slap through it.

The danger to certain racecourses came with the ever-increasing demand for land to build on in urban or semi-urban areas, together with the changing habits of racegoers in the post-war era. In the past it had been generally accepted that it was desirable for a racecourse to be situated close to a large town or at least within easy reach of a main-line railway station. Gradually, though, more and more racegoers travelled by car and they tended to prefer for their day's outing a course in pleasant rural surroundings. Thus courses like Birmingham and Manchester gradually lost their former appeal.

It came as a bitter disappointment in 1944 when the Stewards of the Jockey Club announced that they had approved in principle a scheme by which offers could be made to convert the shares of certain racecourse companies into fixed interest bearing securities but the Treasury, for reasons of financial policy, had refused permission for those offers to be made although the scheme could be implemented as soon as the government's control of capital issues was relaxed.

If the programme of reforms suggested in the report had actually been carried through, this could have been the Jockey Club's finest hour. Alas, the spirit of change that had budded in so promising a fashion gradually withered away and it was not long before a policy of wait-and-see—or, indeed, of downright apathy—reigned supreme. Of course there were very real difficulties to be faced. Money was always a problem and in addition during the austere post-war regime of the Labour Government almost any project of significance was faced by a forbidding list of barriers and restrictions. Moreover, there being little else to spend money on, there was a big boom in racing and gambling, just as there had been after World War I. In the euphoria of the moment a complacency was induced that refused to face up to the problems that would have to be confronted once the boom was over.

The three-year-olds were by no means outstanding in 1943. It could be argued that the pick of them was Lord Derby's Herringbone, bred by her owner and trained by Walter Earl. A strongly made, plainish bay, she was by Blenheim's half-brother King Salmon, exported in 1943 to Brazil, out of Schiaparelli, winner of ten races, by the Swynford horse Schiavoni, who had failed to win until he was four. Herringbone won The One Thousand Guineas by a neck from Ribbon. In The Oaks she was only fourth behind Why Hurry, a Precipitation filly trained by Noel Cannon for Mr J. V. Rank, Ribbon and Tropical Sun. She won The St Leger, though, by a short head from Ribbon with The Derby winner Straight Deal three parts of a length away third. She bred eight winners including Entente Cordiale, a stayer that won a dozen races worth over £9,000.

The real heroine, though, among the fillies and a tremendous favourite with the racing public was Lord Rosebery's Ribbon, trained by Jack Jarvis. She was very small but neat, well-proportioned and full of quality. As a two-year-old she was beaten first time out but then won her next four races. In The Middle Park Stakes she took on the colts and beat them. In that race she had a gruelling battle with Nasrullah.

Ribbon never grew at all during the winter. She started off at three by winning The Upwell Stakes at Newmarket, Herringbone being third. In The One Thousand Guineas she ran a great race but Herringbone was just too good for her and beat her fairly and squarely by a neck. In The Oaks Ribbon was a desperately unlucky loser. As the tapes went up Noontide swerved right across her. Not only did Ribbon lose lengths but she was left facing the wrong way. The situation appeared hopeless but once she got going she made up ground steadily, and putting everything she had into her final effort, she only failed by a neck to beat Why Hurry, who had herself run a very game race.

In The St Leger, run on the July Course, Ribbon was equally unfortunate. She had a terribly rough passage and was bumped and barged all over the place. She refused to give in, though, and battled on with dauntless courage right to the end. Almost everyone on the course reckoned she had just got up to beat Herringbone but the one man whose opinion really mattered, Major Leslie Petch, the Judge, ruled that Herringbone had won by a short head. To the end of his life Jack Jarvis remained utterly convinced that Ribbon had been 'robbed'.

Lord Rosebery was very keen for Ribbon to conclude her career with a win so it was decided to run her in The Jockey Club Cup in October. At that period there was a mass of American Air Force stores parked on the Heath close to the Cambridge road. While being led down to the July Course, Ribbon was scared by a patrolling jeep. She whipped round, reared up and fell. She then galloped back to the town where she was caught. As her injuries appeared trivial and she seemed perfectly sound it was decided to allow her to take her chance. She proved quite incapable of producing her true form and finished unplaced.

Ribbon was by Fairway out of that good staying mare Bongrace, by Spion Kop, whose victories included the Doncaster and Jockey Club Cups. Unfortunately Ribbon proved a very disappointing brood mare.

The Two Thousand Guineas went to Mr A. E. Saunders's Kingsway, trained at Manton by Joe Lawson—he had originally been trained by Bill Smyth—and ridden by Sam Wragg. Bred by Lord Furness, he was a rich dark bay, full of quality, by Fairway, and Mr Saunders had bought him for 1,000 guineas. In The Guineas he just got home by inches from Captain A. Gillson's Pink Flower. It would have been a real romance of the turf if the dapper Pink Flower had won. Bred by Lord Astor, he was by the German sire Oleander and was the last foal of Plymstock, a notable brood mare whose offspring included the Oaks winner Pennycomequick. He was so weak and undersized as a foal that Lord Astor gave him away to Mr W. Holford. In January 1942 he was offered for sale at Newmarket and bought for 18 guineas on behalf of Sir Alec Black. On Derby day 1942 Sir Alec was taken ill in the paddock at Newmarket and died soon afterwards. All his horses were sold in September and Pink Flower, who had been trained by Reg Day and had run

9. Nasrullah being persuaded, with some difficulty, to go to the start for The Two Thousand Guineas in 1943

three times, was bought for 1,050 guineas by Harvey Leader on behalf of his friend Captain Gillson.

Favourite for The Two Thousand Guineas was the Aga Khan's Nasrullah, who finished fourth. Trained by Frank Butters, he was an exceptionally handsome bay colt by Nearco out of Mumtaz Mahal's daughter Mumtaz Begum, by Blenheim. At two he won The Coventry Stakes at Newmarket but went under by a neck to Ribbon in The Middle Park Stakes. He had a really hard race on that occasion and never forgot it, and it was probably unfortunate that he was never able to run anywhere else bar Newmarket. As a three-year-old he was difficult and self-willed. He began by winning a minor event at Newmarket but he gave a lot of trouble before he could be persuaded to go down to the start. In The Guineas he wore blinkers. He might well have won The Derby had he been thoroughly genuine. He ended his career by winning The Champion Stakes in faultless style from Kingsway.

When Nasrullah retired to the stud his reputation was such that there was no great demand for his services. In consequence in 1944 he was bought cheaply by the 'Nasrullah Syndicate', a small but select concern since it consisted solely of Mr G. McElligott and Mr Bert Kerr. The syndicate passed him on to Mr Joseph McGrath for 19,000 guineas.

Nasrullah turned out to be one of the greatest sires of this century, being champion both here and in America. His fee in Ireland soon rose to 500 guineas and in 1950 he was sold for $370,000 to an American syndicate headed by Mr A. B. Hancock. Before he crossed the Atlantic he had sired Musidora (One Thousand Guineas and Oaks), Belle of All (One Thousand Guineas), Nearula (Two Thousand Guineas), Never Say Die (Derby and St Leger), Nathoo (Irish Derby) and Nashua (Irish One Thousand Guineas). Other winners here included the sprinters Grey Sovereign and Princely Gift, both very successful sires, and Noor, who won four races worth £4,700 before being sent to America where he won eight races worth $348,740. In America Nasrullah's winners included Nashua (a colt) who won £1,225,565, Bold Ruler, a great American sire, Bald Eagle, twice winner of the Washington International, and Never Bend, sire of Mill Reef. Nasrullah was particularly successful with mares by Princequillo. He died in 1959.

In The Derby Miss Dorothy Paget's Straight Deal, trained at Epsom by Walter Nightingall, got up on the post to beat the Aga Khan's Umiddad with Nasrullah close up third. He was ridden by the thirty-seven-year-old Tommy Carey who had been the leading jockey under Pony Turf Club Rules up till the war. He won The Northolt Derby on several occasions, once on Miss Paget's Scottish Rifle. He received a licence to ride under the Rules of Racing in 1941. After the war he trained at Epsom. He was a very big gambler and for some time was remarkably successful but then the tide turned and he vanished completely from the racing scene, eventually ending his own life.

Straight Deal, bred by his owner, was by Solario out of Good Deal, by Apelle. He lived till 1968. Perhaps because of the unfashionable blood in the bottom half of his pedigree there was never an unseemly rush on the part of breeders to secure his services. He did, though, sire three good fillies in Ark Royal, Kerkeb and Above Board. Ark Royal won over £12,000 in stakes despite her ill luck in being a contemporary of the brilliant Meld. Kerkeb was second in The Oaks and would probably have won had her rider not made his effort far too soon. Above Board was an easy Cesarewitch winner in the royal colours.

It had been anticipated that there would be considerably more racing in 1944 than during the previous year, but actually the increase was trivial: sixty-eight days as opposed to sixty-seven. There were, though, eighty-five more races as owing to big entries, many events had to be divided. Some well-known trainers found themselves with greatly reduced strings and Harry Cottrill, whose Lambourn stable had dwindled away to five two-year-olds, decided to call it a day. National Hunt enthusiasts were delighted to hear that twenty-eight days of jumping would be permitted between December 26 and March 31. There had been no jumping at all since March 1942.

The Jockey Club handicapper, Mr Arthur Fawcett, retired and was succeeded by Mr Geoffrey Freer whose uncle, Mr T. F. Dawkins, had been a noted handicapper. Few people in the racing world were better liked or knew more about the sport in all its aspects than Geoffrey Freer. He was extremely shrewd, possessed a highly developed sense of the absurd and was famous as a raconteur. Quick to spot villainy on the turf, he could sometimes feel not wholly unsympathetic towards the perpetrators. Both as a handicapper and as a clerk of the course he was first rate. His admirable dictum was: 'Always remember that racing is meant to be fun.' He certainly lived up to it himself. He was made an honorary member of the Jockey Club in 1967.

Among the racing personalities who died in 1944 was the Earl of Lonsdale. With his distinctly individual clothes and his invariable cigar he was an easily recognisable figure as no doubt he intended to be. The public at any rate liked him and used to give him a cheer as he walked down the course to the paddock before The Derby. With jockeys he was a shade less popular owing to the long time he took in coming good with a promised present after a winner. This was probably due less to parsimony than the acute shortage of cash from which he suffered in the later stages of his life. Bobby Jones never got his present for riding Royal Lancer to victory in the 1922 St Leger.

It is seldom that The Two Thousand Guineas is won by a filly but Walter Earl judged Lord Derby's Garden Path good enough to do so and she justified his high opinion of her by winning by a head from Growing Confidence with the Aga Khan's Tehran third. A full sister to the 1942 Derby winner Watling Street, Garden Path started second favourite for The Derby but finished down the course. She was badly struck into and never raced again. She bred five winners of eleven races.

Rarely do both the owner and the trainer of a Derby winner miss seeing the race but that was the case with Ocean Swell. Lord Rosebery could not leave his duties in Scotland, while both Jack Jarvis and his wife were ill in bed at Park Lodge. Ocean Swell ran on with great determination to win by a neck from Tehran with Happy Landing close up third. He was the sixth Derby winner to have been bred at Mentmore. His sire Blue Peter and his dam Jiffy were both bred there too. He was a member of Blue Peter's first crop of runners.

Ocean Swell was a workmanlike bay who never carried much flesh. Slow to come to hand at two, he had shown promise in his final race, the six-furlongs Alington Plate at Newmarket in which he defeated Golden Cloud, later a fine sprinter, and Tehran. In The Two Thousand Guineas he was outpaced and was never a danger. He was ridden in The Derby by Nevett as the stable jockey Eph Smith had a chance of riding the favourite, Growing Confidence, and Lord Rosebery had given him permission to accept the mount. As it happened, Growing Confidence was in the end partnered by Ken Mullins, later a successful jump jockey, who had ridden him in The Guineas. The agreement with Nevett could not be altered so Smith obtained the ride on Tehran.

In one German prisoner-of-war camp for officers, letters from England had provided information about the likely runners for The Derby. On the departure of Captain Hector Christie, who subsequently trained the Cheltenham Gold Cup winner Fortina, for the austerities of Colditz, the position of leading camp bookmaker was taken over by James Marsham, now a stewards' secretary, and he decided to make a book on the race. The secret wireless set was taken from its hiding place and its operators listened to the B.B.C. commentary. The result gave no joy to the captive punters, not one of whom had supported Ocean Swell. True to the traditions of the bookmaking profession, Marsham stated that he had come out 'just about all square'. Some of the more po-faced inmates were not all that pleased to learn that the wireless set, normally only employed to hear news bulletins, had been used for such a trivial purpose. They would have been even less pleased had they known that a valve expired at the end of the broadcast and some rather tricky negotiations had to be concluded with a co-operative German corporal before it could be replaced and normal service resumed.

Ocean Swell's lead horse broke down some time before The St Leger, which was again run at Newmarket. In consequence his preparation fell short of what Jarvis had intended and he could only finish third behind Tehran and Borealis. Tehran, by Bois Roussel, had been bred by Prince Aly Khan and was leased for racing to the Aga Khan. As a sire Tehran proved inconsistent but he did get one really good horse in Tulyar, winner of the 1952 Derby and St Leger. He also sired a fine stayer in Raise You Ten, who won the Yorkshire, Goodwood and Doncaster Cups and would very likely have won The Ascot Gold Cup too had not that race been abandoned due to the waterlogged condition of the course.

Ocean Swell finished the season by winning The Jockey Club Cup, a victory that induced Lord Rosebery to keep him in training at four with The Ascot Gold Cup as his objective. At four Ocean Swell beat Borealis in The April Stakes at Newmarket but Borealis then beat him in both The Wood Ditton Stakes and The Coronation Cup. Though totally unsuited to the very firm ground, Tehran was favourite at 7/4 on for The Gold Cup. Borealis was second favourite and Ocean Swell was on offer at 6/1. Tehran led round the final bend but Ocean Swell produced the better speed in the straight and won by a length and a half. As a sire Ocean Swell was a failure. His offspring tended to inherit his distinctly plain looks but not, alas, his racing ability.

Jack Jarvis, knighted towards the end of his career for his services to racing, was a true professional and knew every aspect of his job. In particular he was a master at getting the very best out of the Mentmore-bred horses. Horses from his stable were trained to race rather than to delight the critics in the paddock and if they failed it was not from lack of fitness. Ocean Swell was trained to the minute for The Gold Cup but to some eyes he appeared to have had several gallops too many and to have run up distressingly light. As the horses were going down to the start a trainer, at that time concerned chiefly with jumpers, commented adversely in ringing tones on Ocean Swell's appearance. Unfortunately Jarvis overheard these observations and contained himself only with extreme difficulty. When Ocean Swell had passed the winning post Jarvis tapped the offender on the shoulder and remarked: 'I understand that you have twice trained the winner of a selling steeplechase at Newton Abbot. This happens to be my fourth Gold Cup.' He then strode off to receive Ocean Swell in the winner's enclosure.

Jack Jarvis's temper could be formidable but the explosions were of brief duration and he was too big a man to harbour grudges and resentments. Keen on almost every form of sport, particularly coursing, he was by nature an exceptionally generous, hospitable and kind-hearted man and many lame ducks at Newmarket had good cause to remember him with gratitude. He loved parties and was scornful of trainers who never celebrated after a big winner. Over money he was exceptionally shrewd and always declared with some satisfaction that he would have done even better as a stockbroker than as a trainer.

Mr Jim Joel, son of Mr J. B. Joel who won The Derby with Sunstar and Humorist, had his first classic success when Picture Play won The One Thousand Guineas in 1944. Picture Play came from a family that served the Joels well as she was descended from Absurdity, dam of The One Thousand Guineas and Oaks winner Jest, who bred Humorist. Sire of Picture Play was Blenheim's son Donatello II who had been imported from Italy. Donatello II was not such a consistent producer of winners as the Italian-bred Nearco but he exerted considerable influence all the same. His offspring included two great horses who both became very successful sires, Alycidon and Crepello. He also sired the dams of both Pinza and Aureole.

Picture Play's trainer was Jack Watts, a member of a famous racing family and a man of wide and varied experience. He himself trained a Derby winner, his son trained a classic winner and his grandson has trained a classic winner, too. He was the son of the famous jockey Jack Watts who rode four Derby winners, one of them being Persimmon. Jack Watts I died intestate at the age of forty-one. As the law then stood, Jack Watts II was entitled to all the bricks and mortar owned by his father, while the very large amount of cash was shared among the younger sons, none of whom came into racing. Jack Watts II certainly got the worst of the bargain. He rode with success for several years and one afternoon at Windsor he was on five of the six winners. He trained his first winner in 1907 and then had a spell training in Germany. He served in the war overseas with the Suffolk Yeomanry and then returned to Newmarket where he trained the 1927 Derby winner, Call Boy. In 1936 he went to France and for two years trained for M. Boussac. When war broke out he was private trainer in France to M. S. Vagliano. He came back to England on the collapse of France in 1940 and two years later took over Mr Joel's stable at Foxhill following the death of Charles Peck. He retired in 1952.

The Oaks was won by Mr William Woodward's Hycilla, a half-sister by Hyperion to Alcazar, winner of The Ebor Handicap and The Chesterfield and Doncaster Cups. She was trained by Captain Boyd-Rochfort and ridden by Bridgland. Bred in Ireland, Hycilla, a chestnut of exquisite quality, was not eligible for inclusion in the Stud Book under the rules then existing. The American-owned Cap and Bells II, winner of The Oaks in 1901, had also been barred from the Stud Book. Hycilla confirmed her excellence by winning The Champion Stakes in which her rivals included Borealis, Kingsway and Growing Confidence.

The Coronation Cup, run at Newmarket, was won by Lady Zia Wernher's four-year-old Persian Gulf who at last justified the faith his trainer Boyd-Rochfort had always had in him. Unfortunately, in his preparation for The Gold Cup, Persian Gulf cracked the lower end of the cannon bone of his left foreleg. He was a half-brother to the Gold Cup winner Precipitation, being by Bahram out of his owner's famous foundation mare Double Life, whose dam Saint Joan, after sojourns in Germany and India, returned to this country and changed hands for 35 guineas.

There was a terrific race for the substitute Gold Cup run at Newmarket, the Aga Khan's four-year-old Umiddad, by Dastur out of the Oaks winner Udaipur, winning by a head from the six-year-old mare Bright Lady, one of the few good performers sired by the 1932 Derby winner April the Fifth. Bright Lady became the dam of that fine stayer Gladness, who in 1958 won The Gold Cup, The Goodwood Cup and The Ebor Handicap with 9st. 7 lb.

4

THE war ended on May 8, 1945, the day The One Thousand Guineas was run. It had been touch and go at times but racing had survived. That it had done so reflected no little credit on the Jockey Club, whose job it had been to keep the sport just ticking over without affording valid grounds for criticism that the war effort was being impeded. Possibly the two men most largely responsible were Lord Sefton, Senior Steward for three vital years, and Sir Francis Weatherby, Secretary to the Jockey Club.

Hugh Molyneux, seventh and last Earl of Sefton, was an unusual and interesting character. Tall, handsome and extremely rich, he was a 'magnifico' who might have stepped from the pages of a novel by Whyte Melville. For some years he served in the Royal Horse Guards. He was a first-class heavy-weight to hounds, a famous Field Master of the Cottesmore and a brilliant shot. He loved coursing and owned Altcar where The Waterloo Cup is run. At one time he owned Aintree, where he was a steward for forty years, and lived to regret having sold it to Tophams. He did win The Waterloo Cup but he never succeeded in winning The Grand National although his favourite chaser, old Irish Lizard, was twice third. Always beautifully dressed, his demeanour verged on the haughty and those who did not know him well were inclined to rate him aloof, even arrogant. He himself rather enjoyed living up to the part and in consequence there were as many stories circulating about him as there are today about Lester Piggott, and the possibility is that some of them were true. At one of his clubs he had to share a table for luncheon with a young man who, having introduced himself and stated that he was in Lloyds, asked Lord Sefton 'what he did'. 'What do I do?' replied his lordship. 'My dear boy, you might as well ask a hottentot who his tailor is.' On one occasion he stayed in a fairly large and comfortable house for Salisbury races. As he left he observed to a fellow guest: 'Great fun, but I'm not really cut out for cottage life.'

Yet there was another side to his character. He was proud to be a Lancastrian, never shirked his many official duties in the county and was reckoned an outstandingly successful Mayor of Liverpool. He was intensely loyal to those who worked for him and was himself much liked in return. As a steward at a meeting he was highly efficient. Courteous, quick-thinking and above all fair, he had the confidence of trainers and jockeys. He was not particularly successful as an owner-breeder, partly because he was reluctant to get rid of even the most disappointing mares, and partly because he was unwilling to concede that Lancashire might not be the ideal county in which to breed bloodstock. Those who judged him to be an aristocrat of the type that was largely responsible for the French Revolution, did not know him well enough to appreciate his true ability or the good he did for racing and for Lancashire.

Sir Francis Weatherby M.C., known to his friends as 'Guggs', was one of racing's most able and devoted civil servants. In many ways typical of the better type of Wykehamist, he joined the family firm when he came down from Oxford and was Secretary to the Jockey Club from 1930 till his retirement in 1952. When World War II broke out he was in sole charge of the secretariat and for the next five years shouldered under testing conditions an immense burden of administrative duties. He was knighted in 1953.

There was racing over the Rowley Mile again in 1945 and other courses to reopen were Brighton, Catterick Bridge, Lanark, Redcar, Worcester and York. The Jockey Club pushed the boat out when the Rowley Mile was opened again and stood lunch to the racing press. Furthermore they appointed Mr J. H. Freeman, formerly sports editor of the Daily Mail, as their P.R.O. The appointment puzzled one or two of the more senior members of the Club who thought that public relations were something you got into trouble for doing in St James's Park after dark. Mr Freeman was also made P.R.O. to the National Hunt Committee and the Racecourse Betting Control Board. Regional racing was abolished and horses could run anywhere rather than being confined to tracks near the locality where they were trained. The Jockey Club abolished the pointless regulation which permitted two-year-olds to race unnamed. The bloodstock market began to boom and it created a sensation when the colt by Nearco out of Rosy Legend, and thus a full brother of the 1945 Derby winner Dante, was bought for 28,000 guineas. Unlike so many high-priced yearlings, this colt, who received the name of Sayajirao, proved a good horse and won The St Leger for his purchaser, the Maharaja of Baroda.

Two men famous in racing died in 1945, Stephen Donoghue and the Hon. George Lambton. Their backgrounds could hardly have been more different, Donoghue being the son of a hard-drinking steelworker in unlovely Warrington, while Lambton was the fifth son of the 2nd Earl of Durham. Donoghue, a great jockey, was the idol of the sporting public and the cry of 'Come on, Steve!' became a national catch-phrase. Endowed with beautiful hands and an iron nerve, he was at his best on a course such as Epsom. He rode six Derby winners though two of these were in war substitute races at Newmarket. His first winner was at a minor French course, Hyères, in 1904; his last mount was at Manchester in 1937. Not once during his entire riding career was he up in front of the stewards for an infringement of the Rules of Racing.

Donoghue had immense charm, of which he made ample use, and was generous to a fault. Over business and money matters, he was as feckless as a child. Habitu-

10.   Steve Donoghue—showing 'his long rein and wonderful hands'

ally unpunctual and not overscrupulous in keeping agreements or appointments, he eventually achieved a reputation for unreliability which cost him dearly during the later stages of his riding career. Never, though, did he lose the affection of the general public.

Lambton, like Donoghue, had an immense amount of charm. Good-looking, elegantly dressed in a dandyish sort of way and possessing perfect manners, he had friends in every section of the racing world and certainly no trainer could have had a more loyal and devoted staff. He was a beautiful rider and rode many winners both on the flat and over fences. When he fancied a horse he was riding, he betted heavily. He is one of the few amateurs to have ridden the winner of the Grand Steeplechase de Paris at Auteuil and on at least one occasion he was very unlucky not to have ridden the winner of The Grand National. After a crashing fall, he took up training at a time when 'gentlemen' trainers were few and far between. He made a success of it, the turning-point coming when he was asked to train the horses of the 16th Earl of Derby, after whose death he enjoyed a long and successful association with the 17th Earl. He loved and understood horses and never underestimated the value of patience. In all he trained thirteen classic winners, including the Derby winners Sansovino and Hyperion. He was a brilliant judge of a yearling and before the Aga Khan had established his own stud Lambton bought for him such good winners as Mumtaz Mahal, Cos, Teresina, Diophon and Salmon Trout. It is generally agreed that his autobiography *Men and Horses I Have Known* is just about the best book ever written about racing.

By far the best two-year-old in 1944 had been Dante, bred and owned by Sir Eric Ohlson and trained in Yorkshire by Matthew Peacock. He was an exceptionally handsome brown colt by the Italian-bred Grand Prix de Paris winner Nearco, by Pharos, out of Rosy Legend, by Dark Legend. Nearco had been imported into this country for £60,000 by the bookmaker Mr M. H. Benson, whose firm, Douglas Stuart, was well known for its motto of 'Duggie Never Owes' and for its advertisements depicting the betting misadventures of a group of feather-brained aristocrats who made a nonsense of the simplest wager but were always paid in full by Duggie in the end.

Dante ran six times as a two-year-old, winning all his races including The Coventry and The Middle Park Stakes. He was the idol of the north where what the French designate *un veritable crack* is somewhat rare. The following spring an immense crowd assembled at Stockton on April 7 to see him win a race of minor significance. Two days before The Two Thousand Guineas he received what was thought to be a minor eye injury but was in all probability the onset of the disease that eventually blinded him. He started a hot favourite for The Two Thousand but to the chagrin of his sanguine Yorkshire admirers he was beaten a neck by Lord Astor's Fair Trial colt, Court Martial, trained by Joe Lawson.

Neither colt ran again before The Derby, the last one to be run over the July Course which on this occasion proved inadequate for the purpose. The crowd was gigantic and there were long queues of cars stretched along the London road. The number of turnstiles was hopelessly insufficient and a good many people found their way in without the formality of paying. As the afternoon progressed, there was an ever-lengthening line under a fence in the paddock of individuals whose refreshment had been of a purely liquid character.

Ridden by Nevett, Dante won like a really good horse by two lengths from Midas with Court Martial third. He was the first Derby winner from the north since Pretender in 1868. There were high jinks in Yorkshire and the famous Bell at Middleham was tolled. A few days later Nevett was carried shoulder-high in triumph at a Dante Ball.

For some time afterwards Dante was odds-on favourite for The St Leger but then rumours to his disadvantage began to circulate. Peacock was harassed morning, noon and night by the press. On August 22 encouraging reports emanated from Middleham but on the 27th Dante was scratched from The St Leger. He was then retired to the stud where he became completely blind. The worries over Dante undoubtedly left their mark on Matt Peacock, the best type of Yorkshireman, forthright and occasionally blunt but very different from those bogus and easily dislikeable Yorkshire characters who regard courtesy and good manners as a

11.   Dante, W. Nevett up, being led in by Sir E. Ohlson after winning the 1945 Derby at Newmarket

mark of weakness. His comments were usually brief and to the point. 'Aye, he goes a bit,' he observed to a friend after Dante had won The Derby. As a sire Dante was a qualified success. A good many of his offspring were not entirely genuine but he got Darius (Two Thousand Guineas and Eclipse Stakes) and Carrozza (Oaks).

It has been noted that Dante was by an Italian-bred sire out of a French-bred mare. The time had arrived when it became increasingly rare for a top-class British-bred winner not to carry imported blood close up in its pedigree.

Midas never ran again after The Derby. He was an indifferent sire and was exported to America in 1956. In the autumn Court Martial won The Champion Stakes, beating M. M. Boussac's Priam II by a short head. Acquired by Mr Jim Joel for the stud, he proved an outstanding success and was twice champion before he was exported to America in 1958.

The St Leger was won by Chamossaire, bred by the National Stud, owned by Mr 'Solly' Joel's son, Squadron Leader Stanhope Joel, and trained by Dick Perryman who had given up riding after injuring his arm badly in a car accident. A big, strongly made chestnut, Chamossaire had a pedigree that combined stamina with brilliant speed as his sire was the Gold Cup winner Precipitation, while his dam, Snowberry, a half-sister to Big Game by Cameronian, was very fast and won The Queen Mary Stakes at Royal Ascot but did not stay an inch beyond five furlongs. As a yearling Chamossaire was bought for 2,700 guineas by Walter Earl acting on behalf of Squadron Leader Joel.

Chamossaire was a consistent and genuine performer that could have done with a bit more of his dam's speed. He was fourth in The Two Thousand Guineas and fourth in The Derby. In The St Leger, run at York, he won comfortably in the hands of Tommy Lowrey by two lengths from the King's Rising Light. He was second to Black Peter in The Jockey Club Stakes and second in The Jockey Club Cup to Lord Astor's Amber Flash, who became the dam of the Oaks winner, Ambiguity. As a sire Chamossaire had his ups and downs. In his old age he achieved the distinction of being champion thanks to his son Santa Claus who won The Derby and The Irish Sweeps Derby.

A fast three-year-old competing in 1945 was Sir John Jarvis's Royal Charger, trained by Jack Jarvis. He was by Nearco out of Sun Princess, a half-sister by Solario to Nasrullah. An extremely handsome and powerfully built chestnut, Royal Charger was very disappointing in his early days. He showed nothing at home and ran badly in his first race. The stable jockey Eph Smith said he was no good and Jack Jarvis advised Sir John to put the colt in the December Sales. Nevertheless, at the back of his mind Jack Jarvis could not help thinking that Royal Charger must be better than his performances indicated. Accordingly he ran him again and told Eph Smith to wake him up. This Smith omitted to do, saying it was pointless to hit a bad horse. Jarvis observed that 'his humanitarian instincts did him credit but it would have been better if he had obeyed my orders'. At the next Newmarket meeting there was a two-year-old event Jarvis expected to win with Lord Milford's Sun Honey who would be ridden by Smith. Jarvis also ran Royal Charger for whom a very strong rider, Bobby Jones, was engaged. In the early stages Royal Charger was a long way behind the leaders but then Jones got busy on him and Royal Charger quickened to such purpose that he finished less than two lengths behind Sun Honey, who won. He was at once withdrawn from the sale.

At three Royal Charger was third in The Two Thousand Guineas and won three nice races including The Challenge Stakes. At four he was even better, winning The Queen Anne Stakes at Royal Ascot and The Ayr Gold Cup with 9 st. 7 lb. on his back. Sir John Jarvis sold him for £80,000 to the Irish National Stud where he sired Happy Laughter (One Thousand Guineas), Gilles de Retz (Two Thousand Guineas) and Sea Charger (Irish Two Thousand Guineas and Irish St Leger). The Irish, with their curious habit of selling for export stallions that would be of the utmost benefit to their own breeding industry, sold Royal Charger to go to America for something like £200,000. There he got Turn-To, the best two-year-old in America in 1954 and grandsire of The Derby winners Sir Ivor and Roberto.

Jack Jarvis also trained the top sprinter of 1954, Lord Milford's Honeyway, by Fairway out of that fine brood mare Honey Buzzard. Honeyway raced till he was five and proved that he was more than a sprinter by winning The Champion Stakes. He in fact won over a mile and a half at Thirsk during his final season in training. Other successes during his career included The Victoria Cup with top weight, The Cork and Orrery Stakes, The July Cup and The King George Stakes at Goodwood.

At the close of his five-year-old season Honeyway was syndicated at a capitalised value of £72,000. It was a trifle unfortunate, therefore, that he happened to be a a double rig. Lord Milford, however, agreed to re-purchase any share in the syndicate from the original purchaser for £1,200 on or before June 30, 1948 if asked to do so. Honeyway covered a few mares but proved to be sterile so back he went into training again and won three more races. At the end of the season he returned to the stud but his testicles had not yet descended and his fertility remained a source of anxiety. He was withdrawn from his duties for treatment and returned, fully cured, in 1949. In 1953 he had a fertility percentage of 91·18. Among his winners was Great Nephew who lost The Two Thousand Guineas by inches and became the sire of the 1975 Derby winner, Grundy.

The 1945 One Thousand Guineas and The Oaks were both won by Lord Derby's Hyperion filly, Sun Steam, trained by Walter Earl. They were her owner's final successes in classic races. Hyperion was champion sire and was responsible for five of the top six two-year-olds in the Free Handicap.

Racing boomed in the immediate post-war years. This was largely because there was plenty of money about and very little to spend it on. Holidays abroad were not permitted; cars were virtually unattainable and in any case the petrol ration was meagre. Drink was scarce while clothes, household goods and so forth were either rationed or totally unobtainable. It was difficult to obtain a building permit or permission to decorate a house, however shabby it had become. The

Bloodstock Breeders' Review Volume XXXV stated: 'There have never been such crowds, such enthusiasm, such big fields, such prosperity, in the sales rings as well as in the stands and enclosures. The reason for it is probably to be found in the abundance of spending money, created by domestic economic conditions.'

The betting turnover was gigantic and at a course like Windsor there were bookmakers on the rails from one end to another whereas nowadays there may be less than ten. The volume of money in circulation was augmented by the huge profits from black market operations. Said a bookmaker at Newmarket in 1975: 'What we need for our business is another war and a flourishing black market.' It was an eldorado era for bookmakers with no levy to worry about, no betting tax and no need felt to sponsor races for the purpose of advertisement. It is sad to think that only a minute fraction of all money betted was ploughed back into racing for its general good.

A lot of new owners came into the game and some of them could hardly be described as an asset; very much the reverse in fact. The worst of them, though, did not stay long. There were rumours that doping was rife, both to improve a horse's chance or to reduce it. It is probable that a fair amount of effective 'nobbling' went on. Security measures were absurdly inadequate and the Jockey Club rules in respect of doping were primitive and capable of leading to grave injustice.

English-trained horses won all the classic races in 1946 but the year marked the start of an era when horses trained in France presented a continual threat in our major races. This became a cause for grave concern and rightly so. Between 1946 and 1966, both years inclusive, horses trained in France, but not all bred there, won The Two Thousand Guineas four times, The One Thousand Guineas six times, The Derby seven times, The Oaks seven times, The St Leger three times, The Coronation Cup eleven times, The Gold Cup nine times, The Hardwicke Stakes five times, The Eclipse Stakes seven times, The King George VI and Queen Elizabeth Stakes five times and The Champion Stakes nine times.

Most, but not all, of the French successes came in races of a mile and a quarter or more and the basic cause seemed to be the general structure of English racing. In this country, right from the very start of the season, there was a high proportion of events for two-year-olds. A lot of betting owners reckon a smart two-year-old the ideal medium for a gamble and the chief demand from commercial breeders was for quick-maturing types likely to win over five or six furlongs during their first season. Except in the case of potential classic colts and fillies, there has never been much demand for animals which, given plenty of time, are likely to make stayers.

In France, on the other hand, there has always been less emphasis on two-year-old racing and there are few opportunities for the older sprinters. Most of the big prizes are for horses capable of staying at the very least a mile and a quarter. Consequently there was a far higher proportion of stayers in France than over here and many more stoutly bred mares capable of producing a high-class mile-

and-a-half horse even when mated with a stallion incapable of staying that distance himself.

Eventually in 1960 the Jockey Club established a committee under Lord Rosebery to examine the effect that the Rules of Racing, as then existing, had on the production of middle-distance horses. The Jockey Club had been spurred into action by a short, red-bearded, articulate ex-schoolmaster, Mr. Philip Bull, who came into racing during the war with horses trained by Cyril Ray, a somewhat unlucky individual who fell foul of the authorities first as a jockey and later as a trainer. Mr Bull has undoubtedly left his mark on racing as breeder, owner, publicist, inventor of the 'Timeform' system and producer of an admirable racing annual that is of the greatest service to all professionally engaged in racing and to punters as well. Apart from which, Mr Bull, mildly radical in outlook, has never been adverse to sticking a sharp pin into the plump flesh of the 'establishment'. In this particular instance Mr Bull felt strongly, and rightly, that the Rules of Racing gave an undue advantage to precocious two-year-olds.

The report of Lord Rosebery's committee recommended an increase in the number of seven-furlongs and mile races for two-year-olds, and permission to stage seven-furlong races as from July 1, two months earlier than had previously been the case. Mr Bull himself initiated the one-mile Timeform Gold Cup, to be run at Doncaster in October, as the counterpart of France's one-mile Grand Criterium. That race, subsequently The Observer Gold Cup and now The William Hill Futurity Stakes, proved a success from the start.

For half a dozen years or so after the war European racing was dominated by M. Marcel Boussac, whose orange jacket and grey cap were certainly held in considerable awe in Britain. This great French industrialist had come into racing in 1918 when he bought all the bloodstock of Mr. H. B. Duryea who had won the 1914 Derby with Durbar II. He quickly extended the scope of his racing activities and between the wars he had horses trained in this country as well as in France. Basically his racing empire was founded on a policy of accumulating mares that represented the best blood lines in France, Great Britain and in the United States, and mating these mares for the most part with his own sires. This was all very well when M. Boussac owned stallions like Djebel and Pharis II whose services were rarely available to other breeders. Suddenly, though, that powerful tide of success began to ebb and, what is more, with astonishing rapidity. M. Boussac was unable to find replacements comparable to Djebel and Pharis. It began to look as if he had paid too much attention to blood lines, not enough to conformation and soundness. In recent years his colours have rarely been seen in this country, while in France his successes in major events have been few and far between.

There came a time when in our major races the Irish posed a more formidable threat than the French. The fact is that the incentive to send a horse over to England declined with the rising level of prize money in France. This level, thanks to the benefits derived from a tote monopoly, is now extremely high. There are breeders' premiums to be won there as well. Despite these benefits, though, the French bloodstock industry has tended to decline, not least because of a short-sighted habit of selling the best French stallions to America. Like the Irish, the French now largely depend for their best horses on ones that were bred in the United States.

In 1976, however, the French challenge to English racing was renewed with outstanding success, French horses winning all our classics bar The Two Thousand Guineas, to say nothing of The King George VI and Queen Elizabeth Diamond Stakes and The Gold Cup. They would also have won The Prince of Wales's Stakes at Royal Ascot and The Eclipse Stakes, but Trepan, first past the post in those events, suffered disqualification following positive dope tests. English retaliation for all these French victories consisted of Gentilhombre dead-heating for the Prix de l'Abbaye—the photo showed he had won but that was not good enough for the judge—and of Hillandale winning an amateur riders' race at Evry. In general, the English racing world had to seek consolation in the circulation of hair-raising stories about the methods of training now alleged to be common usage at Chantilly.

In 1946, for the first time since 1939, The Two Thousand Guineas was run over the Rowley Mile. A surprise winner at 28/1 was Sir William Cooke's Happy Knight who won with singular ease from the Aga Khan's Hyperion colt Khaled, who later on did well as a sire in America. Bred by his owner, Happy Knight was a big, not particularly attractive bay colt by Colombo out of Happy Morn, by D'Orsay. He had run once, unsuccessfully at two. He was trained by the former jockey Henri Jelliss, who, despite this encouraging success, never really succeeded in establishing himself as a trainer. The following season Happy Knight, who failed as a sire, was trained by George Todd. He was ridden in The Two Thousand by Tommy Weston who had served in the Royal Navy during the war. Weston, a cheerful, optimistic character, had a long and successful career in the saddle, riding many winners for Lord Derby, including Sansovino and Hyperion in The Derby. He must have made a great deal of money in his day, but like other fine riders of the same period he failed to keep much of it and his old age has been anything but affluent.

Sir William Cooke, a Yorkshireman, could never have been described as a non-betting owner. Before World War I he had owned Hornet's Beauty who was the unbeaten winner of fifteen races at three, including three races in four days at Royal Ascot. Sir William, rarely seen in an overcoat even on the coldest day, also achieved some fame as an orchid grower.

Happy Knight started favourite for The Derby but failed to stay and finished well down the course. Sir William had not originally intended to run him at Epsom and had written to Weatherbys to declare forfeit. Unfortunately, being a trifle absent-minded, he omitted to sign the form. When it was returned to him he had second thoughts.

The Derby was back again at Epsom and there was a huge attendance that included the King and Queen, Queen Mary and Princess Elizabeth who were given a tremendous reception when they drove down the course in cars from Tattenham Corner. One thirsty turf historian recorded sadly that two large whiskies and soda cost him 8s 6d.

12–13.   The Derby returned to Epsom in 1946 (**Above**) the mile post (**Below**) the finish. The 50/1 winner is the grey, Airborne, with his feet in the air

Winner of The Derby was Mr John Ferguson's grey colt Airborne, trained by Dick Perryman and ridden by Tommy Lowrey. Perryman and Lowrey had both been apprenticed to Fred Leader. Airborne was the fourth grey to win since the inception of The Derby. As he started at 50/1 his victory afforded joy to few except bookmakers and those who were in some way connected with the airborne forces.

Tall and rather lanky, Airborne had been bred by Lt-Col Harold Boyd-Rochfort, brother of the distinguished trainer, and was bought by Mr Ferguson as a yearling for 3,300 guineas. There was an element of chance in respect of his breeding. He was by the Gold Cup winner Precipitation out of Bouquet, a grey mare by Buchan. Owing to the war there was scant demand for Precipitation's services and he was desperately short of mares. His former trainer Captain Cecil Boyd-Rochfort, therefore, had no difficulty in obtaining a free nomination for his brother who sent his mare Bouquet to be covered, the result of this union being the winner of two classics.

Runner-up in The Derby was Lord Derby's Gulf Stream, who won The Eclipse Stakes and did well as a sire in Argentina.

Airborne also won The St Leger which returned to Doncaster, not long cleared of German prisoners of war. He scored comfortably from his stable companion, Squadron Leader Stanhope Joel's Murren. There were 142,000 paying customers at Doncaster that day and tens of thousands more stood out on the course. Today the Doncaster executive would probably not be displeased with 20,000 people paying at the turnstiles.

It was not a vintage year for three-year-olds and Airborne, who proved a disappointing sire, was cut down to size in the two-miles King George VI Stakes at Ascot in October when he was well and truly beaten by the Grand Prix winner Souverain. He never ran again as it was found impossible to train him as a four-year-old.

Mr Ferguson, who was in the plastics industry, had been a close friend of Squadron Leader Stanhope Joel since their Eton days and it was Joel who inspired his interest in racing. In 1954 Ferguson was elected to the Jockey Club and with his business ability and his charming personality he might have become an outstanding administrator. Alas, he died aged fifty-three in 1956.

The One Thousand Guineas was won by the King's filly Hypericum, bred by himself, trained by Boyd-Rochfort and ridden by Doug Smith. She was a strong-quartered bay by Hyperion, many of whose daughters were apt to be a bit tricky, out of Feola, by Friar Marcus. Feola, bred by Lord St Davids, was bought as a yearling on King George V's behalf for 3,300 guineas. Besides being a winner she was second in The One Thousand Guineas. She proved an outstanding brood mare and was largely responsible for the revival in the fortunes of the royal stud.

Hypericum was always high-spirited and she certainly had her fun on the afternoon of The One Thousand. Drawn No. 1, she suddenly darted forward, barging into several other fillies and then slipping under the gate, causing Smith to be swept off by the tapes. She then cantered fairly sedately down the course until reaching the point where the rails begin, when she branched off to the left in

14. Part of the vast crowd that attended The St Leger at Doncaster in 1946

the direction of her home. At this point she was caught and led back to the start where Smith, fortunately undamaged, remounted her. The race started fourteen minutes late. There were people present who reckoned that the starter had been over-zealous in his loyalty to the Crown. Hypericum did nothing wrong in the race which she won by a length and a half from the odds-on favourite Neolight, who may not have appreciated her long wait on a distinctly chilly afternoon.

Hypericum failed to stay in The Oaks which was won by Steady Aim, by Felstead, from Iona and Nelia. Possibly Nelia was unlucky not to win as she had been left many lengths at the start. Steady Aim was bred and owned by Sir Alfred Butt, a former Tory M.P. who at one time was deeply involved in the theatrical world. He had bought Steady Aim's French-bred dam for 700 guineas during the war. Hypericum bred Highlight, by Borealis, whose daughter Highclere won The One Thousand Guineas and the French Oaks for the Queen in 1974.

For M. Boussac it was a rewarding season. He began by winning The Coronation Cup with the five-year-old Ardan, by Pharis out of the French Oaks winner

Adargatis. Ardan won fifteen races, including the French Derby, and sired Hard Sauce who got the 1958 Derby winner Hard Ridden. A brother of Pardal, who sired the Derby winner Psidium, he was eventually exported to America.

M. Boussac next won The White Rose Stakes, then run over a mile and seven furlongs at Hurst Park, with that remarkable stayer Marsyas II, who was by far the best son of the dual Gold Cup winner Trimdon and was out of Astronomie, dam of the great Caracalla II and the Oaks winner Asmena. Marsyas II, who liked to force the pace from the start, also won The Queen Alexandra Stakes at Royal Ascot by six lengths, and The Doncaster Cup, a race no French-bred horse had won since 1870, by eight lengths. By the end of October Marsyas II had gone over the top. Heavily bandaged and clearly not his true self, he was third in The Jockey Club Cup behind another French horse, Baron de Waldner's three-year-old Felix II. In France Marsyas II established a record that will probably never be equalled by winning the Prix du Cadran, the French equivalent of The Gold Cup, on four occasions.

1946 Royal Ascot winners in the Boussac colours included Caracalla II and Priam II. Caracalla II won The Gold Cup from two other French competitors, Chanteur II and Basileus. A bay by Tourbillon out of Astronomie, he was a horse of the highest class and was never beaten. He did not race at two. At three his victories included the Grand Prix and the French St Leger, while at four in addition to The Gold Cup he won the Prix de l'Arc de Triomphe, beating Prince Chevalier by a head. He did not fulfil expectations as a sire. Priam II, who had given Court Martial such a hard race in The Champion Stakes the previous season, won The Hardwicke Stakes. He was a five-year-old by Pharis II and after doing well as a stallion in France he was exported to America.

Not content with successes in weight for age races, the French also won The Cesarewitch with Monsieur l'Amiral and The Cambridgeshire with Sayani. Sayani, who had won The Jersey Stakes at Royal Ascot, was a top-class three-year-old and he put up a superb performance in The Cambridgeshire to win with 9 st. 4 lb. Bred by Mr Benjamin Guinness in Normandy, he was a half-brother by Fair Copy to the Two Thousand Guineas winner My Babu. He was champion sire in France in 1953, in which year he was sold to go to Brazil.

A fine sprinter in 1946 was The Bug, owned by Mr N. Wachman and trained up till July by the Hon. Gerald Wellesley in Ireland and from then on by Marcus Marsh at Newmarket. The change was made because The Bug was a poor traveller and there were no sprint races of any consequence for him to win in Ireland. By Signal Light out of a mare by Flying Orb, his successes included The Wokingham Stakes at Royal Ascot, The July Cup, The Nunthorpe Stakes and The Diadem Stakes.

Everyone was pleased to see Marcus Marsh with a good horse in his stable. His father was the famous Richard Marsh, a great horseman, the trainer of four Derby winners, three of them in the royal colours, and a man of distinguished appearance who liked to do everything *en prince* and never paused, to his ultimate disadvantage, to count the pennies. Marcus Marsh was for some time assistant to that exacting martinet Fred Darling. Setting up on his own, he won the 1934 Derby with a really great horse in Windsor Lad. In World War II he served in the Royal Air Force, was shot down and spent nearly five years as a prisoner of war. One of the first horses he trained after the war was Twenty Players, a filly owned in partnership with nineteen former prisoners of war. She first ran at Folkestone and the arrival of Marsh and the nineteen partners who all wanted passes for the Club Stand caused the Jockey Club to limit the partners in any one horse to four.

The sun seemed to be shining on Marsh when he succeeded Frank Butters as the Aga Khan's trainer but despite the Derby victory of Tulyar, good fortune beat a retreat again and as far as training went, never made a subsequent advance. Happily Marsh can treat life's reverses with dignity and good humour. When he gave up training he compiled a most readable life-story under the title of *Racing With the Gods*.

During this year the Jockey Club committee appointed to look into the matter reported on the advisability of installing the race-finish camera. The report was favourable and the camera was first used at the Epsom Spring Meeting in 1947.

It had been good to see the Royal Ascot Meeting well on the road back to its former glories. There were certain differences, though. Up till the war there had been seven races each day. The first one was at 1.30 and then there was an interval of an hour during which the swells adjourned for luncheon. No one cared about the tedium inflicted on the thousands of racegoers crammed into the cheaper enclosures. The Heath side of the course was then completely unenclosed and facing the stands there was a long line of gaily beflagged club and regimental marquees dispensing refreshment and hospitality, and occasionally badly needed shelter as in the fearful thunderstorm of 1930.

In view of the food shortage after the war, the King felt that it would be unseemly for big Ascot luncheon parties to be staged that would probably arouse considerable adverse comment. The programme, therefore, was reduced to six races a day, and the first event was at 2.30. Today there are still just six races, quite sufficient for anyone. The Heath side is partially enclosed and those friendly tents have completely disappeared with the exception of the White's tent at the far end of the paddock where prices have escalated to such an extent that anyone giving a party there is in dire need of a long-priced winner afterwards.

In 1946 the King gave his approval to plans for the reconstruction of the course at Ascot, while also proposing that in future there should be three extra meetings, known as Heath Meetings, later in the year. Up till the war the course had been used only for the four days of the Royal Meeting. The main alteration was to move the straight mile from the Golden Gates, the right-hand rails of the old straight course becoming the left-hand rails of the new course, thereby almost doubling the amount of space in the enclosures between the stands and the course. The Golden Gates were too heavy to be moved and remained as an historic monument. New lodges, copied from those at Eridge Park, home of the Marquess of Abergavenny, and new gates were built at the entrance of the new straight mile. A new watering system was introduced, the water coming from a reservoir on the

Heath. The new turf was laid in 1947 but plenty of time was given for it to settle and the reconstructed course was first used in 1955. Following the flooding of the course during the Royal Meeting of 1964, it was deemed advisable to call in drainage experts from Holland and twenty-three miles of drains were added. A further five miles were installed at a later date.

The Duke of Norfolk had been appointed His Majesty's Ascot Representative in 1945 following the retirement of Lord Hamilton of Dalzell. Sir Gordon Carter, for so long Clerk of the Course at Ascot, had died during the war and his post-war successor was Major (later Sir) John Crocker Bulteel D.S.O., M.C. A former Jockey Club handicapper and a truly delightful character, Bulteel possessed a thorough knowledge of every aspect of racing. He was also Clerk of the Course at Hurst Park where he paid most careful attention to the narrow strip of the track that owners, trainers and members of the press walked across from the car park to the enclosures, and into which they habitually dug their umbrellas to test the going. He was essentially progressive in outlook and possessed a unique flair for the framing of races attractive both to owners and the public. Till 1957, when he was succeeded by Major-General Sir David Dawnay, he and the Duke formed a singularly happy and effective partnership. One of their joint successes was to stage in 1951 The Festival of Britain Stakes, an event which was finally destined to become the first £100,000 race in this country and is now, sponsored by De Beers, designated The King George VI and Queen Elizabeth Diamond Stakes.

5

NINETEEN-FORTY-SEVEN was a year of extremes in the weather. The spring was exceptionally wet and the programme arranged for the opening day of the season at that very primitive racecourse, Lincoln, had to be abandoned as the course was flooded. It was possible, though, to stage The Lincolnshire Handicap two days later. It had to be run, however, on the round course as parts of the straight mile were under water. As there were forty-six runners and the going was like workhouse porridge, a distinct element of chance can be said to have entered into the contest. The winner was the 100/1 outsider Jockey Treble trained at Rotherham for Mr Syd Oxenham, a Blackpool bookmaker. Carrying 6 stone, Jockey Treble was ridden with splendid dash by little Emmanuel Mercer, a Stockport-born apprentice who was first with Jim Russell of Mablethorpe and then, when Russell's licence was withdrawn, with George Colling. That Lincoln victory was an important stepping-stone on the road to success for 'Manny' Mercer, elder brother of Joe Mercer, and he rode twenty-one winners that season. In due course he became one of the outstanding riders of his time and was at the height of his powers when sadly he met with a fatal accident at Ascot in 1959 riding Priddy Fair. Priddy Fair became the grandam of that good filly Dibidale.

The summer and autumn of 1947 were unusually warm and dry and both The Cesarewitch and The Cambridgeshire were run on ground officially described as 'hard'.

The outstanding two-year-old of 1946 had been Mr J. A. Dewar's Tudor Minstrel, a handsome, powerful brown colt by Owen Tudor out of Sansonnet, by Sansovino. Bred by his owner and trained by Fred Darling at Beckhampton, he won all his four races including The Coventry Stakes—then run over five furlongs and increased to six in 1955—at Royal Ascot, and The National Breeders' Produce Stakes at Sandown. Both those events he won by four lengths. He did not run again after July. It was said that he had proved his speed and that, as his 1947 target would be The Derby, it would be better if he stayed at home and was taught how to settle down in order to make the best use of his stamina.

Superficially at least, Tudor Minstrel was bred to stay. His sire, by Hyperion, had won a wartime Derby and a wartime Gold Cup. His dam was by a Derby winner out of the Jockey Club Stakes winner Lady Juror, a daughter of the great stayer Son-in-Law. Lady Juror, though, was a half-sister to Mumtaz Mahal, being out of Lady Josephine, by Sundridge out of Americus Girl, and the Americus Girl family has always been prepotent for speed.

Another factor that influenced the decision to withdraw Tudor Minstrel from racing so early in 1946 was the precarious state of his trainer's health. Darling was to enter a nursing home for treatment and arrangements had to be made for him to spend the winter abroad. For the time being the stable was taken over by his brother Sam.

In the Free Handicap Tudor Minstrel was given 9 st. 7 lb., two pounds more than Sir Alfred Butt's Fair Trial colt, Petition. During the winter Tudor Minstrel thrived. At three he stood $15.3\frac{1}{4}$ hands and girthed 72 inches. His back and quarters were noticeably strong and the impression he gave was one of exceptional depth and power. He was hardly the cut of a stayer, though. After winning a small race at Bath he started favourite at 11/8 for The Two Thousand Guineas in which Petition, on offer at 5/2, was confidently expected by his connections to give him a good race. Unfortunately Petition, very much on his toes, dashed into the tapes, unseated his rider and fell back on his haunches. He made no attempt, though, to bolt and was soon remounted but he had in fact injured himself quite severely. He ran badly and was off the course afterwards till the end of July.

Tudor Minstrel was never out of a canter and won by eight lengths from Saravan and Sayajirao. Seldom can Gordon Richards have had an easier ride. Few people had taken much notice of the fact, however, that on April 12 at Hurst Park the injured Petition had beaten Sayajirao by ten lengths.

Spurred on by the less thoughtful members of the racing press who insisted on referring to him as 'the Horse of the Century', the public regarded The Derby as no more than a formality for Tudor Minstrel and money poured in for him as if defeat were out of the question. There was, though, one small complication as far as the Beckhampton stable was concerned. Darling also trained the King's colt Blue Train, by Blue Peter out of the triple classic winner Sun Chariot. Blue Train won his only race in 1946 and the following spring he won a ten-furlongs race at Sandown and then the ten-furlongs Newmarket Stakes, an event regarded as a significant Derby trial. It looked as if Richards might have some difficulty in deciding whether to ride Tudor Minstrel or a fancied colt in the royal colours but Blue Train, never a sound horse, had jarred himself at Newmarket. He had to be taken out of The Derby and in fact he never ran again.

Tudor Minstrel started at 7/4 on for The Derby, the hottest favourite since Cicero in 1905. The race was run on a Saturday to afford the minimum disruption to industry. The going was good. Right from the start Tudor Minstrel fought for his head and Richards was never able to settle him down. He was in front at the top of the hill and though still in front at Tattenham Corner he was clearly in dire trouble soon after. Pearl Diver moved smoothly into the lead three furlongs out and, confidently ridden by Bridgland, he won very easily by four lengths from the Aga Khan's Migoli with Sayajirao third. Tudor Minstrel finished a weary fourth.

Racegoers were not then inured to victories by French horses in our major races. The overthrow of Tudor Minstrel caused widespread gloom and was regarded in the light of a national disaster.

Pearl Diver was returned at 40/1. No one had taken much interest in Baron de Waldner's Vatellor colt who was trained by Percy Carter in France and had come to Newmarket to complete his Derby preparation with Claude Halsey. The rest of Pearl Diver's career was somewhat undistinguished. He failed in the Grand Prix and The St Leger but he did win the Prix d'Harcourt at four. For a time he was at the stud in this country but he made no mark and was eventually exported to Japan.

Richards of course was sharply criticised for the failure of Tudor Minstrel by people who declined to face the fact that the colt simply did not stay. After winning The St James's Palace Stakes at Ascot by five lengths, Tudor Minstrel competed in The Eclipse Stakes. He was beaten below the distance and, though he struggled on courageously, Migoli beat him by a length and a half. His class and his speed had proved insufficient to see him through. His final race before retirement was the one-mile Knights Royal Stakes at Ascot in the autumn. He won, although he was beginning to go in his coat and did not look anything like as well as he had done in the spring. Among those he beat were The Bug, who did not stay, and Petition, who had had an attack of heel bug and was not greatly fancied. Probably if Tudor Minstrel had been kept to races of a mile or under, he would never have been beaten.

As a sire he was not the success anticipated and never achieved a higher place in the list than seventh. However he did get King of the Tudors (Eclipse Stakes, Sussex Stakes), Toro (French One Thousand Guineas), Tomy Lee (Kentucky Derby) and Tudor Melody, a very successful sire.

Fred Darling retired at the end of the season and his place at Beckhampton was taken by Noel Murless. Darling died in 1953 soon after Pinza, whom he had bred, had won The Derby. He came from a racing family and his great-grandfather had won the 1833 St Leger on Rockingham. His own father trained the Derby winners Galtee More and Ard Patrick. He himself began training near Newmarket in 1907, one of his patrons being Lady de Bathe (Lily Langtry), for whom he won The Cesarewich with Yentoi. From 1909 to 1914 he trained in Germany, where he got married, returning in 1914 to take over Beckhampton from his father. At the Newmarket July Sales that year he bought Hurry On, probably the best colt he ever trained, for 500 guineas for Mr James Buchanan, later Lord Woolavington.

That Darling was a great trainer is indisputable. A perfectionist who had no use for the second-rate in man or beast, he trained no fewer than seven winners of The Derby. He also enjoyed twelve other classic successes. In the stable he supervised every detail himself. Only the very best was good enough for his horses. He was a master at building up condition and never did his horses expend on the gallops at home energies that would have been better conserved for the race-course. Beckhampton runners carried a special bloom and air of distinction that

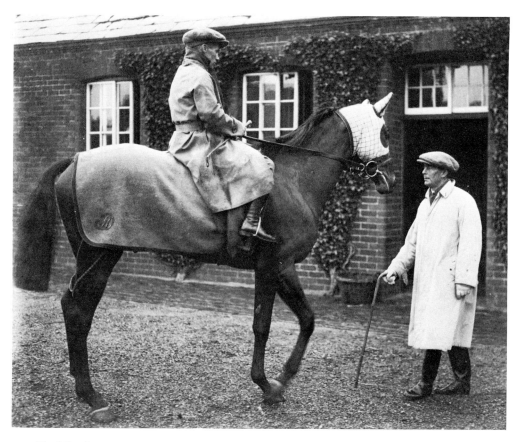

15. Fred Darling, pictured at Beckhampton in 1931 with that year's Two Thousand Guineas and Derby winner Cameronian

rendered them easily recognisable in the paddock. They were almost invariably at their best on the day that really mattered.

As a man Darling was easier to admire for his professional skill than to like for his personal qualities. He was essentially a martinet, ruthless, taciturn, secretive and intolerant. He had no time for fools, bores or importunate members of the press. Owners, too, had to toe the line. It did not worry him in the slightest whether he was popular or not. If there was a clash of wills with a difficult horse or an exacting owner, it was not Darling that emerged second best. Possibly there were excuses for what some people considered to be bloody-mindedness. For years his health was indifferent. In addition his wife had gone back to Germany in 1914 just before the war began and he never set eyes on her again. It is fair to say that those who knew him best, such as Sir Gordon Richards, admired him the most.

The 1947 One Thousand Guineas and The Oaks both went to France, the winner in each case being Madame P. Corbière's Imprudence trained by J.

Lieux. Imprudence, who won The Oaks by five lengths from Major L. B. Holliday's Netherton Maid, also won the French One Thousand Guineas. She was by Canot, whose grandsire was the 1916 Two Thousand Guineas winner Clarissimus, out of the Hurry On mare Indiscretion, whose grandam was Black Gem, a sister of that famous brood mare Black Ray. Sayajirao, Dante's brother, won The St Leger after a desperate battle with M. Boussac's Arbar whom he beat by a head. Sayajirao never attained great popularity as a sire since he committed the almost unpardonable sin of getting stayers. Among his winners were Indiana (St Leger), Gladness (Gold Cup) and Lynchris (Irish Oaks, Irish St Leger).

Chanteur II, a five-year-old from France, won The Coronation Cup, having previously won The Winston Churchill Stakes and The White Rose Stakes, both at Hurst Park. In The Gold Cup, though, he was no match for another French competitor, Souverain. Chanteur II was a tough brown horse by the French Derby winner Château Bouscaut and Mr William Hill, the bookmaker, did British breeders a good turn by importing him into this country. Chanteur II was champion sire in 1953 and among his winners were Pinza (Derby, King George VI and Queen Elizabeth Stakes), Cantelo (St Leger) and Only For Life (Two Thousand Guineas). Souverain was a failure as a sire. At Royal Ascot M. Boussac had to be content with two victories, winning the Chesham Stakes with Djerid and the Hardwicke Stakes with Nirgal. In the autumn the Champion Stakes went to Migoli, a grey by Bois Roussel. The following autumn he won the Prix de l'Arc de Triomphe. He was a thoroughly genuine horse himself but a disappointing sire in that so many of his offspring were unreliable. He did, however, sire Gallant Man, winner of The Belmont Stakes in America.

At the Lincoln Spring Meeting Mr R. Hardy's Boston Boro', trained by J. Russell at Mablethorpe, was subjected to a veterinary test after winning The John O'Gaunt Plate in which he had been backed from 7/1 down to 4/1. The test proved positive and in due course the Stewards of the Jockey Club withdrew Russell's licence. Russell took legal advice and sued the Duke of Norfolk, Lord Willoughby de Broke and Lord Rosebery as Stewards of the Jockey Club and representing all the members, alleging that his licence had been wrongfully withdrawn and claiming damages for alleged breach of contract. He also claimed damages for libel from Messrs Weatherby, publishers of the Racing Calendar.

The case came before Lord Goddard and a special jury on February 24, 1948. Lord Goddard speedily ruled that there was no cause of action in libel, and that the question he intended to leave to the jury was whether Russell had been given a fair and honest hearing when he came in front of the Stewards. On the libel issue, the occasion was privileged and Russell had disclaimed malice. There was therefore nothing to leave to the jury on that score.

In his summing up Lord Goddard said that domestic tribunals such as the Jockey Club were not bound by procedure such as governed the Courts of Law, but in holding an inquiry into the conduct of a person they must act fairly and give the person brought before them fair notice of the charge or complaint against him and an opportunity to defend himself.

After an hour's retirement the jury failed to agree and were accordingly discharged. When he gave judgment on the legal issues the next day Lord Goddard said that he had agreed to leave to the jury the question whether or not the inquiry before the Stewards was fairly held, but that he refused to leave to the jury any question upon the libel issue. 'I left the question to the jury', he went on, 'in the hope that their answer would prevent a new trial if the Court of Appeal should take a different view from me, but unfortunately they were unable to agree. Therefore the question remains unanswered, but, in my opinion, the submission of Sir Valentine Holmes (for the defendants) is right, and there was no case to go to the jury at all.' Lord Goddard dismissed the action with costs, and Russell's appeal against Lord Goddard's decision was dismissed by the Court of Appeal on December 8.

The top three in the two-year-old Free Handicap were My Babu (9 st. 7 lb.), The Cobbler (9 st. 5 lb.) and Black Tarquin (9 st. 5 lb.). My Babu, a half-brother to Sayani by Djebel, was owned by the Maharaja of Baroda and trained by Sam Armstrong. He originally raced under the name of Lerins. When it was changed, the racing correspondent of The Sunday Times observed in his column that Lerins had been re-christened My Babu. The following week he was summoned from the country for an interview with the editor at what was then Kemsley House. On being marched in, he was informed that he had used highly injudicious language and had caused grave offence to many churchmen who had sent in letters of complaint. The racing correspondent was completely puzzled and could not think which words of his had been calculated to cause offence. The editor then pointed out with asperity that it had been improper and offensive to use the term 'christen' in respect of a horse. He took a grave view of the lapse and would have taken a graver one had not the naval correspondent, a far more experienced journalist, recently committed a similar offence in respect of the launching of a battleship. The racing correspondent's observation that at least it was satisfactory that so many devout churchmen read the racing column was not received with any noticeable sign of pleasure.

In 1948 not one of the three classic races in which colts could compete was won by a British-bred competitor. The Coronation Cup and The Gold Cup were won by French horses. Winner of The Two Thousand Guineas was the French-bred My Babu who just got home by a head from The Cobbler, a very handsome colt by Windsor Slipper. As a two-year-old My Babu was unbeaten in his last five races. He had dead-heated in The New Stakes at Royal Ascot with Delirium who later won the Prix Morny at Deauville. It is a striking example of the increase in prize money in France that in 1947 the Prix Morny was worth £1,804 to the winner; in 1975 it was worth £38,546. The Cobbler had won all his races in 1947 including The Middle Park Stakes. He proved to be a top-class sprinter, winning The Wokingham Stakes at Royal Ascot in 1949 with 9 st. 4 lb. He did well as a sire in New Zealand.

The Derby was a disaster as far as British bloodstock was concerned. French horses, My Love and Royal Drake, finished first and second and there were four French-bred competitors in the first six. It was a humiliating situation which of

16–17. The Derby was won by French horses in both 1947 (Pearl Diver) and 1948 (My Love)

course afforded the French considerable satisfaction. My Love was owned jointly by two old men in declining health, the Aga Khan and M. L. Volterra. The Aga Khan had bought a half share at the end of May for something like £15,000. Bred by M. Volterra, My Love was by Vatellor—whom Volterra had acquired when he bought all Captain Jefferson Cohn's bloodstock—out of For My Love, by Amfortas. For My Love, before producing My Love, had been barren to Vatellor the three previous seasons. Trainer of My Love was the sixty-four-year-old Richard Carver who had been born at Chantilly but was a British subject. Carver had never been to Epsom before. He also trained the runner-up, the leggy and distinctly plain Royal Drake, who carried the colours of M. Volterra. My Babu was fourth. He had a rough race but the probability is that he did not quite stay the full distance.

My Love completed a fine double by winning the Grand Prix de Paris. He was stale by the time The St Leger came along and was unplaced behind Mr W. Woodward's American-bred Black Tarquin, by Rhodes Scholar. Trained by Boyd-Rochfort, Black Tarquin was exceptionally good-looking, a fine big brown horse with any amount of quality. As a sire of flat-race horses Black Tarquin was disappointing although he did get that great stayer Trelawny. As a sire of jumpers he was highly successful.

M. Boussac won The Coronation Cup with Goyama, The Gold Cup with Arbar, a half-brother to Caracalla II and Marsyas II by Djebel. At Royal Ascot M. Boussac was also successful in The Gold Vase with Estoc and in The Queen Mary Stakes with Coronation V. Petition proved himself a high class four-year-old. He won The Victoria Cup, in which he carried 9 st. 3 lb., and also The Eclipse Stakes, beating Sayajirao and Noor in a thrilling finish and surprising those who doubted his ability to stay a mile and a quarter. He sired many winners including the sprinter March Past, grandsire of Brigadier Gerard.

One of the last great horses bred by the 17th Earl of Derby was Alycidon, by Donatello II out of the Hyperion mare Aurora, dam of the Coronation Cup winner Borealis and a member of the famous Marchetta family. A long, low chestnut with a tremendous stride, Alycidon was backward at two and Walter Earl did not run him till the autumn, when he was unplaced in a couple of seven-furlong events at Newmarket. In the early part of 1948 he ran in the name of Brigadier T. Fairfax-Ross, Lord Derby having died in February. Lord Derby's death had no impact on Alycidon whose career, though, may have been affected by the fact that Walter Earl was a sick man—he died in 1950—while Doug Smith had been ill, too, and was unable to ride until the latter part of July.

Alycidon started off as a three-year-old by whipping round at the start of The Wren Stakes at Hurst Park and taking no part. After that performance, he was always equipped with blinkers. Shortly afterwards, ridden by R. Shaw, one of Earl's lads, he won the one-mile Classic Trial Stakes at Thirsk, a victory that seems to refute the notion that he was lacking in speed.

Again ridden by Shaw, he was third in The Chester Vase and then won the mile-and-a-quarter Royal Standard Stakes at Manchester. At Royal Ascot he was close up third in The King Edward VII Stakes. On that occasion he was ridden by Lowrey, whose tactics were unenterprising and who signally failed to exploit his stamina. Again with Lowrey in the saddle, he won The Princess of Wales's Stakes at Newmarket, beating among others Sayajirao and M. Boussac's Timor. At the end of July Doug Smith was back in action again. He rode Alycidon to victory in The St George Stakes at Liverpool and partnered him for the remainder of his racing career.

Starting at 20/1, Alycidon was second in The St Leger, beaten a length and a half. This was a very gallant effort as he had to make nearly all his own running and was just beaten for speed at the finish by Black Tarquin. Later that month he won the mile-and-three-quarters Jockey Club Stakes at Newmarket after making every yard of the running. By then he was recognised as a high-class stayer.

His final outing that season was in the two-miles King George VI Stakes at Ascot in October. There was a strong feeling of international rivalry in that event. Alycidon represented England, while from France came Flush Royal, Rigolo and Djeddah. Flush Royal, who started favourite, had beaten My Love at level weights in the spring. In addition he had been third in the French Derby and second in the Grand Prix. Rigolo had won the French Two Thousand Guineas and the Prix Lupin, while Djeddah, destined to win The Eclipse and Champion Stakes the following year, had some good form to his credit. For the first time Alycidon enjoyed the services of Benny Lynch as pacemaker. Benny Lynch set a demanding gallop with Alycidon never far behind. With half a mile to go Alycidon took the lead and then drew clear of his rivals to win by five lengths from Djeddah with Flush Royal third. The cheering began as soon as Alycidon struck the front and increased in volume as he lengthened his lead in the straight. When he entered the unsaddling enclosure he was given a reception that a winning Derby favourite might have envied. For once at least the French had been vanquished in a long-distance race and it really did look as if England would have a worthy Gold Cup candidate in 1949.

Elected to the Jockey Club in 1895, the 17th Earl of Derby was one of the most successful owner-breeders in the history of English racing. Not only that, but horses he bred were influential all over the world. Among stallions he owned and had bred were Chaucer, Swynford, Phalaris, Pharos, Sansovino, Colorado, Fairway and Hyperion. He bred Sickle and Pharamond, both champion sires in America, and also Light Brigade and Heliopolis who were both extremely successful there. In Argentina, Silurian, Bridge of Canny, Hunter's Moon and Gulf Stream all did well. Fair Copy and Plassy sired good winners in France. Pharos stood in France from 1928 and when there sired two great horses in Nearco and Pharis II, both unbeaten.

Lord Derby enjoyed twenty English classic successes including The Derby with Sansovino, Hyperion and Watling Street. George Lambton trained for him till 1926 when Lambton became manager with Frank Butters as trainer. Lambton took over as trainer again from 1931 to 1933, when he was succeeded by Colledge Leader. On Leader's death in 1938 the post of trainer fell to Walter Earl.

Lord Derby was a great Englishman of a type that has become very rare. His services to racing were surpassed by his services to his country. He was succeeded by his grandson whose enthusiasm for the turf has tended to decline over the years. It has become increasingly rare for the celebrated black jacket and white cap to be seen in important races and the glories of the Stanley Stud have, alas, departed.

The 1948 One Thousand Guineas went to Sir Percy Loraine's Queenpot, by Big Game. She was bred by her owner, who had had a distinguished record in the Diplomatic Service, and she was trained at Beckhampton by Noel Murless. On Fred Darling's retirement Beckhampton had been bought by Mr J. A. Dewar and Noel Murless had been persuaded to come down from the north, where he had been very happy, to take over. This was Murless's first classic success. He nearly landed a double as he also trained The Cobbler who so nearly won The Two Thousand Guineas. Queenpot did not really stay a mile but the going was hard at Newmarket and she just lasted out the distance, beautifully ridden by Gordon Richards. On soft ground at Royal Ascot she finished seventeen lengths behind Hyperbole in the Jersey Stakes. She was then retired.

The Aga Khan's Nearco filly, Masaka, ridden by Gethin, had started favourite for The One Thousand Guineas but she was in a highly unco-operative mood. She stood still at the start and declined to budge till the others were lengths in front of her. When she did consent to go, she moved with the utmost reluctance. 'A real cow' was the verdict of her backers.

In The Oaks Masaka was ridden by Nevett and started at 7/1. She showed what she could do when she was not in one of her moods by winning by six lengths from the King's Angelola. She subsequently won the Irish Oaks as well.

In the meantime the rigidities of the so-called 'Jersey Act', originally instituted to safeguard the purity of the Stud Book, had become embarrassing. The post-war successes of the descendants of Durbar II gave rise to a feeling that if the regulations governing admission to the Stud Book were not relaxed they would end up by becoming ridiculous. This feeling was strengthened in 1948 by the successes of My Babu, Black Tarquin and Arbar. Not one of these three was eligible for inclusion in the Stud Book. It was plain that if they were retired to the stud in this country breeders might well not be put off by the 'half-bred' slur and a situation not only absurd but downright chaotic could result.

On July 15, 1948 the following notice of a Jockey Club meeting appeared in the Racing Calendar:

The Senior Steward (the Duke of Norfolk) said that the Stewards had been approached by the Owners of the General Stud Book on the subject of the present conditions of admission to the Book. The Club would remember that Messrs Weatherby, acting on the advice of the Jockey Club, gave up their attempt to widen the scope of the book which they made when Volume XIX was published in 1901, and in 1913, agreeing with what is known as the Jersey Act, they published a restrictive practice when they brought out Volume XXII. That preface holds good today.

They asked whether the Club was in agreement with them that the present preface was too restricted, and whether steps should not now be taken to broaden the scope of the Book so as to allow for outcrossings with certain strains which at present were not admissible.

In order to give Messrs Weatherby the answer to this question, the Stewards asked the Club if they would agree to their setting up a small *ad hoc* committee to discuss the matter.

This had the approval of members present.

The committee appointed consisted of the Duke of Norfolk, Lord Allendale, Lord Rosebery, Mr Peter Burrell, then Director of the National Stud, and Mr Francis Weatherby. At the annual meeting at Newmarket in December of the Thoroughbred Breeders' Association, the Duke of Norfolk stated that some modification was advisable in the qualification at present required. That announcement was received with enthusiasm. In Volume XXXI of the Stud Book published in 1949 the Jersey Act was repealed. Qualification for admission to the Stud Book was altered as follows:

The publishers give notice that as from this date the conditions which have governed admission continuously since Volume XXII are rescinded.

Any animal claiming admission from now onwards must be able to prove satisfactorily some eight or nine crosses of pure blood, to trace back for at least a century, and to show such performances of its immediate family on the Turf as to warrant the belief in the purity of its blood.

All the horses and mares which will appear in Volume XXXII will have been submitted to this test, in which the Publishers reserve to themselves the right of final decision.

Thus ended the Jersey Act which had for years been a source of grievance and ill feeling in America. No gratitude was shown for its removal. The Americans regarded it less as a very long overdue act of justice to American breeders than as a measure taken only because the high quality of so many American and French 'half-breds' was making the Stud Book ridiculous. The Americans in particular had always taken the view that the Act was originally imposed not in the highest interests of the British thoroughbred but as a purely commercial measure designed to give Great Britain a monopoly of the thoroughbred export market throughout the world.

6

THE weather in 1949 was unusually warm and dry. In consequence the ground was firm for long periods and presented trainers with many problems, particularly in respect of two-year-olds who are always more likely to suffer from sore shins than horses of a greater age.

It was encouraging that all five classic races were won by British-bred horses. The French challenge, though, remained formidable. M. L. Volterra's Amour Drake was unlucky not to be the third successive French winner of The Derby, while French fillies were second, third and fourth in The Oaks. French victories included The Queen Alexandra Stakes, The Eclipse Stakes, The Champion Stakes, The King George VI Stakes, The Cheveley Park Stakes and The Dewhurst Stakes. Bar The Queen Alexandra Stakes, those races were all won by horses carrying the orange jacket and grey cap of M. Boussac.

A pleasing feature of the season was the return of Newbury to the fixture list. Newbury racecourse caught it badly in both wars. In World War I it was first occupied by troops, then successively a prisoner-of-war camp, a hay dispersal centre, a munitions inspection depot and finally a tank-testing and repair park. Racing was resumed there in 1919. In World War II racing was possible there till the summer of 1941. In 1942 it was taken over by the U.S. Armed Forces and the Stars and Stripes fluttered from the grandstand flagstaff. The course became one of the main American supply depots. The splendid turf, so carefully tended since John Porter founded the course in the early years of the century, was submerged under concrete roads, hard standing and thirty-five miles of railway lines, while the running rails swiftly disappeared into barrack-room stoves. Prisoners of war inhabited the stables.

Newbury continued to be a supply depot till March 1946 when, under the Lease-Lend agreement, the remaining stores were taken over by the Ministry of Supply for disposal. It was not until June 1947 that the centre land, which included the actual course, was released. Owing to lengthy negotiations, the long and arduous process of clearing the area did not begin until August. The spring of 1949 was made, rather optimistically it seemed, the target date for the reopening of Newbury as a racecourse.

18.   Abernant, with Gordon Richards up

First of all, the railway lines and thousands of sleepers had to be taken up and removed. Then bulldozers, excavators and giant scrapers came into action, supported by fleets of lorries. The utmost care had to be taken to preserve the precious topsoil, buried for five years. Over 200,000 cubic yards of hard-core, ashes and similar substances were scraped off, thus leaving topsoil exposed. This had to be scarified, ploughed and then left idle for a considerable period to give effect to the aeration it had for so long been denied.

A large number of concrete blocks, boulders and huge pieces of metal were constantly being encountered and had to be removed. The whole of the ground was then thoroughly cultivated and the surface graded to even contours. An examination was made of the depth of the soil remaining and in certain places soil had to be brought in. The three separate courses for flat, hurdles and steeple-chasing, which had been planned on paper, were then surveyed in, and an inch of peat was incorporated with the topsoil. It was decided to turf the entire flat course in preference to seeding in order to meet the target date. An enormous quantity of turf was required and the turf nursery laid down in 1944 provided barely half of what was needed. The rest came from a housing estate within the boundaries of

Newbury. The first turf was laid on March 22, 1948. The task was completed by the end of July.

By then 310,000 turves had been put down; 9,000 did not take and had to be relaid. Simultaneously the two jumping courses were prepared for seeding. Six and a half tons of fertiliser were put down and three and a quarter tons of grass seed. Owing to bad weather, the seeding could not be completed. A third of the area was left and, because of drainage troubles, it was not till 1950 that the remainder was turfed.

Apart from work on the course, there was a huge restoration job to be done on the stands. Almost every building had been occupied by troops with results that can easily be imagined. There was no timber available for the white rails enclosing the course so tubular rails and iron posts, once part of the anti-invasion defences, were used instead. The Nissen huts were removed from the lawns which were then re-graded and repaired, and eventually, against all the odds, the course was reopened for racing in April 1949.

The outstanding two-year-old in 1948 had been Major (later Sir) Reginald Macdonald-Buchanan's Abernant, bred by his wife and trained by Noel Murless. Abernant's hocks were rather away from him, but apart from that he was a good-looking colt, grey in colour, strongly made and with a small, lean, intelligent head. His disposition was placid and kindly. He was by the wartime Derby and Gold Cup winner Owen Tudor out of Rustom Mahal, by Rustom Pasha out of that exceptionally fast grey mare, Mumtaz Mahal. Rustom Mahal never ran. She showed brilliant speed but used to dive off the gallops without warning and Fred Darling considered her unsafe to race. In an attempt to keep her straight, she was sent upsides a powerfully built cob but she cannoned into him and broke at least one of his ribs.

Weird things can happen to even the best of two-year-olds first time out and Abernant got beaten at Lingfield by a moderate youngster called Potentate. He then won in succession The Bedford Stakes at Newmarket, The Chesham Stakes at Royal Ascot, The National Breeders' Produce Stakes at Sandown, The Champagne Stakes at Doncaster and The Middle Park Stakes at Newmarket. He had a narrow squeak in The National Breeders' Produce Stakes in which he only got home by inches from Star King, a very fast Stardust colt owned by Mr Wilfred Harvey, a publisher. Mr Harvey later got into severe financial difficulties and retired from the racing scene after winning the 1965 Two Thousand Guineas with Niksar. Star King was eventually exported to Australia where, under the name of Star Kingdom, he established a big reputation as a sire.

At three Abernant began by winning a minor seven-furlongs event at Bath, being returned at the unremunerative price of 25/1 on. He was a 5/4 favourite for The Two Thousand Guineas, second favourite being Star King who, trained by J. C. Waugh, had won The Greenham Stakes at Newbury by five lengths. In the Guineas Abernant led from the start and the scorching pace he set was too much for most of his rivals. Coming into the Dip he looked sure to win but in the final hundred yards his stride began to shorten. In the meantime Nimbus, outpaced early on, was making up ground fast and beginning to look really dangerous. All Gordon Richards could do on Abernant was to sit still and suffer, hoping that the winning post would come just in time. His tactics nearly paid off but the camera revealed that Nimbus, ridden by Elliott, had got his nose in front in the very last stride. It was the first time a photograph had decided the result in a classic. Murless had thus for the second year running lost The Two Thousand Guineas by a very narrow margin. Barnes Park was four lengths away third and Amour Drake fourth. Some backers of Abernant blamed Richards for not having got busy on him near the finish but had he done so the grey might have fallen to pieces completely. Murless was well satisfied with the way Abernant had been ridden.

Abernant was no miler. He was a magnificent sprinter whose only subsequent defeat was at four when he failed by half a length to concede 23 lb. to the three-year-old Tangle in The King's Stand Stakes at Ascot. When he retired he had won fourteen races worth £26,394.

Nimbus was bred by Mr William Hill and was a big bay colt by Nearco out of Kong, by the grey Irish Derby winner Baytown. Kong had won The Woking-ham Stakes with 6 st. 12 lb. Mr Henry A. Glenister bought Nimbus as a yearling for 5,000 guineas and gave him as a present to his wife. Glenister, who possessed a remarkable knowledge of the Stud Book, was always something of a man of mystery to his trainer, George Colling. He liked to describe himself as a farmer and indeed he did farm 700 acres at Sible Hedingham in Essex. He did not invariably choose to inform people that he was in fact a salaried bank official, employed as assistant manager of the London branch of the Midland Bank Executor and Trustee Company in the City. Bank officials closely identified with racing are rare; ones that can fork out 5,000 guineas for a yearling rarer still. On August 16, 1952 Mr Glenister committed suicide in his car in Sussex. At the inquest, it was revealed that he was in default of 'a considerable sum' entrusted to his department at the bank. The full story of that episode has yet to be told; nor has the Midland Bank ever revealed the exact amount that their employee got away with.

As a two-year-old Nimbus won The Coventry Stakes at Royal Ascot but in The Champagne Stakes he was outpaced by Abernant who finished six lengths in front of him. Before the Guineas he won The Thirsk Classic Trial ridden by Elliott, who was to partner him in the Newmarket classic.

Nimbus did not run again before The Derby but his final gallop was thoroughly satisfactory. His preparation had not been helped by the fact that Colling was ill and much responsibility devolved on his head lad, Dick Jones, and on Elliott. Colling was too unwell to go to Epsom and asked Jack Jarvis to saddle Nimbus. In his book of reminiscences entitled *They're Off*, Jarvis gave the following account.

When I went down to the paddock I found Nimbus standing still in the centre of it with a distinctly apprehensive small boy on his back. Nimbus was obviously very much on edge, kicking, sweating and refusing to move. George's head lad was there, too, and so were Mr and Mrs Glenister and George's wife. I told the

19. Amour Drake exercising with jockey Rae Johnstone

boy to dismount and I then got Nimbus to walk quietly down to the saddling stalls that used to stand up against the fence dividing the paddock from the Durdans. Then we dried Nimbus off and settled him down.

Colling had given orders that Nimbus was to be ridden by the boy in the parade ring but Jarvis was sure that Nimbus was happier without the boy on his back. Jarvis, therefore, took the responsibility of ordering the boy to walk along in readiness in case he was needed but not to get mounted. It was not an easy decision for Jarvis to make as it was contrary to Colling's orders and if Nimbus, a high-mettled colt, had played up and got loose, Jarvis would undoubtedly have had to carry the can. It would not have been possible for the head lad to make a similar decision. Luckily, though, everything went well. Jarvis never received a word of thanks from Mr and Mrs Glenister.

It proved to be one of the most exciting and controversial Derbies of this century. With typical boldness, Elliott elected to make the running on Nimbus whom many

20.   The news-reel film of the 1949 Derby shows the dramatic switch to the inside made by Rae Johnstone on Amour Drake in the last 100 yards (1) 200 yards from home—Nimbus (rails) is slightly in front of Swallow Tail, with Amour Drake coming on the outside; (2) Nimbus has edged over to the right and Swallow Tail appears unbalanced; (3) Nimbus seems to be 'leaning' on Swallow Tail; (4) Swallow Tail veers to the right (partially obscuring Amour Drake); (5, 6 and 7) with less than 100 yards to go Johnstone takes Amour Drake to the inside; (8 and 9) at the winning post—a finish of short-heads, 1. Nimbus, 2. Amour Drake, 3. Swallow Tail.

reckoned unlikely to stay the distance on account of the stamina limitations of his dam. At Tattenham Corner Nimbus still led but Lord Derby's Bois Roussel colt Swallow Tail was close up and apparently going every bit as well. At this stage Amour Drake was lying eighth.

Just below the distance, Swallow Tail managed to get his head in front but Nimbus fought back and regained the lead. In the meantime Amour Drake was making up ground fast towards the centre of the course. In the final furlong Nimbus, obviously tiring, began to veer to the right and went very close indeed to Swallow Tail. If he did not actually touch Swallow Tail, he certainly unbalanced him and Swallow Tail, too, edged to the right. It looked as if Amour Drake's powerful challenge might well be impeded by Swallow Tail. Rae Johnstone, Amour Drake's rider, had to make a split second decision. At this late and critical juncture, he switched Amour Drake over to the inside to the left of Nimbus. That manoeuvre looked sure to have put paid to Amour Drake's chance but he finished so fast that he only failed by a head to catch Nimbus—it was the first photo-finish Derby—and he was in front two strides beyond the post. The blinkered Swallow Tail was a head away third.

With ordinary luck Amour Drake would probably have won by a length. If Swallow Tail had been second, his rider, Doug Smith, might well have objected to Nimbus. If Swallow Tail had won and Amour Drake been second, then there might have been an objection by Johnstone. Nimbus, though, had not interfered with Amour Drake. There was no camera patrol in those days and no inquiry was held by the stewards.

There was drama off the course as well. M. Volterra, whose health had suffered during wartime internment by the Germans, was dying in Paris. He was too ill to listen to the broadcast of the race but his wife let him think that Amour Drake had won, thereby giving him a little happiness before he expired the following day.

Brought up with little schooling or money, M. Volterra became, through hard work and quick wits, the king of Parisian theatres and music halls. He took up racing in 1921 and won the Grand Steeplechase de Paris with Roi Belge. In 1933 Captain Jefferson Cohn, son-in-law of Mr Horatio Bottomley, found himself in financial difficulties and Volterra bought all his mares and horses in training. Cohn also passed on the lease of the Bois Roussel Stud, and William Hayton, an acknowledged master of his profession, agreed to stay on there as manager. In 1934 Volterra won the French Derby with Duplex and the Grand Prix with Admiral Drake, sire of Amour Drake, both trained by Émile Charlier. Among the famous horses he bred were Bois Roussel and My Love, both Derby winners; Le Ksar (Two Thousand Guineas); Mary Tudor, dam of Owen Tudor; and Quick Arrow, dam of The Oaks winner, Steady Aim. Of the first fourteen horses to finish in the 1949 Derby, eight were of the stock of stallions Volterra had bred.

The only appearance of Nimbus after The Derby was in The Cromwell Stakes at Haydock Park in which he obtained a walk-over. He was not engaged in The St Leger. During his preparation for the Prix de l'Arc de Triomphe he jarred himself badly and it was decided to retire him to the stud. He was not the success anticipated and in 1962 he was sold for export to Japan. His best winners were Nagami, who was placed in The Two Thousand Guineas, The Derby and The St Leger and who won The Coronation Cup; and Nucleus, runner-up to Meld in The St Leger. Amour Drake, who had won the French Two Thousand Guineas and who won The Coronation Cup at four, was at the stud in Ireland for some time but was not a success and he ended up in Peru. He did get one very fast filly in Sarcelle. Swallow Tail did well as a sire in Brazil.

George Colling was only fifty-five when he died in 1959. He came of a sporting north-country family. His father, Bob Colling, was a trainer and a master of foxhounds. His mother was a daughter of the famous steeplechase rider Robert I'Anson. His brother Jack was for many years a consistently successful trainer. Both Jack, the elder, and George were apprenticed to their father and both rode with success till they became too big. In 1919, while still an apprentice, George rode seventy-two winners. In 1920 he received a retainer from Lord Derby for whom he won The Park Hill Stakes on Redhead. Weight compelled him to retire from the saddle in 1922.

Slight, dark, rather delicate-looking, quiet spoken and with faultless manners, George was plagued from boyhood by indifferent health. His whole life was influenced by this fact and though his friends were apt to make jokes about the anxious care he took of himself, the plain truth is that he very seldom felt well and was often a good deal iller than was generally supposed. Not surprisingly, his disposition was hardly hilarious, but he had great charm, was certainly not without humour and was a really good friend to those whom he liked. He was keen on every form of sport, particularly shooting and golf, and was captain of the Royal Worlington and Newmarket Golf Club, usually referred to as Mildenhall. Strictly brought up himself, he remained old-fashioned in many of his views. His own standards of conduct were high and nothing grieved him more than when individuals he had been brought up to respect, such as members of the Jockey Club or their wives, spoke or behaved in a manner he regarded as deserving of censure.

When he gave up riding he was for a considerable time assistant to his brother who then trained at Newmarket. In 1935 he decided to launch out on his own. To begin with he had few horses and indifferent ones at that. He himself always liked to pretend that he was a singularly unlucky man and he had a story that one of his very first owners sent him a moderate animal but promised, if that particular animal won a race, to buy a couple of really nice yearlings. A race, a very minor affair up north, was duly won and the happy owner was just congratulating George in the unsaddling enclosure when he dropped down dead. However, by 1939 George had built up quite a strong stable, and among his patrons was Mrs Arthur James, whose stud he also managed. In that year he moved into Meynell House, Newmarket, renaming it Hurworth House after Hurworth-on-Tees, where his family had once lived.

George Colling was in the Royal Artillery till 1942, when he was invalided out. He soon re-established his stable but from then on life was all too often a battle against ill health. In 1950 he accepted an offer from Lord Derby to move into Stanley House and train for him and for members of his family. In his first season at Stanley House he trained sixty-one winners. It would not be true to say that he was ever really happy at Stanley House and, though in 1955, his last season there, he trained the winners of over £41,000, he was delighted to return to Hurworth House.

There is little doubt that he was a trainer of the very highest class. Apart from his skill with horses such as Nimbus, Wilwyn and Ark Royal, he was a master at placing less good ones to their best advantage. He much enjoyed bringing off a little coup in a handicap and was apt to remark afterwards: 'Poor old George must think of himself just occasionally.' He was extremely put out when Geoffrey Gilbey used to refer in slightly uncomplimentary terms to some of these little coups in one or other of the publications that he wrote for. George's reputation, though, stood very high and among his patrons when he died were Sir Randle Feilden, Lord Halifax, Major-General Sir George Burns, Mr Richard Hollingsworth and Sir Foster Robinson.

He died the same year as Manny Mercer, who had been apprenticed to him, had ridden many winners for him and was always intensely loyal to him. George always spoke of Mercer, a beautiful natural rider, in the highest terms though he never entirely forgot how Mercer in his Jaguar had driven him at 120 m.p.h. on the way back from Newcastle.

Swallow Tail, who had won The King Edward VII Stakes at Royal Ascot by six lengths, started favourite for The St Leger but had trained off by then and was only fourth behind Ridge Wood, beautifully ridden by Michael Beary. Ridge Wood, by Bois Roussel, was trained by Noel Murless for Mr G. R. H. Smith, a Tadcaster brewer and a former master of the York and Ainsty.

Both The One Thousand Guineas and The Oaks were won by Mr. N. P. Donaldson's Nasrullah filly, Musidora, trained by the most popular and respected trainer in the north, Captain Charles Elsey. Perhaps the most remarkable thing about Musidora, who ran unplaced in The St Leger, is that the first four mares in her tail-female line never saw a racecourse. Her dam, Painted Vale, was sold as an unbroken three-year-old for 220 guineas by Mr Bobby Watson to the Irish breeder Mr F. F. Tuthill. In The Oaks, ridden by the Australian Edgar Britt, the good-looking Musidora got home by a neck from M. Boussac's very closely in-bred Coronation V. In the Irish Oaks Coronation V, much affected by the journey, was beaten by Circus Lady but she finished the season in style by winning the Prix de l'Arc de Triomphe by four lengths from Double Rose with Amour Drake third.

Seldom does The Ascot Gold Cup arouse the intense interest that it did in 1949. The main protagonists were Black Tarquin and Alycidon and there was the keenest rivalry between the partisans of these two fine horses. Admirers of Black Tarquin were inclined to disparage Alycidon as a good one-pacer who would always be beaten by a top-class horse possessing power of acceleration. On the other hand, Alycidon fans declared that Alycidon would have Black Tarquin off

21.   Alycidon being patted by Doug Smith after winning The Ascot Gold Cup, 1949

the bit before the American-bred horse could deliver a challenge. Furthermore, they doubted whether a son of the Eclipse winner Rhodes Scholar was capable of staying the full Gold Cup distance.

Alycidon's preparation was in the hands of dapper Willie Pratt. Poor Walter Earl had collapsed during racing at Newmarket in April. He subsequently underwent brain surgery and remained desperately ill until he died the following year. Willie Pratt was a member of a notable racing family. His father, Francis Pratt, trained at Cheltenham and married Fred Archer's sister. As a boy, Willie often stayed at Newmarket with his famous uncle. Both Willie and his elder brother Fred, who trained for Mr James de Rothschild for nearly forty years, were apprenticed to James Ryan. Willie was only fourteen when he dead-heated for The Cesarewitch on Cypria who carried 6 st. 5 lb. Not long afterwards he became first jockey to the powerful Rothschild stable in France. He won the Grand Prix four times and also rode successfully in Germany. In 1904 he relinquished riding to become trainer to M. Jean Stern and he also trained for Lord Derby, Lady Granard and Mr 'Solly' Joel. On the outbreak of World War II he was training for M. P. Wertheimer. In 1940 he came back to England. He trained the 1947 Cesarewitch winner, Whiteway.

Willie Pratt died in 1957 aged eighty. He had married his cousin Ethel, daughter of Charles Archer and sister of the Fred Archer who trained the Grand National winner Double Chance. Willie's three daughters all married into the racing world and became respectively Mrs Claude Halsey, Mrs Jack Watts and Mrs Humphrey Cottrill. Charles Pratt, Willie's younger brother, trained at Lambourn till he was killed in an air crash returning from a race meeting.

Black Tarquin and Alycidon both won their preliminary races before the Cup. Black Tarquin, Britt up, was favourite at 11/10 while Alycidon, ridden by Doug Smith, was on offer at 5/4. Alycidon had the services of two pacemakers, Benny Lynch and Stockbridge. The pacemakers did their work well. Stockbridge led for eleven furlongs and then Benny Lynch was in front till five furlongs from home when Alycidon, amid terrific cheers from his supporters, headed him.

Meanwhile, Black Tarquin, moving very easily, drew up to tackle the leader. The excitement mounted. 'Now watch the real racehorse come away and win,' observed a confident racing correspondent who had napped Black Tarquin. There was no question, though, of Black Tarquin 'coming away'. The pair raced together for a hundred yards and then Britt was obliged to feel for his whip. It was to no avail; the gallant Black Tarquin had given everything he had. He was a well-beaten horse at the distance whereas Alycidon showed not the slightest sign of weakening and galloped on strongly to win by five lengths. It was the most popular Gold Cup victory since that of Persimmon in the royal colours in 1897. The time was a second outside the record set up by Flares in 1938.

Alycidon went on to win The Goodwood Cup and The Doncaster Cup. Black Tarquin was apparently none the worse for his exertions and he looked magnificent when he turned out for The Princess of Wales's Stakes at Newmarket later that month. He did not run, though, within a stone of his true form and finished unplaced. The Gold Cup had got to the bottom of him. When in 1975 Grundy was beaten at York following his gruelling battle with Bustino at Ascot, a good many people recalled the case of Black Tarquin.

Top trainer in 1949 was Frank Butters, whose brother Fred had trained the 1937 Derby winner Mid-day Sun. It turned out to be Frank's final season. One winter evening he set out on his bicycle to attend a committee meeting at the Rous Memorial Hospital. Not far from his house he was in collision with a lorry. The shock he received was so severe and of such a lasting nature that he was never able to resume training again. He died in 1957.

Like Willie Pratt, Frank Butters came from a racing family. His father, Joseph Butters, had been a jockey before he trained, and he married Janet, daughter of James Waugh and sister of the trainers Willie, Charles, Dawson and Tom Waugh. Frank himself was born in Vienna where his father was then training. He began his own training career in Austria–Hungary and was there when war erupted in 1914. He was interned for the duration but his treatment was fairly lenient. In 1919 he set up as a trainer in Italy and remained till 1926, when he returned to England to assist George Lambton. In 1927 he succeeded Lambton at Stanley House, having been given a four-year contract by Lord Derby. He won The St Leger with Fairway, The One Thousand Guineas with Fair Isle, and The Oaks with Toboggan and with Lord Durham's Beam. The year 1930 was one of economic depression and at the York August meeting Lord Derby told Butters that his expiring contract would not be renewed as he was reducing his racing commitments. In 1931 Lambton took up his old post as trainer at Stanley House.

Thus at the age of fifty-two Butters was out of a job. However, he rented the Fitzroy House establishment and Mr A. W. Gordon and Sir Alfred Butt both sent him horses. In 1931 the Aga Khan quarrelled bitterly with Dick Dawson and before the season was over Butters had the Aga Khan's horses under his care. This was the start of a long, happy and successful association. The Aga Khan described his trainer 'as one of the most delightful men one could ever hope to meet with a nature as clean and clear as a diamond but without its harshness'.

Butters trained fifteen classic winners including the Derby winners Bahram, who carried off the Triple Crown, and Mahmoud. He also won the Prix de l'Arc de Triomphe with Migoli. He was said to be hard on his horses but those with the constitution to stand up to a rigorous preparation were fit to run for their lives on the day that really mattered. He embodied most of the old-fashioned virtues such as loyalty to his employers, integrity and a high standard of duty. He only had one big bet in his life; that was on Fairway in The Derby. His temper was equable but he did show signs of displeasure when a young gentleman, destined to become Senior Steward of the Jockey Club, was bolted with on the Heath and went slap through the Aga Khan's Ascot two-year-olds. The great sorrow of his life was the tragic death of his son Victor, his valued assistant, while on a short winter holiday in Switzerland.

By 1949 the judges had just about got the hang of the photo-finish and could interpret the photographs correctly, not invariably the simplest of tasks. There was, however, a contretemps in The Bentinck Stakes at Goodwood. The judge called for a photograph after a very close finish between High Stakes and Hornet III and after examination he awarded the verdict to High Stakes. It was generally agreed that he had misread the photograph and that Hornet III had been robbed.

High Stakes, bred and owned by Lord Astor and trained by Jack Colling, was exceptionally well bred, being by Hyperion out of the Oaks winner Pennycome-quick. Unfortunately his disposition in his youth was such that it was deemed necessary to have him cut. However, he had a long and honourable racing career, winning thirty-one races, dead-heating in two others, and earning well over £20,000 in stakes. When finishing, he held his head very high which made it look as if he was hating every second of it but in fact he was a thoroughly game performer and was deservedly a favourite with the public.

1950 was not the happiest of years for English racing. As conditions of life became less austere and more consumer goods were available on the market, so did the racing boom recede. During the year attendances dropped by as much as 15 per cent. The golden days for racecourse executives were over.

In addition it was a year of triumph for the French who won every classic bar The Two Thousand Guineas. In The Oaks and The St Leger French horses finished first and second. In The Derby there was only one British-bred competitor in the leading four. Additional French victories included The Coronation Cup, The Gold Vase, The Eclipse Stakes, The Goodwood Cup and The Gimcrack Stakes. For the first time since the great days of Count de Lagrange and Gladiateur in the previous century, a Frenchman, M. Boussac, headed the owners' list and the breeders' list as well. His trainer, the former jockey C. H. Semblat, was leading trainer without having once set foot in this country.

It was common knowledge before the season began that Captain Boyd-Rochfort trained an American-bred colt of exceptional promise for one of his several American owners, Mr William Woodward, a banker. Mr Woodward was Chairman for many years of the New York Jockey Club and was an honorary member of the Jockey Club here. In 1928 he had been introduced to Boyd-Rochfort by Mr Marshall Field and from then on he nearly always sent him two or three yearlings to be trained. On the whole he had been very successful and had won The One Thousand Guineas with the beautiful Brown Betty, The Oaks with Hycilla and The St Leger with Boswell and Black Tarquin. He had also won The Gold Cup with Flares, who thereby avenged the defeat of his brother Omaha at the hands of Quashed in that event two years earlier. Mr Woodward visited this country rarely and so seldom saw his horses run.

Mr Woodward's classic contender in 1950 was Prince Simon, a big, powerful, very good-looking bay colt, possibly a bit straight in the shoulder, by Princequillo out of Dancing Dora. In 1949 he was too big and backward to be risked on the firm ground that persisted for so long. He wintered exceptionally well and the manner in which he worked at home raised the highest expectations of his ability. He was an impressive winner of the one-mile Wood Ditton Stakes at the Craven

Meeting and started favourite at 3/1 for The Two Thousand Guineas. Second favourite was the Middle Park Stakes winner Masked Light and there was a lot of money for the Aga Khan's classy grey Fair Trial colt, Palestine, who was under the care of Marcus Marsh following the retirement of Frank Butters. Palestine had a brilliant record at two, winning six of his seven races. He was probably stale when Masked Light beat him in the Middle Park.

That Palestine, who just stayed a mile but not an inch more, won The Two Thousand Guineas was largely due to the riding of Charlie Smirke whose worst enemy—he had several of them—could hardly have accused him of lacking self-confidence and self-esteem. He was invariably at his best on the big occasion. In this race 'Cheeky Charlie' always had a handy position. He had the grey perfectly balanced at the Bushes and he then drove him down the hill into the Dip as hard as he could go, making the very most of the downhill impetus. He gained a lead of almost three lengths on the much bigger Prince Simon, who did not handle the descent nearly as smoothly. When Prince Simon met the rising ground, however, he fairly flew but, although Palestine was weakening at the finish, he still had a bit in hand and won by a very short head. It had been a brilliant piece of opportunist riding and, according to Marsh, Charlie was quite insufferable for days afterwards.

The Derby, for which Prince Simon, who in the meantime had won The Newmarket Stakes by six lengths, was a 2/1 favourite, did not concern Palestine. Harry Carr, who partnered Prince Simon, was in the lead at half-way, a lot sooner than he had intended, but Lowrey on Pewter Platter who was in front of him had shouted a warning that his mount was beginning to hang and might carry the favourite wide at Tattenham Corner. Under the circumstances Carr felt obliged to go on.

Two furlongs from home Prince Simon was going so well that he looked sure to win but M. Boussac's Galcador, who had been seventh at Tattenham Corner, was making up ground fast. At first Carr did not appear to appreciate the danger fully and perhaps did not drive Prince Simon on quite as hard as he might have done. Below the distance Johnstone asked Galcador for his effort. The chestnut son of Djebel quickened in great style and with a hundred yards left he led by three-quarters of a length. At that point, however, he had shot his bolt and, with Prince Simon staying on gamely enough, the French colt had only a head to spare at the finish.

Poor Harry Carr came in for a lot of wounding criticism and many people thought he had ridden a weak and ill judged race. In the bitterness of defeat, though, Boyd-Rochfort refused to hear a word against his jockey and to his eternal credit defended him resolutely against the many attacks that were made. Johnstone had praise lavished on him by the press and his army of admirers. No one bothered to point out that Johnstone had come very close to throwing the race away by making his effort too soon.

At Royal Ascot Prince Simon started at 8/1 on for The King Edward VII Stakes but was beaten a head by Babu's Pet, a 20/1 outsider. He never raced again as he went wrong in his preparation for The St Leger. As a stallion he was a total failure and in the end was given away as a hack. He had surely been born under an unlucky star. Galcador never ran again and eventually ended up in Japan.

The French filly Camaree, who, trained by A. Lieux, had won The One Thousand Guineas for M. J. Ternynck, was favourite for The Oaks but finished unplaced. The winner was M. Boussac's Asmena, by Goya out of the famous Astronomie, dam of Caracalla II, Marsyas II and Arbar. Asmena did not possess the best of joints and, heavily bandaged, she hobbled down to the start like a hen in handcuffs. It really looked at one point as if she was going to fall over and of course she drifted in the market. She warmed up, though, when she began to race; the stiffness wore off and she battled on gamely to win by a length from another French filly, Plume II.

M. Boussac won The St Leger, too, his Prix du Jockey Club winner Scratch II, a chestnut son of Pharis, getting the better of Baron Guy de Rothschild's Grand Prix de Paris winner, Vieux Manoir. Laumain, who rode Vieux Manoir, was no match for that wily tactician Johnstone on Scratch II. With jockeys reversed, Vieux Manoir would probably have won. He was by Brantôme, a son of Blandford that was one of the best horses in France during the inter-war period. Brantôme was stolen by the Germans but was luckily recovered after the war.

In the Ascot Gold Cup there were thirteen runners, nine of them bred in France and one in America. The 10/1 winner, though, was Mr W. Harvey's Supertello, trained by J. C. Waugh at Chilton. Bred by Mr Herbert Blagrave, he had been bought by his owner for 2,700 guineas as a yearling. Runner-up was the French filly Bagheera, winner of the Grand Prix in 1949. Supertello was a flop as a sire.

The Eclipse Stakes was rather a peculiar affair. Baron de Waldner had high hopes of winning the £9,467 prize with his three-year-old colt Pearl Clip, a half-brother of the Derby winner Pearl Diver. He also intended to run the four-year-old Flocon as pacemaker. On the morning of the race Pearl Clip was discovered lying on the floor of his box in pain and running a high temperature. It was eventually found necessary to destroy him. The cause of his sudden illness was given as acute colic. This was distressing for Baron de Waldner, who did obtain some consolation, however, as Flocon won the race by a head from the Aga Khan's Éclat. The Baron stated after the race that Flocon was ten pounds inferior to Pearl Clip at weight for age.

Palestine, who had won The St James's Palace Stakes by five lengths, failed to stay in The Eclipse and finished unplaced. He ended his career by winning The Sussex Stakes at Goodwood, then worth only £1,017. At the stud he sired the Queen's Two Thousand Guineas winner, Pall Mall.

It gave considerable satisfaction to the racing world when Mr (later Sir) Winston Churchill decided to join the ranks of the owners. His father, Lord Randolph Churchill, had taken up racing at one stage and had won the 1889 Oaks with L'Abbesse de Jovarre, who bred the successful sire Desmond. In 1949 the Epsom trainer Walter Nightingall was charged with the task of buying a horse for Mr Churchill and for a moderate price he purchased for him in France a grey three-year-old called Colonist II, by Rienzo, who had won races in Egypt, out of Cybele. During his first year in this country Colonist II won three minor races which at least gave racegoers a chance of displaying the affection they felt for his owner.

In 1950 Colonist II improved considerably. He ran eleven times, was never out of the first four, and won six races including The Jockey Club Cup. Tough and game, he established himself as the most popular horse in the country. He carried on the good work in 1951, winning, amid scenes of great enthusiasm, The Winston Churchill Stakes at Hurst Park, and then The White Rose Stakes on the same course. He ran a great race in The Gold Cup but found one too good for him in Pan II. He was retired to the stud at the end of the season and was eventually bought by the Queen. He lived on happily till his death at Sandringham in 1973. He sired a lot of good jumpers, including the grey Stalbridge Colonist who beat the mighty Arkle in The Hennessy Gold Cup.

During his fifteen years on the turf, Sir Winston Churchill was remarkably successful. In the mid-1950s he bought the Newchapel Stud near Lingfield. There he bred High Hat, who beat the great Petite Étoile in The Aly Khan Memorial Cup at Kempton and who sired The One Thousand Guineas winner Glad Rags and High Line, thrice winner of The Jockey Club Cup; Vienna, sire of the Prix de l'Arc de Triomphe winner Vaguely Noble; Tudor Monarch, winner of The Stewards' Cup; and Welsh Abbot, who won The Portland Handicap as a three-year-old with 9 st. 2 lb.

The King won the 1950 Cesarewitch with his three-year-old filly Above Board, bred by himself and trained by Boyd-Rochfort. She was by the Derby winner Straight Deal out of the Friar Marcus mare Feola who did such splendid service for the Royal Stud. Above Board had previously won the Yorkshire Oaks and the original intention was to run her in the Newmarket Oaks. However, during the week-end before the Newmarket meeting began, those two shrewd Irishmen Boyd-Rochfort and Captain Charles Moore, the King's racing manager, put their heads together. They decided The Cesarewitch would not take a lot of winning and elected to run Above Board in that race instead. This late decision was not received with three loyal and hearty cheers by punters who had already made their wagers on the 'autumn double' and had of course omitted Above Board from their calculations. Above Board had been languishing at 40/1 in the market and her price was at once reduced to 18/1. Some very big bets were struck and one well-known racing journalist won enough to ensure a reasonably comfortable standard of living for a considerable number of years. Above Board caused no heart tremors to her backers and won by six lengths. At the stud she bred Doutelle, a good horse who looked like making a really good sire and whose unfortunate early death through an accident was a severe loss to breeders, and Above Suspicion, winner of The St James's Palace Stakes at Royal Ascot and The Gordon Stakes at Goodwood.

During this era rumours were rife over the prevalence of doping. Frequently, extreme views were taken. There were some who regarded every doping story as emanating from the minds of individuals who had been over-exposed to the stirring racing novels of Mr Nat Gould during their formative years. Others ascribed the downfall of almost every favourite to the activities of doping gangs.

That a certain amount of doping was going on, chiefly to stop horses winning, was indisputable. Doping to win is almost invariably carried out by someone closely connected with the stable. It is necessary to know the horse's condition and the plans that have been made for it. A little experimentation is desirable, too. A dose that is just right for one horse may send another one raving mad.

On the other hand, no trainer in full possession of his mental faculties would ever stop a horse with dope, there being so many other simpler methods available. However, the primitive standard of security that existed in most stables and on the majority of racecourses made access to a horse by outsiders a not insuperable difficulty.

The ante-post market on big races has throughout racing history proved a source of temptation to villains since in ante-post betting the punter loses his money if the horse he has backed fails to run. It does not matter to the villains, therefore, if the horse in question is severely injured. The object of the exercise is to ensure it cannot take the field in the race for which it has been backed.

Stopping a horse from winning a race in which there has been no ante-post betting demands methods considerably less crude. It is pointless to give a horse so much dope that it is unable to rise from the floor of its box; the horse has got to be able to run, but so far below its true form that those in the know can lay it with complete confidence. The ideal race for the operation is one in which there is a small field with two fancied competitors; then one can be laid and the other backed.

On January 1, 1951 an amendment to Rule 102 came into effect. A new paragraph had been added which read: 'If in any case it shall be found that any drug or stimulant has been administered to a horse for the purpose of affecting its speed in a race, the licence of the trainer of the horse shall be withdrawn and he shall be declared a disqualified person.'

Rule 102 now seemed to leave the Stewards of the Jockey Club with no room to manoeuvre and they were bound to impose a penalty of extreme severity on a trainer whose horse had been 'got at' even though there was no evidence of his complicity and it was in the highest degree improbable that he was involved. It was in fact a deplorably unjust rule. Possibly the authorities felt the situation was of sufficient gravity to warrant legislation that left no doubts at all as to a trainer's responsibilities in respect of his horses, and that any relaxation of the rule might leave the door open to abuses highly prejudicial to the sport as a whole. Obviously it was extremely unlikely that the actual doper would ever be caught red-handed in the act.

Those who preferred not to see the perils inherent in Rule 102 received a nasty jolt on December 7, 1951 when the Press Association announced the receipt of the following letter from Lord Rosebery, one of the shrewdest, most experienced and most influential members of the Jockey Club:

Dalmeny House
Edinburgh

SIR,

There has been a great deal written in the Press concerning the doping of racehorses, and, indeed, several trainers have lost their licences owing to horses in their care having been discovered by the veterinary surgeons, employed by the Jockey Club, to have been doped.

Now there are two methods of doping. One, to make a horse go faster, and the other to make it go slower, or what is commonly known as to 'stop' it.

It is only common sense to realise that nine out of ten of the horses that are given a stimulant to make them go faster have been doped by someone connected with the stable, because no one outside the stable would know if the horse was fit and in proper condition, or fancied by the stable.

On the other hand it seems inconceivable that any owner or trainer would give a horse anything to stop it, because there are so many easier ways of so doing; for instance, giving it a bucket of water, or even telling the jockey to give it an easy race.

I was dissatisfied with the running of one of my horses this season, and instructed a veterinary surgeon to examine it with the usual tests. I now find that the animal had received a dope, causing it to be stopped.

With the approval of my trainer, J. L. Jarvis, in whom I have the utmost trust and confidence, I am offering £1,000 reward for any information that establishes the identity of the offenders.

Yours, etc.,
Rosebery.

The animal in question was the two-year-old filly Snap, who started at 5/2 for The Dalham Stakes at Newmarket on October 31 and finished twelfth. The impact of Lord Rosebery's letter lay in the realisation that if the test carried out had been official rather than private, the Stewards of the Jockey Club would have been left with no option but to deprive of his livelihood a man no more likely to dope a horse than Lord Rosebery was to rob a bank. It would have been a terrible miscarriage of justice; and speculation arose as to whether lesser trainers had, in the past, been in fact unjustly treated.

However, the case of Snap may at least have done something to stir the minds of the authorities and to expedite the changes that were eventually made in the rules pertaining to doping.

In 1951, M. Boussac was again both leading owner and leading breeder. Four of the classic races, though, went to British-bred horses. The top two-year-old of 1950, Big Dipper, trained by Boyd-Rochfort, never ran and the winner of The Two Thousand Guineas was Ki Ming, a seventeen-hands brown colt owned by Mr Ley On, who kept a Chinese restaurant in London, trained by Michael Beary, and ridden by the Australian jockey Arthur Breasley, commonly known as 'Scobie'. Bred in Ireland by the late Mr J. C. Sullivan, Ki Ming did not boast a fashionable pedigree as he was by Ballyogan, who never won beyond five furlongs, out of Ulster Lily, by Apron. As a foal he was sold in Dublin for 370 guineas to Mr Tim Hyde, who had won the 1939 Grand National on Workman. At the same sale, Ulster Lily was knocked down for 50 guineas. A year later Michael Beary's brother John bought Ki Ming at Newmarket for 760 guineas.

Michael Beary came from Tipperary. He spent part of his apprenticeship with 'Atty' Persse, a great believer in old-fashioned stable discipline, and he obtained his first ride in public on the recommendation of Steve Donoghue. He became a stylish and effective rider who was at his best on 'difficult' horses. He won the 1937 Derby on Mid-day Sun. He was far from being devoid of charm but he talked too much, disregarding the possible consequences, and he was liable to get people's backs up. Over financial matters he was singularly inept. Despite this fine start to his training career, he was soon in serious difficulties. He was a poor man when he died in 1956.

When the average member of the public has a bet on The Derby, he (or she) does not give a damn about pedigrees and Ki Ming started favourite at Epsom although his prospects of staying the distance were remote. He never looked like winning. In the autumn he won the six-furlongs Diadem Stakes at Ascot, beating a single opponent. He was no good as a sire.

The Derby had a distinct flavour of National Hunt racing. The six-lengths winner was Arctic Prince, owned by Mr Joseph McGrath, trained by W. Stephenson and ridden by Charlie Spares, who was perhaps more closely identified with Wincanton than with Epsom. Signal Box, who finished third, was ridden by the great Irish steeplechase jockey, Martin Molony.

Mr McGrath, as a patriotic Irishman, had fought for his country's independence during 'the troubles'. He became a minister of the Irish Free State, a man of great influence and a leading participator in the development of the Irish Hospitals Sweepstake. The stud he founded became one of the most powerful in Europe and would have been even more successful had he not sold not only Nasrullah but Arctic Prince as well.

Willy Stephenson had been apprenticed to Major W. V. Beatty. He became a highly competent jockey and was a bold rider to hounds. For many years he has conducted a successful 'mixed' stable at Royston. He trained the Grand National winner Oxo and also that outstanding hurdler, Sir Ken. Spares was never in the first flight either on the flat or over hurdles. There was a story that on entering the winner's enclosure on Arctic Prince he observed: 'The others must be awful, guv'nor, as ours ain't much'; but I fear this comment is apocryphal.

Bred by his owner, Arctic Prince was by the French Derby winner Prince Chevalier out of Arctic Sun, by Nearco. Prince Chevalier had been imported into England in 1947 and Arctic Prince was among his first crop of runners. He also sired Charlottesville, winner of the French Derby and the Grand Prix, and La Paiva, dam of Brigadier Gerard. Arctic Sun had been the best two-year-old in Ireland in 1943 and was out of the Solario mare, Solar Flower, winner of over £10,000. As a two-year-old Arctic Prince had won a race worth £207 at Thirsk but failed badly when fancied for The Gimcrack Stakes. The following spring he was seventh in The Two Thousand Guineas. He may not have beaten a very good field when he won The Derby at 28/1 but he could hardly have scored with greater ease. Unfortunately, he broke down in The King George VI and Queen Elizabeth Festival of Britain Stakes. Before being exported to America he sired the Eclipse winner Arctic Explorer, who did well as a sire in Australia; Exar, winner of the Goodwood and Doncaster Cups; and Nellie Park, dam of that great mare Park Top.

Sybil's Nephew, destined to do well as a sire in South Africa, had finished second in The Derby and started favourite for The St Leger, in which however he was unplaced. This was a truly remarkable race. M. Boussac's candidate was Talma II, a leggy chestnut by Pharis II. In the paddock Talma's conduct and general demeanour could hardly have been less attractive and would have been more appropriate to a stallion during the covering season. Usually when a horse behaves in that manner he tends to drift in the market. In Talma's case the reverse occurred. Money poured in for him and his price came tumbling down from 100/7 to 7/1. Those who backed him certainly knew what they were about. With nearly a mile to go he went clear and left his opponents apparently marking time. The judge's verdict was ten lengths; it looked rather more like twenty. Neither before nor subsequently did Talma II show comparable form. At Ascot the following month he was all out to beat the three-year-old Eastern Emperor, who received 3 lb., by a neck in The Cumberland Lodge Stakes. There was no dope test ordered after Talma's St Leger success.

The One Thousand Guineas went to a beautiful Nasrullah filly, Belle of All, owned by Mr Henry Tufton who had paid 8,000 guineas for her as a yearling. Mr Tufton, later Lord Hothfield, was a type of Jockey Club member that has become increasingly rare. The turf formed a very important part of his life. He attended nearly all the major meetings and a good many of the less important ones, too. He was thoroughly conversant with form and with most of the ins and outs of the game as well. In consequence he was admirably suited to carry out the duties of a steward.

Trainer of Belle of All was Norman Bertie, who had been Fred Darling's head lad and was a first-class stableman. The power behind the throne in that stable was Jack Clayton, who eventually took out a licence and became a trainer himself. He was closely connected with racing in one way or another almost from the time he left Eton. At one period he obtained some notoriety as a big but not particularly successful punter, and at times he was identified with the racing interests of Mr J. V. Rank and Sir Victor Sassoon. He bore the ups and downs of life philosophically. His generous nature made him liked wherever he went and he never said an unkind word about anyone. He died in 1975.

Belle of All found the distance in The Oaks too much for her but she won The Coronation Stakes at Royal Ascot. The winner of The Oaks was Major Lionel Holliday's Neasham Belle, trained by Geoffrey Brooke and ridden by Stanley Clayton.

Major Lionel Brook Holliday was eighty-five when he died in 1965, a few days after his wife. He was head of L. B. Holliday and Co. Ltd, manufacturers of aniline dyes at Huddersfield. He was undoubtedly the most consistently successful of the big owner-breeders during the post-war era. He conducted his bloodstock breeding operations on the very best lines and his racing operations on the best lines, too. His horses were always out to win. 'That man's a menace,' grumbled a professional punter after one of the Major's horses had come up at 25/1. 'Even when his horses aren't fancied they're always trying.'

A Yorkshireman, with certain characteristics not untypical of the inhabitants of that county, Major Holliday could be difficult, even cantankerous. Perhaps for that reason he was not elected to the Jockey Club till he was over eighty, despite his great services to racing. He was a man who apparently never felt the need for friends and was wholly uncompromising in his views and conduct. He knew what he wanted and was determined to have things done the way he liked. Few trainers stayed with him for long and some departed with a permanent feeling of resentment. One who was more kindly in his judgement than others used to say, 'There must be real good in a man who is such a wonderful judge of a fox-hound.' Major Holliday himself did not appear to worry unduly over the rapid turnover in trainers. 'They come to me on bicycles,' he once said, 'but they all leave in Bentleys.' One of his trainers was having his furniture moved into the trainer's house and observed to the foreman: 'Do you think this house is damp? I've got some nice bits of furniture and I don't want them to come to any harm.' 'Don't worry, guv,' replied the foreman. 'They won't be here long enough.' And they weren't.

Sometimes the Major antagonised trainers other than his own. One was apt to give him the Nazi salute and greet him with a cry of 'Heil Holliday'. Another observed bitterly: 'When he dies, they needn't say "No Flowers by Request". There won't be any bleeding flowers.'

Major Holliday's great good fortune was to purchase the mare Lost Soul, by Solario. She and her daughter Phase were the corner-stones of his triumphs as a breeder. He was three times leading breeder and three times leading owner, too. He never won The Derby but would very likely have done so if Hethersett, who subsequently won The St Leger, had not been brought down at Epsom. It was sad that Major Holliday never lived to see the triumphs of the best horse he ever bred, Vaguely Noble.

If Major Holliday was never one of the most genial and popular personalities in the racing world, Geoffrey Brooke most certainly is. For twenty long years he assisted 'Atty' Persse, a form of employment which may have had its advantages but was certainly not lucrative. He soon established his reputation when he took over Major Holliday's horses and when that particular engagement came to an end he was highly successful as a public trainer at Newmarket. Newmarket became a duller place when he retired in 1967 and departed to live in Ireland. Wherever Geoffrey Brooke is, cheerfulness and fun keep on breaking through. He has an apt turn of phrase. Invited to explain a physical peculiarity possessed

22.   Major Lionel Holliday leading in his Neasham Belle, S. Clayton up, after winning the 1951 Oaks

by a former patron he had not much liked, he replied: 'I think they were hanging him when the rope broke.'

Stanley Clayton, ex-miner and budgerigar fancier, had his ups and downs with Major Holliday but was probably the Major's favourite jockey if indeed anyone could be said to have occupied that position. He is now assistant trainer to Dick Hern, having previously assisted Jack Clayton till the latter's death.

1951 was Festival of Britain year and to mark the occasion the Duke of Norfolk and Sir John Crocker Bulteel devised The King George VI and Queen Elizabeth Festival of Britain Stakes for three-year-olds and upwards to be run over a mile and a half at Ascot in July. The total stakes amounted to £30,000 and it was then the richest race ever staged in this country. Not everyone approved. At the Annual General Meeting of the Thoroughbred Breeders' Association in 1950 Lord Derby read out the presidential speech of Lord Rosebery who was indisposed. In this speech Lord Rosebery expressed his dislike of what he termed 'these mammoth races'.

Be that as it may, the race aroused the utmost interest and there was a gigantic crowd to see it run on a perfect summer afternoon. The field included Arctic Prince, Scratch II, the great French four-year-old Tantième, Ki Ming, Belle of All, Wilwyn, Dynamiter, Zucchero and the improving three-year-old, Supreme Court. The pace from the start was terrific. Two riders who adopted a policy of patience and were prepared to wait were the experienced Elliott on Supreme Court and young Piggott on Zucchero. Their tactics paid off as Supreme Court came with a great run in the straight to win by a length from Zucchero with Tantième, a notoriously bad traveller, third. Tantième twice won the Prix de l'Arc de Triomphe. The winner was bred by Mr Tom Lilley and carried the colours of his wife Vera, who, following Mr Lilley's death, married Colonel F. R. Hue-Williams. Trainer of Supreme Court was the former steeplechase jockey Evan Williams, who had won The Grand National on Royal Mail in 1937 and conducted a successful stable at Kingsclere before leaving to become a Master of Fox-hounds in Ireland.

Supreme Court was by Persian Gulf or Precipitation, presumably the latter, out of the Fair Trial mare Forecourt who had belonged to Lt-Col Giles Loder and had been bought by Mr Lilley for 8,100 guineas at the December Sales when she was carrying Supreme Court. Mr Lilley decided to sell Supreme Court as a yearling but as the modest reserve of 2,000 guineas was not attained, he gave the colt to his wife. Supreme Court joined Marcus Marsh's stable but, when he became the Aga Khan's trainer, Marsh requested Mrs Lilley to take the colt back. He was accordingly then sent to Williams.

Slow to develop, Supreme Court won once at two. At three, when he had no classic engagements, he was unbeaten and may have been the best three-year-old in the country, winning The White Lodge Stakes at Hurst Park, The Chester Vase, The King Edward VII Stakes and finally the big Ascot race following which his owner chose to terminate his career. He was not a resounding success as a sire. His daughter, Athene, bred the Arc winner Rheingold and his son, Pipe of Peace, was third in the Derby.

Charles Elliott was a great jockey at his peak, a fine judge of pace and a very strong finisher. His father was travelling head lad to Lord George Dundas. He himself went as a boy to Jack Jarvis who taught him to ride. The boy's progress was one of remarkable rapidity. Within a year of riding his first winner he was Jarvis's stable jockey and in 1922 won The Gold Vase, The Gold Cup and The Eclipse Stakes on Golden Myth. In 1923 he was equal top jockey with Donoghue, who had been champion without a break since 1914. He won The Derby on Call Boy, Bois Roussel and Nimbus. Towards the end of his career he rode marvellous races on Souepi to win The Gold Cup and The Goodwood Cup. Though intelligent, articulate and self-confident, he was never in fact a good judge of horses or of their form; punters who took his advice ended up on the wrong side of the ledger. When he gave up riding, he trained for a few years for M. M. Boussac but unfortunately the Boussac fortunes were then starting to decline. He returned to England in 1956 and for a brief period ran a small stable at Newmarket. Alas, like others among his contemporaries, he was never very careful with his money and sadly the sun has seldom shone on him in his old age.

Up till the early 1950s the English racing world had reckoned little to flat-racing in Ireland, even though there had been one Irish-trained Derby winner earlier in the century, namely Mr R. Croker's Orby whose trainer was that versatile and entertaining member of the medical profession, Colonel Frederick McCabe. In general the standard of flat-racing in Ireland was low, which was hardly surprising in view of the exiguous nature of the prize money. The Irish Classics were fair game for English horses not good enough to win a classic in England.

Times were beginning to change, though, even if it was quite impossible to foresee that the Irish would supplant the French as the most formidable overseas challengers in our most valuable races and that certain Irish stables, strongly supported by American owners, would be numbered among the most powerful in Europe.

There was a hint of things to come in 1951, when the two-year-old Free Handicap was headed by Windy City with 9 st. 7 lb. This unfashionably bred colt was by Wyndham out of a mare by The Satrap and had cost 700 guineas as a yearling. Winner of The Gimcrack Stakes, he was owned by Mr Ray Bell, an American, and was trained in Ireland by Paddy Prendergast. His breeder, incidentally, was Colonel H. G. Alexander, a brother of Field Marshal Lord Alexander.

Paddy Prendergast is a member of a large family hailing from Athy. His father was well known as a 'spotter', meaning that if you wanted a horse, told him the type and the price you were prepared to pay, he would put you in touch with someone owning a horse of the sort that was desired. If the deal went through, he received a modest commission. I found him a most agreeable character and, like so many Irishmen, an accomplished raconteur. My dealings with him were of the happiest nature as for £60 he unearthed a hunter whose homely looks found ample compensation in her tough constitution and admirable performances over a number of years.

Paddy was apprenticed in his youth to Roderic More O'Ferrall, then a trainer and for many years now both a successful breeder and a gardener of no small repute. In due course Paddy went to find fame and fortune in England and rode under National Hunt rules. It is fair to say that as a rider over fences he was probably a shade better than the long-legged Noel Murless, whose feet were liable to drag through the tops of the fences. However, when he returned to Ireland at the start of the war, Paddy was probably no richer than when he left.

When the chance came in Ireland to start as a trainer, though, he took it with both hands. His natural ability, plus some useful backing by the More O'Ferrall family, soon set him on the path to success. Before long he was able to give up jumpers and to concentrate on the flat. One of his main assets was his eye for a yearling and, though later in his career his stable was full of animals that had fetched big prices at the sales, many of his early victories were achieved with horses that had cost little and were far from fashionably bred. In due course he became top trainer in England three years running. There was a time when his many wins in England engendered a certain degree of jealousy but his good nature and lack of conceit eventually overcame most of the hostility that had been felt. In recent years his health has been less robust than it was and his exploits have been overshadowed by those of his fellow countryman, Vincent O'Brien.

7

NINETEEN-FIFTY-TWO was Tulyar's year. Bred and owned by the Aga Khan, he was a brown colt, not striking in appearance but difficult to fault, by Tehran out of the Nearco mare Neocracy whose dam Harina was a sister of the 1929 Derby and St Leger winner, Trigo. Neocracy also bred Saint Crespin III, winner of The Eclipse Stakes and the Prix de l'Arc de Triomphe. A May foal, Tulyar was small and backward as a yearling so he was not sent from Ireland to join Marcus Marsh's stable till six weeks after the remainder. At two he was nothing out of the ordinary but at least he gave proof of stamina in the autumn, winning in succession two handicaps both run over a mile, The Buggins Farm Nursery at Haydock Park and The Kineton Nursery at Birmingham. In his last outing of the season he was second in the seven-furlongs Horris Hill Nursery at Newbury. He was given 8 st. 2 lb. in the Free Handicap, 19 lb. less than Windy City who was exported to America. On the whole Tulyar had given the impression that he might make a useful staying handicapper. During the winter Aly Khan tried to sell him for £7,000 but failed to find a purchaser.

There was not a happy atmosphere in Marsh's stable the following year. Prince Aly Khan was the most charming and generous man in the world when things were going his way but when the luck was out he could be tricky and unreliable. The Aga Khan, old and frail, was apt to leave matters in his son's hands. Aly Khan, without having the grace to inform Marsh, had in fact already arranged to transfer most of the horses to Noel Murless at the end of the season. Marsh discovered this by accident at Goodwood in July when Nesbit Waddington, the Aga Khan's stud manager, said how sorry he was the horses were leaving, assuming that Marsh had been told. Murless had never really settled down at Beckhampton where he did not invariably see eye to eye with his principal patron, Mr J. A. Dewar. He decided, therefore, to move to Newmarket. Beckhampton was put up for sale and was bought by Herbert Blagrave, breeder, owner, trainer and the fortunate possessor of valuable property in Reading. The stables and gallops at Beckhampton were leased to Jeremy Tree, who trains there today, and Dick Warden who had been training at Newmarket. The Dewar horses were moved to Noel Cannon at Druids Lodge.

24.   The Aga Khan's Tulyar, Charlie Smirke up

Tulyar started off at three by winning the seven furlongs Henry VIII Stakes at Hurst Park, beating the Middle Park winner, King's Bench, who looked, though, as if he was very much in need of a race. The going was firm at the end of April and largely for that reason Tulyar was not asked to compete in The Two Thousand Guineas, in which the home-trained runners were made to appear extremely moderate; the five-lengths winner was the French colt Thunderhead II; King's Bench was second and M. Boussac's Argur third. The fact that King's Bench finished second added fuel to the fire in respect of the differences between Marcus Marsh on the one hand and the Aga Khan and his son on the other. The Aga Khan took the view that Tulyar ought to have run and by the end of the season he was able to convince himself he had been robbed of the Triple Crown.

Thunderhead II was owned by M. E. Constant and trained by Étienne Pollet who was destined to gain many more successes on the English turf. M. Constant had bought Thunderhead II, by Merry Boy, as a yearling solely, he said, because Herodiade, the colt's dam, had once been in Pollet's stable. The grandam of Herodiade was Lord Derby's famous mare Gondolette.

It rained hard before the Chester meeting and the going was heavy when Tulyar turned out for the mile-and-three-quarters Ormonde Stakes. He won by half a length from the moderate Nikiforos, later quite a successful long-distance hurdler. Eight days later Tulyar was far more impressive when winning the Lingfield Derby Trial and at last people began to realise his true potentiality. Before Epsom the weather was dry and hot, which worried Marsh as he was doubtful at the time of Tulyar's ability to show his true form on hard ground. There was even some talk of Smirke being transferred to the stable's other Derby candidate, Indian Hemp, a Nasrullah colt that Sir Humphrey de Trafford had sold to the Canadian, Mr Max Bell.

Five days before The Derby, Tulyar had his final gallop. Smirke was supposed to bring him up a peat moss strip but to Marsh's horror he brought Tulyar up a parallel strip where the ground was as hard as the Cromwell Road. Marsh was furious when Smirke pulled Tulyar up, but the imperturbable Charlie quickly assured him that Tulyar was even more effective on top of the ground.

Tulyar started favourite for The Derby at 11/2, an immense volume of money on the day forcing his price down from initial offers of 100/8. He won by three parts of a length from Mrs J. V. Rank's Gay Time with the French colt Faubourg II third. Aly Khan won £40,000 in bets but was not altogether satisfied and inclined to blame Marsh for not having ascertained Tulyar's true merits earlier on.

Gay Time unshipped Lester Piggott after passing the winning post. Piggott returned to the weighing room without the horse which was later caught and brought back by a mounted policeman, entering the unsaddling enclosure twenty minutes after the race was over. Piggott, having weighed in, then alleged that Tulyar had leant on Gay Time in the closing stages and wanted to object, but Mrs Rank, after consulting her trainer Noel Cannon, sensibly decided to take no action. Just before the big Goodwood meeting at the end of July, the National Stud bought Gay Time for £50,000. He turned out to be a bad bargain. His form deteriorated and it was found that he was wrong in his wind. It was deemed expedient, therefore, to export him without delay to Japan.

In the opinion of some of the more experienced jockeys, The Derby had been a very rough race. M. Boussac's Marsyad broke a fetlock and had to be destroyed.

Tulyar went from strength to strength after The Derby. He won The Eclipse Stakes, The King George VI and Queen Elizabeth Stakes and finally The St Leger. It was then announced that he would remain in training as a four-year-old. However, in view of the Aga Khan's record, it caused no surprise when it became known in the winter that Tulyar had been sold to the Irish National Stud for approximately £250,000. The first intimation Marsh received was when listening to the six o'clock news.

Tulyar had won £76,417 in stakes, beating the record of £57,455 established by Isinglass who raced till he was five. Possibly Tulyar was fortunate in that his contemporaries were moderate but he could do no more than keep on winning. At three he won from seven furlongs to a mile and six furlongs, and on ground varying from rock hard to mud. No opponent ever succeeded in getting to the bottom of him that year. He was indolent by nature, was endowed with a placid and easy-going temperament and was never anxious to do more than he had to in order to win. In 1955 he was sold for export to America. He left after the 1956 covering season but his stud career was impaired by a grave illness which nearly cost him his life. He eventually recovered but he never made a great mark as a sire.

In The One Thousand Guineas Sir Malcolm McAlpine's Zabara, a Persian Gulf filly trained by Victor Smyth, just beat the French filly La Mirambule. In The Oaks the distance was just too far for Zabara, who was second to Captain A. M. Keith's workmanlike filly Frieze, trained by Captain Charles Elsey. Frieze was not bred in the height of fashion, being by the Irish Derby winner Phideas out of Cornice, by that fine stayer Epigram. It was necessary to go back ten generations in the tail female line of Frieze's pedigree to unearth a previous classic winner.

The Aga Khan won The Coronation Cup with the Italian-bred Nuccio trained by Alec Head. Nuccio won the Arc in the autumn. Nuccio's Epsom victory meant that for seven years running the winner of this important race had come from abroad, the result of the growing habit in this country of hustling top-class three-year-olds off to the stud at the earliest opportunity.

The Gold Cup winner, Aquino II, was trained by the shrewd Sam Armstrong at Newmarket but this big rangy bay horse, by Tornado, had been bred in France by the Marquis de Nicolay. His dam Apulia, by Apelle, had originally belonged to Sir Hugo Cunliffe-Owen and after winning a selling race for him at Gatwick she was bought by the Epsom trainer Stanley Wootton, for whom she won four sellers before he passed her on to Lord Derby. She won races for Lord Derby, who eventually sent her to his stud in France. When war broke out she was taken over by the Marquis de Nicolay. The Maharanee of Baroda bought Aquino II as a two-year-old. Aquino II had a nasty temper and in The Goodwood Cup he simply refused to race at all. He did, though, retrieve his reputation in The Doncaster Cup. He ended his days in Poland.

Another foreign victory was in The Champion Stakes, won for the second year running by M. Boussac's Dynamiter.

By now the financial situation of racing was beginning to cause serious concern. People were beginning to realise that the days when English racing was dominated by the great owner-breeders, as often as not members of the aristocracy, were drawing to a close. Men and women who, by and large, could afford to race on a big scale without being greatly concerned about the cost were becoming very thin on the ground. Sensible people of course did not take up racing expecting as a right to make money out of it, but the financial side was playing an increasingly important part, and more and more owners were anxious as far as was possible to break even over their racing operations. Racing in fact was ceasing to be a sport; it was becoming more and more common to hear it referred to as a business or an industry.

The cost of maintaining a horse in training was continually rising. Racecourse executives were unable to increase prize money in proportion owing to the burden of taxation, particularly of the Entertainment Tax. Despite the gigantic annual betting turnover, the contribution by betting to the sport was minimal and that only through the tote. The age of sponsorship had not arrived.

No one did more to inform the public about racing's situation than the Hon. (now Sir) J. J. Astor, at that time a Conservative M.P. Mr Astor has in his lifetime played many parts in racing. A son of that great owner-breeder the second Viscount Astor, he rode in his younger days both on the flat and over fences. During the war he was a brother officer of Mr John Hislop in 'Phantom', commanding the squadron attached to the S.A.S. He has been an owner-breeder on a big scale, a Steward of the Jockey Club, a member of the Racecourse Betting Control Board and the Horserace Totalisator Board, President of the Thoroughbred Breeders' Association, the holder of a permit to train jumpers, and eventually in 1975 a public trainer on the flat, counting among his patrons Lord Wigg, a friend since parliamentary days, and the playwright Mr William Douglas-Home. When he received a licence to train, Mr Astor had to resign from the Jockey Club. He was re-elected at the end of the year, though, when he decided to give up training. Unfortunately he also decided to cut down his racing interests in drastic fashion, selling his stud and nearly all his bloodstock.

He has always had a lively and inquiring mind, a bit too lively for some of the older Jockey Club members, and he has never been prepared to sit back and let racing's problems solve themselves. Some of his ideas have been good, others rather less so. In 1952 he unquestionably did racing a service by publishing detailed figures showing on the one hand the annual expenditure by owners and breeders and on the other the amount of money available to be won. The gap between the two amounted to £4,000,000, a figure that could hardly be sustained for an indefinite period and one which was more likely to increase than to decline. The figures produced were accompanied by a number of suggestions for endeavouring to solve the existing problems. It was pointed out that the Royal Commission on Gambling (1949–51) had recommended that off-course cash betting should be legalised in view of the contradictions in the existing laws that were difficult to enforce. It was Mr Astor's opinion that, if the public could lawfully bet with bookmakers and with the tote off the course, and if the figure of the estimated millions of pounds passing through Starting Price offices was remotely correct, there ought to be ample surplus for the Treasury to give a large grant to racing after they had taken a share.

The Astor figures and recommendations certainly provoked discussion which, in one form or another, has been going on ever since. Not everyone was moved to the point of tears by the owners' plight. It has always been a commonly held view that owning racehorses is essentially the pastime of the rich. It is not compulsory and it ought not to be subsidised. This opinion frequently has the backing of bookmakers for obvious reasons of self-interest. In addition, owners have not always been adroit at presenting their own case.

However this was 1952 and there was still a long way to go before the Betting and Gaming Act (1960) which conferred legal status on bookmakers and reformed the system of betting in this country. The Treasury now does very well out of racing, which, unfortunately does not do at all well out of the Treasury. In consequence the quality of English racing is suffering badly. It seems a short-sighted policy on the part of the Treasury not to give a few grains of nourishment every now and then to the goose that has so far produced annually a golden egg of generous proportions.

The Jockey Club, meanwhile, was taking steps to reduce the dangers of doping. Security in stables and at racecourses was tightened up and stable employees were issued with identity cards. The Jockey Club set up a committee under Sir Reginald Macdonald-Buchanan to examine the whole question of doping. As a result of the committee's findings, the Stewards did not recommend any amendment to Rule 102(II) which governs the issue and withdrawal of trainers' licences. The Jockey Club, not surprisingly, came in for some sharp criticism in the press and one or two journalists who had only just missed an O level in History were able to compare the Stewards to the Bourbons.

Mr (later Sir) Francis Weatherby resigned from the office of Keeper of the Match Book and Secretary of the Jockey Club. His place was taken by his nephew, Mr E. W. Weatherby, whose father, Mr E. M. Weatherby, had been Secretary from 1901 to 1930. Like most of his family, Bill Weatherby was a Wykehamist. He had been with the firm since 1921 except for the war years when he served with the Royal Buckinghamshire Yeomanry in France and Burma. Quiet, gentle and extremely conscientious, he held office during a period of major administrative changes in racing and bore a heavy load of work and responsibility. In 1966 his health gave way under the strain and he had to take a long holiday in South Africa. He seemed to recover but the following year he collapsed and died at London Airport while on his way to see the Irish Derby. He had done great services for racing.

Some famous racing personalities died in 1952: the second Viscount Astor, a great owner-breeder; Mr J. V. Rank, a staunch supporter of racing both on the flat and under National Hunt rules; Sir William Bass, at one time owner of Sceptre; Lord Hamilton of Dalzell, who was largely responsible for the introduction of the tote into this country and had been the King's Representative at Ascot; and Felix Leach, a former trainer who had been head lad to Richard Marsh in the great days of Persimmon.

Far younger than these was Gordon Johnson Houghton who, while hunting with the Old Berks, was thrown from his horse in front of a lorry and was killed instantly. After Eton and Oxford he had gone as a pupil to Jack Colling before setting up on his own at Neston in Cheshire. He was just beginning to make a name for himself when war broke out. His horses were dispersed and he himself departed to serve with the Cheshire Yeomanry. On being demobilised he took over the stables at Blewbury formerly occupied by Steve Donoghue. Being both well liked and highly efficient, he soon had plenty of patrons, among them Miss Dorothy Paget and Sir Adrian Jarvis. In 1950 he won fifty races, in 1951 forty. He had married Helen Walwyn, twin sister of Fulke Walwyn. There is very little she does not know about racing[1] and, although under the rules then existing she was not permitted to hold a trainer's licence herself, she managed to keep the flag flying, winning among other races The Two Thousand Guineas with Gilles de Retz, until her son Fulke Johnson Houghton was ready to take over the stable. This he has done to some purpose, winning the Irish Sweeps Derby and The St Leger in successive years with the brothers Ribocco and Ribero.

In 1953 there were two horses in The Derby whose victory would have been extremely popular. On the one hand there was Aureole owned by the Queen who earlier in the week had been crowned at Westminster Abbey. On the other there was Pinza ridden by Gordon Richards, who had just been honoured with a knighthood for his services to racing and whose splendid career lacked only a victory in the greatest race of the year.

Bred by King George VI, Aureole was a high-mettled chestnut with a good deal of white about him by Hyperion out of The Oaks runner-up Angelola, by Donatello II. At two he had run twice and won once. He began his three-year-old career by running a creditable fifth behind Nearula in The Two Thousand Guineas, after which he showed his merit clearly by winning the Derby Trial at Lingfield, a race that so often fell to his trainer, Captain Boyd-Rochfort.

Pinza was a big, burly bay standing over sixteen hands and more impressive for sheer power than for quality. Bred by Fred Darling, he was by Chanteur II out of Pasqua, by Donatello II. As a yearling he was bought for 1,500 guineas by Sir Victor Sassoon, who sent him to Norman Bertie to be trained. Pasqua never won herself and bred only one other winner. Mrs Morriss, whose husband Mr H. E. Morriss owned the Banstead Manor Stud, had Pasqua covered by Chanteur II who was then standing at Banstead, and not having a high opinion of Pasqua's first five foals sent her at the end of the year to the December Sales. Fred Darling, then in South Africa, saw her name in the catalogue, liked her pedigree and asked Mr Dewar to buy her for him. Mr Dewar was able to secure her for 2,000 guineas. When Darling returned to England and saw Pasqua he did not care for her and in December she was back again at the Sales, where an Argentinian breeder bought her for 525 guineas.

Pinza's first racecourse appearance was at Hurst Park in July, when, though still backward, he displayed encouraging promise for the future. At the Doncaster St Leger meeting he won The Tattersall Sale Stakes by half a dozen lengths. In the one-mile Royal Lodge Stakes at Ascot he was favourite at 5/2 on but in a race that was not run at a strong gallop he was beaten by the Aga Khan's Neemah, a lovely filly that failed to train on. However, he redeemed his reputation by a decisive victory in The Dewhurst Stakes. In The Free Handicap he was given 9 st. 2 lb., 5 lb. less than the Middle Park Stakes winner, Nearula.

During the winter Pinza, always inclined to play up, unseated his rider, galloped off and then fell on a gravel path, gashing his forearm. The injury was not

---

[1] Mrs Johnson Houghton is now a member of the Jockey Club.

25. Owner Sir Victor Sassoon offers a reward to his horse Pinza, after winning The King George VI and Queen Elizabeth Stakes, 1953

serious but later he became lame and it was found that a small piece of gravel had not been extracted. This held back his preparation and he was not fit enough to compete in The Two Thousand Guineas, which was won by the handsome Nasrullah colt Nearula, trained in Yorkshire by Captain Charles Elsey. Pinza's sole outing before The Derby was in The Newmarket Stakes. Although he still looked big and backward, he won very easily by four lengths.

Nearula's Derby preparation was interrupted by a minor accident and at Epsom he started at 10/1. Joint favourites at 5/1 were Pinza and Aureole's stable companion, Premonition, owned by Brigadier W. P. Wyatt and ridden by Eph Smith. Premonition, by Precipitation, had won The Blue Riband Trial Stakes at Epsom in fine style but was then beaten in a falsely run race at Sandown. However, he returned to favour when he won The Great Northern Stakes at York. Aureole, ridden by Harry Carr, was on offer at 9/1.

Premonition ran a lamentable race and was never in the picture. Shikampur led into the straight followed by Pinza who headed him with a quarter of a mile to go.

26.   Sir Gordon Richards riding a characteristic finish

From that point Pinza was never in danger of defeat and he went on to win by four lengths from Aureole, who was never able to get close enough to deliver an effective challenge. Thus at his twenty-eighth attempt Gordon Richards had won the race that had for so long eluded him. He was given a tremendous reception and the Queen sent for him to congratulate him on his success.

Pinza only ran once again and then defeated Aureole by three lengths in The King George VI and Queen Elizabeth Stakes. Unfortunately he broke down before The St Leger. Though clearly superior to Aureole as a racehorse, he was a dire failure as a sire, whereas Aureole was twice champion and sired a Derby winner in St Paddy as well as three winners of The St Leger.

Born in 1904 in Shropshire, Sir Gordon Richards was one of the greatest riders in English racing history. When he retired following a nasty accident at Sandown in 1954 he had been champion jockey on twenty-six occasions. He had ridden 4,870 winners, a record unapproached by any other rider, while his 269 winners in 1947 constituted a record, too.

It is arguable that as a big-race rider he was less good than Lester Piggott. Despite his jaunty, self-confident appearance, he was always highly-strung, whereas 'Old Stoneface' seems no more moved by a classic race than by a selling handicap at a night meeting at Wolverhampton. Where Gordon was so good was that he so rarely rode a poor race. No man, in fact, has ever lost fewer races that he ought to have won. Punters have never had a truer friend.

The sporting public loved him and they respected him, too. His integrity was unquestioned. Publicity and adulation never turned his head. His way of life remained unpretentious. Not all champion jockeys have proved worthy representatives of their profession but he was beyond criticism in that respect. His lack of conceit and his humour make him an engaging personality. When he retired from riding he trained till 1970, but in that role, being a perfectionist, he may have worried a shade too much. When he handed in his licence, the Jockey Club made him an honorary member. He now assists Lady Beaverbrook and Sir Michael Sobell in the management of their horses. No man has ever done more to enhance the reputation of horse-racing with the general public.

During his life Sir Victor Sassoon spent a fortune on bloodstock and remained undeterred by many expensive disappointments. Before the war his only classic winner was the Solario filly, Exhibitionnist, who won the 1937 One Thousand Guineas and The Oaks. She was the produce of one of the cheapest mares he ever bought. It is typical of the way luck runs in racing that he first achieved his ambition of winning The Derby with a colt that cost only 1,500 guineas. Moreover his 1958 Derby winner, Hard Ridden, cost only 270 guineas. His two other Derby winners, Crepello and St Paddy, he bred himself. It seems odd that such a lavish supporter of racing was never elected to the Jockey Club but the fact is that a lot of people found him a very difficult man to get on with.

Premonition was sent to run in the Irish Derby. Ridden by Carr, he passed the post a head in front of Chamier, trained by Vincent O'Brien. An objection was lodged on the grounds of boring and Chamier was awarded the race. A lot of

English people who saw the race thought Premonition had been 'robbed', but Bill Rickaby, who rode Chamier, was the very last man to lodge an objection unless there were valid grounds for so doing.

Premonition won The Voltigeur Stakes at York and in The St Leger, ridden by Eph Smith, he started at 10/1. Aureole, Carr up, was favourite at 6/4. Aureole's conduct at home had been getting worse and worse and he had been receiving treatment from Dr Charles Brook, a London neurologist who had been successful with other 'difficult' horses. In Aureole's final work-out on the Limekilns it took him three-quarters of an hour to complete a seven-furlongs stint. At Doncaster he was not in an amenable mood. He played up during the parade and in the race itself he fought for his head and refused to settle down. Not surprisingly, he was a beaten horse two furlongs from home, eventually finishing third behind the placid Premonition and the French colt, Northern Light II.

Aureole finished the season by winning The Cumberland Lodge Stakes at Ascot. Carr was unable to do the weight so Eph Smith rode him instead. The Queen's racing manager, Captain Charles Moore, took the view, one which many others shared, that Aureole had gone better for Smith than he had done for Carr at Doncaster. Accordingly it was decided that Smith would ride Aureole in his races as a four-year-old.

One of the best two-year-olds of 1952 had been Mr J. S. Gerber's Bebe Grande by Niccolo dell'Arca. She was trained by Sam Armstrong and in a strenuous season had won eight of her nine races, some of them hard ones. In 1953 her owner made the bold decision to take on the colts in The Two Thousand Guineas. She ran a brave race but found one too good for her in Nearula, who beat her by four lengths. It was asking a lot of her to turn out again in The One Thousand Guineas a couple of days later. She displayed her customary courage but under the circumstances the task she had been set was too severe and the best she could do was to finish third behind Happy Laughter and Tessa Gillian. She never won another race and was not a success as a brood mare.

Another very game filly was Happy Laughter. Bred by the Ballykisteen Stud, she was an attractive chestnut by Royal Charger and as a yearling she had been bought for 3,500 guineas by Jack Jarvis on behalf of Major David Wills. She was a good, consistent two-year-old, winning five of her seven races including The Sandown Park Stud Produce Stakes and The Acorn Stakes at Epsom. Nevertheless, Jarvis never had her really to his liking. She sweated up a lot and suffered from chronic sinus trouble.

She was sent to pass the winter at her owner's stud but not only did her condition fail to improve but she developed an ugly lump under one eye. Sulphonamide treatment proved quite ineffective so Colonel Douglas Gray, who then managed Major Will's stud, consulted a Harley Street nose and throat specialist. He recommended surgical treatment. Accordingly she was operated on at the Equine Research Station, the orbital bone being trephined and the right maxillary sinus drained.

At the Research Station it was discovered that Happy Laughter was suffering from three separate infections. Two were speedily cleared up but aureomycin was needed for the third and aureomycin was then in very short supply in this country. Colonel Gray decided to cast his net in Ireland. Royal Charger, Happy Laughter's sire, was then standing at the Irish National Stud and a supply of the drug was procured.

It was only in February that Happy Laughter returned to Jack Jarvis. She had a big hole in her head that needed dressing twice daily and it was obviously going to be a battle against time to have her anything like ready for the spring campaign. In fact she did her first sharp canter just a month before The One Thousand Guineas was run. Though she was still very backward she turned out for The Free Handicap at the Craven Meeting and delighted her trainer by running second to Good Brandy, who was receiving 5 lb. In The Guineas Bill Rickaby, the stable jockey, rode Tessa Gillian, a smallish filly of beautiful quality that had won four races at two and had only narrowly been beaten by Bebe Grande in The Cheveley Park Stakes. In The Free Handicap she had been rated 12 lb. above her stable companion, Happy Laughter, who was partnered in The Guineas by Manny Mercer. Bebe Grande, doubtless feeling the effects of her exertions in The Two Thousand Guineas, faltered on the hill and Happy Laughter ran on strongly to beat Tessa Gillian by a couple of lengths. It was Mercer's first classic success.

Happy Laughter failed to stay in The Oaks but then won The Coronation Stakes at Royal Ascot, The Falmouth Stakes at Newmarket and The Nassau Stakes at Goodwood. Unfortunately she was a disappointment at the stud.

The winner of The Oaks was Lord Astor's Big Game filly, Ambiguity, ridden by Joe Mercer, younger brother of Manny and a thoroughly sound and dependable rider. Ambiguity won by half a length from the Aga Khan's Kerkeb and may have been lucky to do so as for once Gordon Richards rode a poor race and made his effort on Kerkeb far too soon. Ambiguity, a real stayer, derived her stamina from her dam, Amber Flash. Like Amber Flash, she won The Jockey Club Cup. She was trained by Jack Colling, elder brother of George. He was an extremely able member of his profession with a record of consistent success over many years. His runners always had to be reckoned with at the big York Meeting in August. He is an exceptionally good judge of a horse and when he gave up training he worked for the British Bloodstock Agency. He has also acquired a local reputation as a highly skilled exterminator of moles. He is a man of exquisite courtesy and addresses even the humbler members of the racing press as 'sir'.

The Gold Cup will be remembered for Elliott's marvellous riding on the five-year-old Souepi, who beat M. Boussac's second string, the four-year-old Aram, ridden by L. Heurteur, by a short head. Souepi was a head behind two strides before the post and a head behind again two strides after.

Souepi, by Epigram, was owned in partnership by his trainer George Digby, who had ridden and trained at one time in Egypt, and Mohammed Bey Sultan. They had also bred him. He never ran at two and when he raced at three his jockey declared with no little assurance that six furlongs was his proper distance. He was unplaced in all his seven races at three but at four he displayed immense improvement, winning The Gold Vase, The Northumberland Plate and The

Sunninghill Stakes at Ascot. After his Gold Cup triumph Souepi won The Goodwood Cup, again largely thanks to the riding of Elliott. He beat Blarney Stone by roughly an inch. In The Doncaster Cup he dead-heated with Nick La Rocca. The contempt in which good game stayers are held in Britain is demonstrated by the fact that in 1954 Souepi was exported to Chile for 2,300 guineas.

It had been expected that Dynamiter, twice winner of The Champion Stakes, would win The Coronation Cup for M. Boussac. A few days before that race, though, he stumbled, broke a fetlock and had to be destroyed. In his absence The Cup was won by Mr G. Rolls's wayward but potentially brilliant Zucchero, by Nasrullah, who beat Wilwyn by a length. In August it was announced that Zucchero had been bought for £60,000 by Baron Guy de Rothschild and would stand at the Haras de Meutry in 1954. There were certain contingencies, though. Firstly Zucchero was to run in the Prix de l'Arc de Triomphe in the name and colours of his current owner, Mr Rolls, a bookmaker; secondly he had to pass a veterinary examination for stud soundness. Alas, he let everyone down. He was left in the Arc and failed in his stud test, the sale being therefore automatically cancelled.

French horses were first and second in The Eclipse Stakes, M. Boussac's Argur, by Djebel, winning easily from Baron Guy de Rothschild's Guersant. Aureole, who had not entirely escaped a coughing epidemic at Newmarket, was third. In the autumn Nearula, though he had gone in his coat by then, won The Champion Stakes.

The best two-year-old seen out during the season was The Pie King, whom Paddy Prendergast trained for Mr Ray Bell. He was an unfashionably bred colt by The Solicitor out of a mare by Diligence and had cost only 1,850 guineas as a yearling. He won successively The Coventry Stakes at Royal Ascot, The Richmond Stakes at Goodwood and The Gimcrack Stakes at York. Prendergast also trained Sixpence, a Ballyogan filly that had cost 2,000 guineas and who won The Cheveley Park Stakes.

The English were still not thoroughly accustomed to Irish stables coming over and winning some of our more important races. Possibly, as was sometimes alleged in Ireland, a certain amount of jealousy had been engendered by Prendergast's successes. At all events, before the season ended there was a clash between the Jockey Club and Prendergast which provoked heated discussion in England and a lot of ill feeling in Ireland.

The animal in question was Blue Sail, a two-year-old colt by Tehran out of a Blue Peter mare that Prendergast trained for Mr J. H. Griffin. As might be expected from his pedigree, Blue Sail took some time to come to hand and he did not see a racecourse till August, when he finished eighth in the six-furlongs Dowth Maiden Plate at Navan. A month later he was seventh in the six-furlongs Railway Plate at The Curragh. On October 10 he was one of eleven runners for the one-mile Cornwallis Stakes at Ascot, the field for which included Arabian Night, who was destined to be second in The Derby; Minstrel, a future Cambridgeshire winner; and a good middle-distance horse, Umberto. Blue Sail was heavily backed and started favourite at 5/2. Ridden by Tommy Gosling, he finished second, beaten a neck by Plainsong to whom he was giving 6 lb.

The Ascot Stewards held an inquiry into Blue Sail's form and, not being satisfied with the explanation offered, passed the case on to the Stewards of the Jockey Club. In due course the Stewards of the Jockey Club published in the Racing Calendar a notice stating that 'the running of Blue Sail in The Cornwallis Stakes on October 10th was inconsistent with his previous running in Ireland and that horses trained by P. J. Prendergast would not be allowed to run under their Rules, and that no entries would be accepted from him'.

This particular penalty did not require reciprocal action from the racing authorities in Ireland, who nevertheless took this slur against the leading Irish trainer very seriously. Obviously the view taken by the Jockey Club Stewards was that Blue Sail had been given a couple of easy races in Ireland and then been the medium for a gamble in England where of course the market was a great deal stronger.

As Prendergast held a trainer's licence both from the Stewards of the Irish Turf Club and the Irish National Hunt Steeplechase Committee, those two bodies decided to hold a joint inquiry into the Jockey Club's ruling. The witnesses examined included Mr Geoffrey Freer, the Jockey Club Handicapper; Mr D. Bulger, the Turf Club's Senior Stewards' Secretary, who saw the races at Navan and at The Curragh; Mr T. Hurley, the Turf Club's Assistant Stewards' Secretary, who also saw those races; Major R. Turner, Handicapper to the Turf Club, who also saw the two races in Ireland; Major A. McMorrough Kavanagh, who saw Blue Sail run at Ascot; Messrs N. W. Waddington and R. More O'Ferrall, who saw Blue Sail run at the Curragh and at Ascot; P. J. Prendergast; the jockeys P. Powell junior, W. Johnstone and T. Gosling; Mr J. H. Griffin; and Mr J. D. Woods, who gave evidence in respect of the betting.

The verdict was as follows:

The evidence before the Irish Stewards showed that their three senior officials were satisfied with the running of Blue Sail in Ireland. The Form Books of both countries were examined and the Stewards took note of the fact that the race at Ascot was over a distance of one mile, and that the race in Ireland, at the Curragh, in which Blue Sail ran, was over six furlongs sixty-three yards.

The Irish Stewards were of opinion that on the evidence given before them there was no unexplained discrepancy.

The Irish were of course jubilant at the verdict which was interpreted there, and by many people in England as well, as a rebuff to the English authorities. In England opinion was sharply divided as to the justice and wisdom of the action taken by the Stewards of the Jockey Club. The radicals regarded Prendergast as an addition to the long list of Irish martyrs; right-wingers saw him as a man who had asked for it and got it. Between the two were many who, while in general backing up the Jockey Club, thought that the punishment had been too severe. Some journalists took the line that the action taken by the Jockey Club could only be justified if similar strictness was applied to certain stables in this country. They felt, not without good reason, that a few trainers with distinguished and influential patrons could get away with murder and never a question asked.

The ban on Prendergast was lifted in August 1954. He celebrated the occasion by sending ten horses to the York August meeting and winning with four of them.

Experiments, which proved successful, were made this year with a new amenity for racegoers, the commentary broadcast on each race. As was only to be expected, a few crusty old die-hards objected and said they could perfectly well read a race without help from anyone, which in most cases simply was not true. For the majority of racegoers, though, it was an undoubted boon, particularly for those without binoculars or who did not pretend to be expert race-readers. The commentary was especially useful in the early stages of races run over a straight mile or in an event like The Cesarewitch in which so much of the running takes place virtually out of sight that spectators have been described as hanging about in Suffolk for a race that is run in Cambridgeshire.

One of the earliest and most consistently accurate of racecourse commentators has been Robert Haynes, a former Coldstream Guardsman who was commissioned into the Essex Regiment during the war. He had had the right sort of training to be a commentator as he had been employed since the war on those invaluable publications, Raceform and Chaseform. For much of that period he had worked in co-operation with the firm's senior race-reader, Jack Topham. A big, burly Yorkshireman who never wore a hat, Jack Topham was hardly the most lovable of men. He was a bit of a bully, dictatorial, opinionated and given to long and extremely tedious monologues. Furthermore he had a chip on his shoulder as, although he possessed a profound knowledge of racing and was an excellent judge of form, he had little facility for writing and the major jobs in racing journalism eluded him. As a race-reader, though, he was beyond criticism. He never committed the error of guessing. If he was not sure of something, he made it his business to find out. His form-book comments were in consequence entirely reliable. Anyone who worked with him for long emerged a thoroughly competent race-reader even though there were times when they were goaded to the very brink of mutiny. Raceform's top race-reader today is John Sharratt, who manages to combine efficiency with a most helpful and friendly personality.

Other successful racecourse commentators include Michael Seth-Smith, who is also a notable turf historian, and Cloudesley Marsham, whose father led Kent to victory in the County Cricket Championship in 1906 and whose brother James is a stewards' secretary.

An obviously unfair rule of racing was the one whereby a disqualified horse was automatically relegated to last place even if the objection had not been based on any accusation of foul or deliberately unfair riding. However, there were still a good many Jockey Club members who thought they heard the distant rumbling of tumbrils if there was the slightest suggestion of change. In October a proposal put forward to ascertain if Rule 173 required alteration was defeated by 13 votes to 12.

The most controversial race in 1954, and one certainly not without its slightly comic side, was The Winston Churchill Stakes run over two miles at Hurst Park on June 7. Among the six runners was the St Leger winner, Premonition, who had opened his season by winning The Yorkshire Cup at York. In that race he had had the services of the seven-year-old Osborne as pacemaker. Osborne had then been ridden by R. Burrows, the lad who looked after Premonition, Osborne, again ridden by Burrows, was in the field at Hurst Park. Premonition started at 8/1 on.

Osborne made the running followed by Royal Task and Prince Arthur. Spectators regarded the race as nothing more than a lap of honour for Premonition and imagined he could quicken and take the lead when ever his rider, Harry Carr, so desired. What in fact happened was a very different matter. Premonition, right from the final bend, was being hard ridden with remarkably little result. He certainly would not have won if Burrows had not seen fit to ease Osborne in the most blatant manner near the finish, thereby enabling the favourite to scrape home by a very short head. It certainly all looked very odd, not only to those present, but to the many thousands who watched the race on TV.

The Stewards sent for Captain Boyd-Rochfort, trainer of the two horses concerned, and Burrows and invited them to explain the circumstances of the running. Having heard their explanation, the Stewards said they were not satisfied and reported the case to the Stewards of the Jockey Club. The fact that Boyd-Rochfort was the Queen's trainer naturally rendered this a meaty sensation for the press.

After hearing further evidence from Brigadier Wyatt and Harry Carr, the Stewards of the Jockey Club informed Boyd-Rochfort that he had neglected his responsibilities as a trainer in not giving Burrows concise orders in accordance with Rule 139. They therefore fined him £100. They informed Burrows that they did not accept his explanation that the horse was hanging and withdrew his licence to ride until July 3.

Rule 139 lays down that every horse which runs in a race shall be run on his merits, whether his owner runs another horse in the race or not.

The trouble at Hurst Park lay in the fact that no consideration had been given to the possibility of Osborne winning. Burrows had been told 'Be second if you can' and he had carried out that order all too literally. The Stewards were criticised in some quarters for having acted with undue severity. They would, of course, have been far more harshly criticised had they been lenient and they would undoubtedly have had to face accusations that certain trainers with distinguished patrons were privileged to get away with anything. Of course no one seriously believed that in this case there had been any deliberate hanky-panky. It was just a regrettable mix-up through failure to issue the appropriate orders and to realise what a very good horse Osborne was. Premonition failed in The Gold Cup, which was won by M. Boussac's Elpenor, by Owen Tudor. Osborne went on to win The Goodwood Stakes with 9 st. 7 lb. He dead-heated in the mile-and-a-half Great Yorkshire Stakes at York and finally won The Doncaster Cup by four lengths. He then unfortunately developed tendon trouble. It is arguable that he would have gone close to winning The Gold Cup had he run in that race. He was

27.   Aureole and jockey Eph Smith after winning The Coronation Cup, 1954

far too good a lead horse at home for Premonition and it may have broken Premonition's heart being constantly asked to concede him weight and distance.

Osborne, by Verso II, had been bred in France and won on the flat and over hurdles in the land of his birth. In 1951 Gordon Johnson Houghton was looking for a horse suitable for Lt-Col James Innes, late Coldstream Guards, to ride in flat-races and he purchased Osborne for that purpose. In the role for which he had been bought Osborne proved a failure and for a time in this country he seemed a very moderate performer. He improved with age, though, winning three times in 1952 and three times again in 1953. It was in the autumn of 1953 that Brigadier Wyatt bought him as a six-year-old to act as Premonition's lead horse.

Considering his age and experience, Boyd-Rochfort did not behave very sensibly after the Premonition–Osborne affair. Silence would have been the wisest and most dignified course but he insisted on making a statement to the press. He was barking up the wrong tree when he declared that his honour and reputation had been impugned. They had not: his dignity had been dented but that was another matter. The racing world as a whole was inclined to treat the affair with a certain levity.

Premonition proved a flop as a sire. Many of his offspring showed early promise but failed to train on. In 1955 the association between Boyd-Rochfort and Brigadier and Mrs Wyatt came to an abrupt conclusion. There was a flare-up on the Heath one morning between the Brigadier and his trainer and in consequence the Wyatt horses left the stable.

On the whole, though, 1954 was a good year for Boyd-Rochfort. He ended the season as top trainer while the leading owner was the Queen whose horses won nineteen races worth £40,944. The Queen's Aureole proved to be a four-year-old of the highest class. He had improved in looks since he was three and had filled out in most of the right places. His first race was The Coronation Stakes at Sandown in April. It was a rough sort of contest and Aureole was distinctly unlucky to go under by a length to the Irish Derby winner, Chamier. The Stewards did not see fit to take any action. Aureole then won in succession The Victor Wild Stakes at Kempton Park; The Coronation Cup, in which one of his victims was Nearula; The Hardwicke Stakes, in which he was flat out to beat M. Boussac's Janitor by a narrow margin; and finally The King George VI and Queen Elizabeth Stakes, which he won from Madame Volterra's Vamos and the Two Thousand Guineas winner Darius. Down at the start Aureole had reared up when a man standing close to him opened an umbrella. He deposited Eph Smith on the ground but happily he did not gallop off and he was soon remounted.

Aureole had run fourteen times and his seven victories had earned him £36,225. Like so many other good winners in the royal colours, he was a descendant of Feola. It is sometimes forgotten that the credit for buying Feola belonged to Brigadier H. A. Tomkinson who secured her as a yearling for 3,000 guineas when he was King George V's racing manager.

As regards the three-year-olds in 1954, The Pie King had been exported to America. The winner of The Two Thousand Guineas turned out to be Sir Percy

Loraine's Dante colt, Darius, bred by his owner at the Kildangan Stud in Ireland, trained by Harry Wragg and ridden by Manny Mercer. He passed the post a length ahead of the French colt Ferriol, with Poona third. In his previous outing that season Darius had been beaten by Tudor Honey in the Two Thousand Guineas Trial at Kempton. Probably he needed that race. In any case, there is a world of difference between seven furlongs on the bend at Kempton and the Rowley Mile.

Darius ran a brave race in The Derby but the distance was a furlong too far for him and he finished third behind Mr Robert Sterling Clark's Never Say Die, trained by Joe Lawson and ridden by Lester Piggott, and Mr J. E. Ferguson's Arabian Night. Piggott was eighteen years old. It is believed that J. Parsons, the stable boy who rode Caractacus to victory in the 1862 Derby was only sixteen at the time. At the other end of the scale, J. Forth was over sixty when he won in 1829 on Frederick.

Mr Clark was an American who had had horses trained in England since 1930. His filly Galatea II won The One Thousand Guineas and The Oaks in 1939. In 1946 he had a dispute with the New York Jockey Club and transferred his racing interests, bar his stud, to this country. His stud in France had been wrecked during the fighting in Normandy in 1944.

In 1952 the yearlings sent over by Mr Clark from America were divided between Joe Lawson and Harry Peacock. Sometimes some were sent to Arthur Budgett. On this occasion Lawson and Peacock tossed for first pick and Peacock won. Never Say Die, a chestnut by Nasrullah, was clearly the best looking but Peacock did not care for Nasrullah's stock so the colt joined Lawson's stable at Newmarket.

At two Never Say Die was nothing out of the ordinary. He ran six times and his only success was in the six-furlongs Rosslyn Stakes at Ascot in July. Lawson treated him tenderly on account of the hot Nasrullah blood but confessed himself disappointed by Never Say Die's lack of progress after his Ascot victory.

In 1954 Never Say Die was backward when he ran second to Tudor Honey in The Union Jack Stakes at Liverpool in the first week of the season. That race was reckoned to have brought him on and he was made favourite for the seven-furlongs Free Handicap at Newmarket. The distance was too short for him, though, and he finished unplaced. His only other race before The Derby was the mile-and-a-quarter Newmarket Stakes. That race was run at a strangely lethargic pace, the time being nine seconds slower than that taken by Pinza the previous year. Elopement, a brother of Gay Time, won by half a length from Golden God with Never Say Die close up third. The favourite, Arabian Night, was not in the first six. The pace had been too slow for Never Say Die to exploit his stamina and in addition Manny Mercer had not ridden one of his better races. Never Say Die had been last at the Bushes and then made ground up so fast that he led coming out of the Dip, at which point he became unbalanced. The racing press took a dim view of the form and concluded that the race would have little bearing on The Derby. In fact horses that took part in it finished first, second and fourth at Epsom.

Never Say Die started at 28/1 in The Derby. The big punters ignored him but all over the country members of the public had their small wagers on him, partly because his name appealed to them and partly because he was ridden by 'wonder-boy' Piggott. In the race Never Say Die was always nicely placed and going well. He outstayed Darius in the straight and, holding off a late challenge from Arabian Night, won by two lengths. Mr Clark was unfortunately unwell and could not come and see his horse win.

Joe Lawson was then in his seventy-fourth year. Born in Durham, he joined the Manton stable in 1898. He became travelling head lad there, then assistant to the great Alec Taylor, whom he eventually succeeded in 1928. In 1931 he established what was then a record by winning £93,899 in prize money for his owners. After the war he left Manton and set up at Newmarket. He had thirteen successes in classic races but Never Say Die was his only Derby winner. A quiet man who was greatly respected in the racing world, he always declared that Sceptre was the greatest racehorse he had ever seen. Next in merit he placed Orwell whom he trained to win the 1932 Two Thousand Guineas but who went wrong afterwards.

Lester Piggott's father was a capable National Hunt jockey and trained Ayala to win The Grand National. His grandfather, Ernest Piggott, rode three Grand National winners and married a Miss Cannon, sister of Mornington and Kempton Cannon who both rode winners of The Derby. Lester's mother was, before her marriage, a Miss Rickaby.

Young Lester was pitchforked into a tough adult world at an early age and rode his first winner at the age of thirteen. For a boy he was precociously brilliant and it is a wonder he was not ruined for life by the frequently nauseating adulation heaped on his youthful head by the press. Unfortunately, his remarkable ability in the saddle was not allied to self-discipline or to any noticeable respect for the Rules of Racing. Sometimes his utter fearlessness and his determination to win degenerated into sheer recklessness that endangered not only his own neck, but the necks of his fellow riders as well. His clashes with authority became all too frequent but it must be conceded that they never affected his popularity with the general public, who took the view that his offences were caused by anxiety to win and that he was fundamentally, therefore, on their side. The jockeys they objected to were those who were economical in effort on well-backed horses.

A turning point in Lester Piggott's career came in Never Say Die's next race after The Derby, The King Edward VII Stakes at Royal Ascot. It was a rough, ugly race and Piggott was by no means the only offender. Never Say Die and Arabian Night, first and second in The Derby, were both unplaced. The Stewards objected to the winner, Rashleigh, and then withdrew their objection. Piggott was suspended for the rest of the meeting and reported to the Stewards of the Jockey Club. In due course the Stewards of the Jockey Club informed Piggott that 'they had taken notice of his dangerous and erratic riding both this season and in previous seasons, and that in spite of continuous warnings, he continued to show complete disregard for the Rules of Racing and for the safety of other jockeys'.

28–29.   Lester Piggott: (**opposite**) winning his first Derby on Never Say Die in 1954 (**above**) the veteran champion, 'one of the greatest riders in racing', pictured by Gerry Cranham

A statement was then issued that before any application for a renewal of Piggott's licence could be entertained, he must be attached to some trainer other than his father for a period of six months. Piggott's fans thought the 'establishment' had a down on their idol but the probability is that this suspension did him a great deal of good. It was arranged for him to be attached to Jack Jarvis's stable. Jarvis had no complaints about his conduct and rather to his surprise even grew quite fond of him, though in later years he would occasionally shake his head sadly over something Piggott had said or done and would murmur 'My biggest failure as a trainer—I never made a gentleman of Lester Piggott.'

That Piggott is one of the greatest riders in racing history few would dispute. On the tall side for a jockey, he rides very short indeed and with his bottom stuck up in the air he is easily recognisable in a race. His style is not one to be copied by riders of less ability and it is one that renders him somewhat easily dislodged if his mount plays up on the way to the start. During a race he is nearly always in a good position and his strength in a finish is phenomenal. At one time he was apt to be hard on his horses but he now places less reliance on the whip than he did. He is quite fearless and excels at Epsom. So far he has ridden eight winners of The Derby. Since the Never Say Die affair, his appearances in front of the stewards have been very much fewer.

He is a 'character'. He has always been hard of hearing and would never win a prize for elocution. The racecourse, in fact, is rather too full of people who fancy they can imitate his manner of speech. He is apparently quite unemotional and to him The Derby is just another race. That may be partly the reason why he is nearly always so good on the big occasion. No one has ever accused him of being the last of the big spenders; he takes money seriously and is reputed to read the Financial Times before he turns to the Sporting Life. He is certainly not without humour of a somewhat cynical and sardonic nature and many stories about him, some of them true, now form part of the lore and legend of racing. Popularity has never meant much to him. One afternoon he was warmly applauded as he entered the unsaddling enclosure after winning a big race but as usual he looked glum and uninterested. 'Can't you give them a smile, Lester?' said the trainer. 'Why should I?', 'Golden Boy' is alleged to have replied. 'If I'd have lost, they'd be throwing shit at me.'

It undoubtedly forms an attraction when Piggott rides at a meeting. The public are very fond of him but they do not respect him in the way that they respected Sir Gordon Richards. Nowadays he is not much interested in being champion. He rides a lot in France where the prize money is higher and where he is typically indifferent to the volatile and excitable nature of Parisian racegoers. He must have an iron constitution as he has a weight problem and he hardly ever takes a day off during the season. He married Susan Armstrong, daughter of that extremely good trainer, Sam Armstrong.

Never Say Die had one more race after the Royal Ascot débâcle, The St Leger, in which he was ridden by Smirke. In that race he showed that the further he went the better he was and he delighted his owner by leaving his rivals standing and winning by a dozen lengths. He would probably have made a wonderful Cup horse as a four-year-old but his owner decided to retire him to the stud. Mr Clark died aged seventy-nine in 1956. Earlier that year he had presented Never Say Die to the National Stud. In appreciation of that gift, he was elected an honorary member of the Jockey Club.

As a sire Never Say Die was certainly not a failure—he was champion in 1962—but he was not quite as successful as had been anticipated. Too many of his off-spring lacked the essential quality of speed. His son Larkspur won The Derby but was one of the least distinguished winners of the race this century. His daughter Never Too Late II won The One Thousand Guineas and The Oaks.

In the One Thousand Guineas Trial at Kempton, Key, trained by Noel Murless, won from Mr J. A. Dewar's Festoon. Ridden by Sir Gordon Richards, Key started favourite for The One Thousand Guineas. It was Sir Gordon's last ride in a classic. An accident at Salisbury prevented him from riding at Epsom. In July he had a far worse accident at Sandown when the Queen's Abergeldie reared up on leaving the paddock, threw him, fell herself and then rolled on him. A month later he announced his retirement, thus bringing to an end a long and honourable career which had conferred nothing but credit on the sport.

Festoon had been backward at Kempton and, ridden by Breasley, she had no difficulty in reversing the form at Newmarket, winning by two lengths from Big Berry with Welsh Fairy third and Key fourth. Bred by her owner and trained by Noel Cannon at Druids Lodge, she was a lovely chestnut filly, full of quality, by Fair Trial out of Monsoon by Umidwar. Monsoon had been bred by Mr Edgar Cooper Bland who had bought her dam Heavenly Wind as a yearling for 30 guineas.

Festoon failed to stay the distance in The Oaks but won The Coronation Stakes at Royal Ascot. Her final appearance was in The Sussex Stakes at Goodwood. She and Big Berry simply could not cope with a gale force wind and finished a long way behind Landau who carried the colours of the Queen. By Dante out of the triple classic winner Sun Chariot, Landau was exported to Australia and sired a lot of winners there.

Mr Dewar died a fortnight after Goodwood. Born in 1891, he had inherited in 1930 from his uncle, Lord Dewar, a million pounds, a two-thirds interest in a £2,500,000 trust, a flourishing stud, and a string of racehorses that included the 1931 Two Thousand Guineas and Derby winner, Cameronian. Mr Dewar maintained the stud with much success and among his winners were Commotion, who won The Oaks, Tudor Minstrel, a great miler, and that excellent sire, Fair Trial. He was elected a member of the Jockey Club in 1941. He bought the Beckhampton establishment on Fred Darling's retirement but resold it in 1952 when Murless moved to Newmarket.

After Mr Dewar's death there was a dispersal sale conducted by Tattersalls of all his bloodstock. Buyers were attracted from all over the world and forty-eight lots were disposed of for a total of 398,595 guineas. Festoon was bought by Mr Anthony Askew, a nephew of Mr J. V. Rank, for 36,000 guineas, then a record price in this country for a filly out of training. The best winner she bred was Atilla, by Alcide, who won over £16,000 in this country as well as the Grosser Preis von Baden and did well as a sire in Australia. She also bred Pindaric who won the Lingfield Derby Trial but unfortunately met with a fatal accident in training.

When Noel Cannon died in 1959 at the age of sixty-one after a long and brave battle against a dire illness, it is doubtful that he left even one enemy in the racing world. He was a man of rare charm and sweetness of nature who bore the reversals of fortune uncomplainingly. Between 1952 and 1958, apart from his own ill health, he had to contend with the deaths, all more or less unexpected, of his main patrons, Mr J. V. Rank, Mr J. A. Dewar and Mr J. Olding.

He belonged to a distinguished racing family that originally came from Eton and where in the first half of the nineteenth century several were watermen—one taught the Eton boys swimming—and one kept an inn on the Brocas. Noel's father, Joe Cannon, won The Grand National on Regal and trained many winners on the flat and over the jumps. Noel himself was commissioned into the Third Hussars on his eighteenth birthday and was subsequently wounded in France. After the war he trained in India for some years before returning to this country to manage a bloodstock agency. When his brother 'Boxer'—they were both good golfers—became private trainer to Lady Yule at Balaton Lodge, he took over Bedford Lodge from 'Boxer' and began training there in 1933.

In 1935 he won five races with a two-year-old of Mr Rank's called Under Thirty. Mr Rank, who had originally concentrated on jumpers, was becoming increasingly interested in the flat. In 1934 he bought Druids Lodge, near Salisbury, a stable where some famous coups were hatched in the early years of the century, and in 1936 he installed Noel there as his private trainer. The association was a happy and successful one that lasted till Mr Rank's death. Among the good winners were Scottish Union (St Leger), Why Hurry (Oaks) and Epigram (Goodwood Stakes, Goodwood Cup, Doncaster Cup, Queen Alexandra Stakes). Noel was genuinely devoted to his horses and his real favourites were old geldings like Knight's Armour, Black Speck, Strathspey and Highland Division.

The Oaks proved a disaster for the home-trained runners. Mme R. Forget's Sun Cap, a light-coloured grey by Sunny Boy, won by six lengths from M. M. Boussac's Altana with M. Paul Duboscq's Philante third. Sun Cap was subsequently bought for Lady Macdonald-Buchanan's stud but the winners she bred were of small account. One of them, Biretta, by the Derby winner St Paddy, won a hunters' chase at Fakenham.

Darius may have been a bit unlucky not to have won The Eclipse Stakes as Manny Mercer seemed to leave him a bit too much to do and he was beaten a length and a half by King of the Tudors, a half-brother by Tudor Minstrel to the 1955 Two Thousand Guineas winner Our Babu. It was a weakness of Mercer's that he could only ride by intuition. He found it difficult to absorb detailed riding orders. Before this Eclipse, Harry Wragg took Mercer up to the top of the stands and gave him exact instructions covering every foot of the ten furlongs. Mercer carried them out to the letter—but in a subsequent race.

King of the Tudors had been bought as a yearling for 5,200 guineas by Mr F. W. Dennis and was trained by Willie Stephenson. Mr Dennis, usually referred to on the racecourse as 'Potato' Dennis, was well known to members of the Thoroughbred Breeders' Association for his somewhat eccentric speeches at the Annual General Meeting.

It is not often that a maiden wins The Champion Stakes but Major Holliday's Narrator, by Nearco out of Phase, had not won before his success in that event. Trained by Humphrey Cottrill, Narrator won The Coronation Cup the following year. Humphrey Cottrill is a son of the former trainer Harry Cottrill and brother of Alec Cottrill, an outstanding amateur rider on the flat who was fatally injured in a race at Lewes. The authorities make better use of trainers in retirement than once they did and Cottrill now acts as a steward at Newbury.

Autumn racing at Newmarket was then very different from what it is now. The First October Meeting, the Second October Meeting and the Houghton Meeting all lasted four days although most people had had enough at the end of three—not least, in days of dwindling domestic help, local hostesses who had guests on their hands from Tuesday till Friday. The big races at the First October Meeting were The Cheveley Park Stakes and The Jockey Club Stakes, the latter then run over a mile and three-quarters. At the Second October Meeting there were The Middle Park Stakes on Tuesday, The Cesarewitch on Wednesday and The Champion Stakes on Thursday. The feature races at the Houghton Meeting were The Cambridgeshire, The Jockey Club Cup and The Dewhurst Stakes. Racegoers had to keep their wits about them as an occasional race was liable to finish in the Dip, or at the top of the hill leading down to the Dip.

8

NINETEEN-FIFTY-FIVE proved to be a year of many inconveniences. By far the worst of these was the coughing epidemic which broke out towards the end of July, which affected virtually every training centre in the country and did much to ruin racing, at least until mid-October. For example there were only three runners for The Champagne Stakes at Doncaster and two of them were coughing. Some horses never really recovered their form properly afterwards. Luckily that great filly Meld only started to cough the day after she won The St Leger. Fields were further reduced by the long spell of fine warm weather that rendered the ground hard from midsummer till well on into the autumn.

There was industrial trouble in the newspaper world and no national newspapers were available from March 25, the day The Grand National was run, till April 30. Off-course betting took a knock but racecourse attendances showed an increase during this particular period.

The railwaymen were out on strike from May 28 till June 14. A State of Emergency was proclaimed on May 31. The Jockey Club stated that racing would continue unless the government directed otherwise. The Royal Ascot meeting, however, was postponed, the opening day being transferred to July 12. Naturally much inconvenience and dislocation resulted. The weather proved to be extremely hot during Royal Ascot which did not distress the ladies unduly but was fairly uncomfortable for men more or less appropriately clad for a funeral in February. On the third day there was a violent thunderstorm. Two racegoers were killed by lightning and others were severely burned. The scene recalled the terrible Ascot storm of 1930 when a bookmaker was killed and the programme was abandoned for the day after The Royal Hunt Cup, the course being waterlogged.

This was the first year of the new course at Ascot and Major John Crocker Bulteel, who, with the Duke of Norfolk, was largely responsible, was knighted just before the original date fixed for the Royal Meeting. For the first time a full straight mile was available: previously The Royal Hunt Cup had been run over seven furlongs and one hundred and sixty-six yards. Spectators in the Royal Enclosure were little better off, but the Silver Ring, for example, was trebled in size.

Attendances continued to cause concern despite certain technical advances and experiments with night meetings and with meetings at which there were both flat-racing and events under National Hunt Rules. Evening meetings could be a bit of a gamble and in bad weather the attendance was liable to be exiguous. On the other hand, a fine summer evening sometimes produced a jackpot for the executive. Windsor, since the construction of the M4, does consistently well with its evening meetings.

On December 5, the Duke of Norfolk, Senior Steward of the Jockey Club, produced figures showing the financial difficulties faced by many racecourse companies. These figures, which were placed before the Chancellor of the Exchequer, showed how every 20 shillings earned by racecourses was, on average, spent. The figures, applicable to 1955, were:

Entertainments Duty	4s	10d
Prize money	5s	7d
Operating costs	7s	5d
Local and national taxation	1s	2d
	19s	0d

The remaining shilling was used to provide a dividend of 5d and a reserve of 7d for development and other contingencies.

The colts were a poorish lot in 1955 and the outstanding three-year-old was Lady Zia Wernher's Meld, a filly worthy to be ranked with such heroines of the turf as Sceptre, Pretty Polly and Sun Chariot. Bred by her owner, she is by the great stayer Alycidon out of the Fair Trial mare Daily Double, a granddaughter of Lady Zia's wonderful foundation mare, Double Life, in honour of whom a memorial stone stands at the Someries Stud.

Bay in colour and of commanding aspect, Meld when in training stood over sixteen hands and combined power and quality to a quite remarkable degree. She soon showed Captain Boyd-Rochfort that she was something out of the ordinary but quite early in her two-year-old career she split a pastern. However, she was ready to race by the autumn and on September 30 she lined up for the five-furlongs Great Foal Stakes at Newmarket. She was friendless in the market at 20/1 and was ridden by Stan Smith, the stable jockey, Harry Carr, being up on the Queen's Corporal. Corporal won with Meld a creditable second. It was the only defeat in her career. Three weeks later she won the six-furlongs Quy Maiden Stakes with great ease from seventeen rivals. Many who saw her win that day came away convinced they had seen the winner of the 1955 Oaks.

Meld thrived in the winter. She looked a picture in the paddock before The One Thousand Guineas and people lined the rails three deep to watch her canter down to the start. On firm ground she quickened up the hill to beat Lord Rosebery's stout-hearted grey, Aberlady, by two lengths. The general election took place during the Epsom Meeting and both The Oaks and The Coronation Cup were

30. Lady Zia Wernher leads in her One Thousand Guineas winner, Meld, in 1955. Her trainer, Captain Cecil Boyd-Rochfort, congratulates her

run on the Friday. Meld won The Oaks by six lengths from Mr Richard Hollingsworth's Straight Deal filly, Ark Royal, trained by George Colling. Ark Royal was good enough to win The Oaks nine years out of ten. She won all her other races at three, these being the Lingfield Oaks Trial, The Ribblesdale Stakes, The Yorkshire Oaks, The Park Hill Stakes and The Newmarket Oaks.

The going was very firm at Royal Ascot for The Coronation Stakes but that did not disturb Meld who won by five lengths from Gloria Nicky. Besides being a fine stayer, Meld had any amount of speed. Harry Carr, who often rode that brilliant sprinter Pappa Fourway, thought that Meld would have been at least his equal over six furlongs.

There remained only The St Leger. Boyd-Rochfort's horses were hard hit by the coughing epidemic and the time came when Meld was the only member of the stable in the clear. Every effort was made to keep her so. She was dosed daily with cod-liver oil and malt, and Boyd-Rochfort declared he had used more disinfectant in a week than he normally did in six years. A lad was posted permanently outside

Meld's box to hear if there was a suspicion of a cough. Luckily she remained free of infection. In the paddock at Doncaster she looked lighter than she had done at Ascot. Despite paddock rumours that she had coughed a couple of times that morning, she started at 11/10 on.

For the first three-quarters of a mile the pace was lamentably slow. When at last it increased the issue seemed to lie between Meld and the French colt Beau Prince who had been third to the Derby winner Phil Drake in the Grand Prix. Carr sensed Meld was not quite her usual self and rode her as tenderly as he could. When she challenged on the outside Meld took the lead without undue difficulty but the superb acceleration showed in previous races was not forthcoming. Luckily Beau Prince was in trouble, but Lester Piggott on Miss Dorothy Paget's big Nimbus colt Nucleus was looming uncomfortably close.

At this point Carr began to flourish his whip and Piggott got to work in typically vigorous fashion on Nucleus. Meld, obviously tiring, veered towards the rails and Nucleus, not much liking the treatment he was receiving, jinked sharply to the left behind the favourite. Carr put down his whip, feeling that Meld was already giving everything she had, while Piggott, seeing that Meld was continuing to drift leftwards, switched Nucleus to the outside again. Nucleus made a brave final rally but Meld held on gallantly to win by three parts of a length with Beau Prince third.

Miss Dorothy Paget was not present to see Nucleus run. Piggott dismounted and, without speaking to Charles Jerdein who held the licence in the stable that Mrs Johnson Houghton actually controlled, stalked into the weighing room, borrowed £10 and lodged an objection to Meld on the grounds of crossing. The period of suspense was brief. The Stewards swiftly overruled the objection and ordered Piggott to forfeit his deposit. Possibly the Stewards were a bit hard on Piggott, who thought he was acting in the best interests of Nucleus's owner. Undoubtedly he would have consulted Jerdein had Jerdein been in the unsaddling enclosure, but it took him a long time to battle his way there from the grandstand. It is arguable that Nucleus would just about have won had he kept a straight course when he came under the whip.

Obviously The St Leger was not one of Meld's more scintillating performances but the reason for it soon became clear. Once she got back home she started to cough and ran a high temperature. She never raced again. She had won five races worth £43,049. She was as handsome a filly as anyone could ever hope to see and was every bit as good as she looked. Of course she had an easy time of it compared with Sceptre and Pretty Polly as she only ran six times. Sceptre and Pretty Polly were both in training for four seasons and had respectively twenty-five and twenty-four races. Sceptre won from five and a half furlongs to a mile and three-quarters; Pretty Polly from five furlongs to two and a quarter miles. Both mares were placed in the Ascot Gold Cup.

For some years Meld was a sad disappointment as a brood mare but past failures were forgotten when her son Charlottown triumphed in the 1966 Derby. Another son, Mellay, by Never Say Die, did well as a sire in New Zealand.

Nucleus, racegoers used to say, possessed a thoroughly unpleasant disposition. If he did, there was a good excuse for it as he probably suffered much pain at times from a brain disease which was the cause of his death the following year. His victories at three included The King Edward VII Stakes and The Jockey Club Stakes, while he won all the three races in which he was able to compete in the spring of 1956.

The top two-year-old of 1954 had been Mr David Robinson's Our Babu, winner of The Champagne Stakes and The Middle Park Stakes. Trained by Geoffrey Brooke, he was a well grown bright bay with black mane and tail and with big ears set well apart. He was a half-brother by My Babu to the Eclipse winner King of the Tudors and had been bought on Mr Robinson's behalf as a yearling for 2,700 guineas.

His first race at three was the Kempton Park Two Thousand Guineas Trial. He was still a bit backward and like Darius the year before he suffered defeat, being beaten by the Queen's Alexander. A week before The Guineas he was formally tried on the Limekilns. He finished behind that redoubtable veteran Durante but was held to have accomplished a satisfactory performance. The fact that the Limekilns was used shows how unusually hard the ground was that spring.

Favourite for The Two Thousand was Lord Porchester's Persian Gulf colt Tamerlane. He nearly brought it off but in a tremendous finish he went under by a neck to Our Babu with Klairon, who subsequently won the French Two Thousand, inches away third. Our Babu did not stay in The Derby and was only third behind Tamerlane in The St James's Palace Stakes. He was exported to America, returned to this country in 1963, and went to Japan in 1967.

Mr David Robinson is a figure of importance in post-war racing though one who through deliberate reticence is little known personally either to the press or to the public. His entry in the 1973 Directory of the Turf amounts to about twenty words. In the 1967 edition he had no entry at all.

He is a self-made man who through hard work and intelligence amassed a splendid fortune in the radio and television business. When he came into racing in the 1940s he seemed quite unable to find a trainer that suited him and changes were made with a regularity that gave him the reputation of being a thoroughly difficult individual. For a time he seemed to get on reasonably well with Geoffrey Brooke, whose rollicking sense of humour no doubt helped to make his job tolerable. However, in 1962 Mr Robinson bought the Carlburg establishment at Newmarket and engaged Bruce Hobbs as his private trainer. Bruce, a quiet and modest individual, had, at the age of seventeen, won The Grand National on the diminutive Battleship. After serving with distinction in the war, he had years of valuable experience as assistant to Captain Boyd-Rochfort. Bruce did well for Mr Robinson but his tenure of office was brief. He was succeeded by Jimmy Thompson from Beverley. Thompson may not have been sorry to return to the north two years later.

Mr Robinson's empire was expanding the whole time and he had also bought Clarehaven from Lord Harrington with the proviso that Geoffrey Brooke stayed

31. Mr David Robinson, pictured in 1971 receiving the trophy after the Johnnie Walker Ebor Handicap at York

there till he gave up training. In 1968 Mr Robinson had over seventy horses and divided them between two private trainers, Michael Jarvis and Paul Davey. Jarvis is the son of Andy Jarvis, who rode many winners over the sticks for the late 'Towser' Gosden, and Davey is the son of the veteran north-country trainer Ernie Davey. At one point Mr Robinson had over a hundred and twenty horses in training and found it expedient to engage a third private trainer. He has recently made drastic cuts in his racing commitments and such horses as he still has are with Jarvis, who is now a public trainer.

On the racecourse Mr Robinson, whose health is far from good nowadays, is usually accompanied by his wife. He seems to prefer to keep himself to himself and even receiving a trophy can be an ordeal. Doubtless he derives satisfaction from the belief that his racing interests are run on business lines, which includes sending horses that have cost five figures as yearlings to pick up small prizes at courses like Pontefract and Catterick Bridge.

Mr Robinson has been described as a well-balanced man in that he has a chip of equal size on both shoulders. Perhaps he was not treated with noticeable tact when he first came into racing. It might have made some difference—though I doubt it—if some of the members of the Jockey Club had congratulated him after Our Babu had won The Two Thousand Guineas and had asked him up for a drink. It is conceivable that he feels a certain contempt for individuals who have not come up in life the hard way. He regards the Jockey Club as unbusinesslike, not realising that, though one or two of the members might have little difficulty in being qualified as drones, there are others with experience in business at least equal to his own. In making the main speech of the evening at the 1969 Gimcrack Dinner he observed:

'It is nonsense to argue as some do that business and sport cannot mix. In another age racing may have been purely a sport. But for a long time now it has been an industry, and as an industry it has declined because the administrators of racing have had neither the business experience to run it effectively, nor apparently the will or even the desire to bring in that experience for the benefit of racing.

'You see before you the spectacle of a once proud sport reduced to utter dependence on public money. A sport that is slowly strangling itself by the foolish expenditure of that money, and yet with a chance—a last chance—to put things right.

'As you may know, I have now bought Kempton Park which from a money-making point of view is a bad investment. But that is not my purpose. As in my stables at Newmarket, I have at Kempton Park an opportunity to put my ideas into practice.

'I firmly believe that with proper business management and a complete change of attitude Kempton can draw the crowds, reach a profitable basis and perhaps show others what is possible if the administration of a course is businesslike and efficient.'

With all this fighting talk about businesslike methods and efficiency, everyone was on the qui vive to see what Mr Robinson could accomplish at Kempton, a course that had been going steadily downhill in the estimation of the racegoing public. It was soon apparent that Mr Robinson's knowledge of racing administration was of an exiguous nature. At one Kempton meeting he asked one of the stewards how much he was paid for the job and seemed genuinely taken aback to discover there were individuals who were perfectly prepared to do the work for nothing.

There were no major changes during the Robinson regime at Kempton. Mr Robinson himself soon seemed to lose interest and the property once again changed hands. With the ignominious collapse of so many big firms in recent times, the demand for experienced businessmen to come and run racing has become perhaps a trifle less insistent.

Mr Robinson has never displayed much interest in bloodstock breeding but he has been one of the most prolific buyers of yearlings, colts rather than fillies, in racing history. His purchases have been chosen by a team of experts headed by Lord Harrington and known as 'the Robinson Rangers'. Yet, despite the immense expenditure and the advice received from acknowledged experts, the fact remains that Our Babu is the solitary classic winner in Mr Robinson's colours.

It could never be claimed that Mr Robinson is one of the turf's more attractive characters but the sport owes him one big debt, nevertheless. At one stage he was providing over five hundred runners in a single season; and every one of them was a tryer.

The Derby yet again went to France, the victor being Phil Drake who carried the colours of the glamorous Mme Volterra and who had been bred by her late husband. It was a truly remarkable race. The favourite was Alycidon's brother, Acropolis, leased by Lady Irwin (now Countess of Halifax) to her grandmother, Alice, Lady Derby, who was then well over eighty years of age. Acropolis was fourth at Tattenham Corner and apparently going well but from that point he showed not a glimpse of acceleration. Turning into the straight, the 100/1 outsider from Ireland, Mr J. McGrath's Panaslipper, ridden by James Eddery, Pat Eddery's father, was tenth. He then quickened to such purpose that with two furlongs to go he was in front. He headed for home as hard as he could go and, although he was tiring at the distance and starting to hang, it looked highly improbable that he could be caught.

At Tattenham Corner there were only five horses behind Phil Drake. He then began an astonishing run, weaving his way through the field like an errand boy on a bicycle dodging heavy traffic. Even so, at the distance he still had five rivals in front of him. He maintained his run, though, in superb fashion and inside the final hundred yards he headed the tiring Panaslipper and won by a length and a half. Acropolis was third.

Phil Drake was trained by François Mathet and ridden by Fred Palmer. Mathet, once a cavalry officer, is a fine horseman and has ridden at Aintree. He is a master of organisation and this enables him to run the biggest stable in France with consistent success. Palmer is French though his father was British. He was apprenticed to Claude Halsey in France and besides being a first-rate rider on the flat he rode many winners over the jumps as well. He is now a successful trainer at Chantilly.

Phil Drake was a brown horse by the Grand Prix winner Admiral Drake out of a Vatellor mare that had bred Bozet, winner of the Prix Morny. He himself was too big and backward to run at two. Thirteen days before The Derby he won the Prix de la Rochette at Longchamp. That evening Rae Johnstone rang up an English owner and told him how much he had been impressed by Phil Drake. In those days the results from France did not automatically appear in the Sporting Life the following day. The owner who had been contacted and some of his friends were able to back Phil Drake on the course at Lingfield at 50/1.

Phil Drake won the Grand Prix but those two victories took a lot out of him and he was unplaced in The King George VI and Queen Elizabeth Stakes. He never ran again.

Major Holliday won The Coronation Cup with Narrator, who beat Darius and Zarathustra in an absurdly slow-run race. The hard ground made it very difficult

32. Madame Suzy Volterra pictured in 1970 at the Newmarket Bloodstock sales, owner of the 1955 Derby winner, Phil Drake

for Humphrey Cottrill to keep Narrator at the top of his form after Epsom and Narrator was far from being at his best in The Eclipse Stakes, which was won by Darius.

There was an Italian victory in The Ascot Gold Cup, the winner being the Marchese Incisa della Rochetta's Botticelli, a four-year-old by Blue Peter that had been bred by the great bloodstock expert Federico Tesio. He won comfortably from the American-bred Blue Prince II with M. Boussac's Elpenor, winner the previous year, third.

One of the outstanding horses seen at Royal Ascot was the sprinter Pappa Fourway who won the five-furlongs King's Stand Stakes. Now The Tetrarch, perhaps the fastest horse ever seen on the English turf, was by Roi Hérode, a French-bred stayer that was hardly more than a plodder. Pappa Fourway was by the French-bred Pappageno II who had been bought for £50 as a yearling at Deauville and proved to be a mudlark that won The Manchester November Handicap. Oola Hills, by Denturius, who was the dam of Pappa Fourway, never raced. Chikoo, dam of Oola Hills, managed to win a race or two under Pony Turf Club Rules. Pappa Fourway's pedigree hardly looked a glamorous one when he was in training, but it looked rather better some years later when Park Top, a granddaughter of Oola Hills, was proving herself one of the finest race mares of the past fifty years.

Pappa Fourway was bred by the Ballykisteen Stud. He came up for sale at Ballsbridge as a yearling and the Malton trainer Bill Dutton bought him for 150 guineas for Mrs E. Goldson. At the time Pappa Fourway was tall and gaunt and looked as if he might conceivably make a jumper provided he was given a great deal of time.

As a two-year-old Pappa Fourway was pretty smart and won four of his seven races. At three he was brilliant. He won successively The Prince of Wales's Handicap at Chester; The Stewards' Handicap at Epsom; The Festival Stakes at Birmingham; The Gosforth Park Cup at Newcastle; The July Cup at Newmarket; The King's Stand Stakes at Royal Ascot; The Diadem Stakes at Ascot; and The Tetrarch Stakes at Manchester. Some of his wins were obtained on very firm ground; it was extremely heavy when he won at Manchester. His victories that year brought him in only £7,842, which drew attention to the lack of remunerative opportunities for top-class sprinters. Before the year was out a big offer from America was received for Pappa Fourway and he was duly exported.

Bill Dutton, who died suddenly in 1958 at the age of fifty-seven, was quiet, modest and gentle and he made friends wherever he went. He was the son of a Cheshire farmer and, after gaining his B.A. and LL.B. degrees at Cambridge, he was articled to his uncle, a Chester solicitor. He was able to do a fair amount of riding under National Hunt Rules and won The National Hunt Chase at Cheltenham, a far more important race then than it is now, on Cloringo, a half-brother to that fine handicapper, Irish Elegance, who won The Royal Hunt Cup with 9 st. 11 lb. and The Portland Handicap with 10 st. 2 lb. Dutton's great triumph as a rider, though, was to win the 1928 Grand National on the 100/1 outsider Tipperary Tim, the only horse that year to get round without a fall.

In 1932 Dutton forsook the law and began training at Hednesford with a small stable of jumpers, mostly indifferent. He did, though, win The Liverpool Hurdle with a horse owned by the wife of a curate who had been a friend of his at Cambridge. During the war he served in the Middle East. Afterwards he began training again, transferring his stable to Malton. He won The Cheltenham Gold Cup with Limber Hill but his interests were becoming more centred on the flat. He won the 1957 Cesarewitch with Sandiacre, who also won The Ascot Stakes, and two excellent sprinters under his care were Vigo and Right Boy, the latter little inferior to Pappa Fourway. With those three his stable was able to win The July Cup three times in four years. On his death his horses were taken over by his son-in-law, Pat Rohan.

The 1955 King George VI and Queen Elizabeth Stakes produced a very exciting finish. Acropolis, who subsequently caught the cough and had to miss The St Leger, ran a brave race but he just lacked a bit of extra speed at the finish and lost by a head to M. P. Wertheimer's three-year-old Vimy, trained by Alec Head. It was in 1947 that Alec Head first came to the notice of English racegoers. He then rode Le Paillon, favourite for The Champion Hurdle at Cheltenham, and partly through lack of experience on that course he was beaten by Danny Morgan on National Spirit. Later that year Le Paillon won the Prix de l'Arc de Triomphe. William Head, Alec's father, had ridden Ballyboggan into second place in the 1919 Grand National.

Vimy, later bought by the Irish National Stud for £105,000, was by Wild Risk, one of France's very best hurdlers, out of Mimi, by Black Devil. Mimi also bred the gigantic Midget II who won The Cheveley Park Stakes in 1955 and the following year The Coronation Stakes and The Queen Elizabeth II Stakes.

Head had a good autumn in England as he won The Middle Park Stakes with Buisson Ardent and The Queen Elizabeth II Stakes and The Champion Stakes with Hafiz II. Both horses belonged to the Aga Khan. Darius may have been a bit unlucky in The Champion Stakes as his pacemaker did not do his job properly and the race was run at a miserable pace. On the other hand Hafiz II had had a long and tiresome journey, his plane having been unable to land at Cambridge owing to fog. Hafiz was a big, powerful chestnut by Nearco. A certain prejudice then existed against chestnut Nearcos on the grounds that they were highly-strung and unreliable. Hafiz II was certainly liable to sweat up profusely before a race but once in action he seemed genuine enough.

It is perhaps worth noting that Lord Derby's presidential speech at the annual general meeting of the Thoroughbred Breeders' Association ended with these words: 'While I certainly hope our racing will become much more prosperous in the future, it is vital that it should retain its character as a sport.' No doubt a similar sentiment would be received with derision by many today.

By 1956 there was a general feeling that in the not far distant future there was going to be a drastic revision of the country's betting laws and that this revision might well enable betting to make at long last a worthwhile contribution to the general benefit of the sport. There was, though, a marked difference between the government's approach to the question and that of the majority of racing organisations from the Jockey Club downwards. The government was greatly concerned with moral principles and seemed content to move slowly, ever careful of offending those who detested the existence of gambling in any shape or form. Racing people, on the other hand, were interested in practical issues and were irritated by what seemed to them to be niggling objections and avoidable delays.

It was announced in the Racing Calendar of May 6 that the Jockey Club was to set up a joint committee in order to agree on basic principles with regard to the proposed legislation on betting. The Senior Steward, Lord Willoughby de Broke, said this would enable the Stewards to inform the Home Secretary that these principles formed the bedrock of their policy. The organisations involved were the National Hunt Committee, the Racecourse Betting Control Board, the National Bookmakers' Protection Association, the Thoroughbred Breeders' Association, the Racehorse Owners' Association, Tattersalls' Committee, Tote Investors Ltd, the Racecourse Association and the racing press.

In August the Home Secretary, Major G. Lloyd George, interviewed the Stewards and requested them to produce by October:

1   a case to show the present economic plight of racing;
2   a case to support the principle—never previously put to any government— that betting on horse-racing should contribute to horse-racing;
3   a skeleton scheme for a body to control betting on and off the course both with the bookmakers and with the totalisator.

As regards the skeleton scheme, the Stewards drafted one with the help and advice of legal experts. They made it perfectly clear to the Home Secretary that they were working to terms of reference that he himself had laid down. The scheme, therefore, could not be interpreted as an expression of the views of the Jockey Club or of the Joint Betting Bill Committee with regard to the advantages and disadvantages of either a tote monopoly or of betting shops.

The Stewards were careful to emphasise that their scheme was based on an assumption that the government had accepted the principle that betting on horse racing ought to contribute to horse racing; and that if that assumption was incorrect, they were not prepared to proceed further in the matter.

In November the Stewards again met the Home Secretary. It was not a satisfactory interview. The Home Secretary put forward a plan for a partial tote monopoly with regard to off-course betting. The Stewards replied that such a plan was not only unworkable but potentially harmful to racing. The Home Secretary then made it clear that there would be no provision in the Bill for betting with off-course bookmakers to contribute to racing. The Stewards replied that they could not support a Bill which made no provision for all betting on horses to contribute to the sport, and that under the circumstance they would await the draft of a Betting Bill put forward by the Home Office before deciding whether they could make further recommendations and support the Bill.

Thus on this vitally important matter the year ended on a note of anxiety and disagreement.

The season of 1956 was for the most part grey, cool and wet, and the rainfall during the month of July was the heaviest for a hundred years. Once again French horses had a wonderful year, winning The Derby, The Oaks, The St Leger, The Gold Cup, The Coronation Cup and The Eclipse Stakes. Apart from which, the great Italian horse Ribot won The King George VI and Queen Elizabeth Stakes.

The driest part of the season came in the spring and the Rowley Mile was very firm, even hard in places, for The Two Thousand Guineas. This race provided an astonishing result, the winner being the 50/1 outsider Gilles de Retz, owned by Mr Tony Samuel and trained by Charles Jerdein, who held the licence in the stable controlled by Mrs Johnson Houghton. Ridden by Frank Barlow, Gilles de Retz won by a length from Chantelsey with Buisson Ardent third. A son of Royal Charger, Gilles de Retz had finished a poor fifth in The Greenham Stakes at Newbury. On the Saturday before The Guineas he had worked in an unsatisfactory manner at home. After The Guineas he ran in the Lingfield Derby Trial,

The Derby and The St James's Palace Stakes and was unplaced on each occasion. He was a very baffling customer indeed. Some people reckoned he must have a kink; others that he was suffering from an undisclosed disability.

The Derby was a wretchedly depressing affair. Run on a cold, wet afternoon, it was won by M. Pierre Wertheimer's Lavandin, trained by Alec Head and ridden by Johnstone. A fast-finishing second, beaten a neck, was Mr R. Strassburger's Montaval and third was Mr J. McGrath's Roistar. Thus there was no English-trained horse in the leading three.

What made the whole business so discouraging was a suspicion that Lavandin, who started favourite, was not a particularly good horse. He was certainly one with a very doubtful leg. He subsequently finished unplaced in the Grand Prix and that concluded his racing career. He made no great mark as a sire and was exported to Japan.

A workmanlike bay, Lavandin had been bred by his owner and was by the Comte de Chambure's Verso II, a good winner in France during the war, out of Lavande, by Rustom Pasha. Lavande was an erratic breeder but in her early days at the stud she got Le Lavandou, by Djebel, who was a good two-year-old in France and a winner in England of The Portland Handicap. He became grandsire of Levmoss and My Swallow. She also got Lavarede, by Verso II, who was second in the Grand Prix. She was barren in 1949 and in the three following years as well so M. Wertheimer, who in his younger days had owned that brilliantly fast horse Epinard, decided to have her put down. The Comte de Chambure, though, persuaded him to give her one last chance. She was mated with Verso II again and this union produced the winner of The Derby.

Lavandin was the last Derby winner ridden by William Raphael Johnstone, commonly known as 'Rae' Johnstone, who was then in his fifty-second year. He was born in Australia, rode his first winner there at fifteen and was top jockey in Sydney at the age of twenty-six. In 1932 he went to France at the invitation of M. Wertheimer and was an immediate success. French racegoers always admired him and gave him the nickname of 'Le Crocodile'. In the first six years he rode in France he was champion jockey three times. In 1934 he accepted an offer to come to England—his nickname here was originally 'Togo' but that was dropped after the war—to ride for Lord Glanely. This did little to enhance his reputation. He won The Two Thousand Guineas on Colombo but was widely, and to some extent unfairly, blamed for Colombo's defeat in The Derby. It must surely be doubtful if Colombo could ever have beaten Windsor Lad over a mile and a half. Johnstone and Lord Glanely parted company long before the season ended. In 1935 Johnstone won The One Thousand Guineas on M. Wertheimer's Mesa but his reputation with English followers of racing suffered another blow when he rode a lamentable race on Mesa in The Oaks, losing a race he certainly ought to have won quite comfortably.

During the war Johnstone was in France and his experiences included a spell in a German prison camp. It was only in post-war racing that his true merit was appreciated in England. In 1947 he won The One Thousand Guineas and The

Oaks on Imprudence, and the following year he won The Derby on My Love. He rode for M. Boussac for three years when the Boussac stable was enjoying a period of wonderful success. In 1950 he won The Derby, The Oaks, The St Leger, the French Derby and the Irish Oaks. In 1952 his association with M. Boussac terminated after the defeats of Auriban in the Grand Prix and of Arbele in The King George VI and Queen Elizabeth Stakes.

All told Johnstone won twelve English classic races. At his peak he was a polished and stylish horseman and, like most Australians, a fine judge of pace, with a preference for riding waiting races. When he gave up racing he set up as a trainer. In 1964 he died after a severe heart attack at Le Tremblay. Cosmopolitan in outlook, at one time a compulsive gambler, he was a sophisticated man of the world who lived his life to the full.

Mr Strassburger made up for Montaval's defeat in The Derby by winning The St Leger with Cambremer, trained by George Bridgland and ridden by Palmer. Cambremer stayed on well to win by three parts of a length from Lord Astor's Hornbeam, with French Beige third. Baron Guy de Rothschild's Pont Levis started favourite but finished last. Cambremer, who had previously won the Grand Prix de Vichy, was a strongly made but plainish chestnut by the 1945 St Leger winner Chamossaire out of Tomorrow II, a mare by the Derby runner-up Easton. In 1940 Tomorrow II, together with other horses owned by Mr Strassburger, had been sent to America from France.

Hornbeam, by Hyperion out of Thicket, by Nasrullah, was a compact chestnut trained by Jack Colling. He was a good honest stayer and nearly always ran a creditable race but he just lacked that bit of extra speed that would have made him very good indeed. Being a stayer, he was not extensively patronised by British breeders and was exported to Sweden in 1966. Possibly his departure was regretted after his son Intermezzo had won The St Leger and his daughter Windmill Girl, second in The Oaks, had bred The Derby winners Blakeney and Morston.

M. Wertheimer had had high hopes of winning The One Thousand Guineas with his big grey filly Midget II, by Djebel, who had won The Cheveley Park Stakes the previous autumn. Midget II raced on the far side of the course and her rider Roger Poincelet returned to the unsaddling enclosure wreathed in a sunny smile of self-satisfaction being under the impression that Midget II had won quite comfortably. The smile, though, was swiftly erased when a somewhat irate Alec Head informed him that Honeylight, racing on the stand side, had won by a couple of lengths. Head, never at his smoothest when things go wrong, was outspokenly vexed at Midget II's defeat. Two days later Poincelet rode Lavandin into third place in the Prix Hocquart. Head was not satisfied with his riding; nor for that matter were the Longchamp Stewards. In consequence Poincelet was taken off Lavandin for The Derby and the ride given to Johnstone instead.

Honeylight, who had previously won The Free Handicap, was bred and owned by Sir Victor Sassoon and was a half-sister by Honeyway to the dual classic winner Crepello and the Gold Cup winner Twilight Alley. Both Honeylight and Arietta, who finished third, were trained by Captain Charles Elsey.

The distance of The Oaks was too far for Honeylight who finished fourth. French fillies occupied the first three places, Madame Volterra's Sicambre filly Sicarelle, who stood out in the paddock and started favourite, winning easily from M. Boussac's Janiari with Prince Aly Khan's Yasmin a distant third. Sicarelle, trained by Mathet and ridden by Palmer, looked a really good filly that day but she failed badly not only in the Grand Prix, but more surprisingly in the Prix Vermeille as well.

The French also won The Coronation Cup with Baron Guy de Rothschild's Tropique, who the following month carried off The Eclipse Stakes, too. Tropique, a good-looking bay by Fontenay, split a pastern at two and did not race until he was three.

At Royal Ascot The Gold Cup was just a benefit match for the French, M. Boussac's four-year-old Macip winning from Mme C. del Duca's Bewitched with Mr R. Strassburger's Clichy third. Macip, winner of the French St Leger, was a chestnut by that fine stayer Marsyas II out of Corejada, by Pharis II. At two Corejada won The Findon Stakes at Goodwood, The Lowther Stakes at York and The Cheveley Park Stakes at Newmarket. At three she won the French One Thousand and the Irish Oaks but in the Yorkshire Oaks was beaten by the King's Above Board. Other French successes at Royal Ascot were the Queen Alexandra Stakes with M. Weisweiller's Borghetto and the King's Stand Stakes with the Aga Khan's speedy Palestine filly Palariva. Palariva had a hard race to beat Vigo by a short head.

Boyd-Rochfort was never averse to having a go in a big handicap and he won The Royal Hunt Cup with the Queen's Alexander backed from 100/9 to 13/2. Boyd-Rochfort also pulled off The Ascot Stakes with Zarathustra who two years previously had won the Irish Derby and was destined to win The Gold Cup. Prendergast produced another very fast two-year-old in Skindles Hotel, who won The New Stakes and, before being sent to America at the end of the season, had also won The Rous Stakes at Doncaster and the Prix d'Arenberg at Longchamp. He was typical of many of his trainer's best two-year-olds at this period as he was unfashionably bred, by Maharaj Kumar out of a Concerto mare, and had been bought cheaply, in his case for 1,500 guineas. Major Holliday and Humphrey Cottrill landed a rewarding double with Pirate King in The St James's Palace Stakes and Pharsalia in The Queen Mary Stakes, while Hugh Lupus, trained by Noel Murless won The Hardwicke Stakes for Lady Ursula Vernon. A four-year-old by Djebel that had won the Irish Two Thousand Guineas in 1955, Hugh Lupus won The Champion Stakes in the autumn. He sired a good horse in the St Leger winner Hethersett.

By far the best horse seen out in England in 1956 was the Marchesa Incisa della Rochetta's four-year-old Ribot, who won The King George VI and Queen Elizabeth Stakes by five lengths from what admittedly was indifferent opposition. He was trained by Ugo Penco and ridden by Enrico Camici.

Ribot was bred by Razza Dormello-Olgiata, a name signifying the Tesio–Incisa della Rochetta partnership. He was actually foaled at the English National Stud

33.   Ribot, who won The King George VI and Queen Elizabeth Stakes in 1956

and was by Tenerani, by Bellini, out of Romanella, by Pharos's son El Greco. Tenerani was a high-class horse that in Italy won the Italian Derby, the Gran Premio di Milano, the Gran Premio d'Italia, the Italian St Leger and ten other races. In England he beat Black Tarquin by inches in The Queen Elizabeth Stakes at Ascot and he also won The Goodwood Cup in which the favourite Arbar broke down. He stood for three seasons in Italy and then came to England where he was at the National Stud till 1960. At the end of that year he was back in Italy where he died in 1965. Signor Tesio had a high opinion of Tenerani and strongly urged British breeders to send mares to him, but breeders here never really took to him. He did, though, sire the dual Gold Cup winner, Fighting Charlie; the Goodwood Cup winner, Tenterhooks; and Tender Annie, winner of The Ribblesdale Stakes. Romanella, Ribot's dam, won five of her seven races at two but then developed a ring-bone and was sent to the stud at three.

As a foal Ribot was so small that he was nicknamed 'il piccolo' and was not entered for the Italian Two Thousand, Derby or St Leger. When fully grown, however, he stood sixteen hands. A light bay with black mane and tail, he was most solidly built, giving the impression of possessing remarkable depth. His quarters were extremely powerful and he had an intelligent head with a fine bold outlook. Some critics thought he lacked quality; none could deny that he looked thoroughly businesslike and purposeful.

He was in training for three seasons and won all his sixteen races. He won £106,514 in prize money, beating the European record then held by Tantième by over £22,000. At three he won the Prix de l'Arc de Triomphe by three lengths; at four by six lengths.

As a sire Ribot spent four seasons in Europe before being sent to America where he died of a twisted intestine in 1973. Originally the Marchesa Incisa della Rochetta had leased him for five years but when that period was up any suggestions of a possible return to Europe were invariably countered with the statement that Ribot's temper made such a journey impossible. He was leading British sire in 1963, 1967 and 1968. He was second in Italy in 1964, third in France in 1966, fifth in America in 1965. He sired four St Leger winners in Ragusa, Ribocco, Ribero and Boucher. All bar Boucher won the Irish Sweeps Derby, and Ragusa in addition won The King George VI and Queen Elizabeth Stakes. His Arc winners were Molvedo and Prince Royal II. Alice Frey won the Italian Oaks, Regal Exception the Irish Guinness Oaks. Tom Rolfe won The Preakness Stakes, was three-year-old champion in America, and has sired the 1970 two-year-old champion Hoist the Flag and the 1971 grass-course champion Run the Gantlet. Arts and Letters won the Belmont Stakes and was 1969 Horse of the Year in America. Graustark, only once beaten, sired the 1972 American three-year-old champion, Key to the Mint, and another good three-year-old in Jim French. Altogether Ribot, who had a gentle enough disposition when in training, is likely to leave his mark on European and United States racing for many more years to come.

The Aga Khan's four-year-old Hafiz II made a fine attempt to win The Cambridgeshire with 9 st. 7 lb. As usual he sweated up before the race like a June bride but he ran with admirable determination and only lost by half a length to Loppylugs who was receiving 27 lb. Loppylugs was owned and trained by John Beary, brother of Michael Beary. Four years previously a mare of his called La Joyeuse was found to have been doped. It was in the highest degree improbable that Beary had anything to do with it but under the rule then existing he was deprived of his licence. Two years later, while still disqualified, he bought Loppylugs as a foal for £150, hoping to sell him at a profit. However, he had not owned Loppylugs long before his licence was restored. He set about re-establishing his stable and accordingly retained Loppylugs, so called because of his huge ears, but later sold a half share to Mr N. Hinds, who farmed near Wantage. Beary had a lot of friends, all of whom felt he had been unfairly treated, and this success was received with much rejoicing. During this year there was an alteration in the rule affecting the administration and detection of drugs. This graciously permitted trainers to test their horses on their own initiative without the fear of losing their licences.

Since 1838 Tattersalls had always held their principal yearling sale at the Glasgow Paddocks, Doncaster, during St Leger week. In 1956 Captain Kenneth Watt, the senior partner in Tattersalls, stated that the last Doncaster sale conducted by his firm would be in 1957 since they found it quite impossible to accept the new terms offered by the Doncaster Corporation. The loss was undoubtedly Doncaster's. Doncaster is a singularly dreary and unattractive town and the sales did a lot to augment the pleasures and interest of St Leger week. A good many visitors came more for the sales, in fact, than for the racing. In particular, the number of visitors from Ireland dwindled sharply once the sales had been transferred to Newmarket. The whole atmosphere of The St Leger meeting has changed and become a great deal less entertaining.

A great figure in European racing vanished in 1957 with the death of the Aga Khan at the age of seventy-nine. In this country he was leading owner thirteen times and leading breeder eight times. In Great Britain and Ireland he won 741 flat-races worth £1,043,934. He won The Derby five times, The St Leger five times, The Two Thousand Guineas three times, The Oaks twice and The One Thousand Guineas once. He also had thirteen successes in Irish classic races. He won the Prix de l'Arc de Triomphe twice.

It would be an exaggeration to say that the Aga Khan was universally popular in England, particularly after war. The sale of his Derby winners irked a good many people. His importance, though, was undeniable and he conducted his racing operations on an appropriately princely scale. He came to know a great deal about bloodstock breeding and he established a reputation for being both extremely astute and totally devoid of sentiment. He was essentially a realist and some of his opinions were unpopular as when he declared that English racing was conducted almost entirely for the benefit of bookmakers. He once had the temerity to refer in a letter to The Times to the injurious effect of the steady flow of our best horses to America. Lord Rosebery replied that in this particular respect the Aga Khan was by far the greatest offender though by no stretch of the imagination could he be called a poor man. Mr A. B. Clements, for many years Editor of the Sporting Life, hit the nail on the head when he wrote: 'The Aga Khan's interest in bloodstock is primarily that of the dealer.'

The Aga Khan had originally been inspired to take up racing by Lord Wavertree, whose own personality was a compound of shrewdness and eccentricity. Many years passed, though, before the Aga Khan actually went into action. In 1921 he asked George Lambton to train for him. Lambton was unable to accept but agreed to buy for him a number of yearlings that would form the basis for a stud. Among the fillies bought were Cos, Teresina and Mumtaz Mahal, while the colts included the classic winners Diophon and Salmon Trout. These were all trained by R. C. Dawson at Whatcombe. Owner and trainer had words at a Newbury meeting in 1931 and all the Aga Khan's horses were removed from Dawson without delay. By the end of the year they were with Frank Butters, who remained his trainer till 1949, when Butters retired after his serious accident. Butters was followed by Marcus Marsh, and Marsh by Noel Murless. In 1954 the Aga Khan transferred his racing interests to France where his trainer was Alec Head. He gave as his reason the lower cost to owners in France in relation to the prize money available. When he died he owned, in partnership with Prince Aly Khan, five studs in Ireland and four in France. His stud managers in Ireland were successively Sir Henry Greer, Colonel T. J. Peacocke, Mr Nesbit Waddington, and Major Cyril Hall.

Top of the two-year-old Free Handicap in 1956 had been Mr Keith Mason's Amour Drake filly Sarcelle, trained by Noel Cannon. At three she failed to train on. The leading colt had been Mr Stavros Niarchos's Pipe of Peace, trained by Sir Gordon Richards. On the 9-stone mark was the Dewhurst Stakes winner Crepello, bred and owned by Sir Victor Sassoon and trained by Noel Murless. Crepello proved to be a three-year-old of the highest class and won The Two Thousand Guineas and The Derby. He was a big, handsome, strongly made chestnut by the Italian-bred Donatello II out of Crepuscule, by the French-bred Mieuxcé. Crepuscule also bred the One Thousand Guineas winner Honeylight and the Gold Cup winner Twilight Alley.

It was a very dry spring and the going everywhere was firm. It had been planned to run Crepello in the Blue Riband Trial Stakes and he was actually taken to Epsom but Murless sent him home when he saw the state of the ground. Pipe of Peace, who had won The Greenham Stakes, was favourite for The Two Thousand Guineas at 100/30. The French colt Tyrone and Crepello were both heavily backed at 7/2. Ridden by Piggott, Crepello, who met with some interference approaching the Bushes, secured the lead close to home to win a very pretty race by half a length from Quorum with Pipe of Peace, who had weakened after leading at the foot of the hill, only a head away third. It was thus clear that Crepello was that rare and highly desirable type, a horse with a stayer's pedigree and top-class speed. If he kept sound he seemed certain to win The Derby. It had been a fine piece of training by Murless who, under conditions not at all favourable for a big horse like Crepello, had produced him fit to win The Guineas without the advantage of a previous outing.

Mr T. H. Farr's Quorum, trained at Middleham by Lt-Col Wilfred Lyde, was a grey by the sprinter Vilmorin out of a mare by Bois Roussel. He subsequently won The Jersey Stakes at Royal Ascot and The Sussex Stakes at Goodwood. He did pretty well as a sire, versatility being one of his characteristics as he got sprinters, middle-distance horses and out-and-out stayers. The most famous of his offspring, though, is the triple Grand National winner Red Rum.

The going remained firm for the Epsom meeting. Crepello, who stood out in the paddock, started a hot favourite at 6/4 for The Derby and won with a bit in hand by a length and a half from the Irish colt Ballymoss, with the fast-finishing Pipe of Peace a length away third. The winning margin would have been greater if Piggott had not dropped his hands in the final fifty yards. Bearing in mind the fine achievements of Ballymoss subsequently, it is fair to assume that Crepello was an above-average winner of The Derby.

As it happened, Crepello never ran again. It was planned to run him in The King George VI and Queen Elizabeth Stakes at Ascot in July and he was listed as a probable in the morning papers. On the assumption that he was to run, other English horses had been taken out of the race. Many people came to Ascot expressly to see him perform. An hour before the race the decision was taken not to run him, a decision that naturally caused disappointment and resentment. There had been a good deal of rain during the week and the state of the ground was given as the reason. The official description of the going was 'dead'. Possibly Murless had never really been keen to run Crepello, whose soundness was not on the same high level as his ability. It is fair to say that Murless always put the interests of his horses first and would not be afraid to do so even if those interests did not happen to coincide with those of the public.

In August Crepello broke down on his off foreleg and was retired to the stud where he proved extremely successful. In his absence, French horses filled the first four places in The King George VI and Queen Elizabeth Stakes, Montaval winning by a short head from Prince Aly Khan's Al Mabsoot with Tribord third and Saint Raphael fourth. Shortly afterwards Montaval, by Norseman, was bought by Lord Harrington to stand at the Mount Coote Stud, Co. Limerick. He was unplaced in The Washington International at Laurel Park.

Noel Murless was born in Cheshire in 1910. Before the war he was attached to Frank Hartigan, an exacting taskmaster if ever there was one, and rode, not with any marked success, under National Hunt Rules first as an amateur and then as a professional. Later he helped Frank Hartigan's brother Hubert—a big man who had nevertheless one year looked like winning The Grand National on Old Tay Bridge—at Penrith and also in Ireland. There is not much Hubert Hartigan did not know about horses and racing and doubtless Murless learnt a great deal during their association. Eventually Murless set up on his own at Hambleton in Yorkshire and very soon began to make a name for himself, among those impressed by his ability being Sir Gordon Richards. On the retirement of Fred Darling, Murless succeeded him at Beckhampton but he was never really happy there and was pleased to move to Newmarket a few years later.

It is generally agreed that as a trainer of high-class horses Noel Murless was second to none. He was very conscientious and above all patient. He was genuinely devoted to his horses and their interests came first. Like most trainers of his age-group, he probably felt that a trainer's life—even that of a top trainer—was not the fun that it used to be and he was distressed by the strike of stable lads in 1975. In appearance he is tall, thin, a poorish mover, and he looks worried as often as not. He does not wear his heart on his sleeve and is possibly not at his happiest at a party but he is certainly not without humour and has some good stories to tell—in particular one about a certain hunter-chase at Colwall Park. His wife Gwen knows as much about running a stable as he does and their daughter Julie is married to Henry Cecil. Murless retired from training at the end of the season in 1976 and was knighted in 1977.

Ballymoss, owned by Mr J. McShain, the head of a big American construction company, and trained by Vincent O'Brien, started favourite at 9/4 on for the Irish Derby and won as he pleased. He returned to England for The Great Voltigeur Stakes at York but finished only third behind Brioche and Tempest. However, it was thought that O'Brien had probably left something to work on before The St Leger and furthermore that Ballymoss had not been suited by the rather dead ground. This view was confirmed when Ballymoss, ridden by T. P. Burns and starting at 8/1, won The St Leger by a length from Court Harwell with Brioche third. It was O'Brien's first success in an English classic. It was, in fact, the first Irish victory in any English classic since Orby won The Derby in 1907. No Irish-trained horse had ever won The St Leger before.

Ballymoss, who subsequently disappointed in The Champion Stakes won by the French-trained One Thousand Guineas winner, Rose Royale II, was bred by Mr R. Ball in Ireland at the same stud where the dual Grand National winner Reynoldstown had been reared. When in training he was a compact, strongly made, medium-sized chestnut with the very best of limbs. He is by Nearco's son Mossborough, who just missed the top class as a racehorse, out of Indian Call, by the St Leger winner Singapore. Bred by Lord Glanely, Indian Call ran twice unplaced and after the outbreak of war she was one of a large draft sent up to the December Sales at Newmarket from the Exning Stud. Despite her pedigree, she was knocked down to Mr Ball for only 18 guineas. Her dam, the Yorkshire Oaks winner Flittemere, by Buchan out of the St Leger winner Keysoe, only made a tenner. Indian Call also bred Guide who won eight races worth over £5,000.

Vincent O'Brien, now one of the most celebrated and successful trainers in the world, was born in 1917 and began training in Ireland in 1944. He made his name with jumpers and English racegoers first realised he was a man to be reckoned with when he sent Cottage Rake to win The Cheltenham Gold Cup three years running. He also won that race with Knock Hard. He won The Champion Hurdle three years running with Hattons Grace and he won The Grand National in 1953 with Early Mist, in 1954 with Royal Tan and in 1955 with Quare Times.

These successes proved beyond a shadow of doubt his remarkable professional ability but his career has not been without its setbacks. In March 1954 the Stewards of the I.N.H.S. committee called him before them to explain the inconsistent running of four horses trained by him—Royal Tan, Lucky Dome, Early Mist and Knock Hard. The witnesses included not only Irish racing officials but also Rear Admiral H. B. Jacomb and Lt-Col J. M. Christian, stewards' secretaries from England. The Stewards were unable to accept O'Brien's explanations and when considering what action was required, they had to take into account the fact that O'Brien had been warned and cautioned on several previous occasions as to the running of his horses. Accordingly they withdrew his licence for a period of three months. O'Brien, in a statement to the press afterwards, said he was completely in the dark as to what, if any, offence he was alleged to have been guilty of. Doubtless, though, there were plenty of people to enlighten him.

In April 1960 Chamour, a three-year-old colt trained by O'Brien, won The Ballysax Maiden Plate at The Curragh. He started at 6/4 on. In his previous race, the Athboy Stakes at Phoenix Park in March, he had started at 100/7 and finished down the course. A dope test taken after The Curragh race proved positive. Chamour was disqualified and O'Brien had his licence withdrawn, his stable being taken over by his brother. As Chamour subsequently won the Irish Derby, beating the 3/1 on favourite Alcaeus, it seemed inconceivable that anyone in his right mind would have pepped him up illegally to win a little maiden race. There was far more sympathy for O'Brien over this case than when he got into trouble over his jumpers.

When O'Brien decided to concentrate on the flat, he proved if anything even more successful than with jumpers. He has won The Derby with Sir Ivor, Nijinsky, Roberto, and The Minstrel; The Two Thousand Guineas with Sir Ivor and Nijinsky; The St Leger with Ballymoss, Nijinsky and Boucher; The One Thousand Guineas with Glad Rags; The Oaks with Long Look and Valoris; The King George VI and Queen Elizabeth Stakes with Ballymoss and Nijinsky; The Gold Cup with Gladness; The Irish Sweeps Derby with Nijinsky; and the Prix de l'Arc de Triomphe with Ballymoss. In addition Roberto, when winning The Benson and Hedges Gold Cup at York, became the only horse ever to beat Brigadier Gerard.

Unlike so many people who have been prominent in Irish racing, O'Brien is essentially Irish rather than Anglo-Irish. Smallish, of youthful features, very neat in his dress, he is quiet-spoken and possesses enough charm at his disposal to gain, if required, the good will of a whole battalion of retired English colonels. For all the charm and the courtesy, though, it is easy to believe he could be tough, even ruthless, if he felt the situation demanded it. He is fully aware of the financial value of his professional services in respect of which he is as much a perfectionist as was Fred Darling. Nothing is too good for his horses and he possesses immense talent for organisation. He has a great admiration—not surprisingly in view of Sir Ivor and Nijinsky—for the modern American thorough-bred. In 1975 thirty-three of the forty-two horses under his care were American-bred.

There was no English-trained filly in the first three for The One Thousand Guineas in 1957, in which the Aga Khan enjoyed his final classic success, with Rose Royale II, a Prince Bio filly trained by Alec Head, who won by a length from Prince Aly Khan's Sensualita with the Irish filly Angelet, a 4/1 favourite, third. There was a gamble on Mr P. Bull's Orycida who was backed from 12/1 to 6/1. She finished seventeenth.

Rose Royale II was a hot favourite for The Oaks but the final furlong was just too much for her and she finished third. There was a desperate finish between the Queen's Carrozza, trained by Murless and ridden by Piggott, and the grey Irish filly Silken Glider, owned by Mr J. McGrath and ridden by J. Eddery. Carrozza

34.   The finish of The Oaks, 1957—Carozza wins from Silken Glider

owed not a little to the strength of Piggott at the finish and she just held on to win by a very short head. Carrozza started at 100/8 and was much less fancied than the Queen's other runner, Mulberry Harbour, an 11/4 chance trained by Boyd-Rochfort. There was in fact a lot of confidence behind Mulberry Harbour, a Sicambre filly that had won The Cheshire Oaks. She was second into the straight but collapsed in a couple of strides soon afterwards. She finished very distressed and with dilated eyes. Unfortunately she was not tested for dope. She failed again at Royal Ascot but after a rest she recovered her form and in the autumn won The Newmarket Oaks.

Carrozza was bred and owned by the National Stud, being leased to the Queen for racing. She was by Dante, who had died of heart failure the previous year, out of Calash, a full sister to the triple classic winner, Sun Chariot. In 1964, at the dispersal sale of the National Stud's mares, she was sold, in foal to St Paddy, for export to America for 20,000 guineas. Her filly foal by St Paddy was bought by Captain Boyd-Rochfort for 16,500 guineas.[1] Silken Glider, who won The Irish Oaks, was one of the very few good animals sired by Airborne.

There was some ill feeling at Royal Ascot this year. Undoubtedly the state of the going was well below the standard required for a meeting of such importance. The new track had brought its crop of troubles and the previous autumn there was a subsidence that caused the October Meeting to be abandoned. During the winter, extensive drainage operations were carried out. Possibly anxiety existed as to what might happen if the course was watered right up to the Royal Meeting and then the weather changed. At all events, the new Clerk of the Course, Major-General David Dawnay, stopped watering a few days before the meeting began and informed trainers that though the ground was firm there was a good covering of grass. In fact the course, usually so green and fresh, looked parched and dry. Many horses sent to the meeting never ran, including some that had been sent at considerable expense from France. Fields were smaller than usual and a number of runners finished very sore indeed.

The Gold Cup went to the Boyd-Rochfort stable, the winner being Mr Terence Gray's black six-year-old Zarathustra, by Persian Gulf, who won by a length and a half from the 1956 St Leger winner Cambremer, with the Italian horse Tissot third. Cambremer pulled up lame and Madame Volterra's Vattel II could only just hobble past the winning-post. It had been intended to run the French horses Macip and Clichy but because of the going they were sent home.

Zarathustra had been bred by the late Sir Harold Gray and was originally trained in Ireland by Michael Hurley. He won there three times at two and the following season he won The Irish Derby, The Desmond Plate and The Irish St Leger. At four he won The Chippenham Stakes at Newmarket and The Royal Whip at The Curragh. In 1956 he joined Captain Boyd-Rochfort and won the Ascot Stakes under nine stone by five lengths. He then won The Goodwood Cup, beating the Gold Cup runner-up, Bewitched III. In The Jockey Club Cup he

[1] Before being exported, he bred Battle Waggon, by Never Say Die, a successful sire in New Zealand.

lost by half a length to Lord Rosebery's Donald. He split a pastern in that race and did not leave his box for seven weeks afterwards. It was a fine piece of training to win such a severe race as The Gold Cup with him subsequently.

Zarathustra did not tun again after Ascot. He was bought by The Curragh Bloodstock Agency for syndication and stood in Ireland. He was a good game horse that had won from five furlongs to two miles and a half, but the Irish also have little time for stayers, however distinguished, and he was packed off to Japan in 1964.

It was a good meeting for Boyd-Rochfort, who won The Royal Hunt Cup with the five-year-old Retrial, The New Stakes with Pall Mall and The Ribblesdale Stakes with Almeria. Pall Mall and Almeria both belonged to the Queen. Retrial, owned by Lady Zia Wernher, had a tough fight to beat by a length that good French filly Midget II, who was giving him a stone. Thus Boyd-Rochfort became the first trainer in history to win The Royal Hunt Cup four times. Retrial was soundly backed at 100/7 despite public form that could hardly be described as encouraging since he had been unplaced in his five previous races. A winner of The Cambridgeshire at three, he was soon afterwards exported to Argentina.

Bred by her owner, Almeria is a lovely big chestnut, full of quality, by Alycidon out of Avila, by Hyperion. She was slow to develop and only ran once at two. At three she made her first appearance in The Lingfield Oaks and finished a most encouraging third. She did not run in The Oaks as she was still backward and in any case it was thought that the Queen's Mulberry Harbour was good enough to win. Before the season ended, though, Almeria had shown herself to be just about the best of her age and sex, winning in succession The Ribblesdale Stakes, The Bentinck Stakes at Goodwood, The Yorkshire Oaks and The Park Hill Stakes. A slight injury sustained in The Park Hill Stakes prevented her from running again that season. At four she ran three times, winning The Coombe Stakes at Sandown and finishing second in The King George VI and Queen Elizabeth Stakes and The Doncaster Cup. At the stud she has bred Magna Carta, who won over £17,000, and Albany, winner of over £8,000. Unfortunately she has been a somewhat erratic breeder and was barren in 1963, 1967, 1969, 1971, 1972 and 1974. She slipped her foal in 1973.

Lord Howard de Walden won The Coventry Stakes with Amerigo, who scored by eight lengths. He certainly looked a smasher that afternoon. Unfortunately his temper got worse and worse and he became more and more difficult to handle. He never won again in this country and after finishing last in The St James's Palace Stakes in 1958, he was exported for a quite modest sum to America and no one was sorry to see him go. He landed in America with the reputation of being a man-eater and indeed he tried to make a meal of one or two people before he had been there very long. Gradually, though, he was tamed without his spirit being broken. Not only was he a great success on the racecourse but during a brief stud career—he died young—he was extremely successful, too.[1] He was a big,

[1] He sired Fort Marcy, twice winner of The Washington International at Laurel Park.

powerful chestnut by Nearco out of the Precipitation mare, Sanlinea, who was third in The St Leger.

Pipe of Peace was favourite at 5/4 on for The St James's Palace Stakes but was only third to the Irish colt Chevastrid and Tempest. He was eventually exported to Australia and sired a lot of winners there. The King Edward VII Stakes went to another horse destined for a successful stud career in Australia, Lt-Col Giles Loder's Arctic Explorer, trained by Murless. A son of Arctic Prince, Arctic Explorer went on to win The Eclipse Stakes. Lt-Col Loder had inherited the racing interests of his uncle, Major Eustace Loder, owner of Pretty Polly and Spearmint. He himself was serving in the Scots Guards when he won the 1920 Derby with Spion Kop. Tall and solidly built, he was a lifelong bachelor, shy and inarticulate, and though fundamentally kind-hearted and by no means averse to having his leg pulled he was very far from rash where the expenditure of money was concerned. He was a member of the Jockey Club, but not a particularly active one, for many years. Apart from racing, his main interests were his garden at his home in Sussex and his stud at Eyrefield in Co. Kildare, managed successively by Noble Johnson, a really wonderful judge of any type of horse, and Peter Burrell, who became Director of the National Stud. Lt-Col Loder was well over eighty when he died on holiday in the South of France. Loyal to those he employed, he understood horses and racing. Owners of his stamp are very thin on the ground today.

M. M. Calmann's Fric, who had won The Coronation Cup, the eighth French victory in that event since the war, won The Hardwicke Stakes. A five-year-old by Vandale, a descendant of Son-in-Law, he was being trained for his Epsom race by P. Lallie, a former officer in the French army who had been wounded in Indo-China. After The Coronation Cup Fric was transferred to Joe Lawson. M. Calmann had been a patron of Manton between the wars both with Lawson and his predecessor Alec Taylor. Two good sprinters were seen out during the meeting, Matador and Right Boy. Matador, a four-year-old by Golden Cloud, had originally belonged to Mr J. E. Ferguson and on his death in 1956 was bought by Mr Stanhope Joel, for whom he won The Stewards Cup with 9 st. 2 lb.—a fine performance for a three-year-old. He sired a fair number of winners but was nevertheless exported to Japan in 1967. Right Boy, an upstanding grey by Impeccable, had been bought by Bill Dutton as a yearling in Ireland for 575 guineas. On this occasion he won The King's Stand Stakes. When he retired to the stud as a five-year-old he had won sixteen races worth over £17,000. His other victories included The Cork and Orrery Stakes twice, The July Cup twice and The Nunthorpe Stakes twice. Unfortunately he has never sired a horse of ability approaching his own.

The big Goodwood meeting took place under perfect conditions. M. Boussac sent his 1956 Gold Cup winner Macip over for The Goodwood Cup but in a fine race the five-year-old was beaten half a length by Lord Allendale's three-year-old Tenterhooks, by Tenerani. Trained by Captain Charles Elsey at Malton, Tenterhooks had previously won The Gold Vase at Royal Ascot.

Midget II made her final visit to England to contest the one-mile Queen Elizabeth II Stakes at Ascot in September. She won by half a length from Bellborough but the margin would have been wider if Breasley had not dropped his hands when she had the race at her mercy.

At the end of the 1957 season Noel Murless headed the trainers' list with a total of £116,898. He thus became the first English trainer to pass the £100,000 mark. Jack Jarvis became the second trainer to win over £1,000,000 in earnings for his patrons, Captain Boyd-Rochfort having been the first. The champion jockey, with 173 winners, was Scobie Breasley. Mr Phil Bull, never averse to airing his views on all aspects of racing, made the big speech at the Gimcrack Dinner as the result of the victory in The Gimcrack Stakes of his colt Pheidippides. This was a task very much to Mr Bull's liking and, apart from a few routine digs at the 'establishment', he advocated starting-stalls, overnight declarations, a cine record of every race, a measure of centralisation, and the abolition of selling races. At the annual meeting of the Racehorse Owners' Association, the Council of that body expressed unanimous disapproval of overnight declarations.

In his Budget speech on April 9, the Chancellor of the Exchequer, Mr Peter Thorneycroft, abolished the duty on all forms of live entertainment. This particular tax had accounted for 4s 10d in every £1 accrued to racecourse executives. At a Jockey Club meeting the following day Lord Howard de Walden, the Senior Steward, said he reckoned racecourse executives would be better off to the extent of nearly £1,000,000 and he hoped that a considerable portion of this would be passed on to the public in the form of lower charges for admission. At Newmarket an excellent example was set by allotting two-thirds of the remission to the reduction of entrance charges.

Another financial gain was the rapid growth of sponsored races. Sponsorship has become the crutch on which English racing, both on the flat and over the jumps, now leans and its removal would be a disaster. Fortunately, even in times of economic stress, there appears to be a never-ending supply of sponsors and if one drops out there is always another waiting to take his place. We can only hope that no well-meaning do-gooder will ever succeed in placing a government ban on sponsorship by tobacco firms, brewers or distillers.

Of course there are disadvantages in sponsorship. It is disconcerting when the sponsors insist on changing the name of an old-established race. Some titles are terribly ponderous, for example The Clerical, Medical Greenham Stakes. Worse still, racecourses have to put up with some unsightly advertising. It is sad when a lovely course like Goodwood is disfigured with hoardings bearing the name of a firm of bookmakers and carefully sited to catch the eyes of the thousands of viewers on TV. Racing, though, is very hard up and beggars cannot be choosers.

As against these financial gains the tote lost an important case involving a decision of the Special Commissioners of Income Tax in respect of profits tax from 1952 to 1954 and income tax for 1953/4 and 1954/5. The amount involved added up to something like £500,000 per annum and the legal costs of the action were heavy as well. In August, as a result of the ever-rising operating costs, the tote increased the minimum stake, which had been the same since 1929, from 2s to 4s. Despite the obvious decline in the purchasing power of 2s, the change was unpopular with the general public, most of whom thought that tote employees got into every meeting free (the Racecourse Betting Control Board paid the admission fee for the particular enclosure in which their employees were working). Nevertheless, despite many difficulties, the annual tote turnover was a rocord one of £27,000,000.

Arguments about racing's financial difficulties continued to drag on. With few exceptions the representatives of the bookmaking profession displayed a lamentable disinclination to co-operate over plans for the future and their selfishness and short-sightedness did them little credit. Moreover, their attempt to present racing's problems as purely imaginary ones conjured up by greedy owners and breeders recruited many adherents to the policy of a tote monopoly.

In 1958 it became clear that there would be no action by the government in respect of betting legislation during the course of the year. A private member's Bill introduced by Colonel George Wigg (later Lord Wigg), a Labour M.P. with a considerable knowledge of, and enthusiasm for, racing was 'counted out' on May 16.

The bookmakers, possibly a little alarmed by the resentment generated by their earlier attitude, changed their tune and instituted 'The Racecourse Amenities Fund'. The plan was for bookmakers to contribute on a purely voluntary basis to a fund designed for the general benefit of the sport, the money raised being spent in a manner approved by the Jockey Club and the National Hunt Committee. The Racecourse Betting Control Board meanwhile continued its costly battle with the Commissioners of Income Tax and was granted permission to appeal to the House of Lords.

For years there had been a demand for a round course at Newmarket to relieve the tedium felt by some racegoers at an unbroken sequence of events over the Rowley Mile. A round course was accordingly laid out and the first race run on it, The Tote Investors' Handicap, took place at the Craven Meeting. Most people seemed to like it but oddly enough this new course, named the Sefton course, became less and less popular over the years and when it was eventually abolished not a voice was raised in protest.

A Jockey Club Subcommittee reported on the possibility of the introduction of overnight declarations. One of its conclusions was as follows:

> Your Sub-Committee, having considered in detail all aspects of the report of the Duke of Devonshire's Committee, are convinced that the advantages to racing are insufficient at this stage to warrant a change in the Rules of Racing by the introduction of overnight declarations in a form which would seriously interfere with the freedom of action of owners and trainers, and compel the former to run under penalty of forfeit.

It was cold in the early part of the spring and the first day of the Kempton Easter Meeting had to be abandoned through snow, except for the Two Thousand

Guineas Trial which was transferred to the Monday. The Queen's Pall Mall was expected to win that event but did not care for the soft ground and finished unplaced behind Sir Harold Wernher's Combat colt Aggressor, a real mudlark trained by J. M. Gosden at Lewes.

However the weather had changed by the time The Two Thousand Guineas was run. The going was good, the temperature was up in the seventies and Lord Rosebery wore a straw hat that normally did not appear before the July Meeting. The big American-bred Nasrullah colt, Bald Eagle, winner of The Craven Stakes and trained by Boyd-Rochfort, was favourite at 7/4 and was ridden by Harry Carr. His stable companion Pall Mall, ridden by Doug Smith, had few friends at 20/1. Pall Mall, a neatly made, well-proportioned chestnut, looked very small compared with Bald Eagle. After four furlongs Bald Eagle was beaten. Pall Mall ran on up the hill like a hero to win by half a length from Mr Jim Joel's Court Martial colt Major Portion, who lacked the advantage of a previous outing that spring.

Pall Mall, bred by his owner, is by Palestine out of Malapert by Portlaw. Malapert was a very moderate performer. She never won and on her final appearance was fourth in a Brighton selling race with 6 st. 9 lb. She was sent to the December Sales where Captain Charles Moore, who was very shrewd where bloodstock was concerned, bought her for 100 guineas for King George VI. It seemed a weird purchase. The reason, though, was this. Malapert carried two lines of The Tetrarch in her pedigree and Moore wanted to inbreed further to this source by sending her to King Salmon's son Kingstone, who then stood at Sandringham and was just about the last tail-male descendant of the Herod line in this country.

Kingstone, not a distinguished sire, did his duty by getting Malapert in foal three years running, the only drawback being that the produce were totally lacking in racing ability. Captain Moore refused to accept defeat, though, and sent Malapert to Big Game, whose dam, Myrobella, was by Tetratema. The result was The Cheetah who won a single race worth £345. In 1954 and 1955 Malapert was covered by Palestine, whose dam, Una, was by Tetratema. After she had foaled Pall Mall, Captain Moore had had enough of her and at the December Sales she was sold to the Clandon Stud for 910 guineas. Her filly foal by Palestine died as a yearling. A year later Malapert was back at the December Sales and was sold for 350 guineas. Before she died she bred two more winners, neither of much account, one being a sister of Pall Mall.

On the home gallops Bald Eagle was Boyd-Rochfort's best three-year-old but though he did win The Dante Stakes at York he was in general extremely disappointing and in this country at any rate just the sort of horse the bookmakers pray for. However, when his owner Captain Guggenheim returned him to America, he proved a very different proposition and he won The Washington International at Laurel Park two years running. He sired the 1972 Arc winner, San San.

In actual performance Boyd-Rochfort's best three-year-old—the best in this country in fact—was Sir Humphrey de Trafford's Alcide, by Alycidon out of the King Salmon mare Chenille, whose grandam was Aloe, a sister of the Gold Cup winner Foxlaw and dam of the Royal Stud's famous mare Feola. Bred by his owner, Alcide was slow to develop at two and did not run until October. On the second of his two outings he won the seven-furlongs Horris Hill Stakes at Newbury rather impressively. It was decided in 1958 not to run him in The Two Thousand Guineas but to concentrate on The Derby and his first race was the mile-and-a-quarter Royal Stakes at Sandown on April 26. In a very rough race he was beaten by the Queen's Snow Cat, trained by Murless and ridden by Piggott. It looked as if Snow Cat deserved to be disqualified but Sir Humphrey was in a difficult position seeing that Snow Cat was owned by the Queen, most of whose horses were trained by Boyd-Rochfort. The obvious solution was for the Sandown Stewards to take action on their own account but this they lacked the gumption to do and in fact they did absolutely nothing. Ten days later Alcide won The Chester Vase. It was not an exhilarating performance, though, and for most of the way he ran sluggishly.

Alcide's last race before The Derby was the Lingfield Derby Trial, a race his stable had won on six previous occasions. His performance was very different from that unconvincing display at Chester. Taking the lead a quarter of a mile from home, he drew clear of his eight rivals in the straight—Snow Cat was among them—and won by a distance the judge declared to be twelve lengths. Seldom can there have been a more encouraging Derby trial and money poured on him. A few days later Alcide was found in his box looking very sorry for himself and obviously in pain. There was a swelling on his nearside back ribs. It is almost certain that Alcide had been got at in his box and had been dealt a blow that broke a rib. It was impossible to run Alcide in The Derby and of course all those punters who had backed him lost their money.

Alcide did not run again till August. Then at York he put up another astonishing performance, winning The Great Voltigeur Stakes by a dozen lengths. He was a hot favourite for The St Leger at 9/4 on and won by eight lengths from Major Lionel Holliday's None Nicer, by Nearco out of Phase. None Nicer, winner of the Lingfield Oaks Trial, The Ribblesdale Stakes and The Yorkshire Oaks, was trained by Dick Hern who had succeeded Humphrey Cottrill as the Major's trainer.

Alcide did not run again that season. It is difficult to believe he was not greatly superior to any of the horses that ran in The Derby.

With Alcide an absentee, the Irish had their first Derby success since 1907. The winner, and a very easy one too, was Sir Victor Sassoon's Hard Ridden, trained at The Curragh by Mick Rogers and ridden by the 51-year-old Charlie Smirke. Hard Ridden, a lean, rangy bay, had a laugh at the expense of the breeding pundits as he was by Sir Victor's sprinter Hard Sauce, who had numbered The July Cup and The Challenge Stakes among his victories. Although by Ardan, who won the French Derby and the Arc, he never raced beyond six furlongs and in fact was never tried beyond that distance for fear of blunting his speed. He also sired the champion hurdler, Saucy Kit.

Probably Hard Ridden derived his stamina from his dam, Toute Belle II, by the Grand Prix winner Admiral Drake out of a mare by Casterari, second in the

Grand Prix and the Prix du Cadran. Toute Belle II was weeded out of the Volterra stud and bought for 460 guineas by Lady Lambart, acting for her son Sir Oliver Lambart, owner of the Beauparc Stud. It was necessary to go back 150 years to unearth a classic winner in Toute Belle II's family. She herself disappointed at Beauparc and was sent to the December Sales. No one wanted her, though, so she stayed at Newmarket and was covered by Hard Sauce. Thus was the 1958 Derby winner produced. In 1955 Toute Belle II was sold for 170 guineas at the December Sales to Colonel Sir William Rowley. The following year, in foal to Patton, she was exported to Peru for £700.

Hard Ridden came up for sale at Dublin as a yearling and Sir Victor Sassoon bought him for 270 guineas because he was by Hard Sauce. Hard Ridden only ran once at two. At three he was second in The Tetrarch Stakes and then won The Irish Two Thousand Guineas by four lengths from Sindon who subsequently won The Irish Derby. Nevertheless, hardly anyone took him seriously as a Derby proposition even when Smirke was engaged to ride him. An exception was the late Derek Barker, 'Ajax' of the Evening Standard and a man who studied form more closely than pedigrees. Despite a lot of teasing by his colleagues, he made Hard Ridden his nap selection.

Possibly the fact that for once The Derby was not run at a fast pace suited Hard Ridden, who afforded not the slightest anxiety to Smirke and won by five lengths from another Irish colt, Paddy's Point, ridden by Willy Robinson who was to win the 1964 Grand National on Team Spirit. Nagami was third. The French colt Wallaby II, who started favourite, was badly hampered coming down the hill and was never a danger.

Hard Ridden was the first colt saddled in The Derby by Mick Rogers, a member of a distinguished Anglo-Irish racing family. He also won the 1964 Derby with Santa Claus. Hard Ridden failed behind Ballymoss in The King George VI and Queen Elizabeth Stakes and never ran again. He was exported to Japan in 1967.

The best two-year-old filly in 1957 had been Mr T. F. Blackwell's Rich and Rare, by Rockefella, but as she held no classic engagements she had been sold to go to America. As things turned out there was no English three-year-old filly in 1958 in the same league as M. F. Dupré's Bella Paola, who not only won The One Thousand Guineas and The Oaks, but The Champion Stakes as well. Bred by her owner and trained by Mathet, Bella Paola was a magnificent big brown filly standing nearly seventeen hands and built in proportion to her frame. She had an intelligent head with big, slightly lopped ears and the kindest of temperaments. She was the first animal of predominantly German blood to win an English classic and was by Ticino, a son of Athanasius, out of Rhea II by Gundomar. Ticino won the Grosser Preis von Berlin three times and was successful in fourteen of his twenty-one races. The fourth dam of Bella Paola was Hesione, by Alcantara II. M. Dupré bought Hesione for 12,000 guineas in 1929 and had her covered by Pharos who was then standing at his stud at Ouilly. The produce of this union, Princesse d'Ouilly, raced in the colours of that glamorous film star of silent days, Miss Pearl White, whose speciality lay in hair-raising adventure stories portrayed in serials. After winning and being placed, Princesse d'Ouilly reverted to M. Dupré who sold her in 1940 to a commission of the German Supreme Racing and Breeding Authority. He was therefore much luckier than many other French owners whose horses were taken without compensation. In 1947 Princesse d'Ouilly was returned to France. Having sold her to the Germans, M. Dupré felt unable to take her back and she was bought by the Haras St Jacques. The Gundomar foal that Princesse d'Ouilly was carrying on her return to France was bought as a yearling by M. Dupré and, duly named Prince d'Ouilly, won The Granville Stakes at Ascot and The Gordon Stakes at Goodwood in England, and the Grosser Preis von Baden in Germany. In 1950 M. Dupré, encouraged no doubt by the promise of Prince d'Ouilly, who was then two, journeyed to Germany and bought from the Waldfried Stud Rhea II, a filly by Gundomar out of Prince d'Ouilly's half-sister, Regina. The following year he bought Regina too. Her owner, Count Spreti, had not been keen to sell her but his assets were blocked and he needed money to buy a French stallion. Regina never bred a live foal for M. Dupré and Rhea II was her only living produce. Rhea II won two races at three and was then covered by Ticino, the result of the union being Bella Paola.

Bella Paola won The One Thousand Guineas by a length and a half from Prince Aly Khan's Amante and The Oaks by three lengths from M. E. Littler's French-bred Mother Goose. In The French Derby, a race no filly had won since 1874, Boullenger rode an ill judged race on her and she lost by three parts of a length to Tamanar. She won the Prix Vermeille but she had run up light before the Arc, in which she was unplaced behind Ballymoss. Nevertheless she was then sent over to Newmarket for The Champion Stakes, which she won smoothly from Sindon and Major Portion. Her daughter Pola Bella won The French One Thousand Guineas and was second in The French Oaks.

Vincent O'Brien had a marvellous season with Ballymoss as a four-year-old. In The Ormonde Stakes at Chester Ballymoss, well short of his best, was beaten by the Queen's good four-year-old Doutelle, by Prince Chevalier, whom he met on level terms. However, he then won in succession The Coronation Cup from the previous year's winner, Fric; The Eclipse Stakes by six lengths from Restoration; the King George VI and Queen Elizabeth Stakes by three lengths from Almeria with Doutelle third; and the Prix de l'Arc de Triomphe by two lengths from Fric. That would surely have been the time to retire Ballymoss, but his American owner insisted on sending him over for The Washington International at Laurel Park. In a rough, unsatisfactory race, Ballymoss was third behind the English-bred Tudor Era and Sailor's Guide. Subsequently the Stewards reversed the placings of the first two. The aftermath of this race was notable chiefly for ill feeling and recrimination and it was sad that the career of Ballymoss, partnered throughout the season by Breasley, ended on a distinctly sour note.

Mr McShain kindly permitted Ballymoss to take up his stud career in England despite very tempting American offers. This arrangement would not have been possible without the financial help of Sir Victor Sassoon and Mr William Hill.

As a sire Ballymoss has hardly done as well as anticipated but at least he has got one really good horse in Royal Palace, who himself experienced difficulty in establishing his reputation as a sire.

It was certainly Mr McShain's year as O'Brien also won for him The Ascot Gold Cup with Gladness, who had previously been second in the Prix du Cadran. Bred in England by Messrs S. McGregor and T. Venn, Gladness was a strong, plainish, workmanlike five-year-old mare by The St Leger winner Sayajirao out of Bright Lady, by April the Fifth. Bright Lady had failed to win a wartime Gold Cup by only a head. Gladness won The Cup by a length from the consistent but luckless Hornbeam, with Doutelle third, and she subsequently won The Goodwood Cup. Her most remarkable achievement, though, was in The Ebor Handicap. Carrying 9 st. 7 lb. and ridden by Piggott, she was backed from 10/1 down to 5/1 and won in a canter by half a dozen lengths. That was a race in which the book-makers certainly took a caning.

At Royal Ascot Bald Eagle met with another defeat, finishing third behind Major Portion in The St James's Palace Stakes. Major Portion had won The Middle Park Stakes the previous autumn from Neptune II. At three Major Portion was a very good miler. He won The Sussex Stakes, beating Pall Mall by a length at level weights, and The Queen Elizabeth II Stakes. At Mr Jim Joel's stud he never quite succeeded in filling the place vacated by Court Martial, who this year was exported to America.

At Doncaster in the autumn there was a sensation when the Queen's Almeria, joint favourite at 5/2, was beaten a neck in the two-and-a-quarter-mile Doncaster Cup by the Queen's second string, Agreement, a 25/1 outsider. There was a good field for The Cup this year and the runners included Hornbeam, Brioche, winner of the Hardwicke Stakes, and French Beige.

Good horses won both The Cesarewitch and The Cambridgeshire. The north-country gelding, Morecambe, trained by Sam Hall, carried 9 st. 1 lb. in The Cesarewitch and won by ten lengths, a truly astonishing performance in such a competitive handicap. Mr (later Sir) Michael Sobell won The Cambridgeshire with London Cry who carried 9 st. 5 lb. In later years it was sad to see the gallant Morecambe plodding round unsuccessfully over hurdles at minor jumping meetings.

9

The general election held in the early autumn of 1959 saw the Conservatives returned with a solid majority. It became clear that before long there would be legislation to reform the betting laws but uncertainty remained as to how far this reform would actually benefit racing. Everything, in fact, hinged on the impending report of a committee set up by the Home Secretary under the chairmanship of Sir Leslie Peppiatt, a former President of the Law Society. This committee was charged 'to investigate whether it is desirable and practicable that persons engaged in betting on horse races, otherwise than by means of the totalisator, should be required to make a contribution for purposes conducive to the improvement of breeds of horses or the sport of horse racing; and if so, to advise on its amount and on the means of securing it'.

The Jockey Club introduced a three-day forfeit rule, which started to operate in August. Owners had to declare forfeit three days ahead or be fined the equivalent of the full running fee. The scheme proved unpopular and the fact that it was initiated at a time when the ground all over the country was hard did not help matters. It had been stated that the scheme would be reckoned successful if the difference between the final acceptors and the actual runners was less than 10 per cent. After a month the figure was found to be 24 per cent. This was certainly not one of the Jockey Club's happier efforts and with singular folly they had omitted to have prior consultation either with the Racehorse Owners' Association or with representatives of the trainers who would be required to implement the scheme. By the end of the season the scheme was generally judged to be a failure. Nevertheless, the Jockey Club, which sometimes equates stubbornness with resolution, decided to continue with it, though remitting the practice of fines for non-runners.

The newly formed Racecourse Amenities Fund, to which bookmakers could subscribe on a voluntary basis, brought in £61,563, of which £45,000 was delivered to racecourses. Pending betting legislation, the Fund lapsed. The Racecourse Betting Control Board's case against the Income Tax Commissioners went to the House of Lords and to no one's surprise the Board lost.

Obviously this was a time when it was vital for the Jockey Club to be strongly and intelligently represented. The weakness of the Jockey Club's system was

35.   The Aga Khan's Petite Étoile ridden by Lester Piggott, September 1961

exemplified by the appointment of the Duke of Roxburghe as Senior Steward. The Duke's chief claim to distinction lay in his unquestioned skill as a shot and as a fisherman. Moreover, a choleric disposition hardly rendered him an individual who, at a point of time crucial to racing, was likely to win friends in high places (or in any other place for that matter) or to influence people whose influence mattered.

The outstanding three-year-old in 1959 was Petite Étoile, owned by Aly Khan and trained by Murless. A perfectly proportioned grey with immense power behind the saddle, she seemed to possess only one fault, namely a pair of rather small and not wholly benevolent eyes. She was by the Eclipse winner Petition out of the Bois Roussel mare Star of Iran. Her grandam, Mah Iran, was a three-parts sister of the grey Derby winner Mahmoud and she was thus a descendant of the 'Flying Filly', Mumtaz Mahal. The pedigrees of Petition and Star of Iran had a common factor in Lady Josephine, grandam of Petition's sire, Fair Trial, and dam of Mumtaz Mahal. It is not surprising that Petite Étoile was generously endowed with speed; more remarkable is the fact that she stayed as well as she did. Possibly her career at three was helped by the conditions that existed. It was one of those rare hot English summers and the ground all over the country was firm or hard from mid-May till mid-October. This suited Petite Étoile's light action. It is said that in England good weather and good racing are incompatible. Certainly it was a difficult season for trainers and a lot of well-bred two-year-olds were not seen out till the late autumn or else did not race at all.

Petite Étoile's first race at two had been in The Prestwich Stakes at Manchester in May. Her solitary opponent was another grey, Chris, who was destined to win The King's Stand Stakes at Royal Ascot in 1959. Always apt to be a bit tricky and skittish, Petite Étoile fooled around before the start and twice dumped Piggott on the floor. By the time the race began her energies were exhausted and Chris beat her by eight lengths. It was not an encouraging start to her career. She had three more races at two, all over five furlongs. She won The Star Stakes and The Rose Stakes, both at Sandown, and was second to the speedy Krakenwake in The Molecomb Stakes at Goodwood. In The Free Handicap she was given 8 st. 6 lb.

In 1959, when Aly Khan had only two horses trained in this country, Petite Étoile had her first race in the seven-furlongs Free Handicap at the Craven Meeting. Partnered by George Moore, who was riding for Aly Khan in France, Petite Étoile accelerated racing down into the Dip and stayed on strongly up the hill to win by three lengths.

Nevertheless, despite this victory Petite Étoile's merits were not yet fully appreciated. In The One Thousand Guineas Piggott elected to ride Murless's Collyria. Moore was on Aly Khan's Paraguana, trained by Head, so Doug Smith, without a superior over the Rowley Mile, was asked to ride Petite Étoile. An 8/1 chance, Petite Étoile quickened from the Bushes in brilliant fashion and won by a length from the favourite, Mr J. J. Astor's Rosalba, with Paraguana four lengths away third. Her time was two seconds faster than that of Taboun in The Two Thousand Guineas two days earlier.

It was now agreed that Petite Étoile was very good indeed up to a mile but doubts remained as to her ability to stay a mile and a half. Thus, ridden by Piggott, she started at 11/2 in The Oaks. Cantelo, a Chanteur II filly that had won The Royal Lodge Stakes the previous autumn and The Cheshire Oaks in the spring, was a 7/4 favourite, while Sir Richard Sykes's Mirnaya, winner of the Lingfield Oaks Trial, was heavily supported at 2/1. It would be hard to exaggerate the ease of Petite Étoile's victory. She won with her ears pricked by three lengths from Cantelo with Rose of Medina five lengths away third.

Petite Étoile had three more races that season, The Sussex Stakes, The Yorkshire Oaks and The Champion Stakes, and won them all. The only excitement came in The Champion Stakes in which in a slow-run race the over-confident Piggott achieved the not inconsiderable feat of getting her tightly boxed in a field of three. It looked as if she was going to be beaten but close to home a very narrow gap appeared and Piggott squeezed her through to win by half a length, leaving one or two big punters, who had chosen to lay the odds, in a condition of almost total collapse. Petite Étoile then retired into winter quarters having won £56,649, more than any other member of her sex had earned in English racing history. Her owner had already announced his intention of keeping her in training in 1960.

The Oaks runner-up Cantelo paid tribute to Petite Étoile by defeating the colts, including the Derby winner Parthia, in The St Leger. She was bred by her owner, Mr William Hill, the bookmaker, and was trained at Malton by Captain Charles Elsey. Her sire, Chanteur II, had been imported into this country by her owner and her dam, Rustic Bridge, was, like the dam of Petite Étoile, by the 1938 Derby winner Bois Roussel.

There was one unfortunate aspect to The St Leger. The gallops at Malton had been very firm and Elsey had been unable to give Cantelo, who had not run since she was fourth in The King George VI and Queen Elizabeth Stakes, all the work that she required. It was therefore decided to run her two days before The St Leger on the well-watered Doncaster course in the Park Hill Stakes over the full St Leger distance. It was hoped that the race would do her good and that she would not be extended to pick up the £5,000 prize. Naturally, Edward Hide, who rode her, was anxious to ensure that she did not have a hard race. In consequence he took matters too easily and Cantelo, favourite at 9/4 on, was caught close home and beaten by the 33/1 outsider Collyria, by Arctic Prince.

Cantelo, starting at 100/7, won The St Leger comfortably from Fidalgo and Pindari, the first Yorkshire-trained winner of Yorkshire's classic since Apology, owned by the Rev. J. King who raced as Mr Launde, won in 1874. The triumph of Apology had been greeted at Doncaster with scenes of unprecedented enthusiasm whereas Cantelo and her connections were booed by a number of racegoers who presumably had lost their money when the filly was beaten in The Park Hill Stakes. Mr Hill's skin was probably of sufficient thickness to bear this undeserved rudeness with equanimity, but nearly everyone at Doncaster was distressed that Captain Elsey, one of the most popular and respected men in northern racing, should be subjected to a hostile demonstration on what ought to have been an occasion for rejoicing.

Aly Khan won The Two Thousand Guineas with Taboun, trained by Alec Head and ridden by George Moore. He had three lengths to spare over Masham who had headed The Free Handicap. Bred by the late Aga Khan, Taboun was a bay colt by Tehran's son Tabriz, a good two-year-old that was unable to race subsequently owing to a broken bone in his foot, out of Queen of Basra, by Fair Trial. As a two-year-old Taboun had won two races including the Prix Robert Papin at Maisons Laffitte, and had been second in The Coventry Stakes at Royal Ascot and the Prix Morny at Deauville. Before winning at Newmarket, he had won the Prix Djebel at Maisons Laffitte in convincing fashion. His subsequent career was disappointing and he was last of five behind the Queen's Above Suspicion in The St James's Palace Stakes.

The fates seldom relent in racing but for once they did so in this year's Derby. There is no doubt that Sir Humphrey de Trafford's Alcide ought to have won

The Derby in 1958. This year Sir Humphrey won that race with Parthia, a colt markedly inferior to Alcide. It was a remarkable achievement to have bred two such horses in successive years at his Hertfordshire stud where there were never more than six or seven mares. Parthia, trained by Boyd-Rochfort, was a brown colt standing 15.3½ hands by Persian Gulf out of Lightning, a half-sister to Alcide by Hyperion. He was too backward to be trained seriously at two and did not run before October. He was then sixth of nine in the one-mile Gainsborough Stakes at Hurst Park, and third to Billum and Traviata in The Dewhurst Stakes at Newmarket. In The Dewhurst Stakes, unbacked at 20/1, he had displayed high promise for the future.

Parthia was indolent by nature and needed plenty of work, while in a race he was seldom inclined to do more than the minimum necessary. However, he was fit enough in April to win the ten furlongs White Rose Stakes at Hurst Park. He did not compete in The Guineas but went for the ten-and-a-half-furlongs Dee Stakes at Chester which he duly won but made terribly heavy weather of his task. His trainer reckoned he needed more racing and accordingly ran him in the Lingfield Derby Trial. Again Parthia won, but if anything less impressively than at Chester. I remember after that race the late James Hilton Park of the Evening Standard, probably the best judge of form among all racing journalists, told me I would be insane to tip Parthia in The Derby.

Starting at 10/1, Parthia, ridden by Harry Carr, won The Derby by a length and a half from Fidalgo ridden by Carr's son-in-law Joe Mercer. The French colt Shantung was third, a length and a half behind Fidalgo. In all probability Shantung was a very unlucky loser. Coming down the hill Palmer, thinking Shantung had injured himself, virtually pulled him up. In fact Shantung was perfectly sound but as a result of this unfortunate episode he was last of twenty coming round Tattenham Corner. He then really got going. He passed horse after horse but the winning-post came just too soon. Jack Jarvis always rated him the unluckiest Derby loser he had ever seen with the possible exception of Lord Rosebery's Sandwich, third to Cameronian in 1931.

Maybe Parthia himself had had one narrow squeak. Three days before the race the door of Alcide's box had been found open and he had been set loose during the night. Luckily he was recaptured unharmed. Parthia's box was three away from that of Alcide and it is conceivable that a mistake had been made and Parthia had been the intended target.

Parthia's only other race that year was The St Leger. He had been coughing and had had to miss York. It was feared that he would not do himself justice at Doncaster but he had been backed by the public ante-post and his owner and trainer thought it fair to give his supporters a run for their money. He finished unplaced behind Cantelo.

This was *annus mirabilis* for Sir Humphrey de Trafford. Alcide, still in training with The Gold Cup as his primary objective, had let down during the winter and his depth of girth and the power of his quarters were impressive. His first outing was in The Jockey Club Cup, then run over a mile and a half in April. He finished sluggishly and went under by a short head to the five-year-old Vacarmé who was giving him 5 lb. The racing press were inclined to be scathing about this effort, so in The Victor Wild Stakes at Kempton, Carr decided to demonstrate just what Alcide could really do. The result was that Alcide won by twenty lengths and lowered the course record. Alcide then won The Winston Churchill Stakes at Hurst Park but after that a mishap in training caused him to miss three vital gallops. In the meantime Harry Carr had had an operation for the removal of stones from his kidneys, so neither horse nor rider was one hundred per cent at his best at Ascot. Alcide ran a brave race but the French four-year-old Wallaby II, owned by Baron de Waldner, beat him by a couple of inches. Apart from the time he was beaten first time out at two, Alcide suffered three defeats, each time by the minimum margin.

It was decided that Alcide's final race was to be The King George VI and Queen Elizabeth Stakes, in the hope that his Gold Cup preparation had not blunted his speed. Ridden by Carr, he won smoothly from Gladness and Balto with Wallaby II unplaced. Carr was taken ill with kidney trouble on the way home and had to spend a fortnight in the London Clinic. Having won over £56,000 in stakes, Alcide retired to the stud. He was not the success anticipated as far too many of his offspring were 'funny' although he had been genuine enough himself. However, his daughters seem to make good brood mares. His son Oncidium, who won The Coronation Cup, was proving an outstanding success as a sire in the Antipodes at the time of his early death in 1975.

There was a hint of the Regency about Sir Humphrey de Trafford who loved every form of sport, helped others—particularly young people—to enjoy it too, and, until at last ill health overtook him, lived his life to the full. Originally he served in the Royal Navy but a life on the ocean wave did not suit him and he transferred to the Coldstream Guards. He went to France with the B.E.F. in 1914 and was subsequently awarded the Military Cross. For fifty years he was involved in racing, firstly as a rider over fences, then as owner, breeder and one of the Jockey Club's livelier administrators. Of medium size, immaculately dressed, he made friends wherever he went and there was no more popular man in the little world of Newmarket and White's. Like his trainer, he never learnt how to drive a car. He was seventy-nine when he died in 1971.

Captain Sir Cecil Boyd-Rochfort, knighted for his services to racing, was born in Ireland in 1887 and it is in Ireland that he is passing his retirement. After leaving Eton he was a learner, first with 'Atty' Persse and then at Newmarket with Captain R. H. Dewhurst. In 1913 he was appointed racing manager to Sir Ernest Cassel, the German-born financier who had been such a close friend of King Edward VII. During the war, in which his brother Arthur was awarded the V.C., he served in the Scots Guards and was wounded and awarded the Croix de Guerre. In 1920 he decided to set up as a trainer at Newmarket, one of his first patrons being a wealthy American, Mr Marshall Field. Among the first yearlings he bought for that owner was Golden Corn, a brilliant filly that won the Middle Park Stakes in 1921. From that moment Boyd-Rochfort's career was one of

36. Captain Sir Cecil Boyd-Rochfort, pictured in 1970

consistent success. He was top trainer five times, won over £1,000,000 in stakes for his owners, had thirteen victories in classic races and succeeded W. R. Jarvis as the royal trainer, an appointment he justified in every respect. Envious persons used to say in disparagement that he had only trained for rich owners, many of them American, who paid their bills regularly and could afford to be patient. However, rich owners like to win races and they are not in the habit of sticking to a trainer who fails to deliver the goods. In fact Boyd-Rochfort was a master of his profession. He excelled at the difficult art of preparing a stayer and he was as adept in getting a horse ready for a gamble in a handicap, a practice he very much favoured, as for a classic.

He has always been an easily recognisable figure, very tall, very erect, impeccably dressed in a slightly old-fashioned way, and looking a good deal younger than his actual age. People who did not know him used to say he was pompous. They were wrong; he has always been dignified, which is entirely different. His relations with the racing press were good. He invariably tried to be helpful and unlike lesser men he did not discard his courtesy when matters were not going his way. I recall that after one of his St Leger victories a journalist who had backed the horse in question insisted on shaking hands with 'the Captain'. The handshake proved to be a lengthy one. The trouble was that whenever 'the Captain' tried to disengage himself the journalist was in grave danger of falling flat on his back. At length the journalist retired to the press room where in some extraordinary fashion he got his index finger, the loop of his mackintosh and a peg on the wall in such a fearful tangle that he was trapped until released by kindly friends. On his retirement in 1968, Sir Cecil handed over his stable to his stepson, Henry Cecil, who shows every sign of being equally successful.

In 1959 The Coronation Cup was won, for once in a way, by a horse trained in this country, the winner being Mrs Arpad Plesch's four-year-old Nagami, trained by Harry Wragg. A son of Nimbus, Nagami had been placed the previous year in The Two Thousand Guineas, The Derby and The St Leger, apart from which he did a fair amount of travelling, winning the Gran Premio del Jockey Club in Milan and the Grand Prix du Printemps at Saint Cloud. At the conclusion of his four-year-old career he was exported to Italy as a stallion.

Poor Major-General Dawnay was in trouble again at Royal Ascot. The going was hard when the meeting started and got harder still as it went on. The quality of the racing fell below the usual high standard and a good many competitors went home sore. Wallaby II won The Gold Cup for France. The Queen won The St James's Palace Stakes with Above Suspicion, whose dam was the Cesarewitch winner Above Board, and the King Edward VII Stakes with Pindari, who was by Pinza out of the triple classic winner Sun Chariot.

At the end of June Harry Wragg sent his Derby runner-up Fidalgo over to The Curragh where he won The Irish Derby with contemptuous ease. Wragg also won the Irish Oaks with Dante's daughter, Discorea, owned by Mrs Plesch. The Eclipse Stakes was a triumph for France, Aly Khan's three-year-old Saint Crespin III, a half-brother by Aureole to Tulyar, winning from Javelot and Vif Argent, both owned by Baron de Waldner. Fidalgo was only fifth. Saint Crespin III, who was trained by Alec Head and who had been fourth in The Derby, subsequently won the Prix de l'Arc de Triomphe. It had been intended to keep him in training at four but he injured a shoulder when colliding with a tree at Chantilly and had to be retired. He ended his days in Japan.

Despite cool and showery weather, the average daily attendance at the big Goodwood meeting was nearly 41,000. The rain was insufficient to improve the going, which was very firm. In consequence the racing, particularly the two-year-old events, was below the customary level. Dickens, by Precipitation, won The Cup for Sir Harold and Lady Zia Wernher in a time fifteen seconds outside the record. Agreement, a stable companion of Dickens, won The Doncaster Cup the following month for the second year running. He was a gelding, having paid the penalty for trying to eat a couple of Boyd-Rochfort's horses on Newmarket Heath some years earlier.

At Ascot in September, when Mr Astor's Rosalba won The Queen Elizabeth II Stakes, Sir Victor Sassoon's two-year-old St Paddy made a most favourable impression when winning The Royal Lodge Stakes and many who saw him that day rated him a potential winner of The Derby.

There was a tragedy on the final day at Ascot. Manny Mercer was killed instantly by a fall from Priddy Fair on his way down to the start of the mile-and-a-half Red Deer Stakes. As Priddy Fair turned round after passing the stands, she reared up, slipped, and fell close to the rails. Mercer not only hit the rails as he fell but was kicked twice in the face by Priddy Fair. Immediately after the race was over, a stunned crowd heard over the loud speakers that Mercer was dead. The remaining race was of course abandoned.

Mercer, who married Susan, daughter of Harry Wragg, came from a working-class family in the north. He was a very likeable character, cheerful and unassuming. He never pretended to know much about pedigrees and conformation, but he was a natural rider who became an extremely good one largely through the tuition he received from Charles Elliott when they were both attached to George Colling's stable. He was nearly always in sympathy with the horses he rode and had the knack of getting the very best out of them. In eight seasons from 1951 to 1958 he four times rode over a hundred winners. He was runner-up for the championship once and was three times third.

Prince Aly Khan had a wonderful year as not only was he leading owner in this country, his horses winning £103,087, but he was leading owner in France as well. His luck held good throughout the autumn as in France he won the Arc with Saint Crespin III, while over here, in addition to the victory of Petite Étoile in The Champion Stakes, he won The Imperial Produce Stakes at Kempton and The Middle Park Stakes with Venture VII, a bay colt trained by Alec Head. Venture VII was by Relic out of The One Thousand Guineas runner-up Rose O'Lynn, whose sire Pherozshah was a half-brother by Pharos to Mahmoud.

The following spring, Venture VII was beaten a head in The Two Thousand Guineas and a fortnight later Aly Khan was killed in a car accident on the outskirts of Paris. Born in 1911, he was the second son of the Aga Khan and of his second wife Teresa Magliano. He was a man very easy to dislike if you did not know him. This was largely the fault of the press who ignored his virtues and chose to portray him as an ageing playboy ruthlessly dedicated to the pursuit of self-gratification. Moreover, his successes with women inspired a degree of sexual jealousy. In fact, few who knew him at all well could resist his charm, friendliness, gaiety and good manners. In a world becoming increasingly grey, he moved with a certain panache and he was very far indeed from being a fool. His father had understood blood lines; he himself understood horses, was a competent amateur rider and realised the importance of conformation. He was a very good judge of a horse and his approach to bloodstock breeding was more flexible than that of his father, who was essentially a theoretician. After the war, in which of all unlikely things he was a lieutenant-colonel in the Wiltshire Yeomanry, he bought a half-share in his father's bloodstock interests. Together they pulled off a couple of notable package deals, buying the entire bloodstock interests of Mr Wilfred Harvey and nearly all the thoroughbred stock of the American, Mr L. L. Lawrence. Part of the attraction of the Harvey deal was five nominations to Nearco. Among the mares was Noorani, who became the dam of Sheshoon and Charlottesville. Included in the Lawrence deal was Green Lodge, Chantilly, situated opposite Alec Head's yard. One of the Lawrence mares was Rose O'Lynn, dam of Venture VII. At the time of his death, Prince Aly Khan had ninety mares and seventy horses in training in Europe. Sixty-four of the horses in training were with Head. He also owned forty mares and three stallions in Venezuela, while in the United States he owned twelve mares in partnership with Mr John W. Galbreath.

It would be wrong to imagine that Aly Khan's life was devoted solely to racing. He was involved in a number of U.N. committees. He was elected a Vice-President of the Assembly and was Chairman of the Afro-Asian group. In his manifold duties of this nature, he managed to combine shrewd political insight with down-to-earth common sense. The best had not yet been seen of him when he died.

1960 was a year of the utmost significance for English racing. It was certainly a memorable day when the committee under Sir Leslie Peppiatt reported that it was both desirable and practicable for persons betting on horse-racing, other than through the tote, to contribute towards the general good of the sport. The Jockey Club was hoping for a levy that would produce £3,000,000 a year; the Peppiatt committee's recommendation was for rather less than half that amount. That was disappointing, but it was felt that the actual sum could be subject to adjustment; what mattered was the establishment of a principle.

The main recommendations of the Peppiatt Report were incorporated in the Betting Levy Bill which passed its third reading just before the Christmas recess. This proposed the formation of a body, the Horserace Betting Levy Board, to collect contributions from the bookmakers and from the tote, and to apply them for the general good of the sport. The Board was to consist of a chariman and two members appointed by the Secretary of State, two members appointed from the Jockey Club and one each from the National Hunt Committee, the Bookmakers' Committee and the Tote.

The first chairman of the Levy Board was a soldier of the utmost distinction. Field-Marshal Lord Harding had deservedly won a great name for himself during the war—in which he was awarded the D.S.O. and two bars—for his efficiency, courage and powers of leadership. He added to that reputation when Commander-in-Chief in Cyprus during the troubles there and as Chief of the Imperial General Staff. He has always possessed immense personal charm and is capable of inspiring the loyalty and affection of those with whom he works. His background is not wholly typical of the military hierarchy of his times as he is the son of a west-country parson, was educated at Ilminster Grammar School and began his army career as a territorial. In appearance a typical light-infantryman, he had ridden at the military race meetings in Italy and Austria at the end of the war but he did not pretend to a profound knowledge of racing. As secretary to the Levy Board he chose another soldier, Major-General Sir Rupert Brazier-Creagh, a tall, intellectual gunner, not as warm a character as Lord Harding but a highly competent staff officer and not a man disposed to put up with any nonsense from anyone.

Perhaps he was too strong a character for this appointment and he was inclined to irk some members of the racing establishment. He has never received the credit due to him for the way he helped Lord Harding to get the Levy Board off the ground.

On the whole Lord Harding's term of office was a successful one and he did not find it difficult to co-operate with the Jockey Club. He did admittedly fall foul of one of the Jockey Club's most influential members, Lord Rosebery, over the proposal to make Edinburgh racecourse redundant. Lord Rosebery felt deeply on that particular subject and it was largely due to him that the proposal was never put into effect. It is true that Lord Harding was less dynamic than his successor, Lord Wigg, but he naturally had to feel his way carefully to start with and in addition he did not possess Lord Wigg's expert knowledge of the betting industry.

One result of the legislation on betting was the replacement of the Racecourse Betting Control Board, which had run the tote since the tote's inception, by a smaller body, the Horserace Totalisator Board. The Racecourse Betting Control Board had been a friendly affair that used to meet once a month in the Board's offices in Euston Road. In a very minor capacity I used to attend some of these meetings and soon observed that certain members of the Board were a shade less deeply concerned than others about the role of the tote in racing. I can recollect a serious discussion on the tote's finances going on at one end of the table while at the other end a member was giving a sotto voce account of the more interesting details in what was known as 'the kiss in the car case' on which he appeared to be remarkably well informed. To avoid giving offence where none is intended, I should perhaps point out that Lord Wigg, who served the Board loyally for a good many years, was at the more serious end of the table.

I used to go to the House of Commons fairly frequently to listen to debates on the Betting and Gaming Bill. My chief impression was of the deplorable ignorance of the subject displayed by most of those who got up to speak and I could only hope they were less ill-informed, though I doubt if that was the case, on matters of greater importance. Lord Wigg, then of course Colonel Wigg M.P., was outstanding in that he knew every aspect of the subject under discussion and it was in no small measure due to him that the Bill was eventually passed.

I have never been to the House of Commons since except once to see the late Mr Richard Crossman. He had plans of a somewhat grandiose nature, which never left their starting-stall, to make Alexandra Park the Longchamp of London.

The Betting and Gaming Act (1960) altered for the better the wagering habits of a great many people. Legal status was conferred on bookmakers, who had to be licensed. In the past it had been simple enough for off-course punters with credit accounts to get their money on simply by ringing up their bookmaker or Tote Investors Ltd. For thousands of less well-off punters it had been a very different matter. They either had to send a postal order to a starting-price book-maker or resort to illegality of some sort, probably by betting with a 'street' bookmaker. Some 'street' bookmakers did very big business indeed. They formed a perpetual problem for the police and were a potent source of police corruption. The establishment of licensed betting offices operating under well-defined regulations made life easier for the police and also for the thousands of off-course punters who have no credit account and who for the most part bet in small sums. The fact that bookmakers were licensed made the collection of the levy, once the amount had been agreed upon by the Levy Board and the representatives of the bookmakers, a comparatively simple matter. It is doubtful if the advent of betting offices made much difference to racecourse attendances as people who patronise betting offices are not as a rule potential racegoers; or at least only on rare occasions. It is undeniable, though, that over the years the on-course betting market has become very much weaker and the number of on-course bookmakers has declined as less and less money is betted on the racecourse and more and more in the offices.

The tote opened betting offices, too. In the autumn of 1962 a man entered a small provincial office operated by the tote. He carried a large suitcase stuffed with bank-notes and expressed the desire to have £10,000 for a place on that good chaser Frenchman's Cove, who was running that afternoon, a Saturday, in The Lyall Optional Selling Steeplechase at Market Rasen. Bar a fall, Frenchman's Cove was certain to be placed and the tote was compelled to pay a minimum dividend of 4s 2d to a 4s stake. The banks were closed and the possession of so much money presented the office manager with a worrying security problem. He was relieved when Frenchman's Cove won—the S.P. was 10/1 on—and the punter departed with his suitcase, his stake and his dividend.

The Jockey Club had annoyed almost everyone by retaining the three-day forfeit rule despite the fact that it was obviously a failure. This year, however, authority bowed its stubborn old head to the storm of disapproval and it was announced that overnight declarations would begin in 1961. No doubt it was felt that as in the future betting was going to make a substantial contribution to racing it was only fair to introduce a measure that would be highly popular with punters although admittedly it curtailed the liberty of action previously enjoyed by owners.

Also to the good were the introduction of patrol film cameras and the plans put forward by a committee under Lord Sefton to revise the racing programme at Newmarket and to make sport there more attractive to the general public. The patrol cameras provided lateral and head-on views of a race within a few minutes of that race having been concluded and greatly eased the task of the stewards in the event of any alleged infringement of the Rules. The films certainly resulted in a decrease in the number of blatant non-triers.

Less agreeable were cases of doping which drew attention to the flagrant unfairness of the existing Rules and to the disturbing lack of confidence in the methods of analysis. This was the year when Vincent O'Brien was deprived of his licence over Chamour. In this country a small jumping trainer, P. V. Doherty, lost his licence following a test, which was stated to be positive, on Précipité after some minor steeplechase. Précipité was eleven years old, had run only once in the past two years on account of chronic leg trouble, started at 20/1 and was pulled up. Not surprisingly many people reckoned Doherty had been unfairly penalised.

There was no appeal against the result of a test undertaken by the Jockey Club analyst. Yet stories abounded of sweat and saliva tests taken on cart-horses and police horses which were stated to be positive. I recollect Peter Cazalet, the distinguished jumping trainer, telling me that he and Lord Mildmay had samples taken from two horses out at grass. Both samples were stated to be positive. During the year a number of horses belonging to distinguished owners, among them the Duke of Norfolk, were found to have been got at after private tests had been taken. If these had been official tests, the Stewards of the Jockey Club would have had no option but to deprive trainers of the highest integrity of their livelihood. Local stewards did not like to order tests, not wishing to be involved in the possibility of depriving an innocent man of his licence.

Four minor villains involved in doping were apprehended, tried and convicted but they were only very small fish from an extremely murky pond. However, their case did at least bring home to many people how simple it was to dope a horse without the trainer knowing anything about it. None too soon the Jockey Club appointed a committee under the Duke of Norfolk to look into the whole question of doping and to examine the Rules of Racing pertaining to that subject.

The 1960 Two Thousand Guineas ended in a victory for Ireland, the winner being Mr R. N. Webster's chestnut colt Martial, trained by Paddy Prendergast and ridden by Ron Hutchinson. It was the very first win in England for the 32-year-old Hutchinson, who had just arrived in Europe from Australia to ride for Prendergast's stable. He had never ridden over the Rowley Mile course before. Bred by Captain Darby Rogers and bought for only 2,400 guineas as a yearling, Martial, who had won The Coventry Stakes at Royal Ascot the year before, was a massive, powerful colt who looked far more like a sprinter than a stayer. He was by Hill Gail out of Discipliner, by Court Martial. During this season his half-brother by Golden Cloud, by name Skymaster, won The Windsor Castle Stakes and The Middle Park Stakes for the Duke of Norfolk, but was successfully 'got at' before The Granville Stakes at Ascot in July. There were only three runners, one of which had no chance. This was a splendid opportunity for the dopers, who could lay Skymaster and back Good Old Days, an easy winner by five lengths. Probably a fair amount of people knew that Skymaster was 'no good' as he opened at 2/1 on and started at evens.

At Newmarket Martial got up in the last two strides to head Venture VII. It was impossible to say which of the two had won and when it was announced that the verdict had gone to the 18/1 Martial a great cheer went up from the bookmakers. Martial, not easy to train, had only one more race. That was The Sussex Stakes in which Venture VII, receiving 6 lb., beat him by half a length with a bit in hand. Martial was exported to Argentina in 1967.

Sixth in The Two Thousand Guineas was Sir Victor Sassoon's St Paddy who had shown such high promise the previous autumn. He had not had a race before The Guineas and no doubt Murless had a nice bit to work on before The Derby.

St Paddy went on to win The Dante Stakes at York in a canter. In The Derby, he was ridden by Piggott, started at 7/1 and won by three lengths from Alcaeus. A bay colt by Aureole out of Edie Kelly, a Bois Roussel mare that went back to Pretty Polly, St Paddy was the pick of the field on looks and far more attractive than the 2/1 favourite, the French colt Angers owned by Mrs Strassburger. Winner of The Grand Criterium at two, the blinkered Angers, by Worden II, had impressed in the spring when winning the Prix Jean Prat over ten furlongs and then the mile-and-a-half Prix Hocquart. At Epsom he went down to the start more like an elderly crab than a Derby favourite. He never seemed to be going well in the early stages of the race and to the consternation of his backers he was not among the runners when the field reached Tattenham Corner. It was later learnt that he had shattered a leg coming down the hill and the vet had been left with no option but to destroy him. It was sheer bad luck and no other horse was involved.

St Paddy was rested till Goodwood where he started favourite for The Gordon Stakes at 11/8 on. He probably needed the race as his preparation was being timed for The St Leger but it was a shock nevertheless when he failed to find anything when tackled close to home by Lord Sefton's Kipling who was receiving 5 lb. and beat him by half a length. Suspicions were aroused that St Paddy, who looked a great horse when everything was going his way, might not be much of a battler when it was necessary to fight hard for victory. He went on to win The Great Voltigeur Stakes in a manner that was not altogether impressive but Murless produced him at his best for The St Leger which he won very easily indeed from Die Hard and Vienna. He did not run again that season.

Both The One Thousand Guineas and The Oaks were won by Mrs Howell E. Jackson's Never Too Late II, trained at Chantilly by E. Pollet and ridden by Roger Poincelet. Bred in America, she was a smallish chestnut filly by Never Say Die out of the British-bred Gloria Nicky, an Alycidon mare that had won The Cheveley Park Stakes. She made up for her lack of inches by being perfectly proportioned and full of quality and courage. Following a victory in the Prix Imprudence at Maisons Laffitte, she started at 11/8 on in The One Thousand Guineas and won comfortably by a couple of lengths. It was a very different matter in The Oaks, for which she was favourite at 6/5. Poincelet had been told to be close behind the leaders at Tattenham Corner but he elected to ignore those orders and both he and J. Boullenger on another French filly, Baron Guy de Rothschild's Imberline, were a hundred yards behind No Saint and Io who were in front at that point. With less than a furlong to go, yet another French filly, Mrs Strassburger's Paimpont, by Chamossaire, took the lead and so well was she going that she seemed sure to compensate her owner for the loss she had suffered over Angers. Never Too Late II and Imberline made up ground rapidly from Tattenham Corner but with only a furlong to go they were still three lengths behind Paimpont. However, in a last valiant effort little Never Too Late II caught and headed Paimpont just short of the winning-post, but the effort had exhausted her and she then veered to the left towards Paimpont. The result was that

37. The Oaks, 1960. Never Too Late II beats Paimpont by a head with Imberline, immediately behind them, third

Imberline, who was by no means out of contention, was badly hampered and passed the post with her rider standing up in his stirrups. The judge's verdict after studying the photograph was that Never Too Late II had beaten Paimpont by a head with Imberline two lengths away third.

The subsequent scenes outside the weighing room were of a lively nature and the factions involved were unrestrained in accusation and recrimination. As this was essentially a French row, the English looked on with the detached and somewhat condescending interest of tourists observing a weird ritual dance by one of the remoter African tribes. Of course if Imberline had been second she could have objected to Never Too Late II and would very likely have got the race. The concluding stages of the contest would certainly have been less traumatic if Poincelet and Boullenger had shown rather better judgement. Never Too Late II failed in the Prix Vermeille and was second in The Champion Stakes to the Italian filly Marguerite Vernaut, by Toulouse-Lautrec.

The biggest disappointment of the year was the defeat of Petite Étoile in The King George VI and Queen Elizabeth Stakes. After winning The Victor Wild

38. The three runners for the 1960 Coronation Cup at Epsom being watched by the Queen and the Queen Mother as they go to the starting post. The Queen's runner, Above Suspicion (left) came in last. The other two horses are Parthia (Harry Carr up) and Petite Étoile, the winner, ridden by Lester Piggott

Stakes at Kempton, she had beaten Parthia in a canter in The Coronation Cup. She started at 5/2 on at Ascot and she ought to have won but Piggott for once rode an indifferent race. Although the going was soft, which did not suit the filly and blunted the edge of her speed, he was last of eight entering the short Ascot straight and left her with a great deal to do. He then initiated his challenge on the inside but found not the glimmer of an opening. He accordingly switched her to the outside and in so doing collided with Kythnos. By the time the last furlong had been reached Petite Étoile had given all she had and she failed by half a length to catch Sir Harold Wernher's five-year-old Aggressor who, conceding 3 lb., beat her by half a length. She did not race again that season. It had been hoped to run her in The Queen Elizabeth II Stakes and The Champion Stakes but she fell victim to a coughing epidemic.

Aggressor, who now stands in Italy, is a strongly made bay, a trifle lacking in quality, by Combat out of Phaetonia, by Nearco. Unbeaten Combat was by no means distinguished as a sire and in 1960 a nomination was readily available at 100 guineas. At the Dewar dispersal sale Captain Boyd-Rochfort had bought Phaetonia, carrying Aggressor, for 15,500 guineas on behalf of the Someries Stud. After being weaned, Aggressor was sent to the Blackhall Stud, Co. Kildare. There he was inspected as a yearling by Sir Harold Wernher and Captain Boyd-Rochfort. Neither of them cared for him and it was arranged for him to be sent up to a September sale at Ballsbridge. Shortly before that sale, Mr Bob Jeffares, the stud manager at Blackhall, rang up the Someries manager and said that Aggressor was doing so well that he advised a reserve of 2,000 guineas being placed on him. Sir Harold somewhat reluctantly agreed to one of 1,000 guineas. In fact Aggressor was led out of the ring unsold at 750 guineas. Boyd-Rochfort could not take all the Wernher yearlings so Aggressor joined Gosden's stable at Lewes. This Ascot victory was the eleventh for Aggressor, who was always at his best when the ground was soft. Earlier in the season he had won The Hardwicke Stakes at Royal Ascot after which he was on offer at £20,000, but no one displayed the slightest interest.

Jack Gosden, commonly known as 'Towser', was the son of a Sussex farmer. In his young days he was a competent amateur rider over fences and acted as assistant to George Poole, a slightly eccentric bachelor never seen without a cigarette attached to his lower lip, who conducted a 'mixed' stable at Lewes. In 1929 Gosden set up on his own and turned out a steady stream of winners, mostly jumpers. In the war he served in the R.A.F. till invalided out. When the war was over he still had a lot of jumpers under his care but gradually his energies became centred on the flat. In this branch of the sport he did extremely well. He had a number of owners who liked to bet heavily and some notable wins in important handicaps were achieved. Unfortunately his health gave way and he was forced to retire in 1965. The following year Charlottown, who had been in his stable, won The Derby. He himself died in 1967.

In one Lewes stable there used to be a top floor room which overlooked Lewes gaol and from which a view was obtainable of the grisly procession from the condemned cell to the building that concealed the gallows. It was said that on execution mornings the trainer concerned used to sell places in this room to morbid individuals and that when 'Brides-in-the-Bath' Smith met his end he had a full house at £5 a head.

There was yet another French victory in The Ascot Gold Cup, the winner being the late Prince Aly Khan's four-year-old Sheshoon, trained by Alec Head. He won by a length and a half from Dr C. Vittadini's Exar with the Comte d'Audiffret-Pasquier's Le Loup Garou third. In the Prix du Cadran Le Loup Garou had vanquished Sheshoon by a short head.

Sheshoon was bred in Ireland and is a handsome chestnut by Precipitation, who won The Gold Cup himself, out of the Nearco mare Noorani, whose son Charlottesville, by Prince Chevalier, this year won the French Derby and the Grand Prix. Sheshoon was a good deal more than an out-and-out stayer; he was a top-class middle-distance performer whose wins included the Grand Prix de

Saint Cloud and the Grosser Preis von Baden. Both he and Charlottesville failed on the soft ground in the Prix de l'Arc de Triomphe. As a sire Sheshoon's record has been rather an odd one. Standing in this country, his record among English-trained horses has been disappointing, with the exception of the surprise Two Thousand Guineas winner Mon Fils. On the other hand his offspring have done well in France and include Sassafras, who won the French Derby, the French St Leger and the Arc, in which he cut Nijinsky down to size; Samos III (French St Leger); Pleben (Grand Prix and French St Leger); and Stintino (Prix Lupin).

The French also won The Eclipse Stakes with Baron de Waldner's four-year-old Javelot, who had been a shade unlucky when second in that event the previous year. Venture VII started favourite for The Eclipse but a heavy storm broke over Sandown not long before the race and rendered the going soft. Venture VII hated the conditions and was beaten three furlongs from home.

A good horse won the mile-and-a-half Princess of Wales's Stakes at Newmarket in the six-year-old Primera whom Murless trained for Mr Stanhope Joel. Primera had been second in this race at four and had won it at five when he carried the colours of Mr C. H. Dracoulis. He was then sold to Mr Joel for whom he won The Bentinck Stakes at Goodwood and The Ebor Handicap at York with 9 stone. He ran the race of his life in the Arc in which, though not in the leading three, he finished within a length of the winner, St Crespin III.

Primera was bred at the Baroda Stud and was by the Two Thousand Guineas winner My Babu out of Pirette, a top class mare that won the French Oaks and the Prix Vermeille. Despite this attractive pedigree, he made only 1,040 guineas as a yearling in Dublin. As a sire he proved inconsistent and his fillies were markedly better than his colts. His winners included Lupe (Oaks, Coronation Cup); Aunt Edith (King George VI and Queen Elizabeth Stakes); Greengage (Coronation Stakes); and Attica Meli (Yorkshire Oaks and Park Hill Stakes). He was eventually exported to Japan.

Exar won The Goodwood Cup and also The Doncaster Cup in which he had a solitary opponent to beat. A very good filly from Ireland, Lynchris, who unfortunately died young, won The Yorkshire Oaks. She had previously won The Irish Oaks very easily and went on to win the Irish St Leger. A tall, rather leggy bay, she was bred by the Baroda Stud and as a yearling she was bought by that excellent judge Mr Bert Kerr for only 480 guineas on behalf of Sam Hall. The Irish trainer John Oxx persuaded Hall to take £100 profit and he himself trained the filly for Mrs E. M. Fawcett, an Ulster hotelier. Lynchris was by Sayajirao out of Scollata, whose grandam was a half-sister to Herringbone and Swallow Tail.

Another good winner that had been bought cheaply as a yearling was Sovereign Path, who won The Queen Elizabeth II Stakes. This grey by Grey Sovereign had cost only 700 guineas and won eight races worth over £10,000. He has proved a highly successful sire, his winners including Humble Duty, who won The One Thousand Guineas, and Wolver Hollow, who won The Eclipse Stakes. The Queen Elizabeth II Stakes was run at Newbury, the rebuilding of the Ascot grandstand having begun immediately after the July Meeting there.

Hyperion died in the last month of the year. This great little chestnut had been a marvellous racehorse at three but his career ended in anticlimax at four. He was essentially a 'character' whose idiosyncrasies had to be respected. Up till the end of his second season he had been trained by George Lambton but at four he was trained by Colledge Leader who had become Lord Derby's trainer. Lambton understood Hyperion and his little ways and Hyperion in return developed a warm affection for Lambton. Leader was probably a bit too tender with Hyperion, who was lazy at home, and did not work him hard enough for his main objective, The Gold Cup. Hyperion did not have his first two-mile gallop till just before Ascot and he became so distressed that Tommy Weston pulled him up. Of course everyone at Newmarket heard about this fiasco and Frank Butters, who trained the Aga Khan's Cup candidate Felicitation, determined to make things hot for Lord Derby's colt.

To warm him up, Butters ran Felicitation in the two-miles Churchill Stakes the day before The Cup. Felicitation made all the running and won by ten lengths. In The Cup Felicitation set a cracking pace to test Hyperion's stamina to the utmost. He was never headed and won by eight lengths from Thor II. Poor little Hyperion trailed in a weary third. Moreover, Hyperion was beaten by his solitary opponent in his only subsequent race, The Dullingham Stakes at Newmarket.

As a sire Hyperion was an outstanding success. He was six times champion, the first time in 1940, the last in 1955. He was four times second and once third. He was twice leading sire of brood mares and five times second. He sired two colts and five fillies that won classic races. His son Aureole proved a highly successful sire in Britain, while Heliopolis, Alibhai and Khaled all did very well in the United States. Owen Tudor was not consistent but got two exceptionally fast horses, Abernant and Tudor Minstrel, and a top-class middle-distance horse in Right Royal V. Helios was champion sire in Australia, Ruthless in New Zealand, Deimos in South Africa. In South America Gulf Stream, Aristophanes, Burpham and Hypocrite all did well. Aldis Lamp had a fine record in Belgium as had Hyperbole in Sweden. Rockefella and High Hat both sired classic winners in this country.

At the time of his death Hyperion had sired the winners of 748 races worth £557,009, a record that would have been much better but for the war. His fillies were on the whole rather better than his colts though the best of them were inclined to be a bit temperamental, Sun Chariot and Godiva being notable examples. Good winners from Hyperion mares included Parthia, Carozza, Alycidon, Supertello and Fair Edith.

'Good trainers, like good wives, are born not made. Without natural flair it is far better to keep away from racing stables and run a garage.' Thus wrote 'Atty' Persse, a great trainer who died in 1960 aged ninety-one. In his younger days he finished third in The Grand National on Aunt May. The most famous horse to come under his care was The Tetrarch, whom he bought for 1,300 guineas as a yearling and who was probably the fastest horse ever seen on an English racecourse. Nevertheless, for all his phenomenal speed, The Tetrarch sired three

St Leger winners in five years. Speed was the quality that Persse was always seeking. He excelled in the training of two-year-olds and had the knack of bringing them out to win the first time they ran. Though he had a highly developed sense of humour and was a famous raconteur, he was a tough taskmaster and maintained a standard of discipline within his stable that would be regarded as quite impermissible today. Among those who learnt the trainer's art under him were Sir Cecil Boyd-Rochfort and Geoffrey Brooke.

The Hon. Dorothy Wyndham Paget died this year at the age of fifty-four. She was not just a leading owner but one of racing's more remarkable and eccentric characters. She was the second daughter of the first and last Lord Queenborough by his first marriage to Pauline Whitney, daughter of Mr W. C. Whitney, at one time Secretary of the United States Navy. She was a cousin of Mr John Hay Whitney, a great supporter of English racing. Her wealth she had inherited from her maternal grandfather.

In appearance she was quite unmistakable. By no stretch of the imagination could she have been described as good-looking or well turned-out. She was heavy in build with an exceptionally large round pallid face and dead straight dark hair. Her uniform consisted of a blue felt hat that owed nothing to the dictates of fashion and a long grey coat that terminated just short of her ankles. On the race-course she never spoke to anyone bar her attendants, all female, her trainer or her jockey and her racing adviser, the late Sir Francis Cassel, a concert pianist and himself an owner and breeder. She had no trouble in keeping the press at arm's length, or rather further. Her shyness impelled her to live almost as a recluse at her home in Chalfont St Giles. The racegoing public sometimes saw her in the paddock or they might catch a glimpse of her tucking into an entire chicken for tea in the Pullman car on the way back from Lingfield. Stories seeped through from time to time of the unconventional hours that she kept; of her gargantuan appetite; of the conferences held far into the night on racecourses long after the last race had been run; of Christmas lunches where there were no sixpences in the pudding but cheques in the mince pies. Despite her oddness and an extremely demanding nature, the few who knew her well were genuinely fond of her. She was generous to those whom she employed and devoted to her horses. Of course she was not easy to serve. She had a will of iron and enough money to insist on having her own way. Hence the many abrupt partings from trainers and jockeys, the most notorious of which was when she removed her great steeplechaser Golden Miller and other horses from Basil Briscoe. However, her stud manager, Charlie Rogers, whom she always referred to as 'Romeo' stayed in her employment for twenty-three years and claimed he had never had a row with her.

In the 1920s she had a brief flirtation with motor-racing but the turf was in her blood. Her grandfather's colours had been carried to victory in The Derby by Volodyovski, known to the bookmakers as 'bottle of whisky'; her father won The Two Thousand Guineas with St Louis. She began with jumpers trained by Alec Law at Findon. She enjoyed beginner's luck as in 1931 she paid Mr Philip Carr, father of England's cricket captain Mr A. W. Carr, £6,000 for Golden Miller and left him with Basil Briscoe who had had the horse since early days when apparently it was of little account. Golden Miller won The Grand National in record time with 12 st. 2 lb., and five consecutive Cheltenham Gold Cups. There is no doubt that her entry into the sport was a welcome shot in the arm for National Hunt racing. The fact that she was always on the look-out for potential jumpers and was not particular over the price increased the value of store horses, while her betting operations, which were liable to be on a formidable scale, pepped up a market that hitherto had all too often been lamentably weak.

Her first transactions on the flat were less successful. Most of the yearlings for which she paid big prices were disappointing and among them were two notorious failures, Tuppence and Colonel Payne. In fact she acquired a reputation for reckless expenditure. She did have her successes and Wyndham, who raced his first season as the Bossover colt, was an exceptionally fast two-year-old. Before the war she was a staunch supporter of pony racing. She was twice leading owner under P.T.C. Rules and won the Northolt Derby with Scottish Rifle. Considering the scope of her bloodstock-breeding operations, she obtained only a moderate return for all the money she spent. However, in 1943 she did win The Derby with Straight Deal, whom she had bred herself and who was trained for her by Walter Nightingall. In that year she won The Coventry Stakes and The Middle Park Stakes with Orestes, a colt by Donatello II that turned temperamental at three. Other winners of note were Aldborough, who won The Queen Alexandra Stakes and The Doncaster Cup; and the ill-fated Nucleus who won over £11,000 in stakes and was second to Meld in The St Leger. All told she had 1,532 winners during her racing career, the majority being under National Hunt Rules.

On May 4, 1961 the Duke of Norfolk's committee, which had been formed to inquire into the question of doping, and particularly into the Rules of Racing pertaining to doping, published its report. This report, which was very well received, recommended, and rightly so, the abolition of the old unjust rule whereby a trainer was automatically disqualified if a horse of his was found to have been doped. The present rule now reads:

> Where any horse has run in any race under these Rules and has been found, on examination under Rule 14(VI), to have received any amount of any substance (other than a normal nutrient), being a substance which by its nature could affect the racing performance of a horse, the trainer of the horse in question shall be fined not less than £100 and, at the discretion of the Stewards of the Jockey Club, his Licence or permit may be withdrawn. However the Stewards may waive the fine if they are satisfied that the substance was administered unknowingly and that the trainer had taken all reasonable precautions to avoid a breach of this Rule.

This existing rule is not only much fairer to trainers but gives the Stewards room to manoeuvre as well. Another recommendation which was adopted was in respect of the taking of tests of certain winners or other runners. Ninety tests had been taken before the joint meeting of the Jockey Club and the National Hunt Committee in December and all of these proved negative.

In the meantime doping by criminal gangs continued, the most notorious cases being those of Pinturischio and Pandofell. Sir Victor Sassoon's Pinturischio was a Pinza colt trained by Noel Murless. He did not run as a two-year-old. His first race at three was The Wood Ditton Stakes at the Craven Meeting. He had by then acquired a big reputation at Newmarket and he duly won on a tight rein. He was then backed for The Two Thousand Guineas at 5/2 and for The Derby at 5/1. He started favourite for The Guineas at 7/4 and finished fourth behind Rockavon. Most people who saw him that day were satisfied with his performance and he continued to be backed for The Derby. It was intended to run him in The Dante Stakes at York on May 16. On the previous day he was 'got at' in his box at home and was of course unable to run. He rallied from that attack, though, and there was a good chance that he would be able to take the field in The Derby. However, a second attack not only stopped him from running in The Derby but was of sufficient severity to prevent him from ever racing again. All those who had backed him ante-post for The Derby lost their money. The instigator of this outrage was never discovered but on the racecourse it was believed that a man very well known in the betting world was responsible.

Pandofell, trained by F. Maxwell and winner of The Gold Cup, was due to run in the Sunninghill Park Stakes at the Ascot July Meeting. On the morning of the race he was found dazed and ill, hardly able to stand in fact, and with his eyes badly cut. Tests showed that he had been given phenobarbitone. No one profited from this crime. There was no ante-post betting on the race and as Pandofell was far too ill to run those who had hoped to lay him were disappointed.

In certain instances these doping cases were very likely an inside job as far as the actual perpetrator went. For a stable employee earning a far from munificent wage, a bribe of £100 or more could offer a very real temptation.

Before leaving the sordid question of doping, it may be said that the methods of analysis are now far more sophisticated than they used to be and there is general confidence in the result of tests conducted at the Equine Research Centre. A great many tests are now taken each year and nearly all of these are negative. An opinion in fact exists that too many tests are taken and these cost a great deal of money that could be better spent elsewhere. Perpetual vigilance is required, though. New drugs are constantly coming into circulation, not only from European sources but from America and South America, too. There is always a danger that dopers could, temporarily at least, be one step ahead of the analysts.

There were two other changes in 1961. In April the Jockey Club decided to allow local stewards to place a disqualified horse in other than last place if they thought it was fair to do so. Secondly, the maximum weight in handicaps was raised from 9 st. 7 lb. to 10 st. except in apprentice races or in nurseries. Jockeys in the past were often products of the industrial revolution. That is to say they came from working-class families in densely populated urban communities where conditions of life were usually hard, sometimes unhygienic, and where under-nourishment among children was all too common. Conscription in World War I revealed all too clearly the stunted growth and poor physique prevalent among so many citizens of this country. Happily the Welfare State and the general rise in the standard of living have done much to diminish, if not to eliminate, cases where children have to suffer on account of the poverty of their parents. In consequence it has become harder and harder to find light-weight lads. It will be no surprise if there is another rise in the range of weights in the not far distant future.

The leading two-year-old colts in 1960 had been an indifferent collection. Top of The Free Handicap with 9 st. 7 lb. was the French filly Opaline II, while there were seven fillies in the leading twelve. There was certainly no colt with outstanding credentials in The Two Thousand Guineas but even so the victory of the 66/1 outsider Rockavon came as a considerable shock. Rockavon certainly did not impress in the paddock and I remember the manager of one of the big Newmarket studs remarking: 'What a waste of time and money sending a horse like that all the way down from Scotland.' The fact remains that Rockavon won, and won comfortably too, by two lengths from Prince Tudor with Time Greine third.

Rockavon was bred in Northamptonshire by Mrs Seton Gordon and is by Rockefella out of Cosmetic, by Sir Cosmo, and is thus a half-brother to the very useful Rock Star. As a foal he was bought for 420 guineas by Mr R. J. Donworth, who resold him nine months later to Mr T. C. Yuill, a Scottish dairy farmer, for 2,300 guineas. Trained at Dunbar by George Boyd, he won three minor races at two but was not reckoned worthy of inclusion in The Free Handicap. His career after The Two Thousand Guineas, in which he was ridden by the northern jockey Norman Stirk, was nothing to write home about though he did beat a solitary opponent in a race of minor significance at Newcastle. He was the first Two Thousand Guineas winner ever to be trained in Scotland. His trainer never saw Rockavon's Newmarket triumph as his plane was fog-bound at Glasgow.

The Derby provided a result every bit as surprising as that of The Two Thousand Guineas, the winner being Psidium who was friendless in the market at 66/1. Favourite at 5/1 was the French colt Moutiers, a half-brother to Montaval and to the Oaks runner-up Paimpont. A tall, lanky chestnut with a lot of white about him, Moutiers was probably ill suited to the firm ground and finished fourteenth.

With just under a furlong to go, the leader was Boyd-Rochfort's representative, Pardao, a Pardal colt owned by Mrs C. O. Iselin who was well over ninety years of age. He was being hard pressed, though, by Madame Volterra's Dicta Drake, who in fact succeeded in heading him close to home. In the meantime Psidium had been making rapid headway since Tattenham Corner, at which point he had had only three or four rivals behind him. In the final fifty yards, continuing his run on the wide outside, he produced a burst of speed that made it look as if the horses he was passing were stationary. Such was the pace at which he was travelling that he had two lengths to spare over Dicta Drake at the winning-post while Pardao was a neck away third.

Psidium entered the winner's enclosure amid a silence that was positively embarrassing. No one had backed him; his owner Mrs Arpad Plesch was little known to the majority of English racegoers, while Poincelet was no hero to English racing crowds. Some writers praised Poincelet for having ridden a brilliant race. It is arguable that he would not have dared to employ similar tactics on a fancied horse. Possibly Psidium's trainer, Harry Wragg, was not totally surprised by the result. He had remarked a few days previously that if the going at Epsom was hard Psidium might well show to better advantage than his other and better fancied runner, Sovrango, who finished fourth. Possibly Psidium was a great racehorse; possibly his victory was one of those weird flukes that occasionally happen in racing. The matter was not put to the test as he developed tendon trouble and never ran again. Before being exported to Argentina, he sired Sodium who won The Irish Sweeps Derby and The St Leger.

Psidium's Derby success was a notable example of the international flavour so prevalent in modern racing. A half-brother to the French Two Thousand Guineas winner Thymus, Psidium was bred in Ireland by his owner, the wife of a Hungarian-born financier resident in France, and is a chestnut by the French-bred Pardal out of the Italian-bred Dinarella, a descendant of Pretty Polly. His jockey was French and the only English thing about him was his trainer. Pardal, who also sired Pardao, had belonged to M. M. Boussac and never won until he was four. His victories included The Princess of Wales's Stakes and The Jockey Club Stakes. Hearing that he was for sale, the late Lord Manton and his brother Mr Bobby Watson bought him one afternoon for £50,000 and he proved cheap at the price.

Born in 1902, Harry Wragg, the eldest and most accomplished of three brothers, had been one of the most consistently successful jockeys of his time. He won The Derby on Felstead, Blenheim and Watling Street. He had ten other victories in classic races to say nothing of five in The Eclipse Stakes. Thoughtful, intelligent and patient, he was a wonderful judge of pace and excelled in waiting tactics: hence his nickname during his riding days of 'The Head Waiter'. He began training at Newmarket in 1947 and among his many good winners have been Darius, Fidalgo, Espresso, Ambergris, Abermaid, Miralgo, Salvo, Sovereign, Full Dress II, Intermezzo and Moulton.

Dicta Drake won the Grand Prix de Saint Cloud impressively in July and Mathet decided to run him in The St Leger, for which he started favourite at 6/4. His rider, M. Garcia, evidently entertained no doubts about his stamina and he was in front before the straight had been reached. He was under pressure, though, three furlongs out and could find no answer when Aurelius, ridden by Piggott, moved up to tackle him. Aurelius stayed on stoutly to win by three parts of a length from Bounteous with Dicta Drake the same distance away third and Pardao fourth.

Aurelius was bred by Mrs Muriel McCall, Sir Cecil Boyd-Rochfort's sister, at the Tally Ho Stud in Ireland and was a very big powerful bay by Aureole out of the American-bred Niobe II, by Sir Gallahad III. The dam of Niobe II was

Humility, a sister of the Oaks winner Hycilla. When Aurelius came up for sale as a yearling, Noel Murless bought him for 5,000 guineas on behalf of Mrs Vera Lilley. He would have made more money, only potential purchasers reckoned he might prove too big to be trained. He naturally needed plenty of time and only ran once at two. The following season he won The Craven Stakes but was beaten a head by The Axe in The Newmarket Stakes. He missed The Derby because of the hard ground. The going was more to his liking at Royal Ascot and he was a comfortable winner of The King Edward VII Stakes. He was then rested till The Great Voltigeur Stakes at York, in which Just Great beat him by a neck with Pardao four lengths away third and Bounteous fourth. Murless had him at his best for The St Leger, which he won like a true stayer. He had one bit of luck, though. Just Great played up at the start and was left a hundred yards.

The outstanding three-year-old filly in 1961 was Mrs S. M. Castello's Sweet Solera, who as a two-year-old had won The Princess Stakes and The Cherry Hinton Stakes, both at Newmarket. At three she was unbeaten, winning the One Thousand Guineas Trial at Kempton, the Thirsk Classic Trial, The One Thousand Guineas and The Oaks. She was probably lucky not to lose the Thirsk race but the connections of Mr Jim Joel's Henry the Seventh declined to object and the Thirsk Stewards were apparently incapable of taking action on their own account.

A big, handsome chestnut, Sweet Solera was bred by Mrs Dorothy Walker who died in 1958. Sweet Solera did not possess a particularly imposing pedigree as she was by Solonaway, exported to Japan in 1958, out of Miss Gammon, by Grandmaster. Her third dam, Bacona, was one of the few descendants of the 1927 Derby winner, Call Boy, who was almost sterile. Solonaway won The Irish Two Thousand Guineas but six furlongs was his best distance and he won The Cork and Orrery Stakes and The Diadem Stakes. As a yearling Sweet Solera was bought for 1,850 guineas by Reg Day on behalf of Mrs Castello. Considering Sweet Solera's pedigree, which stopped many a so-called breeding expert from backing her in the classics, she stayed remarkably well and both in The One Thousand Guineas and The Oaks she beat Ambergris quite comfortably. One of the most popular features of her successes was the fact that she was ridden by Bill Rickaby. She never raced again after The Oaks and her owner turned down a big offer for her to go to America. Unfortunately she has been rather disappointing at the stud.

Few top-class fillies are kept in training for a fourth season and if they are they seldom add much to their reputation. Petite Étoile won four races at five but something of her former brilliance had departed. At Sandown in April she got up in the last few strides to beat Wordpam by a neck in The Coronation Stakes. She won her second Coronation Cup by the same margin from Vienna but it is fair to say that she had a bit in hand at the finish.

At Royal Ascot she had a simple task in The Rous Memorial Stakes and won readily. It was naturally hoped that she would win The Aly Khan Memorial Gold Cup at Kempton run over a mile and a half but she found nothing in the final furlong and was fairly and squarely beaten by Sir Winston Churchill's High Hat. She won The Scarborough Stakes at Doncaster with appropriate ease but in her final race, The Queen Elizabeth II Stakes at Ascot, she went under by half a length to the Irish four-year-old Le Levanstell, who had previously won The Sussex Stakes and was destined to sire a great racehorse in Levmoss.

Petite Étoile had won fourteen races and £67,786, more by £24,735 than the record for her sex established by Meld. She was probably not a genuine stayer but her class and her speed, coupled with the usually brilliant riding of Piggott, combined on most occasions to see her through. She was certainly at her best on fast ground and won both her Coronation Cups on going that suited her. Sadly, she has proved a failure as a brood mare.

St Paddy began his four-year-old career in great style by winning successively The Coombe Stakes at Sandown, The Hardwicke Stakes and The Eclipse Stakes. In The Eclipse Stakes, without being extended, he lowered the course record. The moment of truth for him, though, came in The King George VI and Queen Elizabeth Stakes, in which he was opposed by Mme Couturié's three-year-old, Right Royal V. Handsome as St Paddy was, he was dominated in the paddock by Right Royal V, a magnificent brown colt standing 16.3 hands. Moreover St Paddy displayed disquieting signs of being in a rather sulky mood. He was far from keen to enter his box to be saddled and he was reluctant to leave the paddock for the racecourse as well. In the race itself he put up no sort of a fight at all and hoisted the white flag after a barely token resistance. It was a humiliating defeat for a horse alleged to be England's champion.

Bred by his owner and trained by Pollet, Right Royal V, by Owen Tudor, had won The Grand Criterium at two. At three he was beaten in the Prix de Fontainebleau, Poincelet riding one of his more ridiculous races. However he then won the French Two Thousand Guineas, the Prix Lupin and the French Derby. In his final race he was second to the Italian horse Molvedo, a son of Ribot, in the Arc.

St Paddy won The Jockey Club Stakes, which on this occasion was run over the Sefton Course. He would have had more to do if High Hat, who subsequently only just missed a place in the Arc, had not been ridden in strangely unenterprising fashion. St Paddy's final race was The Champion Stakes. He again showed that he had only a limited inclination towards a battle and was beaten three parts of a length by the French three-year-old Bobar II, by Bozzetto. In all he had won nine races worth £97,193. The best winners he has sired have been Connaught, whose best distance was a mile and a quarter, and that stout-hearted stayer Parnell.

The new grandstand was ready for the Royal Meeting at Ascot. It could accommodate 13,000 racegoers and included 280 private boxes and more than 1,600 reserved seats. In general it met with approval but there was criticism on the grounds that too much attention had been given to box-holders and their friends, too little to ordinary patrons of Tattersalls who did not want to incur the extra expense of reserving a seat.

Because of the long dry spell the course had been liberally watered. The day before the meeting began, though, there was a steady downpour of rain that lasted for twelve hours. The going became soft but the course dried out reasonably well during the progress of the meeting. Unfortunately it soon became clear that horses drawn on the far side of the straight course were at a very serious disadvantage.

One of the features of the meeting was the success of the Irish trainer R. Fetherstonhaugh, who brought over three horses of Mr Stanhope Joel's and won The Cork and Orrery Stakes with Bun Penny, The Windsor Castle Stakes with Prince Tor, and The King's Stand Stakes with Silver Tor. At the Ascot October Meeting he brought over two horses, both of which won, so his Ascot tally for the season was five out of five. Burly and rubicund, 'Brud' Fetherstonhaugh is the younger son of the late Bob Fetherstonhaugh, a very amusing character who trained at The Curragh and numbered Lt-Col Giles Loder and Major Dermot McCalmont among his patrons. In 1919 Bob trained Ballyboggan, who was second in The Grand National. The story goes that Bob was keen to have his elder son christened Ballyboggan, but his wife put her foot down and a compromise was reached, the child being named Aintree instead.

Favourite for The Gold Cup was the French four-year-old Puissant Chef, who in 1960 had won the French St Leger and the Prix de l'Arc de Triomphe. He was unplaced, though, the winner being Piggott's mount Pandofell, a four-year-old owned by Mr Warwich Daw and trained by the former steeplechase jockey F. Maxwell, commonly known as 'Maxie' and a former assistant to Evan Williams at Kingsclere.

Delight at a resounding English triumph in The Cup was mingled with sympathy for that great supporter of English racing Mr Jim Joel, whose horses were then trained by Ted Leader, a member of a highly respected Newmarket family and a great steeplechase rider who had won the 1927 Grand National on the massive Sprig. Mr Joel bred Pandofell, by Solar Slipper, and raced him at two. Pandofell, however, showed scant promise in his two races and was sent up to the December Sales where Mr Warwick Daw obtained him for the trifling sum of 600 guineas. At three Pandofell won four races worth over £1,600 and he was also first past the post in the Craven Stakes at Goodwood, only to suffer disqualification. He would have been a certainty for The Cesarewitch with 7 st. 3 lb. but a cough prevented him from running. As a four-year-old he had won The Queen's Prize at Kempton and The Yorkshire Cup prior to his triumph at Ascot. It has previously been related how he was 'got at' when he was due to run at the Ascot meeting in July. He had to miss The Goodwood Cup but happily he recovered in time to win The Doncaster Cup. He would probably have made a good sire but breeders in this country are absurdly prejudiced against Gold Cup winners and he ended his days in Soviet Russia. Before he left he sired Pandora Bay, who was third in the 1968 Oaks, won The Ribblesdale Stakes and was then exported to France where she won good races, too. He also sired that queer-tempered but very good stayer Piaco, whose victories included The Doncaster Cup and The

Northumberland Plate with 9 st. 1 lb. Both Pandora Bay and Piaco were trained by Geoffrey Barling.

Mr Joel obtained some compensation for having missed The Gold Cup by winning The Goodwood Cup with Predominate. In some respects the race was a bit of a farce. The four runners set off at a walk when the flag fell and for over a mile the pace would not have inconvenienced a large mounted policeman on a warm summer afternoon. However, if the first half of the race was tedious, the finish was exciting and Predominate just held on to win by a short head from Shatter. The time was almost a minute slower than that recorded by Exar the previous year.

Predominate was given a great reception since he was deservedly a Goodwood favourite, having won The Goodwood Stakes in 1958, 1959 and 1960, on the last occasion with 9 st. 5 lb. on his back. In addition he was second in The Cup in 1960. By Preciptic out of a mare by Great Scot, he was nine years old when he carried off The Cup. He had been bred in Ireland and as a yearling Ken Cundell bought him for 1,150 guineas on behalf of Mrs Trimmer-Thompson. He won five races worth £2,580 for her at two, three and four, and he also won twice over hurdles. At five he ran third in The Cesarewitch and he was then bought by Mr Joel, who hoped he would become a top-class hurdler. He was accordingly sent to Bob Turnell but it soon became apparent that he did not really enjoy jumping hurdles. It was therefore decided to concentrate his energies on the flat and he joined Ted Leader's stable with happy results. In all he won fifteen flat races worth £15,896.

The two-year-olds of 1961 were not of outstanding merit, particularly the colts. Top of The Free Handicap were two fast fillies trained in Ireland by P. J. Prendergast, La Tendresse (9 st. 7 lb.), by Grey Sovereign, and Display (9 st. 3 lb.), by Rustam. The victories of La Tendresse included The Seaton Delaval Stakes at Newcastle, The Molecomb Stakes and The Lowther Stakes. Display won The National Stakes at Sandown, a race that took the place of the prestigious National Breeders' Produce Stakes in 1959 after produce races had been abolished. She also won The Cheveley Park Stakes and was third in the Prix Morny behind Prudent. The top colt was Mr G. A. Oldham's Miralgo (9 st. 1 lb.), a son of Aureole trained by Harry Wragg. Miralgo won the first race for the one-mile 'Timeform' Gold Cup, an event devised by Mr P. Bull and run at Doncaster in October. It carried £10,000 in added money and on this occasion its value of £21,893 made it easily the richest two-year-old prize ever competed for in this country. Miralgo's win ensured that the Queen's Aureole was top sire for the second year running.

1962 saw the results of the Betting and Gaming Act becoming fully operative. Betting shops spread in rich profusion all over the country, to an extent in fact that far surpassed official expectation. Magistrates found it extremely difficult to turn down an application within the legal definition and if they did so the applicant almost invariably appealed and more often than not won his case. It may well have been a combination of betting shops and televised racing—sometimes races from three meetings were shown on a Saturday—that caused a further decline in racecourse attendances. Racecourse executives began to realise, none too soon, that the standards provided in the cheaper enclosures were in many cases no longer adequate, and that the incentive to go racing was being swiftly eroded.

At this point of time race courses were alarmingly vulnerable to take-over bids from 'developers' searching for open spaces near urban communities. To the regret of the racing world, Hurst Park fell a prey to 'developers' and vanished from the fixture list for ever. Hurst Park may not have been a great racecourse but sport there was brisk and it was a handy spot for Londoners to get to. A popular event there was The Victoria Cup, a seven-furlongs handicap run in the spring. The start was just out of sight of spectators in the grandstand and there were a few tense moments after the 'off' while waiting for the runners to round the bend and then seeing if the horse one had backed was among the leaders. Apart from the loss of Hurst Park, Manchester by the end of the season appeared in dire peril of extinction.

During the course of the year the Betting Levy Board announced its first allocations of money. A few journalists objected because owners appeared to be the first recipients of funds whereas in their view the money ought to have been employed to reduce admission charges. In 1962 the total amount of prize money available to be won under Jockey Club Rules was £2,115,862, of which £1,711,966 went to actual winners. Of this sum, sponsors contributed £117,000 and owners themselves £708,374 or 33·48 per cent of the whole. This year saw the first running of the Irish Sweeps Derby. It carried a prize in excess of £50,000 and was the richest three-year-old event ever staged in Europe and the highest endowed race ever run in Britain or Ireland.

The field for The Two Thousand Guineas was by no means a distinguished one. The race was won with some ease by Privy Councillor, bred by Major (later Sir) Gerald Glover in Northamptonshire and trained by the very able Tom Waugh at Newmarket. Winner of The Free Handicap at the Craven Meeting, Privy Councillor was stylishly ridden by Bill Rickaby and started at 100/6. At the winning-post he had three lengths to spare over Romulus who was probably the pick of the three-year-old milers but did not come to hand as early as his conqueror, who failed to win again subsequently.

Privy Councillor is by Court Martial's son Counsel out of High Number, by His Highness. Major Glover bought High Number as a foal for 750 guineas. She ran fourteen times without winning at two and three but secured a couple of minor events at four. Counsel had won ten races worth over £9,000 in Lord Astor's colours. He was never a very imposing individual and when his racing days were over the Sussex breeder Mr E. H. Covell was able to buy him for 2,700 guineas. After Privy Councillor's victory, Mr Covell received some big offers for Counsel from abroad. At this point the Levy Board decided on a well-intentioned rescue act and bought a controlling interest of twenty-one shares in the horse for £3,000 per share. As events turned out, they would have been wiser to let Counsel go.

The Derby proved to be one of the most sensational in the long history of that race. There were twenty-six runners, seven of which fell in the course of the descent to Tattenham Corner, among them the favourite, Major Lionel Holliday's Hethersett. The winner was the Irish colt Larkspur owned by Mr Raymond Guest, for some years United States Ambassador to Ireland, trained by Vincent O'Brien and ridden by the Australian jockey Neville Sellwood, who in the autumn was killed when riding the inappropriately named Lucky Seven at Maisons-Laffitte. Larkspur was far from being a great Derby winner and was certainly nothing like as good as Sir Ivor who won for Mr Guest in 1968. Mr Guest can be rated one of the more fortunate owners as he won two Cheltenham Gold Cups and The Grand National with L'Escargot.

The disaster took place about halfway down the hill. It is hard to say exactly what happened as it was all over in a few seconds and occurred at a point where little is visible from the stands. The cause, though, was not a matter for dispute. In any big field for the Derby a fair number of the runners are simply not fit to be in the race and the object of their presence is probably to gratify the egotism of their respective owners. Coming down the hill the mediocre competitors are dropping back beaten while the better ones are striving to improve their position. Inevitably jostling and crowding take place and, with over twenty horses galloping flat out downhill, a nasty accident must always be a possibility.

Romulus was one of the first to fall. Carr on the favourite and Sellwood on Larkspur pulled away from the rails to avoid disaster but, whereas Sellwood just managed to keep Larkspur on his feet, Hethersett's legs caught those of Romulus and down he came. In a trice Crossen, Pindaric, Persian Fantasy, Changing Times and King Canute II were all on the ground too. The only horse badly hurt was King Canute II who broke a leg and had to be destroyed. All the jockeys bar R. P. Elliott were taken to hospital. Carr could not ride again before the end of July and Stan Smith was out of action even longer.

Larkspur ran on like a true stayer and won by two lengths from M. Boussac's Arcor with another French competitor, Madame Volterra's Le Cantilien, third. Thus no English competitor reached the first three. Bred by Mr Philip Love, Larkspur is a chestnut by Never Say Die out of the Precipitation mare Skylarking whose dam Woodlark was a half-sister by Bois Roussel to Alycidon, Acropolis and Borealis. He is, therefore, a member of the very successful Marchetta family and was that family's first winner of The Derby. As a yearling he had been bought at Ballsbridge for 12,200 guineas and at the time he was the most costly yearling ever to win the 'Blue Riband'.

The remainder of Larkspur's career was undistinguished. He failed in the Irish Sweeps Derby and also in The St Leger. He made little mark as a sire and was eventually exported to Japan.

Usually noise and excitement are the concomitants to the finish of a Derby. On this occasion the close of the race was far quieter and less animated than usual. There were loose horses in the straight and no one was sure of their identity. Spectators in the stands had little idea of what had happened. Comparatively

39. Larkspur wins the 1962 Derby—a sensational race in which seven runners fell before they reached Tattenham Corner

little attention was paid to Larkspur when he was led in. Larkspur's victory enabled Never Say Die to become the first American-bred horse to become champion sire.

A thorough investigation was made of the accident and in due course the following statement was issued:

Derby Stakes. The Epsom Stewards enquired into the running of this race where seven horses fell. They interviewed several jockeys who had ridden in the race, and had reports from the jockeys who were still in hospital, of whom Carr was unable to make a statement on account of his injuries. The Stewards also saw films.

The Stewards were satisfied that no individual was to blame. There was no evidence of rough riding.

The general opinion of the jockeys was that too many horses were falling back after six furlongs, and the remainder closed up, and in the general scrimmage some horse was brought down, the rest falling over that horse.

The Stewards accepted that view and regret that such a large number of horses not up to classic standard were allowed by their owners and trainers to start.

The Stewards wish to record their gratitude to the amateur photographers who lent them the film taken near the scene of the accident.

Hethersett next ran in The Gordon Stakes at Goodwood. He clearly did not fancy the firm ground and was unplaced behind the Irish colt Gay Challenger who won in record time. These two met again in The Great Voltigeur Stakes at York. There was plenty of give in the ground and Gay Challenger was in trouble a long way from home. Hethersett looked like trotting up at a mile and a quarter but in the end he was all out to beat Miralgo by a short head. This performance raised doubts of his ability to stay the St leger distance.

Favourite for The St Leger at 7/2 was the Italian colt Antelami, a rather plain lightish bay with four white socks who was by the Gold Cup winner Botticelli. Hethersett was easy to back at 100/8. Antelami ran badly and Hethersett won decisively by four lengths from Monterrico. Larkspur was a moderate sixth. On that form Hethersett would surely have won The Derby.

Bred by his owner, Hethersett was a very good-looking colt by Djebel's son Hugh Lupus out of the speedy Big Game mare, Bride Elect, a descendant of Lost Soul. He looked like making a successful sire—his son Blakeney won the Derby—but unfortunately he died young. He was the first classic winner trained by Dick Hern, who concluded five years with Major Holliday at the end of the season and departed to West Ilsley to take over the Astor horses on the retirement of Jack Colling.

There was no lack of drama in both The One Thousand Guineas and The Oaks. Favourite for The One Thousand Guineas was the Irish filly Display, owned by Beatrice, Lady Granard, trained by Paddy Prendergast and ridden by the Australian, George Bougoure. Winner of The National Stakes and The Cheveley Park Stakes in 1961, Display was a light-framed, greyhoundy chestnut by Rustam out of Commander Peter FitzGerald's famous brood mare Review, whose other winners included Pourparler, winner of The One Thousand Guineas in 1964. Bougoure made plenty of use of Display who was in front at least three furlongs from home. At that point she looked very much like winning but in the final hundred yards her stride began to shorten. By then she was being hard pressed by Abermaid, the mount of Bill Williamson, and West Side Story, ridden by Eph Smith. With fifty yards to go Abermaid got her head in front but she too was tiring. Her head was right up in the air and her tail was making rapid revolutions. She was hanging, furthermore, and veered towards Display with the result that West Side Story, in between them, had to be checked. Abermaid held on to win by half a length from Display with West Side Story three parts of a length away third.

The Stewards at once lodged an objection against Abermaid for interference. They had the patrol camera film to help them in their deliberations and after twenty very tense minutes it was announced that the objection had been over-ruled. The fact is that it was the unfortunate West Side Story who had been hampered, not Display. If West Side Story had been second, she might well have got the race.

Bred by the late Sir Percy Loraine and Mr Roderic More O'Ferrall, owned in partnership between the latter and Lord Elveden, Abermaid, who was trained by Harry Wragg, was a powerfully built, muscular grey who looked a typical sprinter. This was hardly surprising as she was by Abernant out of Dairymaid, by Denturius. Dairymaid was a half-sister to Nella, dam of Miralgo and of that tough stayer Parnell.

The unlucky West Side Story, who carried the popular colours of Mr Jim Joel, started favourite for The Oaks. Eph Smith evidently had implicit confidence in her stamina as he sent her to the front at half-way. In the straight she was strongly challenged by the French filly Monade, who in fact established a lead of rather more than half a length. West Side Story, though, refused to give in and the daughter of Rockefella passed the winning-post almost level with Monade, who most people reckoned had just held on to her lead.

There followed fifteen nerve-racking minutes before the verdict was known. The judge, Mr John Hancock, was unable to give a verdict on the projected negative because there was a white snip on West Side Story's nose. Mr Hancock sent for a print but this was blurred and accordingly he sent for another. At long last he announced that Monade had won by a short head which in fact was about an inch.

Monade, the seventh French post-war Oaks winner, was owned by M. G. P. Goulandris, trained by J. Lieux and ridden by the admirable Yves Saint-Martin. A brown filly by Klairon, she had been bred by M. Achille Fould, a former Minister of Agriculture, who decided to sell her because of his own ill health. M. Goulandris, whose biggest success previously had been to win the Greek Derby with Andros Navigator, bought her for £1,800.

Smith's riding of West Side Story came in for plenty of criticism. A lot of people reckoned he had made too much use of her and that she had been even unluckier than in The One Thousand Guineas. Later in the season she won The Yorkshire Oaks.

The French won The Coronation Cup with Dicta Drake and The Gold Cup with Balto, by Wild Risk, who beat Lady George Cholmondeley's Sagacity, by Le Sage, by less than a length. Sagacity, trained by Boyd-Rochfort, was an out-and-out stayer little suited to the indifferent pace. He took his revenge on Balto in The Goodwood Cup. The One Thousand Guineas winner Abermaid was defeated in the Jersey Stakes at Ascot but Display, blinkered, looking even lighter than usual and apparently not at all on good terms with herself, won The Coronation Stakes. She never ran again afterwards.

A feature of Royal Ascot was the superb double achieved by Mrs L. Carver's six-year-old gelding Trelawny, who had won the Chester Cup two years pre-viously. On the Tuesday Trelawny, trained by George Todd, won The Ascot

Stakes with 9 st. 8 lb. and on the Friday, The Queen Alexandra Stakes with 9 st. 5 lb.

There was a huge crowd at The Curragh for the first running of the Irish Sweeps Derby. Tambourine II, bred in America and trained in France by Pollet, won a thrilling race by a short head from Mrs E. M. Carroll's Arctic Storm, trained by Oxx. Tambourine II, who carried the colours of Mr Howell E. Jackson, had previously been fourth in the Prix du Jockey Club. Arctic Storm was by no means fashionably bred, being by Arctic Star out of Rabina, by Blanding. Rabina had many ups and downs in her lifetime and at one point won a maiden hurdle at Roscommon of all places. There was a story that she had been included for luck in a consignment of cattle that Mrs Carroll had bought. There is no doubt that Arctic Storm was a good colt. He won the Irish Two Thousand Guineas and was a good third in The King George VI and Queen Elizabeth Stakes. He ended the season by winning The Champion Stakes, among his victims being Hethersett. Deservedly, he was placed top of the three-year-old Free Handicap.

Mr Joel obtained some consolation for his ill luck with West Side Story when his four-year-old Henry the Seventh, by King of the Tudors, won The Eclipse Stakes. The previous year Henry the Seventh, bought for 3,600 guineas as a yearling by his trainer Captain Elsey on Mr Joel's behalf, had dead-heated for The Cambridgeshire with Violetta.

The French enjoyed another major success when M. F. Dupré's Match III, trained by Mathet, won The King George VI and Queen Elizabeth Stakes after making all the running. Aurelius was second, beaten by three parts of a length, and Arctic Storm a neck away third. Neither M. Dupré nor Mathet, who had a stomach ache, were present. In the autumn Match III won The Washington International at Laurel Park.

Match III was by Tantième out of Relance, by Relic, a mare descended from Sceptre. He was a full brother to Reliance, who won the Grand Prix, the Prix du Jockey Club and the Prix Royal Oak, and a three-parts brother to the Derby winner Relko. Tantième, by Deux Pour Cent, was a great racehorse that twice won the Arc but he was a bad traveller and could not produce his best form when sent to run in Britain. Deux Pour Cent, who also sired Mandarin, winner of a memorable race for the Grand Steeplechase de Paris and also of The Cheltenham Gold Cup, ended his days in Czechoslovakia.

Mr D. Van Clief's Crocket, a King of the Tudors colt trained by Geoffrey Brooke, won The Coventry, Gimcrack and Middle Park Stakes and headed The Free Handicap with 9 st. 7 lb. The most impressive performance by a two-year-old, though, was the victory of Mrs Olin's Mossborough filly Noblesse in the Timeform Gold Cup. This medium-sized chestnut, trained by Paddy Prendergast, made mincemeat of her rivals and won on the bit by three lengths from Partholon with Star Moss third. In The Free Handicap she was given 9 st. 4 lb.

Some well-known figures in the racing world died in 1962, among them Sir Alfred Butt. He had started off his working life as a clerk in Harrods and eventually became a man of power in the theatrical world both in London and in the provinces. He was Conservative M.P. for Balham and Tooting from 1922 till 1936, when his political career terminated on a low note following involvement with Mr J. H. Thomas in a matter concerning the leakage of Budget secrets. Among the best horses to carry his colours were Steady Aim (Oaks) and Petition (Eclipse Stakes).

Others to die this year were Lord Milford, a successful owner-breeder who was largely responsible for the founding of Tote Investors Ltd; Mr William Christie, who was a hundred and three and had owned horses up to the age of ninety-nine; George Duller, far less adept as a trainer than he had been as a rider over hurdles; and Meyrick Good, one of the best known of racing journalists. Eighty-five when he died, Meyrick Good, a man of exceptionally tough constitution, had worked for the Sporting Life for over sixty years. Immensely industrious, he favoured rather flowery and old-fashioned expressions and was probably the last man to refer to an elderly amateur rider as 'a veteran unpaid knight of the pigskin'. He mystified younger readers by his references to the 'Spagnoletti Board' at Ascot. Junior members of the press room were apt to laugh at his style but I remember that at Eton I read with relish every word that he wrote and thought him a marvellous writer. Unlike most modern racing journalists, he rode well and was an excellent judge of a horse. He could be somewhat cantankerous in the press room but he mellowed with age. Right to the end, though, he carried on a cold war with another crusty veteran whose job was to return the starting prices for the Sporting Life. They loathed each other and there was never the remotest chance of a détente.

Particularly sad was the death of the Lambourn trainer Charlie Pratt in an air crash as he was flying home from Redcar where he had won The William Hill Gold Cup with Songedor. His mother was a sister of Fred Archer.

IO

NINETEEN-SIXTY-THREE proved another bad year for English-trained horses. The one English classic success was that of Only For Life in The Two Thousand Guineas. Apart from four classics, challengers from abroad won The Coronation Cup, The Eclipse Stakes, The King George VI and Queen Elizabeth Stakes and The Champion Stakes.

The most popular horse in the country was Trelawny, a seven-year-old gelding owned by Mrs L. Carver, who had won The Grand National with E.S.B. Trelawny was trained at Manton by George Todd. He had, of course, brought off that splendid Royal Ascot double in 1962 of The Ascot Stakes and The Queen Alexandra Stakes. This year he achieved the same double again, carrying 10 stone in the Ascot Stakes and conceding 49 lb. to the runner-up. No wonder he was given a reception that brought back memories of Brown Jack. Furthermore, Trelawny won The Goodwood Cup by six lengths with his ears pricked, and the cheering that day must have awakened visitors to Bognor Regis from their post-luncheon deck-chair slumbers.

Bred by Mr J. J. Astor, Trelawny was by Black Tarquin, not very successful as a sire of flat-racers, out of the Umidwar mare Indian Night, a descendant of the Astor foundation mare Popingaol and grandam of the St Leger winner Provoke. Trained by Jack Colling, Trelawny was big and slow to develop. At three he won three races of no particular significance and was then sent to the December Sales where Fred Rimell bought him as a prospective jumper for 2,500 guineas on Mrs Carver's behalf. At four he was trained for the flat by Sid Mercer and won The Chester Cup. In The Goodwood Stakes he broke a cannon bone. The course vet wished to put him down but Mercer refused to agree. He took Trelawny home and by skilled attention succeeded in getting the broken bone to mend. In 1961 Trelawny was back with Jack Colling and won The Brown Jack Stakes at Ascot. For the 1961–62 jumping season he was with Fred Rimell. He ran four times over hurdles, being placed on each occasion, but jumping clearly did not appeal to him. When the jumping season was over he began his fruitful association with George Todd. The Trelawny saga did not end in 1963 for he was back at Ascot again in 1964.

Only For Life was bred at the Hanstead Stud, a bay by the tough Chanteur II out of Life Sentence, by Court Martial. I recollect, on my very first visit to Ascot, standing on an orange-box on the course side to see Arabella, a beautiful Buchan filly and great-grandam of Life Sentence, win The Queen Mary Stakes in Lt-Col Giles Loder's colours. Arabella, who was a granddaughter of Pretty Polly, was fourth dam of Only For Life.

Then named Dartmoor Ditty, Only For Life came up for sale as a yearling at Newmarket and Jeremy Tree bought him for 1,600 guineas on behalf of Miss Monica Sheriffe, a very knowledgeable regular racegoer with a sharp wit and formidable power of repartee. In her prime she was one of the best of her sex across Leicestershire. Tree described Only For Life as 'one of the ugliest yearlings I have ever seen'. He bought him largely because he had inherited Life Sentence from the late Mr Peter Beatty and she had won four races in his colours before being sold to Miss Gladys Yule for 5,500 guineas. Miss Yule died in 1957 and the Hanstead Stud passed to Miss Patricia Wolf. There were only five mares at the Hanstead Stud when Only For Life was foaled.

Winner of The Clarence House Stakes at two, Only For Life, ridden by Jimmy Lindley, started at 33/1 in The Guineas. Crocket was favourite at 5/2. It was a typical English spring day with cold, driving rain that reduced the attendance and rendered the going extremely soft. Only For Life battled on up the hill like a hero and got up in the last two strides to beat the Irish-trained Ionian, who faltered close to home, by inches. Crocket was last. The time was six seconds slower than that of Privy Councillor the previous year. It was a first classic victory for owner, trainer and jockey. Lindley was a strong and stylish rider who had considerable trouble with his weight. Possessed of both intelligence and charm of manner, he is now making a name for himself as TV paddock commentator (B.B.C.) in succession to Clive Graham.

Only For Life was not entered for The Derby. He could stay a mile and a half, though, as he won The King Edward VII Stakes at Royal Ascot and was only just beaten by Ragusa in The Great Voltigeur Stakes. In The St Leger the ground was not soft enough for him and he could not show his true form at all. He is ending his days in Japan.

Noblesse was very slow to come to hand in the spring and was not ready to participate in The One Thousand Guineas. In her absence that event was re-garded as a good thing for the French-trained Hula Dancer, winner of the Grand Criterium the previous autumn. Bred in America by her owner, Mrs P. A. B. Widener, Hula Dancer was a big, rather leggy grey with a bold, intelligent head by Native Dancer out of Flash On, by Pharos's son, Ambrose Light. Flash On had no racing ability whatsoever. Trained by Pollet and ridden by Poincelet, Hula Dancer, who on her first appearance at three had won the Prix Imprudence very easily, started at 2/1 on at Newmarket. She duly won but needed to fight hard to hold off Mr J. G. Morrison's Spree by a length. Spree was a Rockefella filly from Tree's stable.

Hula Dancer failed in the Prix de Diane, the one defeat of her career, but then won the Prix Jacques le Marois at Deauville and the Prix du Moulin at Longchamp. She returned to England in October for The Champion Stakes and owing to doubts on the score of her stamina she started at 9/2, The Creditor being favourite at 6/4. Brilliant acceleration from the Bushes enabled Hula Dancer, ridden by Deforge, to lead coming into the Dip and she held on up the hill to beat Linacre by a length with The Creditor third.

M. F. Dupré's Relko, a three-parts brother to Match III by Tantième's son Tanerko, had some smart form at two but in The Grand Criterium he had found Hula Dancer's speed more than he could cope with. He wintered exceptionally well and at three stood 16.1½ hands and girthed 73 inches. He began the season by winning the Prix de Guiche at Longchamp and then won the French Two Thousand Guineas by two lengths. After this victory Mathet announced that Relko would go for The Derby. Relko was at once installed as favourite and never lost that position.

It was not a strong Derby field and more than a third of the runners were maidens. One of the nonentities, Hullabaloo, played up at the start and caused a delay of fourteen minutes on a bitterly cold grey afternoon. This upset the second favourite Duplation who got cross and tried to eat Singer.

The race itself proved a dull one. Relko, partnered by Yves Saint-Martin, won by six lengths from Merchant Venturer with Ragusa third. There was only one English-trained horse in the first four.

The sequel to Relko's victory was both unpleasant and unsatisfactory. Six weeks after The Derby, the Stewards of the Jockey Club and of the National Hunt Committee issued a statement the main points of which were as follows:

> The Stewards are seriously concerned that a number of routine tests have recently shown positive evidence of doping.
>
> There are seven such cases—two under N.H. Rules—covering a period from mid-April to the end of May.
>
> The local Stewards, having received positive confirmation of doping from the analysts, will now investigate each case, and after their enquiries will refer the cases to the Stewards of the Jockey Club and of the National Hunt Committee.
>
> Until the Stewards' enquiries have been completed, no details can be given as the cases are, of course, sub judice.

This statement was injudicious to say the least since it afforded grounds for speculation and rumour, often of the most bizarre and improbable character, without providing any positive information. Diligent and resourceful journalists at once got to work. Before long it was known that one of the horses concerned was Relko. Three weeks later the authorities held a press conference. The names of the seven horses were given as well as the fact that the saliva tests had proved negative, the urine tests positive. A reward of £2,000 was offered for information leading to the conviction of persons engaged in doping.

40. Relko after winning the 1963 Derby

The affair dragged on throughout the summer. There was considerable resentment in France where the age-old dislike of the English is never very far below the surface. On August 29 this notice appeared in the *Racing Calendar*:

The Stewards of the Epsom Summer Meeting held their enquiry at the Registry Office on 28 August, when they heard evidence from the trainer and other parties concerned, including technical witnesses called on their behalf. They also took evidence from the Stewards' Advisory Committee.

The Stewards were satisfied that a substance other than a normal nutrient was present in the horse.

From the technical evidence they were not satisfied that it was administered with the intention of increasing its speed or improving its stamina, conduct or courage in the race.

They adjourned the case for further enquiry in conjunction with the Police.

Finally the matter was settled on October 3 with the following notice in the Racing Calendar:

The Stewards of the Jockey Club, having considered the report on their further enquiries, are satisfied that the trainer and his employees have no case to answer under Rule 102(II).

They found no evidence that would justify a disqualification of Relko under Rule 66(c).

It was most unfortunate that the rumours about Relko had been intensified by what happened in the Irish Sweeps Derby on June 29. Relko was apparently sound in the paddock but Saint-Martin saw fit to walk him down to the start. At the gate Relko was definitely lame. He was examined by a vet and, after telephonic communication with Mathet, he was withdrawn from the race. The source of his lameness remained uncertain. A dope test proved negative.

Relko next ran in the Prix Royal Oak, the French St Leger. He showed what a really good horse he was by winning easily from Sanctus, winner of the Prix du Jockey Club and the Grand Prix. French sentiments in respect of Relko were shown by the fact that he was cheered from the final bend to the unsaddling enclosure even though M. Dupré was very far from being a popular figure on the French turf while Mathet could hardly be described as a prime favourite with the racing public. Relko was favourite for the Arc but sweated up and was unplaced behind Exbury.

Relko remained in training in 1964, a half share in him having meanwhile been bought by Lord Sefton. He won the £18,000 Prix Ganay in fine style but was far less impressive in winning The Coronation Cup by a neck from Khalkis. Probably, though, he disliked the heavy ground. He concluded his career with a victory in the £41,000 Grand Prix de Saint Cloud. He was slow to establish himself as a sire but was fourth on the list in 1977.

Noblesse made her first appearance as a three-year-old in the Musidora Stakes at York on May 15. She showed that she was indeed an outstanding filly, winning in a canter by six lengths. May 15 was quite a good day for Paddy Prendergast as at The Curragh on that same afternoon he won the Irish Two Thousand Guineas with Linacre and the Irish One Thousand Guineas with Gazpacho.

Ridden by Bougoure and starting at 11/4 on, Noblesse made a nonsense of The Oaks, winning on the bit by ten lengths from Spree. Had she been ridden out she might well have won by a furlong. Mr and Mrs John Olin, who had never set eyes on their filly previously, flew in from America to see the race. Mr Olin was too lame to go down to the paddock and the first time he saw Noblesse close up was when he greeted her in the winner's enclosure. Mrs P. G. Margetts, who had bred Noblesse and sold her as a yearling for 4,200 guineas, flew from Canada to see the race.

It had been planned to run Noblesse in The King George VI and Queen Elizabeth Stakes and The Yorkshire Oaks, but she injured a hock and was compelled to miss those events. Her only other race was the Prix Vermeille in which she was fourth to M. Dupré's Golden Girl, by Supreme Court. After that defeat she departed for America.

Yet again the French won The Coronation Cup, the winner this time being Baron Guy de Rothschild's Exbury, who earlier in the month had won the Prix Ganay. In the paddock at Epsom Exbury, a smallish chestnut, beautifully made and of superb quality, earned unstinted praise. In the race itself he slammed Hethersett to the tune of six lengths. He went on to win the Grand Prix de Saint-Cloud and the Arc. He is by Le Haar, a member of the Blandford male line, out of the British-bred Greensward by Noblesse's sire, Mossborough. Baron de Rothschild bought her as a three-year-old for 1,000 guineas at the Newmarket December Sales. Exbury sired the 1976 St Leger winner Crow.

For once in a way The Ascot Gold Cup went to England, the winner being Lady Sassoon's four-year-old Twilight Alley, by Alycidon out of Crepuscule, and thus a three-parts brother to Crepello. Twilight Alley is a gigantic chestnut standing $17.1\frac{1}{2}$ hands and not surprisingly he was by no means an easy horse to train. He never ran at two and at three he made only one appearance, winning a mile-and-a-half maiden race at Ascot in July. In 1963 he ran second in The Henry II Stakes at Sandown to Gaul who was giving him 6 lb. The Gold Cup was only the third race of his career. Favourite for The Cup was the French six-year-old Taine, who had twice won the Prix du Cadran.

In the race Piggott gave an interesting example of the art of waiting in front. He made all the running and still had enough left in reserve to withstand a determined challenge by Misti IV in the straight. It was a skilful piece of riding by Piggott and a fine feat of training by Murless. The French riders on Misti IV and Taine were probably unwise to allow Piggott to dictate a somewhat undemanding pace while they themselves were dawdling behind on tough and experienced stayers. Twilight Alley broke down in The King George VI and Queen Elizabeth Stakes and never ran again. He has made little mark as a sire.

Crocket, who had run so badly in The Two Thousand Guineas, reappeared in The St James's Palace Stakes equipped with a large pair of blinkers. Ridden by Doug Smith, he set off in front and headed for home as hard as he could go. He soon set up a long lead which he never looked like losing and he won by six lengths from Follow Suit with Ionian third. Crocket's only other race was The Sussex Stakes at Goodwood. Similar tactics were attempted but he was never permitted to get far ahead of his rivals and when he was tackled by Linacre over two furlongs out he folded up like a pocket knife. This left Linacre in front a bit sooner than had been intended and he was caught in the last few strides by Lord Carnarvon's Queen's Hussar, a three-year-old trained by 'Atty' Corbett. Queen's Hussar, by the versatile March Past, was a good miler that had previously won the Lockinge Stakes at Newbury. His most fervent admirers, though, could hardly have anticipated that he would sire a great racehorse like Brigadier Gerard, to say nothing of Highclere who won The One Thousand Guineas and the French Oaks for the Queen.

Ragusa has been mentioned as finishing third in The Derby. Bred by Captain H. F. Guggenheim, he was by Ribot out of Fantan II, by Ambiorix. His dam was flown to Italy, where Ribot was then standing, to be covered by that great horse. She proved extremely difficult to get in foal and it was only at the last possible opportunity, on June 15, that she conceived. In 1960 she went to Ireland to be covered by her owner's Red God. There she produced Ragusa, a very small and singularly unprepossessing foal. In March the following year Ragusa was moved to the Middleton Park Stud. Every effort was made to improve his physique but he did not help matters by slipping his stifle and having to be confined to his box for a long period. During the summer Captain Guggenheim asked his trainer in England, Captain Boyd-Rochfort, if he would take Ragusa into his stable. Boyd-Rochfort replied that he had twenty-nine yearlings coming in and politely requested that Ragusa be sent elsewhere. Accordingly the colt was sent to the Ballsbridge September Sales where Paddy Prendergast bought him for 3,800 guineas on behalf of Mr J. R. Mullion.

Prendergast gave Ragusa plenty of time to build up his strength and did not run him till October when he won a seven-furlongs race at The Curragh. At three he was unplaced in The Players Navy Cut Trial Stakes at Phoenix Park and second to My Myosotis in The Dee Stakes at Chester. It was after The Derby that he really began to improve at a fantastic pace. With Relko out of the way he won the Irish Sweeps Derby very comfortably. Of course luck was on his side with Relko being suddenly afflicted by mysterious lameness and luck was on his side again in The King George VI and Queen Elizabeth Stakes in that the favourite, Twilight Alley, broke down. Ragusa won that race very easily by four lengths from Miralgo. He was a little bit short of his best when he turned out for The Great Voltigeur Stakes at York and he beat Only For Life by a mere head. In The St Leger, though, he was never in danger of defeat and starting at 5/2 on he won by six lengths from Star Moss. It was a wonderful season for Prendergast, who had also won The Eclipse Stakes with Khalkis, and he finished up as top trainer with a total of £125,294.

Spree, second in The One Thousand Guineas and The Oaks, gained a little compensation when winning The Nassau Stakes at Goodwood. In the latter half of the season, though, the best of the home-trained fillies that could stay was Outcrop, who, like Spree, was by Rockefella. A 1,700 guineas yearling, she won five races including The Yorkshire Oaks and The Park Hill Stakes. She carried the colours of Major Jack Priestman, a Northumbrian who loved every form of sport, and was trained by Geoff Barling. Priestman had become friends with Barling when they were both serving in the Royal Artillery in North Africa.

As money became an increasingly important factor in racing, so the tendency grew to regard racing less and less as a sport, more and more as a business or industry. Not unnaturally, a good many people began to question whether the Jockey Club was keeping pace with the changes that were taking place and were inclined to think that the outlook and attitude of most of the members were better suited to a more leisurely age.

The more progressive members of both the Jockey Club and the National Hunt Committee were in fact far from being averse to change and modernisation. In 1964 a new step forward of some significance was announced, this being the formation of a new supreme authority, the Turf Board, which was formed from the Jockey Club and the N.H.C. and on which there would be continual representation of the policies and the views of the Betting Levy Board.

Broadly speaking, the Turf Board's job would be to deal with general policy, their decisions being carried into effect by the Jockey Club and the N.H.C. The chairman of the Turf Board would serve for five years and would be assisted by two vice-chairmen, one from the Jockey Club, one from the N.H.C., whose term of office would last for two years. It had been an obvious weakness of the old system that the Senior Steward of the Jockey Club only held office for a year and therefore had to give up his appointment just as he was becoming nicely settled in. In addition, under the new arrangement there would be three Stewards of both the Jockey Club and the N.H.C., who would not be called upon to worry about formulating policy but would be charged with the day-to-day conduct of the sport.

The first Chairman of the Turf Board was Sir Randle Feilden, generally acknowledged to be the outstanding administrator in post-war racing. A Lancastrian by origin, Gerry Feilden, as he is generally known, is a square, immensely solid figure who does not look much different at seventy-two from what he did in his twenties, although he may have put on a few stone. At Eton he was formidable on the football field. He has never been much of a horseman—shooting, stalking and fishing are his sports—but a brother-in-law went within a length of riding the winner of the Grand National. He caught the best catch at cricket I have ever seen, mainly because he would have been decapitated if he had not. A fondness for the turf developed at Cambridge, encouraged by a wager on the 100/1 Cesarewitch winner Charley's Mount. From Cambridge he joined the Coldstream Guards where he enjoyed a reputation for shrewdness, toughness and common sense. When I joined the Third Battalion at Chelsea he was acting adjutant and I can personally testify that very little missed his ear or his eye. His worst enemy could never describe him as an intellectual and at one point the promotion examination from subaltern to captain proved an unexpectedly formidable barrier.

In those happy days officers were only rarely called upon to work after midday. There were plenty of opportunities to go racing and usually at least one carload of racegoers left barracks at 12.30 whenever there was a metropolitan meeting. Like most of his brother officers, Feilden, reputed a successful punter on a modest scale, patronised Tattersalls rather than the Members'.

That first bitterly cold winter of the war found him in France commanding a company. There he was spotted by his Divisional Commander, then Major-General B. L. Montgomery, who whisked him away to his staff. He proved himself a forceful and highly competent administrator. He was a Major-General by VE Day and when his military career terminated he was Vice-Quarter-Master-General. Subsequently he was for some years boss of the NAAFI.

41. Major-General Sir Randle Feilden, the first Chairman of the Turf Board

He was a close friend of the late Duke of Norfolk and the first horses he owned were trained at Arundel. Before long he was elected to the Jockey Club and was a Steward from 1952 to 1955 and again from 1959 to 1961. He was made a K.C.V.O. in 1953 for services in connection with the Coronation.

Most people agree that Feilden has done a fine job for racing. He has certainly been unstinting of his time and his energy. He has a bold, forthright approach both to problems and to individuals and if at times he lacks finesse he makes up for it by the straightforwardness of his methods and by his determination to achieve his objective. He has never been an easy man to eyewash and anyone endeavouring to be a trifle 'warm' at his expense is liable to come off second best. On the whole his public relations have been good and whatever his private views about individual journalists he has succeeded in getting on well with most of them and he was always at pains to make himself accessible. Seldom have his robust sense of humour and his power of repartee failed him. His job was certainly not all beer and skittles and if he was obviously a tired man at the end of it this was probably due to a series of clashes with the Levy Board when the Board was under the chairmanship of Lord Wigg. Feilden's successor was Lord Leverhulme, a man of charm, immense kindness and impeccable manners but perhaps a trifle lacking in steel when the game got a little bit rough.

1964 will be remembered as the year in which the last two days of Royal Ascot had to be abandoned. The financial loss suffered by the executive was considerable and this was all the more regrettable as the new Royal Enclosure stand, costing £1¼ million, had just been completed and much of the money spent had had to be borrowed. There was a certain amount of rain on the opening day but trouble really started late on Wednesday afternoon when it began to rain really hard, and by midday on Thursday ·65 of an inch of rain had fallen. After a brief lull it started to rain again just before the first race, which was put back by fifteen minutes. Soon afterwards it was raining in a way that reminded old colonels of the monsoon in Calcutta. Before long the paddock and most car-parks were submerged. At 3.15 racing was called off for the day and racegoers, many of them soaked to the skin, headed soddenly for home. Plans were made to stage nine races on the Friday and nine more on the Saturday but in fact the course never dried out sufficiently on those days to permit racing to take place. This was rather sad for old Trelawny whose target had been to pull off the Ascot Stakes–Queen Alexandra Stakes double for the third year running. In his ninth year and carrying 10 stone he finished second in The Ascot Stakes giving four years and 40 lb. to Delmere, the winner. For two miles he had been well behind and the probability is that he had been left with rather too much to do. Had The Queen Alexandra Stakes been run, he would have obtained a walk-over.

Once again horses from abroad did well in the big races. The French won The Two Thousand Guineas, The King George VI and Queen Elizabeth Stakes and The Champion Stakes while to the Irish fell The One Thousand Guineas and The Derby.

The Two Thousand Guineas was won by Mrs Howell E. Jackson's American-bred colt Baldric II, one of the first crop of runners by that very good American horse Round Table who won forty-three of his sixty-six races. At two Baldric II had won the Prix Tramp at Le Tremblay but in The Grand Criterium he had sapped his strength by running all too freely. Shortly before that event he had been transferred from Étienne Pollet to the stable of Australian-born Ernest Fellows who, during the winter, concentrated on teaching him to settle down. In his first race at three Baldric II dead-heated for second place with Djel in the Prix Djebel at Maisons-Laffitte, the pair finishing inches behind Takawalk. Baldric II created a favourable impression as he had not been subjected to a hard race. At Newmarket he started at 20/1, and taking the lead well before the Bushes he won by two lengths from Fabergé II, subsequently sire of Rheingold, with Balustrade third. He was ridden by the Australian, Bill Pyers, who had never ridden a winner in Europe before. In The Derby Baldric II ran well for a mile and a quarter but failed to stay the distance. He was second to Ragusa in The Eclipse Stakes and returned to England in the autumn to win The Champion Stakes, worth over £27,000 to the winner, by a length from Linacre.

The One Thousand Guineas went to Beatrice, Lady Granard's Pourparler who had been bred by Commander Peter FitzGerald and is by Hugh Lupus out of Review, by Panorama, thus being a half-sister to her owner's Display, second in The One Thousand Guineas in 1962, and to Mr R. C. Boucher's Fleet, who won The One Thousand Guineas in 1967. Pourparler, who had won The National Stakes and The Lowther Stakes at two, won all out by a length from Lord Rosebery's Abernant filly Gwen. In The One Thousand Guineas Trial Stakes at Kempton, run over seven furlongs, Gwen had beaten Pourparler by three parts of a length. Gwen, the smallest filly in the field, played up in the paddock at

Newmarket and also down at the start. The starter eventually told her rider, Peter Robinson, to take up a position as best he could and Gwen, though drawn No. 3, actually started on the far side. She never ran again.

The Derby proved to be a small breeder's triumph as Santa Claus had been bred by Dr F. Smorfitt, a Warwickshire medical practitioner who owned one other mare at the time.

Santa Claus was a bay by the 1945 St Leger winner Chamossaire out of Aunt Clara, by Arctic Prince. Dam of Aunt Clara was Sister Clara, a half-sister by Scarlet Tiger to the brilliant and temperamental Sun Chariot. Sister Clara, who had appalling forelegs, was sold as a yearling at Ballsbridge for 20 guineas to Major E. C. Doyle, a great rider over fences in his day. She never ran. After the triumphs of Sun Chariot, Major Doyle reckoned that the time was opportune for the sale of Sister Clara. He got her in foal to Dastur and sent her to the 1944 Newmarket December Sales where Miss Dorothy Paget bought her for 11,000 guineas. She produced seven winners but none of any particular account. At the age of fifteen she bred Aunt Clara, her ninth foal. As an unraced two-year-old Aunt Clara was sent to the December Sales and Dr Smorfitt bought her for 130 guineas. For him she raced three times unplaced and was then retired to the stud. Santa Claus was her third foal. As a foal he was sent to the December Sales and Mr A. N. G. Reynolds bought him for 800 guineas. A year later he was offered at the Newmarket September Sales and was bought for 1,200 guineas by the Dublin branch of the B.B.A. As for Aunt Clara, she was sold privately before Santa Claus won the Irish Two Thousand Guineas to Mr Tim Rogers, owner of the Airlie Stud and brother of Mick Rogers who trained Santa Claus at The Curragh for the joint owners, his mother Mrs Darby Rogers and the octogenarian Mr John Ismay. Aunt Clara was in foal to Aureole when she was sold. The produce, a colt named St Christopher, was sold as a yearling for 25,000 guineas but failed to make much mark on the racecourse.

As a two-year-old Santa Claus gave proof of his exceptional merit, and in particular of his striking power of acceleration, when he won the important seven-furlongs National Stakes at The Curragh by eight lengths. After that performance he was made favourite for The Derby. It was a wet spring in 1964 with soggy conditions underfoot and his first appearance was on May 16 in the Irish Two Thousand Guineas, which he won by three lengths, ridden by W. Burke, from Young Christopher. His victory was received with exuberant enthusiasm and every Irishman at The Curragh that day went home convinced he had seen the winner of The Derby.

The Derby this year was worth over £72,000 to the winner, more than double the value of any previous 'Blue Riband'. The going was on the soft side. Santa Claus, whom the paddock critics crabbed for his lean and lanky appearance, for being straight in the shoulder and the possessor of allegedly dubious joints, was favourite at 15/8. He was ridden by Breasley, the experienced Eph Smith, who had ridden Blue Peter to victory twenty-five years previously, being up on the second favourite, Lord Howard de Walden's handsome Alcide colt Oncidium.

42.   Scobie Breasley won his first Derby on Santa Claus in 1964 at the age of fifty. He is pictured here in 1968, just before he retired to become a trainer, with Peter O'Sullevan, the journalist and owner

Trained by Jack Waugh, Oncidium had won the Lingfield Derby Trial by five lengths. Unfortunately for Oncidium's backers, he fought for his head at Epsom, pulled his way to the front after a furlong and was a beaten horse with a quarter of a mile still to go. Breasley, as unhurried as ever, made steady progress up the centre of the course from three furlongs out. In fact Breasley's riding was a shade too confident for the nerves of some of the favourite's supporters and it was only well inside the final eighty yards that Santa Claus headed Mr C. W. Engelhard's Indiana, ridden by Lindley, to win by a length. Dilettante II was two lengths away third. Thus in seven years Mick Rogers had trained two Derby winners, the pair of them costing as yearlings a total of under 2,000 guineas. It was Breasley's first Derby win and was achieved at the mature age of fifty.

Oncidium became increasingly obstreperous at home and eventually Jack Waugh suggested to Lord Howard de Walden that a change of surroundings might prove beneficial. Accordingly, before The St Leger, in which he was fifth, Oncidium was transferred to George Todd at Manton. In his final race that season he won the two-miles Jockey Club Cup in faultless style. Todd was very patient in his handling of Oncidium and did not run him in 1965 till The Coronation Cup, in which he decisively defeated his nine opponents. Todd reckoned him a certainty for The Gold Cup, for which he was an even money favourite, but unfortunately he was 'got at' and trailed in nearly twenty lengths behind the winner. He never recovered his best form subsequently. He was exported to New Zealand and proved an outstanding success there as a sire.

Ridden by W. Burke, Santa Claus won the Irish Sweeps Derby with ease to the delight of all Irish followers of racing who were generously prepared to forgive and forget the unfortunate fact that he had been bred in England. The successful jockey slightly surprised English journalists by saying that as usual he would be 'doing his two' that evening.

There were only four runners for The King George VI and Queen Elizabeth Stakes and the many Irishmen present at Ascot regarded the race as no more than a lap of honour for their hero, who started at the unrewarding price of 13/2 on. The going was firm and Santa Claus went down to the start like an elderly hen that was having trouble with her feet but he was never an elegant mover in his slower paces. Far more imposing than the favourite in the way that he strode out and also in his looks was Mrs Howell E. Jackson's four-year-old Nasram II, a half-brother by Nasrullah to the Irish Sweeps Derby winner Tambourine II. He was in fact the last horse that Nasrullah ever sired, that great stallion expiring the day after he covered Nasram's dam.

Pyers set off in front on Nasram II. Santa Claus, again ridden by Burke, never got close enough to make an effective challenge and Nasram II won comfortably by two lengths, thus providing another major triumph for France. Inevitably Santa Claus's reputation was badly dented. He remained a short-priced favourite, though, for The St Leger until the end of August when the bookmakers began to lengthen the odds. Their intelligence service, which makes the K.G.B. look like a troop of incompetent Brownies, had reported that all was not well with Santa Claus. However it was only five days before the race that Rogers announced that the favourite was not certain to run. Three days later Santa Claus was declared a non-runner. In view of the public money at risk in the ante-post market, it was thought that Rogers might conceivably have been a little bit more forthcoming earlier on.

With Santa Claus out of the way, the race was won by Indiana who in a terrific finish beat Beatrice, Lady Granard's filly Patti by a head with Soderini third. Unplaced were the joint favourites I Titan and Baron Guy de Rothschild's Grand Prix winner White Label II. Indiana had been close up second in the Grand Prix but had been rather unconvincing in beating the 33/1 Fighting Charlie by a head in The Great Voltigeur Stakes. Fighting Charlie was in fact an improving horse and won The Gold Cup in 1965 and again in 1966. Indiana, by Sayajirao, was a good, courageous stayer. As such, breeders did not want to know about him when he retired to the stud and before long he had been issued with a one-way ticket to Japan. Santa Claus's final race was the Prix de l'Arc de Triomphe. Ridden by Lindley he ran a fine race but went under by three parts of a length to Prince Royal II, a British-bred son of Ribot. Santa Claus's stud career was a brief one as he died in 1970.

Looks are not everything in racing and before The Oaks everyone had unkind remarks to make about the Alycidon filly Homeward Bound, bred and owned by Sir Foster Robinson, a former Gloucestershire cricket captain, and trained by John Oxley, previously assistant to the late George Colling. A mean-looking, light-framed chestnut, Homeward Bound was a notoriously bad doer at home. However, ridden by Greville Starkey, she handled the very soft ground far more effectively than most of her rivals and won by two lengths from Windmill Girl. In modern times racehorses are seldom owned by serving soldiers but Windmill Girl carried the colours of Lt-Col Sir Jeffrey Darell of the Coldstream Guards who, in partnership with Miss E. B. Rigden, had leased her for racing from her trainer, Arthur Budgett. She went on to win The Ribblesdale Stakes at Royal Ascot while at the stud she had the rare distinction of breeding two Derby winners, Blakeney and Morston. She had been bred by Major Holliday and Arthur Budgett had bought her as a foal for 1,000 guineas.

In August Homeward Bound carried off The Yorkshire Oaks but both she and Windmill Girl were at the tail end of the field in the Prix Vermeille. John Oxley, an Old Etonian and former Rifleman, had his share of successes but he was a bit too forthright and uncompromising for some tastes, while public relations were hardly his strongest point. He retired from training in 1975.

Ragusa had been beaten in The Royal Whip at The Curragh starting at 10/1 on. However, he recovered his form in The Eclipse, which he won from Baldric II. His only other race was the Arc in which he was unplaced. He retired having won £146,524. Incidentally, The Eclipse this year, thanks to a boost of £15,000 from the Levy Board, was worth double what it had been the year before. Before Ragusa's early death at the age of eleven, he had sired a Derby winner in Morston.

Raise You Ten, a Tehran four-year-old trained by Boyd-Rochfort, had won The Doncaster Cup in 1963. This year he won The Yorkshire Cup and The Goodwood Cup. He would very likely have won The Ascot Gold Cup, too, if that race had not been abandoned. In The Doncaster Cup he was caught close to home by Grey of Falloden (it ought to have been 'Fallodon' but his name was spelt incorrectly on registration) to whom he was conceding 8 lb. This in fact was a good performance by Raise You Ten as Grey of Falloden was an outstanding stayer and this five-year-old by Alycidon, trained by Hern, won The Cesarewitch under the stiff burden of 9 st. 6 lb., a record since the race was instituted in 1839. The Sussex Stakes at Goodwood, worth over £15,000 to the winner, went to Mr T. F. C. Frost's Roan Rocket, a grey by Buisson Ardent from George Todd's stable. A 1,800-guinea yearling, Roan Rocket had previously won The St James's Palace Stakes. Today he is a successful sire.

The saddest death this year was that of Captain Peter Hastings-Bass at the age of forty-three. He was in his first year as the Queen's trainer and looked to have a great future ahead of him. He was the only son of the Hon. Aubrey Hastings who trained four Grand National winners and rode one of them to victory himself. At Stowe and at Oxford Peter was an outstanding athlete and but for the war, in which he was wounded while serving with the Welsh Guards, he would probably have played rugby for England. From 1946 to 1952 he assisted the very shrewd Ivor Anthony who had succeeded Peter's father as trainer at Wroughton. In 1954 he assumed the additional surname of Bass to conform with a clause in the will of his uncle, Sir William Bass, who at one time had been the owner of Sceptre.

In the meantime Peter had bought Kingsclere from Evan Williams and, though previously he had been chiefly associated with jumpers, he soon made a success of training on the flat. When stricken with cancer, he faced the inevitable end with a dignified courage that was typical of his character.

At the end of the 1964 season an American, Mrs Howell E. Jackson, was top owner, while the Bull Run Stud which she and her husband owned in America ranked as top breeder. Prendergast was leading trainer but Lester Piggott just pipped the Australians Ron Hutchinson and 'Scobie' Breasley to be champion jockey. Champion sire was 22-year-old Chamossaire who in fact died on November 17.

The season of 1965 was rendered hideous for trainers by the severe coughing epidemic that persisted from the spring to the autumn, reducing the quality of much of the racing. Stables and studs all over the country were affected and certain stallions had to be withdrawn temporarily from service. A number of horses were never quite the same afterwards. Others took a very long time to recover. It was not uncommon to find a horse winning a race after apparent recovery from the cough and then losing its form again completely. Apart from the disappoint-ment caused to owners and the burden of worry inflicted on trainers, it was also a very tricky period for punters.

The Chesterfield Stakes at Newmarket on July 8, won by Track Spare ridden by Lester Piggott, has its place in English racing history as it was the very first race in this country in which starting stalls were used. Stalls are now an accepted part of racing life and there are liable to be shrill yelps of protest if by chance they are not available for some minor fixture. There was, though, considerable oppo-sition to their introduction, not surprisingly since most people connected with racing tend to be allergic to change. There were complaints that stalls made racing too mechanical and would degrade it to the level of dog racing; that the dividend fairly earned by jockeys who were particularly skilful at the gate would be removed; and that the system imposed a great strain on horses and rendered them liable to injury. However, before very long it was realised that stalls are the fairest and most efficient way of starting a race.

The Jockey Club member entitled to most of the credit for the introduction of stalls was Mr Tom Blackwell, one of the more determined and energetic of racing's administrators. He is a man who very sensibly relishes comfort and the good things of life and when war broke out there was interest among his friends as to how he would react to the austerities of military life. In fact he quite enjoyed Sandhurst and rose to be Brigade Major in a Guards Armoured Brigade. He is (or rather was) a good golfer, though less good than his younger brother John who entered for the amateur championship at the mature age of forty-nine and reached the final. Tom Blackwell achieved a rare double in being Senior Steward of the Jockey Club and Captain of the Royal and Ancient at St Andrews. His brother has also been Captain of the R. and A. but in racing he has not gone further than taking time off from being a schoolmaster to act as steward at

Folkestone. Tom Blackwell is noted among his friends for his jovial hospitality during Newmarket race weeks and not for nothing has his home near Bury St Edmunds become known as 'Cirrhosis Hall'. It is well over forty years since Tom Blackwell had his first runner. It was a hurdler at long-defunct Bungay and was ridden by an unknown claiming amateur called Hislop.

Once again the English failed to produce a horse capable of winning The Derby but at least that race was won by a colt of quite outstanding merit, M. J. Ternynck's Sea Bird II, trained by Pollet. Those who sometimes feel slightly depressed by the uninspiring pedigrees of so many yearlings offered for sale can possibly cheer themselves up by remembering that not one of Sea Bird's five immediate dams won a race under the rules of a Jockey Club in any country. The fourth dam, Colour Bar, ran unsuccessfully in sellers but eventually won under Pony Turf Club Rules. She was 'missing, believed killed' in the Normandy fighting.

Sea Bird stood over 16 hands and was a bright chestnut with a white blaze and two white stockings behind. He had a bold, intelligent head and exceptionally powerful quarters. When he was walking it was noticeable that he 'dished' with his off fore. His sire was Dan Cupid, by the American horse Native Dancer. A strongly made, close-coupled chestnut that looked a typical sprinter, Dan Cupid came over to England at two and ran second to Masham in The Middle Park. At three he was unplaced in The Two Thousand Guineas and The Derby. It was widely agreed that he was being run well beyond his proper distance but he dismissed this theory by running that good horse Herbager very close indeed in the Prix du Jockey Club.

Sea Bird ran three times at two. He won the Prix de Blaison and then the seven-furlongs Criterium de Maisons-Laffitte in which he defeated Carvin, later sire of Pawneese. In the Grand Criterium he finished second to his more fancied stable companion, Grey Dawn. However, many who saw that race were of the opinion that Sea Bird could well prove the better horse of the two.

At three Sea Bird won the Prix Greffulhe in a canter from Diatome who had won the Prix Noailles and was later to win The Washington International at Laurel Park. Sea Bird then won the Prix Lupin by six lengths after which Pollet stated that the main objective was The Derby. Sea Bird was at once made favourite for that race. It would be difficult to exaggerate the ease with which he won at Epsom. He passed the post, ridden by Glennon, two lengths ahead of Meadow Court but the distance would have been very much wider if Glennon had not eased him up when victory was certain.

Sea Bird next went for the Grand Prix de Saint Cloud which he won with his customary facility. His final appearance was in the Prix de l'Arc de Triomphe, a race that will never be forgotten by those who had the good fortune to see it. With two furlongs to go the issue clearly lay between Sea Bird and M. Dupré's Reliance, an exceptionally good horse that had won the Prix du Jockey Club, the Grand Prix de Paris and the Prix Royal Oak. The excitement was tremendous but quite suddenly the duel was over. Sea Bird accelerated and in half a dozen strides he was clear. He went on to win by six lengths from Reliance who in his turn was five lengths clear of Diatome. It was a fantastic performance, certainly one of the greatest achieved on a racecourse within living memory.

The power of the dollar soon made itself felt and the American breeder Mr John Galbreath leased Sea Bird, who had won £225,000, to stand in Kentucky. Sea Bird returned to France shortly before he died in 1973. Some of his offspring were tricky and needed careful handling but Gyr was second to Nijinsky in The Derby and won the Grand Prix de Saint Cloud, while that magnificent filly Allez France numbered the Poule d'Essai des Pouliches, the Prix de Diane, the Prix Vermeille and the Prix de l'Arc de Triomphe among her many glittering victories.

The Two Thousand Guineas winner, Niksar, was French-bred but owned by Mr Wilfred Harvey and trained at Epsom by Walter Nightingall. He was in fact the first Epsom-trained winner of the race this century. Bred by the Marquis de Nicolay, he was bought at Deauville by M. André Beaujean on Nightingall's behalf. He ran three times at two and though he did not win he showed promise when third in The Crookham Stakes at Newbury. He started off in 1965 by winning the Two Thousand Guineas Trial at Kempton by six lengths, starting at 100/6. This did not impress racegoers all that much, and ridden by Duncan Keith he started at 100/8 in The Two Thousand Guineas. The very soft going suited him and he won by a length from Silly Season, the favourite. He never won again but was fourth in The Derby and third behind Silly Season in The Champion Stakes. At the end of the season he was sold for export to Australia.

Ian Balding had succeeded Peter Hastings-Bass, whom he had been assisting, at Kingsclere. A notable all-round athlete—he obtained a rugby blue at Cambridge—and a competent amateur rider, Ian is the younger son of the late Gerald Balding, a great polo player and a successful trainer. Silly Season helped Ian, who married Emma Hastings-Bass, to get off to a good start as a trainer. Bred and owned by Mr Paul Mellon, Silly Season is a brown horse by Tom Fool, whose grandsire was Hyperion's half-brother Pharamond, out of Double Deal, a Straight Deal mare that was at one point owned and trained by Tommy Carey, who had ridden Straight Deal to victory in The Derby. She had been bred by Major Jack Paine, at one time Lord Derby's stud manager, and when Mr R. F. Watson sent her up for sale in foal to Pardal she was bought on behalf of Mr Mellon by Clive Graham, for many years 'The Scout' of the Daily Express. At two Silly Season ran four times, winning The Coventry Stakes at Royal Ascot and The Dewhurst Stakes. At three he was in action throughout the season and it was a fine piece of training on Balding's part to keep him in form throughout. Silly Season's victories were The Greenham, St James's Palace and Champion Stakes. At four he won The Lockinge Stakes and was only narrowly beaten in The Rous Memorial, Sussex and Queen Elizabeth Stakes. He was not an easy horse to ride since he had to be held up for as long as possible as he only had a run of about the length of a boys' cricket pitch. Horses like that are apt to make their riders look foolish and more than once the unfortunate Geoff Lewis was sharply criticised for what appeared to be indifferent judgement.

The Derby runner-up, Meadow Court, originally named Harwell Fool, was bred in Ireland by Mrs E. Parker Poe and is a chestnut by Court Harwell out of Meadow Music, by Tom Fool. At the Ballsbridge September Sales he was bought for 3,000 guineas on behalf of the Canadian partners in Alberta Ranches, Mr G. M. Bell and Mr Frank McMahon. Later Mr Bing Crosby took a share in the horse, who was trained by Paddy Prendergast. Meadow Court ran twice at two, on the second occasion winning The Sandwich Stakes at Ascot. In 1965 he began by running second in the one-mile Gladness Stakes at The Curragh and in mid-May he was on offer at 100/1 for The Derby. His price was reduced, though, to 20/1 after he had finished close up second to Ballymarais, a half-brother by Ballymoss to Larkspur, in The Dante Stakes at York. In fact he was improving fast and there was sufficient confidence behind him for him to start at 10/1 in The Derby. Of course the fact that he was ridden by Piggott also affected his price. He justified that confidence by running an excellent race.

He went on to win The Irish Sweeps Derby from Convamore, also by Court Harwell, and The King George VI and Queen Elizabeth Stakes from Soderini and Oncidium. Not surprisingly, he was a red-hot favourite for The St Leger at 11/4 on. It was an appalling day with the rain coming down in torrents and the heavy ground made The St Leger a gruelling test of sheer, slogging stamina. Three furlongs from home Joe Mercer took Mr J. J. Astor's 28/1 outsider Provoke to the front. Meadow Court tried hard to keep in touch but Provoke forged farther and farther ahead, passing the winning-post ten lengths in front of Meadow Court with Solstice five lengths away third.

Meadow Court's final race was the Arc, in which he finished ninth. His efforts, supplemented by those of Convamore, who won The King Edward VII Stakes, resulted in Court Harwell, by Prince Chevalier, being champion sire. However at this point in time Court Harwell was already in Argentina, having been purchased by Senor Miguel Martinez de Hoz for 40,000 guineas, a price that was only a tenth of the value placed on Meadow Court. Senor Martinez de Hoz's father had bought the disqualified Derby winner Craganour, and Rustom Pasha and Bahram also stood at this stud. It was stated that the reason for Court Harwell's sale was that during the three years he stood in Ireland breeders took little interest in him. This seems a rather odd explanation in view of the fact that during those three seasons he covered 125 mares. When trained by Sir Gordon Richards, Court Harwell had been slow to come to hand and was sluggish in his work. He was greatly improved by a sharp course of hurdling from Bob Turnell. Unfortunately for Meadow Court's stud career, his fertility record was soon giving cause for concern.

Provoke, who had won a handicap at York by a head the previous month, was by Aureole out of Tantalizer, a half-sister by Tantième to that stout-hearted stayer Trelawny. He never raced again. It was proposed to keep him in training at four but in fact he was exported to Russia where he died soon after his arrival. His trainer, Dick Hern, completed a rare double when, ten days after Provoke's success, Lord Astor's Craighouse, by Mossborough, won the Irish St Leger.

The One Thousand Guineas went to Night Off, bred and owned by Major L. B. Holliday, who died later that year. Night Off, a Narrator filly that had won The Cheveley Park Stakes the previous autumn, had been coughing early in the spring but had recovered in time to take her chance at Newmarket. Favourite at 9/2 and ridden by Bill Williamson, an unostentatious but extremely effective jockey known as 'the quiet Australian', Night Off just prevailed by a neck in a driving finish against the French filly Yami, ridden by Desaint, whose methods certainly lacked nothing in vigour. Mabel was third. The time was slow due to the heavy going.

It was proposed to run Night Off, who was trained by W. Wharton, in The Oaks and as a preliminary she competed in The Musidora Stakes at York. She ran a lamentable race and was very ill afterwards. A dope test proved negative and probably the true cause of her collapse was the hard race she had at Newmarket so soon after she had been afflicted with the cough. She had to miss The Oaks but had recovered sufficiently to finish second in The Coronation Stakes at Royal Ascot. She disappointed in her subsequent races. The Oaks was won by the American-bred Ribot filly Long Look, bred and owned by Mr J. Cox Brady, Chairman of the New York Racing Association, trained by Vincent O'Brien and ridden by Jack Purtell. She was O'Brien's first ever runner in The Oaks.

When Oncidium was 'got at' before The Ascot Gold Cup and ran far below his true form, the winner was the four-year-old Fighting Charlie, bred and owned by Lady Mairi Bury, youngest daughter of Lord Londonderry, and trained by the former steeplechase jockey Farnham Maxwell. By Ribot's sire Tenerani out of the Cameronian mare Flight of the Heron who had been foaled in 1941, Fighting Charlie was slow to develop. He did not win at two and in ten outings at three he only won once although he did run Indiana very close in The Great Voltigeur Stakes. Before winning The Gold Cup quite comfortably from Waldmeister, winner of the Prix du Cadran, he had won at Liverpool, Lanark and Kempton.

Old age was taking its toll of Trelawny. Now in his tenth year Trelawny did not compete in The Ascot Stakes and in The Queen Alexandra Stakes he was unplaced behind Grey of Falloden. However, his owner evidently did not consider that Trelawny deserved a rest. During the winter the old horse was with Fred Rimell and won three times over hurdles, his successes including The Spa Hurdle at Cheltenham and The Coronation Hurdle at Liverpool.

Prendergast produced a real flyer at Ascot in Mrs Parker Poe's Young Emperor, a grey by Grey Sovereign. Young Emperor won The Coventry Stakes by six lengths and Prendergast declared him to be the best two-year-old he had ever trained. In his next race, The Richmond Stakes at Goodwood, Young Emperor showed he had inherited some of the less desirable traits of his sire as he gave trouble at the start and was deservedly left. However, his only other race that season, The Gimcrack Stakes, he won in brilliant fashion. He failed to train on at three.

The Coronation Stakes went to Mr R. F. Watson's Primera filly Greengage, who got up in the very last stride to beat Night Off. Her success owed not a little to the artistic riding of Breasley. Greengage also won her other two races during the season, The Ebbisham Stakes at Epsom and The Rank Organisation Stakes at Ascot. In each case Breasley's remarkable split-second timing enabled Greengage, later exported to America, to get her head in front right on the post.

The King's Stand Stakes, then worth only £2,050 to the winner, was won by the north-country sprinter Goldhill who was later to acquire some fame as sire of that distinguished hurdler Comedy of Errors.

The royal colours were successful in The Eclipse Stakes for the first time since the victory of the handsome but evil-tempered Diamond Jubilee in 1900. In a terrific finish the Queen's four-year-old Canisbay, a 20/1 outsider ridden by Stan Clayton, won by a short head from Roan Rocket. It was Boyd-Rochfort's fourth success in this event as he had won it before the war with Royal Minstrel, Loaningdale and Boswell. Canisbay, bred by his owner, is a big chestnut by Doutelle, whose early death represented a severe loss to British breeders, out of Stroma, by Luminary. He never ran at two. The following year he won The Wood Ditton Stakes at Newmarket but after finishing second to Con Brio in the Brighton Derby Trial he suffered from persistent lameness so that it was found necessary to take him out of training and turn him out. He did not run again for over a year when he was third in the mile-and-a-half Churchill Stakes at Ascot. Then came his surprise victory at Sandown, following which his form was disappointing. He has done well as a sire in Italy, among his offspring being Orange Bay who beat Bruni in the 1976 Hardwicke Stakes.

The Queen had another little-anticipated success when her five-year-old Aureole gelding Apprentice won The Goodwood Cup, the other runners being Grey of Falloden, Philemon, Trelawny and Soderini, who had won The Hardwicke Stakes and been second in The King George VI and Queen Elizabeth Stakes. Earlier in the season Apprentice, then still a maiden, had won The Yorkshire Cup at York. He had broken down at the 1963 Ascot July Meeting and had been fired, gelded and turned out. In fact The Yorkshire Cup was his first racecourse appearance for nearly two years. Apprentice's victories represented a fine piece of training by Boyd-Rochfort.

At Goodwood Roan Rocket met with a further disappointment as in The Sussex Stakes he was well beaten by Prendergast's three-year-old Carlemont, by Charlottesville. It is perhaps worth noting that The Arundel Castle Private Sweepstakes—an event commonly if unjustifiably referred to as 'The Castle Carve-up'—was won by Delaunay, a half-brother by Donore to Brigadier Gerard.

Before being exported to Japan, Primera had shown himself to be far more successful as a sire of fillies than of colts and one of the best of his fillies was Lt-Col (later Sir) John Hornung's Aunt Edith, trained by Noel Murless. She was out of Fair Edith, a Hyperion mare bred by Lord Rosebery. A granddaughter of the One Thousand Guineas winner Plack, Fair Edith proved of no account on the racecourse. Lord Rosebery eventually sent her up to the December Sales where the West Grinstead Stud bought her for 3,500 guineas. Her son Domesday, by Supreme Court, who was to win the Rosebery Memorial Handicap at Epsom, was then a foal.

Aunt Edith ran twice without success at two. At three, starting at 25/1, an unusual price for a mount of Piggott, she was beaten a head by Arctic Melody in The Musidora Stakes at York. She did not compete in The Oaks and in fact was not seen out again till The Nassau Stakes at Goodwood in July. She won that event very easily by four lengths. Her only other race in 1965 was the Prix Vermeille at Longchamp, worth on this occasion £30,485 to the winner. In a field of twenty-two she won by no less than eight lengths from Dark Wave with the Oaks winner Long Look third. Doubtless good fortune was on her side as three fillies fell and others suffered considerable interference. All the same, it was a notable success.

It was expected that Carlemont would win The Queen Elizabeth II Stakes at Ascot in September but he fell a victim to the cough. In his absence the race was won by Mrs H. H. Renshaw's four-year-old Derring Do, a Darius colt trained by Arthur Budgett. Bred by the Burton Agnes Stud and a member of the Lost Soul family, Derring Do was a good miler that at two had won The Imperial Stakes and The Cornwallis Stakes. All told he won six races and over £20,000 in stakes. In view of his own marked stamina limitations—his dam was by Abernant—it came as a surprise to find him siring a St Leger winner, certainly a very moderate one, in Peleid. He also sired the Two Thousand Guineas winners High Top and Roland Gardens.

One of the more interesting two-year-olds in 1965 was Lady Zia Wernher's Charlottown trained at Lewes by Gosden who was unfortunately compelled by ill-health to retire at the end of the season, the stable being taken over by Gordon Smyth who had previously trained at Arundel. Charlottown could hardly be crabbed for his pedigree as he is by Charlottesville, winner of the Prix du Jockey Club and the Grand Prix, out of his owner's triple classic winner Meld. By no means as striking in appearance as his dam, Charlottown ran in three seven-furlongs races and won them all, namely The Solario Stakes at Sandown, The Blackwood Hodges Stakes at Ascot and The Horris Hill Stakes at Newbury. Workmanlike rather than brilliant, he clearly stayed well and appeared a possible candidate for the 1966 Derby.

Mr Paul Mellon's Berkeley Springs, an American-bred filly by Hasty Road, won The Cheveley Park Stakes while Track Spare, by Sound Track, won The Middle Park Stakes from a substandard field for his owner-trainer, Ron Mason of Guilsborough, who had only paid 1,600 guineas for him as a yearling. In the autumn Mr J. A. C. Lilley's Pretendre, trained by Jack Jarvis, proved himself a stayer of high promise, winning The Dewhurst Stakes and then The Observer Gold Cup, formerly The Timeform Gold Cup. He was a chestnut by Doutelle out of Limicola, by Verso II, and had been bred by the late Princess Royal, Mr Lilley buying him as a foal for 3,600 guineas.

Besides Major Holliday, some notable figures in the racing world died in 1965, among them Captain Charles Moore C.V.O., M.C. and Mr Archie Scott. Captain Moore, who was eighty-four when he died, was in no small measure responsible for the many racing successes the Queen enjoyed between 1954 and 1960, during which period she was twice leading owner. An Irishman who served with distinction in the Irish Guards in World War I, Moore had been appointed King George VI's racing manager in 1937. Under his shrewd and experienced direction, the royal studs emerged from a period of decline. One of Moore's more notable acts of wisdom was to recommend the appointment of Captain Cecil Boyd-Rochfort as royal trainer. These two Irishmen, both a longish way past the first flush of impetuous youth, formed a formidable and highly successful partnership. It is sometimes stated that Moore, who retired in 1963, was responsible for the purchase of the famous Sandringham foundation mare Feola, but in fact she had been bought by his predecessor, Brigadier H. A. Tomkinson.

Archie Scott had been ill for a long time when he died aged sixty-one. An Old Etonian, very tall, very thin, gentle and quietly humorous, he became a man of great influence in the bookmaking profession. He had begun his career in 1928 by becoming clerk to Mr Sidney Fry, who had been amateur billiards champion. This was followed by a short spell on his own after which he joined Mr Dick Fry (no relation to Sidney). The firm of Scott–Fry was very well known on the rails up till the war when Scott was commissioned into the Green Howards, serving in France and North Africa. After the war he was on his own for a bit but this venture was not wholly successful and in 1961 the business was taken over by Alfred Cope.

Scott's importance lay not in his own bookmaking but in all the arduous work he did on various committees. He was a man of total integrity who was completely trusted and his influence was immense. He was Chairman of the National Bookmakers and Associated Bodies Joint Protection Association, Chairman of the National B.P.A., a member of Tattersalls Committee on Betting, Chairman of the Association of Rails Bookmakers, Chairman of the Bookmakers Betting Levy Committee and their member on the Horserace Betting Levy Board. He served as a member of the Peppiatt Committee that paved the way for the Betting Levy Act. The public image of the bookmaker has never been a very flattering one. No man has ever done more than Scott to improve it.

His closing years were overshadowed by tragedy. His wife was killed in a car accident near Newmarket; his second son, a soldier, was killed on active service at Aden.

Finally, 1965 saw the death of the best known of all racing tipsters, 'Prince' Monolulu, in private life Mr Peter McKay, a coloured man of uncertain age and unknown country of origin. With his baggy trousers and ostrich feathers and his raucous cry of 'I gotta horse' he was an easily recognisable figure and no film even remotely concerned with racing was complete without at least one brief appearance by the 'Prince'.

II

ENGLAND won The Derby in 1966 for the first time since 1961. This gratifying achievement, though, was assisted by the fact that no French horses were allowed to run in this country from mid-May till November 1. The reason for this was an outbreak in Europe of equine anaemia, commonly known as swamp fever. The French were not entirely frank about this outbreak and because of that the authorities here became suspicious. In consequence a long and drastic ban was imposed on all horses from suspect areas of the Continent. The French are great umbrage takers and they certainly took umbrage on this occasion, electing to adopt the view that a largely artificial barrier had been erected to prevent French horses winning the big English races. In this country a particularly unpleasant virus put the unfortunate Dick Hern's stable out of action for a period of months.

The Budget brought bad news for racing in the form of the S.E.T. levy of 25s a week in respect of every male employee in a non-productive industry, and half that rate for women and for boys under the age of eighteen. This hit nearly every section of the racing industry and the total cost to the sport was estimated to be £3½ million.

A new direct tax on betting was applied to turnover at the rate of 2½ per cent on all money staked. The stated aim of the Treasury was to raise £17 million.

The price of bloodstock had slumped in 1965 but 1966 proved a better year. At the main yearling sales there was many a lively duel between representatives of Messrs D. Robinson and C. W. Engelhard, these two between them paying a total of 215,000 guineas for forty yearlings. The December Sales showed a modest improvement on the previous year, though well below the figures for 1964 when there had been a dispersal of stock belonging to the National Stud. The bloodstock market was helped by an agreement on the Capital Gains Tax negotiated between the Joint Turf Authority and the Board of Inland Revenue. Under this agreement a considerably higher proportion of expenditure on horses in training was permitted than had been anticipated.

The Jockey Club had always shown itself in its silliest mood when refusing to give women the right to hold a licence to train even though it was apparently quite in order for a woman to control a stable providing the actual licence was held by a male underling. The precise reason for this attitude by the Jockey Club was never explained. Perhaps it was just an interesting example of male chauvinism. It was hinted that Weatherbys were distressed at the thought of a woman entering the weighing room and catching a glimpse of a jockey without his trousers on. One normally rational member of the Jockey Club declared that a woman trainer might be influenced by an 'undesirable' man; apparently it was not thought possible that a man could be influenced by an 'undesirable' woman. Two indomitable fighters for the women's cause were Mrs Florence Nagle and Miss Norah Wilmot and these two surely deserve a race named in their honour on Oaks day. Finally, under the threat of High Court action, the Jockey Club gave way and nearly everyone was delighted to see them beaten. At Brighton on August 3 Miss P. K. Wolf's Pat, trained by Miss Wilmot, became the first winner on the flat to be officially trained by a woman.

The tote, so often accused of stodginess, had a bright idea and instituted the Jackpot Pool. It got off to a spirited start at Royal Ascot where for a five-shilling stake a widow in Suffolk, an off-course punter, scooped a prize of £63,114.

For the fourth year running an Irishman, on this occasion Vincent O'Brien, was top trainer. Piggott was champion jockey for the third year running. Sad to say, Piggott's long association with Noel Murless ended this year. The split really began when Piggott insisted on riding O'Brien's Valoris in The Oaks. The trouble was patched up temporarily but the real break came when Piggott rode O'Brien's Pieces of Eight in The Champion Stakes. In the future Piggott was to ride as a free-lance, an arrangement that probably best suited his particular characteristics and way of life.

The French won The Two Thousand Guineas with Kashmir II but for patriotic Englishmen the pain was eased by the fact that Kashmir II was owned by a Yorkshireman, Mr Peter Butler, while Irishmen could take pride in the fact that the winner had been bred in Ireland by Mrs Jane Levins-Moore at the Yeomanstown Stud in Co. Kildare. Kashmir II is by Tudor Melody, a son of Tudor Minstrel that had also been bred at Yeomanstown and had been sold as a yearling for only 610 guineas. At two Tudor Melody headed The Free Handicap, having won five of his six races including The Chesham Stakes at Royal Ascot and The Prince of Wales's Stakes at York. He was then exported to America, where he won twice. When his racing career was over, a group of young Irish breeders brought him back to Ireland to stand at the Mount Coote Stud. After Kashmir II had won The Two Thousand Guineas, the National Stud bought fourteen shares in Tudor Melody and the rest of his stud life has been passed at the National Stud at Newmarket.

Dam of Kashmir II was Queen of Speed by Blue Train out of Bishopscourt. He was thus in-bred to Mumtaz Mahal's half-sister Lady Juror, dam of Fair Trial, since Lady Juror was grandam of Tudor Minstrel and also of Bishopscourt.

Kashmir II cost 8,600 guineas as a yearling. Trained by Mick Bartholomew, he won three times as a two-year-old, one of his victories being in the Prix Robert

Papin at Maisons-Laffitte. He was also third behind Soleil in the Prix Morny at Deauville. He started off at three by winning the Prix Djebel at Maisons-Laffitte in impressive fashion after which Jimmy Lindley was engaged to ride him at Newmarket.

Favourite for The Two Thousand Guineas at 9/4 was Pretendre, who had looked a good·stayer in the making the previous autumn when he won The Dewhurst Stakes and The Observer Gold Cup. It had not been the intention to run Pretendre in The Guineas but on his first appearance at three he had won The Blue Riband Trial Stakes at Epsom in such brilliant style that plans were changed and it was decided to let him take his chance at Newmarket. Second favourite was Piggott's mount Young Emperor, while Kashmir II was soundly backed at 7/1.

Approaching the Bushes Young Emperor was in front and going so smoothly that he looked a probable winner, the only visible danger being Pretendre who was handily placed close behind him. By the time the Dip had been reached, though, the position had changed. Young Emperor was in trouble while Pretendre could only keep going at one pace. On the other hand Lindley had brought Kashmir II along with one long run to take the lead from Young Emperor and victory appeared within his grasp. Up the hill, though, Pretendre's unconsidered stable-companion, the 66/1 outsider Great Nephew ridden by Rickaby, put in a tremendous challenge and in the end it was only by a short head that Kashmir II prevailed. Celtic Song was third, just in front of Young Emperor.

Bartholomew had timed Kashmir II's preparation to perfection. Kashmir II was never as good again afterwards and later in the year was syndicated and retired to the stud. Great Nephew, bred and owned by Mr Jim Philipps, is a bay by the great sprinter Honeyway out of Sybil's Niece, an Admiral's Walk mare descended from Pretty Polly through Sister Sarah. At two he had been nothing out of the ordinary, winning once in seven outings. He started off at three by falling in The Coventry Stakes at Kempton. After The Guineas he was narrowly beaten by Silly Season in The Lockinge Stakes and was third in both The St James's Stakes at Epsom and The Queen Anne Stakes. He was then transferred to Étienne Pollet's stable at Chantilly. In France he won a seven-furlongs event at Deauville and was just beaten by Silver Shark in the Prix du Moulin. The following season he came to England for The Eclipse and ran second to Busted. In France he won the nine-furlongs Prix de Paques at Le Tremblay, the mile-and-a-quarter Prix Dollar at Longchamp and the one-mile Prix du Moulin. He was second in the Prix Ganay. Retired to the stud in England, he surprised his most fervent admirers by siring a really good mile-and-a-half horse in Grundy.

Pretendre had been favourite for The Derby at 3/1 but after his Guineas failure his price was extended to 6/1. A new favourite was found in Mr Charles Engelhard's Right Noble, a big, dark brown colt by Right Royal V that was trained by Vincent O'Brien. Right Noble owed his position to a facile victory in The White Rose Stakes at Ascot, an event in which he defeated Sodium, who had run well as a two-year-old in good-class races. Right Noble was not in fact a prepossessing animal. He was lacking in quality and his action was inclined to be laboured. Unkind critics suggested that with a few minor alterations he would be the ideal mount for a trombone player in the Household Cavalry mounted band. Poor Right Noble, he was to meet his death in a novices' hurdle at Sandown.

Lord Rosebery's General Gordon, a Never Say Die colt that had split a pastern at two, came into The Derby reckoning after winning The Chester Vase. He continued to please Jack Jarvis and in his final Derby gallop he was pulling over Pretendre and other horses when he broke a leg and had to be destroyed. Another Chester winner to advance his Derby prospects was Mr Engelhard's Grey Moss, by Mossborough. Trained by O'Brien, Grey Moss won The Dee Stakes by the unusual margin of twenty lengths.

Charlottown was due to make his first appearance of the season in the Brighton Derby Trial on May 9. There was a big crowd at Brighton hoping to see him perform but in fact he never took the field as he had been found to be suffering from a bruised foot that morning. In his absence the Brighton Trial was won by Sodium. Although faced by only three opponents, Frank Durr and Sodium got into a fearful tangle and Sodium had to produce an impressive burst of speed inside the final furlong to beat Crisp and Even by three parts of a length.

With only sixteen days to go before The Derby, Charlottown's injury, trifling in itself, was serious and he drifted in the ante-post betting to 20/1. However, he was found fit to compete in the Lingfield Derby Trial on May 13. The going was soft, particularly on the round course. Actually it was only after a morning inspection by the stewards that racing was declared possible.

Reasonably enough, Ron Hutchinson, who was partnering Charlottown for the first time, was concerned to give his mount as unexacting a race as possible. Consequently he permitted Charlottown to take matters far too easily early on. The unfortunate result was that Charlottown found himself in a hopeless position at the tail-end of the field and by half-way it was clear that only by the most strenuous efforts would he stand a hope of even being placed.

In the meantime Brian Taylor drove Black Prince II into a long lead and headed for home as hard as he could go. He entered the straight at least twenty lengths ahead of Charlottown. From two furlongs out Charlottown really got down to business and made extremely rapid progress but, just as it was beginning to look as if he might conceivably trouble the leader, he started to hang badly to the left. Hutchinson had to stop riding him in order to straighten him out and, though Charlottown staged a final rally, Black Prince II beat him by three lengths. Charlottown had had a hard race and the riders in the stands, who so rarely make a mistake, gave poor Hutchinson a fearful lambasting. It came as no surprise when Breasley was announced as Charlottown's partner at Epsom. As a matter of fact this engagement was almost nullified when Breasley took a crashing fall at Windsor two days before The Derby. The veteran Australian, though, was tougher than he looked and a man whose nerve was not easily shaken. He declared himself fit for duty at Epsom and proved it by riding a couple of winners on the opening day of the meeting.

Joint favourites for The Derby proved to be Right Noble and Pretendre at 9/2. There was no lack of money for Charlottown at 5/1 while Grey Moss was backed down from 100/7 to 8/1. The going was good. Just as Charlottown was being mounted by Breasley, he trod on his own off fore, the plate being torn off. There was a nerve-racking delay of a quarter of an hour while Gordon Smyth's own blacksmith replated Charlottown, a tricky business since Charlottown suffered from thin-soled feet. However, the operation was successfully concluded and Charlottown duly joined the others down at the gate.

The leaders from the start were Right Noble and St Puckle. After half a mile Pretendre was not in the leading fifteen while Charlottown had only three horses behind him, one of them being Grey Moss. It was seldom indeed that Breasley could ever be lured far away from the rails and despite his unpromising position he elected to make his effort on the inside. By a miracle he obtained a completely trouble-free run. Not for a stride did Charlottown have to be checked and nor did he have an opportunity to hang to the left as he had done at Lingfield. Breasley's risky gamble paid a handsome dividend.

Right Noble and St Puckle were both done with early in the straight and their places were taken by Black Prince II and Sodium. With a quarter of a mile still to go Sodium was in trouble and it looked as if Black Prince II was going to emulate his sire, Arctic Prince, and win. Pretendre and Charlottown, though, were both improving their position and at the distance Pretendre, on whom young Paul Cook had ridden a cool and well judged race, headed Black Prince II. The one danger to Pretendre was Charlottown, whose final piece of sheer good fortune had been when Right Noble and Black Prince II both came away from the rails and let him through.

Just inside the final furlong Pretendre led Charlottown by a neck. However, Breasley, as cool-headed as ever, balanced Charlottown and then gave him two taps with the whip. Charlottown responded courageously and got his head in front close to home to win a splendid race by a neck. Jack Jarvis afterwards used to regret that Cook had not seen fit to give Pretendre just one sharp reminder with the whip. 'I don't like seeing a game horse hit,' he was wont to say, 'but after all, this was The Derby.'

Pretendre won The King Edward VII Stakes but failed in The Eclipse Stakes and The St Leger. Before The St Leger he had been sold for something like £150,000 for export to America. After his son Canonero II had won the Kentucky Derby, Pretendre came back to England, it being the intention of his owner, Mr Nelson Bunker Hunt, to give him two mating seasons each year, one in the Northern Hemisphere, one in the Southern. Pretendre had just come back from New Zealand in 1972 when he dropped down dead from heart failure.

There were dope tests after the race on Grey Moss, who had performed in deplorable fashion, and on Sodium, whose rider, Durr, said he (Sodium) had appeared to choke at Tattenham Corner. Both tests proved negative.

It was a popular Derby victory, not least because many people were delighted to see the race won by a son of that great race-mare Meld, whose stud career till then had been disappointing. Charlottown was her fifth foal. Naturally, though, there were regrets that 'Towser' Gosden had been deprived by ill health of the opportunity to saddle a Derby winner.

Charlottown provided a second and final Derby winner for 'Scobie' Breasley, one of the most gifted Australian jockeys ever to ride in this country. Cool, immensely shrewd and with an excellent head for business, he was masterly in his judgement of pace and excelled at split-second timing. Perhaps there was a shade too much finesse in his methods to make him a hero with the general racing public. At times he puzzled the average racegoer who could not make out, after Breasley had won by inches, whether he had been flat out or had had several pounds in hand. No one was superior to him in winning on a two-year-old without subjecting it to a severe race. Like most Australians he hankered for the rails and a certain inflexibility in this respect occasionally resulted in him being boxed in unnecessarily. Toughness and pluck number among his characteristics and his nerves remained unimpaired by some nasty falls he had late in his career. When he retired in 1968, he set up as a trainer at Epsom and soon proved he had a flair for the job. At the end of 1975 he moved to Chantilly to be private trainer for Mr Ravi Tikkoo. In 1976 Breasley won over £300,000 in prize money in France for Mr Tikkoo, who, however, apparently objected to the Rules of Racing being applied by the French authorities to two of his horses. It looks as if Breasley will be on the move again soon with the United States as his destination.[1]

Charlottown was an odds-on favourite for the Irish Sweeps Derby but he lost by a length to Sodium. George Todd had fancied Sodium tremendously at Epsom but, as has been stated, Sodium for some reason or another appeared to choke at Tattenham Corner. At The Curragh Breasley was criticised for leaving Charlottown with too much to do. This was unfair, though, as Charlottown was only half a length behind Sodium at the entrance to the straight.

Bred by the Kilcarn Stud Ltd, Sodium is a bay by Psidium out of Gambade, a Big Game mare that was a full sister of Lord Astor's Oaks winner Ambiguity. Gambade herself was hopeless as a racing proposition. When her racing career, such as it was, was over, Aly Khan bought her for 4,200 guineas but two years later he sold her for 4,500 guineas to Major E. O'Kelly's Kilcarn Stud. In 1964 Mr Radha Sigtia asked Todd to buy three yearlings for him for approximately £10,000. Todd bought one, Sodium, who cost 3,500 guineas.

Sodium's next race was The King George VI and Queen Elizabeth Stakes at Ascot. He was second, beaten half a length, to the year older Aunt Edith who ran her race out with exemplary courage. On August 13 Sodium and Charlottown met again, this time in The Oxfordshire Stakes, run over a mile and five furlongs at Newbury. Charlottown was ridden by Jimmy Lindley as in the first race that afternoon the unfortunate Breasley had a horrible fall which rendered him *hors de combat* for the remainder of the season. There were only four runners but Mr J. J. Astor kindly started Desert Call II to ensure a good pace. The race proved

---

[1] He in fact did move to the United States at the end of 1976.

something of a fiasco as Sodium, the odds-on favourite, could hardly raise a gallop. Charlottown won by five lengths from Desert Call II with Sodium eight lengths in the rear of the runner-up. The inevitable dope test proved negative but it was found that Sodium was suffering from severe kidney trouble. For the time being it seemed he might be unable to run in The St Leger.

Happily Sodium recovered in time to compete at Doncaster. Charlottown was favourite at 11/10, Pretendre second favourite at 3/1. Sodium was easy to back at 7/1. Faultlessly ridden by Durr, Sodium challenged well below the distance and ran on gamely to master Charlottown close to home and win by a head. He was the first classic winner trained by George Todd, one of the ablest and most like-able members of his profession. Neither Sodium nor Charlottown ran again that season but it was decided that both would stay in training at four.

Both The One Thousand Guineas and The Oaks went to Vincent O'Brien's stable. Winner of The One Thousand Guineas was Mrs J. P. Mills's Glad Rags, who had been bred by Captain Darby Rogers and was ridden by Paul Cook. Then just twenty years of age, Cook, like other successful riders including Pat Eddery, had been apprenticed to 'Frenchy' Nicholson at Cheltenham. At this point of time Cook looked like going right to the top of the tree but possibly his rise had been a shade too rapid for his own good and a little later his career went temporarily into rather sharp reverse. After all, it is a demanding test of character for a boy under twenty-one to find himself earning almost as much as the Prime Minister and the recipient of a lot of publicity, too. Fortunately Cook survived his setback and is now well to the forefront again.

Starting at 100/6, Glad Rags won by a neck from Mr Paul Mellon's big American-bred filly Berkeley Springs with the French filly Miliza II third. Miliza II, winner of the Prix Imprudence, was favourite at 11/10 on. In her previous race Berkeley Springs, winner of The Cheveley Park Stakes the previous autumn, had finished nineteenth of twenty in the One Thousand Guineas Trial at Kempton. In this very wet spring the gallops at Kingsclere had become saturated and Ian Balding had had difficulty in getting Berkeley Springs really fit.

The start of The One Thousand Guineas had been delayed for fifteen minutes by the antics of Lady Sassoon's Crepello filly Soft Angels, who in September had won The Royal Lodge Stakes from Sodium, Glad Rags and Black Prince II. Mr Alec Marsh showed remarkable patience with Soft Angels, a patience that the connections of other fillies in the race thought was perhaps a trifle excessive. At all events Soft Angels eventually got off, only losing about four lengths. Miliza II was squeezed for room and lost about half that amount. However, Miliza II soon worked her way into a good position and had every chance entering the Dip, but she just failed to quicken from that point. Glad Rags led over a furlong out but was headed on the hill by Berkeley Springs. She rallied bravely, though, and regained the lead close to home to win by a neck.

Glad Rags is by High Hat, who originally stood at the stud where Glad Rags was bred but was later exported to Japan, out of Dryad, by Panorama. A close-coupled chestnut by no means outstanding in looks, she had been bought for

6,800 guineas as a yearling. She was far more effective on good going than when the ground was soft. This she demonstrated to the consternation of her backers in the Irish One Thousand Guineas when she finished well down the course behind her far less fancied stable companion, Valoris. At Royal Ascot she was third in The Coronation Stakes behind Haymaking after losing a lot of ground at the start, having become involved in the misbehaviour of Soft Angels. In The Sussex Stakes she finished last.

Mathet, trainer of Miliza II, was disgruntled, not perhaps unjustifiably, over the long delay at the start of The One Thousand Guineas and observed with some asperity that it was high time the English got down to using starting stalls. In fact all the classic races were started from stalls the following year.

Following her victory in the Irish One Thousand Guineas, Valoris, owned by Mr (later Sir) Charles Clore, was all the rage for The Oaks, the more so since Piggott had insisted on riding her and had declined the mount on Murless's Varinia, winner of the Lingfield Oaks Trial. Starting at 11/10, Valoris won smoothly from Berkeley Springs with Varinia third. A bay or brown filly by the Italian St Leger winner Tiziano out of Vali by Sunny Boy II, Valoris had been bred in France by M. R. Forget and was purchased at Deauville for approximately £10,000. Grandam of Vali was Carpet Slipper, who bred Godiva and Windsor Slipper. The remainder of Valoris's career was undistinguished. She started at 7/2 on in the Irish Guinness Oaks but could not act on the firm ground and was only fifth behind Merry Mate, a Ballymoss filly whose dam was the Gold Cup winner Gladness.

With no competitors from France The Coronation Cup took less winning than usual. It was won by Mr Louis Freedman's four-year-old I Say, who had been third in the 1965 Derby. Being a stayer by the staying Sayajirao, breeders had no time for him here and he was exported to Brazil.

There were seven runners for The Ascot Gold Cup and the connections of five of them had been doing their best to secure the services of Piggott. Piggott on such occasions does not just play hard to get: he is hard to get and takes time to make up his mind. On this occasion he eventually opted for Aegean Blue whom he had ridden to victory in The Chester Cup and The Usher-Vaux Brewery Gold Tankard at Ayr. This time Piggott's judgement, usually shrewd, was well off target and Aegean Blue never looked like winning.

Favourite at 15/8 was Fighting Charlie, on whom Piggott had won the previous year. He had won a couple of preliminary races and hopes of success ran high till the Sunday before the Royal Meeting began, when it was discovered that both his forelegs were inflamed, the near one being, according to his trainer, 'as big as a telegraph pole'. However, the Lambourn vet, Mr Frank Mahon, then got to work. Fighting Charlie was strapped up in harness and given electrical treatment combined with repeated applications of clay and camphor. He did not leave his box till the Tuesday. On the Wednesday he was given two seven-furlongs canters, and as he pulled up sound it was decided to let him take his chance.

Greville Starkey rode Fighting Charlie, who moved smoothly into the lead half a mile from home. As he did so, a great cheer went up. Suddenly, though, Fighting Charlie's legs began to hurt him. He checked and then swerved so violently that the commentator thought he had run out of the course. Though Starkey managed to straighten him out again, he was half a dozen lengths behind Biomydrin on the final bend. It certainly looked as if he was done for but he pulled himself together and staged a remarkable rally. Lengthening his stride, he produced a turn of speed that swept him past Biomydrin and he passed the winning-post no fewer than eight lengths to the good. No wonder he was given a hero's reception as he entered the winner's enclosure. He never ran again. Breeders had shown little disposition to make use of his services when he died six years later.

The most impressive two-year-old at the meeting was undoubtedly Beatrice, Lady Granard's Bold Lad, winner of The Coventry Stakes. Trained by Paddy Prendergast, this bay colt by the great American sire Bold Ruler, a son of Nasrullah, was exceptionally powerful and mature and might well have been taken for a three-year-old. Later he won The Champagne Stakes and The Middle Park Stakes and headed The Free Handicap with 9 st. 7 lb.

Odds-on favourite for The Hardwicke Stakes was Aunt Edith, who the previous month had won The Yorkshire Cup at York with singular ease, beating Fighting Charlie by four lengths. On this occasion she ran in deplorable fashion, finishing fifth of six behind Prendergast's Prominer, by Beau Sabreur, who won by six lengths. A dope test was ordered but it was not until August 4 that this test was announced to have proved negative. Not surprisingly, it was a common view that something had been found but not in sufficient quantity for a positive result to be declared.

Aunt Edith next ran in The King George VI and Queen Elizabeth Stakes. Ridden by Piggott, she was on offer at 7/2, Sodium being favourite at 6/4. With two furlongs to go Piggott dashed Aunt Edith into a two lengths lead. Sodium went in hot pursuit and steadily narrowed the gap. The filly was desperately tired in the final hundred yards but she battled on with marvellous courage and had half a length to spare at the finish. In her final race she was unplaced in the Arc. She was then bought for $185,000 by Mr Ogden Phipps, Chairman of the New York Jockey Club, and departed to America to be mated with Bold Ruler.

Pretendre was made favourite for The Eclipse but the distance was too sharp for him. A decisive winner was O'Brien's handsome black three-year-old, Pieces of Eight, owned by the Countess de la Valdene, sister of Mr Raymond Guest. By Relic out of Baby Doll, Pieces of Eight had cost 7,500 guineas as a yearling and was something of a late developer. His grandam was that fast and gallant mare Bebe Grande who was placed in both The Two Thousand and The One Thousand Guineas. In the autumn Pieces of Eight won The Champion Stakes from Ballyciptic who had also been runner-up in The Eclipse Stakes.

Another valuable race to go to Ireland was The Sussex Stakes, won by Paveh, bred and owned by Mr P. A. B. Widener and trained by T. D. Ainsworth. A son of Tropique and winner of the Irish Two Thousand Guineas, Paveh was in front a furlong out but was soon afterwards headed by Silly Season who looked certain to win. Silly Season, though, once again showed that he possessed a very short run. He faltered close to home and Paveh was able to rally and get his head in front again on the post. The riders in the stand criticised Geoff Lewis for having made his effort too soon.

For the third year running the Queen won The Goodwood Cup, this time with the three-year-old Gaulois whose pedigree, as his name suggested, had a strong French accent since he was by Auriban out of Gallega, by Galcador. Gallega was a half-sister to that fine race-mare Almeria who, however, possessed some curious quirks, one being a marked reluctance to pass her stable-companion Agreement on the gallops at home or on the racecourse. This little peculiarity cost her The Doncaster Cup in which Agreement acted as her pacemaker.

The 1966 Doncaster Cup was won by a horse of distinctly peculiar temperament, Mrs O. V. Watney's Piaco, by Pandofell out of Pink Parrott, by Pardal. Trained by Geoff Barling, Piaco ran a couple of times at two and was so thoroughly obstreperous that he was cut. This operation seemed to produce little beneficial result and in the following spring he was as bloody-minded as ever. In fact, there was talk of sending him up to the sales, an idea reinforced by his first racecourse appearance at three when he sweated up, gave trouble at the start and ran indifferently. Thereafter, however, he became a reformed character, at least as far as actual racing was concerned. He won six of his seven remaining races, these including, besides The Doncaster Cup, The Kenneth Robertson Stakes at Newbury and The Michael Sobell Handicap at Sandown. The following year he won the Northumberland Plate with 9 st. 1 lb. That popular number 'Raindrops keep falling on my head' would hardly have appealed to Piaco as he objected strongly to being out in inclement weather and getting his head wet.

Ryan Price gave proof, if any was required, of his skill as a trainer by winning The Cesarewitch with Lord Belper's eight-year-old gelding Persian Lancer. This patched-up veteran was scoring for the first time since his three-year-old days yet carried immense confidence and landed a considerable gamble.

In addition to Bold Lad, two-year-olds of obvious ability and high promise for the future were Royal Palace, Reform and Ribocco. A bay by Ballymoss out of Crystal Palace, by Solar Slipper, Royal Palace was bred and owned by Mr Jim Joel and trained by Noel Murless. At Royal Ascot he was obviously still backward when he ran in The Coventry Stakes but greatly pleased his trainer by the speed he showed for nearly five furlongs even though he finished unplaced. He did not run again till he won The Acomb Stakes at York in August. His final outing of the season was in the one-mile Royal Lodge Stakes at Ascot. This he won despite being caught flat-footed at the start and losing half a dozen lengths so that he was last on the final bend. Many who watched him that day reckoned they had seen the winner of the 1967 Derby.

A bay by Pall Mall out of Country House, by Vieux Manoir, Reform was bred and owned by Sir Michael Sobell and trained by Sir Gordon Richards. As a yearling he was a mean and undersized specimen. Accordingly he was excluded from the Ballymacoll Stud yearlings being sent up for sale as it was thought he would be a poor advertisement for the draft. His start was a modest one. Friendless in the market at 25/1, he finished sixteen lengths behind the speedy Manacle in The Half Moon Stakes at Kempton in April. He then proceeded to win all his next six races ending up with The Clarence House Stakes at Ascot. By the end of the season it was being regretted that the former ugly duckling held no classic engagements.

Mr C. W. Engelhard's Ribocco, a bay by Ribot out of Libra, by Hyperion, was bred in America and cost 35,000 dollars as a yearling. Trained by Fulke Johnson Houghton, Ribocco, a neatly made colt that did not appear to hold much scope for physical development, ran four times. On his first appearance he won The Ecchinswell Stakes at Newbury, starting favourite at 5/4. The following month he won The Washington Singer Stakes at Newbury. At the St Leger meeting he took on the formidable Bold Lad in The Champagne Stakes and ran him to three-quarters of a length. Opinions greatly varied as to how much, if anything, Bold Lad had in hand. Ribocco's final race that autumn was The Observer Gold Cup. The opposition did not appear to be particularly strong and he started at 9/4 on. He did not have matters all his own way, though, and in the end he was flat out to beat Starry Halo by three parts of a length.

Among those who died in 1966 was Captain Charles Elsey, aged eighty-four. Never has there been a northern trainer more widely liked or so greatly respected. Though his long career was interrupted by World War I, in which he served in the Yorkshire Dragoons, and restricted in its scope by World War II, he nevertheless saddled the winners of 1,548 races worth nearly £800,000. He never trained a Derby winner but won The Two Thousand Guineas with Nearula, The One Thousand Guineas with Musidora and Honeylight, The Oaks with Musidora and Frieze, and The St Leger with Cantelo. He was a man of total integrity, a sportsman in the true sense of that brutally mistreated word, a fine judge of bloodstock and the most loyal of friends. His elder brother took orders and became a bishop. On his retirement Captain Elsey's stable was carried on by his son Bill.

Other deaths in 1966 were those of Colonel Giles Loder, owner-breeder of the 1920 Derby winner Spion Kop, and of Mr Joseph McGrath, who did so much to improve the prestige and prosperity of Irish racing and who won The Derby in 1951 with Arctic Prince.

The season of 1967 was a good one for home-trained horses. For once there was not a single success by an overseas challenger in the classics, and in fact there was not a winner from the Continent throughout the entire season. In the four previous seasons an Irishman had ended up as top trainer. This time no Irish trainer figured among the leading twelve.

It was a memorable year for Noel Murless, who won three classic races and whose winnings for his owners added up to a then record total £256,899, the previous

43.   Doug Smith, five times champion jockey who rode 3,111 winners, retired in 1967 to become a trainer; and the Newmarket trainer Geoffrey Brooke to whom Smith was first jockey for many years

best figure having been £145,899 established by himself in 1959. With Piggott riding free-lance, Murless's jockey was the Australian George Moore. This rather highly-strung individual soon proved himself to be a beautiful horseman and a rider of the very highest class. He enjoyed many notable successes, including The Derby on Royal Palace, but it is doubtful if his sojourn here was really a happy one. In September he revealed that threats were being made against his wife and daughter and that his flat had been ransacked. Those responsible were never discovered. He did not return to England in 1968.

Piggott missed some big winners by going it alone but he ended up as champion again. Joe Mercer was in the lead in mid-August but then injured his spine badly in a fall at Folkestone and was out of action for the rest of the season. Breasley missed a month's riding after a fall at Ascot.

Doug Smith, younger brother of Eph, retired to take up training. Five times champion, he had ridden his first winner as far back as 1931 when he was fourteen years old and apprenticed to Major F. B. Sneyd, reputed to be a tough master but a good trainer of jockeys. Doug never rode a Derby winner or an Oaks winner— Epsom was probably a longish way from being his favourite course—but he was without a superior over the Rowley Mile. He won The Two Thousand Guineas twice and The One Thousand Guineas twice, too. A fine judge of pace, he excelled in long distance races, winning The Gold Cup twice, The Goodwood Cup three times, The Doncaster Cup seven times and The Cesarewitch five times. A genuinely popular character who was never bothered by problems of weight, he rode 3,111 winners, a figure surpassed only by Sir Gordon Richards, whose total was 4,870.

The sport's financial problems continued to grow. Grants from the Levy Board had enabled many courses to spend money on building and improving the standard of comfort available but it was soon discovered that expenditure on bricks and mortar did not result in increased attendances. It could be argued, though, that attendances might have declined disastrously if racecourses had not made some effort to conform to the general rise in the standard of living.

The introduction of starting stalls, though widely approved by punters, did not bring about an increase in the volume of betting. At the start of the season the English handlers were assisted by a team of experienced men from France and television viewers with sharp ears were able to add some unusual words to their French vocabulary. Another innovation designed to please punters was the Jockey Club's decision to publish the overnight draw in 1968.

At the termination of the government's first full year of betting taxation, the sum realised turned out to be £31,650,000, whereas the yield anticipated had been put at between £11 million and £17 million. Some £27 million had been derived from horse-racing. With rather naïve optimism, the rulers of the sport expressed hopes that some of the money raised would be ploughed back into racing. Of course nothing of the sort happened despite warnings of the folly of killing the goose that laid a golden egg of such generous dimensions.

The Turf Board came to the conclusion that the condition of racing demanded a really thorough investigation and accordingly it established the Racing Investigation Committee under Sir Henry Benson to make a detailed study of the financial structure and requirements of the sport. Sir Henry, a former President of the Institute of Chartered Accountants, was to be assisted by Lord Abergavenny (Joint Turf Authorities), Sir Rex Cohen (Jockey Club) and Major W. D. Gibson (National Hunt Committee).

A committee under Lord Porchester looked into the question of race planning. In particular the conditions for, and the timing of, prestige races were reviewed to ascertain whether they were really suited to the needs of high-class horses, both at home and abroad.

It was a blow to the administration of racing during this period of many changes when Bill Weatherby, Secretary to the Jockey Club, died from a heart attack at London Airport. Weatherbys were then in the throes of modernisation and in November a computer designed to handle the bulk of their clerical work came into operation.

In the spring the National Stud was opened to the public. The stud had the right sort of director for this innovation as Lt-Col Douglas Gray, who had ridden in the Grand National and won the blue riband of pig-sticking, the Kadir Cup, was not averse to a touch of showmanship in addition to maintaining a high level

44.   Lord Wigg, who succeeded Lord Harding in 1967 as Chairman of the Horserace Betting Levy Board, talking to jockey Jimmy Lindley, now a BBC commentator, in 1968

of professional competence. A new stallion was acquired in the American-bred Stupendous, who was purchased jointly by the National Stud and Wing-Commander Tim Vigors for about £220,000. There was a quick return on this outlay as Stupendous won two nice races before being sent off to England. Unfortunately, Stupendous, a son of Bold Ruler, found scant favour with most breeders, some of whom passed uncivil remarks to the effect that he looked ideally suited to sire Household Cavalry chargers. His sojourn in this country was not of a lengthy duration and in 1972 he was packed off to Japan.

Lord Wigg was appointed to succeed Lord Harding as Chairman of the Levy Board. This was an appointment of the utmost significance since the Levy Board controlled the purse-strings of racing at a time when financial considerations were of paramount importance. Racing tends to be a conservative sport in every sense of that adjective and few individuals deeply involved in it—Mr William Hill, the bookmaker, was an exception—could be said to hold left-wing views.

Lord Wigg's appointment, therefore, was not received with tumultuous applause, particularly as he was reckoned to be a very outspoken individual—though perhaps unduly sensitive to criticism of himself or of his views—with strongly expressed dislikes and no noticeable compunction in treading weightily on toes that happened to be in his way. However, there were plenty of factors in his favour. He knew a lot about racing, particularly about the betting side, from his experiences as punter, racegoer, owner, and one-time member—a very diligent one, too—of the Racecourse Betting Control Board and the Horserace Totalisator Board. Because of his knowledge and the customary thoroughness of his homework, he had been of the utmost value in the passage of the Betting and Gaming Act. Above all he had always been a doughty fighter with few holds barred if ever things got a bit rough. Even those who liked him least admitted his determination to help racing, and not least to assist those in the racing industry who were at the foot of the wage scale or who had suffered misfortune through sickness or injury.

Obviously it was desirable that Lord Wigg worked in amity and co-operation with the Jockey Club and the National Hunt Committee. Equally obviously there were dangers of a clash of personalities and of basically differing viewpoints on how the bulk of the levy was going to be spent.

Of the fancied candidates for The Two Thousand Guineas, the first to make his reappearance was Ribocco. Favourite for The Craven Stakes at Newmarket, he disappointed in the paddock as he hardly seemed to have grown at all, nor was he conspicuous for muscle. He ran a mediocre race and was only fourth behind Mr Hollingsworth's Sloop, to whom he was conceding 13 lb. His price for The Two Thousand Guineas was at once extended to 33/1 and three days subsequently it was announced that he would not compete in that event. A few days later Bold Lad mortified his admirers by his display in The Tetrarch Stakes at The Curragh when he scraped home by a neck from Mark Scott, whose handicap rating was 16 lb. lower than that of the winner. In the meantime it looked as if there was going to be a strong challenger from France when Mme G. Courtois's Taj Dewan, by Prince Taj, won the Prix Montenica at Maisons-Laffitte in pleasing style.

Joint favourites on the day of the race were Royal Palace, who had had no preliminary outing, and Bold Lad, while Taj Dewan was a popular each way chance at 4/1. The massive Bold Lad was the pick on looks. Taj Dewan, rather of the lean, greyhound type, did not give the critics much to enthuse about; nor did Royal Palace who was backward in his coat, sweating over his loins, and conveying a certain disquieting air of nervous tension. Approaching the Bushes the leader was Golden Horus with Taj Dewan and Bold Lad hard on his heels and Royal Palace handily placed. At the top of the hill Freddie Head on Taj Dewan and Des Lake on Bold Lad challenged more or less simultaneously. Taj Dewan at once accelerated and shot into the lead but Bold Lad's response was less enthusiastic and he veered to the right as Golden Horus closed the gap on the rails. Lake was compelled to snatch Bold Lad up and then switch him, after which manoeuvre the Irish colt stood no chance. Some people reckoned Bold Lad had been desperately unlucky but his head was twisted sideways and he was not travelling like a winner before the worst of his troubles occurred.

In the meantime Moore balanced Royal Palace and asked him for his effort. Royal Palace immediately quickened and went in hot pursuit of Taj Dewan whom he caught and headed half-way up the hill. At one point Royal Palace led by a neck but Taj Dewan refused to give in and the photograph showed that Royal Palace was only a short head to the good at the winning-post. Missile was third and Golden Horus fourth. Thus Royal Palace had emulated Crepello who ten years previously had won The Two Thousand Guineas on his first appearance of the season.

Royal Palace had shown that he possessed excellent speed while his pedigree suggested that he was likely to stay a mile and a half. He did not run again before The Derby, for which he was favourite at 7/4. He looked better and above all calmer than he had done on Guineas day. Piggott's mount, Ribocco, was on offer at 22/1. He had failed in The Dee Stakes at Chester and then in the Lingfield Derby Trial. However, his appearance was certainly more pleasing than in the spring and with the advent of warmer, sunnier weather he was clearly beginning to thrive.

Fifth at Tattenham Corner, Royal Palace moved smoothly into the lead just over a quarter of a mile from home and seemed assured of victory. Piggott, however, was not going down without a struggle. He steered Ribocco wide at Tattenham Corner and then began to make steady progress up the centre of the course well away from any other competitor. At one point, amid growing excitement, Ribocco must have almost drawn level with the favourite, but Royal Palace still had a bit in reserve and when Moore gave him a couple of taps with the whip he quickened to win by two lengths and a half. Dart Board finished strongly to take third place behind Ribocco.

It was a genuinely popular victory quite apart from the not unimportant fact that the winner was a heavily backed favourite. Mr Jim Joel, born in 1894, is one of the best liked members of the Jockey Club—quiet, unassuming and generous, a great supporter of racing under both Rules. He is of a markedly different type from his father, the late Mr J. B. Joel who won The Derby with Sunstar and Humorist. Joel senior was a self-made man who had amassed a fortune quite early in life in South Africa, making a certain number of enemies in the process. He did not believe in luck but in hard work and plenty of it. His son, a lifelong bachelor, is a very much gentler character and it is difficult to believe he has an enemy in the world. During World War I he served in the 15th/19th Hussars. He happened to mention in a letter home from France that he was short of a charger. His father promptly sent him out a horse that had been second in The Middle Park. It was just before the battle of Arras and a breakthrough by the cavalry was part of the plan. Fortunately the animal was tired after a bad journey as it had to move up, too, with the rest of the regiment to the battle area. It was entrusted with a good deal of its owner's kit and Mr Joel had no great hopes of seeing his horse or his belongings again. He was unduly pessimistic as the new charger took to warfare like a duck to water, and survived till the Armistice, after which he returned to England and won a couple of handicaps at Nottingham.

At his stud at Childwickbury, near St Albans, Mr Joel has always aimed to produce the high-class middle-distance horse. Unfortunately, Major Portion proved an inadequate successor to Court Martial, whom Mr Joel had bought from Lord Astor, while Royal Palace until 1977 failed to come up to expectations as a sire. Royal Palace's victory was very much a Joel family triumph as he is descended from Mr J. B. Joel's mare Absurdity, who was foaled in 1903 and whose descendants have won every classic race for either Mr J. B. Joel or his son. Among these classic winners was Absurdity's son, the unpredictable St Leger winner Black Jester, whose daughter Black Ray has become one of the most famous mares in the Stud Book.

Royal Palace missed tempting engagements to concentrate on The St Leger and the chance of becoming the first Triple Crown winner since Bahram. Ribocco, though, went for the Irish Sweeps Derby, which he duly won from Sucaryl and Dart Board. He started favourite for The King George VI and Queen Elizabeth Stakes but could do no better than finish third to Busted and Salvo. He was beaten, too, in the mile-and-three-quarters March Stakes at Goodwood which Dart Board won by a head from Tumbled with Ribocco six lengths away third. This was a rather unsatisfactory race in which neither Breasley on Dart Board nor Piggott on Ribocco were seen to their usual advantage.

It had been intended to run Royal Palace in The Great Voltigeur Stakes, a recognised St Leger trial, but he rapped himself at home and, though the injury was not serious, he did not run. That event was won very easily by Prendergast's Great Host, by Sicambre out of The One Thousand Guineas winner Abermaid. Despite the supposedly trivial nature of Royal Palace's injury, adverse rumours about his well-being began to circulate. However, he worked well on the morning of September 2. Newspapers carried headlines stating that Royal Palace was certain to run in The St Leger. Murless himself tended to be less optimistic. He emphasised that the worries were by no means over and that the leg was still being hosed twice a day to keep it cool. On September 9 Royal Palace worked in a thick mist which reduced visibility to a furlong. It was reported that he had gone well but in fact he blew so much afterwards that his trainer doubted his ability to race three days later. After a conference with Mr Joel, Royal Palace was taken out of The St Leger. Murless was chided by certain sections of the press for not having been more communicative.

In Royal Palace's absence, Ribocco started joint favourite for The St Leger with Hopeful Venture, an Aureole colt that belonged to the National Stud but was leased to the Queen for racing and was trained by Murless. Hopeful Venture did not run at two. He started off at three by winning The Wood Ditton Stakes at Newmarket and The Grosvenor Stakes at Chester. At Royal Ascot he lost The King Edward VII Stakes by inches to Mariner but then won The Princess of Wales's Stakes at Newmarket and The Oxfordshire Stakes at Newbury. In The St Leger Hopeful Venture ran a good race but Ribocco had a bit too much pace for him at the finish and beat him by a length and a half. Ruysdael was third just in front of Dart Board, who had anything but a clear run.

Ribocco ran twice after The St Leger. He ran a great race in the Prix de l'Arc de Triomphe to finish third behind Topyo and the English-trained Salvo, beaten a neck and a short head. Had he enjoyed a trouble-free run he might just about have won. In his previous race Salvo, whom Harry Wragg trained for Mr G. Oldham, had won the Grosser Preis von Baden. Ribocco was then sent to America for The Washington International at Laurel Park. He was probably feeling the effects of his hard battle at Longchamp as he was never going well and finished unplaced behind the British-bred Amerigo's son, Fort Marcy.

Ribocco was bred in Kentucky by Mrs Julian G. Rogers but his pedigree is essentially European as he is by Ribot out of Libra, by Hyperion. Libra was bred by Mrs R. Digby and won a two-year-old race at Folkestone in 1956. At the end of that year she was sent to the December Sales and was bought for 8,300 guineas by the Anglo-Irish Agency. Dam of Libra was the speedy Portlaw mare, Weighbridge, whose granddaughter Never Too Late II won The One Thousand Guineas and The Oaks. As a yearling Ribocco was bought for 35,000 dollars at the Keeneland Summer Sales by Mr Engelhard's racing manager, Mr David McCall.

On October 1 Hopeful Venture was first past the post in the Prix Henry Delamarre, worth over £11,000 to the winner, at Longchamp, but was disqualified and relegated to second place, first place going to the English filly In Command from Harvey Leader's stable. The decision was a just one. Hopeful Venture returned to France for the Prix du Conseil Municipal but ran poorly. It was decided to keep him in training for another season.

Murless and Moore landed the Two Thousand Guineas–One Thousand Guineas double, the winner of the fillies' race being Mr R. C. Boucher's Fleet, who had won The Cheveley Park Stakes the previous autumn. In her preliminary outing before The Guineas Fleet had disgraced herself and shocked her trainer by refusing to line up for the Classic Trial Stakes at Thirsk. She was left and took no part. At Newmarket, Fleet, a magnificent bay with tremendously powerful quarters, was certainly the pick of the field on looks. She was second favourite at 5/1, the hot favourite at 11/10 being the American-bred, French-trained Fix the Date, by Swaps out of the dual classic winner Never Too Late II. Fix the Date looked dangerous at the Bushes but failed to stay and was in trouble in the Dip. Fleet went to the front with just over a furlong to go and kept going well to beat Mr Stanhope Joel's 66/1 outsider St Pauli Girl by half a length with Lacquer a head away third, inches in front of Pia who had just lacked a little bit of extra speed in the closing stages. Lacquer may indeed have been a somewhat unlucky loser of this extremely exciting race as she was flying at the finish after meeting with considerable interference. Bred and owned by Mr R. B. Moller and trained by Harry Wragg, she is by Shantung out of the Molecomb Stakes winner Urshalim, by Nasrullah. Subsequently Lacquer won the Irish One Thousand Guineas and The Cambridgeshire. In The Cambridgeshire she carried 8 st. 6 lb. and gave 5 lb. to Wolver Hollow who was third.

Fleet ran a good race in The Oaks but the final furlong was too much for her and she finished fourth. However, she won The Coronation Stakes at Royal Ascot, in which Lacquer was fourth and, after failing in The Eclipse Stakes behind her less fancied stable-companion Busted, she ended her career by winning The Michael Sobell Stakes at Ascot. This was run over a mile, her best distance. In due course her owner chose to sell her for export to America.

Fleet was bred in Ireland by Commander Peter Fitzgerald and was bought as a yearling at Newmarket for 11,000 guineas by Mr Boucher. She is by Immortality out of that illustrious mare Review, by Panorma out of a half-sister to the speedy Careless Nora. Immortality, by Never Say Die, showed promise at two when trained by Boyd-Rochfort but split a pastern and never ran. Sold for 600 guineas as a prospective stallion, he stood for some years in Ireland before being exported to Argentina. He is the only unraced horse to have sired an English classic winner this century. Why, one may well ask, was Immortality selected as the mate for Review? It so happened that Review was one of those rare but eminently desirable mares which, in the words of the old saying, would produce a winner by a book-maker. She was, however, difficult to get in foal and came into season very late. The important thing in her case was getting her in foal rather than the careful selection of a mate. As soon as she came into season, she was hustled off to Immortality who was then conveniently stationed just up the road.

Commander FitzGerald, late of the Royal Navy, had bought Review for 1,550 guineas, chiefly because his father had owned her great-grandam, a mare called Traverse. Rarely indeed do racing or breeding transactions prove so profitable. Fleet was Review's sixth foal and sixth winner. Previous winners had included Spithead, by Guersant, who topped the Irish Free Handicap in 1958; Display, by Rustam, second in The One Thousand Guineas, winner of the National, Cheveley Park and Coronation Stakes; and Pourparler, by Hugh Lupus, winner of The One Thousand Guineas, the National and Lowther Stakes. Following the successes of Fleet, three of Review's offspring were sold as yearlings for what was then a record price in this country. In 1967 Democratie, by Immortality, made 36,000 guineas. She won four races in France, including the Prix de la Forêt. Two years later, La Hague, by Immortality, made 51,000 guineas. She was a winner in France. In 1971 came Princely Review, a colt by Native Prince that Sir Douglas Clague bought for 117,000 guineas. Unfortunately, Princely Review proved a singularly moderate racehorse though he did eventually succeed in winning a small handicap at Salisbury as a four-year-old.

The Oaks provided a rare classic success for the north, the winner being Pia, the very first animal that Bill Elsey trained at Malton for Countess Margit Batthyany, owner of the Erlenhof Stud in Germany. A 100/7 chance, Pia was ridden by Edward Hide and ran on gamely to win by three parts of a length from St Pauli Girl. At two Pia had won The Cherry Hinton Stakes and The Lowther Stakes. She was rather disappointing after The Oaks but dead-heated with Pink Gem for The Park Hill Stakes. She is by Darius out of Peseta II, by Neckar. The German-bred Peseta II won races in France and is a descendant of the famous Plucky Liège.

The Derby winner Charlottown reappeared in the mile-and-a-half John Porter Stakes at Newbury in April. He duly won but was flat out to beat Salvo by a head.

As Salvo, by Right Royal V, later won The Yorkshire Cup, the Hardwicke Stakes and the Grosser Preis von Baden, besides being second in The King George VI and Queen Elizabeth Stakes and only just losing the Arc, Charlottown had nothing of which to be ashamed. At Epsom Charlottown won a slow-run race for The Coronation Cup by two lengths, despite hanging to the left, from the 1966 Prix du Jockey Club winner, Nelcius. Sodium, running for the first time that season, was sixth of seven. In the Grand Prix de Saint-Cloud Charlottown ran the only poor race of his career and was down the course behind Taneb who beat Nelcius by a short head. Unfortunately Charlottown never had a chance to redeem his reputation as he never ran again. Never an imposing individual, he failed to make his mark as a sire in Britain and was exported to Australia in 1976.

The Ascot Gold Cup was reckoned a good thing for Madame F. Dupré's four-year-old Danseur, by Tantième. This handsome, massive bay colt had won the 1966 Grand Prix and in 1967 he had won the Prix du Cadran. What few Ascot punters knew was that he had had leg trouble between the Prix du Cadran and Ascot. Moreover the Ascot going, firm for the first three days, was all against him. He broke down on his off foreleg in the straight, finishing third behind Parbury and Mehari, who fought out a desperate battle. Parbury, powerfully ridden by Joe Mercer, got up in the very last stride to win by a short head. Danseur never ran again.

Parbury, by Pardal out of a mare by the great stayer Alycidon, was bred and owned by Major H. P. Holt and trained by Derrick Candy whose very first Gold Cup runner he was. Candy, whose stable is now carried on by his son Henry, was originally a regular soldier in the Sherwood Foresters. After three years as assistant to Miss Nora Wilmot, he took out a licence on his own account in 1936. A man of great charm and high competence, he won a lot of races before his retirement, including The Cambridgeshire with King Midas and Negus. Parbury, who remained in training in 1968, eventually went to Chile as a stallion, while Mehari, a son of Lavandin, subsequently won the Prix Kergorlay at Deauville before being sent off to Poland.

Reform had started the season by getting narrowly beaten by Play High in The Greenham Stakes at Newbury. He then won The St James Stakes at Epsom on Derby day by a length from Golden Horus and followed that up by winning The St James's Palace Stakes at Ascot by a head from the 20/1 outsider Chinwag with Bold Lad and Wolver Hollow close up third and fourth respectively. This was a most exciting race and the nerves of some of Reform's bolder supporters were strained to an almost intolerable extent. It was, as it happened, not one of Breasley's more brilliant efforts. Thinking he had the race firmly in his grasp, he eased Reform inside the final furlong, not noticing Chinwag who came with a great run and almost caught him. An enormous sigh of relief could be heard when it was known that the photo was in favour of Reform. Reform's trainer, Sir Gordon Richards, observed: 'Scobie would have been on the first boat to Melbourne if it had gone the other way.'

Reform won The Sussex Stakes quite comfortably but in The Wills Mile at Goodwood a month later he was beaten a length by Mrs Murless's St Chad, to whom he was conceding 5 lb. Breasley was inclined to blame the moderate pace at which the race was run but if the pace was not to his liking it was really up to Breasley to adopt more enterprising tactics. As it was, he tried to give St Chad not only weight but a start as well.

Reform won The Queen Elizabeth II Stakes by ten lengths from Track Spare, but his crowning triumph came in The Champion Stakes, which he won decisively by two lengths from Taj Dewan with Royal Palace third and Pia fourth. From the manner in which Reform finished he might well have been able to stay a mile and a half. What a pity it was that because of his own apparent lack of promise in his youth and the early closing dates that then existed for the classics, he was never entered for The Two Thousand Guineas and The Derby.

As far as Royal Palace was concerned, the writing was on the wall before the race began. In the paddock he was not on good terms with himself at all. He was sweating over his loins and was dull and heavy in his coat. He looked thoroughly tucked up and wintry. Reform on the other hand was the very picture of health and condition, a striking tribute to his trainer's skill.

Reform was retired to the stud and among his winners have been Polygamy (Oaks) and Admetus (Washington International). Royal Palace remained in training to redeem his reputation the following year.

Returning to Royal Ascot, St Pauli Girl, beaten by less than a length in both The One Thousand Guineas and The Oaks, suffered another vexatious defeat, going under by half a length to the Duke of Devonshire's Park Top, trained by Bernard van Cutsem, in The Ribblesdale Stakes. In fact Park Top won a great deal more easily than the narrow margin indicated.

A fine big bay, Park Top was bred by Mrs Leonard Scott at the little Buttermilk Stud near Banbury. There were only four mares there and 1967 was a memorable year for the Stud as, apart from Park Top, Mrs Scott had also bred Luciano, the best three-year-old in Germany. Sire of Park Top was Alycidon's son Kalydon, whom van Cutsem owned, while her dam was Nellie Park, by Arctic Prince, who had at one time carried the Duke's colours though without distinction. Nellie Park was out of Oola Hills, by Denturius, and was thus a half-sister to that fine sprinter Pappa Fourway. As a yearling Park Top was bought for only 500 guineas by van Cutsem who passed her on to the Duke. She never ran at two. Before her Royal Ascot success she had won at Windsor and at Newbury. Subsequently she competed against older horses in the mile-and-a-half Brighton Cup at Brighton and won comfortably carrying 8 st. 2 lb. It was intended to run her in The Yorkshire Oaks and the Park Hill Stakes but she fell lame and was compelled to miss those events. She was not at her best when she failed in the Prix Vermeille, after which it was decided to keep her in training the following season.

It poured with rain on the Thursday night of the Royal Ascot meeting and the going was soft on the Friday. This suited Salvo, who was taking on Sodium in The Hardwicke Stakes. Sodium conceded his rival 4 lb. It proved to be a terrific race between these two. In the straight they went right away from the other runners and indulged in a duel on their own. First one and then the other appeared to hold the advantage and, though both were obviously weary, Sodium may have been just the more weary of the two as he was inclined to hang and inflicted on Salvo at least one fairly severe bump. With fifty yards to go, Sodium drew on his final reserves and obtained a very narrow lead, but Salvo refused to accept defeat and in the last few strides he staged a courageous rally that deservedly secured him the prize. It was a memorable battle between two very game horses. Probably the race got to the bottom of Sodium who ran without distinction four times subsequently. At the end of the season he was sold privately to go to France as a stallion.

It was pointed out that Salvo's victory was a striking example of the international character of modern racing. Salvo himself, a plainish chestnut, was bred in America and cost only 9,500 dollars at the Saratoga Summer Sales. His sire was the French-bred Right Royal V, his dam the Italian-bred Manera. His owner, Mr Gerry Oldham, is an Englishman who served in the Coldstream Guards but is now a financier resident in Switzerland. The jockey was the Australian Ron Hutchinson but at least the trainer Harry Wragg is thoroughly English!

The King's Stand Stakes went to a very good and exceptionally stout-hearted sprinter in the three-year-old Be Friendly, trained in the little Epsom stable of Cyril Mitchell for Mr Peter O'Sullevan, probably the most consistently well-informed racing journalist of his time, not least in respect of French racing, and known to millions for his high level of professional expertise as the B.B.C.'s main race commentator on television. By Skymaster out of Lady Sliptic, by Preciptic, Be Friendly cost only 2,800 guineas as a yearling and proved a wonderful bargain. At three, in addition to The King's Stand Stakes, he won The Two Thousand Guineas Trial at Kempton, The Ayr Gold Cup and The Vernons November Sprint Trophy at Haydock, which he had also won at two. The following year he dead-heated for the Prix du Gros-Chêne at Chantilly and won the Prix de l'Abbaye de Longchamp. At five he won The Sceptre Stakes at Kempton and The Palace House Stakes at Newmarket. As a sire he has so far been perhaps a shade less successful than his many admirers anticipated.

The Eclipse Stakes and The King George VI and Queen Elizabeth Stakes were both won by Mr Stanhope Joel's Busted, a bay four-year-old by Crepello out of Sans le Sou, by Vimy. Mr Joel bought Sans le Sou as a yearling for 750 guineas. She won a minor event at Baldoyle at three and then started to break blood vessels. Busted was her second foal.

At two and three Busted was trained at The Curragh by 'Brud' Fetherstonhaugh. He was a useful performer and receiving 10 lb. he beat Pieces of Eight in the Gallinule Stakes but he was not rated among the pick of his age in Ireland in 1966 and the best that Ireland could produce were inferior to Sodium and Charlottown. As a four-year-old Busted, little known at the start of the season to the English racing public, was trained by Noel Murless. By the end of July 1967 he was by common consent rated the best middle-distance horse in Europe.

He began in April with a comfortable victory in The Coronation Stakes at Sandown. Not long afterwards he pulled a muscle at home—he was said to have been working well with Royal Palace—and could not run again till The Eclipse

45.   Trainer Noel Murless, owner Mr Stanhope Joel and jockey George Moore talking after the latter's success on Busted in The King George VI and Queen Elizabeth Stakes in 1967

Stakes which, as far as he was concerned, was regarded chiefly as a tuning-up race for The King George VI and Queen Elizabeth Stakes. The stable jockey, Moore, was up on Fleet at Sandown, while Rickaby had the mount on Busted who won in authoritative fashion by two and a half lengths from Great Nephew with Appiani third. At Ascot, Moore rode Busted, who won decisively from Salvo with Ribocco third. This was a most impressive performance as with three furlongs to go he was eight lengths behind Salvo whom he defeated by three.

Not surprisingly in view of his Ascot triumph, Busted was then prepared for the Arc. As a preliminary he went to Longchamp on September 3 to run in the Prix Henri Foy. He won by four lengths. It was a great disappointment when not long afterwards he injured a tendon. He never raced again and was retired to the stud where he has done well, among his winners being Bustino who carried off the 1974 St Leger.

At Goodwood there was fun with the Jackpot. Nobody found all six winners on Tuesday, Thursday or Friday. The result was a total of £127,157 to be carried forward to Friday's pool. On Friday followers of racing went Jackpot mad and the aggregate soared to £380,898 even though telephone lines to tote offices were jammed for hours on end and probably more than half the people who wanted to try their luck were unable to get on.

It looked a very easy card on the Friday with small fields and several favourites likely to start at odds on. The dividend in fact would have been a small one but for Caergwrle, a Crepello filly trained by Noel Murless for his wife. A hot favourite at 5/2 on for The Findon Stakes, she unseated Moore in her stall and, dropping to her knees, she somehow managed to squirm out underneath the front gate. She then bolted the length of the track, was caught, led back, put back in her stall and eventually took part in the race. She finished twelve lengths behind the winner. The eventual dividend paid to 409 lucky punters was one of £745. The following year Caergwrle won The One Thousand Guineas.

The Gold Cup winner Parbury did not add to his reputation in The Goodwood Cup, finishing more than six lengths behind Wrekin Rambler, trained by Sir Gordon Richards.

Top of the Two-Year-Old Free Handicap with 9 st. 7 lb. was Petingo, trained by Sam Armstrong for the Greek shipping magnate Captain Marcos Lemos. Captain Lemos had been unfortunate in 1965 when he paid 27,000 guineas for Grecian Sea who was killed in an accident before he ever saw a racecourse. Petingo was bought by Armstrong for 7,800 guineas and was a big bay colt of outstanding quality by Petition out of Alcazar, by Alycidon. Undefeated in three races in 1967, Petingo's victories included The Gimcrack Stakes and The Middle Park Stakes. There seemed every prospect that he would prove a high-class miler at three.

Next to Petingo in The Free Handicap came Vaguely Noble (9 st. 6 lb.) and Remand (9 st. 5 lb.). Trained by W. Wharton for Mr Brook Holliday, son of the late Major Lionel Holliday, Vaguely Noble is a bay by Hyperion's stout-hearted son Vienna, not otherwise a notably successful sire, out of Noble Lassie, a Nearco mare descended from the Oaks winner Brulette, a sister of the Prix du Jockey Club and Grand Prix winner Hotweed. Vaguely Noble made a fairly modest start to his career by finishing second in The Sandgate Stakes at Newcastle in August. On his next appearance he was second in The Feversham Stakes at Doncaster. It was in his third race, the seven-furlongs Sandwich Stakes at Ascot that Vaguely Noble for the first time looked something out of the ordinary, winning by the rare margin of a dozen lengths from seventeen opponents. His final outing of the season was in The Observer Gold Cup, worth over £16,000 to the winner. He made mincemeat of his rivals, who included Connaught and Lorenzaccio, and won by seven lengths in the manner of a future champion. It was clearly a matter for regret that he held no classic engagements.

Because of heavy duties incurred by the death of Major Holliday, Vaguely Noble came up for sale at Newmarket in December. His disposal naturally aroused immense interest and at least half an hour before he was led in there was not a spare inch to be found in Tattersalls' spacious new sale ring at Park Paddocks. The bidding opened at 80,000 guineas, a sum in itself a long way above the record of 47,000 guineas established by Solario in 1932. The B.B.A. dropped out of contention at 100,000 guineas and the issue then lay between the World Wide Bloodstock Agency and Godolphin Darley, the latter representing the American oil tycoon Mr Nelson Bunker Hunt. Finally, at 136,000 guineas, the World Wide

46. Vaguely Noble wins the Sandwich Stakes at Ascot in 1967 by twelve lengths from seventeen opponents

Agency won and it became known that the purchase had been made on behalf of Dr Robert Franklyn, a Hollywood plastic surgeon.

Vaguely Noble was sent to Ireland to join Prendergast's stable. Early in 1968, though, Mr Bunker Hunt acquired a half share and Vaguely Noble was transferred to Étienne Pollet at Chantilly. It was obviously a daring gamble to pay so much money for a horse with no English classic engagements and it looked as if Vaguely Noble would need to win the Arc to justify such a heavy outlay.

Remand, bred and owned by Mr J. J. Astor and trained by Dick Hern, won all his three races, these including The Solario Stakes and The Royal Lodge Stakes. A thoroughly workmanlike chestnut, he was by Alcide out of Admonish, by Palestine, his dam being a half-sister to that great hurdler Persian War. Remand was not engaged in The Two Thousand Guineas and his first major target in 1968 was to be The Derby.

Arguably the equal of any two-year-old trained in Britain was Mr Raymond Guest's Sir Ivor, trained by Vincent O'Brien. Bred in America, Sir Ivor is by Sir Gaylord, a grandson of that fine sire Royal Charger whom the Irish foolishly exported to the United States, out of Attica, a mare by Mahmoud's son Mr Trouble. In Ireland Sir Ivor won The Probationers Stakes and The National Stakes. The success, though, that really drew attention to him was his victory in The Grand Criterium, a race he won in masterful fashion by three lengths. With his class and speed he was obviously going to be a formidable opponent for Petingo in The Two Thousand Guineas the following spring.

Sam Darling and Jack Fawcus both died in 1967. A member of a famous English racing family, Darling, who was eighty-six, had always been overshadowed by his brother Fred. He was, though, an extremely able trainer and one of his achievements was to pull off the Cesarewitch–Cambridgeshire double. This he did in 1925 with Forseti and Masked Marvel, both owned by Mr A. K. Macomber, who landed a considerable gamble. In fact for many years a framed cheque for £100,000—a lot of money in those days—made out to Mr Macomber used to hang on the wall of Ladbroke's main London office.

Jack Fawcus died after a car crash on the way to Uttoxeter races. He was fifty-nine. Before the war he was a highly successful rider over fences and hurdles, first as an amateur and then as a professional. A beautiful horseman who had learnt a lot about tactics from Tom Coulthwaite, he was seldom to be found bashing along in front. He never won The Grand National but from nine rides in that event he was second once, third once, and fourth twice. He won the Scottish Grand National three times, the Welsh Grand National four times. His principal patron was Mr J. V. Rank.

At the start of the war he was one of the few professional jockeys holding a commission in the Territorial Army. As a captain in the Northumberland Fusiliers he was taken prisoner in 1940. He had little spare flesh on him when he was captured and he suffered more than most from the privations of the first twelve months. Nor did his ill concealed feelings towards his captors make life any easier for him. His health seemed irretrievably ruined when he got back to England in 1945. With typical courage he picked himself up off the floor and started to establish himself as a trainer with a 'mixed' stable of horses. The victories of that fine chaser Cool Customer were a great help, while on the flat he won The Cesarewitch with Flush Royal and The Zetland Gold Cup with Tale of Two Cities. He had his ups and downs, the downs including two bad car accidents, but he never ran out of courage and when things were going anything but well he was never without loyal friends. What he had needed was just a bit more luck.

12

EFFORTS continued to be made to streamline the administration of racing. A significant change took place in 1968 with the amalgamation of the Jockey Club and the National Hunt Committee. As these two bodies shared a secretariat and moved largely on parallel lines, while quite a number of Jockey Club members were also members of the N.H.C., this was obviously a sensible move. The new organisation was known as the Jockey Club and Sir Randle Feilden was appointed Senior Steward with nine Stewards to assist him. Brigadier S. H. Kent was made General Manager of the Secretariat with Mr Peter Weatherby as Chief Executive. To improve public and press relations, a Racing Information Bureau was set up under Mr Anthony Fairbairn.

The Rowley Mile course at Newmarket had never been a particularly popular one with the general public, one reason being that the general standard of comfort and convenience tended to be low. The gaunt and hideous grandstand looked like part of some ancient and neglected railway siding in industrial Lancashire. When the wind was blowing from the north-east—there is said to be no barrier between Newmarket Heath and the Ural mountains—conditions could be very bleak indeed.

The Jockey Club decided that something must be done to improve racing at the headquarters of English flat-racing, and acting on a plan originally sketched out by the Duke of Norfolk, a complete and entirely successful transformation was achieved between the spring and the autumn at the very reasonable cost of £614,000. This represented far better value for money than the far more expensive rebuilding scheme that took place at Sandown. Approval of Newmarket's new look was almost unanimous, the exceptions being one or two sour radicals who could not bring themselves to utter a word of praise about anything connected with the Jockey Club.

Racing politics and racing economics continued to be subjects for warm discussion. The Government increased the betting tax to 5 per cent and Lord Wigg announced that in future bookmakers were to be levied on turnover rather than on profits. The objective was to raise £4,300,000 from bookmakers and the tote in the financial year 1969–70. The bookmakers reacted in the manner anticipated at the thought of an increase of £1,500,000 in their contribution, even though the charge in fact represented only $\frac{1}{2}$ per cent of turnover. There were rumblings of revolt that left Lord Wigg totally unmoved. Talk of illegality faded quietly away when Lord Wigg suggested that the bookmakers might care to test the validity of his scheme in the courts of law.

The Report of the inquiry by Sir Henry Benson's Committee into the Racing Industry was submitted in June. The main findings were summarised in paragraphs 512 and 513 of the Report:

512 There is insufficient money circulating in the industry to maintain or improve the present standard of racing; to match competition from overseas; and to maintain the bloodstock industry. In consequence the racing industry in this country is deteriorating and it is losing ground as compared with racing in overseas countries.

513 Recent increases in taxation here have placed exceptional burdens on the racing industry which are greater than those borne by other industries.

With the growth in the importance of the financial background to racing and the increase in the amount of money derived from betting available for the general benefit of the sport, it was only natural that the role of the Jockey Club was frequently called into question. It was clearly undesirable that levy money should be handed over piecemeal for disposal by the Jockey Club, a self-elected, self-perpetuating body composed for the most part of individuals drawn from a narrow sector of the racing world, a sector, moreover, that was playing a far less significant part in bloodstock breeding and ownership than in the past. It came as no surprise, therefore, that the Benson Committee recommended that a new Authority be established to control and develop the racing industry, this new Authority taking over the functions of both the Levy Board and the Totalisator Board. The Authority would assess and collect the levy needed to place the finances of the industry on a proper basis and administer the funds so raised.

Approval was given in the Report to the amalgamation of the Jockey Club and the N.H.C. It was suggested that the new Jockey Club ought to be more broadly based than the old one and should carry out, under powers delegated from the Authority, the functions previously carried out by the old Jockey Club and the N.H.C. It would also carry out the present duties of the Joint Administrative Authority. The Committee emphasised that each section of the racing industry ought to ensure that the body formed to safeguard its interests fully represented all the members of that section and was constituted on sound lines.

The summary contained 29 paragraphs pertaining to racecourses. Among the more interesting were the following:

521 There is room for improvement in the quality of the management of some racecourses.

522 The Racecourse Association should be organised and administered so that in future it can speak with authority on behalf of all racecourses.

525   The average attendances at racecourses per day's racing have fallen during the past fifteen years. The trend has been accelerated since the introduction of betting offices in 1961.

526   Subject to re-examination when reliable evidence has been accumulated, the present coverage of racing by television is, on balance, advantageous.

528   Racecourses should be relieved of the responsibility for providing all prize money in future, which should be taken over by the New Authority.

529   The relief thereby afforded to the racecourses should in part be used to enable them to show a better financial return, and in part passed on to the public in the form of better amenities and reduced charges.

532   Enclosures at some courses should be merged. Where space permits, members' enclosures should be open to day visitors and the voucher system abolished.

534   The present financial results achieved by racecourses and the return on capital employed are altogether inadequate.

535   In consideration of the Authority assuming full responsibility for providing all prize money, the Authority should receive the revenue from the betting shop commentary fund and from television, sound broadcasting and cinema newsreel rights.

537   No closure of any racecourse is at present recommended but racecourses which have no reasonable prospect of becoming financially viable should be allowed to go out of existence.

545   Every effort should be made to remove the present restrictions on Sunday racing.

550   The new Authority should in future exercise surveillance over the admission charges, the condition of the track, the amenities and the catering facilities at each racecourse.

The Committee was strongly of the opinion that the whole future depended on fixing an adequate level of prize money and that the Authority should, in conjunction with the racecourses concerned, fix the total prize money appropriate to each racecourse.

Demands for increased prize money are invariably ill received by bookmakers and by a few dedicated anti-establishment journalists who can be relied on implicitly to trot out that weary old complaint about rich men expecting their hobby to be subsidised by the public. Of course the majority of people who own horses do not expect to make a profit; in these difficult times they just do not want to lose too much. Gone, doubtless for ever, are the days when there was no shortage of English owners who were not greatly concerned with matters of profit or loss as long as they had some fun. In any case, increased prize money benefits not just owners but trainers, jockeys and stable employees too.

The Committee suggested the percentages which ought to be deducted from prize money and paid to trainers, jockeys and stable staff respectively. It also made a recommendation that breeders' premiums should be paid to breeders of British-bred horses which win a pattern race on the flat.

By and large the Report of the Benson Committee was well received as indeed it deserved to be. Unfortunately, like other plans for turf reform, it has never been implemented and no doubt it is now tidily stacked away on a shelf in Portman Square next to the Report of the Ilchester Committee, both accumulating a layer of rarely disturbed dust. Lack of money is the accepted reason for failing to put the major reforms that were suggested into actual operation. Meanwhile the Treasury extracts a huge sum annually from betting and is deaf to all appeals to plough just a small proportion of it back into the sport. American-bred horses play an ever-increasing role in English racing and the once accepted superiority of the British thoroughbred is called in question; too much of our best blood is exported overseas; and the increased prize money available for our major races is all too frequently carried off by challengers from abroad.

Men who were leading figures in racing between the wars were beginning to become all too thin on the ground. Sir Jack Jarvis died very suddenly one December morning just before his eightieth birthday and on the eve of his departure for his annual holiday in South Africa. A trainer for fifty-four years, he represented the traditions of Newmarket at their best. His father was a Newmarket trainer, his mother a Newmarket trainer's daughter. His brothers Basil and William both trained at Newmarket and his wife was a member of the Leader family. He richly deserved his knighthood, awarded in 1967 for his services to racing.

As a boy he was a promising rider. During his first season as a jockey he rode a score of winners and partnered Hackler's Pride when she landed a tremendous gamble in The Cambridgeshire for the Druids Lodge 'confederacy'. Before long, though, he had weight problems and after a brief spell riding over hurdles he assisted his father for five years. He took out a trainer's licence in 1914. After the war, in which he served in the Royal Corps of Signals, he took a chance and purchased Park Lodge although it was still under military occupation and a field kitchen stood smoking in the centre of the stable yard. The horse that did most to establish his reputation in those early days was Sir George Bullough's Golden Myth, who as a four-year-old won The Queen's Prize, The Gold Vase, The Gold Cup and The Eclipse Stakes. Jarvis used to say that Golden Myth first made him and then nearly ruined him as Golden Myth was a dire failure at the stud and at one point Park Lodge was full of Golden Myth's offspring that either could not go at all or were unwilling to do so if they could.

In the early 1920s he succeeded Frank Hartigan as trainer to the 5th Earl of Rosebery, the former Prime Minister. The hand-over was not a very happy one as Hartigan refused to allow any of Jarvis's lads inside the yard and the horses were led out and taken over outside. There were eighteen horses, every single one of which was to win a race, and they were conveyed from Weyhill to Newmarket by special train. Lord Rosebery was not such a good judge of horses or of racing as his elder son and was inclined to be impatient and difficult. His letters to his trainer invariably started 'Jarvis' and he never signed them more fully than 'R'

47. Lord Rosebery and Sir Jack Jarvis

The following is a sample after a horse of Lord Rosebery's had been unplaced at Lincoln on the opening day of the season:

> Jarvis,
>> I fear we have got into a vein of also-rans.
>>> R.

With the 6th Earl, Jarvis formed a happy and successful association, based on mutual trust and friendship, that lasted for forty-five years. Both were men of strong and determined character but they nevertheless were able to work together in harmony. Lord Rosebery never consulted Jarvis about his stud at Mentmore but Jarvis knew just how to get the best out of the Mentmore stock, members of which tended to be tough, wiry and game. Jarvis rarely earned unstinted praise from the critics for the appearance of his horses in the paddock but they were trained to win races, not rosettes in the show-ring. A fancied Jarvis horse never failed from lack of fitness.

Jarvis had an explosive temper which once got him into quite serious trouble when he abused a jockey who he thought had roughed up Fearless Fox in The Ascot Gold Cup. The Ascot Stewards fined Jarvis £25 and he was sued furthermore for slander by the jockey, though eventually the case was settled out of court.

It would have been an expensive one, with Sir Patrick Hastings appearing for the jockey and Sir Norman Birkett (later Lord Birkett) for Jarvis. Jarvis subsequently admitted he ought not to have used the expression 'Irish bastard' as the jockey in question had been born in Scotland.

Jarvis's outbursts, though, were of brief duration and he was never vindictive. He was in fact an exceptionally kind and generous man and a good many lame dogs at Newmarket missed his helping hand after his death. He loved parties and could hardly conceal his contempt for trainers who did not push the boat out after a big win. Almost every form of sport gave him pleasure, particularly coursing—he won the Waterloo Cup—and shooting. He was into his car and off to Fenner's Ground at Cambridge in a flash if he heard that Ted Dexter was batting. He was shrewd over money and was apt to claim that he would have been a better stock-broker than trainer. At the time of his death he had saddled just short of 2,000 winners and had won over £1,000,000 in stakes for his owners.

Walter Nightingall, who died aged seventy-three, was as closely associated with Epsom as Jarvis was with Newmarket, the Nightingall family having established themselves at South Hatch in 1860. Walter, whose riding career had been virtually terminated in 1909 when he fractured his skull badly at Windsor, was a quiet, modest and essentially likeable man. He took over the South Hatch stable on the death of his father in 1926 and in his first full year as a trainer he turned out fifty-five winners on the flat, twenty under National Hunt Rules. His horses rarely figured in top-class races but he was a marvel at placing them to their best advantage. However, he did win a wartime Derby with Miss Dorothy Paget's Straight Deal and in 1965 he won The Two Thousand Guineas with Mr W. Harvey's Niksar. In 1948 he became trainer to Sir Winston Churchill, for whom, on the advice of Mr (later Sir) Christopher Soames, he purchased the French-bred grey, Colonist II, a stout-hearted stayer that became the most popular horse in the country. Other horses to carry the Churchill colours included Vienna, later the sire of Vaguely Noble, High Hat, and Welsh Abbot. On Nightingall's death the stable was carried on for the time being by his sister Margery, who had always been of great assistance to him, until Scobie Breasley was ready to take it over.

Other deaths in 1968 were those of the Gaekwar of Baroda, Mr Geoffrey Freer and Major Dermot McCalmont. The Gaekwar of Baroda, who was at one time said to enjoy an income of £2,000,000 a year, made a big splash in English racing between 1945 and 1951. In 1945 he created a stir by paying 28,000 guineas for the yearling brother of Dante. Subsequently named Sayajirao, this colt did far better than most high-priced yearlings, and trained by Sam Armstrong he won the Irish Derby and The St Leger. Another good horse the Gaekwar owned was the Two Thousand Guineas winner My Babu whom he bought from Aly Khan. Unfortunately the Gaekwar's racing triumphs in England did nothing to increase his prestige and popularity in India. In August 1948 there were demands that he be deposed and the following year he was pensioned off, being permitted an annual allowance of £14,000. His huge racing establishment had to be cut down and before very long he had vanished from the racing scene.

Mr Geoffrey Freer was the outstanding racing official of his day, a man whose advice was constantly sought right up to his death. Witty as well as wise, he knew the racing game inside out. As a handicapper he was both fair and exceptionally shrewd, while as clerk of the course he possessed the knack of pleasing the race-going public and also people professionally engaged in racing. It was largely due to him that Newbury recovered so quickly after being used as an American supply base during the war. For many years he maintained a small stud and there he bred Tofanella, who became the dam of Ribot's sire Tenerani. He was always at pains to emphasise that, above all, racing is meant to be fun. He was made an honorary member of the Jockey Club in 1967.

Major Dermot McCalmont, born in 1887, had the good fortune to inherit while a boy at Eton most of the fortune of Colonel Harry McCalmont who had owned the Triple Crown winner Isinglass. As a subaltern in the 7th Hussars he won The Grand Military Gold Cup in 1911 on Vinegar Hill. The following year, returning from India, he agreed to buy a weirdly marked grey yearling colt by Roi Hérode that his cousin, the trainer 'Atty' Persse, had bought for 1,300 guineas at Doncaster. Named The Tetrarch, and known to the public as 'The Spotted Wonder', this colt showed himself to be just about the fastest horse ever seen on an English racecourse. Despite his phenomenal speed and the fact that his career as a stallion was curtailed by his reluctance to carry out stud duties, he sired three St Leger winners in five years. He also sired that famous mare Mumtaz Mahal.

Major McCalmont, the most generous and hospitable of men, was a great supporter of hunting and racing in Ireland, and of racing in England. He won The Two Thousand Guineas with Tetratema, by The Tetrarch, and with Mr Jinks, by Tetratema. He enjoyed many successes in Irish classic events. His son by his first marriage, Major Victor McCalmont, has inherited his father's love of hunting and is also one of Ireland's most capable and progressive racing administrators.

The 1968 Two Thousand Guineas was regarded as virtually a match between Sir Ivor and Petingo. Piggott had the choice of riding either of those two. He delayed making a decision till mid-March, when he opted for Sir Ivor. Both colts won their preliminary races. Petingo was the more impressive but his rival had appeared the more backward.

The going was soft at Newmarket on May 1. Sir Ivor was favourite at 11/8 and Petingo was on offer at 9/4. There was quite a lot of support for Murless's candidate, the big, burly Connaught, who carried Mr Jim Joel's colours. Connaught could be a thoroughly awkward customer and he had refused to start in one race at two and more recently in The Greenham Stakes at Newbury. On this occasion he firmly declined to enter a loose box to be saddled and this operation had to be conducted outside in the pouring rain. However, he caused the starter little bother down at the stalls. Petingo was the pick of the field on looks but Sir Ivor had obviously done extremely well in a physical sense since he ran at Ascot early in April.

The race proved unexpectedly tame. So Blessed led for over six furlongs, then Mercer took Petingo to the front. Sir Ivor, though, had always given the impression that he was travelling a bit better than Petingo and there he was, ideally placed and ready to pounce. When Piggott asked him to go, the favourite immediately accelerated and swept past Petingo to win smoothly by a length and a half. Jimmy Reppin was third. It was O'Brien's first success in The Two Thousand Guineas. Horses trained by him had already won the other classic events.

The rest of Petingo's form—he retired at the end of the season—was inconsistent. He flopped behind Luthier in the Prix Lupin but then won The St James's Palace Stakes. He won The Sussex Stakes at Goodwood but in The Wills Mile at Goodwood was soundly beaten by Jimmy Reppin, to whom he was giving 6 lb. He looked like making a good sire with winners such as Satingo (Grand Criterium) and English Prince (Irish Sweeps Derby) but unfortunately he died all too young. His daughter, Fair Salinia, won the 1978 Oaks.

Sir Ivor did not race again before The Derby, for which he was favourite at 5/4 on. In the parade ring he paid tribute to O'Brien's professional skill, looking even bigger and better than he had done at Newmarket. Second favourite at 4/1 was Remand, who had given Connaught 4 lb. and a half-length beating in The Chester Vase. When he made his appearance in the Epsom paddock, those of his backers who were there to see him immediately realised their fate. He had run up conspicuously light and was on anything but good terms with himself. It was known that an epidemic had struck Dick Hern's stable and it looked ominously as if Remand was sickening for the cough. He did in fact start coughing not long after his return home. Connaught, ridden by Sandy Barclay, looked big and well but compared with Sir Ivor he was markedly deficient in quality.

The race was indeed a memorable one to watch. Connaught led round Tattenham Corner. At this point Remand was fifth and Sir Ivor on the rails not far behind him. Once the straight had been reached Connaught went flat out as hard as he could go. At one stage he was five lengths clear and, though Remand and Sir Ivor were improving their positions, it really looked as if they both had too much to do and The Derby was going to be won by a maiden. Remand, who had fought most gallantly considering his condition, was in trouble with a quarter of a mile to go and from then on Sir Ivor represented the one danger to the leader. At this juncture Piggott, typically cool-headed at a moment of crisis, switched Sir Ivor to the outside. Then, having got him nicely balanced, he delivered his challenge. For a second Sir Ivor seemed to hesitate and then he flew. He had three lengths to make up with just under a furlong in which to do it but such was his acceleration that he not only caught Connaught but beat him by a length and a half. Seldom can The Derby have produced a more dramatic or spectacular finish and no wonder horse and rider were cheered to the echo as they entered the winner's enclosure. The 45/1 outsider Mount Athos, not a horse with the sweetest of tempers, finished strongly to take third place in front of Remand.

Sir Ivor's victory owed not a little to Piggott's brilliant riding. Sir Ivor's ideal distance was probably a mile and a quarter and Piggott, despite Connaught's commanding lead, resisted the burning temptation to make his challenge too early and with iron nerve waited until the time was really ripe. Sir Ivor's class and speed did the rest, just as the class and speed of Nearco, from whom Sir Ivor was descended, enabled him to win the Grand Prix de Paris although he was not in fact a true stayer.

The Irish Sweeps Derby was regarded as a walk-over for Sir Ivor, who, ridden by Liam Ward, was a red-hot favourite at 3/1 on. Piggott was up on Mr Engelhard's Ribero, a brother of Ribocco who had won the race the previous year. Ribero had been disappointing up till then and at Royal Ascot Connaught, receiving 4 lb., had beaten him by a dozen lengths in The King Edward VII Stakes. Like his elder brother, though, Ribero was beginning to thrive with the advent of warmer weather and some sun on his back.

Ribero beat Sir Ivor by two lengths with Val d'Aoste third. Ward did nothing wrong on Sir Ivor who, for some unascertainable reason, ran well below his true form. 'He just died in my hands,' said the unhappy Ward afterwards. Undeterred by this totally unexpected reverse, Mr Guest and O'Brien made the bold decision not to wait for The King George VI and Queen Elizabeth Stakes at the end of the month but to send Sir Ivor to compete in The Eclipse Stakes at Sandown the very next Saturday.

There were five runners for The Eclipse Stakes, which was to produce the finest race for this event since 1903 when Ard Patrick narrowly beat Sceptre with the Triple Crown winner Rock Sand a soundly defeated third. Those three great horses won eight classic races between them. On this occasion the runners included, in addition to Sir Ivor, the dual classic winner Royal Palace, and Taj Dewan, who had just been beaten by Royal Palace in The Two Thousand Guineas but had finished in front of him in The Champion Stakes. At four Royal Palace had won The Coronation Cup, Taj Dewan the Prix Ganay. The going was firm. In the paddock Sir Ivor dominated his rivals. By comparison Royal Palace looked almost small, Taj Dewan light and leggy.

The outsider Franc Castel weakened on the final bend whereupon Saint-Martin took Taj Dewan to the front and headed for the winning-post as hard as he could go. It appeared as if these enterprising tactics were going to succeed as inside the distance Sir Ivor was under pressure and failing to produce acceleration comparable to that which had gained him the day at Epsom, while it looked as if Royal Palace had just a little bit too much still to do. Royal Palace, however, was battling on in most resolute fashion, and to roars of encouragement from his supporters he steadily closed the gap. Taj Dewan for his part showed no sign of weakening, let alone of accepting defeat. These two game horses were almost level crossing the line with Sir Ivor, the 5/4 on favourite, three parts of a length away third. Nineteen out of every twenty people at Sandown that day were pretty sure that Taj Dewan had won. His connections were utterly convinced of his success. Bookmakers offered 8/1 freely against Royal Palace securing the verdict. The photograph, though, showed that Royal Palace had prevailed by a very narrow margin. Members of the French contingent were dumbfounded and reluctant at first to accept the evidence placed before their eyes. It was an occasion when one was thankful for the camera. There would have been the worst Anglo-French row since

48.   The finish of the Eclipse Stakes, 1968—Royal Palace beating the French horse Taj Dewan and the Derby winner Sir Ivor

Fashoda if the judge had named Royal Palace the winner on his own initiative.

O'Brien and Piggott were inclined to blame the going for Sir Ivor's defeat. It is arguable, though, that Piggott had been a shade overconfident. He had left Sir Ivor with a lot of ground to make up in the last two furlongs on Taj Dewan and Royal Palace, horses of a different and superior calibre from any he had met in The Derby.

Sir Ivor, a bit sore after The Eclipse, was rested prior to his preparation for the Prix de l'Arc de Triomphe. His preliminary race, a mere week before the Arc, was the Prix Henry Delamarre at Longchamp. He obviously needed that outing and failed by half a length to beat Prince Sao, to whom he was giving 9 lb. In the Arc Sir Ivor was back to his best and ran a fine race although he was beaten by three lengths by Vaguely Noble. Behind him were opponents such as Roselière (Prix de Diane, Prix Vermeille), La Lagune (Oaks), Dhaudevi (Prix Royal Oak), Samos III (Prix Royal Oak), Luthier (Prix Lupin), Luciano (Grosser Preis von Baden) and Ribero (Irish Sweeps Derby, St Leger).

Mr Guest was evidently a believer in the dictum of that great trainer the late Mat Dawson—'Let 'em sweat for the brass'—as only thirteen days after the Arc Sir Ivor lined up for The Champion Stakes at Newmarket. This was over his best distance, a mile and a quarter, and he won very easily from Locris, Taj Dewan finishing fifth of six. Even then Sir Ivor's campaign was not concluded and it says much for his temperament and the robustness of his constitution that he was able to travel to America and win The Washington International at Laurel Park from Czar Alexander and Fort Marcy. Piggott did not in fact ride one of his more brilliant races and the American racing press indulged in a number of uncivil comments at his expense. These 'Old Stoneface' accepted with a composure amounting to total indifference.

Sir Ivor was then retired to the stud and it was arranged for him to stand for a single season in Ireland (£4,000; no foal, no fee) before being transferred to the Claiborne Farm, Kentucky. He has done well as a stallion and in 1976 his daughter Ivanjica won the Arc. He himself was voted the 1968 Horse of the Year, to the chagrin or derision of admirers of Royal Palace who pointed out that Sir Ivor had been beaten in four consecutive races, whereas Royal Palace was unbeaten at four and had defeated Sir Ivor fairly and squarely the only time they met.

Royal Palace's crown of laurels had become slightly defoliated in 1967 through his defeat in The Champion Stakes. In 1968 he regained everything he had lost. He began by winning The Coronation Stakes at Sandown, The Coronation Cup at Epsom and The Prince of Wales's Stakes at Royal Ascot. That was all very satisfactory but in each case the opposition was frankly too mediocre to test him. Then came his superb win in The Eclipse Stakes. His final appearance was in The King George VI and Queen Elizabeth Stakes. At one point he looked like winning that race without undue difficulty but a furlong from home he suddenly faltered and veered away to the left. In the end he only just managed to hang on to beat Felicio II by half a length with Topyo a short head away third. He had in fact torn a suspensory ligament in his near foreleg and as he hobbled into the unsaddling enclosure it was evident that only sheer courage had kept him going. He never ran again and retired to the stud having won nine of his eleven races, those victories being worth £163,950. He disappointed as a sire till 1977 when Dunfermline won The Oaks.

Ribero, who had cost 50,000 dollars at the Keeneland Yearling Sales, emulated his brother Ribocco by winning The St Leger, thereby giving Mr Engelhard his third success in that race. Following the Irish Sweeps Derby, Ribero had run somewhat indifferently in The King George VI and Queen Elizabeth Stakes after unseating Piggott on the way to the stalls and cantering down to the Old Mile start where he waited placidly for recapture, nibbling away at the grass and some adjacent shrubs. He also ran poorly in the Prix Kergorlay at Deauville, won by Pardallo. In The St Leger Connaught was favourite at 11/10. Ribero was weak in the market, drifting from 5/2 to 100/30. Connaught failed to stay and was beaten three furlongs from home. At the distance Ribero looked like winning comfortably but in fact he only just lasted home with a mere short head to spare at the finish over Canterbury, a Charlottesville colt trained by Prendergast. As Canterbury rapidly closed on Ribero, Piggott never lost his nerve. He nursed Ribero until the last few strides when he gave him the full treatment—a masterly piece of riding.

It was sixty-eight years since two full brothers won The St Leger, Persimmon and Diamond Jubilee having achieved this double in 1896 and 1900.

Ribero competed in the Prix de l'Arc de Triomphe but was kicked at the start and made no show. He was kept in training at four but added nothing to his reputation. Consistency had never numbered among his virtues and he was now extremely temperamental. After refusing to enter his stall at Epsom prior to The Coronation Cup, he was retired to the stud.

Turning to the fillies, The One Thousand Guineas was won by Caergwrle, bred and owned by Mrs Noel Murless and trained by her husband. A strong-quartered chestnut, Caergwrle is by Crepello and the second foal of the Abernant mare Caerphilly, whose first foal was that good miler St Chad. Grandam of Caerphilly was Malapert who bred the Two Thousand Guineas winner Pall Mall.

Caergwrle had won the One Thousand Guineas Trial at Kempton very easily. Ridden by twenty-year-old Sandy Barclay, who had a highly successful first season with Murless and whose handling of Royal Palace in his races earned him much well deserved praise, Caergwrle was favourite for The One Thousand Guineas at 4/1, second favourite at 5/1 being Mr R. B. Moller's strongly made Pardao filly Sovereign, whose four victories the previous season had included The Queen Mary Stakes. Lalibela, winner of The Cheveley Park Stakes, wore blinkers, in addition to which she did not appear to have done at all well physically. Last into her stall, Caergwrle was first out but Barclay settled her down and took up a handy position behind Sovereign, who made the running. Approaching the Bushes, Caergwrle moved smoothly into the lead and had no great difficulty in withstanding the challenge of Mr Jim Joel's light-framed Match III filly Photo Flash, whom she beat by a comfortable length. Sovereign, who, because of the cold, dry weather had not been given a preliminary outing, was a short head away third.

Caergwrle only ran once more, failing by a length to give 4 lb. to Ileana in The Ebbisham Stakes at Epsom. She undoubtedly possessed great speed. Murless had bought her grandam Cheetah, by Big Game, for only 1,000 guineas. He was attracted by the concentration of The Tetrarch blood in Cheetah, who had inherited one strain from Big Game, two more from Malapert. He reinforced this concentration by mating her with Abernant.

In The Oaks our fillies were put in their place, a relatively humble one, in no uncertain fashion by M. H. Berlin's La Lagune, trained by François Boutin. She won in a canter by five lengths from Glad One, a daughter of the Gold Cup winner Gladness, with Pandora Bay a short head away third. Pandora Bay, trained by Geoff Barling for Major C. H. Nathan, went on to win The Ribblesdale Stakes. At the December Sales this big Pandofell filly was sold for 22,000 guineas to go to France, where she won the important Prix Kergorlay at Deauville and two other nice races as well. At the Deauville December Sales she was sold for £30,000.

La Lagune was bred by the Marquis du Vivier and cost her owner only £2,000. She is by Val de Loir out of a non-winning daughter of Sicambre. Those who made the long trek down to the paddock saw an immensely powerful bay with a white face and four white socks. Not everyone liked her and some critics voted her rather coarse. She could certainly gallop, though, at any rate on this occasion. She never won again. She flopped in the Prix de Diane and was a poor third in the Prix Vermeille. She did, however, run reasonably well in the Arc, in which she was fifth behind Vaguely Noble.

If our fillies were crushed at Epsom, so were our stayers in The Ascot Gold Cup. The Prix du Cadran had not been run because of the strikes and riots that brought France seemingly to the brink of revolution. Accordingly the French stayers paraded in strength at Ascot and were rewarded by taking the first three places in the Cup, Madame Volterra's Pardallo, who had previously won the Prix Jean Prat and subsequently won the Prix Kergorlay, winning from Samos III and Petrone. Like the previous year's winner, Parbury, who on this occasion was seventh, Pardallo is by Pardal. In 1966–67 he raced with success over hurdles and, but for a bad fall in the Grande Course de Haies de Quatre Ans at Auteuil, he would very likely have been sent to Cheltenham to contest The Champion Hurdle. He remained in training in 1969, winning the Prix de Barbeville. He failed, though, in the Prix du Cadran after which he was exported to America.

Spectacular three-year-old winners at Royal Ascot were Sovereign and Connaught. In The Coronation Stakes Sovereign turned the tables on Ryan Jarvis's Front Row, by Epaulette, who had beaten her in the Irish One Thousand Guineas, and defeated her with the utmost ease by half a dozen lengths. She only ran once subsequently, finishing fourteen lengths behind Petingo in The Sussex Stakes at Goodwood after spreading a plate.

Connaught, clearly none the worse for his exertions in The Derby, won The King Edward VII Stakes by twelve lengths from Ribero with Karabas four lengths away third. At Goodwood he was declared a runner for the Gordon Stakes but, never a sticker for conventional conduct, he parted company with his lad on the way from the stables to the paddock and went off by himself for a romp in the woods. By the time he was recaptured in a somewhat dishevelled condition, the race was over. He was clearly short of an outing when he paraded in the paddock before The Great Voltigeur Stakes at York and his portly form suggested something designed to draw the Lord Mayor's coach. In the final furlong he indulged in a bumping match with Riboccare, and the latter, much the smaller, probably came off second best. However, Piggott drove Riboccare home to win by a neck. Naturally there was an inquiry. The Stewards, having examined the film, decided that Riboccare was chiefly to blame, and to Piggott's tersely expressed indignation, awarded the race to Connaught.

Favourite for The St Leger, Connaught failed to stay and was beaten a long way out. His reputation did not stand high when he retired into winter quarters but he eventually made amends once it was realised that his proper distance was a mile and a quarter.

The Queen's four-year-old Hopeful Venture had begun the season by beating Park Top easily in The Ormonde Stakes at Chester. At Royal Ascot he won The Hardwicke Stakes without difficulty. His big triumph, though, came in the Grand

Prix de Saint Cloud, worth over £54,000 to the winner, which he won from nineteen opponents, among them Vaguely Noble. In the autumn he returned to France for the Prix Henri Foy at Longchamp. He ran badly and finished down the course behind Petrone. He had in fact been cast in his box the night before and after the race his hock was badly swollen. He never ran again and was retired to the National Stud. A big, strong bay, he is by Aureole out of White House, a half-sister to Chamossaire by Supreme Court. He was not a success as a sire. His stock tended to be slow to develop, and when they did develop were more noticeable for stamina than speed. There is no place for a stallion like that in modern British bloodstock breeding and he was exported to Australia.

There were no great excitements at Goodwood. The standard of the sport at the main meeting there was not as high as it had been in pre-war days. This was due to increased competition, firstly from the Ascot July Meeting, secondly from Deauville where the high level of prize money was attractive to English owners. This year, for instance, The Goodwood Cup was worth £3,259 to Ovaltine, who beat Parbury by two and a half lengths, whereas Pardallo earned £14,439 for winning the Prix Kergorlay. The Richmond Stakes at Goodwood was worth £6,421 to Tudor Music, the Prix Morny £19,632 to Princeline. However, in point of numbers Goodwood seemed to maintain its popularity with the public though the purely social side suffered through large houses in Sussex tending to be staffed by a Lithuanian au pair girl or a Filipino couple as opposed to a staff of eight, or probably a good many more, in the old days. Five-day meetings are not entirely popular with hostesses who like to go racing themselves and are nevertheless expected to do work in the kitchen formerly reckoned just within the scope of an experienced cook and two kitchen maids.

Mr David Robinson's So Blessed, by Princely Gift, won the five-furlongs King George Stakes at Goodwood. He was a high-class sprinter that had previously won The July Cup and went on to win The Nunthorpe Stakes. Colonel Peter Payne-Gallwey's little Lambourn stable enjoyed a triumph in winning that highly competitive handicap, The Stewards' Cup, for the second year running with Sky Diver, a Skymaster horse that was later exported to Australia. Colonel Payne-Gallwey, who died after a long illness in 1971, had been one of the best amateur riders of his day over fences when serving in the Eleventh Hussars. His war record was one of singular distinction and he was awarded the D.S.O. and two bars.

At Doncaster in September Ribofilio won The Champagne Stakes. Trained by Fulke Johnson Houghton, he was yet another good American-bred Ribot colt to carry Mr Charles Engelhard's colours. He had previously won The Chesham Stakes at Royal Ascot but had failed in the Prix Morny. Subsequently he won The Dewhurst Stakes and headed The Free Handicap with 9 st. 7 lb. Next in The Free Handicap came Right Tack (9 st. 5 lb.), who had won The Imperial Stakes at Kempton and The Middle Park Stakes; and Tower Walk, winner of The National Stakes at Sandown and The Norfolk Stakes at Doncaster. Right Tack was by Hard Tack and Tower Walk by High Treason, so both were likely to have stamina limitations at three. The French won The Cheveley Park Stakes with Mige, a filly of Madame Wertheimer's by Saint Crespin III out of that fine race-mare Midget II, who had herself won The Cheveley Park Stakes as well as The Coronation Stakes and The Queen Elizabeth II Stakes. Mige was Midget II's eighth foal and the first to approach her dam's high standard of excellence.

The Observer Gold Cup went to Miss Monica Sheriffe's The Elk, hardly the most distinguished winner of that race but a colt that had improved rapidly throughout the season. Earlier in the month he had won The Rowley Mile Nursery at Newmarket with 8 st. 9 lb. Bred in Ireland, he was by Only For Life out of Sambur, by Big Game, and both his sire and his dam were exported to Japan. He was bought for Miss Sheriffe, who had owned Only For Life, by Jack Clayton for only 700 guineas. Clayton had been prepared to bid up to 3,000 guineas and when he obtained the colt so cheaply he thought there must be something seriously wrong with him.

Sir Cecil Boyd-Rochfort retired at the end of the 1968 season, handing over his stable to his son-in-law, Henry Cecil. He had been a trainer for forty-seven years, leading trainer on four occasions. He was the first English trainer to win £1,000,000 in stakes for his owners. His duties as royal trainer, firstly to King George VI and then to the Queen, he carried out with the utmost distinction. He was knighted for his services to racing in 1968. He possessed high professional ability and excelled in the preparation of stayers, winning The St Leger six times, The Gold Cup three times, The Goodwood Cup six times and The Doncaster Cup seven times. Nor was he averse to having a tilt at the major handicaps as the bookmakers sometimes discovered to their cost.

'Scobie' Breasley retired to take over the South Hatch stable at Epsom. He was a mature and experienced rider when he came to England in 1950. He was four times champion jockey and rode two Derby winners, the first one when he was fifty years of age. Few riders as stylish have been seen in England this century. His split-second timing was fantastic and he knew to an inch the position of the winning-post, whereas too many English jockeys seem to think it is sited two furlongs from home. Behind the finesse was the toughness and courage that enabled him to take some horrible falls without losing his nerve.

The cheering broke out a long way from home when Mr Tom Blackwell's Silver Spray won The Birdcage Nursery at Newmarket. The reason for this was that it was Bill Rickaby's final ride before retirement and departure to take up a racing appointment in Hong Kong. A member of a famous racing family, Rickaby is deservedly popular. Good-looking, immaculate, courteous and full of charm and humour, he has always made friends wherever he goes. His integrity has never been questioned and without being a great rider he was a good, sound one who was apt to respond according to the degree of confidence that was placed in him. He was not at his best with owners or trainers who made a habit of blaming the jockey when things went wrong. It is sad indeed that a disastrous car crash in Hong Kong not only nearly cost him his life, but has left its mark on him ever since.

Over in France Vaguely Noble proved well worth the 136,000 guineas paid for him at the December Sales. His objective, which he duly achieved, was the Prix de l'Arc de Triomphe. He began his career in France by winning the Prix de Guiche at Longchamp and the Prix du Lys at Chantilly. He was confidently expected to win the Grand Prix de Saint Cloud but Deforge rode one of his more indifferent races, leaving him far too much to do against good horses on fast ground from the final bend. Vaguely Noble was only third to Hopeful Venture and Minamoto.

Vaguely Noble's last race before the Arc was the Prix de Chantilly at Longchamp. In that event, which he won by eight lengths, and also in the Arc, he was ridden by that excellent jockey Bill Williamson. He won the Arc decisively by three lengths from Sir Ivor, thereby proving himself the best mile-and-a-half horse in Europe. He never ran subsequently. An extremely handsome horse of notable size and strength, he stands in America but his offspring have been more successful in Europe than in the United States. They include Dahlia, twice winner of both The King George VI and Queen Elizabeth Stakes and The Benson and Hedges Gold Cup; and Empery, winner of the 1976 Derby.

Racing politics were sometimes rather disagreeably to the fore in 1969. Mr David Robinson won The Gimcrack Stakes with Yellow God. In his speech at the Gimcrack Dinner in December he saw fit to blame the Jockey Club for many of racing's current difficulties. A few days later, Lord Wigg, Chairman of the Levy Board, could not resist adding a little fuel to the fire when, in a post-luncheon speech, he made certain observations about the Jockey Club, among which he compared that institution to a well kept veteran car.

This was a bit more than the Duke of Norfolk was prepared to stand and he counter-attacked Mr Robinson and Lord Wigg in a speech—which made Lord Wigg very cross indeed—over the public address system during a jumping meeting at Ascot. Most people tended to agree with the sentiments expressed by the Duke but thought they would have been better suited to a letter in The Times, thereby ensuring a far wider audience. It was left to Sir Randle Feilden to smooth ruffled feathers as best he could. Followers of racing did not really much care for this bickering between members of two bodies that ought to have been co-operating for the general good of the sport.

During the year Mr Robinson bought Kempton Park for a sum in the region of £750,000. Kempton had not been making money in recent years. Of its two best known races, The Jubilee, once the most popular of all the spring handicaps, had lost almost all its former prestige, while The Imperial Stakes, once The Imperial Produce Stakes, has now disappeared from the programme altogether. Mr Robinson had boldly announced his intention of making the track pay by sticking strictly to commercial principles. Those who expected a new and dynamic approach at Kempton under the direction of a man rightly proud of his prowess in business were doomed to total disappointment. During Mr Robinson's brief tenure of power at Kempton, no major changes took place. Today Kempton is, so to speak, in the same stable as Sandown and Epsom and this once charming course, where until recently a day's shooting in November might produce eighty pheasants, is chiefly notable for the hideous gravel excavations there.

It was in this year that the Levy Board, raising money from commercial sources as well as using its own means, took control of two famous metropolitan courses, Epsom and Sandown. Sandown had been in considerable peril at times both from commercial exploitation and from transport planners who wished to construct a new road through it. Lord Wigg's enterprising action in respect of these two famous tracks deserved high credit.

The poor old tote had a very unhappy year. In the early 1960s things had gone pretty well for the tote, so much so that there were sporadic if ineffectual demands for the establishment of a tote monopoly. In 1969, though, the tote was uncomfortably perched on the very brink of insolvency. This was due to the cumulative effect of various financial demands made in recent years. The ultimate blow was the Rateable Value Tax which decreed that all premises used for betting should be subject to an additional tax of three times the rateable value. The tote was compelled to dispose of various betting offices that could no longer be run at a profit. Nor was that all; in September the Levy Board declared that the tote was indebted to the board to the tune of £693,072.

Nor was 1969 all a bed of roses for trainers. A horribly wet winter with water-logged gallops was followed by a wet spring. Worse was to come, though, as in July and August stables all over the country were hit by a coughing epidemic which almost brought racing to a halt.

The Two Thousand Guineas was sensational in the worst sort of way. Favourite at 15/8 was Ribofilio, who had cost Mr Engelhard $100,000 as a yearling and whom his owner was apt to describe as 'the last of the cheap Ribots'. Ribofilio had started off at three by winning the Ascot Two Thousand Guineas Trial in funereal time from a couple of drab opponents. It was less of a race than an exercise canter. At Newmarket, ridden by Piggott, he looked bright in his coat and well in himself. In the race itself he was never going at all at any stage. Always at the tail-end of the field, he was virtually pulled up at the Bushes. Naturally a dope test was ordered. This proved negative. Ribofilio's abject performance remains one of racing's great unsolved mysteries. To this day, though, there are people, whose opinion is worthy of respect, who are utterly convinced that, despite the total lack of supporting evidence, somehow or other Ribofilio was got at.

The winner of The Two Thousand Guineas was Mr J. R. Brown's 15/2 chance Right Tack, trained at Epsom by John Sutcliffe junior and ridden by Geoff Lewis. He won comfortably by two and a half lengths from Tower Walk with Welsh Pageant close up third. The well backed French candidate, M. D. Wildenstein's Yelapa, finished very lame. Lewis was able to settle Right Tack down and wait with him until he challenged Tower Walk coming into the Dip. In The Greenham Stakes at Newbury Tower Walk, receiving 5 lb., had beaten Right Tack by a length and a half. The going was faster at Newbury than at Newmarket.

A very good-looking bay, Right Tack, who had won his first race at two at Alexandra Park, hardly a course where future classic winners were likely to be observed, was bred in Ireland and sold as a foal for 700 guineas. A year later he was bought for 3,200 guineas at Doncaster on behalf of Mr Brown. His pedigree is not one of noticeable distinction. His sire, Hard Tack, by Hard Sauce, was a tearaway who started off by winning a couple of five-furlongs events at the Curragh but never won again subsequently. Polly Macaw, Right Tack's dam, was a speedy plater whose six victories were all achieved over five furlongs. To unearth a classic winner in Polly Macaw's female line, it was necessary to go back to the 1861 St Leger winner Caller Ou. At the 1969 December Sales Polly Macaw, in foal to Takawalk, was sold for 20,000 guineas.

Right Tack inherited his sire's speed but his willingness to settle down enabled him to stay a mile and he was in fact a very good horse up to that distance. Three weeks after The Two Thousand Guineas he won the Irish Two Thousand Guineas very comfortably from Hotfoot, while at Royal Ascot he beat Habitat by half a length in The St James's Palace Stakes, despite having been left with a great deal to do in the straight and getting bumped by the runner-up in the final furlong.

After Ascot Right Tack developed the cough and did not run again till September, when he failed to stay in the ten-furlongs Peter Hastings Stakes at Newbury and was slammed by the four-year-old Principal Boy. His final race was the Prix du Moulin at Longchamp, in which he and Welsh Pageant were both unplaced behind Habitat. He was then retired to the stud. In 1976 he was offered at the December Sales and bought for 70,000 guineas to go to Australia.

Well as the big, handsome Tower Walk ran in The Two Thousand Guineas, his main successes came when Geoff Barling decided that sprinting was his game. He then won The Nunthorpe Stakes and, better still, the Prix de l'Abbaye at Longchamp, worth over £9,000 to the winner. At four Tower Walk ran three times, winning The Palace House Stakes at Newmarket. He has done pretty well as a sire and was particularly successful with his two-year-olds in 1975, when Nagwa, Venus of Stretham and Western Jewel won twenty-five races between them.

There were no Derby trials at Chester as the three-day May Meeting there was washed out. At York, where the going was very holding, The Dante Stakes was won by the Duke of Sutherland's Activator, who, like most of the stock of his sire, Aggressor, relished the mud. The Lingfield Derby Trial marked the first appearance of Blakeney as a three-year-old. Bred by the Whatcombe trainer, Arthur Budgett, Blakeney is a bay by Hethersett, who died all too young, out of Windmill Girl, by Hornbeam. In 1964 Windmill Girl was second in The Oaks and won The Ribblesdale Stakes. She had the rare distinction of producing a second Derby winner in Morston. Windmill Girl had been sent up to the 1962 December Sales but failed to reach her reserve of 5,000 guineas. As a yearling Blakeney was offered for sale but he too failed to reach a similar reserve. Budgett therefore retained Blakeney and trained him himself but sold quarter shares to Mrs Diana Carnegie and Mr Horace Renshaw.

At two Blakeney had run twice, winning the seven-furlongs Houghton Stakes at Newmarket. In April 1969 he suffered a minor ailment which delayed his reappearance. He certainly ought to have won at Lingfield but Geoff Lewis, who rode him that day, got into all sorts of trouble and just failed to catch The Elk, who had had two previous races and was certainly the fitter of the two.

The racing public are quick to forgive and forget and Ribofilio, Piggott up, was favourite for The Derby at 7/2. He had had a gallop at Sandown on May 27, when the press and the public were welcome to attend if they wished. Some observers were not much impressed with what they saw but clockwise Ribofilio was stated to have done well. One bold punter who, the previous October, had had a bet of £20,000 to £4,000 about Ribofilio for The Derby at once increased his liabilities by striking a bet of £7,000 to £2,000. Second favourite for The Derby at 11/2 was Mr Jim Joel's Paddy's Progress, a big, lanky colt by St Paddy that hardly looked the ideal type for the course, while there was plenty of money for the French-trained Prince Regent and for Blakeney. On this occasion Blakeney was partnered by young Ernest Johnson who had been promised the ride the previous autumn after Blakeney's victory at Newmarket. Originally apprenticed to Ian Balding, Johnson had proved himself a strong and capable light-weight. He had been top apprentice in 1967 and had ridden over sixty winners in 1968.

There can be little doubt that the Comtesse de la Valdene's Prince Regent, ridden by Deforge, ought to have won, but his rider seemed to take him everywhere on the course bar the ladies' cloakroom. With half a mile to go Prince Regent's position looked hopeless but in the straight he made rapid headway, passing horse after horse to gain third place only two lengths behind the winner. The Comtesse de la Valdene's other runner, Moon Mountain, made the running until a furlong from home and only missed third place by a neck. Another unlucky horse besides Prince Regent was Intermezzo, who was badly hampered coming down the hill.

In the early stages Blakeney was nearly last. From half-way, though, he began to improve. Johnson, like Breasley on Charlottown three years earlier, elected to make his effort on the inside and like Breasley he had the good luck to experience a trouble-free run. It is to Blakeney's credit, though, that when a narrow opening presented itself a furlong out he went through it with not a moment's hesitation. Running on stoutly, he headed Mr P. G. Goulandris's Shoemaker inside the furlong to win by a length.

Arthur Budgett is a member of a well-known hunting and polo-playing family and is the third Old Etonian to train a Derby winner this century. He took out a licence to train in 1939 but then came the war and six years' service in the Indian Cavalry. When he resumed training, his first winner was Fair Mile, who in 1947 carried off a steeplechase at Newton Abbot. The following year Budgett won The Lincoln with the eight-year-old Commissar, owned in partnership with his brother. Commissar had won The Stewards' Cup at Goodwood in 1946 but had then been trained by Eric Stedall. Once established, Budgett was consistently successful and in particular he had many successes with horses bred and owned by Lt-Col Percy Wright. Quiet, friendly and unassuming, he himself has always been a much liked member of the racing world, and in his press and public relations he was greatly assisted by his wife, a sister of the breeding expert and racing journalist Major Peter Towers-Clark. He retired in 1975 and was doubtless not sorry to do so. Like others of his generation he had found that a trainer's life was not the fun it used to be, not least because of the constant worries over labour.

Blakeney's subsequent record that season was disappointing. In the Irish Sweeps Derby he finished fourth behind Prince Regent, who beat the favourite, Ribofilio, by a length with Reindeer five lengths away third. Prince Regent, who before The Derby had just beaten Mr Stanhope Joel's Caliban in the Prix Lupin, was on this occasion ridden by Geoff Lewis and duly demonstrated how unlucky he had been at Epsom. In The St Leger Blakeney, who admittedly had anything but a clear run, was unplaced behind Intermezzo, while he finished the season by running unplaced in the Arc. It was decided to keep him in training in 1970.

As for Ribofilio, he started at 7/1 on in The March Stakes at Goodwood and successfully defeated a solitary and indifferent opponent. He was a hot favourite for The St Leger but for once Piggott rode a very poor race and got into every sort of trouble with the result that Ribofilio was beaten a length and a half by Intermezzo on whom Ron Hutchinson had employed intelligent and enterprising tactics. Thus Ribofilio, doubtless in the opinion of the bookmaking profession 'The Horse of the Year', had been favourite for three classic races in England and one in Ireland and had lost the lot. He was unplaced in his last two races, the Arc and The St Simon Stakes at Newbury. There were no protests when he was returned to America at the end of the season.

Intermezzo, by Swedish-based Hornbeam out of Plaza, by Persian Gulf, was bred and owned by Mr G. A. Oldham and trained by Harry Wragg. It was Wragg who thought out the plan that Hutchinson carried out to perfection. Wragg knew that Ribofilio had become an extremely hard puller and he therefore ordered a slow early gallop in order to make Piggott's task of getting the favourite to settle down just a little bit harder. Then, when there was a mile still to go, Hutchinson's instructions were to accelerate suddenly, secure a vital lead, ensure a clear run for himself and probably confuse the opposition. The scheme worked to perfection. Piggott tried to make headway through the centre of the field, was blocked, forced to drop back and to switch firstly round Reindeer and then round Prince Consort. On the completion of these manoeuvres Ribofilio found himself five lengths behind Intermezzo and with only a furlong to go. Ribofilio fairly flew for about a hundred and fifty yards but then the effort suddenly fizzled out. Mr David McCall, Mr Engelhard's racing manager, took Ribofilio's defeat philosophically. 'Lester does not owe us anything,' he said. 'He won the Leger for us on Ribocco two years ago and on Ribero last year when any other jockey would never have won. How can we complain?' Ribofilio's backers were inclined to take a less charitable view.

Intermezzo remained in training in 1970 but failed to win. In the autumn of that year he was exported to Japan.

The One Thousand Guineas was won by Intermezzo's stable-companion Full Dress II. She had the numerals after her name because a horse called Full Dress had won races for Mr Jim Joel and had then done well as a sire in Colombia. Full Dress II, owned and bred by Mr R. B. Moller, was by Shantung out of Fusil, by Fidalgo. Fusil was a descendant of Sceptre and Full Dress II was her first foal. In April Full Dress II had won the One Thousand Guineas Trial at Ascot. At

Newmarket she scored by a length and a half from Piggott's mount, the French-trained Hecuba, by Relic, with Motionless third. The favourite, Anchor, did not please in the paddock and ran poorly.

Coming into the Dip, Hecuba led and looked like winning, particularly as Full Dress II, though full of running, appeared to be shut in on the rails. Hutchinson in fact was forced to switch Full Dress II round three opponents before he could deliver his challenge. When Full Dress II saw daylight she accelerated in great style and headed Hecuba about fifty yards from home. Once in front, though, she veered sharply to the left and in so doing crossed Hecuba, who was snatched up by Piggott in the final fifteen yards. Piggott immediately objected on the grounds of boring and crossing. After seeing the film, the Stewards overruled the objection. The film certainly suggested that the proximity of the two fillies when Full Dress II passed Hecuba was rather more the fault of the latter; and that the result was not affected by Full Dress II's swerve.

It was afterwards stated, no doubt correctly, that winners had been disqualified in this country for doing less than Full Dress II had done, and that Full Dress II would certainly have lost the race in France. No one seemed absolutely certain if a winner should be disqualified in the event of an offence having been committed, or only if the result was affected by that offence.

Full Dress II failed in The Oaks and The Coronation Stakes and was then retired to the stud.

Just before his sudden death, in his very last telephone conversation in fact with Lord Rosebery, Sir Jack Jarvis had said: 'Don't be surprised if I win The Oaks for you with Sleeping Partner.' This forecast must at the time have appeared a distinctly optimistic one as Sleeping Partner had run seven times at two and her solitary success had been in a maiden race at Ayr.

Light grey in colour and by no means outstanding in looks, Sleeping Partner was by Parthia, exported to Japan, out of Old Dutch, by the Victoria Cup winner Fastnet Rock. Old Dutch was a member of the influential Pearl Maiden family and Lord Rosebery had bought her dam Donah, by Donatello II, for only 430 guineas. Donah also bred Donald, winner of The Ebor Handicap and The Jockey Club Cup.

Following Sir Jack's death, Sleeping Partner was transferred to Doug Smith, who had just completed his first season as a trainer. At three she made her first racecourse appearance in the Lingfield Oaks Trial, ridden by the young South African John Gorton. She lost nearly ten lengths at the start, but owing to the slow pace she was able to make up the lost ground and win. This performance, however, made no marked impression on the critics and in The Oaks she started at 100/6. Admirably ridden by Gorton, she won by three parts of a length from Frontier Goddess with Myastrid four lengths away third. The fact is that Sleeping Partner stayed every yard of the distance whereas most of her rivals, including the favourite, Full Dress II, did not.

The victory of Sleeping Partner was exceptionally popular as Lord Rosebery, then aged eighty-seven, was justly regarded as the doyen of the English turf. He and his filly were cheered to the echo as she made her way to the winner's enclosure. Lord Rosebery had never won The Oaks previously though fillies carrying his colours had been four times second.

Sleeping Partner was only the second horse Doug Smith had ever saddled in a classic event. Despite this auspicious beginning, the association between Smith and Lord Rosebery was not to prove of lengthy duration. There was no row; they just happened to see racing in somewhat different lights. In any case Sir Jack Jarvis must have been a very difficult man to follow. John Gorton, then aged twenty-three and looking younger, was in his first season as No. 1 jockey to an English stable. He had made many friends here through his charm, intelligence and good manners. A neat and stylish rider, he was sometimes criticised on the grounds that he was not such a strong finisher as the best of his rivals.

Sleeping Partner showed her victory was no fluke by winning The Ribblesdale Stakes but she then developed the cough and was never as good again afterwards, failing in The Yorkshire Oaks and The Park Hill Stakes. She remained in training at four but only ran once, finishing down the course in The Jockey Club Stakes.

It will be remembered that the Duke of Devonshire's Park Top, trained by van Cutsem, had been one of the best staying three-year-old fillies of 1967. In 1968 she won The Brighton Cup for the second time, on this occasion under 9 st. 10 lb., and the Prix d'Hedouville at Longchamp. In addition she ran extremely well when just beaten by Levmoss and Canterbury in The Oxfordshire Stakes at Newbury. Now it rarely pays to keep a high class filly in training beyond the age of four—some would say beyond the age of three—but the Duke of Devonshire, acting on the advice of the Duchess, did just that and the gamble paid off in no uncertain fashion. Park Top reached the peak of her form at five when, splendid as her record was, with a little bit of luck on her side it could well have been even better.

She started off in 1969 with a trip to Paris and won the mile-and-a-half Prix de la Seine, beating that good filly Pandora Bay, who had been third in the 1968 Oaks, by two and a half lengths at level weights. Her next race was The Coronation Cup, for which Remand, reputed to be back in his best form, was favourite while other runners were Connaught and Mount Athos, second and third respectively in the previous year's Derby. Ridden with the utmost confidence by Piggott, she won with a nice bit in hand by three parts of a length from Mount Athos with Connaught third. At Royal Ascot she was ridden in The Hardwicke Stakes by Geoff Lewis, Piggott being under suspension. In a race that was run at a ludicrously slow pace, she had far too much speed for Chicago and Bringley.

By the time The Eclipse Stakes was run the coughing epidemic was playing havoc with racing. It had been intended to run Right Tack in The Eclipse but then he started to cough. When it became known that Right Tack could not run, it was decided to let Park Top and Ribofilio take their chance. Piggott was required for Ribofilio so Lewis was booked for Park Top. Then Ribofilio began to cough so Piggott was engaged for Wolver Hollow who appeared to have little chance of beating Park Top since he had been slammed by Connaught in The Prince of Wales's Stakes at Ascot.

Park Top certainly ought to have won The Eclipse but Lewis rode a very indifferent race and got into a terrible tangle in the straight. Gamely as Park Top struggled, she had no hope of catching Wolver Hollow, a big, tall five-year-old by Sovereign Path. Wolver Hollow's victory gave Henry Cecil, successor to his stepfather Sir Cecil Boyd-Rochfort, his first important success as a trainer. Owner of Wolver Hollow was Mrs C. O. Iselin, who was a hundred and one years old at the time and who died the following year. She presented Wolver Hollow to Sir Cecil Boyd-Rochfort, a useful sort of present as Wolver Hollow sired the 1976 Two Thousand Guineas winner, Wollow.

Compensation for Park Top's vexatious defeat came not long afterwards as later that month, with Piggott back in the saddle, she was a comfortable winner of The King George VI and Queen Elizabeth Stakes by a length and a half from the 28/1 outsider Crozier, with the Italian horse Hogarth third. Fourth was Felicio II, who had been second to Royal Palace in this race the previous year and more recently had won the Grand Prix de Saint Cloud.

Park Top's autumn objective was the Prix de l'Arc de Triomphe. As a preliminary she went to Longchamp on September 7 for the Prix Foy run over eleven furlongs and won with a ton in hand from Felicio II and Pandora Bay. There were twenty-four runners for the Arc. As the field turned for home, Williamson sent Levmoss to the front and went for the winning-post as hard as he could go. At this point Park Top must have had more than a dozen horses in front of her. There was no opening for her on the inside and Piggott was compelled to switch her to the outside in order to initiate his challenge. Once she saw daylight, Park Top responded with her customary courage and passed half a dozen horses as if they had conveniently consented to mark time. Just for a few seconds it looked as if she was going to pull it off but she had given Levmoss too long a start and furthermore the stout-hearted Levmoss showed not the slightest sign of stopping. He beat her by three parts of a length and Williamson did not feel called upon to use his whip. Grandier was three lengths away third.

Most of those who saw the race reckoned that Park Top had been unlucky and that Piggott had left her with a bit too much to do. An alternative view was that Piggott was compelled to hold her up in order to conserve her finishing speed, and that if he had been in closer touch with the leaders during the race he might well have blunted her power of acceleration. In any case, holders of this opinion added, Levmoss, an out-and-out stayer, had won with a bit in hand. The fact is that horses which finish fast to take second place nearly always look unlucky; but that does not invariably mean that they are.

It would have been just about the most wonderful day of Piggott's career if only Park Top had won. As it was he rode four winners that afternoon: Tower Walk in the Prix de l'Abbaye; Shaft in the Prix des Champs-Élysées; Vela in the Criterium des Pouliches; and Habitat in the Prix du Moulin. Tower Walk, Shaft and Habitat were all trained in England.

After her exertions in France it was asking rather a lot of Park Top to compete so soon afterwards in The Champion Stakes. She ran below her best form and was

49. Levmoss, with Bill Williamson up

beaten by the French three-year-old Flossy, a weedy, mean-looking, blinkered filly trained by François Boutin. In the paddock she was sweating profusely and appeared thoroughly tense and strung up. She could evidently gallop on her day, though, and she did to some purpose on this occasion.

The Irish had reason to feel slightly aggrieved when Park Top was voted Horse of the Year rather than Levmoss, who not only beat her the only time they met during the season but had other fine achievements to his credit as well. After all, he proved himself the best long-distance horse in Europe and then came down to a mile and a half and beat the best middle-distance horses as well. In the Arc, in which he started at 52/1, he beat the first three in The Derby (they all started at a longer price than he did), the first three in the French Derby, the first two in the Irish Sweeps Derby, the winner of the Italian Derby, the winner of the Grand Prix, the first two in the French Oaks, and Park Top, the best of her sex in Europe. Having done that, he had no more worlds to conquer and was retired to the stud.

Bred by the McGrath Trust Company and trained by his owner, Seamus McGrath, Levmoss is a bay by Le Levanstell out of Feemoss, by Ballymoss. By

Le Lavandou out of a Ballyogan mare, Le Levanstell was bred to be a sprinter but proved to be a very good miler. Feemoss won over twelve and fourteen furlongs and was out of Feevagh who won The Yorkshire Oaks and bred Laurence O, winner of The Queen Alexandra Stakes. Grandam of Feevagh was the Brownstown Stud's foundation mare Astrid, whose daughter Panastrid won the Irish One Thousand Guineas and bred Panaslipper, second in The Derby and winner of the Irish Derby.

Levmoss took time to develop and only ran twice at two, winning a maiden race at Gowran Park on his second appearance. It was half-way through his second season that he really began to improve. He then won The Oxfordshire Stakes at Newbury from Canterbury and Park Top; was third in the Prix Royal Oak; and won The November Handicap at Leopardstown under 9 st. 4 lb.

He started off at four by running unplaced over a mile at The Curragh. On April 20 he went to Longchamp for the Prix Jean Prat run over a distance just short of two miles. He ran an excellent race to finish three-quarters of a length behind Samos III, who had himself been beaten the same distance by Zamazaan. The Gold Cup winner Pardallo was fourth. A month later Levmoss returned to Longchamp for the Prix du Cadran, worth over £25,000 to the winner. The runners chose to ignore the well-meant efforts of Mouriez who acted as pacemaker for Samos III and it was Levmoss's speed combined with the intelligent riding of Williamson that enabled Levmoss to win by a neck from Zamazaan with Samos III a neck away third. Pardallo was seventh. The French were rather put out and claimed that the race had been a farce.

A prize worth over £11,000 to the winner was insufficient to lure the French to Ascot for The Gold Cup. Levmoss had a simple task and won as he pleased from Torpid. Mount Athos was in a sulky mood. After trailing the field for a mile, he did his best to run out of the course. The decision was then taken to train Levmoss for the Prix de l'Arc de Triomphe. As a preliminary he ran in The Leinster Handicap at The Curragh with the not unsubstantial weight of 10 st. 10 lb. He won very easily by three lengths. The rest of the story has been told. He was a horse of which the Irish had every reason to feel proud.

An outstanding performance at Royal Ascot was the victory of Mr L. Freedman's Crepello filly Lucyrowe in The Coronation Stakes by a margin of twelve lengths. Trained by Peter Walwyn, she was a neatly-made bay whose grandam, Lady Sybil, had won The Cheveley Park Stakes, in which race she herself had finished second. She began in 1969 by winning the One Thousand Guineas Trial at Kempton. Second favourite for The One Thousand Guineas, she was probably the worst suffer in what looked to be a roughish race and her chance was ruined in consequence. At the Epsom Summer Meeting she won The Ebbisham Stakes in which Motionless, third in The One Thousand Guineas, was fourth. After her Ascot triumph, Lucyrowe had three more races and all of them proved to be hard fought. At Goodwood in July she won the Nassau Stakes but needed all her pluck to scrape home by inches from her stable-companion Seventh Bride, the outsider at 33/1 in a field of five. On that occasion it looked as if Lucyrowe barely stayed the distance, a mile and a quarter. A month later she turned out for The Wills Mile at Goodwood but in receipt of 8 lb. she found Habitat just too strong for her and went under by half a length. Her final appearance was in the Sun Chariot Stakes at Newmarket. Finishing as usual with her tongue hanging out, she battled on gamely to beat Nedda, who received 3 lb., by a neck. It had been intended to run her in the Champion Stakes but her form in the Sun Chariot Stakes hardly seemed to justify that and she was retired to the stud instead.

The American-bred Habitat, who cost Mr Engelhard $105,000 at the Keeneland Sales, is a bay by Sir Ivor's sire Sir Gaylord out of Little Hut, by Occupy. Trained by Fulke Johnson Houghton, he did not run as a two-year-old. At three he took some little time to find his form but by the end of the season he could claim to be the best miler in Europe. His first appearance was in The Royal Stakes at Sandown in April. He started slowly and was unplaced behind Shoemaker, subsequently second in The Derby. He next ran at Windsor and was second in the mile-and-a-quarter Robert Wilmot Handicap. He won an unexacting contest, The Willows Plate at Haydock Park, and then moved into more exalted company, winning The Lockinge Stakes at Newbury, in which his opponents included Jimmy Reppin, Tower Walk, Lorenzaccio and Wolver Hollow. Then came his controversial battle with Right Tack in The St James's Palace Stakes in which, ridden by Piggott, he was beaten by half a length in an ugly, scrambling finish. Piggott was reported to the Stewards of the Jockey Club and suffered suspension for seven days, while Lewis, who rode Right Tack, was cautioned for not having been frank at the inquiry. Habitat ran three times subsequently, winning the Prix Quincey at Deauville, The Wills Mile at Goodwood and finally the Prix du Moulin at Longchamp, in which his victims included Right Tack and Welsh Pageant. He was then syndicated for the stud at a value equivalent to £400,000. He has proved an outstanding success and among his winners have been Rose Bowl, Habat, Roussalka and the 1976 One Thousand Guineas winner Flying Water.

Connaught, as unpredictable as ever, had his failures but he won The Prince of Wales's Stakes at Royal Ascot in record time, beating Wolver Hollow by five lengths, while previously he had beaten Jimmy Reppin by six lengths in The Coronation Stakes at Sandown.

The big Goodwood meeting was hit by the coughing epidemic. Jimmy Reppin beat a substandard field for The Sussex Stakes and Richmond Fair, who was later to run over fences, won The Goodwood Cup.

As a three-year-old Lord Iveagh's Karabas, by Worden II, had been trained in Ireland by Paddy Prendergast and had proved himself quite a useful performer, one of his two successes being in The Warren Stakes at Goodwood. Towards the end of the year he was transferred to Bernard van Cutsem's stable at Newmarket. The change certainly seems to have done him good as he made quite astonishing improvement in 1969.

His first race at four was The City and Suburban which he won under 9 st. 2 lb., and the following week he won The Turn of the Lands Handicap at Newmarket with 9 st. 7 lb. He failed in The Jubilee on heavy ground and was second in The

Zetland Gold Cup. After those two defeats he was rested till September when he re-emerged and proceeded to win six races in succession, namely The Fetcham Handicap at Epsom; The Scarborough Stakes at Doncaster, in which he beat Hotfoot and Connaught; La Coupe de Maisons-Laffitte; The Mitre Stakes at Ascot; the Prix du Conseil Municipal at Longchamp; and finally The Washington International Stakes at Laurel Park. Both the Prix du Conseil Municipal and the Washington International had been won by his sire. At one time Karabas's racing career was handicapped by a rheumatic condition. At Newmarket he always wore a copper band round one fetlock and the rheumatism virtually disappeared.

There was an old-fashioned gamble in The Cambridgeshire on Mr A. Swift's Prince de Galles, a three-year-old trained by the former jockey Peter Robinson. In a field of twenty-six Prince de Galles started at 5/2 and trotted up by four lengths, not having given his supporters a single second of anxiety. A fortnight previously he had won a race over the Cambridgeshire course by ten lengths in record time. He did not incur a penalty for that success and in The Cambridgeshire carried 7 st. 12 lb. The following year he carried 9 st. 7 lb. in The Cambridgeshire and trotted up again. Peter Robinson took over Teddy Lambton's stable at Newmarket in the course of the 1969 season. Lambton, once one of the more proficient amateur riders on the flat, inherited a fair measure of both the charm and the ability of his father, the late George Lambton, but when he was training certain other qualities essential for consistent success were unfortunately less in evidence.

For the third time in six years a two-year-old belonging to Mr Charles Engelhard topped The Free Handicap. In this case it was the Canadian-bred Nijinsky, trained by Vincent O'Brien. An exceptionally powerful, impressive-looking bay, Nijinsky was bred in Ontario by Mr E. P. Taylor and was bought at the Canadian Thoroughbred Horse Society's Sale for $84,000 by Mr George C. Scott on behalf of Mr Engelhard. He is by Northern Dancer out of Flaming Page, by Bull Page. Northern Dancer, a grandson of Nearco, won the Kentucky Derby and The Preakness Stakes but failed to stay a mile and a half in The Belmont Stakes. Flaming Page won the important Queen's Plate in Canada and the Canadian Oaks.

Nijinsky began his racing career by winning the undemanding Erne Stakes at The Curragh on July 12. He then won successively at The Curragh, The Railway Stakes, The Anglesey Stakes and The Beresford Stakes. In October he came to Newmarket for The Dewhurst Stakes and accounted for some rather feeble opposition without the slightest difficulty. He then retired into winter quarters, regarded in general as a good thing for The Two Thousand Guineas and the probable winner of The Derby.

The winner of The Observer Gold Cup was Sir Humphrey de Trafford's Approval, trained by Henry Cecil. This handsome Alcide colt was making only his second racecourse appearance, having previously finished second in The Waterford Stakes at Ascot. The way he came from a long way back to win his race at Doncaster was encouragingly reminiscent of his sire.

Deaths in 1969 included those of Sir Francis Weatherby, whose services to racing have already been mentioned; Sir Felix Cassel, the concert pianist, who was one of Miss Dorothy Paget's few male friends and was at one point her racing manager; Major A. E. Allnatt; three well-known racing journalists, all eighty years of age or over, namely Geoffrey Gilbey, 'Sam' Long and Walter Meeds; and Tom Masson.

Before 1914 Major Allnatt, son of a village shopkeeper in Berkshire, was a master at Ardingly College in Sussex. After war service in the Royal Inniskilling Fusiliers, he went into the property business and made a fortune. It was typical of him that he went into racing in 1940 when everyone else was trying to get out or at least reducing interests. He bought twelve yearling colts from the Aga Khan for £4,800 and among them were winners such as Mehrali, Ujiji and Shahpoor. Two years later he bought the late Lord Glanely's bloodstock—134 animals—for £115,000. He resold them all, bar the stallion Colombo, shortly afterwards for a total of 135,570 guineas. Colombo he sold privately for £24,000. Ujiji, having won a substitute Gold Cup, was sold for something like £30,000. Major Allnatt did not profess to know anything about horses or racing, his temporary interest being purely in the nature of a business speculation. He later burst into the art world and paid £275,000 for Rubens's 'Adoration of the Magi', which he gave to King's College, Cambridge; and £182,000 for Franz Hals's 'Portrait of an Unknown Man'.

Geoffrey Gilbey was a man of many parts. At Eton and at Oxford he was a noted athlete. Always deeply religious, he proposed to enter the Church but changed his mind at the last moment and went on the stage instead. In the war he served in the Sixtieth (K.R.R.C.) and was awarded the Military Cross for saving life under fire. From 1919 onwards he found his niche in journalism, mostly racing journalism. His best work was done between the wars for the Sunday Express when in a manner both fearless and witty he attacked the worst abuses prevalent in racing at that period. He made some enemies in high places but earned the admiration of thousands of readers. He was largely responsible for Clive Graham, whom he had met as a boy at Eton, going into racing journalism and joining the Daily Express at the age of eighteen.

Geoffrey Gilbey was a good talker, a brilliant after-dinner speaker, but a somewhat inattentive listener, vain, witty, and ready to go to any lengths to help someone in trouble. A tremendous enthusiast, his enthusiasm could lead him to see indifferent horses, and indifferent human beings, too, through rose-tinted glasses. He was as keen on racing at eighty as he had been at twenty. He was the first racing journalist to broadcast a commentary on a race.

'Sam' Long was employed successively by The Sportsman, The Sporting Chronicle and The Sporting Life. He was not a notably stylish or imaginative writer but he was a wonderfully good judge of form and was on terms of genuine friendship with a number of leading trainers who were happy to receive his advice. He was a man entirely without malice or jealousy and even among his colleagues it is doubtful if he possessed a single enemy. Walter Meeds held the responsible job of chief starting-price reporter for The Sporting Life for over thirty years. He belonged to the old school of journalists, a professional of professionals. He did not wear his heart on his sleeve, nor in any other visible position either, but though he could be remorseless as an enemy he could be a good friend to those who succeeded in winning his confidence.

Tom Masson, whose stables were close to the prison at Lewes, never recovered from serious injuries received in a car crash when motoring home after Newbury races. A Scottish farmer's son and himself for some years a farmer, he made a name for himself both in show-jumping and in point-to-points. For some years he was associated with Mr Bertram Mills of circus fame and had many successes on Mr Mills's horses in the show-ring, in jumping competitions and in point-to-points. In later years if one sent him a horse that could not win, it would be at least taught to bow as the owner entered the box.

Tom was something of a genius with difficult or obstreperous horses and in fact he became a trainer after successfully reforming two erratic horses sent to him by George Lambton. Eventually the Queen became one of his patrons. He was a notable trainer of jockeys, too, and among his successful pupils were Jimmy Lindley, Bobby Elliott and Mr John Hislop. He himself combined shrewdness with joviality and his reputation as a raconteur was justly earned.

13

NINETEEN-SEVENTY proved a memorable racing year what with Nijinsky becoming the first triple crown winner since Bahram, and My Swallow, Mill Reef and Brigadier Gerard being just about the best three two-year-olds in a single season since Ormonde, Minting and The Bard in 1886.

Nijinsky started the season by winning The Gladness Stakes at The Curragh early in April, beating Deep Run and the Coventry Stakes winner Prince Tenderfoot with impressive ease. In The Two Thousand Guineas, in which he had completely dominated his rivals in the parade ring, he started at 7/4 on. Second favourite was Lord Derby's Tamil at 13/1. Nijinsky never gave Piggott a second of anxiety and won with any amount in hand by two and half lengths from Mr David Robinson's Yellow God, who in 1969 had won The Gimcrack Stakes and had been beaten by a very narrow margin by Huntercombe in The Middle Park Stakes, with Roi Soleil the same distance away third. He was the shortest priced winner of The Two Thousand Guineas since Colombo in 1934.

Nijinsky did not run again before The Derby. The main danger to him at Epsom was the possibility that, like his sire Northern Dancer, he might not stay a mile and a half. That possibility, though, appeared somewhat remote and his apparent superiority reduced the number of his opponents to ten. He started at 11/8 and the fact that he was not an odds-on favourite was largely due to the volume of money for Mr Winston Guest's French-trained Gyr, a heavily backed second favourite at 100/30. Gyr, a big, tall, gangling chestnut by Sea Bird, had won the mile-and-a-half Prix Hocquart as well as the Prix Daru. The less generous paddock critics at Epsom were inclined to compare him to a camel, but the very shrewd Étienne Pollet held a high opinion of him and was said to have delayed his own retirement for a year in order to prepare him for The Derby. Popular each-way choices were Approval, who had followed up a dismal display at Sandown by winning The Dante Stakes, and Mr G. A. Oldham's French-trained Sheshoon colt Stintino, winner of the Prix Lupin.

Approval's action went to pieces coming down the hill and he was beaten before Tattenham Corner. On the other hand Gyr, who hardly looked the ideal type for the Epsom gradients, bowled down the hill like a polo pony and when he went into

50. Nijinsky

a clear lead with two furlongs to go he looked very much like winning. Nijinsky, though, was nicely placed and obviously far from being near to the end of his resources. When Piggott shook him up, he immediately lengthened his stride and swept past the gallant Gyr in majestic fashion to win easily by two and a half lengths. Stintino was third, the same distance behind Gyr. Thus there was no English-trained horse in the leading three. It was Piggott's fifth Derby winner, O'Brien's third. The time very nearly equalled the record set up by Mahmoud in 1936 but the course rode much faster in Mahmoud's day when the covering of grass was a great deal sparser.

Gyr, probably good enough to win The Derby eight years out of ten, went on to win the Grand Prix de Saint Cloud despite sweating up profusely before the start and being in a thoroughly excitable condition. He did not race again before the Prix de l'Arc de Triomphe. Again he worked himself up into a state before the off and under the circumstances did well to finish fourth. He did not run again. A major share in him as a stallion was bought by Mr William Hill, the bookmaker, and he was brought to stand in England. So far he has failed to make much mark.

Nijinsky, on this occasion ridden by Liam Ward, next won The Irish Sweeps Derby from Meadowville and Master Guy. His success was achieved without difficulty but it was noticeable that he got a bit hot and bothered before the race, and that during it Ward had some trouble in settling him down. None the worse, though, for these exertions, Nijinsky next lined up for The King George VI and Queen Elizabeth Stakes. Once again partnered by Piggott, he won easily by two lengths from Blakeney with the French filly Crepellana third and Karabas fourth. It is probably true to say that at this point of the season Nijinsky reached his peak. In his three remaining races he was not the horse he had been in July.

Bids for Nijinsky's stud services had begun immediately after The Derby. An offer by Mr Peter Burrell on behalf of the National Stud proved insufficient and it looked a safe bet that the power of the dollar would prevail in the end. So indeed it turned out and in August it was announced that Nijinsky had been syndicated for $5,440,000 (then £2,266,666) and would go to Mr 'Bull' Hancock's Claiborne Farm in Kentucky. It was at this stud that Mr Engelhard's American mares were boarded.

The original plan had been for Nijinsky to miss The St Leger and to concentrate on the Prix de l'Arc de Triomphe. However the lure of the triple crown proved too strong, particularly as The St Leger looked as if it would be anything but a difficult race to win. Unfortunately during August Nijinsky was afflicted by a severe attack of ringworm which deprived him temporarily of all the hair on one flank. This ailment did not prevent him from winning The St Leger with a great deal in hand but it may well have taken more out of him than was thought at the time.

It came as a painful blow to Irish and English followers of racing when Nijinsky went under by a head in the Arc to Mr Arpad Plesch's Sheshoon colt Sassafras, trained by Mathet and ridden by Saint-Martin. Sassafras, a real stayer, had previously won the Prix du Jockey Club and then, on the disqualification of Hallez, the Prix Royal Oak. He had never been reckoned in quite the same league as Nijinsky, though.

The immediate reaction was to blame Piggott for leaving Nijinsky with too much to do. A cool and careful examination of the film, however, showed that Nijinsky had three lengths to make up on Sassafras when he launched his challenge. With a hundred and fifty yards to go he drew level and he must have won had he maintained his effort. That, however, he failed to do. He faltered, and when Piggott applied the whip with his right hand, he veered to the left. Nijinsky had every chance but when the vital moment came he was unable to seize his opportunity. It was certainly not Piggott's fault that he lost.

The decision to run Nijinsky in The Champion Stakes only thirteen days after the Arc was a classic case of taking the pitcher to the well just too often. Nijinsky looked well enough—O'Brien would obviously not have run him had his physical condition deteriorated—but he got into a terrible state before the off and it is true to say that he had lost the race before it even began. His usual zest and dash were sadly lacking and a huge crowd saw him trounced by the five-year-old Lorenzaccio, whose racing record clearly indicated that he was only on the fringe of the very top class. It was a sad conclusion to the career of a great racehorse.

Top filly in the 1969 Free Handicap had been Humble Duty, owned by Jean, Lady Ashcombe and trained at Lambourn by Peter Walwyn. She had been bred in Ireland by Mr F. F. Tuthill, her sire being Sovereign Path, her dam the Abernant mare Flattering, a descendant of Lost Soul's sister, Venturesome. She had cost her owner 17,000 guineas as a yearling. At two she won three of her four races including The Lowther Stakes and The Cheveley Park Stakes. Her first appearance at three was in The Fred Darling Stakes at Newbury. The going was very dead and there were only four runners, one of these being Mr Brook Holliday's Highest Hopes trained by Dick Hern. By Hethersett out of the speedy Verdura, Highest Hopes had won her solitary race at two. A robust, powerful filly, she was said to be well suited to the conditions at Newbury whereas Humble Duty, a grey, much less substantially built, was not. In addition Humble Duty was believed to be badly in need of a race. Had she not been so and The One Thousand Guineas so close, she would hardly have run. The race turned out to be a travesty of competitive sport. Highest Hopes, favourite at 11/4 on, won hard held by a length from Humble Duty who likewise came under no pressure at all. If the primary objective of the jockeys concerned was to avoid giving their mounts a hard race, they can be said to have been brilliantly successful.

In The One Thousand Guineas Highest Hopes and Humble Duty were joint favourites at 3/1. Highest Hopes ran a lamentable race and finished eleventh of twelve. Humble Duty, ridden by Piggott as the stable jockey Duncan Keith was ill, won in brilliant fashion by the unusual margin of seven lengths from Gleam with Black Satin third. It was Peter Walwyn's first classic success. A dope test on Highest Hopes proved negative.

Humble Duty went on to win successively The Ebbisham Stakes at Ascot, The Coronation Stakes at Royal Ascot, The Sussex Stakes and The Wills Mile, both at Goodwood. She had trained off when unplaced behind Welsh Pageant in The Queen Elizabeth II Stakes at Ascot in September. There can be no doubt that she was a very good miler indeed.

Highest Hopes, who before The Fred Darling Stakes had won the One Thousand Guineas Trial at Ascot by eight lengths, redeemed her reputation in the Prix de Diane, in which she ran an excellent race to finish second to the Irish filly Sweet Mimosa, a sister of Levmoss. She returned to France in July and at Saint Cloud won the ten-furlongs Prix Eugène Adam from the French Two Thousand Guineas winner Caro who was giving her 12 lb. In The Yorkshire Oaks she was beaten fairly and squarely by Lupe, but she enjoyed a triumph at Longchamp on September 20 when she won the Prix Vermeille, worth £47,661 to the winner, from Miss Dan and Parmelia. Among those she beat were the Oaks winner Lupe, the French Oaks winner Sweet Mimosa, and the Irish Oaks winner Santa Tina. All told Highest Hopes's three trips to France earned her £84,000. In her final race she was well down the course in The Champion Stakes behind Lorenzaccio and Nijinsky.

Bred by the Snailwell Stud Company, Mrs Stanhope Joel's Lupe is a bay, rather ordinary-looking when in training, by Primera, a better sire of fillies than of colts, out of the Alycidon mare Alcoa who was just beaten in the 1961 Cesarewitch. Trained by Noel Murless, Lupe ran once at two, winning the six-furlongs Devonshire Stakes at Doncaster in September. She began at three by winning The Cheshire Oaks. She did not really thrive between Chester and Epsom and Murless was unable to give her as much work as he would have liked. Never-theless, ridden by Barclay, she started favourite at 100/30 for The Oaks. Second favourite was Mr Nelson Bunker Hunt's Prime Abord, who was bred on the same lines as Lupe, being by Primera out the Alycidon mare Homeward Bound, winner of the 1964 Oaks. Lupe was always going like a winner and, taking the lead more than two furlongs from home, she won by four lengths from State Pension with Arctic Wave third. It was a rough, scrambling sort of race and Lupe was fortunate in avoiding the trouble that ruined the chance of Piggott's mount Prime Abord. There was no excuse, though, for the Arundel-trained winner of the Irish One Thousand Guineas, Black Satin, who pulled desperately hard and was beaten a quarter of a mile from the winning-post.

Lupe did not run again till The Yorkshire Oaks in August. In that race she looked beaten when Highest Hopes headed her below the distance but her courage and stamina enabled her to stage a rally that pulled her through by two lengths in the end. Highest Hopes, though, obtained her revenge in the Prix Vermeille. Lupe did not run again after her failure at Longchamp but it was then decided to keep her in training for another season.

Now in her seventh year, Park Top showed that she was no back number when at Longchamp on May 7 she won the thirteen-furlongs La Coupe by half a length from the 1969 Grand Prix winner Chaparral, who was conceding her 3 lb. She ought to have won The Coronation Cup for the second time but Piggott's judge-ment was sadly at fault and in a race that progressed at much the same pace as a royal funeral—the time was 15 seconds slower than that of Nijinsky in The Derby—he gave Caliban too much start and Mr Stanhope Joel's Ragusa colt beat the mare by three parts of a length. The 1969 Derby runner-up Shoemaker was close up third.

During the summer Park Top had some tendon trouble and she did not run again till the end of September when she won The Cumberland Lodge Stakes at Ascot. It was then stated that she would have two more races, the Prix de Royallieu at Longchamp and The Washington International at Laurel Park.

The Prix de Royallieu, run over a mile and five furlongs, was run at a pace comparable to that in The Coronation Cup. Piggott had evidently derived no profit from his Epsom lesson and entered the short Longchamp straight eight lengths behind Hazy Idea and Prime Abord. He never looked like catching them. Prime Abord won, Hazy Idea was second, and Park Top dead-heated for third place with La Java.

The Longchamp crowd took the view that Piggott had ridden an appalling race and reacted accordingly. Piggott and Park Top had a most unpleasant journey back to the unsaddling enclosure and all in all it was an ugly and rather frightening scene. Nor was the situation helped in any noticeable way by Park Top's owner feeling that 'noblesse oblige' compelled him to give the old two-finger salute to the booing crowd. The Stewards requested Park Top's trainer and jockey to account for her running. They could only say that the going was softer than she really liked.

Park Top's retirement was announced on her return to England. She had won thirteen races and over £137,500 in win and place money, a remarkable total in view of the fact that with a bit of luck, or at least with the avoidance of bad luck, she might well have won in addition The Eclipse Stakes, the Arc and one Coronation Cup. However, although this 500-guinea yearling was unfortunate at times, she had had the luck to belong to an owner who, throughout her career, scorned to kick for touch and was always ready to adopt a fighting policy.

The Royal Ascot meeting was split into two by the general election. There was no racing on the Thursday, which was polling day, and Thursday's programme was transferred to the Saturday. There were broad smiles and high morale on the last two days, the Tories having defied the opinion polls and gained a surprising victory.

The Gold Cup was reckoned to be a good thing for M. D. Wildenstein's Le Chouan, winner of the Prix Royal Oak and the Prix du Cadran. M. Wildenstein had bought this four-year-old by Le Tyrol for £34,000 at the April dispersal sale of the late Baron de Waldner's horses. Le Chouan, however, finished unplaced and possibly the firm ground did not suit him. Saint-Martin stated that Le Chouan had been struck into from behind five furlongs from home, at which point Le Chouan had lost his place, but a careful examination by the Stewards of the patrol camera films failed to produce any evidence to support the allegation.

The winner was Mr R. J. McAlpine's roan or grey four-year-old Precipice Wood, by Lauso out of Grecian Garden, by Kingstone. A useful stayer, Kingstone had belonged to King George VI and was by King Salmon out of that famous and influential mare Feola. Like Park Top, Precipice Wood had been bred at the little Buttermilk Stud near Banbury. He had been sold for 1,200 guineas as a foal and was resold for 2,800 guineas a year later. As a three-year-old he won four races and was fourth in The St Leger. At four he won The Paradise Stakes at Newmarket early in May but was lame for some time afterwards and it was a fine performance by his trainer, Mrs Rosemary Lomax, to get him fit to win such an exacting test of stamina as The Gold Cup. It was the first success by a licensed woman trainer in a race of primary importance and the achievement of Mrs Lomax, once a leading point-to-point rider, was extremely popular.

Precipice Wood played up in the parade ring and, after some violent bucking had got rid of Lindley, he made off at a brisk pace but was luckily caught before he had gone very far. In the actual race he did nothing wrong and in the straight he battled on with his customary courage to defeat Blakeney by half a length. Clairon, a French seven-year-old, was third. In his only subsequent race Precipice Wood was beaten a neck by Reindeer in the Prix Kergorlay at Deauville. Unfortunately, his main characteristics, stamina and courage, are not those most likely to attract modern British breeders.

51.   Rosemary Lomax trained Precipice Wood, winner of the Ascot Gold Cup in 1971. This was the first success of a licensed woman trainer in a race of primary importance

Blakeney had obtained his first victory since The Derby when he won The Ormonde Stakes at Chester. He did not win again afterwards though he ran good honest races to finish second in The Gold Cup and The King George VI and Queen Elizabeth Stakes. He was very far from disgraced, too, when fifth in the Prix de l'Arc de Triomphe, his final appearance. He is the sire of Juliette Marny, who won The Oaks and the Irish Guinness Oaks in 1975.

Notable Royal Ascot winners included Welsh Pageant and Connaught, both bred and owned by Mr Jim Joel and trained by Murless, and Karabas. Welsh Pageant was a tall bay four-year-old by Tudor Melody out of the Court Martial mare Picture Light, a member of the Amuse family. Before winning The Queen Anne Stakes by five lengths, Welsh Pageant had won The Victoria Cup, run this year at Newmarket, under 9 st. 6 lb., and The Lockinge Stakes. In The Sussex Stakes he was well beaten by Humble Duty but on the other hand he finished seven lengths in front of her in The Queen Elizabeth II Stakes. It was decided to keep this good and genuine miler in training in 1971.

Many disobliging remarks had been made about Connaught during his first three seasons in training but as a five-year-old he gave the critics little cause for complaint. He had a simple task in The Westbury Stakes at Sandown in May. At Royal Ascot he broke the course record when beating Hotfoot by four lengths in The Prince of Wales's Stakes. His final race was The Eclipse Stakes, in which he was opposed only by Karabas and Nor. It was generally thought that Karabas would beat him for speed at the finish and Karabas was accordingly favourite at 6/4 on.

Connaught was always liable to play the fool at the start and for a long time he declined to enter his stall, backing away at the last moment just when it seemed that he had decided to be co-operative. However, the starter was very patient and at long last Connaught entered his stall. That was not the end of the trouble, though, as when the stalls opened Connaught swerved sharply to the left, shooting the unfortunate Barclay up round his neck. For a few seconds Barclay was in jeopardy but somehow he managed to regain his irons and very soon Connaught was in front. There Connaught remained. Karabas never succeeded in getting at him and Connaught won by two and a half lengths, breaking the course record established in this race nine years previously by his sire, St Paddy.

Connaught never raced again. He had had his ups and downs but over a mile and a quarter on a galloping course he was a difficult horse to beat.

Karabas's only victory this season came in The Hardwicke Stakes, in which he beat Intermezzo and Reindeer, winners of the English St Leger and the Irish St Leger respectively. He did, though, go close to winning the valuable Prix Dollar at Longchamp, going under by a mere nose to the German six-year-old Priamos. In The King George VI and Queen Elizabeth Stakes he was badly struck into and he never ran again.

The King's Stand Stakes at Royal Ascot went to Mr Arpad Plesch's American-bred, French-trained Amber Rama who beat Huntercombe by a length and a half. Huntercombe, trained by Arthur Budgett, had his revenge in the autumn when he beat Amber Rama by the same distance in the six-furlongs Prix de Seine-et-Oise at Maisons-Laffitte. Amber Rama was brought to England as a sire but the son of Jaipur, by Nasrullah, has so far proved rather less successful than anticipated.

The unsuccessful favourite for The King's Stand Stakes was the five-year-old Raffingora by Grey Sovereign out of Cameo, by Como. Bred at the Eveton Stud owned by Mr Tony Samuel, he raced for two years in Mr Samuel's colours and was trained by Doug Smith. His record was unremarkable. At two he won The Caterham Stakes at Epsom and The Lavant Stakes at Goodwood, and at three the Rouge Croix Stakes at Ascot. As he seemed to have no particular future ahead of him and had in fact been showing a certain lack of enthusiasm in his more recent races, he was offered for sale at Newmarket in November and was bought for 1,800 guineas by Mr A. G. M. Stevens, a Wiltshire farmer and bloodstock breeder who sent him to be trained at Marlborough by Bill Marshall, a former National Hunt rider who had been awarded the D.F.C. when serving in the R.A.F. as a fighter pilot.

The change of surroundings had a most remarkable effect on Raffingora and in due course this big, immensely powerful grey became one of the most popular horses in the country. At four he ran fourteen times and won eight races. At York he won The Rievaulx Handicap and The Harewood Handicap, on both occasions shouldering 10 stone. At five he was better still. He won The Cicero Handicap at Epsom with 10 stone, giving 29 lb. to the useful Trillium who was second; The Micklegate Handicap at York with 10 stone, giving 30 lb. to the runner-up; The Temple Stakes at Sandown with 9 st. 4 lb., beating The Brianstan, Tower Walk and Jukebox; The Cherkley Sprint Handicap at Epsom with 10 stone; The Great Central Handicap at Haydock Park with 10 stone, giving 38 lb. to the runner-up; The John Banks Gold Cup at Lanark with 10 st. 1 lb., giving 36 lb. to the runner-up; The King George Stakes at Goodwood, beating The Brianstan and Realm; The Park End All Aged Stakes at Chepstow; and The Executives' Sprint Stakes at Beverley with 9 st. 7 lb. In addition he was third in The Palace House Stakes at Newmarket, The Nunthorpe Stakes and the Prix de l'Abbaye de Longchamp. All told, this very gallant sprinter won twenty races and £24,261 in England and 24,000 francs in France. His record during his last two seasons was a tribute to the skill of his trainer, who transformed a horse that had apparently lost interest in racing into a model of courage and consistency. Marshall was also wonderfully successful with another grey, My Swanee, by Petition, who had belonged to Mr David Robinson till sold at Newmarket as a four-year-old for 5,800 guineas. In the next two seasons Marshall trained My Swanee to win nine races including The City and Suburban Handicap; The Northern Handicap at Doncaster with 10 stone; The Sandown Anniversary Handicap with 10 stone; The Magnet Cup at York with 9 st. 7 lb.; and The Rose of York Handicap at York with 9 st. 13 lb.

Raffingora was retired to the stud in 1971 but sad to say his gallant exploits were insufficient to prevent him from being exported to Japan. His daughter Pasty won The Cheveley Park Stakes in 1975.

A mid-summer event that caused almost as much controversy as Craganour's Derby was The Weyhill Maiden Stakes for two-year-old fillies at Salisbury in July. Among the runners was the Duke of Norfolk's Skyway who had never run before and who was ridden by Ron Hutchinson. She did not appear to be much fancied as she drifted in the market from 5/2 to 9/2. She was well up with the leaders for two furlongs but then lost her place. However, she ran on strongly in the final furlong to finish third to Velvet Sheen and Royal Topper, both making their first appearance, beaten a neck and a length and a half.

From the stands it appeared as if Ron Hutchinson had been somewhat economic in effort and had rather overdone things if his objective had been to give the filly a gentle introduction to racing. The Stewards were certainly not satisfied and, after a most careful examination of the patrol camera films, John Dunlop, Skyway's trainer, and Hutchinson were reported to the Stewards of the Jockey Club. It must have been highly disagreeable for the Salisbury Stewards, at least one of whom was a close personal friend of the Duke's, to take this action over a horse belonging to a much respected owner who had done great services for racing. There is no doubt, though, that if they had taken the easy way out and turned a blind eye they would have been severely mauled by the press.

The upshot was that Dunlop was fined £500 and Hutchinson suspended for a fortnight. For once the Duke, whose health was then beginning to deteriorate, failed to display his customary wisdom and made statements which were later withdrawn. It would have been better had he adopted an attitude of dignified silence. If, however, he overreacted, this was because both he and also the Duchess, who played a leading part in running the stable, were grievously hurt by the result of the case, and furthermore the Duke felt impelled to speak his mind out of loyalty to his trainer and his jockey.

Probably there was no more to it than a filly being given an easy race first time out. After all, the great Myrobella was beaten first time out at Salisbury. Skyway was no Myrobella but in fact a very moderate animal that ran five times subsequently without winning and was sold at Newmarket in December for 1,900 guineas. It was bad luck as far as Skyway and her connections were concerned that the form in The Weyhill Stakes was extremely bad. Velvet Sheen ran five times afterwards that season without winning again, while Royal Topper ran three times more without even gaining a place.

Of course the press made a meal of the whole business. The sad part was that feelings were so badly bruised and a number of old friendships damaged almost beyond repair.

At the big Goodwood Meeting The Molecomb Stakes was won by Cawston's Pride, a tall, rangy chestnut trained by Maxwell. She was unquestionably the season's outstanding two-year-old filly and was unbeaten in eight races, her victories including The Queen Mary Stakes which she won by six lengths, The Star Fillies Stakes at Sandown, The Lowther Stakes and The Cornwallis Stakes. Such was her speed that she was liable to frighten away opposition. She was by no means fashionably bred, being by Ribot's son Con Brio, exported to Argentina, out of Cawston's Tower, by Maharaj Kumar.

Mrs Hue-Williams's Rock Roi, by Mourne, achieved a Goodwood double, winning both The Warren Stakes and The Gordon Stakes. Trained by Peter Walwyn, he was destined to make turf history by twice winning The Ascot Gold Cup and twice being disqualified.

Parthenon won The Goodwood Cup for Sir Reginald Macdonald-Buchanan, beating the Queen's Magna Carta, but Magna Carta, trained by Ian Balding, reversed the form in The Doncaster Cup, which he won by four lengths. Magna Carta was certainly bred to stay, being by Charlottesville out of that good mare Almeria, by Alycidon. His other victories in 1970 included The Ascot Stakes, The Greenall Whitley Trophy and The W. D. & H. O. Wills Trophy. He might have achieved great things in 1971 but unfortunately he met with a fatal accident.

At the St Leger meeting Lord Howard de Walden's Parmelia, a half-sister to St Paddy by Ballymoss, showed what a good stayer she was when winning The Park Hill Stakes by ten lengths. She had previously won The Ribblesdale Stakes.

The top two-year-olds in The Free Handicap were My Swallow (9 st. 7 lb.), Mill Reef (9 st. 6 lb.) and Brigadier Gerard (9 st. 5 lb.). A powerful, impressive bay, My Swallow was bred in Ireland by Mr M. A. Walshe and was bought for 5,000 guineas by Lord Harrington on behalf of Mr David Robinson at Goffs September Sale. He is by Le Levanstell, a good miler that sired an outstanding stayer in Levmoss, out of Darrigle, by the July Cup and Portland Handicap winner Vilmoray. Darrigle won a couple of five-furlongs races in Ireland as a three-year-old. Vilmoray was by the sprinter Vilmorin whose name occurs in the pedigree of Brigadier Gerard, and also in that of the famous steeplechaser Red Rum.

Trained by Paul Davey, one of Mr Robinson's three private trainers, My Swallow made his first racecourse appearance in the five-furlongs Zetland Stakes at York in May. His promise at home had not passed unnoticed by the watchers on Newmarket Heath and he started at 13/8 on. He won impressively by three lengths. He was a shade less impressive in his next race, the six-furlongs Woodcote Stakes at Epsom on Derby day but the course was not altogether to his liking. He did not run again in England till the following season.

My Swallow's first race in France was the five-furlongs Prix du Bois at Longchamp on June 27. Ridden by Swinburn—Piggott rode him in all his other races—he won easily by four lengths. He had a much tougher task in the five-and-a-half furlongs Prix Robert Papin at Maisons-Laffitte as he was opposed by Mr Paul Mellon's Mill Reef who had won The Coventry Stakes at Royal Ascot by eight lengths. My Swallow, drawn on the rails, led from the start but Mill Reef pressed him hard and steadily closed the gap so that in the end it needed everything that Piggott had to offer to enable My Swallow to win by a short head. It was Mill Reef's only defeat that season.

My Swallow's remaining victories that season were more easily achieved. He won the six-furlongs Prix Morny at Deauville by two lengths, the seven-furlongs Prix de la Salamandre at Longchamp by two lengths, and the one-mile Grand Criterium by half a length. The Grand Criterium concluded his brilliant campaign. He headed the Free Handicaps in both England and France. He won £3,189 in England, £88,295 in France. He was the first horse since Nirgal in 1945 to win the Robert Papin, the Morny and the Grand Criterium; the first ever to add the Salamandre to those three. It certainly looked, provided that he made the normal improvement, as if it would take an exceptionally good horse to beat him in The Two Thousand Guineas, his one classic engagement.

Mill Reef, bred in America by his owner Mr Paul Mellon, was a compact, beautifully proportioned bay, full of quality and with a delightful temperament, by Never Bend, a son of Nasrullah, out of Milan Mill, by Princequillo out of Virginia Water, by Count Fleet. Never Bend was the champion American two-year-old of 1962. He was placed in The Kentucky Derby and The Preakness Stakes but ran poorly the only time he was asked to tackle a distance longer than a mile and a quarter. Milan Mill, who only raced at two, was a half-sister to Berkeley Springs, second in The One Thousand Guineas and The Oaks. Fifth dam of Mill Reef is the celebrated Black Ray, Mr Mellon having bought her granddaughter Red Ray, who bred Virginia Water, for 12,000 guineas at Lord Portal's dispersal sale in 1949.

Mill Reef began his racing career in The Salisbury Stakes at Salisbury on May 13. At that point of time an American-bred colt named Fireside Chat was rated the best two-year-old seen out and he started at 9/2 on. Mill Reef had him beaten a long way out, and receiving 7 lb., won as he pleased by four lengths. He won The Coventry Stakes at Royal Ascot by eight lengths and then came his memorable duel with My Swallow at Maisons-Laffitte, when My Swallow, the better drawn of the two, beat him all out by a short head. His next race was The Gimcrack

Stakes at York. It was a dreadful day with the rain teeming down without a break. The going was heavy. Mill Reef was never off the bit, though, and in the last two furlongs he went right away from his opponents to win by ten lengths from Yellow God. It was a wonderfully impressive performance.

He was far less impressive in The Imperial Stakes at Kempton and Geoff Lewis had to work really hard on him before he mastered Hecla, a filly by Henry the Seventh, inside the final furlong. Ian Balding was inclined to blame himself for having given Mill Reef too easy a time at home since The Gimcrack. Hecla was in fact quite a formidable opponent as she was very fast and had won The Cherry Hinton Stakes at Newmarket by eight lengths. Mill Reef completed his racing for the season with an easy victory in The Dewhurst Stakes. He was obviously a very good colt indeed but, because of his sire, doubts existed of his ability to stay a mile and a half the following year.

Mrs Hislop's Brigadier Gerard, a big, handsome powerful bay, was bred by Mr John Hislop and is by Queen's Hussar, a good miler that won The Sussex Stakes, out of the non-winning La Paiva, by Prince Chevalier. Brigadier Gerard was the fifth foal of La Paiva, a descendant of Pretty Polly, and her fifth winner. La Paiva had not been mated with the more fashionable sires. The Traveller's, for example, who won four races, was by Gratitude, while Delaunay, who won seven races, was by Donore. Brigade Major, winner of The Jubilee, was by Major Portion. The selection of Queen's Hussar as a mate for La Paiva may have been influenced to some extent by his (at that time) modest fee and also by his proximity, since Lord Carnarvon's Highclere Stud, where Queen's Hussar stands, is within easy bicycling distance of the Hislops' stud at Easy Woodhay.

I recall John Hislop telling me in the spring of 1970 that Brigadier Gerard was the best two-year-old in Dick Hern's powerful stable. I was inclined to accept that statement as yet further evidence of that rather touching optimism that is typical of so many owners and without which racing could hardly exist at all. I certainly did not then visualise Queen's Hussar as a potential sire of classic winners.

I had reason to start reversing my opinion at Newbury on June 24. Brigadier Gerard took the field in the five-furlongs Berkshire Stakes and, starting at 100/7 in a field of five, he won with singular ease by five lengths. Shortly afterwards, carrying 9 st. 7 lb., he won the six-furlongs Champagne Stakes at Salisbury by four lengths. In August he won the six-furlongs Washington Singer Stakes at Newbury without difficulty. His final appearance for the season came in The Middle Park Stakes. There were some fast colts opposing him including Mr J. H. Whitney's American-bred Swing Easy, winner of The New Stakes at Royal Ascot, The July Stakes at Newmarket and The Richmond Stakes at Goodwood. Furthermore Swing Easy, by Delta Judge, had been third in the Prix de la Salamandre, three and a half lengths behind My Swallow. Also in the Middle Park field was Mummy's Pet, winner of The Hyperion Stakes at Ascot and The Norfolk Stakes at Doncaster. Brigadier Gerard won very comfortably by three lengths from Mummy's Pet. Clearly Brigadier Gerard was a very good colt but there was a tendency to rate him as not quite in the same league as My Swallow and Mill Reef. In addition, doubts were expressed over his ability to stay more than a mile at three. Obviously, though, The Two Thousand Guineas had the makings of a race of absorbing interest.

Mr David Robinson was not the leading owner—first place went to Mr Engelhard—but his 130 horses won for him 109 races, thereby establishing a new English record. During the year Mr Robinson submitted plans for the development of the Kempton Park area, not merely for racing but as part of a grandiose commercial scheme. However, the local authorities turned them down flat. Mr Robinson promptly lost interest and resold Kempton at cost price to the Levy Board, which already controlled Epsom and Sandown.

Alexandra Park, which more than one Bishop of London had tried without success to have closed down, shut its gates for good in 1970. The scheme adumbrated by Mr Richard Crossman to convert it into a Londoners' Longchamp had never got off the ground at all. 'Ally Pally' was really rather an awful racecourse from every point of view, its only advantage being its accessibility from central London. In the 1930s a well filled taxi from St James's Street only cost roughly a pound. Sometimes the crowd there was slightly boisterous and in the 1960s the stewards were given a rough time one evening and had their bowler hats crammed down over their noses. Years earlier the starter there managed to get the favourite hopelessly 'left' and was subjected to a fierce barrage of bricks and stones. Mr Geoffrey Freer was much struck by the starter's coolness under fire and remarked on it. The starter replied that he was inured to such treatment, having been for several years starter at Ostend where he had built himself quite a nice villa on the sea largely out of the bricks and missiles hurled at him on the racecourse in the course of his duties.

There were certain horses like Cider Apple and Auction Pool that loved Ally Pally and always produced their best form there and it was the only course at which Friar's Daughter, dam of the triple crown winner Bahram, ever won a race.

Lord Wigg turned down the offer of a year's extension of his job as Chairman of the Levy Board but accepted a two-year extension. His first term of office was on the whole very successful and his energy and determination, combined with a marked disrespect for pointless traditions, brought about some much-needed changes. His deep understanding of betting and bookmakers was invaluable. His second term proved less rewarding. He seemed to have become more abrasive, less tolerant of views sincerely held that happened to differ from his own. There were constant rumours that he was at loggerheads with the Jockey Club. Tact and urbanity had never been numbered among his more noticeable virtues and he eventually forfeited much of the good will he had enjoyed in the racing world. It was not just racing's 'establishment' that viewed his eventual departure if not with actual relief, then with indifference.

In some parts of the country attendances continued to cause concern. Doncaster's Dickensian old grandstand had been pulled down and a luxurious new one erected but despite that, and despite the presence of Nijinsky, the St Leger day attendance was only 29,000. When Airborne won in 1946, it was 143,000.

Sandy Barclay had appeared to have the world at his feet but in 1970 came the surprise announcement of the end of his association with Noel Murless's stable. In 1971 he was going to France to ride for François Boutin. Despite Barclay's obvious talent, his career since he left Murless has been one of consistent disappointment. Perhaps there is some element in his character that renders him ill suited to the stresses and strains of a top-class jockey's life.

My Swallow's first race in 1971 was the seven-furlongs Usher Stakes at Kempton. He looked as if he had wintered extremely well and won comfortably from three second-rate opponents. Mill Reef had rather more to do in The Greenham Stakes at Newbury and fully satisfied his admirers in beating Breeder's Dream, winner the previous September of The Champagne Stakes, by four lengths with Swing Easy three lengths away third. Brigadier Gerard had no preliminary outing before The Two Thousand Guineas.

The big three frightened the opposition away at Newmarket and there were only six runners for The Two Thousand Guineas. Mill Reef was favourite at 6/4 with My Swallow at 2/1 and Brigadier Gerard at 11/2. Backed from 10/1 to 15/2 was Nijinsky's brother Minsky, who had been narrowly beaten in The Observer Gold Cup the previous autumn by Linden Tree. My Swallow, impressively powerful, was widely regarded as the pick of the field on looks. Mill Reef, admired for his quality and his faultless proportions, seemed almost small alongside My Swallow and the well muscled-up Brigadier Gerard. The blinkered Minsky, winner of his two preliminary races, behaved in the parade ring in a manner suggesting that his mind was not altogether concentrated on racing.

My Swallow, Durr up, forced the pace from the start with Mill Reef in close attendance. Mercer on Brigadier Gerard was content to track these two and close behind him was Piggott on Minsky. The first horse beaten was Minsky whose tail began to revolve at a brisk rate three furlongs from home. Just as everyone was wondering whether My Swallow was going to be able to hold off Mill Reef, Mercer suddenly set Brigadier Gerard alight. Brigadier Gerard immediately responded. With a furlong to go he swept past the two leaders and ran on strongly up the hill to win by three lengths from Mill Reef. My Swallow was three parts of a length away third and Minsky five lengths behind My Swallow.

My Swallow only ran twice subsequently. He was beaten six lengths by Faraway Son in the seven-furlongs Prix de la Porte Maillot at Longchamp, and second, beaten half a length, to Realm in The July Cup at Newmarket. He was then sold for £400,000 as a stallion to Mr Irving Allen. So far Mr Allen does not appear to have obtained a bargain.

The Guineas victory of Brigadier Gerard had been a brilliant one. He had fairly and squarely beaten two high-class horses and had beaten them decisively, too. His success was extremely popular, not least because Mr and Mrs Hislop, who owned him in partnership, had bravely turned down an offer of £250,000 from M. D. Wildenstein and the Hislops were not in the millionaire class—at any rate not then.

Born in 1911, John Hislop came into racing more or less by chance. A soldier's son, he was himself destined for the army after leaving Wellington but a serious operation while at Sandhurst put paid to that particular plan. If his health had not compelled him to leave the R.M.C., he would very likely have departed to India and been lost to racing, at least for a considerable period. As it was, he became assistant to Victor Gilpin, firstly at Newmarket, later at Findon. With typical thoroughness and determination, he made himself into a really good rider. On the flat he was thirteen times leading amateur and could have held his own against professionals. Over fences his best effort was to finish third in The Grand National on Kami. During the war he served firstly with the Royal Artillery (T.A.) and later with 'Phantom' (attached to the S.A.S.), being awarded the M.C.

After the war, when he rode a lot of winners for Tom Masson and George Todd, he took up racing journalism. He is a naturally good writer with a proper respect for the English language, and this, combined with his knowledge of racing from the inside, makes him extremely readable. After many years with The Observer, he had a spell with the News of the World where his talents were shamefully wasted. From its inception he has been closely connected with The British Racehorse. He is an acknowledged expert on bloodstock breeding and the author of a number of widely enjoyed books. Smallish, well-read, impeccably turned out, very keen still on physical fitness and keeping his weight down, he has borne success with Brigadier Gerard and election to the Jockey Club with dignity and without losing or forgetting old friends in many branches of the racing world. If he has made a fortune out of racing, he has worked hard for it, and what he has achieved is largely due to his own expertise and enterprise, though of course a bit of luck is needed for a 'small' breeder to produce a champion like 'The Brigadier'.

Immediately after The Guineas it was at once made clear that Brigadier Gerard would not contest The Derby but would be kept for races over a less exacting distance. The Derby, though, was the objective of Mill Reef. There were many lively discussions about his stamina. He was inclined to run freely but he was not a hard-pulling front-runner like his sire, Never Bend, whom many Americans simply could not visualise getting a high-class winner over a mile and a half.

Until quite recently it was accepted that The Derby would in all probability be won by a horse whose sire had either won, or had been placed in, a top-class race of a mile and a half or more. The influx of American blood into Europe, though, seems to have altered this and Sir Ivor, Nijinsky, Mill Reef and Roberto are all by horses that did not come into that category. Those four, incidentally, are all male-line descendants of Nearco who won the Grand Prix de Paris but was not, in the opinion of his owner, the great Federico Tesio, a genuine stayer but reliant on his class and his courage to see him through. Both Sir Ivor and Roberto are descended from Nearco through The Ayr Gold Cup winner Royal Charger, one of several highly influential stallions unwisely exported by the Irish to America.

Mill Reef did not run again before The Derby, for which he started favourite at 100/30. He ran a delightfully smooth race and Lewis was able to settle him down without apparent difficulty. Fourth at Tattenham Corner, Mill Reef gradually closed on Linden Tree in the straight, and taking the lead at the distance, he ran

52. Mill Reef, after winning the 1971 Derby

on stoutly to win by two lengths from the plucky but somewhat one-paced Linden Tree with Irish Ball two and a half lengths away third. From a long way out Mill Reef had looked so certain to win that the closing stages were somewhat lacking in excitement.

Mill Reef's victory was a notable triumph for Ian Balding, who had taken out a licence as recently as 1964. No doubt it afforded him particular satisfaction to win the race for Mr Paul Mellon, who had been a patron of the stable for many years, having had jumpers with it when it was at Wroughton and under the control of Ivor Anthony. Born in 1907, Mr Mellon, who took a degree at Cambridge, is a member of one of the richest families in the world. He is a leading figure in the differing spheres of banking, the arts and sport—sport in his case including fox-hunting and sailing as well as racing. Quiet and modest, he has owned a number of good winners in this country such as Midsummer Night II, the grey sprinter Secret Step, Silly Season and Berkeley Springs.

Linden Tree, bred and owned by Mrs Dermot McCalmont and trained by Peter Walwyn, had won The Chester Vase before running so well in The Derby. With Mill Reef not a competitor, he looked a good thing for the Irish Sweeps Derby. In that event, however, he appeared to stop as he left his stall and then swerve away to the left. By the time that Duncan Keith had straightened him out, the remainder had covered a furlong. He never ran again and eventually departed to carry out stud duties in France. Winner of The Irish Sweeps Derby was Mr Emile Littler's French-trained Irish Ball, by Baldric II, who had three lengths to spare over Lombardo.

Mill Reef's next race was The Eclipse Stakes, in which his five opponents included the four-year-old Caro and the five-year-old Welsh Pageant. Caro, owned by Countess Margit Batthyany and trained in France by Albert Klimscha, was an extremely good-looking grey by Fortino II, a successful and versatile sire whom the Irish foolishly sold to the Japanese. At three Caro had won the French Two Thousand Guineas and the Prix d'Ispahan as well as finishing third to Sassafras in the French Derby. At four he was even better, winning the Prix d'Harcourt, the Prix Ganay and the Prix Dollar. The French reckoned him capable of beating Mill Reef and he started at 11/8, Mill Reef being favourite at 5/4.

As things turned out, Mill Reef had far too much finishing speed for Caro and went right away from him in the closing stages to win by four lengths. Welsh Pageant was two and a half lengths away third. The French were astonished at the ease with which Caro had been defeated. Klimscha, though, offered no excuses, merely observing that it was no disgrace to be beaten by a great horse and that Mill Reef was better than Nijinsky. Three weeks later Mill Reef produced his most brilliant form to win The King George VI and Queen Elizabeth Stakes by six lengths from Ortis, who, on his previous appearance, had won The Hardwicke Stakes by eight lengths, with Acclimatization three lengths away third. Irish Ball finished fifteen lengths behind the winner.

Mill Reef's final objective was the Prix de l'Arc de Triomphe. Without him, Linden Tree and Irish Ball, The St Leger was very much a second eleven affair but at least it provided an exciting finish, Mrs John Rogerson's Athens Wood, trained by Tom Jones and ridden by Piggott, winning all out by a neck from Homeric with Falkland a neck away third. Athens Wood, a bay colt by Celtic Ash that had cost only 3,100 guineas as a yearling, made all the running and his victory was largely due to Piggott's wonderful judgement of pace and his own courage. There have been many better St Leger winners, few more stout-hearted. In his two previous outings he had won The Gordon Stakes at Goodwood and The Great Voltigeur Stakes at York.

It was a first classic success both for Mrs Rogerson and for Tom Jones. Up till then the most important victory for Mrs Rogerson, a daughter of the late Mr 'Solly' Joel, had been when Salmon Spray won The Champion Hurdle. Tom Jones is a cheerful character, who, after Eton and the First Royal Dragoons—he still retains a trace of what used to be known as 'the cavalry spirit'—received further and doubtless more profitable education in the form of four years with Sam Armstrong. Since 1951 he has conducted a mixed stable at Newmarket with considerable success. He won The Whitbread Gold Cup with Frenchman's Cove owned by Mr Stanhope Joel, whose daughter Solna was his first wife, and The Ribblesdale Stakes and The Yorkshire Oaks with Fleet Wahine. He endures life's little vicissitudes with apparent equanimity assisted by a lively sense of humour which frequently finds an outlet in verse. Not for nothing is he known as the Dylan

Thomas of Newmarket. At times his light-hearted manner has tended to blind people to his undoubted professional ability.

Athens Wood remained in training as a four-year-old but failed to win. After a brief spell as a stallion in this country he was exported to Russia.

Mill Reef fully lived up to his reputation in the Arc. Fifth into the straight, he quickened to lead over a furlong out and ran on without the slightest sign of weakening to win by three lengths in record time from a very good filly in Pistol Packer, who had won the Prix de Diane, the Prix de la Nonette and the Prix Vermeille. The fast-finishing Cambrizzia was third and Caro fourth. Lewis, who as usual rode Mill Reef, also won the Prix de l'Abbaye on Mrs B. Attenborough's sprinter Sweet Revenge, trained by 'Atty' Corbett.

Mill Reef, who was to stay in training for a further year, was voted Horse of the Year, a distinction that caused pain and grief to some of Brigadier Gerard's admirers on the grounds that on the only occasion the two had met, Brigadier Gerard had proved himself unquestionably the superior, at any rate over a mile.

Brigadier Gerard's next race after The Two Thousand Guineas was The St James's Palace Stakes at Royal Ascot. It was a horrible day with the rain teeming down and the going became extremely soft, which did not suit Brigadier Gerard at all. A good many owners would have played safe and taken him out of the race but the Hislops took the view that conditions were no worse for him than for the other runners and let him take his chance. Fortune, quite rightly so, favours the brave and Brigadier Gerard won, but it was sheer courage on his part that enabled him to get his head in front in the last few strides to beat Mr J. R. Mullion's Sparkler, a Hard Tack colt trained by Sam Armstrong, by a short head. Bought as a foal for 1,400 guineas, Sparkler was a good, tough miler whose victories that season included the Thirsk Classic Trial, The Diomed Stakes at Epsom, the Prix Quincey at Deauville and the Prix Perth at Saint-Cloud. The third dam of Sparkler was Hatton, a Mr Jinks mare that produced that remarkable gelding Hatton's Grace, who won the Irish Cesarewitch twice, the second time at the age of ten, and The Champion Hurdle three years running, the first time when already nine years of age.

At Goodwood the ground was soft but it was not ideal for snipe as it had been at Ascot. Brigadier Gerard certainly did not seem to be inconvenienced and won The Sussex Stakes by five lengths from the American-bred, French-trained Faraway Son, who was conceding him 11 lb. On his previous appearance Faraway Son had given My Swallow 7 lb. and beaten him by six lengths over seven furlongs at Saint-Cloud. At Ascot in September the going was firm and Brigadier Gerard won The Queen Elizabeth II Stakes in a canter by eight lengths from the four-year-old Dictus, who was giving him 7 lb. In the Prix Jacques le Marois at Deauville, Dictus had given Sparkler 9 lb. and had beaten him by half a length.

Brigadier Gerard's final race of the season was The Champion Stakes. This was the first time he had tackled a distance longer than a mile. Unfortunately for him, there had been a lot of rain during the previous twenty-four hours and there was a heavy storm while the runners were in the paddock. As at Royal Ascot, the

53. Brigadier Gerard

conditions were all against Brigadier Gerard and as at Ascot, there was no question of shirking the issue. For the second time Brigadier Gerard's superlative courage pulled him through and he won by a short head from the Irish four-year-old Rarity, who was useless on firm ground but a pretty good horse if it happened to come up mud. Fifty yards from home Rarity looked very much like winning but then came a supreme final effort by Brigadier Gerard and Joe Mercer. There was an agonising wait of ten minutes before the judge announced Brigadier Gerard as the winner. A great cheer went up in appreciation of a very gallant victor and soon afterwards John Hislop announced that never again would 'The Brigadier' be asked to race on the soft.

Like Mill Reef, Brigadier Gerard was to remain in training in 1972. Everyone hoped to see these two giants of the turf in opposition for a second time and The Eclipse Stakes seemed to be the most probable race.

Inevitably in 1971 the three-year-old fillies were overshadowed by the colts. Cawston's Pride, the best of her age and sex in 1970, won the One Thousand Guineas Trial at Ascot and started favourite at 6/4 for The One Thousand Guineas. Unfortunately she was not in a co-operative mood and when she got out on to the course after leaving the parade ring nothing would induce her to canter down to the start. She dug her toes in with a resolution worthy of a nobler cause and the combined efforts of her trainer, Farnham Maxwell, and a band of helpers could not induce her to.change her mind. Just when it seemed as if the favourite would take no part, along came Jimmy Lindley riding a plump, shaggy Welsh cob named Billy who had been borrowed from Harvey Leader to escort Cawston's Pride to the track. Lindley steered Billy at the best pace he could muster, which was slow, towards the start. Cawston's Pride gave the matter a few seconds thought and then quietly followed her friend down to the stalls.

In the race Cawston's Pride was travelling smoothly and ideally placed just over two furlongs from home. As soon as she was asked for her effort, though, round went her tail and she took no further interest in the proceedings, finishing fifth. She only ran once afterwards, though 'ran' is perhaps the wrong word as she refused to start in The King's Stand Stakes. Her son Cawston's Clown won the Coventry Stakes at Royal Ascot in 1976.[1]

Second favourite for The One Thousand Guineas and the main hope of Murless's stable was Lord Howard de Walden's Magic Flute, a rather angular, mean-looking Tudor Melody filly that had won The Cheveley Park Stakes. Murless's other runner was the 25/1 outsider Altesse Royale, owned by Colonel F. R. Hue-Williams. She was ridden by Yves Saint-Martin. At the Craven Meeting Altesse Royale had finished second in The Nell Gwyn Stakes to Super Honey who was giving her 4 lb.

Magic Flute looked very dangerous racing down into the Dip but found nothing on the hill and eventually finished fourth. On the other hand Altesse Royale, who had led from the start, ran on like a true stayer to win by a length and a half from Super Honey with Catherine Wheel third.

A big, rangy chestnut with plenty of scope about her, Altesse Royale was bred by Mrs Vera Hue-Williams. Her sire, Saint Crespin III, a half-brother by Aureole to Tulyar, won the Prix de l'Arc de Triomphe and The Eclipse Stakes. He was eventually exported to Japan. Bleu Azur, Altesse Royale's dam, is by Crepello and a member of the famous Marchetta family.

Geoff Lewis rode Altesse Royale in The Oaks. She started favourite at 6/4 and won easily by three lengths from Mr Jim Joel's Maina, likewise trained by Murless. The official electrically recorded time for The Oaks was 2 minutes 36·95 seconds. This made Altesse Royale the fastest of all Oaks winners. Furthermore, her time was a fifth of a second better than that of Mill Reef in The Derby. However, skilled and experienced watch-holders in the stand, among them Mr Phil Bull and Mr Alec Bird, flatly refused to accept the official time and, despite repeated official statements that the course apparatus was entirely reliable, they stuck firmly to their view that the official time was inaccurate to the extent of between one and two seconds. Eventually, months later, it came to light that the electric timing mechanism had not been functioning automatically on Oaks day and that for the big race it had been started manually, clearly later than it should have been. The Managing Director of Racecourse Technical Services resigned.

[1] Another son, Solinus, won The Coventry Stakes in 1977, and The King's Stand Stakes and The William Hill Sprint Championship in 1978.

Altesse Royale ran only once afterwards, winning the Irish Guinness Oaks from M. D. Wildenstein's Vincennes.

Geoff Lewis established a new record at Epsom by winning not only The Derby and The Oaks, but also The Coronation Cup. The 1970 Oaks winner, Lupe, was his mount in The Coronation Cup and she won by a neck from the 11/8 on favourite Stintino. Barclay was widely blamed for the favourite's defeat on the grounds that he had left him with too much to do, but Stintino, who had to be ridden from behind, was reluctant to stride out on the firm ground. Lupe had one more race before retirement to the stud, winning The Princess of Wales's Stakes at Newmarket. Unbeaten in England, she is one of three fillies to have won The Oaks and The Coronation Cup, the other two being Pretty Polly and Petite Étoile.

At Royal Ascot the main event, The Gold Cup, was won by Mrs Vera Hue-Williams's four-year-old Rock Roi, trained by Peter Walwyn. He had previously been second to Ramsin in the Prix du Cadran. A routine dope test followed his victory. This disclosed traces of phenylbutazone, a pain-killer more commonly known as Butazolidin. When the case came up before the Stewards of the Jockey Club, Rock Roi was disqualified and the race awarded to Random Shot, owned by Mrs J. Benskin and trained by Arthur Budgett.

After Relko had won The Derby in 1963 and the test revealed traces in his urine of butacaine and benzocaine, the lengthy inquiries ended with Relko retaining the race and the exoneration of his trainer. At that time Rule 66(c) stated: 'Any horse that has been the subject of fraudulent practice may, at the discretion of the Stewards of the Jockey Club, be disqualified for such time and for such races as they shall determine.' Thus the prosecution had then been required to prove that Relko's trainer had administered a substance other than a normal nutrient in order to increase the horse's speed or improve its stamina, courage or conduct in the race. That rule was altered after the Relko affair with the result that a horse could be disqualified without the necessity of proving that the trainer had been guilty of malpractice. Rule 180(II), which caused the disqualification of Rock Roi, stated: 'When a horse has been the subject of an examination under Rule 14(VI) and has been found to have received any substance (other than a normal nutrient) which could alter its racing performance at the time of racing, the horse shall be disqualified for the race in question and may, at the discretion of the Stewards of the Jockey Club, be disqualified for such time and such races as they shall determine.'

What happened in the Rock Roi case was this. In the week before The Gold Cup Walwyn, on veterinary advice, gave a short course of Equipalazone to remedy some slight initial exercise stiffness. The manufacturers recommended that the use of Equipalazone be stopped 72 hours before a race. Walwyn had stopped using the preparation 118 hours before The Gold Cup and, whereas the normal course of treatment lasted for a week and consisted of 20 grams, Rock Roi had received 6 grams over a period of three days.

Walwyn had every reason for thinking he had acted in a reasonable and circumspect manner. It was put forward in his defence at the hearing that the quantity of the drug revealed by the test was so small that Rock Roi's performance could hardly have been affected; that the stiffness from which Rock Roi suffered in fact had persisted; and that without any treatment Rock Roi had beaten Random Shot more easily in The Goodwood Cup than at Ascot. However, the Stewards decided that the drug, as revealed in the test, could have affected the performance of the horse at the time of running. Accordingly Rock Roi was disqualified. The Stewards expressly exonerated Walwyn and his head lad from any suggestion of corrupt practice and fined Walwyn £100, the minimum for a breach of this particular rule.

Some people reckoned that Rock Roi and his connections had been harshly treated. The Stewards, though, had taken the line that Rock Roi's performance could have been affected, and under the relevant rule they had no alternative but to disqualify him. The fact is that the Jockey Club cannot afford any laxity over the question of doping. It would be disastrous if the racing public—and that includes the betting public—came to believe that doping was prevalent and that in consequence they were not getting a fair run for their money. The harm that might be done to racing in such circumstances is incalculable. In addition, a permissive attitude over the use of drugs would reduce the dividends paid by soundness, and also the effectiveness of the racecourse test which, after all, forms the basis for selection in thoroughbred breeding.

The price to be paid for freedom, or at least comparative freedom, from doping is eternal vigilance, and that means a costly system for security and analysis. Some critics think that the price, particularly in these hard times, is too high but the very small proportion of positive tests reflects the efficiency of the anti-doping measures. Every year new drugs come on to the market and there is always a danger that, temporarily at least, the doper may be a step ahead of the analyst. In addition there are problems connected with the use of anabolic steroids[1] and forms of blood treatment rumoured to be in current use in certain major European stables.

Rock Roi had two races subsequently in 1971. He won The Goodwood Cup very easily, finishing eight lengths in front of Random Shot, who was third; and The Doncaster Cup by a length from Russian Bank. More distinctions and misfortunes lay ahead of him in 1972.

On the first day at Royal Ascot The Queen's Vase was won by Mr Roderic More O'Ferrall's Parnell, who was gaining his sixth victory in succession. A tough, game half-brother by St Paddy to Miralgo, Parnell later this season won the Irish St Leger and was third in the Prix Royal Oak. Sun Prince, trained by Dick Hern for Mr (later Sir) Michael Sobell, won The Coventry Stakes. This handsome chestnut by Princely Gift won The St James's Palace Stakes in 1972 and The Queen Anne Stakes in 1973. It must be rare indeed for a horse to win three different races at three successive Royal Ascot meetings. Waterloo, destined to win The One Thousand Guineas the following year, won The Queen Mary Stakes in brilliant style by six lengths, and Magic Flute, as usual looking as if she needed a

---

[1] The problem of anabolic steroids has apparently been solved.

square meal, won the Coronation Stakes with comparable facility. The American-bred Fleet Wahine, by Fleet Nasrullah, won The Ribblesdale Stakes and another American-bred winner was Mr J. H. Whitney's Swing Easy in The King's Stand Stakes. His time, ten seconds slower than that of Amber Rama the previous year, reflected the state of the going. A wonderful bargain at $13,000 as a yearling, Swing Easy went on to win The David Prenn Stakes at Doncaster and then The Nunthorpe Stakes. In The Nunthorpe Stakes Green God finished first but was relegated to second place for bumping.

The Queen owned a nice staying three-year-old filly in Example, a daughter of Exbury trained by Ian Balding. She followed up her victory in The Park Hill Stakes at Doncaster by winning the Prix de Royallieu at Longchamp. The following season she won the Prix Jean de Chaudenay at Saint-Cloud. It was a sad loss to the Royal Stud that she died so young.

The Derby winner St Gatien won The Jockey Club Cup in 1884, 1885 and 1886. This feat was equalled in October by Mr W. Barnett's five-year-old High Line who, trained by Derrick Candy, won that event for the third year running. By High Hat, exported to Japan, High Line was a good genuine stayer that won nine races, but his entire career was restricted to seventeen appearances since he was handicapped by various injuries, a dislike of firm ground and a marked aversion to starting stalls. He is now at the stud but being a stayer he is unlikely to find breeders queueing up to secure a nomination.

The top two-year-olds were less distinguished than those of the previous season. At the head of The Free Handicap with 9 st. 7 lb. was Mr Frank McMahon's American-bred Crowned Prince, trained by van Cutsem. A strongly made, very impressive chestnut by Raise a Native out of Gay Hostess, by Royal Charger, Crowned Prince is a brother of Majestic Prince, winner of The Kentucky Derby and The Preakness Stakes, and he had created a sensation as a yearling when he realised the then record price of $510,000. He made his first racecourse appearance in the six-furlongs Park Lodge Maiden Stakes at Newmarket in August. He started at 7/2 on but on yielding going, to the chagrin of his owner and his breeder who had flown from America to see him run, he faded out in the final furlong and finished sixth behind the 33/1 outsider Jeune Premier.

His next race was the seven-furlongs Champagne Stakes at Doncaster. Equipped with blinkers, he made nearly all the running and won, easing up, by a length from Rheingold. His only other race was The Dewhurst Stakes in which, unblinkered, he beat Rheingold by five lengths.

High Top, second in The Free Handicap with 9 st. 5 lb., was likewise trained by van Cutsem. He had been bred in Warwickshire by Mr Bob McCreery, once a leading amateur rider, and is by Derring Do out of Camanae, by Vimy. Madrilene, dam of Camanae, was a half-sister to Hard Sauce by Court Martial. High Top was offered for sale as a yearling but failed to reach his reserve and was bought privately for 9,000 guineas on behalf of the industrialist, Sir Jules Thorn. He started off by winning The Aylesbury Plate at Sandown. He was an odds-on favourite for The Washington Singer Stakes at Newbury but failed by half a length to concede

3 lb. to Murless's Yaroslav, who went on to win The Royal Lodge Stakes at Ascot.

High Top had no difficulty in winning The Champion Trophy at Ripon and finished the season with a victory in The Observer Gold Cup, in which he ran on in the most determined fashion to beat Steel Pulse, who had only lost the Grand Criterium by a neck, to Hard To Beat. Pentland Firth was third in The Observer Gold Cup and Rheingold well down the course.

Another good two-year-old trained by van Cutsem was Sharpen Up, bred and owned by his wife. Sharpen Up, by Atan out of a mare by Rockefella, won all his five races and in The Middle Park he just held on to win by a head from Philip of Spain with Sun Prince close up third. In the Free Handicap Sharpen Up, who seemed certain to have marked stamina limitations, was given 9 stone.

Rated the top filly was Mr Jim Joel's Rose Dubarry, trained by Tom Waugh. A daughter of Klairon, she had cost 30,000 guineas as a yearling. She won all her three races including The Lowther Stakes and The Norfolk Stakes. In The Norfolk Stakes she beat Deep Diver by two lengths. In The Free Handicap Rose Dubarry was given 9 st. 1 lb., 5 lb. more than the Cheveley Park Stakes winner Waterloo.

Notable deaths in 1971 were those of Mr Charles Engelhard and Mr William Hill. No doubt the role of industrial tycoon in America takes a lot out of a man and it was a shock to learn that Mr Engelhard, who looked every bit of seventy, was in fact only fifty-four. The son of a German who had emigrated to the United States, he was chairman of the Engelhard Minerals and Chemicals Corporation and a man of immense wealth. He took up racing when he was forty and he certainly went into it in a big way. He had racing interests in America, England, Ireland, France and South Africa, and when he died he owned some 300 thoroughbreds worth about $30 million. At the beginning of 1971 he had horses in this country with Jeremy Tree, Fulke Johnson Houghton, Jack Watts and Bill Watts; and in Ireland with Vincent O'Brien. What he sought in racing was simply the pleasure of owning a good horse. He was tremendously pleased when he won a big race; defeat or disappointment he accepted in the manner of a true sportsman and his colours were deservedly popular. He was greatly assisted by his European racing manager, David McCall, a nephew of Sir Cecil Boyd-Rochfort. McCall thoroughly understood the racing game and was extremely skilful in the matter of public and press relations. Of course Nijinsky was the best horse Mr Engelhard raced over here but he also won good races with Romulus, Ribocco, Ribero, Indiana and Habitat.

Mr William Hill, one of the most successful bookmakers of his time, was the son of a Birmingham coachpainter employed by the Daimler Car Company. He himself ran away from school at twelve to work on a farm. A few years later he was working at a tool factory in Birmingham, augmenting his wage packet by collecting bets from his workmates for local bookmakers. By the time he was nineteen he was a bookmaker and married. In 1929 he began operating in the cheap ring at the White City greyhound stadium. What he saw there of his fellow bookmakers did not impress him: he was convinced he could do better than they did. In the 1930s he was a leading bookmaker at the well-run Northolt Park pony-racing meetings, and he also did a bit on the side, illegally, at the Coventry Club in London. When the war came he took a chance, extending his business and his advertising while his rivals were busy cutting down. It was during the war that he became generally recognised as the leader of the ring.

The money came rolling in and he bought the Whitsbury Manor Stud in Wiltshire and the Sezincote Stud in Gloucestershire. By then he was associated with Mr Phil Bull, who helped in the selection of his mares. He bred Nimbus, who won The Two Thousand Guineas and The Derby for Mrs Glenister, and Cantelo, who won a controversial St Leger for himself. In 1947 he bought Chanteur II on the morning of The Coronation Cup, a race that Chanteur II proceeded to win. It was a wonderful Epsom for Hill as he had laid Tudor Minstrel fearlessly, confident that this brilliant horse would not stay. Chanteur II sired three classic winners in Pinza, Cantelo and Only For Life. Together with Sir Victor Sassoon, Hill was largely instrumental in seeing that Ballymoss was retained in this country as a stallion. Hill gave up betting on the rails in 1955. In 1960 the business of William Hill (Park Lane) was merged with Holders Investment Trust, Hill staying with the joint concern till 1970.

Hill died suddenly in his Newmarket hotel during Houghton Sales week. He was a socialist all his life and great wealth never altered his radical outlook. He could be abrasive, and when in the mood was liable to make disobliging comments about people in the racing world who had not come up the hard way as he had done. It would be absurd to pretend that for much of his racing career he was popular. He certainly was not. A good many people reckoned he was hard, stubborn and ruthless. In his closing years he mellowed considerably and was well on the way to becoming a genial father-figure of the turf.

During 1971 the Jockey Club announced that there would be a limited number of races for women riders in 1972. These races were to be all-amateur but girls employed in racing stables were to be permitted to take part. The news was well received, it being felt that some little recognition ought to be made of the debt owed to the many women and girls who worked in racing stables all over the country and who certainly merited the opportunity for a bit of fun.

Benson and Hedges gave news at a press conference of their intention to sponsor an entirely new race, the mile-and-a-quarter Benson and Hedges Gold Cup, to be run over ten furlongs at York in August. The original initiative in the sponsorship of races came from Colonel W. H. Whitbread, who in 1957 sponsored The Whitbread Gold Cup, a steeplechase run in April at Sandown Park. From the start that race proved immensely successful and set the fashion. Sponsorship is now a crutch on which English racing, both on the flat and over jumps, tends to lean very heavily indeed, and the sport would be in a distinctly sorry plight without it. One can only hope that the businesses that go in for it will continue to find it a satisfactory medium for advertising. Some sponsors drop out after a few years but there always seem to be plenty of others queueing up to take their place. Nor is it only the major courses that benefit. Many of the smaller ones have their quota of sponsors, probably local concerns. Brewers, distillers, tobacco firms and bookmakers tend to go in for sponsorship in a big way and one can only hope that parliamentary do-gooders will not succeed in banning this form of advertising because some people do themselves harm by smoking too much, drinking too much and betting beyond their means.

Of course there are disadvantages in sponsorship. The most beautiful race-courses in the country are liable to be disfigured by hideous hoardings advertising the sponsors and sited to catch the attention of television viewers. Important races are liable to have their names changed in confusing fashion. Some names are awkward or unattractive, such as The Clerical, Medical Greenham Stakes or The Burton Rubber Company Limited Novices Chase. Still, in hard times one must not be too particular.

In November a Bill was introduced into Parliament designed to help in finding a solution for the tote's financial problems. The four main points were as follows:

1   The tote should be given the power to bet on events other than horse-racing.
2   It should be allowed to compete directly with bookmakers by offering fixed odds as well as pool betting.
3   It should be allowed to open betting shops in any area, even if there are plenty of others there already.
4   It should be allowed to receive financial aid from the Levy Board, whether by way of grant, loan, guarantee or otherwise.

Of course the bookmakers were furious and counter-attacked forthwith. They rallied their adherents on both sides of the House and ultimately the Bill came to nothing. It is amusing to recall that a man prominent in turf politics, and later closely identified with the bookmakers, observed to me one afternoon at Sandown: 'I shall never forgive the Tories for going soft on the Bill. If it had gone through, we would have had the bookmakers on the run in five years time and you know that has always been my big objective.'

Mr Alec Marsh resigned as Jockey Club starter and was succeeded by Major Peter Thin. Alec Marsh had been an outstanding amateur rider between the wars. Tall, slim and upright, he was a beautiful horseman and will long be remembered for the elegant figure he cut when, mounted on a horse that did him justice, he cantered in his top hat and black overalls down to the start at Royal Ascot. Alas, the reign of the genial, forthright Peter Thin was a brief one as he died suddenly from a heart attack in 1972.

Before turning to the classic three-year-olds of 1972, it would be as well to complete the racing careers of those two heroes of 1971, Mill Reef and Brigadier Gerard. It was the fervent hope of all followers of racing that the two would meet in what journalists were already terming 'the race of the century'—very likely The Eclipse Stakes. Unfortunately, on account of the ailments and injuries suffered by Mill Reef, this meeting never took place.

Mill Reef's campaign at four began with the ten-and-a-half-furlongs Prix Ganay run at Longchamp on April 30 and worth over £30,000 to the winner. In the paddock Mill Reef did not entirely satisfy many of the critics but his perform-

54.   Mill Reef, ridden by Geoff Lewis, winning the Prix Ganay, 1972

ance in the race could hardly be faulted as he won by ten lengths. Possibly the opposition was not unduly formidable but it was an impressive victory nevertheless. It had been intended to run that fine filly Pistol Packer in the Prix Ganay but, after winning the Prix d'Harcourt on April 9, she had been badly struck into when pulling up and a hind leg was severely gashed, requiring five stitches. The antibiotics administered affected her internally and she very nearly died. She could not race again till August. Two outings showed that she had not recaptured her old form and she was retired to the stud.

Mill Reef's next race was The Coronation Cup. He had three opponents. These were Homeric and Wenceslaus, runners-up in The St Leger and the Irish St Leger respectively, and his own pacemaker, Bright Beam. Those who thought this contest would be a repetition of the Prix Ganay were in for a sharp surprise; in fact Mill Reef abbreviated the life-expectancy of one or two bold punters by having to struggle hard to defeat Homeric by a neck. Lewis may not have actually hit Mill Reef but he had to show him the whip and ride him hard in the final

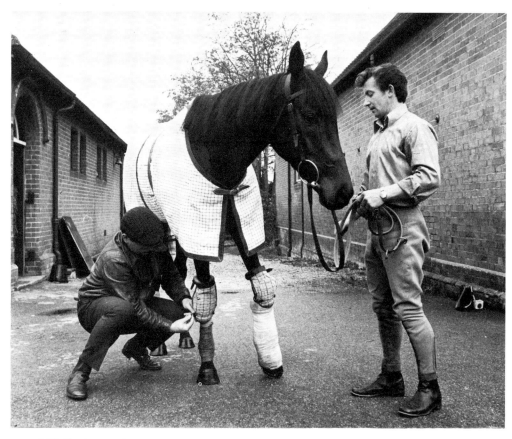

55.   Mill Reef, convalescent, wears a felt support on his left foreleg which he had fractured. His trainer, Ian Balding, and lad John Hallam prepare him for a walk around the stable yard

furlong. Ian Balding's explanation was that because of the atrocious weather Mill Reef had missed a couple of gallops. Soon afterwards, almost every horse in Balding's yard was afflicted by a virus that swept stables throughout the country and it is conceivable that Mill Reef was sickening for it at Epsom. On the other hand, Homeric may have been an underrated horse. Admittedly he failed in The Hardwicke Stakes at Royal Ascot, being third behind Selhurst, but on July 14 he won the £14,700 Prix Maurice de Nieuil at Saint-Cloud. He was then transferred from Dick Hern's stable to that of J. Cunnington junior and on August 6 he won the £11,500 Prix Kergorlay at Deauville. It is more than likely that he would have won the Prix de l'Arc de Triomphe, in which he was third, if he had not broken down badly a furlong from home.

It had been intended to run Mill Reef in The Eclipse Stakes but ten days before that event it was stated that he was not quite himself and would not take part. His target was therefore altered to The Benson and Hedges Gold Cup at York but a slight hock injury prevented him from competing. It was then said that he would run in The Cumberland Lodge Stakes at Ascot prior to endeavouring to gain his second victory in the Arc. In a rather odd attempt to entice Brigadier Gerard into competing in The Cumberland Lodge Stakes, the Ascot executive changed the distance of that event, a pattern race, from a mile and a half to a mile and a quarter.

On August 30 Mill Reef, doing an exercise canter at Kingsclere, fractured his near foreleg. Fortunately veterinary skill of the highest order enabled him to be saved for the stud. He had won twelve of his fourteen races, earning for Mr Mellon £172,259 in England and 1,891,050 francs in France. A horse whose good looks were combined with a gentle and delightful disposition, he had proved himself a great middle-distance horse. He, Ribot and Sea Bird, not one of them British-bred, are probably the three best winners over a mile and a half seen in this country since the war.

Once it was certain that Mill Reef would be able to begin his stud duties in 1973, it was announced that he would stand at the National Stud. In his first season he was limited to twenty mares. Six nominations were offered through the National Stud to British breeders, the fee being 25,000 dollars payable on production of a live foal except for one nomination of £10,000 payable to the National Stud without the foal proviso. Eight nominations were to be sold by Mr Mellon himself, while six he retained for his own mares.

Mill Reef had his first runners in 1976. On the whole they were somewhat disappointing. Million, bought by Lady Beaverbrook for 202,000 guineas, ran once and displayed no observable promise. Teddington Park, who cost 75,000 guineas, showed promise early on but rapidly deteriorated and seemed to lose interest in racing.[1]

It was a wet spring in 1972 and, in order to obtain suitable going, Brigadier Gerard's first appearance at four was delayed until May 20, when he ran in The Lockinge Stakes at Newbury. He gave a thoroughly satisfactory performance in beating Grey Mirage by two and a half lengths with Gold Rod eight lengths away third. Nine days later he ran in the ten-furlongs Westbury Stakes at Sandown. He had quite a tough struggle on this occasion and the four-year-old Ballyhot, receiving 14 lb., kept going gallantly to run him to half a length. At Royal Ascot Brigadier Gerard's target was The Prince of Wales's Stakes in which he gave 19 lb. and a five lengths beating to Steel Pulse, who shortly afterwards won the Irish Sweeps Derby. For The Eclipse Stakes, the going was far softer than he liked following a heavy fall of rain. It is unlikely that he would have run had the opposition been of a more demanding nature. As it was, he never gave the impression that he was really enjoying himself when beating Gold Rod by a length.

Brigadier Gerard's only race over a mile and a half was The King George VI and Queen Elizabeth Stakes. He started favourite at 13/8 on. Among the other runners were the Italian Derby winner Gay Lussac; Riverman, winner of the

[1] In 1978 Shirley Heights, by Mill Reef, won The Derby and the Irish Sweeps Derby, Acamas, also by Mill Reef, won the French Derby.

French Two Thousand Guineas and the Prix d'Ispahan; Steel Pulse; Selhurst, winner of The Hardwicke Stakes; and Parnell, who this season had won the Prix Jean Prat and been second to Rock Roi in the Prix du Cadran. The going was good.

Brigadier Gerard was second and going well, just behind Parnell, as the runners turned for home. With a furlong and a half to go he struck the front and the race looked as good as over. The pace and the distance, though, were beginning to tell and he started to veer to the right towards the rails. Willie Carson snatched Parnell up and switched him to the outside. Gamely as Parnell fought on, he made no impression on Brigadier Gerard in the final two hundred yards, Brigadier Gerard winning by a length and a half. Riverman was five lengths away third. Riverman, on whom Freddie Head was seen to little advantage, had been left with far too much to do and ran very wide on the final bend as well. The time was 0·35 seconds outside the course record established the previous year by Mill Reef.

Inevitably there was an inquiry by the Stewards. Thirteen minutes elapsed before it was announced that the placings would remain unaltered. The films showed that although Brigadier Gerard had indeed veered to the right, there had always been room for Parnell to continue his run on the rails. Futhermore, Parnell himself had been hanging slightly to the left.

Parnell, who had run the race of his life at Ascot, subsequently won a minor race at Windsor as a preliminary to competing in the Arc. He was found to be lame ten days before Longchamp and, though he was sound again three days later, this mishap may have contributed towards a disappointing display. He finished the season by running second to Droll Role in The Washington International. In 1973 Parnell had another good season, winning the Prix Jean Prat again and also The Campari Stakes at Ascot. He was first past the post, too, in the Prix Gladiateur, only to be relegated to third place by the Longchamp Stewards. He remained in training at six and was narrowly beaten in The Queen Alexandra Stakes at Royal Ascot. Tough, genuine little horses of his stamp make scant appeal to modern breeders and in 1976 he was sold for export to South America.

Brigadier Gerard had now won sixteen races in succession and over £200,000. As he seemed none the worse for his Ascot exertions, it was decided to run him in the mile-and-a-quarter Benson and Hedges Gold Cup at York. At one point there was talk of Mill Reef competing in that event but in the end it came to nothing. However, Brigadier Gerard was opposed by Roberto and Rheingold, first and second in The Derby. Roberto was not expected to give much bother. He had had a punishing race in The Derby and had subsequently been twelfth of fourteen in the Irish Sweeps Derby. More trouble was anticipated from Rheingold, who had won the Grand Prix de Saint Cloud by three lengths from Arlequino with Hard To Beat, winner of the Prix Lupin and the French Derby, third. Brigadier Gerard started at 3/1 on, Rheingold at 7/2 and Roberto at 12/1. Roberto was partnered by the American jockey Braulia Baeza, born in Panama, who had never ridden in Europe before. He was not reckoned likely to improve Roberto's chance.

The race proved to be a sensational one. Bright Beam led for four furlongs, after which Baeza sent Roberto to the front. The pace Roberto then set was tremendous. He established a lead of four lengths and soon had most of his rivals in trouble. Joe Mercer was careful not to let Brigadier Gerard get too far behind and with three furlongs to go 'The Brigadier' looked comfortably poised to make his challenge. When Mercer began to ride him, though, there was no response and long before the finish it was clear that the favourite was beaten. Roberto ran on strongly to win by three lengths. Gold Rod was third, ten lengths behind Brigadier Gerard. The time easily beat the course record.

Of course it had been a first-rate piece of opportunist riding by Baeza but that is hardly sufficient explanation for the defeat of a great racehorse by a good one. Brigadier Gerard looked superb in the paddock and he had been greeted by spontaneous applause as he entered the parade-ring. All the same, that Ascot race may have taken more out of him than was thought at the time. Not that he ran badly; his time, too, was better than the previous course record and, though the judge reckoned he had finished ten lengths in front of Gold Rod, the distance in fact was far nearer twenty. He had well and truly slammed Rheingold who had found the pace too hot and had been under pressure a long way out. Really it was not so much a case of Brigadier Gerard running well below his best form as Roberto running far above his. Neither before nor afterwards did Roberto display comparable form. He ran twice after his York triumph, both times ridden by Baeza. In the Prix Niel at Longchamp he was beaten by Hard To Beat and he was then unplaced in the Arc. Mrs Hislop suggested after the York race that Roberto must have been stung by a bee and that seems as likely an explanation as some of the other weird guesses made to account for Roberto's form. At any rate the sponsors had no cause to complain of lack of publicity.

Brigadier Gerard had two races after his defeat by Roberto, The Queen Elizabeth II Stakes and The Champion Stakes. He was brilliant in The Queen Elizabeth II Stakes, giving 7 lb. to a good miler in Sparkler and beating him by six lengths. Sparkler previously this season had won The Queen Anne Stakes at Royal Ascot and the Prix Quincey at Deauville. In The Champion Stakes Brigadier Gerard gave 7 lb. to Riverman and beat him by a length and a half. He was cheered to the echo as he entered the winner's enclosure.

Brigadier Gerard had won seventeen of his eighteen races and £253,000, that money being won entirely in England. As a miler he was worthy to rank with Tudor Minstrel but of course he was a far better stayer than Tudor Minstrel who found even a mile and a quarter beyond him. He was deservedly voted Horse of the Year for 1972. His successes certainly offered encouragement to small breeders as Queen's Hussar's fee was £250 when he covered La Paiva, while Brazen Molly, dam of La Paiva, had cost only 400 guineas at the 1945 December Sales.

The Americans would willingly have paid a couple of million pounds for Brigadier Gerard but the Hislops were determined to keep him in England. Twenty-four shares in him were sold to selected breeders for £25,000 each, thereby giving him a value of £1,000,000. Shares were only sold to breeders who race their own stock. The first of Brigadier Gerard's runners appeared in 1976. The most promising was Baron Guy de Rothschild's Général, trained in France by Mathet.

Général won at Longchamp on the same day that his stable-companion Blushing Groom won the Grand Criterium and he recorded a slightly faster time than Blushing Groom did.[1]

The three-year-old career of Crowned Prince proved brief and disappointing. Favourite at 9/4 on for The Craven Stakes at Newmarket on April 11, he finished unplaced behind Leicester. Shortly afterwards he was found to be suffering from a soft palate. It was decided to take him out of training and retire him to the stud as an operation would keep him off the racecourse for too long and in any case its success could not be guaranteed. It doubtless helped to ease the pain as far as Crowned Prince's owner was concerned that, despite Crowned Prince's modest racing record of two wins in four races, he was sold for a sum alleged to be well in excess of $100,000.

As for Crowned Prince's trainer, Bernard van Cutsem, his consolation came when High Top, who had previously won the Thirsk Classic Trial very easily, won The Two Thousand Guineas, beating Roberto by half a length with Sun Prince no fewer than six lengths away third. High Top, a very strongly made, deep-bodied colt, made all the running and, vigorously urged on by Carson, ran on up the hill in most courageous fashion. He had four more races subsequently and was beaten in the lot. He proved a dire flop in the Irish Two Thousand Guineas but there was a genuine excuse for that failure as he was a sick horse when he got back to England. He did not run again till the end of the July when the fast-improving Sallust beat him by a head in The Sussex Stakes at Goodwood. He ran another good race in the Prix Jacques Le Marois, worth over £19,000 to the winner, at Deauville but went under to Lyphard by a nose. In the Prix du Moulin he was close up fourth behind Sallust and Lyphard. He was then retired to the stud.

The American-bred Roberto, owned by his breeder Mr J. W. Galbreath, is a bay by Royal Charger's grandson Hail to Reason, who never raced at three, out of Bramalea, by Nashua, a son of Nasrullah. Bramalea won eight races and displayed notable resolution in winning The Coaching Club American Oaks. The successes of Roberto emphasised yet again the world-wide influence of Nearco blood.

Trained by Vincent O'Brien, Roberto had proved a high-class two-year-old. He won all his three races in Ireland including The Anglesey Stakes and The National Stakes, but was only fourth behind the Irish-bred Hard To Beat and Steel Pulse in The Grand Criterium, in which, however, he might have been a shade unlucky. As a two-year-old he had been liable to run rather too freely so that in the spring of 1972 O'Brien took a lot of trouble in teaching him to settle down. Roberto learnt his lesson a bit too well. In The Two Thousand Guineas he settled down to such effect that he only really got going when the race was almost over. Coming down into the Dip, he suddenly lengthened his stride and he finished so strongly up the hill that High Top, who had seemed to have the race at his mercy, had to pull out all the stops in order to hold him at bay.

---

[1] Général proved a disappointment at three.

56.   Vincent O'Brien and Lester Piggott together at Epsom on the morning of Roberto's Derby

Roberto did not run again before The Derby, for which he was favourite at 3/1. Ten days before The Derby, Williamson had a fall and hurt a shoulder. However, he was passed fit by his doctor on the Monday of Epsom week. Mr Galbreath, though, elected to take off Williamson and put Piggott up on Roberto instead. Most people judged Mr Galbreath's action to be unsportsmanlike to say the least and Piggott himself was criticised for accepting the mount in such circumstances. It was a common view that if owners are incapable of displaying loyalty to their jockeys, then they have not got the slightest right to expect loyalty in return and it is entirely their own fault if they fail to get it. Mr Galbreath explained that Williamson would receive his percentage of the stake if Roberto won and appeared to think he was acting in a perfectly reasonable manner. There are other aspects, though, about riding a Derby winner besides mere money. A minority opinion was that owners are entitled to put up whom they like in a race, and that racing is a business in which there is no room nowadays for sentiment or good manners. In the entry on Roberto in Racehorses of 1972 comes the following observation: 'It's no use complaining about the demise of old-fashioned values such as sportsmanship. Racing is now a business, like it or not; the difference between winning and losing The Derby nowadays could well be over a million pounds.' It would be difficult to compose a couple of sentences more calculated to make racing look so thoroughly unattractive.

Second favourite in The Derby was Madame P. Wertheimer's Lyphard trained by Alec Head and ridden by his son. By Nijinsky's sire Northern Dancer out of a Court Martial mare, Lyphard had won the Prix Daru very easily by four lengths but was only fourth behind the Irish-bred Hard To Beat and Steel Pulse in the Prix Lupin. Freddie Head, though, rode a very poor race in the Lupin and left him with far too much to do.

At 22/1 was Mr H. Zeisel's Rheingold, trained by Barry Hills at Lambourn and ridden by Ernest Johnson, who had won The Derby on Blakeney. Rheingold is a bay by Princely Gift's son Fabergé, not a horse reckoned likely to sire a Derby winner, out of Athene, by Supreme Court. Athene was sold for 140 guineas as a yearling. She showed scant promise at two and was offered as a prize in a £1 raffle. At three she was sold for 300 guineas in January, for 700 guineas in December. Rheingold, a very attractive bay, realised 3,000 guineas as a yearling.

At two Rheingold had been twice well beaten by Crowned Prince. He started off at three by an uninformative victory in the one-mile Rosebery Stakes at Redcar. Failure to reach the first three in the Blue Riband Trial Stakes at Epsom hardly suggested he was up to classic standard. However he earned his place in the Derby field by winning The Dante Stakes at York despite being the recipient of at least one hefty bump inside the final furlong.

At Tattenham Corner Head appeared unable to control Lyphard who ran so wide that he had no chance whatsoever afterwards. The leader at this stage was Geoff Barling's good-looking Crepello colt Pentland Firth, ridden by Pat Eddery, neither Roberto nor Rheingold being in the leading six. In the straight, though, both these two began to make rapid progress. With two furlongs to go they were almost level and it was at this juncture that Rheingold bumped into Roberto, who was thrown off balance and passed the bump on with interest to Pentland Firth. Pentland Firth had no chance afterwards but he was being hard ridden before this occurred and looked a beaten horse at the time.

This little contretemps left Rheingold in front and he would have been in a winning position if only he had not continued to hang to the left. In the meantime Piggott's situation was a tricky one. He did not want to make his effort too soon in view of Roberto's unproven stamina, but on the other hand the gap between Rheingold and Pentland Firth was becoming narrower not only because of Rheingold, but also because Pentland Firth was hanging to the right away from the rails. A furlong from home Piggott squeezed through the gap, slightly inter-fering with Pentland Firth in the process. Over the final two hundred yards it was a terrific battle between Roberto and Rheingold. Piggott can rarely have ridden a more powerful and effective finish and he certainly did not spare Roberto. Johnson, on the other hand, had his work cut out trying to keep Rheingold balanced and was thus unable to assist him to the extent that Piggott was driving on Roberto.

57.   The tremendous duel between Roberto (Lester Piggott) and Rheingold (Ernie Johnson) in the 1972 Derby. The photograph shows how close they came to each other

Close home, Piggott forced Roberto to the front to win by a short head. Pentland Firth was three lengths away third. An inquiry by the Stewards was a foregone conclusion. After a long interval it was announced that the placings would remain unchanged. If Rheingold had been the winner, he might well have lost the race as he had undoubtedly hampered Roberto two furlongs from home.

The coolness of Roberto's reception was embarrassing, particularly as he had started favourite and Piggott had ridden a marvellous race. There was hardly a cheer. On the other hand when Williamson won The Woodcote Stakes half an hour later he was given the sort of reception that usually only a winning Derby favourite receives.

From the stands it looked as if Roberto had had a really gruelling race. O'Brien, however, did not agree with that view. The fact remains that Roberto gave a singularly lifeless display when unplaced behind Steel Pulse in the Irish Sweeps Derby and most people, rightly or wrongly, were inclined to attribute his failure to his strenuous exertions at Epsom. The rest of his three-year-old career has been covered when dealing with Brigadier Gerard. He may not have been a particularly good Derby winner but he was unquestionably an exceptionally game one and he has a place in history as the only horse ever to conquer Brigadier Gerard. Moreover Rheingold was destined to win the Arc the following year. Rheingold did not run again this season after his failure at York. Pentland Firth was soundly beaten by the four-year-old Falkland in The Princess of Wales's Stakes at Newmarket. Leg trouble prevented him from running in The St Leger. At the end of the season he was sold for export to South Africa.

Without Roberto, Rheingold and Pentland Firth, The St Leger was a very dim affair. The going was soft, patchy and rather treacherous and the pace would hardly have inconvenienced a particularly well-nourished mounted policeman, the time being 24 seconds outside the course record and 20 seconds above the average time for the distance. Steel Pulse, who started favourite, finished last of the seven runners. The winner was Mr O. Phipps's American-bred Ribot colt Boucher, trained by O'Brien and ridden by Piggott. Boucher lost lengths at the start but this really did not matter since the rate of progress was more in keeping with a state funeral than a classic. He won by half a length from Our Mirage with the Oaks winner Ginevra five lengths away third. It was Piggott's seventh St Leger victory, his fifth in six years.

Rose Dubarry, top two-year-old filly of 1971, did not grow at all during the winter and proved a disappointment at three, being defeated in all her three races. She started favourite for The One Thousand Guineas but ran as if the distance was too far for her and the best she could do was to finish third behind Mrs Richard Stanley's chestnut filly Waterloo, trained at Richmond in Yorkshire by Bill Watts and ridden by Edward Hide. By Bold Lad out of the Hyperion mare Lakewoods, Waterloo was bred by the New England Stud. Lakewoods was sold in 1969 for 3,700 guineas at the December Sales to go to America. She never won herself and at the time of her sale none of her offspring had won. Hyperion was in his twenty-eighth year when he covered Lakewoods's dam Holwood.

Compact and strong, Waterloo came to hand nice and early in the spring. After running third behind High Top in the Thirsk Classic Trial, she was at her best for The One Thousand Guineas, in which she started at 8/1. Always going well, she took the lead racing into the Dip and ran on strongly to win by two lengths from the French filly Marisela, who had been second to her in The Cheveley Park Stakes in the autumn. At Royal Ascot Waterloo was beaten a neck by the Irish-trained Bold Ruler filly Calve in The Coronation Stakes, but she just managed to win The Falmouth Stakes at Newmarket from three opponents. She was beaten in her final race, The Strensall Stakes at York. At the end of the season she was sold for a sum said to be in excess of £100,000 to go to America.

Bill Watts, born in 1942, is the son of Jack Watts who won The St Leger with Indiana, and grandson of J. E. Watts who won The Derby with Call Boy. His great-grandfather was the famous jockey Jack Watts, who rode four winners of The Derby.

The Oaks went to Mr Charles St George's Ginevra, trained by Ryan Price and ridden by Tony Murray, son of a former steeplechase jockey. A rather highly-strung filly, she was bred by Lord Suffolk and is by Shantung out of the non-winning Crepello mare Zest whom Lord Suffolk bought in 1965 for 1,200 guineas. Zest was a descendant of the late Mrs Arthur James's mare Figliastra, and Waterloo was a descendant of another mare that carried Mrs James's colours, Beausite. At the Houghton Sales Ginevra was led out unsold at 1,300 guineas but was subsequently bought privately for 2,000 guineas. At two she hardly looked to have classic potential and there was a tendency towards misbehaviour as well. At three she improved immensely and after winning the Lingfield Oaks Trial she started at 8/1 for The Oaks, in which the joint favourites at 6/1 were Mrs Engelhard's Arkadina, a Ribot filly trained by O'Brien, and the French-trained Lady Jones, by Dan Cupid. Ginevra sweated up during the preliminaries but that did not affect her running adversely. She made steady progress in the straight and, taking the lead a furlong out, she won by a length and a half from the French-trained Regal Exception, by Ribot, with Arkadina close up third.

Ginevra never won again subsequently. She was third in the Yorkshire Oaks behind Attica Meli, third in The St Leger, and fourth in the Prix Vermeille. She was offered for sale at Newmarket in December and, though she was anything but an outstanding Oaks winner, the Japanese paid 106,000 guineas for her. This was a record price for a filly out of training, the previous best being 38,000 guineas for Prudent Girl in 1971. A prominent figure in modern racing and allegedly a particularly warm admirer of Piggott, Mr St George patronises a number of stables including those of Barry Hills and Vincent O'Brien.

It was Ryan Price's first victory in a classic race. Born in Sussex in 1912, he was well known in the point-to-point and hunter-chasing world before the war, during which he attained the rank of Captain in the Commandos. He had actually taken out a licence to train in 1937 but it was in the post-war era that he worked his way up from the bottom, or somewhere very near it, to become a leading trainer of jumpers. In his ascent to fame and fortune he was greatly assisted by the fact that for a good many years Fred Winter was his stable jockey, and when Winter retired Josh Gifford took his place. Races that Price won included The Grand National, The Gold Cup, The Champion Hurdle three times, The Whitbread Gold Cup twice, and The Schweppes Gold Trophy four times. Eventually he decided to concentrate on the flat after a period of success with a 'mixed' stable. Besides The Oaks and The St Leger, he has won The Cesarewitch three times, The Chester Cup, The Ascot Stakes, The Gimcrack Stakes, The Champion Stakes, and The Nunthorpe Stakes. His story has not been one of unbroken triumph. There has been controversy, as for example over the remarkable Hill House affair; and disaster, as when he lost his licence temporarily following Rosyth's second victory in The Schweppes Gold Trophy. He has plenty of pluck, though, and a reversal of fortune never keeps him down for long.

Price is liable to arouse strong feelings, both for and against. Friends and enemies, however, agree on one point: he is a great trainer, a marvellous stableman

58. Captain Ryan Price, the Findon trainer, pictured at the Newmarket sales in 1971

with a genuine devotion to his horses. He often seems brash and conceited and even now that he has reached his sixties he has not yet learnt when it is expedient to keep his mouth shut. He is liable to talk far too much far too loud. A fair amount of what he says is exceptionally foolish but only individuals naïve to the point of idiocy take his more outrageous statements without a pinch of salt. Despite his obvious weaknesses, he has no lack of friends who swear by him and he is certainly capable of great kindness. He can, too, be very funny but most of his more memorable comments would not look quite so good on paper. Appearances can be very deceptive but his own does him absolute justice. The patrons of his stable repay study as they form a really interesting cross-section of the racing world. All in all, Ryan Price is what Edwardians used to call 'a card' and racing can never be wholly dull when he is around.

The best staying three-year-old filly in 1972 was not Ginevra but Mr Louis Freedman's Attica Meli, trained by Murless. A bay by Primera, exported to Japan, out of Come On Honey, by Never Say Die, she is a granddaughter of Honeylight, who won The One Thousand Guineas and was a half-sister by Honeyway to Crepello. At two Attica Meli was very backward and only ran once.

At three she started off with a promising display in The Fred Darling Stakes at Newbury but was then afflicted by the virus and was off the course till July when she won a mile-and-a-quarter maiden race at Sandown. Later that month she won a mile-and-a-half handicap at Goodwood.

She was now improving fast. At York she won The Yorkshire Oaks with Ginevra a long way behind her. She concluded the season with victories in The Park Hill Stakes at Doncaster and The Princess Royal Stakes at Ascot. She had thus won five races in succession. In The Three Year Old Free Handicap she was rated 10 lb. superior to Ginevra and only 2 lb. below Roberto. It was decided to keep her in training in 1973.

Rock Roi, the outstanding stayer of 1971, soon proved he was as good at five as he had been at four. His first race was the mile-and-a-half John Porter Stakes at Newbury. He relished the soft ground and won by four lengths from Selhurst, who was receiving a stone, with Example fifteen lengths away third. In The Jockey Club Stakes he started at 7/2 on, but found one too good for him in Major Victor McCalmont's four-year-old gelding Knockroe, who had too much speed for him at the finish. Knockroe, a grey by Fortino II, combined high ability with an eccentric temperament which was apt to be seen in its least favourable light if he came close to other horses in a race. At home he was reluctant to gallop with his stable-companions and preferred to do his work alongside the car of his trainer, Peter Nelson. This season Knockroe, who possessed a fine turn of foot, also won The Yorkshire Cup, The Cumberland Lodge Stakes and The St Simon Stakes so Rock Roi suffered little loss of prestige through this defeat.

On May 21 Rock Roi went to Longchamp for the Prix du Cadran, worth over £23,000 to the winner. On soft ground he won a fine race by a length from the stout-hearted Parnell to whom he was giving 6 lb. Parnell would have had to meet him on worse terms in The Gold Cup and was withdrawn from that race the day before it was run. There was no competitor from France or Ireland for the Cup and Rock Roi started at 11/4 on, the only opponents reckoned to stand even a remote chance against him being Irvine and Erimo Hawk, both grey four-year-olds by Sea Hawk.

For some time past Rock Roi had been giving Peter Walwyn cause for concern over the matter of sore shins and the fast Ascot going did not suit him. In the straight his backers soon began to feel anxious and when Erimo Hawk headed him he looked a beaten horse. He refused to give in, though, and, hard ridden by Duncan Keith, he rallied to regain the lead close to home and win by a head. Unfortunately in so doing he had veered to the left and had interfered with Erimo Hawk. An inquiry was inevitable and after examining the films the Stewards disqualified Rock Roi and awarded the race to Erimo Hawk. Naturally a great deal of sympathy was expressed for Rock Roi, his owner and his trainer but the decision of the Stewards was a just one and was rightly not swayed in the slightest by Rock Roi's misfortune in the race the year before.

The following month M. D. Wildenstein bought a three-quarter share in Rock Roi and took him off to France to be trained for the Prix Kergorlay and the Prix de l'Arc de Triomphe. Unfortunately Rock Roi hurt himself in his box not long after his arrival in France and never ran again. He had proved himself a fine stayer under any conditions but an outstanding one when there was plenty of give in the ground.

Mr Y. S. Yamomoto's Irish-bred Erimo Hawk, a 10,000-guineas yearling, is by Sea Hawk II out of Nick of Time, a half-sister to the Two Thousand Guineas winner Kashmir II by Nicolaus, a half-brother by Solario to Nearco. Trained by Geoff Barling, Erimo Hawk had won The Queen's Prize at Kempton and The Paradise Stakes at Ascot in the spring. After his victory in the Gold Cup he won The Goodwood Cup by a mere half length from Parthian Plain but with a great deal in hand. He was a disappointing failure when confidently expected to win The Doncaster Cup, won by Lady Beaverbrook's Biskrah. In the Prix de l'Arc de Triomphe he was hopelessly out of his class. At the end of the season his owner took him off to Japan.

Sun Prince did not let the Guineas form down at Royal Ascot and was a comfortable winner of The St James's Palace Stakes. On the following day Ryan Price's stable brought off a rewarding double, winning The Queen Mary Stakes with Truly Thankful, by Majority Blue, and The Ribblesdale Stakes with Star Ship, by Dicta Drake, who on her next appearance won The Lancashire Oaks at Haydock Park. Selhurst, a four-year-old half-brother by Charlottesville to Royal Palace that lacked Royal Palace's finishing speed, won The Hardwicke Stakes, having previously won The Ormonde Stakes at Chester. He was eventually exported to Australia. The five-year-old Sweet Revenge, who had won the Prix de l'Abbaye in 1971, won The King's Stand Stakes. He jarred himself badly in so doing and never ran again. A typical high-class sprinter in appearance, he was retired to the stud, a three-quarter share in him having been bought by a group of breeders.

A much improved horse in 1972 was Sir Michael Sobell's three-year-old Sallust, trained by Dick Hern. As a two-year-old he had won The Richmond Stakes at Goodwood but he was inclined to be excitable and to sweat up before a race. On three occasions he wore blinkers. His first race at three was the Ladbroke Two Thousand Guineas Trial at Kempton on April 1. He sweated up in the paddock and ran badly. He was never beaten subsequently. He did not run again till June, when he won The Diomed Stakes at Epsom. He then won successively the Prix de la Porte Maillot at Longchamp, The Sussex Stakes at Goodwood, The Goodwood Mile, and the Prix du Moulin at Longchamp. He twice beat High Top and he also defeated Sparkler and Lyphard. At the end of the season the Irish National Stud obtained him cheaply for £250,000. A chestnut by Pall Mall, he did not boast a noticeably fashionable bottom half to his pedigree, among the names appearing being that of The Font, a now almost forgotten grey handicapper by the non-winning Son and Heir.

A brilliant five-furlongs horse in 1972 was Mr David Robinson's three-year-old Deep Diver, a strong, compact chestnut half-brother to the Irish Two Thousand Guineas winner King's Company by Gulf Pearl. At two he had shown himself to be not only extremely fast but remarkably tough as well, winning seven of his eleven races. Among his victories were The Cornwallis Stakes and two races at Longchamp, the Prix d'Arenberg and the Prix du Petit Couvert. As a three-year-old he reached his peak form in the second part of the season after he had recovered from the virus that attacked so many horses during the summer. He certainly ought to have won The King George Stakes at Goodwood but Piggott rode a poor race and Deep Diver was narrowly beaten by Stilvi, subsequently dam of the Middle Park Stakes winner Tachypous. He then won The Nunthorpe Stakes, beating Stilvi by two lengths, and the Prix de l'Abbaye by four lengths. As a result of these victories he was sold as a stallion for £400,000. His yearlings sold very well in 1975 but were, by and large, disappointing on the racecourse in 1976.[1]

The two-year-old colts were far from being an inspiring collection and The Free Handicap was headed by Lady Butt's Red God filly Jacinth, trained by Bruce Hobbs. Jacinth won The Cheveley Park Stakes in great style by five lengths but nevertheless a small question mark remained beside her name as she had stubbornly refused to enter her stall in The Lowther Stakes at York.

Bernard van Cutsem, who had won the 1971 Observer Gold Cup with High Top, this time saddled the first two in that event, Mr Nelson Bunker Hunt's Noble Decree, by Vaguely Noble, beating Lady Rotherwick's Ksar, by Kalydon, by half a length. Tudenham was a depressingly substandard winner of The Middle Park Stakes and in The Free Handicap his modest ability was clearly shown by the fact that he was rated 16 lb. inferior to Jacinth. A brighter prospect for the future was the Dewhurst Stakes winner Lunchtime, a Silly Season colt bred and owned by Colonel Dick Poole and trained by Peter Walwyn.

In 1972 Ribot, a great racehorse and a great sire, died in America. Thanks to Brigadier Gerard, Queen's Hussar was the leading sire here. I wonder what odds Ladbrokes would have offered when Queen's Hussar first took up stud duties against him ever achieving this distinction. He was the first British-bred sire to head the list since Hethersett in 1969, Northern Dancer having been top in 1970 and Never Bend in 1971. Never Bend, who died in America in 1977 from heart failure, emulated his own sire Nasrullah in having been champion both in Britain and in the United States as well.

The top trainer was Dick Hern, who won £206,767 for his owners; when top in 1962 he had won £70,206. Born in Somerset in 1921, Dick Hern is a quiet man who, unlike some of his colleagues, likes to think first before he speaks. He is in fact the very reverse of the talkative, self-advertising type. He is a good horseman and for a period after the war, during which he had served in the North Irish Horse, he was chief instructor at the Porlock Riding School and instructor to the British equestrian team which won an Olympic Gold medal. Today he prefers a holiday spent hunting in Leicestershire to one passed lolling about on a sunny beach somewhere in the West Indies.

His first racing job came in 1952 when he took up the post of assistant to his former brother officer, Michael Pope. Five years later the big opportunity arrived

[1] He was sold for 10,000 guineas in 1977.

59.   The driving style of Willie Carson

and he succeeded Humphrey Cottrill as private trainer at Newmarket to Major Holliday. Dealing with Major Holliday required tact and forbearance as the old man could be very difficult and crotchety at times, but he was a great bloodstock breeder and his trainer was in charge of high-class horses. Hern established his reputation with Major Holliday before leaving in 1962 to take over from Jack Colling at West Ilsley, where his chief patrons to start with were Lord Astor and Mr J. J. Astor. Today the Astor family has almost vanished from racing and the power at West Ilsley rests in the hands of Sir Michael Sobell and his son-in-law, Sir Arnold Weinstock.

Hern has had many triumphs at West Ilsley and has trained two classic winners for the Queen. But sometimes the stable has seemed alarmingly prone to virus epidemics, and there have been some difficult owners, too. As he is not the owner of the stables or of the house in which he lives, he may feel less independent than those leading trainers who are absolutely free to pick and choose their own patrons. In good times and bad, though, he has so far always managed to keep his cool.

After being top for eight years running, Piggott lost the championship to Willie Carson, who rode 132 winners. Tony Murray came second with 122 and Piggott third with 103. It is highly unlikely that slipping down the list meant much to Piggott, who was by now inclined to ride more and more in France where the level of prize money was higher. Joe Mercer, who rode 91 winners, distinguished

60.   Start of a ladies' race at Lingfield; but not all the criticism came from men. Mrs Louie Dingwall, the eighty-year-old trainer, threatened to apply for a licence because she could 'ride the backside off these girls'.

himself by quick thinking and resolute action after an air crash at Newbury in which his presence of mind probably saved the life of the trainer Bill Marshall.

Willie Carson, a hardy, cheerful Scot who could go to scale at 7 st. 9 lb., was first of all apprenticed to Gerald Armstrong, himself a good rider on the flat, and then to Sam Armstrong, a demanding master but an excellent trainer not only of horses but of young jockeys, too. Carson made steady progress and the turning point came in 1967 when he was chosen by Bernard van Cutsem to be Lord Derby's stable jockey. 'I have had three tough bosses,' observed Carson after achieving his first championship; 'Mr Gerald Armstrong, Mr Fred (Sam) Armstrong, and Mrs Carole Carson.'

1972 saw the introduction of races for women riders. Len Scott wrote in Ruff's Guide: 'In a year or two—when the fact of their presence is accepted and the flood of drivelling facetiousness has subsided—they will probably make a small but useful contribution to the racing scene. Obviously they need more opportunities to improve their riding ability.' There were occasions when the word 'improve' was a piece of masterly understatement. Not all the criticism came from jealous, sex-discriminating men. The amazing Mrs Louie Dingwall, the eighty-plus grandmother and trainer, threatened to apply for a licence because she could 'ride the backside off these girls'.

Lord Wigg retired from his position as Chairman of the Levy Board. As has been said earlier, the latter part of his term of office was far less successful than the earlier years when he unquestionably did racing a lot of good. It was sad that when the end came few people were at all sorry to see him go, and he himself no longer appeared to experience the pleasure he had once derived from going racing.

Lord Wigg's successor was Sir Stanley Raymond. Brought up in an orphanage, he had at one time been in control of all the railways in this country and he was Chairman of the Gaming Board. It is a weakness of the system that a thoroughly worthy individual may be appointed Chairman of the Levy Board who has no knowledge whatsoever of racing and who in consequence has to spend the first half of his term of office in learning the most elementary facts of life about the sport. Sir Stanley Raymond obviously knew nothing about racing and some of the naïve ideas he expressed were liable to cause nothing but hilarity. It is probably true to say that he never really took to racing or to racing people, and that the racing world never really took to him. It was not considered an intolerable deprivation when he resigned before his term of office had been completed.

Two Newmarket personalities died this year in Reg Day, who was eighty-eight, and Harvey Leader, commonly known as 'Jack' Leader, who was seventy-eight. Reg Day was the son of 'Bushranger' Day, so called because before returning to England to train the Oaks winner Airs and Graces he had been veterinary adviser to the Governor-General of New South Wales. Reg Day had a long innings as a trainer as he started when he was seventeen—no licences were required then—and retired only when he was eighty-five. He was reported to be the last man living to have ridden in a steeplechase at Newmarket. During a spell in Germany he trained three German Derby winners for the Kaiser and then came back to Newmarket in 1912 to take over from his father. He trained two of the finest stayers of this century in Son-in-Law and Solario. Son-in-Law was one of the few Cesarewitch winners to become champion sire; Solario's victories included The St Leger, The Coronation Cup and The Gold Cup. Day had the reputation of being rather severe on his horses but he was very successful with stayers that could stand up to an exacting preparation. For many years he trained for Sir Abe Bailey. His last major triumph was to win The One Thousand Guineas and The Oaks in 1961 with Sweet Solera.

Harvey Leader was the youngest son of Tom Leader senior who trained the 1874 Derby winner George Frederick. At one time four of Tom's sons were training at Newmarket. Harvey rode his first winner at twelve and with a rapid increase in weight he rode for a time under National Hunt Rules. He started training after World War I and enjoyed his one classic success in 1920 when Mr M. Goculda's grey colt Caligula won The St Leger. However, in 1926 he won The Grand National with Mr A. C. Schwartz's Jack Horner, ridden by W. Watkinson who was killed not long afterwards.

Leader trained an outstanding sprinter in Mr S. W. Beer's Diomedes, who was unbeaten at two and won seventeen of his nineteen races. He also trained Major J. B. Walker's Shalfleet, a son of Diomedes that won The King's Stand Stakes, The July Cup and The Portland Handicap twice. After World War II he won The Cambridgeshire with Dites and Hidden Meaning. A man of great charm, hospitable and kind-hearted, he was a fine judge of bloodstock and at one time relished a tilt at the Ring. Sport of every kind appealed to him and in his younger days he was Master of the Cambridgeshire Harriers and played polo. Between the wars he was well known for the encouragement and wise advice he gave to Cambridge undergraduates who were keen to ride over fences or take up ownership in a small way.

Jack Leach, who at one time rode for Leader and was a great friend of his, died within a few hours of him. He was a son of Felix Leach senior who trained at Newmarket after being head lad to Richard Marsh. He himself was a most talented individual, charming and companionable but sadly lacking in self-discipline. He rode a lot for Harry Cottrill in the 1920s, winning The Two Thousand Guineas on Adam's Apple, but he always reckoned the best horse he ever rode was Diomedes, whom he partnered when Diomedes won The Portland Handicap as a three-year-old, carrying 9 st. 2 lb. and breaking the course record against a head wind.

After a losing battle with his weight, Jack took up training—Fred Astaire was one of his patrons—and landed a nice little coup when Figaro won The Stewards' Cup. One late autumn day in 1933, a team of Cambridge undergraduates and Sandhurst cadets went to Eton to play football against the boys. One member of the side was a friend of Jack's and had a tip for Figaro who was running in the first race at Windsor. There was just time for the team to go to Windsor and back Figaro before the match was due to begin. In a terrific finish Figaro got home by a head at 12/1. All the betting had been done in ready money and the footballers duly took the field full of champagne and with the pockets of their shorts stuffed with £5 notes.

After war service in the York and Lancaster Regiment, Jack resumed training and won the Prix Morny with Delirium. He had the skill to be a successful trainer but hardly the ideal temperament and he gave up in 1952. He then took to the pen. His articles in The Observer showed him to be one of Nature's journalists and furthermore he wrote a very funny book on racing entitled *Sods I Have Cut On The Turf*. He could have made a very good living out of journalism but unfortunately he was terribly unreliable and the despair of his editors. If he could not keep a job, though, he never lost his friends.

Lord Sefton, an outstanding member of the Jockey Club, died this year and on August 12 Eph Smith was found dead in a shallow brook near Newmarket. He was fifty-seven years old. At the inquest a verdict of misadventure was recorded.

The son of a sporting Berkshire farmer and the elder brother of Doug Smith, Eph was taught to ride as soon as he could walk. He was apprenticed to Major F. B. Sneyd, not a particularly lovable man and certainly not the last of the big spenders but an effective trainer of jockeys. Eph rode his first winner in 1930 and soon proved he had immense natural ability. When he left Major Sneyd he joined Sir Jack Jarvis's stable and there he stayed till 1948. He was then first jockey for Mr Jim Joel till 1963. His deafness seemed no handicap when he was riding and all told he had 2,313 winners from 18,401 mounts. Perhaps the best horses he ever rode were the 1939 Derby winner Blue Peter and the highly-strung Aureole, on whom he won The King George VI and Queen Elizabeth Stakes. A fine judge of pace, he excelled in long-distance races, winning The Gold Cup twice, The Goodwood Cup twice, The Ascot Stakes five times, The Goodwood Stakes five times and The Cesarewitch four times. He never had weight problems and for his weight he was extremely strong. At times he came in for criticism on the grounds that he was rather too hard on his horses.

When he gave up racing, he shot a bit, bred and trained gun dogs and sometimes rode out for Noel Murless. He had always been careful with his money and had no financial problems. At times, though, he seemed lonely and depressed and no doubt his deafness did not make day-to-day existence any easier for him. It was a very sad ending to the life of a man who had made such a substantial contribution to the English turf.

14

IN all probability Thatch, owned by Mr John A. Mulcahy and trained by
Vincent O'Brien, was unlucky not to win The Two Thousand Guineas in 1973.
On good going he was an excellent miler but on soft ground he was far less effective
as he had shown when only fourth in the Prix Morny after winning his three
previous races. Bred in America by the Claiborne Farms and bought privately by
Mr Mulcahy, he is a bay by Forli out of Thong, by Nantallah. Forli, bred in
Argentina, is by Hyperion's son Aristophanes who won races in this country for
Mr J. A. Dewar. Thong is an own-sister to three good American horses: Ridan
(thirteen races and a successful sire), Lt Stevens (nine races and a successful sire),
and Moccasin (Champion Two-Year-Old filly, Horse of the Year, and dam of
Apalachee, winner of The Observer Gold Cup). Rough Shod, dam of Thong, was
by Gold Bridge out of the Yorkshire Oaks winner Dalmary, a mare whose name
appears in the pedigrees of a number of well-known winners such as Sarcelle,
Sammy Davis, Le Sage, Lorenzaccio and Tudor Era.

Thatch won the seven-furlongs Vauxhall Trial Stakes at Phoenix Park on
March 31 and, ridden by Piggott, he started favourite for The Two Thousand
Guineas at 5/2. Second favourite was Targowice, an American-bred Round Table
colt trained by Alec Head. None of the home-trained runners seemed much
fancied but there was a bit of money for Murless's Owen Dudley, who had won
The Wood Ditton Stakes, and for Lunchtime, despite his failure to concede 5 lb.
to Lady Beaverbrook's gelding Boldboy in The Clerical, Medical Greenham
Stakes at Newbury.

Unfortunately for Thatch, it rained hard overnight and the going at Newmarket,
good when the meeting began, became very soft indeed. Thatch looked to have
every chance at the Bushes but found nothing from that point and finished fourth.
The 50/1 outsider Mon Fils won by a head from Noble Decree with Sharp Edge,
who later won the Irish Two Thousand Guineas and the Prix Jean Prat at Chantilly,
three lengths away third. All the first three had failed in their previous race. Mon
Fils had been third behind Boldboy and Lunchtime at Newbury; Noble Decree
a very disappointing fourth in the Ladbroke Two Thousand Guineas Trial at
Kempton; and Sharp Edge a moderate fifth in The Craven Stakes.

Thatch, an extremely good-looking colt, ran three times subsequently. He beat Owen Dudley by fifteen lengths in The St James's Palace Stakes. At Newmarket he displayed exceptional speed in winning the six-furlongs July Cup by three lengths. Finally he beat Jacinth by three lengths in The Sussex Stakes. He was then retired to the stud in Ireland, being syndicated at £25,000 a share.

Mon Fils, despite his long price, was by no means unfancied by his owner-breeders, Mr and Mrs Jack Davis. Mr Davis in fact claimed that he had won £30,000 in bets. Richard Hannon, who trained the colt near Marlborough, had backed Mon Fils at 200/1 before The Clerical, Medical Greenham Stakes. Mon Fils hardly seemed ideally bred to win The Two Thousand Guineas as he is by the Gold Cup winner Sheshoon out of a mare by the St Leger winner Premonition, both Sheshoon and Premonition being by the Gold Cup winner Precipitation. Nor had Mon Fils's form at two offered much encouragement as far as the classics were concerned. He had won twice in seven outings and easily his best performance was in the newly established six-furlongs Mill Reef Stakes at Newbury, when he narrowly beat Tudenham who went on to win The Middle Park Stakes. Tudenham, though, was well below the average standard for winners of that race.

Tall, lanky, and brown in colour, Mon Fils thus appeared to be that rare but highly desirable type, a colt with a stayer's pedigree and top-class speed. He did not run again before The Derby, in which, with Durr up, he started second favourite at 11/2. The weather was perfect, the crowd enormous and the going firm. Mon Fils performed in very disappointing fashion and, after being second at Tattenham Corner, he faded right away to finish eighteenth. He certainly ran like a non-stayer but it is only fair to add that Durr had made a great deal of use of him. It seemed a bit hard on Hannon that after this failure Mon Fils was transferred to Vincent O'Brien. However, Mon Fils developed tendon trouble in Ireland and never saw a racecourse again.

It was anything but a strong Derby field. The favourite, ridden by Carson, was Ksar, who had won the Ladbroke Classic Trial Stakes at Kempton (Sandown was out of action due to rebuilding) and then, not in the least impressively, the Ladbroke Derby Trial at Lingfield. At that particular Lingfield meeting Arthur Budgett's three-year-old colt Morston made his first racecourse appearance in the ten-furlongs Godstone Maiden Plate and this rather leggy chestnut, half-brother to Blakeney by Ragusa, won comfortably by three lengths.

Ksar, who in August won the Prix de la Côte Normande at Deauville, raised the hopes of his supporters when he took the lead from Freefoot two furlongs from home but he proved quite incapable of acceleration from that point. He was soon headed by the 25/1 chance Morston who, in the experienced hands of Edward Hide, ran on strongly to hold off by half a length the determined challenge of O'Brien's Sir Ivor colt Cavo Doro, ridden by Piggott. Freefoot was third and Ksar fourth. Neither Cavo Doro nor Freefoot won subsequently during the season.

The race was a resounding triumph for Arthur Budgett. He had bred, part-owned and trained the 1969 Derby winner Blakeney; and now he had bred,

61. Edward Hide, leading Northern jockey for many years, here riding Mrs McArdy

owned and trained a second winner of the greatest race of the year. He thus emulated Mr William I'Anson who bred, owned and trained the 1857 Derby winner Blink Bonny, and also the 1864 Derby winner Blair Athol, Blink Bonny's son. Sadly, Windmill Girl, dam of Blakeney and Morston, had fallen heavily and fractured her skull while galloping in her paddock the previous winter. She was the ninth mare to breed two Derby winners and the first to achieve two Derby winners during this century.

Morston, like Blakeney, had been named after a village in Norfolk. He had been slow to develop and was in fact still so backward that Budgett was in two minds about running him at Epsom and only finally made up his mind just before the final forfeit stage. The stable jockey, Baxter, was on Projector so Budgett engaged Hide who set eyes on Morston for the first time in the parade-ring before The Derby. With so much scope for improvement still, Morston might have been a really good horse by the autumn but he injured a tendon in his St Leger preparation and never ran again. Of the Derby winners since World War I, Humorist, Call Boy, Felstead, Blenheim, Dante, Galcador, Nimbus (bar a walk-over), Crepello and Psidium were others who never raced again after securing the Blue Riband.

Edward Hide, born in 1937, served a seven-year apprenticeship with his father, who trained at Ludlow. A thoroughly sound and dependable jockey, he has largely been associated with northern racing, riding many winners for the late Captain Charles Elsey and for Bill Elsey. He won The St Leger for the former on Cantelo, The Oaks for the latter on Pia.

Bill Elsey won The St Leger this year with Colonel W. E. Behrens's Peleid, who was surely one of the least distinguished winners of the Doncaster classic this century. As a two-year-old he was no more than humdrum middle-class, running seven times and winning one race, an affair for maidens at York in July. At three be began by winning a handicap at Liverpool on Grand National day. He failed in the Thirsk Classic Trial and The Chester Vase, after which he reverted to handicaps. He won The Zetland Gold Cup at Redcar by a head from the year older Jimsun, who was giving him 25 lb., and he also won The John Smith's Magnet Cup at York. He was second in The King George V Stakes at Royal Ascot and he was fourth in The Ebor, in which a good deal of use was made of him and he was unable to quicken near the finish.

Peleid had few backers in The St Leger and, ridden by Durr, he started at 28/1. Apart from the fact that he did not seem a class horse, his pedigree was hardly encouraging as he is by the miler Derring Do out of Winning Bid, by the American-bred Great Captain. As a matter of fact, Winning Bid, who changed hands at two for 300 guineas, was destined to be credited with the 1974 Eclipse winner, Coup de Feu. Cavo Doro, despite his defeat at The Curragh in The Blandford Stakes, was favourite at 9/4 and others well backed were Buoy, Ragapan, Duke of Ragusa and the Prix Kergorlay winner Valuta. Cavo Doro and Valuta both ran in deplorable fashion and Ragapan appeared lacking in stamina. Duke of Ragusa, in Lord Rosebery's colours, led into the straight but he could do no more than keep plodding along at one pace. A quarter of a mile from home he was headed by Mr Hollingsworth's big Aureole colt Buoy, but Buoy was hardly better off for acceleration than Duke of Ragusa. He certainly could produce no effective answer when Peleid, who had been pulled to the outside with two furlongs to go, delivered a nicely timed challenge, having been ridden far more patiently than at York. Peleid sailed past Buoy to win by two and a half lengths, Buoy just beating Duke of Ragusa for second place.

Hardy, compact and courageous, Peleid had won entirely on his merits. He did not run again this season but he remained in training at four. He added nothing to his reputation and was sold for export to Hungary.

Jacinth, who had headed The Free Handicap, did not run prior to The One Thousand Guineas, for which she was favourite at 5/4 on. She ran well but in the last two furlongs she never looked like beating Mr George Pope junior's 11/1 chance Mysterious, who defeated her decisively by three lengths. The 66/1 outsider Shellshock was two lengths away third. Bred by her American owner, a patron in this country of Noel Murless's stable, Mysterious is a chestnut by Crepello out of Hill Shade, by Khaled's son Hillary. Hill Shade, who herself won The Nassau Stakes and The Sun Chariot Stakes, also bred J. O. Tobin, who looked a real smasher in 1976 until cut down to size by Blushing Groom in The Grand Criterium.

At two Mysterious ran but once, beating a couple of opponents in The Cherry Hinton Stakes at Newmarket. In 1973 she started off by winning The Fred Darling Stakes at Newbury. After her Newmarket triumph she naturally started a hot favourite for The Oaks and, again ridden by Geoff Lewis, she won with singular ease from Where You Lead and Aureoletta. She was reckoned a certainty for the Irish Guinness Oaks and it came as a painful surprise when she was beaten by the American-bred, French-trained Dahlia. It was assumed at the time that Mysterious had run below her true form; after The King George VI and Queen Elizabeth Stakes it was realised she had been conquered by a better filly.

Mysterious won The Yorkshire Oaks but she lost her form in the autumn. In The Sun Chariot Stakes she was beaten by Cheveley Princess, while by The

Champion Stakes she had gone in her coat and was only fifth behind Hurry Harriet, Allez France and Sharp Edge.

Rheingold's next race was the Benson and Hedges Gold Cup at York. Saintleg was noticeably better looking at four than he had been at three. He began the season like a champion, beating fourteen opponents in The John Porter Stakes at Newbury very easily indeed. On April 29 he flew to Longchamp for the ten-and-a-half furlongs Prix Ganay, worth over £31,000 to the winner. He won by a length and a half in a field of sixteen. In The Hardwicke Stakes he did not have a great deal to do and won by six lengths from Attica Meli, who later won The Geoffrey Freer Stakes at Newbury and The Doncaster Cup. In July he returned to France where he invariably produced his peak form and won the Grand Prix de Saint-Cloud, worth £48,111 to the winner, for the second year running. He started favourite for The King George VI and Queen Elizabeth Stakes at 13/8 but Dahlia showed herself to be beyond doubt a superlative filly and beat him with the greatest possible ease by six lengths. In addition to Rheingold she beat Weavers Hall (Irish Sweeps Derby), Parnell, Scottish Rifle (Eclipse Stakes), Hard To Beat (1972 French Derby) and Roberto (1972 Derby, 1973 Coronation Cup). It was a performance memorable for its sheer brilliance.

Rheingold's next race was The Benson and Hedges Gold Cup at York. Saint-Martin came over to ride him. Piggott had been engaged to ride Roberto but when O'Brien decided the ground was too soft for Roberto, Piggott agreed to ride Moulton. On arriving at York, Piggott met his friend Mr Charles St George, a member of the syndicate that owned Rheingold, and St George offered him the ride on Rheingold which Piggott immediately accepted. Thus Saint-Martin, a very fine rider and arguably not inferior to Piggott, was 'jocked off' in the crudest manner possible. Saint-Martin had partnered Rheingold in his victories before the big race at Ascot and the way he was treated was rightly resented by the racing public. A good deal of satisfaction was expressed when Moulton won by two and a half lengths from Scottish Rifle with Rheingold four lengths away third. At this stage of his career a mile and a quarter was not really far enough for Rheingold.

Those two defeats dented Rheingold's reputation but it was more than restored, it was embellished when, with Piggott in the saddle, Rheingold won the Prix de l'Arc de Triomphe by two and a half lengths from Allez France with Hard To Beat four lengths away third. Dahlia finished sixteenth. She really ought not to have run as she had been injured in the Prix Vermeille and her preparation for the Arc had been interrupted. Her failure on this occasion is best ignored. She was back to her best in November when she became the first filly to win The Washington International at Laurel Park. She won that event by three and a quarter lengths from Big Spruce with Scottish Rifle a length away third.

Rheingold's victory left him with a big reputation in France which was not in the least surprising since he had run four times in that country and had never been beaten. In England there was perhaps a slight tendency to play down his success and he was not voted Horse of the Year, that distinction falling to Dahlia.

This somewhat lukewarm attitude was partly due to his defeats at Ascot and York; partly to the still smouldering resentment over the way Saint-Martin had been treated at York; and, even more illogically, because some of the members of the syndicate that owned him were not much liked in the racing world.

No one could deny, though, that the Arc was a triumph for Barry Hills, who was only in his fifth year as a trainer. Slim, neat, and looking younger than his true age—he was born in 1937—he comes from a racing family as his father had been head lad to George Colling. He himself is a good horseman; he rode nine winners when apprenticed to Colling and nowadays he goes like a bird with the Quorn. After National Service in the King's Troop, R.H.A. he returned to Colling's stable. When Colling died, John Oxley took over the stable and Hills served him for ten years as travelling head lad. He took out a licence to train in 1969 and quickly showed that he had a talent for his profession. In 1976 he had 104 horses under his care at Lambourn, and according to Horses in Training, fifty-eight owners, among them such notabilities as Mr P. Bull, Sir Charles Clore, Lord Ranfurly, Mr R. Sangster, Mr C. St George, Mr Cyril Stein and Lord Suffolk.

Rheingold, whose sire Fabergé had been sold to Japan, ran no more after the Arc and was retired to the stud in Ireland. He had won five races and £74,439 in England, four races and 3,192,000 francs in France. Rumours abounded that Wing Commander Tim Vigors had paid over £1,000,000 for him but in fact a number of shares had been retained by Mr H. Zeisel and by other members of the syndicate. Nominations for 1974 were advertised at £7,000; or alternatively at £4,000 on the signing of the contract, with a further £4,000 on October 1 if the mare was in foal.

France had two exceptionally good three-year-old fillies this season in Allez France and Dahlia, owned respectively by two of the most powerful, if not the most popular, figures in modern European racing, M. D. Wildenstein and Mr Nelson Bunker Hunt.

Allez France, trained by A. Klimscha, was bred in America and bought privately there as a yearling for $160,000. She is a bay by Sea Bird II, who died in 1973 soon after being repatriated from America to France, out of Priceless Gem, by Hail to Reason. It is true that Allez France lost four of her seven races at three but she won the Poule d'Essai des Pouliches, the Prix de Diane and the Prix Vermeille. In addition, she was second in the Arc. She met Dahlia on four occasions and never once finished behind her.

Dahlia, likewise bred in America, was trained by M. Zilber and is a chestnut by Vaguely Noble out of Charming Alibi, winner of sixteen races, by Honey's Alibi. In 1973 she won the Prix de la Grotte, the Prix Saint-Alary, the Irish Guinness Oaks, The King George VI and Queen Elizabeth Stakes, the Prix Niel and The Washington International. Judged by the fact that four times she finished behind Allez France and never once in front of her, she seems to have been clearly inferior to her rival. In the Prix de Diane, though, in which she was second, she was brought to her knees rounding the final bend. She was injured in the Prix Vermeille and she was far below her best when she failed in the Arc.

62.   French trainer Angel Penna (right) with Allez France

Roberto failed to enhance his reputation in 1973. It had been intended to run him in the Prix Ganay but he was withdrawn from that event at the last moment on the grounds of a minor injury sustained during the journey to France. On May 7 he ran in the ten-furlongs Nijinsky Stakes at Leopardstown but was beaten three parts of a length by Ballymore, a son of Ragusa, who was taking him on at level weights. Roberto won The Coronation Cup easily enough but the opposition was weak and Attica Meli, the only runner that appeared to stand some chance of beating him, had not yet run into form.

Roberto was declared to run in both The Eclipse Stakes (run at Kempton) and The Benson and Hedges Gold Cup but on each occasion was withdrawn on the day of the race because O'Brien considered the going to be unsuitable. These withdrawals did not increase O'Brien's popularity with the English racing public nor the esteem in which Roberto was held. Inevitably comparisons were made between the policy that had been applied to Roberto and the much bolder one adopted with Brigadier Gerard; naturally to Roberto's disadvantage. A lot of people sincerely thought that Roberto's connections had been over-cautious, to put it politely; only a minority took the line that O'Brien's first duty had been to look after the horse's interests and that he had acted accordingly.

Roberto's final appearance was in The King George VI and Queen Elizabeth Stakes. He was in front nearly five furlongs from home but was a beaten horse early in the straight and finished at the tail end of the field.

There was one significant change at Royal Ascot this year. The Queen's representative for so many years, the Duke of Norfolk, had retired and been succeeded by the Marquess of Abergavenny. At Ascot the Duke had always seemed the benevolent monarch of a small and happy kingdom. He loved Ascot and it was his declared objective to make it the best racecourse in Europe and to stage there racing of the very highest class. Impervious to radical proddings, he made few significant alterations at the Royal Meeting, wisely regarding it as unique and a fixture that would derive no benefit from fundamental change. He therefore maintained the traditional features while making a number of minor concessions to modernity. He was far from being a diehard in every respect, though, and during his term of office there were important changes to the course itself, changes that brought with them some difficult problems over drainage, while the stands were rebuilt on modern lines as well. It was of the greatest value to the Duke that during the first half of his tenure of office he had the shrewd and immensely popular Sir John Crocker Bulteel as Clerk of the Course. They proved a highly efficient combination and under their direction the quality of the sport was constantly improved, The King George VI and Queen Elizabeth Stakes, for example, developing into one of Europe's most prestigious races.

It would be a gross error to think that the Duke was concerned only with pleasing the swells at Ascot. He was at great pains to extend and improve the bus and coach trade and he made it his personal concern to ensure that coach parties were properly looked after and went home feeling they had received good value for money.

Very few people, particularly those in authority, care for journalists, but the Duke got on reasonably well with the press though occasionally irked by anti-Ascot radicals. The press facilities at Ascot are far in advance of those provided by the majority of courses. Some comment has already been made on the Duke's little speech over the public address system at Ascot, the speech that had very much annoyed Lord Wigg. It is difficult to think of two men with less in common except for their love of racing.

National Hunt racing at Ascot is not to everyone's taste but it must be remembered that when Ascot's jumping course was constructed, Hurst Park had been taken over by developers while Sandown's future looked anything but secure. If Sandown had gone, there would have been an urgent need for another jumping course within easy reach of London.

The Duke's reign at Ascot had indeed been a memorable one, and the esteem and affection in which he was held were clearly demonstrated when his horse Ragstone won The Gold Cup in 1974.

The 1973 Gold Cup went to Mr Zenya Yoshida's four-year-old Lasalle, trained in France by R. Carver. He had previously won the Prix du Cadran but Parnell had given him 9 lb. and beaten him by three lengths in the Prix Jean Prat. It cannot be said that his task in The Gold Cup was a severe one as the opposition was in fact depressingly mediocre. Starting favourite and ridden by Lindley, he won very easily indeed from Celtic Cone. In the autumn he won the Prix Gladiateur but only on the disqualification of Parnell who had been first past the post. Bought for £23,000 as a yearling at Deauville, Lassalle is by the Prix de l'Arc de Triomphe winner Bon Mot III, exported to Japan, out of Windy Cliff, by Hard Sauce. Grandam of Windy Cliff was the famous Sandringham mare Feola.

Jacinth paid generous tribute to Mysterious by the ease of her victory in The Coronation Stakes at Royal Ascot but the probability is that she was a considerably better filly in June than she had been in the spring. In The Falmouth Stakes at Newmarket the following month she beat Silver Birch, runner-up in The Coronation Stakes at level weights, almost as easily conceding her 10 lb. In The Sussex Stakes she found Thatch too strong for her in the final furlong but she completed her career with an easily gained victory in The Goodwood Mile against not unduly formidable opposition. At her best she was a very good filly up to a mile.

The favourite for The Eclipse Stakes at Kempton was Mr J. J. Astor's Silver Shark colt Sharp Edge, who, after finishing third in The Two Thousand Guineas, had won firstly the Irish Two Thousand Guineas and then the nine-furlongs Prix Jean Prat at Chantilly. He needed plenty of give in the ground and the conditions at Kempton appeared likely to suit him. In fact he finished last in a field of seven. He was the recipient of a hefty bump from Moulton when nicely placed in the straight and had no chance afterwards.

The winner was Mr A. J. Struthers's four-year-old Scottish Rifle, trained by John Dunlop at Arundel. By no means fashionably bred, he is by the handicapper Sunny Way, eventually exported to Venezuela, out of Radiopye, by Bright News. Costing only 3,600 guineas as a yearling, he proved a tough and thoroughly genuine performer. He won four times at three, his victories including The Gordon Stakes at Goodwood, and he was second in The Irish Sweeps Derby. He started off at four by winning the nine-furlongs Earl of Sefton Stakes at Newmarket and then two ten-furlongs races at Kempton, The Brigadier Gerard Stakes and The Westbury Stakes. He certainly ought to have won The Prince of Wales's Stakes at Royal Ascot, but Ron Hutchinson's judgement for once was sadly at fault and he went under by a neck to Gift Card.

Hutchinson made amends in The Eclipse Stakes, giving an admirable exhibition of the art of waiting in front. Scottish Rifle led from start to finish and held on gamely to win all out by a length from Moulton with Sun Prince inches away third and Toujours Prêt close up fourth. It had not been a pretty race by any means but Scottish Rifle himself was not concerned in the various incidents that had taken place. Moulton, who had sweated up in the paddock, hung persistently to the right in the straight and, in addition to bumping Sharp Edge, barged into Toujours Prêt as well. Apart from detracting from his own chance, Moulton had blatantly impeded others as well and was fortunate to be allowed to retain second place. Sun Prince was perhaps even more unfortunate than his stable-companion Sharp Edge and suffered considerable interference just below the distance.

After being unplaced behind Dahlia at Ascot, Scottish Rifle ran second to Moulton in The Benson and Hedges Gold Cup and then won The Cumberland Lodge Stakes at Ascot. He was unplaced in The Champion Stakes but ended his racing career creditably enough by finishing third behind Dahlia in The Washington International. He was syndicated for the stud at £7,000 a share, having won ten races and £87,567 in England and Ireland, $10,000 in America.

Ascot staged its first race for women riders in July, this being The Cullinan Diamond Stakes, worth £1,140 to the winner. It was won by Mr T. F. Blackwell's Hurdy Gurdy very stylishly partnered by his daughter Caroline who had never ridden in a race before but had been riding out a lot for Bruce Hobbs. It was a rewarding day for the Blackwell family as Le Patron won The Virginia Water Stakes in the colours of Caroline's brother, Charles.

At Goodwood Lt-Col John Chandos-Pole's three-year-old Proverb, a big, long-striding chestnut by Reliance II, won The Goodwood Cup. Bred by his owner and trained by Barry Hills, he had created a big surprise earlier in the season when he won The Chester Vase at 33/1.

The season's best sprinter was Mr C. Olley's three-year-old Sandford Lad, trained by Ryan Price. A chestnut colt by St Alphage out of a non-winning mare by Djebe, Sandford Lad cost only 1,800 guineas as a yearling. At two he won three of his four races. First time out he started at 14/1 in a field of four for The Berkshire Stakes at Newbury and was narrowly beaten by Quintilian. He then won The Erroll Stakes at Ascot, The Pilgrim Stakes at Goodwood and The Prince of Wales's Stakes at York. In The Free Handicap he was given 8 st. 13 lb.

In 1973 he did not run till July when he won The Sheffield Handicap at Doncaster by five lengths, giving the runner-up 34 lb. At Goodwood he won The King George Stakes but had to fight hard to defeat the four-year-old Workboy; nor did he have matters all his own way when winning The Nunthorpe Stakes from Balliol. His final appearance was in the Prix de l'Abbaye at Longchamp. In a field of twelve he won by two lengths from the King's Stand Stakes winner Abergwaun, to whom he was giving 3 lb. He was then retired to the stud at a 3,000-guinea fee. Recently there has been a substantial increase in the prize money available for top-class sprinters and there is therefore more incentive to keep them in training beyond the age of three.

The many English visitors to Longchamp to see the Prix de l'Arc de Triomphe this year ought to have returned with bulging pockets as, apart from the victories of Rheingold and Sandford Lad, Sparkler, trained by Robert Armstrong and ridden by Piggott, won the Prix du Moulin, worth over £19,000 to the winner. Among the horses Sparkler beat was Kalamoun, winner of the French Two Thousand Guineas, the Prix Lupin and the Prix Jacques Le Marois. Earlier in the season Sparkler had won The Lockinge Stakes at Newbury.

Allez France came to Newmarket for The Champion Stakes, for which she started a firm favourite. Possibly the race came a bit soon after her exertions in the Arc; possibly Saint-Martin made too much use of her. At all events she was in front approaching the Bushes but tired up the hill and was caught and beaten by the 33/1 outsider Hurry Harriet.

Hurry Harriet, bred and owned by Mr M. Thorp and trained in Ireland by P. Mullins, was having her eleventh race of the season. She had won The Pretty Polly Stakes at The Curragh and had been third to Dahlia and Mysterious in The Irish Guinness Oaks. Allez France may not have been at her best at Newmarket and Saint-Martin may not have ridden one of his more intelligent races, but Hurry Harriet, ridden by J. Cruguet, also beat Sharp Edge, who was third, Moulton, Mysterious, Scottish Rifle, and Ksar. She was a bad last in The Washington International at Laurel Park. She is by the little known sire Yrrah Jr, an American-bred Ribot horse that stood for two seasons in Ireland at a fee of 98 guineas before returning to Texas. Somnabula, dam of Hurry Harriet, is a non-winning daughter of Chanteur II.

American-bred two-year-olds occupied the first two places in The Free Handicap. These were Apalachee (9 st. 7 lb.) and Mississipian (9 st. 2 lb.).

Apalachee, owned by Mr J. A. Mulcahy and trained by O'Brien, could boast a distinguished pedigree, his sire being Round Table, not only a high-class racehorse but a tough one that won forty-three of his sixty-six races, while his dam Moccasin, by Nantallah, was the top two-year-old in America in 1965 and altogether won eleven races. She is a sister of Thong, the dam of Thatch, and of the Stakes winners Ridan and Lt Stevens. A powerful, well-grown bay with a devouring stride, Apalachee made his first appearance in the six-furlongs Lee Stakes at the Curragh in August and won on the tightest of tight reins by six lengths. The following month he won The Moy Maiden Stakes at The Curragh with comparable facility.

Apalachee faced far sterner opposition in his final race of the season, The Observer Gold Cup. Among his opponents was Mr Nelson Bunker Hunt's Vaguely Noble colt Mississipian, who had won The Grand Criterium by a nose from Nonoalco, winner of the Prix Morny and the Prix de la Salamandre. Coming into the straight at Doncaster Mississipian was seventh, Apalachee ninth. Both made rapid headway and eventually drew right away from their opponents. Mississipian led just over a quarter of a mile from home but soon afterwards Piggott sent Apalachee to the front and, despite showing signs of inexperience, Apalachee won without undue difficulty by a couple of lengths. The third horse to finish, Alpine Nephew, was ten lengths behind Mississipian.

This was an impressive performance by Apalachee and he successfully captured the imagination not only of the racing public but of the entire racing press as well.

No one seemed prepared to look further afield when it came to forecasting the winner of the 1974 Derby. His entry in Racehorses of 1973 concluded as follows: 'Quite frankly we can see nothing to stop him from winning both The Two Thousand Guineas and The Derby. We have not seen a horse as promising as this for years.'

On the 9 st. 1 lb. mark in The Free Handicap were Habat and Cellini. Habat, a very good-looking grey by Habitat out of Atrevida, by Sunny Boy III, had been bought for 14,500 guineas as a yearling by Mr Keith Freeman on behalf of the Italian owner Dr C. Vittadini. Atrevida, who was third in the Irish One Thousand Guineas, was a descendant of Mumtaz Mahal through Rivaz, a very fast half-sister to Nasrullah. Trained by Peter Walwyn, Habat made his first appearance in The Portsmouth Road Stakes at Kempton in May. Largely due to lack of experience he was caught in the last stride by Dragonara Palace. He then won The Berkshire Stakes at Newbury by five lengths and The Norfolk Stakes at Royal Ascot by six lengths. He certainly looked a smasher in The Norfolk Stakes so it came as a bitter disappointment when he was only sixth behind M. D. Wildenstein's American-bred filly Lianga in the Prix Robert Papin at Maisons-Laffitte. For some un-explained reason he ran well below his true form. His next race was the six-furlongs Mill Reef Stakes at Newbury in September. He won by five lengths but appeared to hesitate momentarily when Eddery asked him for his effort. Habat's last race of the season was The Middle Park Stakes. He won by two and a half lengths from Pitcairn but again one or two critics had their reservations.

Mr Charles St George's Cellini, who had cost $240,000 at a yearling, was a stable-companion of Apalachee and bred on similar lines, being by Round Table out of Gamely, by Bold Ruler. Gamely, winner of sixteen races up to a mile and a quarter and of $574,961, was a granddaughter of Rough Shod, the grandam of Apalachee. Cellini won both his races in Ireland, one being the important National Stakes at The Curragh. In this country he won The Dewhurst Stakes very smoothly from Pitcairn. Obviously O'Brien was going to hold a powerful hand in the 1974 classics.

Top owner in 1973 was Mr Nelson Bunker Hunt. Second came Mr David Robinson, whose total of 115 races won constituted a record for an owner in this country. It was certainly a year that Mr C. St George could look back on with satisfaction. He was a member of the Rheingold syndicate; he had shares, too, not only in Apalachee and Cellini, but also in Giacometti, who, trained by Price, had won The Gimcrack Stakes and The Champagne Stakes. Despite the fact that his stable was particularly hard hit by the virus epidemic in the summer, Noel Murless was leading trainer for the ninth time. He was closely followed by Peter Walwyn who had 87 winners as opposed to Murless's 34. Carson held on to the jockeys' championship with 163 winners against Piggott's 123. He had many more rides than Piggott in this country, Piggott as usual making many profitable visits to Ireland and France. Champion sire was the British-bred, American-based Vaguely Noble; second came Ragusa who had, alas, died early in the year.

Trainers who retired included Derrick Candy, who handed over the stable to his son Henry, George Todd, Geoffrey Barling, and Jackie Sirett. Two great public favourites who vanished from the racing scene were Mr Paul Mellon's Morris Dancer and Mr G. P. Williams's Be Hopeful. Morris Dancer, trained by Ian Balding, had won twenty-five races. A remarkably crusty character, he had not grown any more amenable with age and even in retirement anyone entering his box in the hope of a cosy chat is in for a painful surprise. Be Hopeful met with an accident at Lambourn and had to be put down. He had won twenty-six races and was the very first horse sent to Peter Walwyn when he started training.

The tote, so often criticised for lack of enterprise, launched a new pool entitled the Roll Up. It got off to a very shaky start from the point of view of press and public relations and it always seemed to be fighting a losing battle. Public support proved tepid and the Roll Up passed peacefully away, regretted by few, in November.

Sandown Park reopened in the autumn on the completion of an extensive and costly rebuilding programme. The new grandstand enclosure, which combined Tattersalls and the Silver Ring, looked remarkably good value for £1 but it has been found impossible to maintain admission at that price, and in 1976 it was £2. Members of the Sandown Park Club were not exactly enthusiastic about their new accommodation. They complained of shortage of space on days when important races were run, and of a thoroughly soulless and uncosy atmosphere all too reminiscent of Heathrow Airport. In general it was thought that Sandown's face-lift had been a good deal less successful than the one that had taken place at Newmarket at a fraction of the cost.

It was during this year that Sir Randle Feilden relinquished his post as Senior Steward. Naturally his long term of office had not been devoid of mistakes and clearly towards the end of it he was a tired man, but in the post-war era no one had worked harder or to better effect for the general good of racing. It was certainly not his fault that relations between the Jockey Club and the Levy Board became so strained. His successor was Lord Leverhulme. A man of infinite kindness and courtesy with whom it would never be easy to have a row, Lord Leverhulme possibly lacked the toughness and that hint of ruthlessness that a Senior Steward needs today if he is not going to stand in constant peril of being trampled underfoot. At Ascot Lord Abergavenny was beginning to show that in racing it is possible to be progressive and efficient without being abrasive, and he and Captain Nicholas Beaumont, the Clerk of the Couse, have formed a most effective partnership with excellent public relations.

In October Lord Leverhulme announced that in 1974 women would be permitted to ride in amateur riders' races against men, and that in 1975 they would be able to apply for professional licences and thus be eligible to take a mount in The Derby. In addition, girls would be able to start an apprenticeship at the age of sixteen.

In December 1973 the Chairman of the Levy Board, Sir Stanley Raymond, announced his retirement. His successor was Sir Desmond Plummer, who had headed the Conservative opposition in the G.L.C. Sir Desmond's knowledge of racing when he was appointed could have been written in block letters on the back of a stamp, and very sensibly he played himself in with caution for at least a year, talking to many people and being the recipient of a great deal of advice, some no doubt excellent, some from slightly dubious sources. Once he had got his eye in, he began to play some attractive shots all round the wicket and most people professionally engaged in racing were pleased when his term of office was extended. Now that he fully understands the facts of life about racing, he is proving quite a tough nut without ever being deliberately aggressive or quarrelsome.

Deaths during the year included those of Joe Marshall, Fred Templeman and Sir Harold Wernher. Originally apprenticed to Stanley Wootton, Marshall rode the 1929 Derby winner Trigo but he never became firmly established as a leading jockey. He was deprived of his licence in 1954 on account of his betting operations. Fred Templeman, who was eighty-three, had been apprenticed to F. Hallick. His great success as a rider came in 1919 when he won The Derby on Lord Glanely's Grand Parade. For many years he trained with success at Lambourn, among his winners being Diolite and Lambert Simnel, who both won The Two Thousand Guineas, and Chatelaine, who won The Oaks. Sir Harold Wernher's greatest success as an owner was to win The King George VI and Queen Elizabeth Stakes with Aggressor, trained by Gosden. The most famous horse that he owned, though, was that marvellous stayer Brown Jack, whose victories included The Champion Hurdle, The Queen Alexandra Stakes six years running, The Ascot Stakes, The Chester Cup, The Goodwood Cup and The Doncaster Cup.

There was no slackening in the demand from abroad for British bloodstock and Steel Pulse, winner of the 1972 Irish Sweeps Derby, went to Australia for £370,000. The Levy Board granted a boost to prize money of £2½ million, The Derby, The Oaks and The St Leger being the principal beneficiaries. A trainer called Ken Payne made quite a stir in the north by training forty-four winners in his first year at Middleham. By 1976 he was dead broke and in serious trouble.

Racing correspondents who visited Apalachee before the 1974 season began wrote him up as if he had already proved himself a combination of St Simon and The Tetrarch. On April 6 he won The Gladness Stakes at The Curragh, a race that did not in fact provide any valuable information. Ridden by Piggott, he started favourite at 9/4 on in The Two Thousand Guineas, the shortest-priced runner in that event since Colombo in 1934. Habat, who had won the Two Thousand Guineas Trial at Ascot, was second favourite at 9/1, while there was money, too, for Nonoalco and Giacometti. Apalachee had been drenched with praise to such an extent that it came as rather a shock to racegoers to find that he was by no means outstandingly handsome. Rather the reverse in fact: he looked distinctly leggy and his hocks were very far from being his strongest point. Moreover, there were persistent rumours that he was wrong in his wind. The pick of the field on looks was unquestionably Nonoalco.

There is not a great deal to be said about the race. Apalachee was in front at the Bushes and his supporters were beginning to count up just how much money they had won. This state of contentment, though, proved to be of disappointingly brief duration. It was anticipated that he would now lengthen his stride and draw away to win with dignified ease, but when Piggott started to ride him he proved incapable of acceleration. He was soon headed by Nonoalco who, strongly ridden by Saint-Martin, ran on stoutly up the hill to hold Giacometti at bay by a length and a half with Apalachee a length behind Giacometti. There were some very sad Irish faces as Apalachee was led into the unsaddling enclosure.

Apalachee never saw a racecourse again and was packed off to America as a stallion. The three-year-old career of the alleged 'wonder-horse' had ended in sad anticlimax.

His stable-companion, Cellini, won The Vauxhall Trial Stakes at Phoenix Park but only scraped home by inches from Furry Glen, who was meeting him on level terms. He next won the seven-furlongs Tetrarch Stakes at The Curragh by a length from Red Alert. He started favourite for the Irish Two Thousand Guineas but was beaten a furlong out, finishing third behind Furry Glen and Pitcairn. His final race was The St James's Palace Stakes at Royal Ascot in which he was second to Captain Lemos's Sing Sing colt Averof. He never ran again either and shortly afterwards followed Apalachee to America.

Nonoalco belonged to the Mexican film actress Mme Maria-Felix Berger and was trained by François Boutin, who had won the 1968 Oaks with La Lagune. Bred in America, by Nearco's son Nearctic out of Seximée, by the Preakness winner Hasty Road, he had been bought at the Keeneland Fall Sales for $30,000 by the English bloodstock agent Mr George Blackwell. As has already been stated, he was a top-class two-year-old, winning the Prix Yacowlef, the Prix Morny and the Prix de la Salamandre and only losing The Grand Criterium by about an inch to Mississipian. As he had shown not the slightest sign of weakening at the end of the Rowley Mile, and as his sire Nearctic had got Northern Dancer, sire of Nijinsky, it was generally reckoned that he stood a good chance of staying a mile and a half. Accordingly he started favourite for The Derby at 9/4. His stamina, though, proved insufficient and he was a beaten horse early in the straight. Subsequently he only raced over a mile. He won the Prix Jacques Le Marois at Deauville and the Prix du Rond-Point at Longchamp, in the latter race beating the speedy Lianga. He started at odds-on for the Prix du Moulin but ran in deplorable fashion and finished at the tail-end of the field behind Mount Hagen, a three-year-old by Bold Bidder.

The Derby was won by the 50/1 outsider Snow Knight by two lengths from Imperial Prince with Giacometti a length away third. The fast-finishing Bustino was close up fourth. In one way this Derby was unique. Snow Knight, Imperial Prince and Giacometti were first, second and third respectively at Tattenham Corner and continued in that order to the finish.

Snow Knight carried the colours of Mrs Sharon Phillips, the wife of a Montreal lawyer. In 1972 Mrs Phillips light-heartedly asked the Lambourn trainer Peter Nelson to buy her a horse to win The Derby but limited the price to 5,000 guineas. At the Newmarket October Sales, Mrs Nelson bought her Snow Knight for 5,200 guineas.

As a two-year-old Snow Knight ran five times. He won a maiden race at Kempton and The Donnington Castle Stakes at Newbury. His best performance, though, was to run Giacometti to a short head in The Champagne Stakes. He finished well down the course in The Observer Gold Cup. In The Free Handicap he was given 8 st. 7 lb.

At three he ran a good race first time out as, on firm going at Sandown, he ran Lady Beaverbrook's Bustino, to whom he was giving 5 lb., to half a length in the ten-furlongs Classic Trial Stakes. In the Lingfield Derby Trial he was less appealing in finishing third to Bustino, whom he met on level terms, and Sin Y Sin. Until the final bend had been reached he was held back in last place by Brian Taylor, and when he was asked for his effort in the straight he hung badly to the left. It was not a performance that advertised his chance in The Derby.

The going at Epsom was firm and this suited Snow Knight, who was at his best on top of the ground. Furthermore, Taylor made no attempt to hold Snow Knight up as he had done at Lingfield but permitted him to stride along freely from the start. At half-way Snow Knight went to the front and there he remained to the finish. It was not a great Derby field by any means but Snow Knight had won on his merits, out-galloping and out-staying his opponents. His victory had astonished both students of the form book and the breeding pundits. It had been generally agreed that he was not classically bred, being by the City and Suburban winner Firestreak out of an unraced daughter of the Cesarewitch winner Flush Royal, even if his great-grandam was Snowberry, who produced Chamossaire. A mile was probably the ideal distance for Firestreak, who had also been trained by Nelson.

Snow Knight's victory was a popular one in that most followers of racing were delighted to see Peter Nelson train a winner of The Derby. As a boy at Marlborough and at the R.M.C. he had been an outstanding games-player. From 1932 to 1946 he was a regular soldier in the Royal Berkshire Regiment and he began training in 1948. Relaxed and friendly, he sometimes conveyed the impression on the racecourse that he would sooner have been at the Royal Berkshire or at Sandwich. Throughout his training career he was greatly helped by his wife, a very good judge of a thoroughbred. Besides Snow Knight and Firestreak, he trained good winners such as Whistler, Victorina and Bay Express. He retired at the end of 1975, the stable being carried on by his elder son John. He was probably the best golfer among trainers of his time, and Brian Taylor, who rode such an enterprising race on Snow Knight, is certainly one of the best golfers among modern jockeys.

Snow Knight was sixth behind Dahlia in The King George VI and Queen Elizabeth Stakes, third behind Dahlia in The Benson and Hedges Gold Cup. Early in September he was shipped off to race in Canada. His career there was not immediately successful[1] and he met with three defeats in quick succession. He was apt to be a bit temperamental. In the parade before The Derby he unseated Taylor and had to be taken down to the stalls before the others. At Ascot, Taylor, entirely without permission, took him out of the paddock early and missed the parade altogether. For this bit of cheek he was fined £200 by the Stewards of the

[1] At four Snow Knight won two Grade I Stakes races in North America and was voted United States Champion Grass Horse.

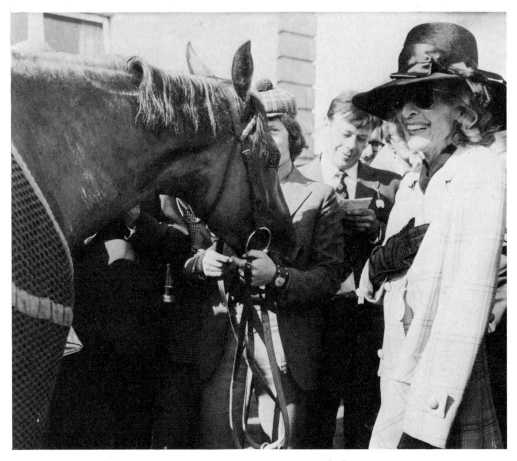

63.   Lady Beaverbrook with Bustino after they won the 1974 St Leger

Jockey Club. In Canada Snow Knight gave a good deal of trouble before one of his races.

At one point it had seemed likely that Mississipian would run in The Derby and that Piggott would ride him rather than the very able stable jockey, Bill Pyers. Not surprisingly, Pyers was not very keen about being 'jocked off' and kicked up a fuss. The result was that Mr Nelson Bunker Hunt took Mississipian out of The Derby and ran him in the Prix du Jockey Club instead. In that race, ridden by Pyers, Mississipian was fourth behind Caracolero.

Bustino had found the early pace in The Derby a bit too hot for him and he just missed a place. Hern had warned after Bustino's victory in the Lingfield Derby Trial that Lady Beaverbrook's colt would probably be better suited to The St Leger. Bustino's next race was the Grand Prix de Paris, a tough test for three-year-olds in early July, being run over a distance only just short of two miles. In a field of eighteen he made a brave effort to secure this prize, worth over £100,000, but found one too good for him in Mr G. A. Oldham's Irish-bred Sagaro, by Espresso, who beat him by two lengths. Sagaro was a high-class stayer and subsequently won The Ascot Gold Cup three times, as well as the Prix du Cadran.

Bustino did not run again till The Great Voltigeur Stakes at York. There were only three runners and English Prince, winner of The Irish Sweeps Derby, was favourite at 7/4 on. English Prince had, in fact, been stopped in his work and was not at his best. He was beaten by four lengths by Bustino, being eased up by Eddery when it was obvious that he could not win, and he never saw a racecourse again.

Bustino was favourite for The St Leger at 11/10. At one point he was 5/4 on but adverse rumours caused him to weaken in the market. He had the services of a pacemaker, Riboson, who was ridden by the experienced and skilful Jimmy Lindley. An excellent judge of pace, Lindley carried out his task to perfection. He was in front till two and half furlongs out when Bustino assumed the lead and, vigorously ridden by Joe Mercer, stayed on strongly to win by three lengths from Giacometti with Riboson four lengths away third. Thus Giacometti had been placed in The Two Thousand Guineas, The Derby and The St Leger, a distinction achieved by Nagami in 1958. The St Leger distance was too far for him and, after looking very dangerous, he weakened in the final furlong and started to hang.

Bustino's victory was a popular one apart from the not unimportant fact that he was favourite. Lady Beaverbrook, whose late husband's venture into racing between the wars had proved both costly and of brief duration, had spent a great deal of money on yearlings and up till then had been a good deal less successful than she deserved. Bigivor, a Sir Ivor colt for whom she paid 81,000 guineas, proved about as fast as an old man crossing a ploughed field in gumboots, while Million, a Mill Reef colt that cost 202,000 guineas, showed little promise as a two-year-old in 1976.

Bustino did not race again at three. A strong, handsome bay that cost 21,000 guineas as a yearling at Newmarket, he was bred by Mr Edgar Cooper Bland and is by Busted out of Ship Yard, by Doutelle. Ship Yard is a member of the famous Marchetta family and her grandam Rosetta was a half-sister to the dam of Alycidon.

Any suggestion that Brigadier Gerard was a mere flash in the pan as far as Queen's Hussar's stud career was concerned was banished when the Queen won The One Thousand Guineas with Highclere, by Queen's Hussar out of Highlight, by Borealis out of the One Thousand Guineas winner Hypericum. Thus once again Feola, Hypericum's dam, demonstrated her immense value to the Royal Stud. Trained by Dick Hern, Highclere, a bay, was a lengthy, racinglike filly that never carried much flesh when in training. At two she began by running second to Polygamy in The Princess Maiden Plate at Newmarket in July. In her next race, The Princess Margaret Stakes at Ascot, she finished two lengths in front of Polygamy who was giving her 4 lb., but was herself beaten a head by Celestial Dawn who was giving her 7 lb. Her third and last race that season was The Donnington Maiden Stakes run over seven furlongs at Newbury. Starting at 5/2 on, she was all out to win by a neck from Reigning Grace. In The Free Handicap she was given 7 st. 11 lb., 11 lb. less than the top-rated fillies Melchbourne, Bitty Girl and Gentle Thoughts. It seemed unlikely that she would ever attain classic standard.

Her first race in 1974 was The One Thousand Guineas. Wearing blinkers for the first time and ridden by Joe Mercer, she started at 12/1. Favourite was Mr Louis Freedman's Polygamy, trained by Walwyn, and second favourite was the same owner's Mil's Bomb, trained by Murless. Polygamy had won the One Thousand Guineas Trial at Ascot. Coming down into the Dip nothing was going better than Mr Tom Blackwell's Silly Season filly Mrs Tiggywinkle but she tired on the hill and, hanging away to the left, may have slightly interfered with Polygamy. Highclere had taken the lead two furlongs from home, and despite occasional swishings of the tail ran on under pressure with the utmost gameness. She was strongly challenged by the equally courageous Polygamy and, as these two brave fillies passed the post, it was impossible to say which had won. A great cheer went up when it was announced that the Queen's filly had prevailed by a short head. Mrs Tiggywinkle was four lengths away third.

It was reckoned that the Epsom course and the distance of The Oaks would be unlikely to suit Highclere and that accordingly her next objective would be the Prix de Diane run over ten and a half furlongs at Chantilly. This decision was fully justified when, in the Queen's presence, Highclere won this rich prize worth over £93,000 by two lengths from Comtesse de Loir, who had won the Prix Saint-Alary and was later to run Allez France to a head in the Prix de l'Arc de Triomphe.

In The King George VI and Queen Elizabeth Stakes Highclere ran another good race and finished second to Dahlia who beat her, very easily it must be admitted, by two and a half lengths. Highclere herself finished six lengths in front of the Derby winner Snow Knight. In the second half of the season Highclere trained off completely. She was only sixth behind Dahlia in The Benson and Hedges Gold Cup. That surely would have been the moment to retire her. It certainly seemed an error of judgement to send her to Paris for the Arc, in which she finished eighteenth in a field of twenty. At her best, she was unquestionably a very good filly indeed.

Bred by her owner, Polygamy, by Reform out of Seventh Bride, by Royal Record II, was only a little filly but what she lacked in inches she made up for in courage. She started favourite for The Oaks, second favourite being the Queen's Musidora Stakes winner Escorial, trained by Ian Balding. Also well backed was Mr N. J. Robinson's Dibidale, trained by Barry Hills. A chestnut by Aggressor out of Priddy Maid, by Acropolis, she had won The Cheshire Oaks at Chester by seven lengths from Mil's Bomb. It is probably true to say that in The Oaks Polygamy was never on the bit from start to finish and Eddery must have had an extremely fatiguing ride. However, she kept battling away with typical tenacity and in the end she mastered Furioso inside the final furlong to win by a length. It was not a brilliant performance but it was certainly a plucky one.

64. The Oaks 1974—Dibidale's saddle has slipped but Willie Carson manages to stay aboard. They were disqualified because a weight cloth was lost and of course Carson was short of weight when he weighed in

In one respect at least Polygamy was fortunate. Dibidale, ridden by Carson, had been sixth at Tattenham Corner and went on to make steady progress in the straight. With two furlongs to go, her backers had good reason for believing that she was going to win. At that point, however, disaster struck. Her saddle slipped right round and Carson had to complete the course riding bareback, a feat he accomplished so skilfully that Dibidale finished third, a mere half length behind Furioso. Unfortunately, though, the weight-cloth had fallen to the ground when the saddle slipped and inevitably the Stewards were compelled to deprive the luckless Dibidale of her place.

On July 20 Dibidale won the Irish Guinness Oaks by five lengths from Gaily with Polygamy a length and a half away third. This result, of course, emphasised

Dibidale's misfortune at Epsom but it is possible that Polygamy trained off after her victory in The Oaks. In The Yorkshire Oaks Dibidale was less impressive and scrambled home by a neck from Mil's Bomb, by Crepello. Mil's Bomb, however, was a much better filly then than she had been in the spring. She had won The Lancashire Oaks at Haydock Park and The Nassau Stakes at Goodwood and she subsequently won The Park Hill Stakes. It was intended to run Dibidale in the Prix Vermeille and the Prix de l'Arc de Triomphe but she jarred her near fore early in September and had to miss both those engagements. The following season this unlucky filly was injured in The Geoffrey Freer Stakes at Newbury and had to be destroyed later that month.

Dahlia was slow to come to her best in 1974. In the Prix d'Harcourt in April she was fourth behind Allez France, who this season was trained by Angel Penna. In the Prix Ganay early in May Dahlia did no better, finishing fifth, fourteen lengths behind Allez France. Despite these failures, Dahlia was favourite for The Coronation Cup, second favourite being the French four-year-old Tennyson, winner of the Grand Prix in 1973. English hopes, such as they were, rested on the representative of Dick Hern's stable, Mr Hollingsworth's Buoy, who the previous month had won The Yorkshire Cup. In the early stages not one of the Coronation Cup competitors was prepared to make the running and the field proceeded at a gentle amble. After a bit, Joe Mercer got tired of this and sent Buoy to the front. The pace gradually increased but there seemed little disposition to chase the leader, who was ten lengths clear at Tattenham Corner. In the final furlong Buoy was a very tired horse but his opponents had given him far too much rope and he won by a length and a half from Tennyson with Dahlia three lengths away third. He had really been presented with the race through the folly of the opposition. He was subsequently second in The Hardwicke Stakes, beaten half a length by Relay Race to whom he was giving 4 lb., and won The Princess of Wales's Stakes. He was by no means disgraced when fourth in The King George VI and Queen Elizabeth Stakes and concluded his career by finishing down the course in the Grand Prix de Deauville. He injured a tendon in that race and was taken out of training. He might have made a magnificent Cup horse but of course there is no stud future nowadays for horses that win over two miles or more. In the autumn he was sold to go to Australia for a sum said to be in the region of £100,000.

Dahlia won the Grand Prix de Saint-Cloud but it was not one of her more convincing performances and furthermore she had seemed nervous and tensed up before the start. By the end of July, though, she was back at her best and it would be difficult to exaggerate the ease with which she won The King George VI and Queen Elizabeth Stakes. She was still on the bit as she passed the winning-post and Piggott had never felt obliged to make a move on her. It was a superb performance. She was back again in England in August and won The Benson and Hedges Gold Cup from Imperial Prince and Snow Knight. It was a decisive enough victory but she had to be pushed out and it is doubtful if she could in fact have pulled out much more had she been required to do so. Presumably at this stage of her career a distance short of a mile and a half was not quite far enough for her.

As a preliminary for the Arc, Dahlia ran in the Prix du Prince d'Orange at Longchamp and in a photo-finish was beaten by On My Way and Toujours Prêt. She failed to produce her usual strong finish and some spectators claimed they detected a certain lack of enthusiasm in her effort. Piggott blamed himself for delivering his challenge too soon. Following that defeat, there were persistent rumours that Dahlia would miss the Arc but it was not until a week before that event that it was announced that she was bound for North America to contest three races there, two in the United States, one in Canada.

Despite the long journey and some rather crude quarantine arrangements on arrival, Dahlia won The Man o' War Stakes at Belmont Park ridden by Ron Turcotte. Piggott arrived to partner her in The Canadian International Championship at Woodbine Park, Toronto, and she duly won by a length, breaking the record for the course in the process. Snow Knight finished unplaced. After these victories she started a hot favourite for The Washington International at Laurel Park but was beaten by Sir Michael Sobell's French-trained Admetus and Desert Vixen. Zilber, greatly disappointed, was inclined to blame Piggott for overdoing the waiting game, and the American press, no lovers of Piggott at the best of times, were scathing in their criticism. Piggott, true to form, appeared unmoved: 'They're not machines, you know. They can't win all the time.'

Thus, although defeated in her final race of the year, Dahlia had again proved herself a superlative middle-distance filly. She was clearly an exceptionally tough one too, bearing in mind her strenuous racing against top-class opponents and the amount of travelling she was called upon to do. It is hardly surprising that on more than one occasion she gave hints of becoming just a little bit temperamental.

Admetus was a four-year-old gelding by Reform that had been trained as a three-year-old by Hern and had then been transferred to J. Cunnington jr. He improved immensely at four and his other victories included the Grand Prix d'Evry, The Prince of Wales's Stakes at Royal Ascot, and the Prix Maurice Nieuil at Saint-Cloud. In addition he was first past the post in the Grand Prix de Deauville but suffered disqualification, his rider having been imprudent enough to hit Ashmore over the head with his whip.

The most popular victory beyond a doubt in 1974 was that of the Duke of Norfolk's Ragstone in The Ascot Gold Cup. Bred by the Duke, Ragstone is by Ragusa out of the Right Royal V mare Fotheringay, a descendant of the dual classic winner Herringbone. An attractive bay, Ragstone was the unbeaten winner of four races at three. He was carefully placed and by no means severely tested. At four he won both his races prior to Ascot, The Aston Park Stakes at Newbury and The Henry II Stakes at Sandown. He clearly possessed excellent acceleration; the question to be answered at Ascot was whether he would stay the distance in a true-run race of two miles and a half. The opposition in The Cup was far from negligible. The favourite, Lassalle, had won The Cup and the Prix du Cadran in 1973. This year he had only lost the Prix du Cadran by a narrow margin to the British-bred Recupere, a Reliance colt bought at Newmarket as a yearling for 2,300 guineas. Also in The Gold Cup was the Irish-bred Authi, a half-brother

by Aureole to Hard To Beat. He had finished close up third in the Prix du Cadran.
Among the outsiders was Proverb, winner the previous year of The Chester Vase
and The Goodwood Cup.

Both Ragstone and Authi had pacemakers but, despite that, the pace to begin
with was far from being an exacting one. Ragstone was apt to take a very strong
hold and Hutchinson had some difficulty in settling him down. At the final bend,
the runners were still closely bunched up together. Once in the straight, Piggott
took Lassalle to the front and headed for home as hard as he could go. Hutchinson,
for his part, was intent on holding up Ragstone for as long as he could in order to
make the most of his speed. When at length he did deliver his challenge, Ragstone
swept past Lassalle and a great cheer went up. The race, though, was not yet over.
Proverb came on the scene with a storming late run and Ragstone had only three
parts of a length to spare at the finish. Lassalle was a neck away third. The reception Ragstone was given reflected the affection that was felt for his owner who had
served English racing, and Ascot in particular, so well for a great many years.

It was proposed to run Ragstone in the Prix de l'Arc de Triomphe but after he
had run poorly on soft going in The Geoffrey Freer Stakes at Newbury, it was
decided to retire him to the stud. Not even the most prejudiced breeder can take
the view that he is a mere plodder devoid of speed.

Proverb, trained by Barry Hills, had a good season. He won The Paradise
Stakes at Ascot, The Goodwood Cup for the second time and The Doncaster Cup.
He was third in the Prix Gladiateur but was out of his proper league when com-
peting in the Arc. Lassalle was taken to Japan by his owner at the end of the season.

Royal Ascot started off on a somewhat bizarre note. Confusion won The Queen
Anne Stakes in a tight finish with Gloss and Royal Prerogative. Brook was six
lengths away fourth. It had not been a pretty race to watch in the closing stages,
being unpleasantly reminiscent of the less savoury incidents liable to be seen in
'Match of the Day'. The Stewards at once initiated an inquiry at the conclusion
of which the first three horses to finish were all disqualified and the race awarded
to Brook. The jockeys concerned, Starkey, Eddery and Goreham, were all suspended for four days. It was generally agreed that justice had been done.

Old Lucky, owned by Mr Nelson Bunker Hunt and trained by Bernard van
Cutsem, was backed from 12/1 to 8/1 in The Royal Hunt Cup and duly landed an
old-fashioned gamble. Vincent O'Brien won The Coronation Stakes with the
American-bred Lisadell, a sister of Thatch, and The Cork and Orrery Stakes with
the American-bred Saritamer, a grey by Dancer's Image that subsequently won
The July Cup and The Diadem Stakes. The King's Stand Stakes went to Peter
Nelson's exceptionally good-looking three-year-old Bay Express, by Polyfoto.
Unfortunately Bay Express developed a large splint and was unable to run again
that season.

Winner of The King Edward VII Stakes was Mrs Vera Hue-Williams's English
Prince, a big, handsome bay by Petingo out of English Miss, by Bois Roussell.
Virelle, dam of English Miss, was a half-sister to Sayani and My Babu by Casterari.
English Prince began the season by running second in a mile maiden race at

Newbury. He showed encouraging promise for the future on that occasion and on his next appearance he won the ten-furlongs White Rose Maiden Stakes at Ascot. He followed up that success by an impressive six-lengths victory in the mile-and-a-half Predominate Stakes at Goodwood. Peter Walwyn reckoned that English Prince still needed time and that in any case Epsom would not suit him so it was decided to give The Derby a miss and to go instead for The King Edward VII Stakes followed by The Irish Sweeps Derby.

The decision proved a wise one. English Prince won at Ascot in record time and then won The Irish Sweeps Derby from Imperial Prince with Sir Penfro third. Mississipian in fact finished third but his progress under the guidance of Head, never a lucky jockey outside France, had been of a somewhat erratic nature. The Stewards relegated him to fourth place and Sir Penfro moved up into third.

It was a memorable race for the Hue-Williams family as they had bred not only the winner but also the runner-up who was a half-brother by Sir Ivor to Altesse Royale and carried the colours of Mrs Hue-Williams's husband. Trained by Noel Murless, Imperial Prince had begun the season by winning The Wood Ditton Stakes at Newmarket. It proved to be the only race he won. He was second in The Chester Vase to Mr T. F. Blackwell's Aureole colt Jupiter Pluvius; second in The Derby; second in The Irish Sweeps Derby; second in The Benson and Hedges Gold Cup; and fourth in The St Leger. His trouble was that he did not stay beyond a mile and a half, while over middle distances he lacked the ability to produce that bit of extra speed at the end of a race that would have made all the difference.

Unfortunately English Prince was difficult to train after his triumph in Ireland and he had done little fast work before his defeat by Bustino in The Great Voltigeur Stakes. It was that contest that terminated his active career.

Horses beaten in a handicap for apprentice riders at Wolverhampton in the spring seldom go on to win The Eclipse Stakes the same season. However, this was the accomplishment of Coup de Feu, owned by Mr F. Sasse and trained by his son Duncan at Lambourn. A five-year-old by White Fire III out of Winning Bid, dam of the St Leger winner Peleid, Coup de Feu had been bought for 26,000 guineas at the 1973 Newmarket December Sales. Up till then he had been trained by Jack Watts. Following his Wolverhampton defeat, he showed good form in winning The Newbury Spring Cup with 9 st. 11 lb. His whole record before The Eclipse showed five wins in twenty-two races and none of his form suggested he was capable of winning an event of such importance. Probably there have been few less distinguished winners of this great race. Later in the summer he ran really well, though, to finish close up third behind Nonoalco and Toro in the Prix Jacques Le Marois at Deauville. He was unplaced in the Arc, The Champion Stakes and The Washington International.

Giacometti and Averof were favourite and second favourite respectively for The Eclipse. Giacometti ran poorly and, at the request of the stable jockey Tony Murray, it was arranged for Piggott to ride the horse in subsequent engagements. Averof was knocked for six when Forsetti suddenly went into reverse on the final bend. Other sufferers were Mount Hagen and Rose Laurel. A 33/1 outsider, Coup de Feu won by three lengths from Ksar with Mount Hagen three parts of a length away third. Ksar subsequently won the Prix Gontaut-Biron at Deauville, Mount Hagen the Prix du Moulin.

At Goodwood the Irish three-year-old Red Alert, trained by D. K. Weld, put up a splendid performance to win The Stewards Cup under 9 st. 2 lb. He had previously won The Jersey Stakes at Ascot with considerable ease. A son of Red God, he never ran again after Goodwood. The time was clearly ripe for cashing in and he was sold for around £200,000 for stud purposes.

Averof started favourite for The Sussex Stakes but he pulled very hard and ran all too freely, eventually finishing fourth behind Mr Nelson Bunker Hunt's four-year-old Ace of Aces, who beat Habat by a couple of lengths. Due to various vexatious minor misfortunes, Habat was running for the first time since his failure in The Two Thousand Guineas. He had a disappointing season at the end of which he was retired to the National Stud. Ace of Aces, by Vaguely Noble and trained by Zilber, was a substandard winner of The Sussex Stakes. Earlier in the season he had acted as Dahlia's pacemaker in the Prix Ganay.

Doug Marks's outsider Singing Bede won The King George Stakes, in which the Forlorn River filly Melchbourne, winner of six races at two, was a desperately unlucky loser. The stout-hearted Proverb was put to little bother in beating King Levanstell and Parnell in The Goodwood Cup. Mr A. Villars's Take A Reef, trained by Hobbs, clearly showed what a high-class middle-distance performer he was when winning The Extel Handicap under 9 st. 11 lb. He had previously won The Epsom Handicap and The John Smith's Magnet Cup, his one defeat during the season coming in The Cosmopolitan Cup at Lingfield in which he met with a lot of interference. Shrewd judges rated him the best of his age trained in this country. He was, however, never tested in top-class company as he broke down in his preparation for The Champion Stakes. A neatly-made, well-proportioned bay, he is by Right Tack out of the unraced Nigthingale (*sic*) II by Sicambre.

There was no really outstanding English-trained sprinter in 1974. Possibly the best, at any rate on fast ground, was the four-year-old Blue Cashmere who, in The Nunthorpe Stakes at York, inflicted a decisive defeat on Rapid River and Saritamer. The previous year his successes had included The Ayr Gold Cup.

The Queen Elizabeth II Stakes was not run this year. The last two days of this important Ascot meeting had to be abandoned because the course was waterlogged after heavy rain.

Allez France just held on to beat Comtesse de Loir in the Prix de l'Arc de Triomphe. Her rider, Yves Saint-Martin, had injured a thigh two days previously and it was found necessary to give him a pain-killing injection before the race. As she seemed none the worse for her Longchamp exertions, it was decided to run Allez France in The Champion Stakes. The day before that race was run, Newmarket was buzzing with rumours about Allez France and a lot of people professed to know that she was not going to take the field. In the end, late on the eve of the race, it was announced that she would not run as she had sustained a slight injury while being loaded on to the plane for Newmarket. It would have been sensible as well as courteous if Penna had explained all the circumstances to the Newmarket Stewards but he just flew Allez France back to Paris without bothering to give any reason for her absence. The matter was the subject of a Jockey Club inquiry which resulted in Penna being fined £100. The whole business did nothing to increase M. Wildenstein's popularity in Britain.

In the absence of Allez France, The Champion Stakes was won by Giacometti from Northern Gem and Pitcairn. It was a tribute to Price's professional skill that he produced Giacometti so fresh and well at this late stage of the season. A 5,000-guinea yearling, Giacometti is by Fabergé out of Naujwan, by Ommeyad.

The leaders in The Two-Year-Old Free Handicap were Grundy (9 st. 7 lb.), Green Dancer (9 st. 6 lb.), Cry of Truth (9 st. 5 lb.), No Alimony (9 st. 1 lb.) and Steel Heart (9 st.). Grundy was bred by the Overbury Stud in Gloucestershire owned by Messrs E. and T. Holland-Martin. A rather light-coloured chestnut with flaxen mane and tail, he is by the Guineas runner-up Great Nephew, a son of the champion sprinter Honeyway, out of Word From Lundy, by Worden II. He was sent up for sale at Newmarket as a yearling and Mr Keith Freeman bought him for 11,000 guineas on behalf of the Italian owner Dr Carlo Vittadini. He was sent to Peter Walwyn to be trained and made his first appearance in The Granville Stakes at Ascot on July 26. It was widely known that he had shown a bit at home and he was second favourite in a field of seventeen. He was a bit squeezed for room at one stage but won comfortably enough in the end from his stable-companion No Alimony, an Alcide colt owned by Mr Louis Freedman. Grundy's manner of racing, and in particular his power of acceleration in the final furlong, strongly suggested that he had a distinguished future ahead of him.

At the end of August he had no difficulty in winning The Sirenia Plate at Kempton but a severer task faced him in The Champagne Stakes at Doncaster. At half-way he seemed to be in some difficulty as he was last but one and it looked as if he might have trouble in finding an opening. However, his class and his speed saw him through in the end and in beating Whip It Quick and Bold Pirate Pat Eddery did not feel compelled to draw his whip.

Grundy's last race that season was The Dewhurst Stakes. On soft ground he made mincemeat of Mr Ravi Tikkoo's speedy Habitat colt Steel Heart, winner of The Gimcrack Stakes and The Middle Park Stakes, and beat him by half a dozen lengths. A few people were prejudiced against Grundy because they did not care for his colour, but it was widely agreed that he looked an outstanding prospect for The Two Thousand Guineas. Opinion with regard to his chance in The Derby was less sanguine. Not everyone could visualise Great Nephew as the sire of a top-class mile-and-a-half horse.

Madame P. Wertheimer's Green Dancer, trained at Chantilly by Alec Head, was one of the first crop of runners by Nijinsky. A slightly leggy bay, he was second in the Prix des Chênes, beaten a neck by Mariacci who subsequently won The Grand Criterium. Green Dancer started second favourite for The Observer Gold Cup and won rather impressively from the Irish colt Sea Break and No Alimony.

Winner in his two previous races of minor events at Haydock Park and Goodwood, No Alimony started favourite.

Bred by her owner, Miss Pearl Lawson-Johnston, a former Master of Foxhounds who keeps one or two mares at the Langham Hall Stud of her cousin Mr T. F. Blackwell, Cry of Truth, the best of her age and sex in 1974, is by no means fashionably bred, being by Town Crier, a smart miler by Sovereign Path, out of False Evidence, by Counsel. When it came to racing, False Evidence, to give her the benefit of the doubt, was a shade better than useless. She ran fifteen times on the flat and the best she could do was to be placed in maiden events at Lanark and Edinburgh. Nor was she any better over hurdles. Her first foal, an extremely moderate animal by Acer, won a minor event in France at the age of four. Her second foal died and then came Melchbourne, by Forlorn River. She was a very fast two-year-old and won half a dozen races. At three she only ran three times, winning a handicap at Doncaster with 9 st. 7 lb. and being a most unlucky loser of The King George Stakes at Goodwood. Unfortunately she died soon after being retired to the stud.

The third living foal of False Evidence was Cry of Truth, a grey like her sire. Through sheer inexperience she disappointed Bruce Hobbs on her first appearance, being narrowly beaten in the Wills Embassy Stakes Qualifier at York. She then won successively The Grimthorpe Maiden Stakes at Doncaster by four lengths; The Wills Embassy Stakes Final at Goodwood by five lengths; The Lowther Stakes at York by five lengths; The Champion Trophy at Ripon, her first race over six furlongs, breaking the two-year-old course record; and The Cheveley Park Stakes, in which she made all the running, by two lengths. Obviously she was never going to make a stayer but there seemed a fair chance that she would be able to last out a mile, in which case she would take a lot of beating in The One Thousand Guineas.

Steel Heart had cost Mr Tikkoo 71,000 guineas as a yearling. Trained in Ireland by D. K. Weld, he showed fine speed in winning The Gimcrack Stakes and The Middle Park Stakes but his limitations were brutally exposed when he clashed with Grundy in The Dewhurst Stakes.

Thanks chiefly to Dahlia, Mr Nelson Bunker Hunt was leading owner for the second year running and this year he was leading breeder, too. His American-based stallion Vaguely Noble was champion sire as he had been in 1973. Dahlia was voted Horse of the Year for the second time. Peter Walwyn was top trainer with Dick Hern second, both winning over £200,000 in stakes for their owners. Walwyn won ninety-six races, the biggest total since Matt Peacock's hundred in 1932. John Dunlop, who has been so consistently successful since he succeeded Gordon Smyth at Arundel in 1966, actually won a hundred and one races but only eighty of these were in Britain. He had started off the season by winning eight races at Cagnes-sur-Mer and he also won races in Belgium and Germany. After completing his National Service with the Royal Ulster Rifles, he had been assistant firstly to Neville Dent and then to Gordon Smyth.

With a hundred and forty-eight winners, five more than Lester Piggott, Pat Eddery became champion jockey at the age of twenty-two, the youngest since Sir

65. Champions—Pat Eddery, who became champion jockey for the first time in 1974, and Willie Carson, who held the title before him

Gordon Richards topped the list in 1925 when he was twenty-one. Eddery was the first Irish-born rider to be champion. He is the fifth of the twelve children of Jimmy Eddery, who rode for Seamus McGrath and was twice champion jockey in Ireland. Pat Eddery owes much to 'Frenchie' Nicholson, to whom he was apprenticed and who is something of a genius in the production of jockeys, other examples of his handiwork being Tony Murray and Paul Cook. Eddery has never let success go to his head. He is always willing to learn and in consequence is always improving. It is seldom indeed nowadays that he loses a race he ought to have won.

Jimmy Lindley decided to retire after a long and difficult battle against his weight. He is now racing manager to Mr and Mrs Mullion and B.B.C. television paddock commentator. Originally apprenticed to Tom Masson, he had retired once before because of weight problems and went to work in a Brighton factory, but the former Lewes trainer Matt Feakes enticed him to Lambourn to help school his hurdlers. Lindley rode some winners over hurdles and eventually started riding on the flat again. He won six races in 1957, fifty-one in 1958. In 1959 he married Matt Feakes's daughter. He had successful associations firstly with 'Towser' Gosden and later with Jeremy Tree. He won The Two Thousand Guineas twice and The St Leger once. Other jockeys to retire were John Gorton, who returned to South Africa to train for Mr Harry Oppenheimer; Willie Snaith; and Mickey Greening. The Dorking trainer Alec Kerr decided to retire, having reached the age of seventy. In his final season he gave a reminder of his skill by winning five races in succession with that highly-strung filly Calaba. Humphrey Cottrill, who at one time had trained for Major Holliday and subsequently won many races for Mr Stanhope Joel, decided to call it a day and now graces the panel of stewards at Newbury. Cyril Mitchell of Epsom handed over to his son Philip and Paul Davey was a victim of Mr David Robinson's decision to slash his racing empire, a decision at least partially actuated by Mr Robinson's indifferent health.

One of the outstanding personalities in English racing this century, Albert Edward Harry Meyer Archibald Primrose, 6th Earl of Rosebery, died on May 21 at the age of ninety-two. It would be foolish to pretend that for the first half, at any rate, of his long life he was either greatly liked or widely admired. He was far too inclined to be arrogant and overbearing. In addition he had a quick brain and a power of repartee that was apt to be wounding. Two factors were largely responsible for these unlikeable characteristics. His mother, Hannah Rothschild, daughter of Baron Meyer de Rothschild, died when he was a child. His father the 5th Earl, the only man ever to have won The Derby when Prime Minister of England, made no secret of his preference for his younger son Neil who took after his father in looks, whereas Harry's heavier features were more reminiscent of his mother. The 5th Earl could be charming when in the mood but, partly because he had been flattered and atrociously spoilt as a boy at Eton, he was selfish, exacting, easily bored and frequently rude. His wit more often than not was caustic. The attitude adopted by his elder son was no doubt a form of defence against the father whom he greatly admired but whose love he was unable to win.

The second factor was his war record. On the face of it he did exceptionally well. Apart from being badly wounded, he was awarded the D.S.O., the M.C., the Legion of Honour and was four times mentioned in dispatches. The trouble was that these distinctions were gained on the Staff and not with the Grenadier Guards, the regiment in which he had served as a young man. He was in fact on very close terms indeed with the great but explosive General Allenby, to whom he was not just Assistant Military Secretary but trusted friend. That he had served on the Staff and risen to comparative eminence caused jealousy and resentment in the more narrow-minded military circles. These sentiments were rarely concealed and cannot have been easy or pleasant to endure.

At Eton Harry Dalmeny, as he then was, proved an outstanding athlete. In his twenties he captained the Surrey cricket team for a couple of seasons and did it well. He was essentially an attacking batsman and rarely needed more than two hours for the compilation of a century. It was he who gave Sir Jack Hobbs his county cap. He was up to international class at polo, one of the best heavy-weights to hounds in the country, a fine shot and a useful golfer who knew how to adapt his game with age.

For a short time he served in the Grenadier Guards but perhaps his father felt he was enjoying himself too much. Pressure was put on him to send in his papers and to take up politics. His father was not over-generous with regard to money and it may have been because of this that Harry's name became involved in a distasteful racing episode that gave his father additional cause for complaint. For some years Harry was Liberal M.P. for Midlothian. He did not really care for political life but just as he was beginning to make some sort of name for himself his father began to show signs of jealousy and to put barriers in the path of his progress.

Neil Primrose was killed in 1917 and it was made plain to Harry by his father that he would sooner it had been Harry's fate to die. However, in the closing years of the 5th Earl's life there was something like a reconciliation, and father and son became very much closer, particularly in respect of matters connected with the Mentmore Stud and the running of the horses. It was largely due to Harry that Jack Jarvis became his father's trainer in succession to Frank Hartigan. When his father died, the 6th Earl continued the association, which proved one of the happiest and most successful in English racing. It was Jarvis who trained his classic winners Blue Peter, Ocean Swell and Sandwich. Sleeping Partner was trained by Doug Smith.

As a steward Lord Rosebery had the reputation of being tough but fair. He was a good deal more sympathetic than might have been imagined to the less affluent and successful individuals professionally engaged in the sport. He had a profound knowledge of racing based on experience and on what he had read. He seemed to have read, and to remember, every book ever written on racing, and almost every newspaper article too. He greatly admired the writers in that once famous publication, The Pink 'Un. As he grew older he certainly mellowed. To young people he was invariably kind and thoughtful and he was a delightful and highly entertaining host at Mentmore, particularly when the talk turned to racing and his skill as a raconteur came into full play. He suffered a great sorrow when his son by his first marriage, a young man who had inherited his athletic prowess and his love of sport, died while an undergraduate at Oxford.

Outside his racing activities, Lord Rosebery was Regional Commissioner for Scotland and Secretary of State in World War II; Chairman of the Fine Arts Commission in Scotland; President of the MCC; a member of the Royal Commission on Justices of the Peace; and President of the Committee of Inquiry into the export of horses.

He saw his first Derby in 1892 and had his first placed horse in a classic in 1906. His extraordinary knowledge of sporting, social, political and military life over a long period made it regrettable that he could never be lured into writing his reminiscences. Up to the end of his life his memory rarely failed him. I remember sitting with him at Ascot not long before he died and listening to his stories of Surrey cricket nearly seventy years previously; how his role as captain was made extremely difficult by a parson at a lunatic asylum who was always interfering on behalf of his son, one of Surrey's more distinguished players; and how a very gifted amateur left Surrey for good owing to a dispute as to who should pay the laundry for washing his white flannel trousers.

George Todd, who died in his late seventies, came from a farming family in Lincolnshire and through his skill as a trainer and his shrewdness as a punter was able to purchase and maintain the famous training establishment of Manton, near Marlborough. As a boy he worked on a farm but he was mad about horses and decided to transfer his energies from agriculture to racing. World War I saw him in Kitchener's army but, though his tall erect figure would have made him an ideal right-hand man in the King's Company, First Battalion Grenadier Guards, his outspoken and individual nature hardly rendered him ideally suited to a soldier's life. He was wounded on the Somme and his experiences on the western front gave him a distaste for 'abroad' that lasted till his death. He invariably declined to leave England and did not even go to Ireland to see Sodium win The Irish Sweeps Derby, while for his annual holiday the Imperial Hotel at Torquay met his needs. He would never consent to enter an aeroplane.

He was head lad, first to Bert Lines and then to Tom Coulthwaite at Hednesford. Coulthwaite, who never got on a horse's back in his life and trained three Grand National winners, knew all there was to know about training racehorses and possibly a bit more besides. The late Jack Fawcus, who rode for the stable between the wars, told me the value of a Coulthwaite education, and Todd learnt a good deal there as well. When Coulthwaite said a horse would win it usually did and Todd made enough money to set up on his own at Royston, subsequently moving to West Ilsley. It was not until after World War II that he acquired Manton.

Todd loved horses, understood them, did his own feeding and was infuriated by any suggestion of cruelty. His stable invariably contained a number of veterans that most other trainers would have culled years previously. It does not require a high degree of professional skill to win races over five or six furlongs with two-year-olds. Todd excelled at the more difficult business of training stayers and his memorable triumphs with Trelawny have already been recorded. He also did well with his hurdlers. Owners he was inclined to regard as a tiresome necessity but his feelings on the subject were less acute if he owned a share in the horse himself. Quite early in his career he had been badly 'carted' by a fashionable jockey and his reverence for the leading riders was of a somewhat qualified nature. He did not necessarily employ one of the top jockeys when he indulged in one of his larger bets. There is no doubt that he made a lot of money by betting during the closing stages of the war and in the immediate post-war era.

Todd could be—and frequently was—outspoken about people he disliked and he hardly had the temperament to suffer fools gladly. However, he was intensely loyal to his friends, very generous and the best of company. He knew how to lose gracefully. 'Win or lose, there's always booze,' he used to observe as he opened a bottle of his favourite Bollinger for some friends after a short-head defeat. All in all, he was a great trainer, a 'character', and a man who added not a little, as far as his many friends were concerned, to the pleasures of racing.

Clive Graham, 'The Scout' of the Daily Express and one of the best known and best liked of racing journalists, died after a long illness aged sixty-one. He developed, as others have done, a passion for racing while at Eton. It was during his Eton days that he met Geoffrey Gilbey, who was then writing for the Sunday Express, and it was through Gilbey that he joined the Daily Express as soon as he had left school, writing under the nom de plume of 'Bendex'. He was soon dabbling in ownership and in partnership with Michael Strutt, a stepson of Lord Rosebery who was killed flying during the war, he owned a very useful horse called Bendex, who was trained by Jack Leach. Except for the war years, when he served in the Army till 1944 and later as a war correspondent, Graham remained with the Daily Express till he died.

In Graham and Peter O'Sullevan, so different from each other both in character and in their approach to the sport, the Daily Express had a racing partnership unequalled by any other newspaper, and of course they were furthermore known to millions as paddock commentator and race commentator respectively on television for the B.B.C. Graham was essentially a gregarious character who liked late nights and was comfortably at home chatting away to a steward of the Jockey Club or to one of the less reputable patrons of the Silver Ring. There was not an ounce of snobbishness or pomposity in his personality. Nor was he easily over-awed, as one senior member of the Jockey Club and a certain chairman of the Levy Board both discovered. He worked hard to improve the status of racing journalists and it was due to his efforts that the Horserace Writers' Association was formed. As a writer he tended to be erratic but at his best he was without a superior and he could at times be very funny, being singularly unhampered by any undue respect for those in authority.

The influence of the racing press on the sport is not wholly without significance. My comments are largely based on personal experience. In 1947 my military career, which had lasted for seventeen mostly happy years, drew peacefully to its close. One sunny Saturday in June I rode a chestnut gelding, inappropriately named Virile, on the King's Birthday Parade and the following Monday I was in darkest Battersea helping to compile the index to Chaseform, a former brother officer, the late Roger de Wesselow, having kindly offered me a job with Raceform and also with a publication called The Racehorse which then appeared twice a week. A few weeks later I was greatly surprised to receive a letter from the Sunday Times inviting me to pay a call. I did so with alacrity and was duly appointed racing correspondent under the nom de plume of 'Fairway'. I was then 'Martin Murray' in The Racehorse. I remained with the Sunday Times for twenty-eight years and I am still churning out articles for The Racehorse. When I took up racing journalism I was thirty-seven years old, a time of life when many journalists have passed their peak and are just beginning to detect the symptoms of cirrhosis of the liver. I knew a little about racing, far less in fact than I thought I did, and absolutely nothing about journalism and newspapers. No one for whom I worked ever mentioned trade unions to me, and the subject did not crop up for about ten years. It was a great bit of luck for me that, because of the war and national service, racing journalists were in short supply: I do not flatter myself that I would have found such congenial employment but for the exceptional circumstances.

The work to start with was fairly arduous and I usually raced six days a week and went to the Racehorse office in Curzon Street on the Sunday. Pay was exiguous by modern standards and the two jobs combined brought in roughly £1,000 a year. In this post-war era cars were in short supply and petrol severely rationed. Racing people were inclined to travel by train and to stay away in hotels. It was certainly far easier then for a journalist to get to know owners, trainers, jockeys, officials and so forth than it is today when everyone goes by car and is off at 70 m.p.h. down the motorway as soon as the last race but one has been run. On the whole it was a very friendly and companionable atmosphere and there were some good parties at meetings like York, Goodwood, Liverpool, Doncaster and Manchester. I soon found that covering the lesser fixtures for Raceform and Chaseform involved me in some fairly complicated itineraries and I would never have got to Buckfastleigh on one occasion if I had not done the last ten miles on a borrowed bicycle. Nor was it much fun to arrive at a deserted Ludlow station at 2 a.m. on a cold winter morning. In those early days when I knew nothing about the business at all, I received much help and kindness from Geoffrey Hamlyn of The Sporting Life, Peter Willett of the Sporting Chronicle and Robert Haynes, who was then with Raceform but later became a racecourse commentator. Hamlyn is the most conscientious journalist I have ever met and one who still resolutely believes in outmoded virtues such as loyalty, integrity and hard work. Willett I had met racing in Italy where he was handicapper and I was clerk of the scales. Haynes and I had served in the same battalion in Alexandria before the war.

Some of the old hands in racing journalism were slightly forbidding characters who had come up the hard way themselves and were inclined to resent newcomers who were perhaps a shade better educated than themselves and had never had to fill inkpots in the provinces or report inquests at Stoke-on-Trent. A few of them seemed to exist on a largely liquid diet and were apt to be unplayable by the time the second leg of the tote double was run. One who was usually generous and friendly when sober used to become objectionable and aggressive when sloshed and apt to accuse people of stealing his race-glasses, which in fact were invariably found suspended from his own neck. Less inconvenient, because he was much quieter, was a former military gentleman who preferred to get stoned on his own. At Kempton he favoured a table by the door in that rather dirty little bar behind the weighing room. One summer afternoon he was sleeping there peacefully when some noisy individuals came in after the first race and woke him up. Possibly he was slightly confused and imagined himself at home as his reaction was to put his hand up to his mouth, remove his teeth and drop them in the glass containing the dregs of his gin. He then went to sleep again.

One got to know one's colleagues much better in those days as nearly every racecourse provided lunch, sometimes a very good one, for journalists in a special room, and during this meal there was a general exchange of gossip and information. Despite the rivalries, the inevitable tensions and petty jealousies, feeling on the whole was good and most people were friendly and helpful. I can only recollect two fights in the press room. One was between two very large elderly men in the old press room at Kempton. Luckily there was insufficient space for much damage to be inflicted and in the end little was lost bar dignity and breath. Some journalists used to get—they probably still do—terribly worried when in the throes of a run of ill fortune and in consequence occupying a low position in the Sporting Life nap table. It was a sad and common sight to see some harassed middle-aged man anxiously scanning the midday Evening Standard in the hope of finding that the naps of his rivals had been as unsuccessful as his own.

I have already mentioned Meyrick Good and Walter Meeds of The Sporting Life and Jack Topham of Raceform. Meeds was an expert on professional athletics and used to come into his own when he covered The Powderhall Sprint every year. It was a great disappointment to his admirers if he failed to describe some competitor as 'the most promising lad to don spiked pumps north of the Tweed for many a long day'. James Park of the Evening Standard was an exceptionally good judge of form and anything he wrote about a big race was invariably well worth reading. Of distinguished appearance, he did not wear his heart on his sleeve but personally I found him kind and helpful. Cyril Luckman, for many years before Clive Graham 'The Scout' of the Daily Express, seemed to be having a permanent meal and the area where he sat was usually littered with unappetising scraps of food and rows of sauce bottles. To me he always appeared a very unattractive character. Norman Pegg, 'Gimcrack' of the Daily Sketch, was very solidly built and somewhat deaf. He had had a distinguished record as a sergeant in the Gloucestershire Regiment in World War I. He could be maddeningly stubborn on occasions but was essentially good-hearted and rather enjoyed having his leg pulled. He might have made a successful trade union leader of the old-fashioned sort.

There was an elderly character known for some reason as 'the old lamplighter' who contributed to a publication not unconnected with the liquor trade. On Derby day he was allowed to write two articles. The first was under his own name; the second, under an alias, was apt to start 'I cannot altogether agree with the views of my distinguished colleague' and end up by tipping a different horse.

Recently there have been complaints that there are too many Old Etonians in the Jockey Club. There was a phase not very long ago when a similar complaint might have been made about the racing press since the proportion did seem inordinately high, what with Geoffrey and Quintin Gilbey, John Oaksey, Richard Baerlein, Tom Nickalls, Clive Graham, Bill Curling, Charles Benson, Ivor Herbert, Michael Seely, Peter Towers-Clark, Philip Clifford, John Hanmer and myself. I hesitate to add the former Tory M.P. Sir David Llewellyn, who contributes to The Sporting Life under the names of Jack Logan, John Bliss and A. Skinner, as he does not use the press room or concern himself with horses, preferring to nag away ceaselessly at the establishment. An apparently uncritical admirer of Lord Wigg and Mr Jack Jones, he can be said to have achieved a *succès d'animosité* in that many people read his column every Friday in the hope of being provoked; a hope that is rarely unfulfilled.

Probably, what with closed shops and N.U.J. militancy, the job of a racing journalist is less attractive now than it once was. Certainly a somewhat different type of individual tends to be lured to it. Sports editors, usually liable to be more deeply concerned with football than with racing, seldom feel that it is necessary for a racing correspondent to know very much about horses. Consequently only a few outmoded veterans now bother to inspect the runners carefully in the paddock before an important race. What most sports editors want are 'quotes' from owners, trainers and jockeys, enlivened by the occasional 'human interest' story. Most journalists have the sense to soldier on and not worry overmuch when their Derby story suffers severe cuts to make room for an account of the Turkish Womens' Cycling Championships.

Some racing correspondents are very well informed, some are excellent judges of form, others are consistently entertaining. A few fall into none of these categories. A run of successful tips may have an influence, temporary at least, on circulation figures. At one time the patients in a large lunatic asylum were dedicated followers of 'Hotspur' in the Daily Telegraph and a prolonged run of success by 'Hotspur' resulted in the patients attaining such a condition of hilarious excitement that the staff were literally on their knees praying for 'Hotspur' to have a long run of losers.

Whether any racing journalists can be said to possess real influence is a matter of opinion. It is probably true that some are experienced enough and respected enough for criticism on their part to induce the authorities to sit up and pay attention. In the field of race planning, Peter Willett has played a not inconsiderable part and his successor in that role, Peter Scott, can be expected to attain a similar high standard of usefulness. It must be remembered, too, that Brigadier Gerard's part-owner, John Hislop, was for many years a working journalist. The dedicated anti-establishment naggers carry virtually no weight at all. If there is a corporate weakness among racing journalists it is a reluctance to criticise jockeys (except foreign ones) with the result that some jockeys develop a very false estimation of their true ability. Some journalists, too, have a tendency to write about all individuals penalised by the authorities as if those individuals were invariably innocent.

It would be invidious for me to pontificate on the journalistic merits of colleagues past and present. I will restrict myself to saying how much I have enjoyed John Hislop and Peter Willett on racing policy and bloodstock breeding; Tom Nickalls for his lively style and descriptions of individual horses; Frank Byrne when he used to do the 'turnover' article in The Times before The Derby or The Grand National; Peter Scott for his invariable common sense and fairness; Peter O'Sullevan for his accurate and up-to-date knowledge of English and continental racing; John Oaksey on steeplechasing; and the Gilbey brothers, at their best, for their wit.

Little need be said further in connection with the season of 1974. Geoff Lester summed it up in Ruff's Guide as follows:

Another smack in the eye for punters came in the opening week of the season via the spring budget when the Chancellor increased the rate of off-course betting tax to $7\frac{1}{2}\%$. The bookies, as expected, levelled it out to 8%. The regular punter now has about as much chance of making a profit as Clement Freud has of becoming Prime Minister and the summer of 1974 saw racing at a low ebb. Perhaps the government looks upon betting as an evil pastime, but as the Treasury receives approximately £70 million in betting tax they should think again.

The present slump is causing smaller owners to leave the sport and even the more wealthy ones, such as David Robinson, have had to cut down drastically. The autumn budget failed to give the racing industry any reason to cheer, either, and Mr Healey didn't even bother to mention the sport. Britain is the only country in the world which applies Value Added Tax to bloodstock at the full rate. None of the other important branches of animal breeding are smitten by VAT to this extent. These injustices, combined with world-wide inflation, have ensured a wholesale slump in racing, and the comparatively inactive sales rings during the autumn bore out this view.

The Beckwith-Smith family were finding it increasingly difficult to run Lingfield Park as a private concern and it looked as if this agreeable course might well disappear from the fixture list. The threat of extinction was, however, removed, when Ladbrokes bought Lingfield for £500,000.

The decision was taken to introduce graded racing in 1975, the objective being to make the sport more competitive and to reduce the number of really bad horses in training. It was planned to start with handicaps in 1975 and to extend grading to certain selected condition events in 1976.

The report of Mr T. F. Blackwell's Committee, which included among its members a former Labour Minister of Labour, Mr Ray Gunter, on the future requirements of racing made a number of valuable recommendations but the trouble nowadays with committees of that type is that they are liable to be overtaken by events before their conclusions have been completed and published.

15

LABOUR troubles are rare in English racing. People who work in stables are not, as a rule, union-minded. In 1975, however, there was a strike by stable lads. Two points about the strike must be emphasised. Firstly, it was confined to Newmarket and received no support from other training centres. Secondly, one hundred per cent support for the strike was not forthcoming at Newmarket and enough lads remained at work to enable stables to carry on though sometimes under conditions of considerable difficulty. Perhaps rather worse than its actual effects at the time was the legacy of resentment and distrust that the strike left behind. Inevitably life was not easy for the lads who chose to stay at work and, apart from the constant abuse, there were cases of actual intimidation. Some of the strike leaders were sincere men of excellent character; others, including one just recently released from gaol, were the riff-raff of Newmarket. It is arguable that Mr Sam Horncastle, district organiser of the Transport and General Workers' Union, was a bit too heavy-handed to deal with a tricky and potentially explosive situation.

It is imprudent to generalise about stable labour. There are many variations both with regard to employers and to employees. There are rich stables that can afford to pay more than the minimum wage, that provide excellent accommodation and where a steady stream of winners throughout the season ensures more money being available for distribution among those who work there. There are desperately poor stables, run on a shoestring, where conditions are apt to be rough and winners few and far between. Fringe benefits vary from stable to stable. Some trainers, not all in a big way of business, know how to look after their lads. There are others who could not care less. Some have got the gift for man-management; in others this is conspicuously lacking.

As for the lads, there are those who are dedicated to what can be a demanding job, who genuinely love horses and find being part, albeit a humble part, of the racing world with all its meretricious glamour is a way of life thoroughly congenial to them. They do not hanker after a different form of employment despite their comparatively meagre rewards. After all, it is rare for a lad to have the luck to look after a really outstanding horse, and the present of £5,000 a lad received not long ago for his care of a Derby winner was equivalent to a big win on the pools.

The dedicated lad is worth his weight in gold to his employer and any trainer in full possession of his faculties does his utmost to ensure that such a lad remains in his service. There is no need for a first-class lad to remain with a second-class employer.

On the other hand, due to labour shortage, trainers too often have to fill the gaps in the ranks with undisciplined, uninterested, unreliable clock-watchers who are not even worth the minimum wage and ought never to be in charge of a valuable thoroughbred. Some trainers have mistakenly endeavoured to make do by using their apprentices as a form of cheap labour.

One of the odder features of the strike was that in general it had the sympathy, if not the actual support, of all those elements in racing that are opposed to a higher level of prize money although more money would mean that owners could afford to pay their trainers a more realistic fee, while trainers could then offer those who worked for them a more attractive wage. Furthermore, bigger prizes result in more money being available for distribution in the yard.

The older generation of trainers, with experience of racing in the 1930s, are apt to compare modern lads to their disadvantage with those who worked in stables between the wars. Certainly there has been a deterioration in discipline and turn-out but that is only a reflection of life in England as a whole. A Newmarket trainer of the old school would have a stroke if he could see some of the strings at work on Newmarket Heath today.

Matters came to a head in the spring of 1975 when the Newmarket Trainers' Federation, headed by John Winter, refused to grant lads an additional £1.47 per week. The Federation, rightly or wrongly, took the view that many owners would not stand for yet another rise in the basic fee, and that the less affluent owners would be forced out of the game with the consequence of lads having to be made redundant. On the other side, Mr Horncastle was not prepared to give an inch.

The public were made to feel the gravity of the situation on One Thousand Guineas day at Newmarket. The picketing of the approaches and entrance to the course did not greatly matter. More important were the strikers assembled at a point down the course since it soon became clear that they intended to interfere with the racing, if not stop it altogether, by the simple drill of forming a line across the Rowley Mile course and then sitting down. Soon the mood of the majority of racegoers changed from indifference or mild amusement to active hostility. The climax came when, in a race prior to The One Thousand Guineas, Willie Carson was cantering down to the start. Some strikers closed in on him, dragged him off his horse and started to beat him up. This violent act incensed the nearest spectators, who happened to be those in the Silver Ring, some of whom crossed the rails and joined battle with the strikers. One or two trainers who had walked down the course to see what was happening became involved as well. Such was the 'Battle of Newmarket'. It was not pretty to watch but it was brief and no one was reported injured, although it was rumoured that a solitary black eye was on public display afterwards. There is no doubt that some of the more militant lads were determined

66. The 'Battle of Newmarket', 1975

on action, appreciating the presence of TV cameras and that any incident that took place would be sure to receive the widest publicity.

Needless to say the media made a meal of the Battle of Newmarket. Reports in a number of newspapers appeared to be written by individuals who had not themselves been present and knew singularly little about racing. An attempt was made to prove that it was patrons of the members' enclosure who had grappled with the strikers, although in fact the members had been farthest from where the action took place. There were allegations that a prominent member of the Jockey Club had been involved and subsequently several newspapers, as a result of legal action, had to pay for their inaccuracy. Rather surprisingly, the two most spiteful and untruthful articles appeared in what are commonly referred to as 'quality' newspapers.

There was trouble before The Two Thousand Guineas, too. Geoff Lester recorded in the 1976 Ruff's Guide: 'Striking stable lads, as well as hired strong-arm trouble makers who cared as little about horses as many so-called soccer fans do about football, bulldozed fifteen holes in the course in a pre-dawn raid.' Fortunately the damage was far less serious than might have been the case. The bulldozer had been stolen from the Newmarket bypass.

The strikers allowed the runners for The Two Thousand Guineas to go down to the start. When the runners were nearly all in the stalls, they repeated the tactics employed two days earlier and sat down in a line extending across the course. Mounted police and policemen with dogs gradually cleared the course. While this was being done the starter, Major Eveleigh, had the horses unloaded from the stalls. He then lined them up fifteen yards in front of the stalls and despatched them by flag. Happily, the start was a good one. The few lads still fooling about on the course made a quick dart for safety when they saw the runners bearing down on them.

The strike dragged on but in fact the worst was over. People who enjoyed watching racing on TV were deprived of that pleasure because the TV cameramen acted in sympathy with the strikers. Thanks largely to intercession by Lord Wigg, the Epsom Summer Meeting was televised but Royal Ascot was missing from the screens. The trainers, perhaps unwisely, saw fit to reject arbitration while Mr Horncastle remained equally obdurate. Eventually, on July 24, after the help of the Advisory Conciliation and Arbitration Service had at last been sought, an agreement was reached, the main point being that as from August 1 the minimum wage of a lad would be fixed at £37. The Levy Board, to help matters out, announced a prize money grant for 1976 of £1,000,000 but insisted that machinery was set up to enable a minimum wage scale for stable staff to be established. Many stable lads now felt they needed representation but had no desire to be involved with a big, politically motivated organisation like the T.G.W.U. Helped by Lord Oaksey, journalist and former amateur rider, and Mr Jimmy Hill of football fame, they set about establishing an association of their own.

Some of the strikers got their jobs back; others were less fortunate. Trainers were naturally reluctant to sack lads who had helped them during the period of trouble in favour of others whom they felt had let them down. In some stables the number of horses had been reduced and there were simply no jobs available.

Early in 1975, before that unhappy episode, Grundy had the misfortune to be kicked in the face by a stable-companion. It was a nasty blow that could easily have been very serious indeed; as it was, his preparation was interrupted for several days. To add to Walwyn's worries, it was an exceptionally wet spring. The going at most courses tended to be heavy while many home gallops were water-logged. Grundy was some way short of his best when he turned out for The Clerical, Medical Greenham Stakes at Newbury. The ground was another instance of being more suitable for snipe than for thoroughbreds. Starting at 6/4 on, Grundy was beaten two lengths by Captain Lemos's Supreme Sovereign colt Mark Anthony, trained by Clive Brittain. Mark Anthony seemed to revel in the conditions.

Grundy was much straighter in condition for The Two Thousand Guineas, for which he was favourite at 7/2. The going was good. He ran an excellent race and hopes ran high when he led at the Bushes, but coming down into the Dip he was headed by Mr C. d'Alessio's Bolkonski, ridden by Gianfranco Dettori. A 33/1 outsider, Bolkonski held on resolutely to his lead and kept the favourite at bay by a margin of half a length. Dominion was third.

A well-grown, handsome chestnut, Bolkonski was bred by the Woodpark Stud in Ireland and sold as a foal at the Newmarket December Sales for 7,000 guineas. He is by the sprinter Balidar out of the Dante mare Perennial, whose eleventh foal he was. Calluna, great-grandam of Bolkonski, was also great-grandam of the 1976 Champion Stakes winner Vitiges. At two Bolkonski was trained in Italy where he won the valuable Premio Tevere in Rome by eight lengths. He was sent to join Henry Cecil's stable at Newmarket early in 1975. He was a bit on the big side when he turned out for The Craven Stakes at Newmarket but nevertheless ran an encouraging race to finish second to Grundy's stable companion No Alimony, to whom he conceded 4 lb. Considering the promise he showed on that occasion, it is surprising there was not more support for him in The Guineas.

Bolkonski certainly looked a high-class miler when winning The St James's Palace Stakes by three lengths from Royal Manacle. He was less impressive in The Sussex Stakes. He was always prone to be a bit excitable and at Goodwood he was upset by a loose horse on the way to the paddock, where he sweated up profusely and looked in anything but the ideal frame of mind for racing. In fact he ran his race out gamely enough, Dettori having been hard at work on him from two furlongs out, but at the winning-post he had only a neck to spare over Mrs Engelhard's Rose Bowl, while the July Cup winner Lianga was a mere short head behind Rose Bowl.

By the autumn Bolkonski had lost his form and in The Queen Elizabeth II Stakes he finished thirteen lengths behind Rose Bowl. That failure terminated his racing career and he was retired to the stud in France.

Grundy, having started off the season with a couple of defeats, went to The Curragh for the Irish Two Thousand Guineas, worth over £21,000 to the winner. He won very easily from Monsanto and Mark Anthony. In The Derby he started favourite at 5/1. He had not yet proved his ability to stay beyond a mile unlike the 6/4 favourite Green Dancer, winner the previous autumn of The Observer Gold Cup. Green Dancer had earned £41,000 by winning the French Two Thousand Guineas and £68,000 by winning the ten-and-a-half-furlongs Prix Lupin. At Epsom Green Dancer gave Freddie Head an indifferent ride and never looked like winning. Grundy, on the other hand, was in his very best form and never afforded Pat Eddery any serious cause for concern. Fourth at Tattenham Corner, he moved smoothly into the lead below the distance and showing not the slightest tendency to stop he won by three lengths from Mr Nelson Bunker Hunt's Vaguely Noble

filly Nobiliary, winner of the Prix Saint-Alary, with Hunza Dancer four lengths
away third. Piggott's mount Bruni, trained by Price, was fourteenth.

It was a great triumph for Peter Walwyn. Born in 1933, he comes from a 'horsey'
family as his father Major 'Taffy' Walwyn, a Gunner, rode Admiral Sir Hedworth
Meux's White Surrey to victory in The Grand Military Gold Cup, while Fulke
Walwyn and Mrs Helen Johnson Houghton are his cousins. Educated at
Charterhouse, he did his National Service not as one might expect as an officer in
the Hussars or the Lancers but as a corporal in the Intelligence Corps. His racing
career began in 1953 when he went as learner-assistant to Geoffrey Brooke. He
remained there for three rewarding years and then from 1956 to 1960 he was a
partner of Mrs Johnson Houghton. He set up on his own in 1961, the first horse
sent to him being Mr Percival Williams's Be Hopeful, a marvellous servant who
raced till he was fourteen and won over a score of races. In 1961 Walwyn won £971
in stakes; in 1975, £382,527.

In 1976 he had 105 horses under his care at Seven Barrows. He is a man of
remarkable energy and enthusiasm, and these qualities, combined with a certain
flair for organisation, enable him to cope with all the work, practical and administrative, that such a large number of horses—and their owners—entails. A stable
of this size means that there are comparatively few days during the season when he
does not have a runner and the amount of motoring he must get through is ex-
hausting even to think of. His wife, 'Bonk', sister of the neighbouring jumping
trainer, Nick Gaselee, helps out with the driving and can handle press and public
relations with charm and skill. Walwyn is not a calm man by nature and would
never win a prize for keeping his cool under trying circumstances. His eruptions,
though, if fairly frequent, are seldom of lengthy duration. Fundamentally he is a
friendly, cheerful and hospitable character and it must be good fun having a horse
trained in his stable.

Grundy went to The Curragh for the Irish Sweeps Derby. On firm going he
started at 10/9 on and won comfortably by two lengths from O'Brien's King
Pellinore with Anne's Pretender third. Both King Pellinore and Anne's Pretender
are American-bred. It was Walwyn's second win in succession in this race which
this year earned Grundy's owner £64,063.

Grundy's next race was The King George VI and Queen Elizabeth Stakes. This
proved to be the climax of his career and one of the finest races on the English
turf within living memory. Grundy had ten opponents of which the most formidable were Bustino, Dahlia and Star Appeal. Bustino had only run once this season,
winning The Coronation Cup in record time. Unfortunately Riboson, who had
been his highly effective pacemaker in both The Coronation Cup and The St
Leger, was not available, having cracked a cannon-bone. To make up for this loss,
Hern decided to run two pacemakers, Highest, who was a miler, and Kinglet, a
stayer. Both were horses of modest ability but it was hoped they would assist
Bustino to test Grundy's stamina to the utmost in the same manner that Alycidon's
two pacemakers contributed to the defeat of Black Tarquin in The Gold Cup.
Dahlia, now five, was not as good as she had been but she had hinted at a return

67. Grundy, with Pat Eddery up

to form in the Grand Prix de Saint-Cloud in which she was fourth after meeting with a lot of interference. The German-trained Star Appeal had won The Eclipse Stakes and was destined to win the Prix de l'Arc de Triomphe.

The pacemakers carried out their task to the best of their ability but Bustino was in front four furlongs from home, perhaps rather sooner than Joe Mercer really wished. From this point Bustino headed for home as hard as he could go and on the final bend he must have been nearly four lengths in front of Grundy, on whom Pat Eddery was already vigorously at work. For a time it looked as if Bustino was too far ahead to be caught but Grundy, responding in the gamest possible fashion to Eddery's relentless driving, was gradually closing the gap. At the distance the two horses were neck and neck and at this critical stage, with so much at stake, Mercer, to his eternal credit, refrained from hitting Bustino with his whip because he realised that Bustino was already giving everything he had. This tremendous duel went on till fifty yards from the winning-post when Bustino could find no more and Grundy, summoning his last reserves of strength to master his gallant opponent, won by half a length, leaving the crowd temporarily speechless from excitement and admiration. Dahlia was five lengths away third and the course record had been lowered by more than a couple of seconds.

Of the two Grundy looked the more exhausted and he really seemed at the end of his tether as, cheered again and again, he entered the unsaddling enclosure. If you get to the bottom of a high-mettled horse—and that race certainly got to the bottom of Grundy—that horse takes a long time to recover as a rule, if indeed he ever recovers at all. Grundy seemed none the worse for his exertions when he returned home and as he was soon working again in his best form it was decided to run him in The Benson and Hedges Gold Cup the following month. He proved but a dim shadow of his true self, finishing a poor fourth behind Dahlia, Card King and Star Appeal. He never raced again. It is always easy to be wise after the event and Walwyn was criticised for having taken a chance and run Grundy so soon after Ascot. If Grundy had missed the York race, the same critics would have accused Walwyn of wrapping Grundy up in cotton wool and refusing to run the risk of a defeat. As for Bustino he met with a mishap in training and never saw a racecourse again.

After The Derby, the Levy Board had bought a three-quarter share in Grundy for £750,000 and planned to stand him at the National Stud. Evidently the Levy Board reckoned with so much of their money invested a degree of caution was necessary and accordingly stipulated that Grundy would be retired at the end of the season and would take part in no more than four more races, all of them in the British Isles. An American offer for Bustino was rejected and it was arranged for him to stand at the Wolferton Stud, King's Lynn, his syndication value being £600,000.

Walwyn went very close to winning the French Derby as well. He had in his stable Dr Vittadini's Patch, a chestnut colt by St Paddy out of Palatch, by Match III. Palatch had won The Musidora Stakes and The Yorkshire Oaks. Patch raced in Italy at two and was about a stone behind the best of his age in that country.

At the end of the season he was sent off to England. His first race in England was The Craven Stakes in which he finished a somewhat distant fifth behind No Alimony and Bolkonski. He left that form far behind in the Lingfield Derby Trial, making all the running and winning by ten lengths from Anne's Pretender who was subsequently just over seven lengths behind Grundy in The Derby.

As Grundy was to represent Dr Vittadini in The Derby, it was decided to let Patch take his chance in the Prix du Jockey Club. He ran a great race and lost by only a head to Val de l'Orne. Unfortunately he was never as good again. He was only seventh in the Grand Prix and he was all out to score a somewhat unconvincing half-length victory over Sea Anchor in The Great Voltigeur Stakes. He ended the season with a weak display behind Calaba when favourite for The Cumberland Lodge Stakes at Ascot. His career as a four-year-old did nothing to restore his reputation.

Favourite for The St Leger was Mr J. A. Mulcahy's American-bred King Pellinore, a half-brother by Round Table to Thatch and a member of Vincent O'Brien's stable. His best performance had been to finish second to Grundy, beaten two lengths, in The Irish Sweeps Derby. Like all the other St Leger runners he proved no match for Bruni, who won by ten lengths. King Pellinore was second and Libra's Rib third.

Bruni was bred by the Barrettstown Castle Stud in Ireland and is a very light-coloured grey by Sea Hawk II out of Bombazine, by Shantung. Sea Hawk II, so unwisely exported by the Irish to Japan, has been mentioned in connection with the Gold Cup winner Erimo Hawk. In 1974 he sired the Prix Vermeille winner Paulista, and in 1975 the Grand Prix winner Matahawk, whose grandam was the Oaks winner Carrozza. As a yearling Bruni was bought for 7,800 guineas by Mr Charles St George who sent him to Ryan Price to be trained. At two Bruni was leggy and unfurnished. He only ran once, finishing well down the course in a maiden race at Warwick, a somewhat unglamorous start for a colt destined to win a classic.

At three his first race was The Tudor Maiden Stakes run over a mile at Sandown in April. The distance was too sharp for him but he finished close up second in a big field. Early in May he won a ten-furlongs event for maidens at Salisbury. Later that month he moved up in class and demonstrated his improvement by running No Alimony to a short head in the mile-and-a-quarter Predominate Stakes at Goodwood. It was decided to run him in The Derby and with Piggott, a close friend of Mr St George, in the saddle he was well supported at 16/1. The venture proved an unfortunate one. He was carried wide at Tattenham Corner, finished fourteenth, returned home sore and shortly afterwards contracted a virus. Nothing more was seen of him till August 30 when he won the mile-and-a-quarter Friends of the Variety Club Stakes very easily indeed in record time. His next race was The St Leger, in which he was ridden by Murray. Starting at 9/1 after opening at 7/1, he had the race at his mercy a long way out and proved that he was a very fine stayer indeed. Price wanted to retire him for the season but his owner wanted to run him in the Arc and his owner's will prevailed. At Longchamp

Bruni looked as if he had run up a bit light and he certainly lacked the quality of some of his opponents. He ran fairly well to finish seventh behind Star Appeal.

Staying was really Bruni's game and he might well have made an exceptionally good Cup horse at four but of course victories in races over two miles or more do nothing to help a horse's stud career; the reverse in fact. Possibly Bruni just lacked the speed to succeed in the major European races run over a mile and a half and his record at four was a little disappointing in consequence. He started off well enough by an impressive victory over Mr Bigmore and Sea Anchor in the mile-and-three-quarters Yorkshire Cup but he was beaten a head by Orange Bay in The Hardwicke Stakes and a length by Pawneese in The King George VI and Queen Elizabeth Stakes. In both those races he lost ground at the start and on both occasions there was criticism of Piggott's riding. In September he won The Cumberland Lodge Stakes without difficulty but once again he was not good enough in the Arc, in which he had every chance. He ran quite a good race, though, to finish fifth to Ivanjica. He was then sold for a sum said to be in the region of £1,000,000 to go to America.[1]

Cry of Truth, the top two-year-old filly of 1974, unfortunately failed to train on. She failed in The Nell Gwyn Stakes at the Craven Meeting and never ran again. Mrs Engelhard's Habitat filly Rose Bowl, trained by Fulke Johnson Houghton, won The Nell Gwyn Stakes, and ridden by Piggott, she started at 7/4 favourite for The One Thousand Guineas. She was desperately unlucky not to win. Lester Piggott had her poised to challenge on the inside but unfortunately the expected opening failed to materialise. Eventually Piggott had to switch her in order to give her any chance at all. Even then she did not appear to have all that much room yet she finished only a little more than a length behind the winner.

Victory went to Nocturnal Spree, who carried the colours of Mrs Anne O'Kelly, was trained in Ireland by Noel Murless's brother Stuart and ridden by Johnny Roe. Bred by Mr Gerry Dillon and bought for 6,300 guineas by the B.B.A. (Ireland) on Mrs O'Kelly's behalf, she is by Supreme Sovereign out of the non-winning Night Attire, by Shantung. Night Attire is a member of the famous Marchetta family through Moonstone. Nocturnal Spree ran only once at two, showing encouraging promise for the future when third behind her stable-companion Sea Break at The Curragh. Shortly afterwards she split a pastern. The following April she won the April Maiden Stakes at The Curragh. Light grey in colour and well grown, she was considered lacking in quality in the paddock before The One Thousand Guineas and one paddock critic summed her up as 'more Uttoxeter than Newmarket'. Starting at 14/1, she made steady headway from three furlongs out and running on most gallantly up the hill she caught the French-trained Girl Friend a few strides from the post to win by a short head. The Queen's Joking Apart, trained by Ian Balding, was a length behind Girl Friend while the unlucky Rose Bowl was inches behind Joking Apart.

Nocturnal Spree ran only once subsequently, finishing fourth behind Miralla in the Irish One Thousand Guineas. During the summer she again split a pastern.

[1] He failed in America, returned to England and was beaten in The Gold Cup.

She was sent up to the Newmarket December Sales where a Canadian purchaser paid 96,000 guineas for her.

Rose Bowl strained a muscle in her quarters and did not race again till The Sussex Stakes. Last on the final bend, she ran on to such purpose in the straight that she only failed by a neck to catch Bolkonski. Her performance was all the more creditable as she needed the race. On that running she looked sure to win The Waterford Crystal Mile at Goodwood at the end of August but for some unexplained reason she ran far below her true form and was beaten three lengths by O'Brien's American-bred three-year-old Gay Fandango, by Forli. However, Rose Bowl concluded the season in great style. At Ascot she slammed Gay Fandango and Bolkonski in The Queen Elizabeth II Stakes, while at Newmarket she put up the best performance of her career in winning The Champion Stakes from Allez France, Ramirez and Star Appeal. Allez France met with a little inter-ference at one stage but it is doubtful whether the result was affected. Allez France, who retired at the end of the season, was not quite as good at five as she had been at four but she nevertheless won the Prix Ganay, the Prix Dollar and the Prix Foy. Her thirteen victories earned M. Wildenstein £493,100. By her victory in The Benson and Hedges Gold Cup Dahlia had increased the money gained by her victories to £497,741.

Rose Bowl stayed in training at four but the long spell of hot, dry weather in the summer did not suit her. In the spring she was close up fourth in the Prix Ganay and in May won the ten-furlongs Clive Graham Stakes at Goodwood. She did not win again till the autumn, when on soft ground she won The Queen Elizabeth II Stakes by four lengths. There was an unusually big field of nineteen for The Champion Stakes and the runners included Wollow (Two Thousand Guineas), Malacate (Irish Sweeps Derby) and Crow (St Leger). Rose Bowl accounted for those three without difficulty but found one too good for her in Mme Laloum's three-year-old Vitiges who had just joined Peter Walwyn's stable. Pat Eddery succeeded in getting the free-running Vitiges, by Phaeton, to settle down and he produced a turn of speed at the finish that enabled him to head Rose Bowl on the hill and beat her by a neck. In The Two Thousand Guineas Vitiges had led till headed by Wollow coming down into the Dip.

Rose Bowl's final race was The Washington International Stakes at Laurel Park. She finished a distant fifth behind Mr Nelson Bunker Hunt's Prix du Jockey Club winner Youth, who won by ten lengths from On My Way with the Arc winner Ivanjica third.

Blakeney was a thoroughly genuine and somewhat unlucky horse but not even his dearest friends could claim that he was one of the great Derby winners. There was not exactly a mad stampede to secure his services when he was retired to the National Stud, where, however, he proceeded to delight his admirers by getting a classic winner, Juliette Marny, among his first crop of runners. She was in fact his very first runner in a classic. She was bred by the Fonthill Stud near Salisbury, a stud started in 1956 with mares bought as yearlings by Lord Margadale. The stud is managed by Lord Margadale's son, Mr James Morrison, and it was his colours that Juliette Marny, trained by Jeremy Tree at Beckhampton, carried. An attractive, well-made bay, she is out of Set Free, by Worden II, a half-sister to Spree who ran second in The One Thousand Guineas and The Oaks. Worden II had a fine season as a sire of brood mares as also among his daughters were the dams of Grundy, Wollow and Duboff.

Juliette Marny was backward at two and only ran twice, on the second occasion finishing second in a maiden race at Salisbury. Her first race in 1975 was the eight-and-a-half-furlongs Princess Elizabeth Stakes at Epsom. Backed from 20/1 to 16/1 and ridden by Starkey, she won by two lengths from Persian Market but Starkey had been apparently unable to stop her hanging badly to the left inside the final furlong. Inevitably she was disqualified as she had seriously interfered with Persian Market. She was relegated to last place and Starkey was stood down by the Stewards. In her next race, the Lingfield Oaks Trial, she was ridden by Piggott and won all out by a head from Harmonise. As she was receiving 5 lb. from Harmonise and appeared to have the harder race of the two, her prospects for The Oaks did not look to be particularly bright.

Mr Jim Joel's Musidora Stakes winner Moonlight Night, by Levmoss, was favourite for The Oaks. Juliette Marny, despite being Piggott's mount, was weak in the market at 12/1. She won, though, with the utmost ease. Sixth into the straight, she was in front below the distance and won by four lengths from Val's Girl with the favourite third. The fast ground clearly suited Juliette Marny, who was wearing blinkers for the first time.

Piggott had the choice of three mounts in The Irish Guinness Oaks: Juliette Marny, the Derby runner-up Nobiliary, and O'Brien's improving American-bred Herbager filly Tuscarora. Usually a pretty shrewd judge, Piggott elected to stick to Juliette Marny, who won all out by a neck from Tuscarora with Nobiliary two lengths away third. It was only inside the final fifty yards that Juliette Marny gained the lead. Her final race was The Yorkshire Oaks. She hurt a leg in the course of it and probably because of that she ran below form and finished third behind May Hill. It had been hoped to run her in The St Leger but instead she was retired to the stud and covered in 1976 by Queen's Hussar.

May Hill was a really good staying filly bred and owned by Mr Percival Williams, a sportsman of the old school, and trained by Peter Walwyn. By Hill Clown out of that very genuine mare Mabel who was placed in The One Thousand Guineas and The Oaks, May Hill ran fourth in The Oaks and besides winning The Yorkshire Oaks she also won The Park Hill Stakes, defeating Tuscarora a good deal more easily than Juliette Marny had done at The Curragh. In the Prix Vermeille she was third behind Ivanjica, winner of the Arc in 1976, and Nobiliary. She remained in training in 1976 but failed to add to her reputation.

Followers of Vincent O'Brien's stable enjoyed a rewarding four days at Royal Ascot, with victories in The Queen Anne Stakes (Imperial March), The Ribbles-dale Stakes (Gallina), The Jersey Stakes (Gay Fandango), The Queen's Vase (Blood Royal), The Cork and Orrery Stakes (Swingtime) and The Wokingham Stakes (Boone's Cabin). All six winners were American-bred. This was a fine achievement by O'Brien, whose Irish fans were quite surprised to hear that Frank Barling had trained seven winners for Lord Glanely at Royal Ascot in 1919.

The Gold Cup was won with consummate ease by Mr G. A. Oldham's Irish-bred Sagaro, trained in France by Boutin. Winner of the Grand Prix in 1974, Sagaro was to win the Prix du Cadran in 1976 and The Gold Cup in 1976 and 1977. Mr Hollingsworth brought off a double on Gold Cup day, winning The King Edward VII Stakes with Sea Anchor and The King George V Stakes with Zimbalon. A big, handsome, long-striding chestnut by Alcide, Sea Anchor failed in The Irish Sweeps Derby and The St Leger but did well as a four-year-old, winning The Henry II Stakes at Sandown, The Goodwood Stakes carrying 10 stone, and the Doncaster Cup. There is of course no demand by breeders in this country today for a horse of Sea Anchor's stamp and accordingly he has been exported to New Zealand.

There was a gamble in The King's Stand Stakes on Mrs Hausman's four-year-old Flirting Around, trained in France by R. Carver. Bred in America and a son of Round Table, Flirting Around won in brilliant fashion by five lengths and on that form he must have been a very good sprinter indeed. Unfortunately nothing more was seen of him. He had been sold shortly before the race and soon after-wards was exported to South Africa. At Ascot he finished seven lengths in front of Bay Express, winner of The King's Stand Stakes in 1974 and The Nunthorpe Stakes in 1975. The French also won The July Cup at Newmarket, the winner here being M. D. Wildenstein's Lianga, a four-year-old American-bred filly by Dancer's Image. In addition Lianga won the Prix de l'Abbaye and The Vernons Sprint Cup. As a two-year-old she had won the Prix Robert Papin and at three the Prix Maurice de Gheest. Apart from her excellence as a sprinter, she was also a very good miler as was shown by her form in The Sussex Stakes.

One of the most remarkable performers in 1975 was the five-year-old Star Appeal. Bred by the Gestüt Rottgen, he is a compact, deep-bodied bay by the Italian sire Appiani II, a member of the Son-in-Law male line, out of the German mare Sterna, by Neckar. He began his racing career with John Oxx in Ireland. In his first race he behaved indifferently and he always wore blinkers afterwards. He was quite a useful three-year-old but not up to classic standard. Early in the autumn of that year he was sent to Baden Baden where he won his race and was bought for £10,000 by Mr W. Zeitelhack. He was subsequently third in the Irish St Leger and thirteenth in the Arc. At four he was trained in Germany by T. Greiper, running fourteen times and winning but twice. He campaigned at Cagnes-sur-Mer in the winter of 1974 and was placed in minor events behind the German mare Blabla and My Brief.

In 1975 he showed spectacular improvement. He won a race at Baden Baden and followed that up by winning the Gran Premio di Milano. These successes failed to impress English racegoers and he started at 20/1 in The Eclipse Stakes, the last Eclipse to be sponsored by Benson and Hedges. The Derby runner-up Nobiliary was a short-priced favourite but failed to finish in the first three, Star Appeal, who showed fine acceleration in the closing stages, winning decisively from Taros and Royal Manacle. He was the first German-trained horse to win in England for 125 years.

In The King George VI and Queen Elizabeth Stakes Star Appeal finished twenty lengths behind Grundy and he was a moderate third behind Dahlia in The Benson and Hedges Gold Cup. Not surprisingly, he was not much fancied in the Arc against opponents such as Allez France, Dahlia, Comtesse de Loir, Green Dancer, Bruni and Ivanjica. It proved to be a rough and unsatisfactory contest. Coming down the hill Dahlia struck into Allez France, the favourite, and nearly fell. Shortly afterwards Allez France was badly hampered when Carolus, just in front of her, suddenly weakened. Star Appeal had plenty to do from the final bend. He was full of running, though, and darted like a snipe from one opening to another. In the words of one writer, 'he zoomed under Piggott's nose and almost knocked Cordero out of the saddle'. Finally Greville Starkey, who had ridden him to victory at Sandown, steered him through a narrow gap between Comtesse de Loir and Nobiliary and such was the speed at which he finished that he only needed to be hand-ridden to score by three lengths from the fast finishing On My Way. Comtesse de Loir was third. The tote dividend in respect of the winner represented odds of 119/1. It may have been of considerable assistance to Star Appeal that so many of the fancied competitors met with considerable interference.

Star Appeal was fourth in The Champion Stakes and unplaced behind Nobiliary in The Washington International. It was then decided to retire him and arrangements were made to stand him in 1976 and 1977 at the National Stud, the fee being 1,000 guineas payable on July 15, and a further 2,000 guineas on October 1 provided the mare was in foal.

At Goodwood Proverb was unable to attempt to win The Goodwood Cup for the third year running as he had broken down badly in The Gold Cup. The Goodwood Cup was won by Girandole, whose task was rendered easier when the favourite, Crash Course, fell after going a mile. Girandole, who has since performed over hurdles, is by the Goodwood Cup winner Raise You Ten.

One of the more interesting Goodwood winners was Mrs C. Radclyffe's Duboff, who, trained by Barry Hills, won The Extel Stakes. A three-year-old filly by So Blessed out of a mare by Worden II, Duboff had been bred at Mr John Baillie's Crimbourne Stud in Sussex and was sold as a yearling for 9,400 guineas. At two she ran three times unplaced. In 1975 she made phenomenal improvement, winning nine races and ending up with a victory in The Sun Chariot Stakes at Newmarket. Her only defeats were in The Irish Guinness Oaks and in the Prix de la Nonette, in which she was third behind Ivanjica. She stayed in training at four, winning firstly The Dalton Holme Stakes at Beverley and then the one-mile Child Stakes at Newmarket, in which, carrying 9 st. 6 lb., she ran on with exemplary courage to get her head in front in the last few strides. She was sent up to the December Sales and realised 100,000 guineas.

The two-year-olds did not appear to be a great collection by any means and easily the best of them was Mr C. d'Alessio's Wollow, trained by Henry Cecil.

68. A trainer (Barry Hills) in his office

Bred by the Tally Ho Stud in Ireland, managed by Sir Cecil Boyd-Rochfort's sister Mrs Muriel McCall, Wollow is by the Eclipse winner Wolver Hollow out of Wichuraiana, by Worden II. He is a member of the distinguished Black Ray family and his third dam, Infra Red, is the fourth dam of Mill Reef. He came up for sale as a yearling and was bought by the Newmarket Bloodstock Agency for 7,000 guineas on Mr d'Alessio's behalf.

Wollow, tall and rangy, had four races at two and won them all. His most impressive success was in the Dewhurst Stakes, in which he fairly and squarely beat O'Brien's much fancied Sir Ivor colt Malinowski. Wollow was anything but a tearaway and gave the impression that he might well be able to stay the Derby distance. In fact the entry on him in Racehorses of 1975 included the following sanguine observation: 'Should Wollow beat Manado and win The Two Thousand Guineas, The Derby, barring accidents, will be as good as over. For Wollow will be much more of an effective force at a mile and a half.' Manado had won the Prix de la Salamandre and the Grand Criterium. In The Two Thousand Guineas Wollow was the winner and Manado only ninth but alas, Wollow, favourite at

11/10, was very disappointing in The Derby, finishing fifth behind the American-bred, French-trained Empery.

Henry Cecil also won the 1975 Observer Gold Cup, the horse in question being Mr d'Alessio's American-bred Take Your Place, by Round Table, who won by a head from the French colt Earth Spirit with Gallapiat third. There was not a British-bred competitor in the leading four. Take Your Place was a flop at three and failed to win a race.

The top two-year-old filly was Mr Percival Williams's Pasty, trained by Walwyn. A grey by Raffingora, she won all her five races, including The Lowther Stakes and The Cheveley Park Stakes. Unfortunately she failed to maintain her form at three.

Deaths in 1975 included those of the Duke of Norfolk, of whom much has already been written, Bernard van Cutsem and Victor Gilpin.

Bernard van Cutsem, who was fifty-nine, was a man of outstanding courage. The manner in which he faced up to a dire illness and to the truly fearful operation which that illness involved was typical of him. His parents died when he was a boy and he was brought up by relatives and educated at Ampleforth and Cambridge. Quite early in life he decided that racing was going to be his career, and after a spell with Harvey Leader he set up on his own shortly before the war at Beechwood House, Exning. This venture was cut short by the war, in which he served with the Life Guards. Afterwards he decided to concentrate on bloodstock breeding and established the Northmore Stud at Exning, later buying the Side Hill Stud at Newmarket in partnership with Mr Richard Stanley and acquiring the success-ful stallion Mossborough. All the time, though, he was hankering after a closer contact with actual racing. He installed Jack Leach at the Graham House stables at Newmarket, and, when Leach proved temperamentally unsuitable, he took over the stable himself with immediate success. Later he moved to Stanley House where he trained until he died. His best winners were Park Top, Kalydon, High Top, Karabas, Sharpen Up, Parnell, Decies, Noble Decree and Ksar.

People who did not know van Cutsem well were apt to find him forbidding, even a trifle alarming. They took him to be a hard man, and his remarkable calm as a gambler, combined with a certain intolerance of fools, increased the suspicion that fundamentally he was ruthless. He was, however, greatly loved and admired by his friends, who came from all walks of life, not merely the racing 'establish-ment'. He himself was notably loyal to those whom he liked, sympathetic and generous, while as regards his profession he was in truth a dedicated professional and a man always prepared to speak his mind on racing politics even when he knew that his views would be unpopular with the majority. It is above all, though, his courage in fighting a long losing battle by which he will be remembered.

Victor Gilpin was in his eighty-sixth year and his death removed the final link with the great days of the famous Clarehaven stable. He took over Clarehaven in 1928 from his father, Peter Gilpin, trainer of Pretty Polly, Spearmint and Spion Kop. He was never in quite the same league as a trainer as his father had been but he won good races with Colorado Kid, Finglas, Bonny Boy II and Arabella. On the opening day of Royal Ascot in 1930 he won The Ascot Stakes with Bonny

Boy II, The Queen Mary Stakes with Atbara and The St James's Palace Stakes with Christopher Robin. A few years before the war he moved to Michel Grove, retiring for good not long after hostilities had started.

Pattern Races and the Group System now form an integral part of English racing. The first steps directed towards a carefully planned programme were taken by Lord Ilchester's Racing Reorganisation Committee way back in 1943. It was the view of that Committee that the programme then existing was liable to place too great a strain on horses before they had attained maturity, and that the provision of rich prizes for two-year-olds early in the season encouraged breeders to produce sharp, early-developing animals. In fact the policy in general was contrary to the best interests of the British thoroughbred. It was accordingly recommended that restrictions be placed on two-year-old races before June, and that to counteract the temptation given to breeders to produce precocious animals valuable races should be instituted for horses of four years of age or more.

To the discredit of the Jockey Club, which appears to have fallen, as it had so often done before, into a fat and comfortable slumber, the main recommendations of the Ilchester Committee were ignored and no review of the English racing system in the light of its effects on the British thoroughbred was undertaken. However, better later than never: twenty-two years subsequently the Duke of Norfolk, who had served on the Ilchester Committee, was appointed Chairman of the Pattern of Racing Committee which was charged with looking into the programme of racing as organised on a national basis in respect of its relationship with the breed of the racehorse itself.

The terms of reference of the Norfolk Committee were as follows:

To make recommendations on the general programme of all races, with special attention to the top class horses of all ages, the Prestige races, and the improvement of the Thoroughbred.

In its report, the Committee posed the question 'Why is the Thoroughbred important?' and replied in these words: 'It is because the Thoroughbred is a British creation, and is a part of our national heritage which is worth preserving. It is the duty of the Turf Authorities to try and preserve the supremacy of the British Thoroughbred as far as possible.'

The report also said it was the duty of the turf authorities to ensure that a series of races, over the right distances and at the appropriate time, were available to test the best horses of all ages. Furthermore, they must try and ensure that the best horses stayed in training long enough, and ran with sufficient frequency, to be tested for constitution and soundness.

Among the specific recommendations of the Norfolk Committee were these:

1 Prize money for two-year-old races should be limited until June. After the end of May the prize money for two-year-old races should rise, and the programme

should culminate in championship races over five, six and seven furlongs in the autumn.

2   The Classic races were supreme in the programme for three-year-olds, but should be supplemented by well-endowed weight-for-age races over distances from a mile to one and three-quarter miles throughout the season.

3   The situation in respect of four-year-olds had deteriorated since the publication of the Ilchester Report, and should be redressed by the provision of up to thirty well-endowed races over distances from a mile to one and three-quarter miles in which they would be eligible to run.

4   There should be a series of five-furlongs and six-furlongs weight-for-age sprints spread over the whole season.

The Committee defined the ideal horse as follows: 'The ideal racehorse has more speed than the best specialist sprinter, although he may never in fact race over a shorter distance than seven furlongs, and is supreme over distances from one to one and three-quarter miles at three years old and upwards.'

This view differs from that widely held in the latter half of the last century, when the ideal horse was expected to win over five and six furlongs at two and over two miles or more at four. The modern 'ideal horse' is essentially a middle-distance performer and it is for middle-distance horses that the major European events are staged.

The Jockey Club accepted the Norfolk Report and so did the Levy Board, who agreed to base their prize money scheme on the Report's general line of thought. Two years later a Race Planning Committee, with Lord Porchester as Chairman, was formed for the purpose of applying the principles established by the Norfolk Committee to the actual racing programme. Its terms of reference were to examine the whole picture of classic, prestige and feature races, taking into account other valuable weight-for-age races, including important races abroad, and as a result of this scrutiny to make recommendations for the avoidance of the overlapping of these races and as to how deficiencies in the Pattern programme could be remedied.

The Planning Committee's report listed a programme of 130 races needed for the proper testing of the best horses. These events were named 'Pattern Races', the terms 'Prestige Races' and 'Feature Races' being abandoned.

The Race Planning Committee was appointed to keep an eye permanently on the Pattern of Racing. It is charged with making recommendations for improvement, keeping in close touch with the authorities in France and Ireland, and with making periodical reports to the Jockey Club for consideration by the Joint Racing Board. An annual Pattern Race Book is now published giving details of Pattern Races in Great Britain, France, Ireland, Germany and Italy, as well as a list of 'Graded Stake Races' in the United States.

The Group System came into existence owing to the disparity between prize money levels in different countries. This led to glaring inequities in the calculation of penalties and allowances. There was understandable disgruntlement in France, a high prize level country, because horses could come from England, a low prize level country, and gain an advantage over French horses of comparable status. Feelings in France on this point became so intense that the French authorities came under pressure from French breeders and owners to bar French Pattern Races to foreign horses. An unpleasant situation was relieved by introducing a method for calculating penalties based, not on the actual monetary value of a race but on its intrinsic importance. Pattern races were accordingly divided into three categories:

Group I: championship races, including classic races, in which horses meet at weight-for-age without penalties or allowances.

Group II: races just below championship standard whose conditions may include some penalties and allowances.

Group III: the rest of the races, including classic trials, required for testing the best horses of all ages.

Introduced in 1971, the Group System has been a success and of considerable advantage to international racing. One of the benefits is that success in Group races provides a convenient method of assessing a horse's merit and a means of classification that transcends national frontiers. It would be a great help to breeders if the Pattern and Group System was extended to include all the main thorough-bred-producing countries. The system has not been introduced in Britain entirely without opposition, chiefly from sponsors, particularly bookmaker sponsors, who wish to manipulate the Pattern or to stage valuable handicaps in competition with Pattern Races. There has been opposition, too, from racecourse executives more concerned with their own interests than with the interests of racing as a whole; and occasionally from members of the Levy Board who are not invariably competent to judge on a matter of this description.

For the future, it is essential that the Pattern race system does not become too rigid. For example, it might one day be necessary to check the current swing away from stamina if the trend towards sheer speed is proving detrimental to the breed.

16

A JOURNALIST of sixty-five, particularly a gouty one, is an anachronism. On attaining that age I handed over my duties at the Sunday Times to Brough Scott, and apart from doing occasional jobs I withdrew to a considerable extent from the racing scene. Good horses give me as much pleasure as ever but most of the bread-and-butter racing I now find rather less interesting than when I used to drive half way across the country in a deplorable motor to watch indifferent horses compete at minor courses. Being less directly involved than previously, therefore, I will abridge my comments on the seasons of 1976 and 1977.

1976 was chiefly notable for the successes in important races gained by horses trained in France though not necessarily bred there. Flying Water won The One Thousand Guineas, Empery The Derby, Pawneese The Oaks and The King George VI and Queen Elizabeth Diamond Stakes, Crow The St Leger, Sagaro The Gold Cup and Vitiges The Champion Stakes. Vitiges had in fact joined Peter Walwyn's stable in the autumn but only a fortnight before winning at Newmarket. Wollow prevented an English washout in the classics by winning The Two Thousand Guineas.

Partly, but by no means entirely, due to chagrin over the French successes, the English racing world was buzzing with rumours about illegal methods allegedly employed by certain trainers in France. Confirmation of these rumours appeared to be forthcoming when François Mathet observed to a leading English racing journalist: 'Horses are being doped throughout Chantilly. I know what is used and how it is being done.' Mathet subsequently asserted that the words he used had been distorted. One of the more persistent rumours claimed that in a certain stable horses were given transfusions of their own blood, a form of treatment said to impart a temporary improvement to performance.

In the middle of the season occurred the sensational Trepan affair. Trepan, a four-year-old trained by François Boutin, won The Prince of Wales Stakes at Royal Ascot with singular ease in record time. The following month he won The Eclipse Stakes at Sandown with comparable facility, also in record time. After both those races Trepan was subjected to a routine test and in each case the test proved positive. Boutin appeared before the Stewards of the Jockey Club on

August 12. His contention was that the traces of caffeine and theobromine found in Trepan's urine after Ascot were due to an employee having mistakenly given the horse a dose of the diuretic drug Hepatorenal only twenty-four hours before the race. Normally, Boutin explained, when a diuretic was deemed advisable, it was administered three days before the race. In respect of that offence Boutin was fined £1,000, the stable employee £100. After The Eclipse, traces of theobromine were found in Trepan's urine but the source of this was not discovered. In this instance Boutin was fined £250, the Stewards evidently envisaging a possibility of traces of theobromine remaining in Trepan's system between the two races. The nature of the punishments showed that the Stewards regarded the cases, though serious, as essentially technical. Had they thought otherwise, they could have declared Boutin a disqualified person and have asked the French authorities to withdraw his licence to train. Trepan returned to England in August and ran last behind Wollow in The Benson and Hedges Gold Cup at York.

Wollow began the season with a smooth victory in The Clerical, Medical Greenham Stakes at Newbury. Starting an even-money favourite, he won The Two Thousand Guineas by a length and a half from the French colt Vitiges with the 66/1 outsider Thieving Demon two lengths away third. Thus Mr C. d'Alessio, Henry Cecil and G. Dettori repeated the success gained the previous year with Bolkonski. Evidently a believer in striking while the iron is still hot, Mr d'Alessio swiftly syndicated Wollow at £31,000 a share.

Wollow started favourite for The Derby at 11/10 but in what was regarded as a sub-standard field he performed disappointingly and finished only fifth behind Empery. No blame for his failure could be attached to Dettori. In The Eclipse Stakes Wollow was well and truly slammed by Trepan but secured the prize following Trepan's eventual disqualification. At Goodwood Wollow turned out for The Sussex Stakes. There are some verses by the late Captain Harry Graham which contain the following lines:

> or dachshunds, of the thin and wan sort,
> retrieving grouse for the Prince Consort.

Wollow certainly looked a bit thin and wan in the paddock at Goodwood but nevertheless he was successful in winning. He looked very much better at York where he put up an excellent performance in defeating Crow, Patch, Twig Moss and Trepan in The Benson and Hedges Gold Cup. It was a pity his racing career ended on a low note with a feeble display in The Champion Stakes.

Mr Nelson Bunker Hunt's American-bred Empery, trained by Zilber and ridden with faultless judgement by Piggott, was one of the less glamorous Derby winners. A son of Vaguely Noble, his top card was his stamina and he ran on strongly at Epsom to score by three lengths from Lady Beaverbrook's Relkino with Oats third. Relkino's subsequent form that season was lamentable but he retrieved his reputation as a four-year-old. Empery only ran once after Epsom, finishing second to Malacate, trained by Boutin, in The Irish Sweeps Derby.

Empery was inferior to his owner's Youth and had in fact finished third behind Youth in the Prix Lupin. A plainish colt by Ack Ack, Youth was so long in the back that he looked half empty with only one man in the saddle. However, likewise trained by Zilber, he won the Prix Greffulhe, the Prix Daru, the Prix Lupin, the Prix du Jockey Club, the Canadian International Championship, and finally The Washington International by ten lengths. In the Prix de l'Arc de Triomphe he was third to Ivanjica. His one real failure was in The King George VI and Queen Elizabeth Diamond Stakes in which he was ninth behind Pawneese. He was ridden on that occasion by Head who may well be brilliant in France but has an unfortunate tendency to bog it in England. He took Youth so wide on the final bend that it looked as if he intended to call on friends in Bagshot. Not surprisingly Youth had no chance thereafter. Mr Bunker Hunt brought off a nice stroke of business when twenty investors consented to pay $300,000 for a share in both Youth and Empery.

M. D. Wildenstein gained his first English classic success when his charming little Habitat filly Flying Water won The One Thousand Guineas. Trained by Angel Penna, Flying Water had made a most favourable impression when winning the Nell Gwyn Stakes at Newmarket three weeks earlier and she started favourite at 2/1 for the Guineas, the firm ground being expected to favour her low, daisy-trimming action. She was ridden with rather cheeky confidence by Saint-Martin who left her with a formidable amount to do in the last four furlongs. In the last quarter of a mile, though, she fairly flew and took the lead on the hill to win by a length from the Canadian-bred Konafa with the American-bred Kesar Queen close up third. At half-way Kesar Queen must have led Flying Water by at least a dozen lengths.

In the Prix Saint-Alary, Flying Water was said to be amiss and finished unplaced behind the Luthier filly Riverqueen, winner of the French One Thousand Guineas. Not long afterwards Flying Water met with an accident and raced no more that season. However she staged a successful comeback in 1977.[1]

It was a wonderful season for M. Wildenstein. In The Oaks he was represented by Pawneese, a filly of the highest class by the far from fashionable sire Carvin. Pawneese, a lithe, active bay that never carried much flesh, won the Prix la Camargo at Saint-Cloud early in March and later that month the Grade III Prix Pénélope over the same course. More informative, though, in respect of her chance in The Oaks was the sound beating she handed out to some useful fillies in the Prix Cléopatre, also at Saint-Cloud, in May. At Epsom she started at 6/5, took the lead after half a mile and won with almost impertinent ease by five lengths. She was in a totally different class to her opponents. Only nine days later she took the field in the Prix de Diane for which Riverqueen was favourite. Pawneese led from start to finish and won smoothly from Riverqueen and Lagunette, the latter of whom subsequently won the Irish Guinness Oaks and the Prix Vermeille.

Pawneese returned to England for The King George VI and Queen Elizabeth Diamond Stakes, in which Youth started favourite. Once again she made every

---

[1] She met with a fatal accident racing in America in 1978.

yard of the running and held on bravely to win by a length from Bruni with Orange Bay and Dakota close up third and fourth respectively. Probably her exertions on this occasion took a good deal out of her. She certainly trained off in the autumn and finished unplaced in both the Prix Vermeille and the Arc.

M. Wildenstein's third English classic winner in 1976 was Exbury's son Crow in The St Leger. Crow never ran at two, and it was not till half-way through his second season that his true merit began to become apparent. In July he won the mile and a quarter Grade II Prix Eugène Adam, worth over £27,000 to the winner, at Saint-Cloud and the following month he ran an excellent race to finish only a length behind Wollow in The Benson and Hedges Gold Cup. His running on that occasion suggested a longer distance might well suit him better. Co-favourite for The St Leger, he moved smoothly into the lead three furlongs out and won comfortably from another French colt, Secret Man, with the gigantic grey, Scallywag, who had gone in his wind, a neck away third. The going was very much on the soft side and Paquet, who suffered a little by comparison with Saint-Martin on the winner, was unable to prevent Secret Man from hanging to the left. Crow ran another fine race to finish second to Ivanjica in the Arc but a return to ten furlongs in The Champion Stakes was not a success and he was never going well at any stage. In that race Eddery persuaded the free-going Vitiges to settle down, Vitiges running on really well to defeat the previous year's winner, Rose Bowl, by a neck.

At Royal Ascot Mr G. A. Oldham's Sagaro, who the previous month had won the Prix du Cadran, again won The Gold Cup, this time by a length from Crash Course with Sea Anchor third. He was ridden with supreme confidence by Piggott and it would be hard to estimate just how much he had in hand.

The crack sprinter of 1976 was Mr C. Spence's big, powerful bay four-year-old Lochnager, trained in Yorkshire by M. W. Easterby. Besides winning The King's Stand Stakes at Royal Ascot, he won The Temple Stakes at Sandown, The July Cup and The William Hill Sprint Championship (formerly The Nunthorpe Stakes) at York. Bought privately as a foal for quite a small sum, Lochnager looked likely at one stage to become a store horse for jumping. He is certainly not bred in the height of current fashion, being by Dumbarnie out of a mare by Le Dieu d'Or. His grandam was by a virtually unknown stallion named Punt Gun, by Roar, while his third dam was by an almost forgotten son of Tetratema named Thyestes.

The best two-year-old colts to run in this country in 1976 appeared to many to be the American-bred J. O. Tobin, the American-bred Godswalk and the Canadian-bred The Minstrel. J. O. Tobin, whom Noel Murless trained for Mr G. A. Pope, is by Mill Reef's sire Never Bend and was thought to be what the French call 'un véritable crack' after his victories in The Richmond Stakes at Goodwood and The Laurent Perrier Champagne Stakes at Doncaster. However when he went over to Longchamp for The Grand Criterium, he was cut down to size in no uncertain fashion by the Aga Khan's brilliant Red God colt Blushing Groom. J. O. Tobin's owner then returned him to the land of his birth where he has experienced both triumphs and disappointments.

Mr P. Gallagher's Godswalk, trained this season by C. Grassick, is a grey by Dancer's Image and looked a flyer when he won The Norfolk Stakes at Royal Ascot by four lengths. It came as a considerable shock when, in The Phoenix Stakes at Phoenix Park in August, a Sir Ivor filly of Vincent O'Brien's named Cloonlara beat him to the tune of six lengths. Cloonlara on that form appeared to be an exceptional filly but she did not run again that season and was a failure in 1977. After that defeat, Godswalk won The Waterford Testimonial Stakes at The Curragh by four lengths.

Mr R. Sangster's The Minstrel, trained by O'Brien, is by Nijinsky's sire Northern Dancer out of Nijinsky's half-sister Fleur. A rather light-coloured chestnut with a lot of white about him, he did not please everyone by his appearance but he looked a pretty good colt when he won The Dewhurst Stakes by four lengths.

As regards the fillies, Mr R. Sangster's Lyphard filly Durtal, trained by Barry Hills, won The Cheveley Park Stakes in fine style and seemed a possible winner of The One Thousand Guineas. When assessing fillies for the following season's classics, it is doubtful if much thought was ever given to a couple named respectively Mrs McArdy and Dunfermline.

M. Wildenstein was leading owner with ten races worth £244,500. Henry Cecil was top trainer with fifty races worth £261,301. Just over a thousand pounds behind him came Peter Walwyn who won more than double the number of races. M. W. Easterby became the first northern trainer to top the £100,000 mark. Pat Eddery was again leading jockey. In June it became known that the fourteen-year association between Joe Mercer and Dick Hern's stable was to be concluded at the end of the season. It was widely believed that the instigators of this move were Sir Arnold Weinstock and his father-in-law Sir Michael Sobell, owners of the West Ilsley stable. Other patrons of Dick Hern were apparently quite satisfied with Mercer who accepted the post of first jockey to Henry Cecil's stable.

Noel Murless, now Sir Noel and a member of the Jockey Club, retired at the end of the season at the age of sixty-six. He had been nine times leading trainer and had been responsible for such famous winners as Crepello, Royal Palace, St Paddy, Petite Etoile and Abernant. A true lover of horses, he cared little for popularity and it was the interest of the horses under his care that always came first. In the closing years of his career he gave the impression that worries over labour were among the several factors that were making a trainer's life more worrying and less pleasurable for him than had at one time been the case.

Mr Woodrow Wyatt succeeded the urbane and witty Lord Mancroft as head of the Tote. The appointment of this former Labour M.P., who at one time had horses in training with David Hastings, surprised a good many people and dismayed quite a few as well but in fact Mr Wyatt shows every sign of proving the most imaginative and successful boss that the Tote has yet been blessed with.

The ever-increasing influence of the American thoroughbred in European racing continued in 1977 and The Minstrel was the sixth Derby winner since 1968 (inclusive) to have been bred the other side of the Atlantic. However three of the classics were won by horses bred and trained in this country and it gave immense satisfaction that, in the year of Her Majesty's Silver Jubilee, the Queen won The Oaks and The St Leger with Dunfermline.

The black day, racingwise, in 1977 came on Friday, May 13, when it was announced that cases of an unusual genital infection in mares had been discovered at the National Stud, Newmarket. The stud had to be closed and all covering suspended. The stallions then located there were Mill Reef, Grundy, Blakeney, Tudor Melody, Habat and Star Appeal.

The disease, contagious metritis, was believed to have originated in Ireland. It affected about a score of studs in this country and it is estimated that the cost to the breeding industry was about £10,000,000. As a result of the outbreak, there was a temporary ban imposed on the export of our thoroughbreds to the United States, Canada, Australia, New Zealand and Brazil.

On the other hand, highly satisfactory was the advance in technique that enabled the Newmarket forensic scientists to detect the administration of anabolic steroids. Cases heard by the Stewards of the Jockey Club early in the year showed that the authorities were determined to stamp out that pernicious practice.

Racing politics tend to be a bore and possess only tepid interest for the racing public. Mr Phil Bull enjoys the esteem of a man who has been a good friend to punters. He likes airing his views on the administration of racing and from time to time has something interesting to say, but it is not to his own advantage, still less to that of his readers or listeners, that he has always tended to underestimate the virtues of brevity. In a lengthy submission to the Royal Commission on Gambling, he gave his view that there was no place for the Jockey Club in the future of British racing, an opinion that came as no surprise to anyone with even a slight knowledge of Mr Bull. Of course there were three dutiful cheers from the radical fringe of the racing world, but the 'Establishment' retained its composure and in general the reception tended to be on the cool side.

The Jockey Club took a notable pace forward by electing three women members, Lady Halifax, her half-sister Mrs Priscilla Hastings, and Mrs Helen Johnson Houghton, mother of Fulke Johnson Houghton and twin sister of Fulke Walwyn who rode a Grand National winner and who has been a leading jumping trainer for many years. It was generally agreed that all three had merited their distinction.

Two very successful trainers who died during the year were Sam Hall and Staff Ingham, the former a Yorkshireman, the latter always associated with Epsom. The burly, genial Sam Hall, full of good stories and a man that it was impossible not to like, was the son of a breeder of hackneys and shire horses. To begin with he assisted firstly his brother Tom, and then another brother, W. A., commonly known as Charlie. After serving as a seaman in the Royal Navy, he took out a licence soon after the war and quickly began to make a name for himself. He won a lot of big handicaps including The Ebor Handicap (twice), The Cesarewitch, The Manchester November Handicap (four times), The Lincolnshire Handicap (twice), The Wokingham Stakes (twice) and The Royal Hunt Cup. There was no more popular character in northern racing.

Staff Ingham was apprenticed to Stanley Wootton whose influence and advice was of great help to him throughout his career. He was a good rider as a boy and in 1925 won The Royal Hunt Cup on the King's Weathervane (6 st. 12 lb.). In the 1930s, despite being six feet tall, he was just about the best and most stylish hurdle race rider in the country. He only rode once over fences, finishing second in a chase at Plumpton. He had just started to train when the war broke out. He joined the RAF and achieved the rank of Squadron Leader. When hostilities were over he resumed training and his Epsom stable was very soon a force to be reckoned with. Slim, immaculate and reserved, he was an expert in every aspect of the racing game and achieved some big coups, particularly with Richer in The Cambridgeshire and Chantry in The Cesarewitch. He had a good many victories over hurdles too, including the winners of The Imperial Cup and The Daily Express Triumph Hurdle. His stable is being carried on by his son Tony.

Gordon Smyth, who had succeeded his father at Arundel in 1961 before setting up as a public trainer at Lewes in 1965, decided to leave this country and try his luck as a trainer in Hong Kong. He had the good fortune to train the Derby winner Charlottown in his first season at Lewes but had experienced one or two lean years there since.

It was a cool damp spring in 1977 and the going at Ascot was heavy on April 2 when The Minstrel took the field for the Ascot Two Thousand Guineas Trial Stakes. He won by a length and a half from Gairloch, winner of The Royal Lodge Stakes the previous autumn, but by and large he failed to raise much enthusiasm among those who saw him. With the ground as it was, it was excusable that he hung to the left near the finish. In The Two Thousand Guineas, run on good going, he started a hot favourite but the best he could do was to finish third, beaten a length and a length, behind Nebbiolo and Tachypous. It was said in extenuation of his defeat that he had been badly drawn and had started slowly. He certainly did not look to be a great racehorse that day and in the paddock he compared ill with some of his opponents, particularly with Tachypous who had beaten Nebbiolo in The Middle Park Stakes the previous autumn.

A tough, strongly made chestnut by Yellow God, exported to Japan, out of the German-bred Novara, by Birkhahn, Nebbiolo belonged to Mr Niels Schibbye, a Dane engaged in the motor-car business. He was trained in Ireland by Kevin Prendergast and ridden by Gabriel Curran. Novara was just about the best two-year-old in Germany in 1967 and won a good mile-and-a-half race there the following season. Unfortunately she developed a cyst in her womb, was operated on and seemed unlikely to be able to breed. Accordingly Mr Schibbye sold her, but in point of fact she produced a couple of foals and when she was offered at the December Sales, carrying Nebbiolo, Mr Schibbye bought her back for 16,000 guineas. Nebbiolo himself was offered for sale as a yearling but was led out unsold at 1,900 guineas. Mr Schibbye therefore asked Kevin Prendergast to train the colt. Mr Schibbye had never before had a horse in training in the British Isles.

Nebbiolo was a hardy and consistent performer at two, winning five races including The Gimcrack Stakes. On the whole, though, he gave the impression that he might be a shade below classic standard at three. Also, he had a very hard race, which some feared he might always remember, when second in The Middle Park Stakes. He did not win any of his three races after his Newmarket triumph but was close up third, after meeting with some interference, in the Irish Two Thousand Guineas behind Pampapaul and The Minstrel. At the end of the season he was retired to the Ballygoran Stud in County Kildare.

Despite a fiasco in the Ascot One Thousand Guineas Trial in which she was left in a flag start and took no part, Cloonlara was favourite for The One Thousand Guineas at 6/4. Durtal was not a runner, her target being the Poule d'Essai des Pouliches. Cloonlara showed speed for six furlongs but, when challenged by Mrs McArdy, she swished her tail and showed a disinclination for further exertion, eventually finishing fourth behind Mrs McArdy, Freeze The Secret and the Irish-bred, French-trained Sanedtki—a daughter of Sallust that had won the Ascot Trial, was sold in the autumn for £116,500 and then won the Prix de la Forêt. Sanedtki had cost 1,050 guineas as a yearling. Mrs McArdy was going well throughout and from the Bushes she always looked like winning. Though she started at 16/1, she was by no means unbacked.

Bred by Lord Grimthorpe, Mrs McArdy can hardly be said to boast a typical classic pedigree as she is by Tribal Chief, now in Japan, out of Harina, by Darling Boy who was exported to Holland. A few years previously Lord Grimthorpe had decided to dispose of his racing interests and sold all his bloodstock to Mick Easterby, who re-sold them with the exception of Mrs McArdy who later was transferred to the ownership of his patron, Mrs Kettlewell. She ran four times at two, winning her last four races which included the Prince of Wales's Nursery at Doncaster. There was, however, no disposition to regard her as a potential classic winner. The following spring she won The Tote Free Handicap, a race in which the form frequently works out well, carrying 8 stone and starting co-favourite. Those who knew her best were by no means surprised by her victory in The One Thousand Guineas. She failed to stay in The Oaks, which was hardly surprising in view of her pedigree, but she subsequently won the one-mile Fen Ditton Handicap at Newmarket and the seven-furlongs Strensall Stakes at York. She was out of her depth competing against the colts in The Sussex Stakes at Goodwood, while old Boldboy gave her four years, 10lb. and a six-and-a-half-lengths beating in the seven-furlongs Sanyo Stakes at Doncaster. An attractive, well-made bay, she came up for sale at Newmarket in December and was bought by Mr B. Firestone for 154,000 guineas, a record price at Tattersalls for a horse in training. Her new owner said he planned to run her in America.

Blushing Groom, who had grown very little since his two-year-old days, won the French Two Thousand Guineas without difficulty and started favourite for The Derby despite the obvious fact that it was highly improbable he would stay a mile-and-a-half. Moreover his jockey H. Samani was not familiar with Epsom. Fortunately for certain acknowledged breeding experts who had promised to carry out a number of improbable and humiliating forfeits if Blushing Groom won, the son of the non-staying Red God was well and truly beaten with two furlongs to go and finished a weary third behind The Minstrel and Hot Grove. He only ran once subsequently, being narrowly beaten by Flying Water in an absurdly slow-run race for the one-mile Prix Jacques le Marois at Deauville. He was then shipped off to the United States, the syndication arranged before his Derby failure giving him a value of six million dollars. It only remains to congratulate the Aga Khan on what appears to have been a brilliant stroke of business.

Second favourite for The Derby at 5/1 was The Minstrel who had been narrowly, and perhaps a shade unluckily, beaten by Pampapaul, a tough son of Yellow God, in the Irish Two Thousand Guineas. The Minstrel had a very hard race, as indeed he had also had at Newmarket, but he was none the worse for it afterwards. That shrewd judge Lester Piggott was convinced that The Minstrel could stay and it was in no small measure due to Piggott's persuasive powers that O'Brien decided to allow The Minstrel to take his chance at Epsom.

In the paddock at Epsom The Minstrel showed he had improved considerably in a physical sense since the spring. Ridden by Piggott with a combination of faultless judgement and remarkable strength, he was fourth and ideally poised at Tattenham Corner. In the straight he had a terrific duel with Lord Leverhulme's Chester Vase winner Hot Grove, the mount of Willie Carson, who had gone to the front early in the straight. Hot Grove battled on with admirable resolution and it is doubtful if any rider bar Piggott could have forced The Minstrel up close home to win a gruelling race by a neck. There is traditional prejudice against chestnut horses of The Minstrel's type but in fact The Minstrel's outstanding characteristics were toughness and courage. The manner in which he responded when Piggott really got at him was beyond praise. It was Piggott's eighth Derby victory, O'Brien's fifth.

The Minstrel ran twice subsequently. He won The Irish Sweeps Derby from the Nijinsky colt Lucky Sovereign but he had not kept a straight course in the closing stages and had to survive an objection. In The King George VI and Queen Elizabeth Diamond Stakes he gave another exhibition of toughness and pluck, winning by a short head from Orange Bay, on whom the application of blinkers had a highly beneficial effect, with The Coronation Cup winner Exceller third and Crystal Palace, winner of the French Derby, fourth. Two St Leger winners Bruni and Crow were unplaced. Both Bruni and Crow had a disappointing season. Possibly Bruni, who eventually broke down in The Doncaster Cup, was feeling the effects of his abortive winter trip to America.

There was talk of running The Minstrel in the Prix de l'Arc de Triomphe but in September he was shipped off to America at short notice in order to beat the ban on imports shortly to be imposed because of the outbreak of contagious metritis in Britain. Bought as a yearling for $200,000, he had won £315,211, a record amount for a horse trained in England or Ireland. His joint owners, Mr R. Sangster, Mr Simon Fraser and Vincent O'Brien, accepted an offer from Mr E. P. Taylor of $4,500,000 for eighteen of the thirty-six shares in him. The current astronomical prices paid for bloodstock in America bear no relation to those that breeders in this country can afford.

Mr Sangster was less fortunate in The Oaks. His filly Durtal had begun the season with an easy victory in The Fred Darling Stakes at Newbury, after which she dead-heated for second place in the French One Thousand Guineas behind the brilliant Madelia, by Caro, who later won the Prix Saint-Alary and the Prix de Diane de Revlon. Durtal was a heavily backed favourite for The Oaks. On the way to the start, however, her saddle slipped. She took fright and galloped off, dragging Piggott with her. Fortunately the stirrup leather broke and released Piggott's foot or else he might well have been gravely injured. As it was, he was badly shaken and no wonder. Durtal herself collided with a post and cut herself so badly that she had to be withdrawn. She could not race again till the autumn when it was apparent that she had lost her form completely.

Among the runners in The Oaks was the Queen's Dunfermline who had shown promise at two without winning. In her only race in 1977 prior to The Oaks she had won the ten-furlongs Pretty Polly Stakes at Newmarket by four lengths from Olwyn who subsequently won the Irish Guinness Oaks. Well backed in The Oaks at 6/1, Dunfermline sweated up in the paddock beforehand but this did not affect her performance. Carson brought her with one long run from Tattenham Corner and she finished like a true stayer to secure the lead close home and won by three parts of a length from Freeze The Secret with Vaguely Deb third. She was trained by Dick Hern who had won The One Thousand Guineas and the French Oaks for the Queen in 1974 with Highclere. Coming as it did at the end of Silver Jubilee week, Dunfermline's victory was both popular and appropriate; the only regret was that the Queen herself was unable to be present.

Bred by her owner, Dunfermline is a rangy, racinglike bay by Royal Palace, who very badly needed a good winner, out of Strathcona, by St Paddy. Strathcona's dam Stroma, by Luminary, cost only 1,150 guneas as a yearling and though she did not win herself she bred four winners including the Eclipse victor Canisbay, sire of Orange Bay. Unfortunately from the point of view of the Royal Stud, it was decided to send Strathcona to the December Sales in 1976 and she was sold for 7,600 guineas. She is now in America, the Mylerstown Stud having re-sold her after Dunfermline had won The St Leger for 150,000 dollars. Her colt foal by Town Crier realised 38,000 guineas at the December Sales. Tartan Pimpernel, Strathcona's daughter by Blakeney, showed high promise as a two-year-old in 1977.

Dunfermline disappointed in The Yorkshire Oaks, finishing third to Busaca, by Busted, but she was obviously not suited to the modest pace at which the race was run. In The St Leger, in which she started at 10/1, she had the services of Gregarious as pacemaker. This race was looked upon as a good thing for Mr J. R. Fluor's American-bred Alleged, by Hoist The Flag, a grandson of Ribot. A member of O'Brien's stable, Alleged came to Doncaster the unbeaten winner of five races and in The Great Voltigeur Stakes at York he had put up a tremendous performance, winning by seven lengths from a field that included not only the

Derby runner-up Hot Grove, but also Lucky Sovereign and Classic Example, second and third respectively in The Irish Sweeps Derby. It is true, though, that Hot Grove, who missed The St Leger, did not recapture his Derby form till late October when he won The St Simon Stakes at Newbury.

Gregarious did his work to perfection and led at a good pace till half a mile from home when Piggott took Alleged to the front. Alleged was going so well at that point that it seemed merely a question of just how far he was going to win by, but excitement mounted when it was seen that Carson and Dunfermline were in resolute pursuit. Gradually the gap was closed, and after a glance over his shoulder, Piggott began to ride Alleged really hard. Alleged was courageous enough and gave everything he had but he was unable to quicken and a Yorkshire cheer that must have been heard for miles went up when Dunfermline got her head in front just below the distance. Once in the lead she ran on stoutly to the finish to win by a length and a half. The others were hardly at the races at all: Classic Example, who was third, was no less than ten lengths behind Alleged. It had been an unforgettable duel between two very game horses.

The excitement was not all over, though. At one stage Dunfermline and Alleged had come very close together and an inquiry by the Stewards, whose task was hardly an enviable one, was deemed necessary. The inquiry lasted for a good twenty minutes before it was announced that the placings would remain unaltered, at which another great cheer went up. Unfortunately once again the Queen had been unable to be present.

Alleged took his revenge over the shorter distance of the Arc, Piggott riding one of his best races to win by a length and a half from the New Zealand champion Balmerino with Crystal Palace third and Dunfermline close up fourth. Dunfermline had no pacemaker on this occasion, the moderate pace early on did not suit her, and she seemed to be ridden for speed rather than for stamina which is her strongest point. In finishing third in the Prix Royal Oak, Dunfermline did not show her best form. The ground was softer than she likes, she had had a long and tiring journey, and possibly she had trained off just a bit. It will be disappointing if she fails to win some good races in 1978. She will always, though, find Alleged hard to beat over a mile and a half.

The outstanding performance at Royal Ascot, where the weather was more appropriate for a jumping meeting in February, was Sagaro's third successive victory in The Gold Cup, a unique performance. Superbly trained by Boutin, Sagaro was at his very best and won on a tight rein by five lengths from Buckskin who had beaten him in the Prix du Cadran. Buckskin, by Yelapa, now in Japan, and himself now a member of Peter Walwyn's stable, had also beaten Sagaro in the Prix de Barbeville and the Prix Jean Prat. There was general approval when soon after Ascot it became known that the Levy Board had bought Sagaro for the very reasonable price of £175,000. He will eventually stand at the National Stud but is beginning his stud career at the Lockinge Stud near Wantage.

Godswalk had been bought since the previous season by Mr Sangster for a sum said to be over £300,000 and was now trained by O'Brien. He looked a high-class sprinter when he won The King's Stand Stakes despite having stumbled and lost several lengths at the start. It came as a nasty shock to several big punters when he was beaten a head by Haveroid, a Tycoon II colt trained by Adam, in The William Hill Sprint Championship at York in August. There seemed to be no excuse for that defeat. He terminated his career with an easy victory at The Curragh in The Airlie, Castle Hyde, Coolmore Sprint Championship run over six furlongs and worth over £10,000 to the winner. He was then retired to the Castle Hyde Stud at a fee of 4,000 guineas with an October 1 concession.

Haveroid's stable-companion Gentilhombre did not find his best form till the autumn. He did win The July Cup but only on the disqualification of O'Brien's Marinsky, a half-brother by Northern Dancer to Thatch. Marinsky's three-year-old career was crammed with controversy and ended in tragedy. His first race was the seven furlongs Lumville Stakes at The Curragh in May. Starting at 7/1 on, he finished five lengths behind the 20/1 Sun Rod. The Stewards had Piggott up and warned him to be more vigorous and persistent in his riding. It was Piggott's view that Marinsky did not stay and maybe he was right. In The Diomed Stakes at Epsom, Marinsky finished third but was disqualified, having made a resolute attempt to eat Relkino approaching Tattenham Corner. Blinkered and muzzled, he was caught close home in The St James's Palace Stakes at Royal Ascot and beaten a head by the north-country Don. The general view was that he had chucked it. Again blinkered and muzzled, he won The July Cup very easily but was disqualified for interfering with Gentilhombre though it was very unlikely that the result was in any way affected. O'Brien undertook not to run Marinsky in this country again and a month later Marinsky died of a twisted gut. He might have proved a brilliant sprinter. Had he done so, his value, bred as he was, would have been at least £500,000.

Gentilhombre, looking a picture, won The Diadem Stakes at Ascot very easily in September and then put up the best performance of his career to win the Prix de l'Abbaye de Longchamp by four lengths. Haveroid was six lengths away third. Gentilhombre remained in training in 1978 but had been moved to N. Callaghan's Newmarket stable.

Quite one of the best horses in the country over six and seven furlongs was Lady Beaverbrook's gallant old warrior Boldboy, whose career is a tribute to Dick Hern's skill as a trainer. At seven years of age Boldboy, a gelding, was better than ever before, winning The Abernant Stakes at Newmarket for the third time, The Challenge Stakes at Newmarket for the second time, The Duke of York Stakes at York, The Sanyo Stakes at Doncaster and The Vernons Sprint Cup at Haydock Park. In addition, with 9 st. 10 lb. on his back, he was beaten a head in The Victoria Cup at Ascot and also in The Beeswing Stakes at Newcastle. He has now won over £91,000 and with luck will pass the £100,000 mark in 1978. No wonder his owner has made provision for him in her will!

O'Brien's three-year-old Artaius, by Round Table out of a mare by My Babu, had been bought for 110,000 guineas as a yearling for Mrs George F. Getty II. He started off his second season by winning The Classic Trial Stakes run over a mile-and-a-quarter at Sandown in April. At that point O'Brien hoped he was going to make a high-class mile-and-a-half horse. After running unplaced in the Irish Two Thousand Guineas, Artaius put up an excellent performance in the Prix du Jockey Club to finish second to Crystal Palace, beaten only by half a length.

Artaius, however, was to show that a mile or a mile-and-a-quarter suited him better than a mile-and-a-half. He made mincemeat of his opponents in The Eclipse Stakes in which he led from start to finish. He was never headed, too, in The Sussex Stakes, winning by a length and a half from Free State with Relkino six lengths away third. After two such scintillating performances he was reckoned sure to win The Benson and Hedges Gold Cup in which he started at 11/8 on, but he was clearly lacking the zip he had shown in July and was well and truly beaten by Relkino who had finished so far behind him at Goodwood. Owing to being afflicted with ringworm, Artaius did not run in the autumn and was retired to the Airlie Stud, having been syndicated at no less than £55,000 a share.

The four-year-old Relkino, who had been the top-priced yearling in England or Ireland in 1974, had lost his form after finishing second to Empery in The Derby. However Hern succeeded in getting him back to his best form in 1977 when it was clear he was best suited by distances under a mile-and-a-half. Besides The Benson and Hedges Gold Cup, he won the one-mile Lockinge Stakes at Newbury and ran admirably to finish second to Flying Water in The Champion Stakes. By the Derby winner Relko out of that game mare Pugnacity, Relkino was syndicated at the end of the season at £8,000 a share, giving him a valuation of £320,000.

North Stoke, trained by John Dunlop for Mrs M. Lequime, cost only 820 guineas as a yearling. By Northfields out of a mare by Whistler, he proved one of the best three-year-olds in the country, winning six races in succession, including the mile-and-a-quarter Joe McGrath Memorial Stakes at Leopardstown worth over £19,000 to the winner. He also won valuable prizes in Belgium and Germany. He was greatly fancied to win The Champion Stakes but found Flying Water and Relkino too good for him which was certainly no disgrace. It will be surprising if he fails to win more good races in 1978.

American-bred colts and fillies dominated the two-year-old scene. O'Brien's American-bred Dewhurst Stakes winner Try My Best, by that great sire Northern Dancer, headed The Free Handicap with 9 st. 7 lb. and looked the ideal type for The Two Thousand Guineas. The American-bred Middle Park Stakes winner Formidable, by Forli, who seemed to improve with every race, received 9 st. 3 lb. An American-bred son of Secretariat, Dactylographer, won The William Hill Futurity Stakes but this distinctly plain colt was given a comparatively modest place in the Handicap with 8 st. 8 lb. The two top fillies were the American-bred Cherry Hinton, a really beautiful daughter of Nijinsky, and the American-bred Sookera, by Roberto, winner of The Cheveley Park Stakes. The top British-bred colt was Sexton Blake (9 st. 4 lb.) who won The Champagne Stakes but was no match for Try My Best in The Dewhurst Stakes.

One of the most pleasing performances by an English-trained two-year-old was that of John de Coombe, a Moulton colt trained by Paul Cole that had failed to reach his reserve when offered for sale as a yearling. To everyone's surprise, John de Coombe won the seven-furlongs Group I Prix de la Salamandre worth over £29,000 to the winner. Among those he beat was the American-bred Prix Morny winner Super Concorde, by Bold Reasoning out of a daughter of the Oaks winner Homeward Bound. Bold Reasoning, though, had his revenge in The Grand Criterium.

Mr R. Sangster, an Isle of Man resident, was the most successful owner with a total of £348,023. Then came Lady Beaverbrook, The Queen and Mrs G. Getty II. As recently as 1961 the late Major L. B. Holliday was top owner with £39,227. Vincent O'Brien headed the trainers' list with £439,123 and Pat Eddery was champion jockey for the fourth year running. In the past fifty years there have only been eight champion jockeys. Northern Dancer was leading sire for the second time, a remarkable feat by a stallion that has never stood in this country and therefore has had few runners here.

How pleasant it would be to be able to forecast that the 1978 Derby and the 1979 Derby will be won by British-bred, British-trained colts! On the whole, though, such a desirable eventuality seems, though far from impossible, to be improbable. In the current economic climate, our big races are likely to go on falling in rich profusion to American-bred horses belonging to owners not resident in this country.[1]

It would be foolhardy to make any forecasts with regard to the future of English racing. It is passing through a period of profound change in which the prophecies of one year are liable to be overtaken by actual events in the next. For those who can remember racing between the wars, the greatest change has been the transformation of what was formerly a sport into what is mainly a business or an industry, a transformation that hardly tends to make it more attractive. Death duties mean that a great stud is usually dispersed when its owner dies and the choicest lots offered are liable to fall to the bids of purchasers from abroad. The aristocracy, such as it is today, has largely opted out of racing and the owner-breeders on whom for so many years we so largely depended for our best horses have almost ceased to exist. At the yearling sales it is not English owners as a rule who pay the top prices and in addition too many of our best mares and fillies out of training are exported. The power of the dollar since 1945 has been a dominating factor in bloodstock breeding and few would deny that the American thoroughbred is now supreme. The weakness of English-trained horses was demonstrated with brutal clarity in 1976 when horses from abroad won The One Thousand Guineas, The Derby, The Oaks, The St Leger, The Gold Cup and The King George VI and Queen Elizabeth Stakes. The substantial increase in prize money, particularly for Group races, is indeed welcome but it will prove of scant advantage if our horses are simply not good enough to resist the challenge of invaders from Ireland and France.

[1] In fact the 1978 Derby was won by the British-bred Shirley Heights by a head from the American-bred Hawaiian Sound.

There is no shortage of owners despite ever-increasing costs. Few, though, of those who come into racing today have been brought up with horses and many scarcely know which end bites and which end kicks. Too many are inclined to believe that money guarantees success and are liable to walk off in a huff when they find that it does not. Up till World War II, few stables contained more than forty horses. Now, despite the shortage of labour, there is a growing number of trainers who take on double that number and some who take over a hundred. With all those owners, one imagines the telephone bell never stops ringing. It is permissible to speculate on whether, even with intelligent organisation and a measure of decentralisation, all the horses in these huge concerns get properly trained. The best ones probably do, but doubts surely exist with regard to some of the less talented animals.

The labour situation is unlikely to improve until a lad's wages are at least noticeably superior to National Assistance. It seems absurd to buy a yearling for 25,000 guineas and then place it in the care of a lad who would probably be little worse off if he gave up working. In the end trainers may feel compelled to raise their fees substantially. This would certainly drive some owners out of the game and not necessarily those that could best be spared; but it might prove in the long run to be the lesser evil. The future may see more horses owned by syndicates or by businesses and companies.

For a long time the bloodstock market favoured sellers and any yearling with legs of a sort at each corner and the conventional number of heads was reasonably sure to find a purchaser. Because of the economic situation, buyers have become choosier and recently the ordinary bread-and-butter yearling has not been easy to dispose of, particularly as some breeders are apt to impose a reserve that could only be justified if the animal in question had swallowed a diamond tiara. The market for the moderate yearling is almost wholly domestic but it is international for classically bred colts and fillies and prices for them are still liable to be high. A price of 10,000 guineas for a yearling looks very nice in the columns of the Sporting Life but it is sometimes overlooked that it may have cost the breeder that amount to put that particular yearling into the sale ring. If the present financial climate means a falling off in the number of brood mares at stud that are never likely to produce anything but an equine disaster, racing will be all the better for it.

It would be an exaggeration to describe the Jockey Club as groggy but its position is perhaps less assured than at any time in its history. This is less due to actual resentment at its existence than to the increasing difficulty in finding men with suitable qualifications who can afford to give their time, unpaid, to the administration of racing. Of course a certain degree of opposition does exist to what has been described as 'the last bastion of the aristocracy' and radicals are undoubtedly hostile to a self-elected, self-perpetuating body, of which more than half the members happen to be Old Etonians. Most of the opposition, though, comes from individuals who do not carry much weight in the racing world or whose own track record might not stand up well to intensive scrutiny. The strength of the Jockey Club's position is based not a little on the fact that many followers of racing reckon that any body formed to take its place could so easily be very much worse. There are few who ardently desire nationalised racing, and control by a statutory body composed of failed politicians and time-expired trade union leaders could easily prove a disaster. In recent years in a gallant attempt to make the control of racing seem, at least superficially, more democratic, a number of bodies have been formed and are afforded the privilege of consultation. No doubt this is all to the good but the public does not seem to care much and gets somewhat confused between BRIC, RILC, BOLA and a new organisation known as PRIC (The People's Racing Information Centre).

The Jockey Club is constantly being advised to broaden the basis for membership but it would be pointless electing men successful in business or in industry who could not undertake to pull their weight in respect of the many administrative duties that have to be carried out. Contrary to what some journalists seem to believe, not everyone in racing wishes to belong to the Jockey Club. There is certainly a strong case for electing certain retired trainers and officials, although a good many people who retire after a lifetime of racing wish to give it up completely and for ever.

English racing is likely to continue short of money. It is totally unrealistic to imagine that any Chancellor of the Exchequer would hand back to racing a fair whack of the large sum of money derived annually from the betting tax. The traditional system of betting in this country may suit off-course punters but it is of limited assistance to racing's finances. Nevertheless, it is difficult to visualise any political party giving parliamentary time to legislation that would establish a tote monopoly, particularly as that legislation would be unpopular with the great mass of punters. It is just conceivable though, that a time may eventually come when it will be a question of racing with a tote monopoly or no racing at all. In the meantime racing must struggle on as best it can with what it has got and the sport must rely on competent housekeeping by the Levy Board, who must not shrink from reducing the number of racecourses and taking steps that would discourage the breeding and maintenance of bad horses. The aim ought to be directed towards quality. There are some who think that the quality of our horses is of scant significance but, if that is indeed the case, why do huge crowds assemble year after year at Royal Ascot, Goodwood in July and York in August? The fact is that there is no greater draw in racing that an outstanding horse, a notable example being the steeplechaser Arkle. Admittedly racing could not exist without betting but there are, I am glad to say, other aspects to it as well.

Certainly English racing today is beset with many complex problems and, human nature being what it is, the various interests concerned in the sport all apparently think that their own problem is the most important. In the meantime, however, the dogs bark and the caravan moves on, and let it never be forgotten that racing is meant to be fun.

INDEX

NOTES:

1. Where a reference occurs frequently, eg Ascot, minor mentions have been omitted.
2. References to the English classics (Derby, Oaks, One Thousand Guineas, St. Leger, Two Thousand Guineas) have been sub-divided into (a) each year and winner from 1940 onwards; (b) general references.
3. Where the name of a race has changed, eg due to sponsorship, references to the race have been listed for the sake of continuity either under the title by which it has been commonly known, eg Eclipse Stakes, or under the most recent title, eg Great Voltigeur Stakes.
4. 'i' means illustration, eg Abernant 68i.
5. 'p' means passim (here and there), sometimes more than one mention on a page, eg Goodwood, p.
6. To assist the reader, cross references are frequent.